Insight and Psychosis

Insight and Psychosis

Awareness of illness in schizophrenia and related disorders

SECOND EDITION

Edited by

Xavier F. Amador

Columbia University, Teachers College and the
National Alliance for the Mentally Ill, Arlington VA, USA

and

Anthony S. David

Institute of Psychiatry, King's College, London, UK

OXFORD
UNIVERSITY PRESS

OXFORD

UNIVERSITY PRESS

Great Clarendon Street, Oxford OX2 6DP

Oxford University Press is a department of the University of Oxford.
It furthers the University's objective of excellence in research, scholarship,
and education by publishing worldwide in

Oxford New York

Auckland Cape Town Dar es Salaam Hong Kong Karachi
Kuala Lumpur Madrid Melbourne Mexico City Nairobi
New Delhi Shanghai Taipei Toronto

With offices in

Argentina Austria Brazil Chile Czech Republic France Greece
Guatemala Hungary Italy Japan Poland Portugal Singapore
South Korea Switzerland Thailand Turkey Ukraine Vietnam

Oxford is a registered trade mark of Oxford University Press
in the UK and in certain other countries

Published in the United States
by Oxford University Press Inc., New York

First published 2004

Reprinted 2005
Edition for Janssen–Cilag Ltd, 2005

A catalogue record for this title is available from the British Library

Typeset by Newgen Imaging Systems (P) Ltd.,
Printed in Great Britain
on acid-free paper by
Biddles Ltd., King's Lynn

ISBN 10: 0 19 929910 2
ISBN 13: 978 0 19 929910 2

Preface

It has been over 12 years since we first conceived the idea of collecting together articles on the topic of insight in serious mental disorders, and 6 years since the first edition of *Insight and Psychosis* was published. We could not have predicted the speed with which the field has developed and the breadth and diversity of the issues it has encompassed.

Like most first-time projects the immediate satisfaction of contemplating the finished article was soon tempered by a growing awareness that things could have been done better, and that several areas were insufficiently covered or even omitted altogether. This awareness was sufficient to prompt us to plan a second edition and we were pleasantly surprised to learn that our publishers at Oxford University Press shared our vision. As well as consolidating the knowledge summarized in the first edition, there were three main areas that we felt this new edition should seek to address.

The first is the now substantial body of research literature on neuropsychological studies involving insight and indeed the more general application of techniques from the cognitive neurosciences to this previously thought esoteric topic within psychopathology. The second main area concerns clinical relevance. Some critics of the concept of insight have drawn attention to this matter, which has served as a stimulus to us and others in the field. What is the point of attempting to understand some aspect of psychopathology if, in the end, it makes no difference to the lives of the people we are caring for? The third, though related aspect was to broaden out the "stakeholders" who could contribute to the debate and discussion on the sort of topics we chose to cover in the book. There has been a quiet revolution in both the theoretical and practical aspects of mental health care, namely the rise of the consumer movement in the US, or "user movement" as it is called in the UK. This is particularly apposite in discussions of insight. Notions of insight have been caricatured as merely "agreeing with the doctor", thus neglecting the validity of other perspectives, particularly those of the individual labelled as the patient. So not only is the consumer voice relevant in this area as in all area of mental health, it is actually central to our concept of what constitutes insight into the psychoses.

As mentioned, the publishers were very supportive of this new edition, but did lay down certain constraints. They advised that the second edition should be substantially new in comparison to the first, with brand new chapters and updates on all "old" chapters. So far so good. However, they also insisted that the total length of the second edition should not exceed, by too great a margin, that of the first. Inevitably this meant that certain chapters had to go to make room for new ones. The decisions on how this was to be effected were difficult and complex, although in most cases they were made for us by the contributors themselves, invariably driven by pressures of work and other commitments.

Before going through the contents of the second edition, we should start with noting that we have a new sub-title: "Awareness of illness in schizophrenia and related disorders". This is because the term insight is still subject to many different definitions and we did not want to lose potentially interested readers through a misunderstanding of the nature of the contents of the book. Furthermore, we have found that the term "psychosis" is generally falling out of favour in North American psychiatry, while it is still regarded as useful as a broad class of disorder in Europe and other parts of the world. Hence, as a compromise the sub-title serves to emphasize the breadth and scope of the clinical conditions we wish to discuss within the book, but also to underline the centrality of schizophrenia in these discussions. Presumably if we ever get to a third edition we may have to broaden the remit to take account of research and activity in other areas of psychiatry and neurology.

The first chapter is by Amador and Kronengold. This again outlines, in more detail, the issue of description and definition of the term insight in its different guises. Since the first edition there are now a number of semi-structured interviews, rating scales and other research instruments for researchers to choose from. Indeed, there is a sufficient array of assessment instruments that a cool and objective assessment of the relative strengths and weaknesses of each of these is long overdue. The conceptual history of insight and psychosis is, paradoxically, an area which continues to evolve. And the old adage regarding those who fail to acknowledge history being condemned to repeat it is as true in this context as any other. The same could be said for the philosophical interrogation that Bill Fulford gives insight in this new edition. Professor Fulford makes explicit his debt to German psychopathologists, Jaspers and Kraepelin, as well as British philosopher J. L. Austin.

We are delighted to include in this new edition a chapter from the doyen of cognitive approaches to psychopathology, Tim Beck. In his chapter (co-authored with Debbie Warman) we see how Beck's immense clinical experience allows him to tease out the mechanisms underlying the appreciation and acceptance of psychotic symptoms in a way that has previously revolutionized the field of affective disorders. For Beck this represents, in some ways, a return to familiar territory, since his very first and tentative steps into what became cognitive therapy back in the 1950s (Beck, 1952). Suzanne Jolley and Philippa Garety have developed a cognitive approach, which at least implicitly owes much to thinkers such as Beck. In this completely rewritten chapter on delusions they add an important review of a range of theories from social psychology, which forms the basis of a new appraisal of delusional thinking. In particular, it is situated within a continuum model of the normal psychology of belief and attribution. Whatever the rights or wrongs of this theoretical position, there is no doubt that it paves the way for psychological approaches to treatment which might have seemed hopeless and misguided merely a decade ago.

One area that was perhaps neglected in the first edition was a full discussion of insight in affective disorders. This problem has been remedied by a brand new chapter from Ghaemi and Rosenquist. Nassir Ghaemi and colleagues have led an important conceptual attack on insight and awareness in relation to mood, and his group is undoubtedly most influential in this regard. The authors combine both a quantitative meta-analytic approach to the published work in this field as well as a particularly enlightening philosophical stance to the existential dilemma of self-knowledge.

The second section of this edition of *Insight and Psychosis* deals with neuropsychology. This includes the study of people with neurological or neurobehavioral disorders who have difficulties in the area of insight and awareness, a neurological approach to similar difficulties in people with so-called functional disorders, as well as a discussion of the application of neuroscientific tools, particularly neuroimaging in the understanding of insight. The previous edition had two companion chapters by Bill Barr and Richard Keefe, which, in the interests of healthy integration and economy, we felt could be usefully combined into a single overarching essay. Frank Larøi was able to do this with the original authors' help, as well as bringing his own fresh perspective into this important aspect of insight research. Laura Flashman and Robert Roth, who have a background in neuropsychiatry, review neuroimaging work, particularly structural MRI, which has been employed to study people with schizophrenic disorders. They have then tried to relate measures of brain structure to various metrics applied to the insight concept. Flashman and colleagues have contributed original work to this field, which is bound to expand further in the coming years and will probably include more functional neuroimaging studies in the not too distant future. Perhaps the biggest explosion in terms of published research in this field has been in neuropsychological studies examining general and specific cognitive functions in people with psychotic disorders in relation to insight. Although the idea that insight in psychosis might be analogous to a neuropsychological deficit, perhaps of frontal lobe functioning, has been around at least since Aubrey Lewis's review in 1934, it was with landmark studies in the early 1990s that the field really took off. For example, Young and colleagues (Young *et al.*, 1993) found a correlation between various measures from the Wisconsin Card Sorting test, a classical executive function test, and a measure of insight derived from Amador's scale for the assessment of unawareness of mental disorder. There have now been over 30 studies of this kind, which have been systematically reviewed and summarized by Morgan and David in another new addition to this volume.

In part three we look at the wider aspects and implications of insight. Again, critics of some formulations of insight see it as ignoring important cultural and sociological influences. Laurence Kirmayer and colleagues have refined their previous chapter and show how an anthropological perspective allows constructive questioning of the meanings psychiatrists and patients might attach to their experience, which can be summarized in assessments of insight, while at the same time showing the diversity of such experiences in different settings. To quote:

> Viewed this way, an individual may reject a medical explanation, not because they lack insight but because they are giving priority to maintaining social relations and positions that otherwise might be damaged or lost.

Similarly, a particular setting, namely Japan, allows a fascinating "case study", so to speak, where eastern and western concepts of psychopathology have met and have at times rubbed against each other in not wholly constructive ways. Dr Yoshi Kim outlines the sociopolitical context to these phenomenological debates and adds some recent empirical data on the opinions of psychiatrists in the UK and Japan on the importance of insight in their clinical work and classificatory schemes.

While on the one hand we may seek to demonstrate that insight is not an all or none phenomenon, nevertheless, lack of insight or poor insight is a reality with very important and at times destructive consequences. Different perspectives on this are offered by psychiatrist and activist Fuller Torrey. He discusses the relationship between insight as a predictor of violence and also as an element in public understanding or misunderstanding of psychiatric disorders, which might be called stigma. Finally in this section, Ken Kress offers a very provocative proposition, namely that insight or the lack of it is, in his view, the best justification for involuntary treatment, superior, he argues, to notions of competence and capacity. Many may question Kress's faith in the reliability and validity of insight as currently conceived in psychiatry, but few will deny the clarity and force of his arguments.

In the fourth and final part of the new edition of *Insight and Psychosis*, Alec Buchanan and Simon Wessely update their chapter on delusions, action and insight. This deals with some of the same issues considered by Torrey in the previous chapter, but is avowedly clinical in orientation. The relationship between actions, including aggression, as motivated by for example, delusions, is a particular clinical problem faced by general and forensic psychiatrists. Buchanan and Wessely's thorough treatment of this issue will satisfy both academics and clinicians. The same can be said of Joe McEvoy's revised chapter on compliance or adherence with medication and its relationship to insight. This is perhaps the most obvious area of clinical relevance where research and conceptual understanding of insight can have a tangible influence on clinical psychiatry. Lack of adherence to medication is a pervasive problem throughout the whole of medicine and needs to be understood from all sides. Beliefs and understanding about one's illness are a crucial motivator in seeking medical help, and have recently been the target of therapeutic interventions in their own right. Of course, treatment of schizophrenia and related disorders is not merely a matter of taking the appropriate medication. Psychosocial rehabilitation is just as essential and is equally prone to the beliefs and motivations of individuals concerned. Paul Lysaker and Morris Bell have contributed a considerable programme of empirical work on this very question, which they review in a thoroughly updated chapter. As noted earlier on in the Introduction, the views of consumers in this area are crucial and were unfortunately overlooked in the first edition. Fred Frese has the dual qualification of being a psychologist and a consumer, and his description of his own experiences and struggle to understand them are both moving and informative.

Pulling some if not all of these strands together has been a challenging, but rewarding task. We thank all of the contributors for their creativity and discipline in helping us meet our targets and fulfil our aspirations for this volume. Finally, we acknowledge the part played by our publishers, Richard Marley initially, and later Carol Maxwell for their support.

A.S.D.

X.F.A.

References

Beck, A. T. (1952). Successful out-patient psychotherapy of a chronic schizophrenic with a delusion based on borrowed guilt. *Psychiatry*, **15**, 305–12.

Young, D. A., Davila, R. and Scher, H. (1993). Unawareness of illness and neuropsychological performance in chronic schizophrenia. *Schizophrenia Research*, **10**, 117–24.

Contents

Contributors

Xavier F. Amador
Columbia University, Teachers College
and the National Alliance for the
Mentally Ill,
Arlington VA, USA

William B. Barr
New York University School of Medicine,
New York University,
New York NY, USA

Aaron T. Beck
Department of Psychiatry,
University of Pennsylvania,
Philadelphia PA, USA

Morris D. Bell
Psychology Service,
Connecticut Healthcare System,
West Haven CT, USA

German E. Berrios
Department of Psychiatry,
Addenbrooke's Hospital,
Cambridge, UK

Alec Buchanan
Department of Psychiatry,
Yale University,
New Haven CT, USA

Ellen Corin
Departments of Psychiatry and
Anthropology,
McGill University,
Montréal, Québec,
Canada

Anthony S. David
Institute of Psychiatry,
King's College,
London, UK

Laura A. Flashman
Neuropsychology and Neuroimaging,
Program, Dartmouth Medical School,
Dartmouth-Hitchcock Medical
Center,
Hanover NH, USA

Frederick J. Frese III
Summit County Recovery Project,
Summit County ADM Board,
Akron OH, USA

Bill (K. W. M.) Fulford
Department of Philosophy and
Mental Health, University of
Warwick, and
Honorary Consultant Psychiatrist,
University of Oxford,
Oxford, UK

Philippa A. Garety
Academic Psychology Department,
St Thomas' Hospital,
London, UK

S. Nassir Ghaemi
Department of Psychiatry,
Harvard Medical School,
Cambridge Health Alliance,
Cambridge MA, USA

G. Eric Jarvis
Department of Psychiatry,
McGill University, and
Cultural Consultation Service,
The Sir Mortimer B. Davis – Jewish
General Hospital,
Montréal, Québec,
Canada

Suzanne Jolley
Adamson Centre for Mental Health,
St Thomas' Hospital,
London, UK

Richard S. E. Keefe
Duke University Medical Center,
Durham NC, USA

Yoshiharu Kim
Division of Adult Mental Health,
National Institute of Mental Health,
Chiba, Japan

Laurence J. Kirmayer
The Sir Mortimer B. Davis – Jewish
General Hospital, and
Division of Social and Transcultural
Psychiatry,
McGill University,
Montréal, Québec,
Canada

Ken J. Kress
University of Iowa College of Law,
Iowa City IA, USA

Henry Kronengold
Department of Psychology
Soloman Schechter School of Manhattan
New York NY, USA

Frank Larøi
Cognitive Psychopathology Unit,
Department of Cognitive Sciences,
University of Liège,
Liège, Belgium

Paul H. Lysaker
Indiana University School of Medicine,
Rudebush VA Medical Center,
Indianapolis IN, USA

Ivana S. Marková
Department of Psychology,
University of Stirling,
Stirling, UK

Joseph P. McEvoy
Duke University Medical Center,
Durham NC, and
Department of Psychiatry and
Behavioral Science,
John Umstead Hospital,
Butner NC, USA

Kevin D. Morgan
Department of Psychological
Medicine,
Institute of Psychiatry,
Kings College London,
London, UK

Klara J. Rosenquist
Harvard Medical School and
Cambridge Hospital Bipolar Disorder,
Research Program,
Cambridge MA, USA

Robert M. Roth
Neuropsychology Program and
Brain Imaging Laboratory
Neuropsychiatry Section,
Dartmouth Medical School,
Dartmouth-Hitchcock Medical Center,
Hanover NH, USA

E. Fuller Torry
The Stanley Medical Research
Institute,
Bethesda MD, USA

Debbie M. Warman
School of Psychological Sciences,
University of Indianapolis,
Indianapolis IN, USA

Simon C. Wessely
Department of Psychological
Medicine,
Institute of Psychiatry,
King's College London,
London, UK

Part 1

Phenomenology and psychology

Chapter 1

Understanding and assessing insight

Xavier F. Amador and Henry Kronengold

When speaking to individuals with schizophrenia and other psychotic disorders about their illness and the need for treatment, clinicians and family members alike are often frustrated by the patient's extreme lack of insight. People diagnosed with psychotic disorders have similarly been frustrated with their friends, family members, and doctors who insist they have a serious mental illness when they are absolutely certain that they do not. Poor insight frustrates attempts by clinicians and concerned family members to help. Such patients, feeling coerced into accepting medication and services for a condition they do not believe they have, do what any of us would do: they refuse the help if possible, or if not, they accept it only for as long as it takes to gain their freedom (from hospital or social pressures). Owing to its prevalence and disruption of relationships with therapists and family caregivers, this dramatic discrepancy in perspective or what we in the mental health field have labeled "poor insight" – has increasingly become the subject of scientific, legal and clinical attention.

To understand insight in psychotic disorders, one must start from a historical perspective. For many years, the published literature reflected a largely theoretical and psychoanalytic perspective. This literature offered few guidelines regarding the phenomenology or measurement of the psychological processes that were thought to constitute insight (Amador, Strauss, Yale and Gorman, 1991). Furthermore, the analytic literature's almost exclusive reliance on the subjective interpretation of case studies resulted in a premature consensus that poor insight was the result of an unconscious psychological defense or a conscious coping strategy. Until relatively recently the lack of empirical methods and data, coupled with preconceptions as to the causes of poor insight, have hampered progress in this area. However, over the past 15 years, the topic of insight has become increasingly popular among researchers studying psychotic disorders. Indeed, since the publication of the first edition of *Insight and Psychosis*, more than 200 studies focused on insight and schizophrenia have been published in the peer reviewed scientific literature.[1]

Whereas most articles about insight used to rely on quite interesting but nonstandardized clinical anecdotes, there is now a substantial literature devoted to the empirical

---

[1] MEDLINE search from 1998 through November 2003 using key words/terms "schizophrenia", "insight into illness" and "awareness of illness."

examination of insight in psychotic disorders. At the time of the first edition of *Insight and Psychosis*, the empirical literature regarding insight was just beginning to emerge and some of the critical questions concerning the phenomenology, measurement and etiology of insight were just taking form. In addition, the literature of that time was dominated by studies and discussions of insight that often lacked standardization with respect to research design and measurement. Today the literature has grown and matured, and with it our understanding as well as continued questions about insight and psychosis have both deepened and become more refined.

As we survey the growing interest in insight, we begin to consider why this area of study has emerged and grown so rapidly. One factor undoubtedly has to do with the fact that in the early 1990's investigators began to develop more reliable and valid methods to assess insight leading to an explosion of new studies that illuminate the role that poor insight plays in the prognosis, course, and treatment of these disorders. Among the findings consistently reported is that deficits in insight most often stem from the disorder itself, from brain dysfunction, rather than from defensive coping strategies (DSM IV-TR, APA press, 2000; see below). Another common finding is that poor insight is among the best predictors of nonadherence and partial adherence to medication. With nonadherence rates continuing to hover at around 50% despite the improved side-effect profiles of second generation antipsychotics, increasing interest in psychological/behavioral interventions aimed at either improving insight and/or compliance has also flourished (see McEvoy, Chapter 15).

In this chapter, we begin by briefly reviewing the history of the use of the term "insight" in psychiatry, followed by a review of current methods and challenges related to its assessment. We then consider the relationship between insight and symptoms of psychosis before moving on to suggest the unique role of poor insight in schizophrenia. We conclude by discussing the etiological factors underlying the development of deficits in illness awareness, or poor insight, and discuss the implications for therapeutic strategies designed to either improve insight and/or remedy the serious problems created by it (e.g., nonadherence to treatment and services and estrangement from caregivers).

What is insight?

Any survey of the literature on insight requires the skill to navigate through an often bewildering sea of terms that have been applied to the observed unawareness of illness (or lack of a consensual perspective) so common in psychotic disorders. Descriptors such as "poor insight", "sealing over", "defensive denial", "attitudes about illness", "indifference reaction", "evasion", and "external attributions" (David, 1990; Greenfeld, Strauss, Bowers and Mandelkern, 1989; Wciorka, 1988; McGlashan, Levy and Carpenter, 1975) reflect important underlying conceptual differences in addition to semantic differences. On one end of the spectrum poor insight is understood as a psychological defense mechanism, while at the other extreme it is conceptualized as a neurocognitive deficit. In between lies a quagmire of related constructs that vary with the orientations of their authors.

Researchers grounded in cognitive psychology have examined the "external attributions about illness" (Wciorka, 1988), while psychodynamically oriented authors have distinguished emotional versus intellectual forms of insight (Richfield, 1954). A more detailed discussion of the conceptual history of insight in psychotic disorders can be found in the chapter by Berrios and Markova in this volume. One fact emerges when reviewing the various terms and conceptualizations that have been reported over time – insight is a complex and multidimensional phenomenon.

Wciorka et al. (1988) and others (Greenfeld et al., 1989; David, 1990; Amador et al., 1991) have argued that insight comprises a variety of phenomena, including retrospective and current insight. As we shall discuss in greater detail, Amador et al. (1991) and David (1990) have stressed the distinction between awareness and attribution, or labeling, of psychotic symptoms, as some patients may recognize signs of illness but attribute their presence to reasons other than mental dysfunction. Furthermore, some patients may recognize certain symptoms while remaining unaware of others. Markova and Berrios (1993) proposed further complexity by conceptualizing awareness of illness as a subcategory of self-knowledge rather than an independent feature of psychotic disorders. Finally, any discussion of insight raises epistemological presumptions about the nature of reality (David, 1990). Philosophical considerations aside, the phenomenon of insight relevant to mental health professionals is one in which an individual's perception of him or herself is grossly at odds with that of his or her community and culture. Indeed, as we shall discuss with particular reference to individuals with schizophrenia, this perception may even differ from the views of similarly affected psychiatric patients (Wing, Monck, Brown and Carstairs, 1964).

At the most fundamental level, poor insight in psychosis has been described as a seeming lack of awareness of the deficits, consequences of the disorder, and need for treatment. We will use the term *unawareness of illness* in this broadest sense (see Amador et al., 1991) unless we are describing specific methods and definitions used to assess insight.

The measurement of insight

Much of the early literature on insight in schizophrenia relied heavily on case material describing patients' beliefs regarding their illness. While this method offered a rich context in which to view each patient's self-assessment, it offered little in the way of replicable research. As a result, investigators began to devise standardized interviews or systematized scoring methods to assess insight. Unfortunately, few researchers combined a standardized interview with a systematic scoring system, and many early studies struggled with either a continued reliance on subjective clinical observations or a preconceived scoring system that did not always do justice to patients' free responses. In addition, early attempts to rate insight typically relied on crude global ratings that classified patients as having "good" or "poor" insight based on whether the patient "vigorously denied he was disturbed". Over the past fifteen years, semi-structured interviews with systematized scoring systems and proven psychometric strengths have been devised to measure insight.

The first such measure to be used widely was The Insight and Treatment Attitudes Questionnaire (ITAQ) developed by McEvoy et al. (1981). The ITAQ has been used in large samples of patients with schizophrenia and has been shown to be reliable and valid. An 11 item questionnaire, the ITAQ assesses patients' attitudes (or beliefs) about whether they have a mental illness and whether they need treatment. Though predictive of several measures of clinical outcome and compliance (McEvoy et al., 1981; McEvoy, Apperson et al., 1989; McEvoy, Freter et al., 1989), the ITAQ fails to assess many of the psychological domains that other investigators believe constitute "insight". Indeed, although this scale represented significant progress in the assessment of insight, it continues in the tradition of viewing insight as a unitary phenomenon.

Adopting a multidimensional view, both Amador et al. (1991; Amador, Strauss, Yale; Gorman and Endicott, 1993; Amador and Strauss, 1993), and David (1990) have proposed a more complex view of insight as comprised of overlapping but distinct factors. David's Schedule for the Assessment of Insight (SAI) assesses insight based on a patient's recognition of having a mental illness, compliance with treatment, and ability to label unusual events, such as delusions and hallucinations, as pathological. This measure does not, however, consider how insight may vary from symptom to symptom, nor does it consider differences between current and retrospective insight into illness.

Amador et al. (1991) take the multidimensional view further by distinguishing two main component dimensions of insight: awareness of illness and attribution regarding illness. *Unawareness* of *illness* reflects an individual's failure to acknowledge the presence of a specific deficit or sign of illness even when confronted with it by an examiner. Incorrect *attribution* reflects the individual's expressed belief that the specific deficit, sign, or consequence of illness does not stem from mental dysfunction. For example: a patient with severe flat affect who does not recognize the presence of this negative symptom illustrates unawareness of flat affect; a patient who is aware that her or his expressions of emotion were flattened, but is certain that this was due to a recent course of antibiotics, would be said to be aware but would display incorrect attribution regarding this sign of illness.

Consistent with this conception of insight, Amador and Strauss (1990) developed the Scale to assess Unawareness of Mental Disorder (SUMD). In addition to the independent assessment of awareness and attribution, the SUMD distinguishes current and retrospective awareness of (1) having a mental disorder, (2) the effects of medication, (3) the consequences of mental disorder, and (4) the specific signs and symptoms. The SUMD, therefore, represented a departure from other published measures that assess whether the patient accepts a diagnostic label or whether the patient believes in the benefit of treatment.

The assessment of insight regarding specific symptoms offers at least two important benefits: first, it can provide data on moderating variables useful for studies of psychoeducational strategies (e.g., are patients more likely to be unaware of particular symptoms?); second, these assessments are of importance theoretically, as they can provide data on the nature and pervasiveness of poor insight. Since its development, the SUMD has gained widespread acceptance as a *multidimensional* measure of insight and has been validated and studied on a range of clinical samples. It has been translated into fourteen languages by investigators in non-English speaking countries interested in studying insight. Nevertheless, as we will argue below, the SUMD may often not be the appropriate measure of insight one should use in their study.

Individuals with psychosis express subtle variations of insight that defy easy categorization. Complicating matters is the fact that some patients flatly refuse to answer what they perceive as intrusive questions about their past and present experiences with mental illness, especially if these experiences leave the patient feeling stigmatized. To circumvent these and other problems Selten and colleagues and Markova and Berrios have each developed self-rating scales to assess insight. Interested in negative symptoms, Selten, Sijben, vanden Bosch, Omloo-Visser and Warmerdam (1993) developed a self-rating scale that measures the patient's Subjective Experience of Negative Symptoms (SENS). An interviewer describes each symptom to the patient and then asks the patient to rate him or herself compared to other people who have not been admitted to the hospital. Designed to complement the Scale for the Assessment of Negative Symptoms (SANS) (Andreasen, 1989), the SENS allows for a fairly simple measure of insight that can be readily compared, to an interviewer's clinical ratings.

Markova and her colleagues also developed a self-rated Insight Scale (Markova and Berrios, 1992). Consisting of 32 items that are answered yes, no, or don't know, the Insight Scale attempts to broaden the measurement of insight by assessing deficits in self-knowledge not only related to illness, but also to how the illness affects a patient's interaction with the world. While most measures of insight focus on having a "mental disorder" or assess symptoms such as hallucinations, Markova *et al.* present the patient with statements such as "I feel different from my normal self" or "I want to know why I am feeling like this" to address the process of insight along a continuum of self-knowledge. Patients may realize that a change has occurred within them without being able to label this change as a mental disorder. Markova and Berrios's emphasis on insight as a dynamic process offers an important contribution to the understanding of poor insight. Recent research has attempted to establish insight as an identifiable symptom of psychotic disorders, and later in this chapter we will present evidence to support this contention. At the same time, poor insight may reflect a broader disturbance of a patient's self-representation or self-schema, as Markova and Berrios imply. In that spirit, the Insight Scale has encouraged further research into insight as it relates to the complexity of self-experience in individuals with psychotic disorders.

Any method of assessing awareness of illness must take the individual's culture and subculture into account. While early studies by the World Health Organization which we will discuss shortly suggested that insight can be consistently measured cross-culturally, a study by Johnson and Orrell (1995) argues for greater sensitivity to sociocultural bias in the assessment of insight. Johnson and Orrell examined the case records of 357 inpatients and compared demographic variables including gender, age, previous psychiatric history, and ethnic origin with comments describing the patient's levels of insight. Classifying these comments as indicating either little or no insight, partial insight, or full insight, Johnson and Orrell found that Caucasian patients were rated as displaying significantly greater insight than patients from ethnic minority groups. Only 47% of the Caucasian British patients, compared to 70% of the patients from other ethnic groups, were viewed as having little or no insight. Furthermore, when entered into a regression analysis with the other variables, ethnicity emerged as the most significant independent factor influencing perceived insight.

Discussing various explanations to account for these results, Johnson and Orrell consider the possibility that patients from social groups where mental illness is especially stigmatized may be more likely to deny their illness or that different sociocultural groups may entertain different models of mental illness from that of Western psychiatry. They also suggest that patients from ethnic minorities may not be admitted to the hospital unless they are more severely ill than Caucasian British patients, and that more severely ill patients display poorer insight – a debatable position that we will discuss in the next section of this chapter.

The most important possibility from a methodological perspective concerns the possible sociocultural bias related to ratings of insight. Perhaps, as Johnson and Orrell point out, patients from ethnic minorities are more likely to be viewed by clinicians as lacking insight. If so, we need to understand the causes of such distortions as well as the means with which to correct them. Clearly, further research into the cross-cultural aspects of insight is needed. Sociocultural factors may influence patients' views of themselves, and in the process affect the levels of insight that are perceived by Western-trained clinicians and raters. These factors may also influence our understanding of what we consider psychotic symptoms. Though sociocultural factors should be examined as they relate to all aspects of psychiatric assessment, they seem especially pertinent to the measurement of an individual's potentially cultural-bound experiences of self that constitute our understanding of insight in psychotic disorders.

Different measures of insight

Researchers must employ precise terminology and methodology if the field is to progress further. It is unfortunate that through nonspecificity and inconsistency in using standardized measures a substantial portion of the studies that have been published since the last edition of this book have yielded results that are often difficult to interpret and/or compare to other studies. Some studies of the relations between aspects of insight and clinical variables such as outcome, medication adherence, psychosocial functioning and neuropsychological performance have yielded *seemingly* contrary results. More often than not such divergent results are because differences between measures used in studies have not been clarified. Comments made by investigators when comparing their results to that of others without first articulating the similarities and differences in terminology and methodology used are often at the root of the problem. This impedes progress by causing confusion and erroneous claims of "failure to replicate".

Similarly, it has been difficult to generalize from the results of various studies because many did not use reliable and valid measures of insight. Although significant progress has been made in this area, the problem still persists. Our hope is that by comparing various methods of assessing insight with special focus on the psychometric strengths and weaknesses of each, researchers will be able to more easily compare and contrast the results of their studies to those of others that used differing measures.

Ghaemi and Pope (1994, p. 31) are exceedingly clear in emphasizing this very point "the definition and measurement of insight in various studies are not standardized, so comparing studies with one another may be misleading. Also, insight measures are frequently not systematic or particularly detailed". It is perhaps more useful to note examples that contain aspects of the clarity we are encouraging. One such example can be found in a report by Michelakeas *et al.* (1994). In this report, the authors start by highlighting issues surrounding the concept of insight and put their own methodology into a historical and conceptual perspective. Their description of the methods used to investigate the relationship between particular aspects of insight and important clinical variables was detailed and concise: e.g., when interpreting differences in "insight" between patient groups they note: "This [finding] may be due to the instrument used ... (ITAQ), which concentrates on the issues of being ill and in need of treatment ... (p. 48)." Their discussion included references to scales developed since their investigation commenced and the relative strengths and limitations of their measure of insight was discussed.

It behooves us all to follow the example set by David *et al.* (1995) when they wrote: "*Insight, as estimated by the PSE* ... (p. 626)." One would not write about "cognitive deficits" or "negative symptoms" without at some point clarifying which deficits/symptoms and the instrument used to measure it. An equally laudable example comes from Swanson *et al.* (1995) who made a well-defined observation regarding the fact that aspects of insight differed in patients with mania versus schizophrenia. In their discussion of their results they note that "*when acutely ill, manic patients are especially unlikely to attribute any symptom to a mental illness*..." (p. 754) and that this aspect of poor insight was not as severe in the patients with schizophrenia.

Over the past decade it has become widely accepted that there are indeed numerous dimensions to insight into illness. What we have learned from the problems we have described is that the assessment of insight and its description in the literature must be targeted and specific to be meaningful and useful (Amador and Seckinger, 1997). Obviously, precision in describing the aspects of insight one is interested in evaluating has

Table 1.1 Measures of insight and their basic characteristics

Measures of insight	Number of items	Type of scale
The Scale to Assess Unawareness of Mental Disorder (SUMD) *Amador and Strauss, 1990 (26)*	74	Not all items rated for every patient Likert
Insight and Treatment Attitude Questionnaire (ITAQ) *McEvoy et al., 1989 (33)*	11	All items relevant Dichotomous
Schedule to Assess the Components of Insight (SAI) *David, 1990 (37)*	3	Not all items rated for every patient Likert
Positive and Negative Syndrome Scale (PANSS) insight item (G14) *Kay et al., 1987 (38)*	1	Item relevant to all patients Likert
Present State Exam (PSE) item 104 *Wing et al., 1974 (39)*	1	Item relevant to all patients Likert
Manual for the Assessment and Documentation of Psychopathology (AMDP System) *Guy and Ban, 1982 (52)*	3	All items relevant Dichotomous
Soskis Scale *Soskis and Bowers, 1969 (43)*	6	All items relevant Dichotomous
A self-report Insight Scale for psychosis (IS) *Birchwood et al., 1994 (53)*	3	All items relevant Likert
The Insight Scale (self-report) *Markova et al., 1992 (40)*	32	All items relevant Dichotomous

advantages over labeling insight broadly. In an effort to facilitate the choice investigators must make when designing studies we provide a comparative chart listing various measures of insight that have been reported in the literature (Table 1.1). Our choice of scales to highlight was guided by their frequency of use and the availability of published data on their reliability and validity. To our knowledge, no widely used scales have been published since this table was first published (see Amador and Seckinger, 1997). We have not presented data on reliability and validity as this is covered in reports by the instrument's authors and in our previous paper (Amador and Seckinger, 1997).

We focus here on a discussion of the core characteristics of those instruments in Table 1.1 that are the most widely used. The Insight and Treatment Attitudes Questionnaire (ITAQ) (McEvoy *et al.*, 1989), is comprised of eleven items designed to assess patients' recognition of illness and the need for treatment. The response of the patient is scored as 2 = good insight, 1 = partial insight and 0 = no insight. The ITAQ employs a narrow definition of insight and does not assess many of the psychological domains that are believed to comprise insight into illness more generally. That said, the ITAQ is particularly useful for evaluating acceptance of a diagnostic label and views about whether or not treatment is needed.

The Scale to assess Unawareness of Mental Disorder (Amador and Strauss, 1990), is a semi-structured interview that evaluates insight as a multidimensional phenomenon. Items are rated on a five point Likert scale. The SUMD distinguishes between two main dimensions of insight – awareness of illness and attribution regarding illness. In addition the SUMD allows for the independent assessment of current and retrospective awareness of having a mental disorder, awareness of particular signs and symptoms, benefit from treatment, and the psychosocial consequences of having a mental disorder. The SUMD can be used to assess either current or retrospective insight and like nearly all measures of insight cited above, it is useful for evaluating patients' endorsement of the diagnostic label (e.g., I have bipolar disorder). Unlike other scales the SUMD assess patient's understanding of how the psychiatric medication has affected them and their awareness of the consequences of having a mental disorder. This measure is also unique in its detailed assessment of patients' awareness of, and attribution for, a wide range of signs and symptoms. Because of this last feature, the SUMD can be cumbersome and lengthy. On the other hand, the scale is modular and can be shortened in a number of different ways (e.g., rate only general items and not awareness of symptoms or rate only awareness of positive symptoms, etc.). The SUMD does not rate the patient's belief about whether treatment is needed, which can be a major limitation depending on the focus of the planned study.

David (1990) proposed that insight is comprised of three overlapping dimensions: the recognition that one has a mental illness, compliance with treatment and the ability to relabel unusual mental events, such as delusions and hallucinations, as pathological. The Schedule to Assess Insight (SAI) explores insight beyond the acknowledgment of illness and the need for treatment. It includes the assessment of attributions: e.g., the patients' ability to classify the morbidity of their psychotic experience. However, the original SAI does not evaluate patients' awareness of, and attribution for, specific signs and symptoms. Its focus centers on the assessment of a patient's awareness of having a mental disorder, the need for treatment and the ability to relabel certain experiences, common in psychosis, as pathological. This has been remedied by the expanded version (Sanz et al., 1998; see David Chapter 18).

The Positive and Negative Syndrome Scale has a single item assessing insight (PANSS, [s2]) which appears on the General Psychopathology subscale (item G12). The patient is rated on a scale from 1 to 7 with 1 signifying the *"absence or lack of judgment and insight"* and 7 representing *"extreme lack of judgment and insight"*. Although the PANSS has recommended interview probes designed to elicit different dimensions of insight, the rating scale itself defines the degree of insight unidimensionally. For example, although a particular rating provides a general idea of where the patient is with respect to awareness and attributions, it does not break these dimensions out separately. Because it consists on a single item, as a measure of insight it is inherently less reliable and lacking in construct validity compared to other measures reviewed here. On the other hand, a unique advantage is that many studies that did not focus on insight have already been completed with this instrument (e.g., many drug trials) consequently, there are literally tens of thousands of patients who have had a rough assessment of insight that has never been analyzed (i.e., archived data sets exist).

The Present State Exam (PSE;) also has a single insight item (item 104) that scores responses to probe-questions such as "Do you think there is anything the matter with you?" on a scale from 0–3 with 0 signifying perfect insight, 1 indicating limited insight, and 2 denoting that the patient "agrees to a nervous condition but...does not really accept the explanation in terms of nervous illness (e.g., gives delusional explanation)", and 3 signaling a complete "denial" of the condition. Like the PANSS, the drawbacks of the PSE measure for insight are its inability to detect and record nuances and its reliance on a single item making it an inherently weak measure psychometrically.

Studies reliant on chart review for their dependent measures have used the clinical mental status exam (MSE) to categorize the patient's insight. Insight, as generally assessed by the MSE, is considered present "*if the patient realizes that he is ill and the problem is in his own mind*" (MacKinnon and Yudofsky, 1986). From one clinician to the next such evaluations of insight vary and at times include "judgment" in the assessment. Lacking standardization, a MSE evaluation of insight is truly a measure of last resort.

Markova and Berrios (1992) developed a self-rated Insight Scale based on the premise that insight is a subcategory of self-knowledge rather than an independent feature of psychotic disorders. This measure of insight is conceptually broader than the others discussed above as it goes beyond insight into illness. Their emphasis on the concept of insight as a dynamic process adds another important dimension which suggests that deficits in insight could potentially be indicative of a broader disturbance of a patient's self-representation or self-schema.

Choosing between instruments

When deciding between instruments the first step involves understanding what the various scales assess and what they do not. Table 1.2 is provided to help in this endeavor. In instances where previous studies exist, it behooves the researcher to begin with instruments that have already been used to increase comparability between studies.

For example, if one were particularly interested in studying the effects of motivational enhancement therapy on insight and compliance, one should start with using the SAI which has been used in previous studies of this intervention. Also, one should choose the insight instrument that is relevant to the study hypotheses. If one is studying compliance with medication, for example, insight measures that address a patient's attitudes and/or experiences with medication may be more relevant than those that do not.

The good news is that as a field we now have an array of reliable and valid insight instruments from which to choose. The bad news is that if we choose an instrument based on its

Table 1.2 Dimensions of insight assessed by method

Dimension of insight assessed and reflected in scoring	SUMD	ITAQ	PANSS	SAI	PSE
Acceptance of illness label	√	√	√	√	√
Awareness of having a mental disorder	√			√	
Perceived need for treatment		√		√	
Awareness of the benefits of treatment	√				
Attribution of benefits to treatment	√	√			
Awareness of signs and symptoms	√			√	
Attribution of signs and symptoms to having a mental disorder	√				
Relabeling psychotic experiences correctly				√	
Awareness of social consequences of having a mental disorder	√				
Lack of judgment (acting on one's awarenessof having a mental disorder)			√		
Temporal aspects					
One or more aspects of insight are assessed currently	√	√	√	√	√
One or more aspects of insight are assessed for past periods	√	√			
One or more aspects of insight are assessed with regards to patient's prediction for the future		√			

SUMD – Scale to Assess Unawareness of Mental Disorder (Amador and Strauss, 1990)

ITAQ – Insight and Treatment Attitude Questionnaire (McEvoy *et al.*, 1989)

PANSS – Positive and Negative Syndrome Scale (Kay *et al.*, 1987)

DSAI – Schedule for Assessing the three components of Insight (David, 1990)

PSE – Present State Exam (Wing *et al.*, 1974)

popularity or some other equally irrelevant factor, rather than its relevance to our planned research, we will weaken the design of our study. A final word about choice. To increase comparability between studies it is often preferable to use more than one measure of insight. We have done this on a number of occasions and find that using complimentary measures of insight involves minimal additional effort while the advantages are many.

The relationship between insight and symptoms of psychosis

In the first edition of this book, the relationship between level of insight and severity of symptoms was seen as questionable, with a variety of studies yielding inconsistent results. Over the intervening years, a host of new studies, utilizing standardized and multidimensional measures of insight, have been undertaken to examine the relationship between insight and symptom severity. As reported in the first edition of this book, the earliest studies to examine this relationship yielded inconsistent results (Whittman and Duffey, 1991; Small, Small and Gonzalez, 1965). Subsequent reports, using standardized assessments of symptoms, e.g., Brief Psychiatric Rating Scale (BPRS), (Overall and Gorham 1962); Scale to Assess Positive Symptoms (SAPS), (Andreasen, 1984); and Scale to Assess Negative Symptoms (SANS), (Andreasen, 1984) suggest that insight and severity of symptoms are independent factors (Bartko, Herczeg and Zador, 1988; McEvoy, Apperson *et al.*, 1989; Amador *et al.*, 1993). These studies found no significant correlations between insight and positive or negative symptoms, general measures of symptoms, depressive symptoms, or manic symptoms. However, the issue became clouded by findings of a relationship between poor insight and more severe scores of general psychopathology (Markova *et al.*, 1992; Takei, Uematsu, Ueki and Sone, 1992; Young, Davila and Scher, 1993).

As reported in the first edition of this book, Amador *et al.* (1994) reported on a large scale study conducted as part of the DSM-IV field trails that assessed the nature of the symptom and insight relationship. In patients with schizophrenia, increased delusionality, thought disorder, and disorganized behavior were all modestly correlated with decreased awareness of mental disorder, the social consequences of mental disorder, and several positive symptoms. While these correlations achieved significance, they remained rather modest, with r's ranging from +0.18 to +0.24. The statistical significance of the findings may have been a function of the large sample size (schizophrenia N = 224) and the fact that insight and symptom ratings were not blinded to one another. Amador *et al.* concluded that level of awareness was generally unrelated to symptom severity.

The relationship between insight and symptom severity has important ramifications for our understanding of insight. One may view poor insight as a reflection of symptom severity or delusional beliefs – in other words, more symptomatic or delusional patients would display less awareness of having a mental disorder. If so, poor insight would qualify as an important consequence of psychopathology rather than as a sign of illness in its own right. However, many studies suggest that poor insight is not related or only modestly to moderately correlated to the severity of symptoms, leading one to consider that insight may be an independent phenomenological feature. While we should continue to examine this possible relationship, the studies cited above that support poor insight as independent of symptom severity, coupled with some of the evidence we will present regarding the prevalence of poor insight in psychotic disorders, indicate that severe and persistent unawareness of illness is clearly a symptom of at least schizophrenia if not other psychotic disorders.

Though not necessarily related to general symptomatology, diminished insight appears characteristic of schizophrenia patients with the deficit syndrome. These patients had been previously assessed with respect to the deficit syndrome. Utilizing the SUMD to assess insight, we found that schizophrenia patients with the deficit syndrome displayed significantly poorer insight compared to nondeficit schizophrenia patients. The associations between poor insight and primary negative symptoms were much stronger than the associations found previously between poor insight and both positive and negative symptoms Such findings suggest that while poor insight may not simply reflect global severity of symptoms, it may nonetheless relate to individual or specific groups of symptoms From a theoretical vantage point, the relationship between insight and primary negative symptoms may suggest that poor insight is reflective of an individual's inability to experience emotion, a potentially vital and challenging breakthrough for research that has thus far emphasized the cognitive aspects of insight. As will be discussed later, lack of emotional response to illness, the "la belle indifference" reaction, has potentially identifiable neuropsychological underpinnings. We have hypothesized that the neuropsychological deficits associated with the deficit syndrome, resulting in part in an inability to experience emotion, may also account for the indifference reaction seen in schizophrenia (Amador et al., 1994).

In summary, while recent studies have offered more rigorous methodology, they have not yet offered definitive answers to the question of how insight and the presence and/or severity of symptoms are related in schizophrenia and psychotic disorders (see David Chapter 18). Mintz et al. (2003) examined 40 studies that had been conducted to determine the relationship between insight and symptom severity in schizophrenia. They found that overall, there was a significant, but small, relationship between both positive and negative symptom severity and insight, with age of onset and acute vs. chronic patient status serving as moderating variables.

Our interpretation of the literature to date suggests that studies focusing on different aspects of insight, using differing methods, accounts for the uneven results across studies. Also, in many instances rater bias may account for the relationships found. That is, in studies where the interviewer rates both symptoms of psychosis and awareness of illness, the inherent bias to see sicker patients as having less insight may produce spurious correlations. Nevertheless many studies, including those utilizing blinded insight ratings, find modest correlations between insight and both positive and negative symptoms. If we understand *severe and persistent unawareness* of illness in its various manifestations to be a symptom of the illness, rather than a coping strategy, then correlations with other symptoms, even if only modest, would be expected. Reviews of this literature, if they are to be informative, must distinguish studies being compared to one another with respect to both the *insight measure* (aspects of insight evaluated) used and *whether symptom/insight ratings were blinded* to one another. Otherwise, the third edition of this volume will have nothing new to report with respect to the question of how unawareness of illness relates to other symptoms of psychosis.

Are particular aspects of poor insight unique to schizophrenia?

We agree with those investigators who view schizophrenia as a disorder involving multiple domains of psychopathology (e.g., Carpenter and Kirkpatrick, 1988; Andreasen, 1990; David Chapter 18). In this section, we will examine the question of whether poor insight can be conceptualized as a sign of schizophrenia. As reviewed previously by Amador *et al.* (1991) and Amador and Strauss (1993), and as discussed in this volume by Dr Anthony David, research suggests the prognostic value of insight with regard to treatment compliance and course of illness. However, in order to establish insight as a sign of schizophrenia, we still need to answer two more questions: What is the prevalence of poor insight in schizophrenia? And, is poor insight unique to schizophrenia?

In an attempt to better identify more distinct subtypes of schizophrenia, Carpenter and his associates (1976) employed cluster analytic techniques on quantified sign and symptom data. This study, based on data collected from the International Pilot Study on Schizophrenia (IPSS) (WHO, 1973), provided a unique opportunity to determine whether subtype diagnoses effectively categorize groups of patients across culture. Examining the data from 811 subjects, 680 of whom were diagnosed as schizophrenic, Carpenter *et al.* (1976) found poor insight to be a prevalent feature of schizophrenia as well as an important discriminating factor in making subtype diagnoses.

Along these lines, Carpenter *et al.* (1976) identified four mathematically defined subtypes culled from the 27 dimensions of the Present State Examination (PSE). They labeled these four subtypes, consisting of 573 patients, as typical, flagrant, insightful, and hypochondriacal schizophrenia. Typical schizophrenia was characterized by poor insight, persecutory and passivity delusions, auditory hallucinations, restricted affect, and withdrawal. Flagrant schizophrenia included aberrant, agitated, or bizarre incomprehensibility, unkempt appearance, incongruent or restricted affect, and the absence of anxiety or depression. Insightful schizophrenia shared many of the characteristics of typical schizophrenia, but had good rather than poor insight and did not include behavioral aberrance other than social withdrawal. The fourth subtype, hypochondriacal schizophrenia, was characterized by intermediate insight and was distinguished by increased somatic concerns and visual hallucinations. The authors highlight several methodological difficulties regarding the use of cluster analytic techniques to define diagnostic groups and cautioned that their results should be considered preliminary, pending replication and validity studies. Despite these limitations, Carpenter's findings strongly support the importance of insight as a common feature of schizophrenia.

In a multinational study, entitled Classification of Chronic Hospitalized Schizophrenics (CCHS), the 12 signs and symptoms of the Flexible System Criteria (Carpenter, Strauss and Bartko, 1973) were assessed in a relatively chronic sample of 768 patients (Wilson, Ban and Guy, 1986). The results of this study replicated the IPSS finding of high rates of poor insight in schizophrenia. Across both the CCHS and IPSS samples, poor insight occurred more often than did any other dimension and ranked among the least variable dimensions of schizophrenia across subtypes. While the study by Johnson and Orrell discussed earlier raised the question of sociocultural bias in the assessment of insight, both of these multicultural studies found comparable rates of insight and, as such, support the notion of insight as a cross-culturally stable identifiable characteristic of mental illness.

In both the CCHS and the IPSS studies, insight was defined as present "if there was some awareness of emotional illness" and absent if the patient "vigorously denied he was disturbed" (WHO, 1973). Such a conservative definition of insight requires only that the patient express some awareness of emotional illness. In the IPSS, awareness did not need be accompanied by correct attribution for specific signs and symptoms (e.g., aware that they have specific symptoms and accurately identify these as a consequence of mental illness) in order to be called insight. Similarly, their definition of insight did not include recognition of the need for treatment. One can argue that a patient who vigorously denies the existence of a mental illness may display a defensive response to escape the depressing reality of his or her situation (Van Putten, Crumpton and Yale, 1976). Consequently, the definition of insight used in these studies may have identified something other than lack of awareness. Furthermore, as a result of the global and unitary definition of insight used in the above studies, we cannot determine if any of the patients displayed at least partial awareness of various aspects of the disorder. We also cannot determine whether any of the patients were aware of the particular signs or symptoms of schizophrenia, the consequences of the disorder, or the effects of medication.

Such limitations aside, these studies offer clear support for a consideration of poor insight as a common feature of psychotic disorders. Moreover, Carpenter et al. (1973) reported that poor insight was one of 12 signs and symptoms that were "especially discriminating between schizophrenia and other psychiatric disorders" (p. 1275). Though not clear-cut, this finding at least suggests that poor insight is a unique feature of schizophrenia.

In 1994 a collaboration with the Schizophrenia and Psychotic Disorders Work Group was empanelled by the American Psychiatric Association to revise the diagnostic criteria for schizophrenia in the Diagnostic and Statistical Manual for Mental Disorders (DSM-III-R) (APA, 1987). An abbreviated version of the SUMD was used in the assessment procedure for the DSM- IV field trials. In this study, more than 400 patients from geographically diverse regions of the United States were evaluated for a wide range of symptoms. The main objective of the insight study was to determine the prevalence of poor insight in psychotic disorders and to examine its specificity to schizophrenia (Amador et al., 1994).

The results indicated that nearly 60% of the patients with schizophrenia displayed moderate to severe unawareness of having a mental disorder. This finding replicates the IPSS report and the CCHS study results, which both indicated that a majority of patients with schizophrenia believe they do not have a mental disorder. In addition, in the DSM-IV field trial sample, between 27 and 87% of the patients with schizophrenia were also unaware of specific symptoms, for example, delusions, thought disorder, blunt affect, anhedonia, asociality, and other dimensions of illness. The prevalence of unawareness of symptoms has not previously been reported in the literature. Importantly, patients with schizophrenia were significantly less aware of having a mental disorder, the efficacy of medication, various aspects of delusion, and anhedonia, than were mood-disorder patients. Similarly, patients with schizophrenia also had poor awareness of various symptoms (hallucinations, delusions, anhedonia, and asociality) relative to schizoaffective patients. Furthermore, patients with schizophrenia had poor insight into many aspects of their illness compared to patients with a psychotic or nonpsychotic major depressive disorder. Items where these two groups did not differ tended to have small sample sizes that drastically reduced the statistical power necessary to adequately compare the two groups. These results suggest that at least some aspects of poor insight (i.e., severe and pervasive deficits in self-awareness) are uniquely characteristic of schizophrenia when compared to other psychotic disorders – the one exception to this rule being patients with bipolar disorder. These conclusions were partially supported by a more recent study where Pini et al. which found that patients with schizophrenia displayed poor insight relative to patients with schizoaffective disorder, though schizophrenia patients did not differ from mood-disorder patients with respect to insight (Pini et al., 2001).

Qualifications in hand, the literature on insight reviewed earlier and the DSM-IV field trail data support the commonly held belief that patients with schizophrenia, as well as other psychotic disorders, display poor insight and that level of insight is an important dimension on which patients can be subtyped. The field trial data also provide the first direct evidence suggesting that poor insight, or self-awareness deficits, is more severe and pervasive among individuals with schizophrenia. These results, taken together with the data reviewed above regarding the relations between level of insight and severity of psychopathology, suggest that poor insight is not simply a consequence of increased symptom severity. If poor insight appeared solely on the basis of psychotic symptoms, we would not expect to find any difference between patients with schizophrenia and other patients with psychotic disorders. We would also have expected to find at least moderate correlations between unawareness and symptoms. We did not. Instead, poor insight in this sample appeared to be an independent feature of the schizophrenia.

More recently, we have elaborated on our thesis that unawareness of illness may help distinguish schizophrenia from other psychotic disorders and further help to subtype patients with schizophrenia (Amador and Gorman, 1998; Ratakonda et al., 1998). In particular, we have proposed that severe and persistent unawareness of illness is another manifestation of the frontal lobe pathology that is so common in schizophrenia. A further rationale and exploration of this conceptualization will be presented in the next section, where we discuss the possible causes of poor insight.

The etiology of poor insight in schizophrenia

While a variety of hypotheses exist to explain poor insight in schizophrenia, two approaches tend to predominate in the literature. One of these approaches considers poor insight in schizophrenia as a psychological defense or adaptive coping mechanism. The other, more contemporary view suggests the role of neurological abnormalities and neuropsychological deficit in the etiology of poor insight in schizophrenia. While recent studies have clearly favored neuropsychological deficit as the likely root of severe and persistent unawareness of illness, a thorough examination of both factors offers a richer perspective of the phenomenon of poor insight.

Psychological defense

Historically, self-awareness deficits in schizophrenia have typically been understood as stemming from psychological defenses or adaptive coping strategies (e.g., Lally, 1989; Levy *et al.*, 1975; Mayer-Gross, 1920; McGlashan and Carpenter, 1976; Semrad, 1966; Searles, 1965; Van Putten *et al.*, 1976). In 1920, Mayer-Gross classified the defensive strategies of patients with schizophrenia and offered two categories highly relevant to the present discussion: denial of the future and denial of the psychotic experience. In the denial of the future category, patients were observed to deny the possibility of positive future events (i.e., they expressed "despair"), even when such events were of high likelihood. Meanwhile, in the denial of the psychotic experience category, patients were typically unaware of the signs and symptoms of the illness. This latter stage is of direct relevance to the present discussion; while the former combines unawareness phenomena (e.g., denial of relevant data for making predictions about the future) with attributional processes. Essentially, Mayer-Gross identified various domains for which patients with schizophrenia displayed awareness deficits and interpreted this finding as evidence for distinct categories of psychological defense.

Similarly, McGlashan and Carpenter (1976) identified the relationship between postpsychotic depression (PPD) and denial in schizophrenia. In their review of the literature, they cite several authors who consider PPD as a stage of recovery from psychosis that either follows a more "primitive" defensive state characterized by denial or precedes the reinstatement of psychotic denial. Despite their differences, these authors share the view that PDD stems from a lessening of defensive denial, resulting in the patient's awareness of the tragic circumstances of his or her illness. In short, this view states that patients who accept rather than deny the reality of their psychotic experiences are prone to depression. In the process, this view of PPD implies a defensive function for denial in schizophrenia.

In other work, McGlashan, Levy and Carpenter (1975) have suggested a continuum of recovery styles: on one end lies integration, and on the other sealing over. Fourteen neuroleptic withdrawn, "generally nonpsychotic" patients with schizophrenia were interviewed 12 months following an acute psychotic episode. Patient responses during a taped structured interview were reliably categorized into either the integration or sealing over categories. The raters employed the following criteria for making this distinction: (1) Some patients prefer not to think about their psychotic experience during recovery and adopt an attitude of "the less said the better". Such individuals were referred to as sealing over patients. (2) Some patients manifest an interest in their psychotic experiences during recovery and are willing to discuss their experiences in an effort to learn more about themselves. These patients would be considered integrators (McGlashan *et al.*, 1975, p. 1270). Responses from each group were evaluated and led the authors to conclude that integrators displayed an awareness of the continuity of their personality before, during, and after their psychotic episode. These patients "took responsibility" for their psychotic symptoms and were flexible in their thoughts about them. Meanwhile, patients that sealed over were either unaware of their psychotic experience or viewed their psychotic experiences as alien, caused by some force outside themselves.

While psychoanalytic approaches emphasize the role of unconscious defense in poor insight, more cognitively oriented research emphasizes the importance of attribution in understanding poor insight. Evidence suggests that depressed college students and psychiatric outpatients may be more accurate than normal controls in some aspects of self-evaluation, such as in judging social competency and evaluating contingencies between their own behaviors and certain outcomes (Alloy and Abramson, 1979; Lewinsohn, Mischel, Chaplain and Barton, 1980). Similarly, in a study contrasting depressed with nondepressed college students (i.e., mean Beck Depression Inventory Scores for depressed = 16.12, and nondepressed = 1.19), Sackeim and Wegner (1986) found that depressed subjects were more accurate in their self-evaluations (i.e., did not utilize the same self-serving biases) than nondepressed subjects. In a second study, they contrasted depressed inpatients and outpatients with inpatients with schizophrenia and of normal controls. Sackeim and Wegner found that the latter two groups utilized "self-serving biases" in their appraisals of their behaviors and their outcomes, the depressed patients did not. The self-serving biases were characterized as follows: "If an outcome is positive, I controlled it, I should be praised, and the outcome 'good'. If an outcome is negative, I did not control it (as much), I should not be blamed and it was not so bad anyway." The authors go on to say that the cognitive distortions displayed by normal controls and patients with schizophrenia represent a "normal" pattern of functioning. In fact, there is an abundance of work with nonpsychiatric samples that supports this position (see Taylor and Brown, 1988, for a review).

Interestingly, Sackeim and Wegner found no differences between normals and patients with schizophrenia. This finding suggests that in at least some areas of self-awareness, patients with schizophrenia, like most people, utilize a generally adaptive bias to evaluate their behaviors and their outcomes. Taken a step further, these finding may influence our theories about the etiology of poor insight in schizophrenia. The gross unawareness of illness observed in schizophrenia could be explained as a result of the disinhibition of normally adaptive cognitive biases rather than as a cognitive or psychodynamic deficit state. Meanwhile, the more accurate self-appraisals identified in depressives can be understood as a failure of these cognitive biases to influence their normal inhibitory effect on dysphoric mood. In other words, the deficits evident in schizophrenia may result from overuse of normally adaptive cognitive biases. Indeed, Sackeim (1983) has proposed that self-deception (or denial) is adaptive and essential to the regulation of euthymic mood states. Interestingly, a report on insight and medication compliance from Van Putten et al. (1976) seems to support this view. They found a significant inverse relation between grandiosity and insight, leading the authors to hypothesize that medication refusers may prefer a grandiose psychotic state (i.e., extreme self-serving cognitive bias) to the more normal state induced by psychotropic medicine. Recent studies have examined the relationship between insight and symptoms of depression. Smith et al. (1998, 2000), conducted two studies examining the relationship between insight and depression. In their 1998 study of 33 individuals with schizophrenia or schizoaffective disorder, they found that higher levels of depression were associated with both improved awareness and attribution of symptoms. In their 2000 study, Smith et al. examined a sample of 46 individuals with chronic schizophrenia or schizoaffective disorder who had recently been discharged from an inpatient unit. They found that higher levels of depression were strongly associated with good awareness of illness though not with awareness of attribution of symptoms. In a related study, Amador et al. (1996) examined the relationship between insight and suicidality, and found that while schizophrenia patients with recurrent suicidal thoughts and behavior were more aware of certain specific symptoms, they were not generally more aware of having a mental illness. Overall, these studies are somewhat inconsistent in their findings. That said, they do offer qualified support for a relationship between insight and depression, a finding supported by Mintz et al. (2003) in their meta-analysis of the insight literature. The relationship between insight and depression may suggest that poor insight, at least in part, is a consequence of either psychological defense or cognitive coping mechanisms (see Ghaemi et al., Chapter 6).

Neuropsychological deficit

The role of neuropsychological deficit has received the greatest attention of all the areas covered in the initial volume of *Insight and Psychosis*. In earlier papers, Amador et al. suggested that more severe and trait-related problems with insight stem from neuropsychological deficit (Amador et al., 1991, 1993). They noted the similarities seen in patients with schizophrenia and those with anosognosia. Babinski's description of anosognosia, the unawareness of illness in neurological disorders, bears a striking resemblance to poor insight in schizophrenia. He characterizes the anosognostic patient as displaying a lack of knowledge, awareness, or recognition of disease. This has most frequently been observed in patients suffering from hemiplegia and hemianopia following stroke. Gerstmann (1942) offers the following description:

> The hemiplegia is usually on the left side of the body. The patient behaves as though he knew nothing about his hemiplegia, as though it had not existed, as though his paralyzed limbs were normal, and insists that he can move them and walk as well as he did before.
>
> (Gerstmann, 1942, pp. 891–892)

As in schizophrenia, unawareness of illness in neurological disorders is largely intractable to direct confrontation. For example, when an anosognostic patient with hemiparesis is confronted with the affected limb, the patient may express indifference (Gerstmann, 1942) or confabulate (e.g., insist that the limb is not his) to account for the evidence that runs contrary to his belief. As with unawareness of illness in schizophrenia, anosognosia has been understood in varying ways. Terms used besides anosognosia include lack of insight, imperception of disease, denial of illness, and organic depression. McGlynn and Schacter (1989) have provided an extensive review of this literature and the theoretical implications of the various terms. In this volume, the chapter by Larøi, Keefe and Barr provides a comprehensive and up to date review of the neuropsychology of such unawareness.

However, in this introductory chapter we would like to draw attention to some observations in the neurology literature which we think are particularly pertinent to understanding the nature of insight in schizophrenia and related disorders. In neurological disorders, neuroanatomically based theories of anosognosia can be broadly divided into those that attribute this deficit to focal brain lesions and those that emphasize diffuse brain damage (McGlynn and Schacter, 1989). Researchers subscribing to the focal lesion viewpoint generally attribute anosognosia to right-hemisphere lesions of the parietal area and its connections (Gerstmann, 1942; Geschwind, 1965; Von Hagen and Ives, 1939; Warrington, 1962; Critchley, 1953; Stuss and Benson, 1986). Although some reports of anosognosia implicate left-hemisphere insult, the bulk of evidence suggests right-hemisphere lesions (McGlynn and Schactner, 1989; Stuss and Benson, 1986). The findings implicating right-hemisphere involvement in self-awareness deficits have led to several theories suggesting that anosognosia may stem from the isolation of cortical speech areas (Geschwind, 1965), a disconnection from awareness of body schema or image representation (e.g., Gerstmann, 1942; Schilder, 1935), or a neurologically-based affective disturbance (e.g., Bear, 1982).

The frontal lobes have also been implicated in anosognosia. Stuss and Benson (1986) suggest that awareness deficits share an inability to self-monitor or self-correct, and that self-awareness demands intact prefrontal function. They note the similarities among different forms of anosognosia, Capgras syndrome, reduplicative paramnesia, and confabulations frequently seen in Korsakoff syndrome. Specifically, they suggest that these deficits in reality testing stem from a disorder of self-awareness and the ability to self-correct. Although structural damage to the frontal lobe has not been demonstrated in reported disorders of awareness, Stuss and Benson cite a large body of literature implicating prefrontal function as necessary for self-awareness.

Anosognosia has also been observed in patients who have had diffuse brain damage, usually following a stroke (Cole, Saexinger and Hard, 1968; Sandifer, 1946; Ullman, 1962). In these patients, self-awareness deficits are most often understood as stemming from an overall decline in cognitive function. This seems unlikely, however, since anosognosia has been observed in patients without general intellectual impairment

(Gerstmann, 1942; Cutting, 1978; Babinski, 1914) and in patients with unawareness of specific dysfunctions coinciding with intact awareness of other deficits (Von Hagen and Ives, 1939). If anosognosia stemmed from general intellectual impairments, then we would expect awareness deficits for multiple rather than for specific defects.

Of particular interest as it relates to what is commonly observed in schizophrenia is the finding of domain specificity for anosognosia (e.g., Bisiach, Valler, Periani, Papogano and Berti, 1986). For example, Von Hagen and Ives described a 76-year-old patient who denied paralysis of the left leg and yet was aware of the paralysis of the left upper limb and of severe memory impairment. Such observations led some investigators to postulate that these deficits involve modality specific disorders of thought that arise from a dysfunction of a modular central processing system rather than a single higher order system responsible for self-awareness. Schachter (1989) disagrees with this view, and offers a descriptive model for unawareness phenomena referred to as Dissociable Interactions and Conscious Experience (DICE). This model involves a centralized conscious awareness system (CAS) that interacts with modular systems concerned with language, memory, perception, and so forth. In order to occur in a particular domain, the input to the CAS from the relevant module would need to drop to a sufficiently low level of activation to become functionally disconnected from awareness.

The literature on unawareness of tardive dyskinesia in schizophrenia (Tremeau *et al.*, 1997; Rosen *et al.*, 1982; Caracci *et al.*, 1990) suggests that self-awareness deficits in schizophrenia may also be domain specific. Rosen and his associates (1982) found that of 70 patients with schizophrenia who displayed tardive dyskinesia, 47 (67%) were unaware of the deficits produced by the movement disorder. Similarly, Caracci *et al.* (1990) found that 15 of 20 (75%) patients with schizophrenia with tardive dyskinesia (TD) were unaware of their movement disorder. As in the study by Caracci and his colleagues, we found that patients who were unaware of their TD were not could be aware of having schizophrenia and vice versa (Tremeau *et al.*, 1996). In other words, for many of the patients the unawareness of illness could be domain specific: i.e., for movement disorder and/or schizophrenia.

Also of interest is that verbal and visual feedback via videotape resulted in a short-term increase in awareness of TD that was not sustained for longer than two weeks (Caracci *et al.*, 1990). This suggests that denial was not a likely factor in these patients being unaware of their movement disorder. If it were denial, why would cessation of the video feedback result in an immediate regression of knowledge and ability to correctly identify TD?

From the literature reviewed, we can draw clear parallels between the unawareness phenomena described in neurological disorders and what is commonly observed in schizophrenia. In both types of disorder the unawareness is: (1) severe, (2) persists despite conflicting evidence and (3) is often accompanied by confabulations. Confabulations are particularly telling with respect to the nature and severity of the unawareness.

For example, in a letter addressed to his friend Lucilius (Liber V, Epistula IX), L. A. Seneca, writing on the moral implications of self-beliefs 2,000 years ago, described what appears to be a case of anosognosia following hemianopia: "Incredible as it might appear . . . she does. ": she is blind. Therefore, again and again she asks her guardian to take her elsewhere. She claims that my home is dark." Similarly, individuals with schizophrenia are frequently observed to confabulate claiming that they were hospitalized to "get a physical" or solely because "of a fight with my mother".

Affective unawareness has also been described in neurological patients – for example, "Other cases exist in which deficient knowledge of illness is inferred from the apparent lack of adequate emotional reactions, the condition Babinski named 'anosodiaphoria' " (Bisiach *et al.*, 1986, p. 19) – and in schizophrenia – for example, "What always surprises the observer anew is the quiet complacency with which the most nonsensical ideas can be uttered by them and the most incomprehensible actions carried out" (Kraepelin, 1919/1971, p. 25), and "the patients have, at first at least, no real understanding of the gravity of the disorder . . . To all representations of the incomprehensibility and morbidity of their conduct the patients give as answers explanations which say nothing" (Kraepelin, 1919/1971, p. 151). Finally, as described above, the unawareness phenomena observed are frequently heterogeneous in their presentation in both anosognosia and schizophrenia. For example, the anosognostic patient may be aware of a memory deficit but unaware of paralysis. Similarly, we have found that patients with schizophrenia can be aware of having hallucinations and delusions, but not of having a thought disorder or negative symptoms. Or aware of having TD but unaware of having schizophrenia.

Over the past several years, studies have been focused on directly measuring the relationship between poor insight and neurological deficit. This is reviewed comprehensively by Morgan and David (Chapter 9). However, it is worth recalling one of the first studies in this area to see how thinking on this topic has evolved. In a study of 31 chronic patients, Young *et al.* (1993) found a significant correlation between unawareness of illness as measured by the SUMD and two variables on the Wisconsin Card Sorting Task (WCST), a neuropsychological test sensitive to frontal lobe dysfunction. The percentage of perseverative responses and number of categories completed on the WCST were found to significantly correlate with the total symptom awareness and total symptom attribution scores as measured by the SUMD. Young *et al.* also classified the sample into high and low awareness groups and performed a discriminant function analysis to determine which of a set of variables most significantly distinguished the high and low groups. From a group of variables including inpatient vs. outpatient status, IQ, WCST categories completed, WCST percentage perseverative responses, and average symptom severity, Young *et al.* found that a combination of perseverative errors and average symptom severity correctly categorized 83.9% of the high and low awareness groups. This study offered the first empirical support of Amador *et al.*'s (1991) hypothesized relationship between poor insight and frontal lobe dysfunction.

In more recent years, while several studies have offered additional support for the relationship between insight and frontal lobe dysfunction (Young, Zakzanis *et al.*, 1998; Mohamed, Fleming *et al.*, 1999; Flashman, McAllister *et al.*, 2001; Buckley, Hasan *et al.*, 2001; Rossell, Coakes *et al.*, 2003), others have not (McCabe, Quayle *et al.*, 2002) or have only offered partial support, finding an association between insight and attribution of illness rather than awareness of illness (Smith, Hull *et al.*, 2000) or with only particular measures of frontal lobe dysfunction (Drake and Lewis, 2003). That said, these apparent failures to replicate are typically the result of using very different measures of insight so that "apples and oranges" are being compared and of small sample sizes that do not provide sufficient statistical power to detect the relationship (see Morgan and David, Chapter 9). It is our opinion that at this time the data collected over the past decade clearly support the hypothesis we suggested in 1991: i.e., that in those schizophrenia patients with *severe and persistent* unawareness of illness, the lack of insight is a symptom of the disorder stemming from neuropsychological deficit.

Two recent studies have suggested a bridging of the gap between theories emphasizing neuropsychological deficit or psychological defense. Lysaker and Bryson *et al.* have reported findings indicating that patients with poor insight display weaker performance on the WCST, indicating frontal lobe dysfunction, as well as a preference for an "escape-avoidant" manner of coping as measured by the Ways of Coping Questionnaire (Lysaker, Bryson *et al.*, 2003). This finding implicates both deficit and defense models in an understanding of the insight. Taking these results a step further, Lysaker and Lancaster *et al.* suggest that rather than choosing between insight as neuropsychological or defense driven, we may be better served by seeing two distinct groups of patients with poor insight: those with frontal lobe dysfunction and those with an avoidant coping style. We agree and suggest that in patients with severe and persistent unawareness who also evidence poor frontal lobe function (and other anosognosia-related neuro-cognitive deficits) we are dealing with anosognosia, or unawareness that is neuropsychologicaly based.

During the last revision of the DSM in which the accompanying text was revised, suggested changes were subjected to peer review. Data in support of any text deletion or addition was presented and recommendations were made based on whether there was ample scientific evidence to support the change. The schizophrenia and related disorders section of the DSM IV-TR (American Psychiatric Association Press, 2000, p. 304) now states:

> A majority of individuals with schizophrenia lack insight regarding the fact that they have a psychotic illness. Evidence suggests that poor insight is a manifestation of the illness itself, rather than a coping strategy. It may be comparable to the lack of awareness of neurological deficits seen in stroke, termed anosognosia. This symptom predisposes the individual to noncompliance with treatment and has been found to be predictive of . . . increased number of involuntary hospital admissions, poorer psychosocial functioning, and a poorer course of illness.

The text just cited emphasizes that poor insight in schizophrenia is *a symptom of the disorder.* Today, there is widespread consensus in the field that schizophrenia is a biologically based brain disorder and that the symptoms of the illness (delusions, hallucinations, negative symptoms, etc.) stem from brain dysfunction. Thirty years of empirical research clearly place severe unawareness of illness in schizophrenia as a common feature of the disorder and it is for this reason, as well as the studies finding correlations between unawareness and neuropsychological deficit, that we can state with confidence that severe and persistent unawareness of illness in schizophrenia is a symptom of schizophrenia. Furthermore, we believe that as we label false beliefs that persist over time despite evidence to the contrary "delusions", *the time has come to label unawareness that is severe, persists over time despite evidence to the contrary and is associated with cognitive deficits, "anosognosia"*. In other words, patients with such severe deficits in insight should be diagnosed as having anosognosia for schizophrenia.

Conclusions

As we mentioned in the first edition of this book, insight is a complex and multi-dimensional phenomenon. In the past decade, investigators have increasingly turned their attention to poor insight as an important feature in schizophrenia. In the process, research has demonstrated that poor insight is a prevalent feature of psychotic disorders in general and of schizophrenia in particular. While the etiology of poor insight in schizophrenia remains unclear, recent studies have particularly strengthened the hypothesis that neuropsychological deficits are at the root of those cases of very poor insight that persist over time.

Studies of poor insight have blossomed over the past decade. As investigators continue to report their findings, we should be able to paint a clearer picture of the nature of this symptom in a range of psychotic disorders. As we bolster our own awareness of this problem, we hope to begin to consider new ways in which we can help patients' who suffer from anosognosia for psychosis. One thing is certain, severe and persistent unawareness of illness is damaging not only to the afflicted person's relationship with loved ones and mental health professionals, but also to their chances to recover and lead more satisfying and productive lives. It is for this reason that interventions aimed at either improving insight directly or, addressing the negative consequences of poor insight (noncompliance, social isolation, estrangement from loved ones and the healthcare system) must be developed. We can think of no more important avenue for research in the years ahead.

References

Alloy, L. B. and Abramson, L. Y. (1979). Judgment of contingency in depressed and nondepressed students: Sadder but wiser? *Journal of Experimental Psychology*, **108**, 441–85.

Amador, X. F. and Gorman, J. M. (1998). Psychopathologic domains and insight in schizophrenia. *Psychiatric Clinics of North America*, **20**, 27–42.

Amador, X. F. and Seckinger, R. A. (1997). The assessment of insight: a methodological review. *Psychiatric Annals*, **27** (12), 798–805.

Amador, X. F., Friedman, J. H., Kasapis, C., Yale, S. A., Flaum, M. and Gorman, J. M. (1996). Suicidal behavior in schizophrenia and its relationship to awareness of illness. *American Journal of Psychiatry*, **153**, 1185–8.

Amador, X. F. and Strauss, D. H. (1990). *The Scale to assess Unawareness of Mental Disorder (SUMD)*. Columbia University and New York State Psychiatric Institute.

Amador, X. F., Strauss, D. H., Yale, S. A. and Gorman, J. M. (1991). Awareness of illness in schizophrenia. *Schizophrenia Bulletin*, **17**, 113–32.

Amador, X. F. and Strauss, D. H. (1993). Poor insight in schizophrenia. *Psychiatric Quarterly*, **64**, 305–18.

Amador, X. F., Strauss, D. H., Yale, S., Gorman, J. M. and Endicott, J. (1993). The assessment of insight in psychosis. *American Journal of Psychiatry*, **150**, 873–9.

Amador, X. F., Andreasen, N. C., Flaum, M., Strauss, D. H., Yale, S. A., Clark, S., *et al.* (1994). Awareness of illness in schizophrenia, schizoaffective and mood disorders. *Archives of General Psychiatry*, **51**, 826–36.

APA (**American Psychiatric Association**) (1987). *Diagnostic and Statistical Manual of Mental Disorders*, 3rd edn, revised. Washington, DC: American Psychiatric Association.

Andreasen, N. C. (1984). *The Scale for the Assessment of Negative Symptoms (SANS)*. Iowa City, IA: University of Iowa.

Andreasen, N. C. (1989). Scale for the assessment of negative symptoms (SANS). *British Journal of Psychiatry*, **155**, 53–8.

Andreasen, N. C. (1991). *Schizophrenia*, DSM-IV Update. Washington, DC: American Psychiatric Association.

Babinski, J. (1914). Contribution a l'etude des troubles mentaux dans l'hemiplegie organique cerebale (Anosognosie). *Revue Neurologique*, **27**, 845–88.

Bartko, G., Herczeg, L. and Zador, G. (1988). Clinical symptomotology and drug compliance in schizophrenic patients. *Acta Psychiatrica Scandinavica*, **77**, 74–6.

Bear, D. M. (1982). Hemispheric specialization and neurology of emotion. *Archives of Neurology*, **40**, 195–202.

Bisiach, C., Valler, G., Periani, D., Papogano, C. and Berti, J. (1986). Unawareness of disease following lesions of the right hemisphere: Anosognosia for hemiplegia and anosognosia for hemianopia. *Neuropsychologia*, **24**, 471–82.

Buckley, P. F., Hasan, S., Friedman, L. and Cerny, C. (2001). Insight and schizophrenia. *Comprehensive Psychiatry*, **42**, 39–41.

Caraccii, G., Mukherjee, S., Roth, S. and Decina, P. (1990). Subjective awareness of abnormal involuntary movements in chronic schizophrenic patients. *American Journal of Psychiatry*, **147**, 295–8.

Carpenter, W. T. Jr., Bartko, J. J., Carpenter, C. L. and Strauss, J. S. (1976). Another view of schizophrenia subtypes. *Archives of General Psychiatry*, **33**, 508–16.

Carpenter, W. T., Jr. and Kirkpatrick, B. (1988). The heterogeneity of the long term course of schizophrenia. *Schizophrenia Bulletin*, **14**, 645–51.

Carpenter, W. T., Jr., Strauss, J. S. and Bartko, J. J. (1973). Flexible system for the diagnosis of schizophrenia: Report from the WHO International Pilot Study of Schizophrenia. *Science*, **182**, 1275–8.

Cole, M., Saexinger, H. G. and Hard, A. (1968). Anosognosia: Studies using regional intravenous anasthesia. *Neuropsychologia*, **6**, 365–71.

Critchley, M. (1953). *The Parietal Lobes*. New York: Hafner Publishing.

Cutting, J. (1978). Study of anosognosia. *Journal of Neurology, Neurosurgery, and Psychiatry*, **41**, 548–55.

David, A. S. (1990). Insight and psychosis. *British Journal of Psychiatry*, **161**, 599–602.

David, A. S., van Os, J., Jones, P., Harvey, I., Foerster, A. and Fahy, T. (1995). Insight and Psychotic illness: cross-sectional and longitudinal associations. *British Journal of Psychiatry*, **167**, 621–8.

Drake, R. J. and Lewis, S. W. (2003). Insight and neurocognition in schizophrenia. *Schizophrenia Research*, **62**, 165–73.

Flashman, L. A., McAllister, T. W., Johnson, S. C., Rick, J. H., Green, R. L. and Saykin, A. J. (2001). Specific frontal lobe subregions correlated with unawareness of illness in schizophrenia: a preliminary study. *Journal of Neuropsychiatry and Clinical Neuroscience*, **13**, 255–7.

Gerstmann, J. (1942). Problem of imperception of disease and of impaired body territories with organic lesions. Relation to body scheme and its disorders. *Archives of Neurology and Psychiatry*, **48**, 890–913.

Geschwind, N. (1965). Disconnexion syndromes in animals and man. *Brain*, **88**, 237–94.

Ghaemi, S. N. and Pope, H. G., Jr. (1994). Lack of insight in psychotic and affective disorders: a review of empirical studies. *Harvard Review of Psychiatry*, May/June, 22–33.

Greenfeld, D., Strauss, J. S., Bowers, M. B. and Mandelkern, M. (1989). Insight and interpretation of illness in recovery from psychosis. *Schizophrenia Bulletin*, **15**, 245–52.

Johnson, S. and Orrell, M. (1995). Insight and psychosis: A social perspective. *Psychological Medicine*, **25**, 515–20.

Kraepelin, E. (1919/1971). *Dementia Praecox and Paraphrenia*. Huntington, NY: Robert E. Krieger.

Lally, S. J. (1989). Does being in here mean there is something wrong with me? *Schizophrenia Bulletin*, **15**, 253–65.

Lewinsohn, P. M., Mischel, W., Chaplain, W. and Barton, R. (1980). Social competence and depression: The role of illusory self-perceptions? *Journal of Abnormal Psychology*, **89**, 203–12.

Lysaker, P. H., Bryson, G. J., Lancaster, R. S., Evans, J. D. and Bell, M. D. (2003). Insight in schizophrenia: associations with executive function and coping style. *Schizophrenia Research*, **59**, 41–7.

Lysaker, P. H., Lancaster, R. S., Davis, L. W. and Clements, C. A. (2003). Patterns of neurocognitive deficits and unawareness of illness in schizophrenia. *Journal of Nervous and Mental Disorders*, **191**, 38–44.

Markova, I. S. and Berrios, G. E. (1992). The assessment of insight in clinical psychology. *Acta Psychiatrica Scandinavica*, **86**, 159–64.

Mayer-Gross, W. (1920). Ueber die Stellungnahme zur abgelaufenen akuten Psychose. *Zeltschrifte fur die Gesmata Neurologie und Psychiatrie*, **60**, 160–212.

McCabe, R., Quayle, E., Beirne, A. D. and Anne Duane, M. M. (2002). Insight, global neuropsychological functioning, and sympomatology in chronic schizophrenia. *Journal of Nervous and Mental Disorders*, **190**, 519–25.

McEvoy, J. P., Aland, J. Jr., Wilson, W. H., Guy, W. and Hawkins, L. (1981). Measuring chronic schizophrenic patients' attitudes toward their illness and treatment. *Hospital and Community Psychiatry*, **32**, 856–8.

McEvoy, J. P., Apperson, L. J., Appelbaum, P. S., Ortlip, P., Brecosky, J. and Hammill, K. (1989). Insight in schizophrenia. Its relationship to acute psychopathology. *Journal of Nervous and Mental Disorders*, **177**, 43–7.

McEvoy, J. P., Freter, S., Everett, G., Geller, J. L., Appelbaum, P., Apperson, L. J., *et al.* (1989). Insight and the clinical outcome of schizophrenics. *Journal of Nervous and Mental Disorders*, **177**, 48–51.

McGlashan, T. H. and Carpenter, W. T. Jr. (1976). Postpsychotic depression in schizophrenia. *Archives of General Psychiatry*, **33**, 231–9.

McGlashan, T. H., Levy, S. T. and Carpenter, W. T., Jr. (1975). Integration and sealing over. Clinically distinct recovery styles from schizophrenia. *Archives of General Psychiatry*, **32**, 1269–72.

McGlynn, S. M. and Schacter, D. L. (1989). Unawareness of deficits in neuropsychological syndromes. *Journal of Clinical and Experimental Neuropsychology*, **11**, 143–205.

Michalakeas, A., Skoutas, C., Charalambous, A., Peristeris, A., Marinos, V., Keramari, E., *et al.* (1994). Insight in schizophrenia and mood disorders and its relation to psychopathology. *Acta Psychiatrica Scandinavica*, **90**, 46–9.

MacKinnon, R. A. and Yudofsky, S. C. (1986). *The Psychiatric Evaluation in Clinical Practice.* Philadelphia: J. B. Lippincott Company.

Mintz, A. R., Dobson, K. S. and Romney, D. M. (2003). Insight in schizophrenia: a meta-analysis. *Schizophrenia Research*, **61**, 75–88.

Mohamed, S., Fleming, S., Penn, D. L. and Spaulding, W. (1999). Insight in schizophrenia: its relationship to measures of executive functioning. *Journal of Nervous and Mental Diseases*, **187**, 525–31.

Overall, J. E. and Gorham, D. R. (1962). The brief psychiatric rating scale. *Psychological Reports*, **10**, 799–812.

Pini, S., Cassano, G. B., Dell'Osso, L. and Amador, X. F. (2001). Insight into illness in schizophrenia, schizoaffective disorder, and mood disorders with psychotic features. *American Journal of Psychiatry*, **158**, 122–5.

Ratakonda, S., Gorman, J. M., Yale, S. A. and Amador, X. F. (1998). Characterization of psychotic conditions: Use of the domains of psychopathology model. *Archives of General Psychiatry*, **55** (1), 75–81.

Richfield, J. (1954). All analysis of the concept of insight. *Psychoanalytic Quarterly*, **23**, 390–408.

Rosen, A. M., Mukherjee, S., Olarte, S., Varia, V. and Cardenas, C. (1982). Perception of tardive dyskinesia in outpatients receiving maintenance neuroleptics. *American Journal of Psychiatry*, **139**, 372–3.

Rossell, S. L., Coakes, J., Shapleske, J., Woodruff, P. W. and David, A. S. (2003). Insight: its relationship with cognitive function, brain volume, and symptoms in schizophrenia. *Psychological Medicine*, **33**, 111–19.

Sackeim, H. A. (1983). Self-deception, depression, and self-esteem: The adaptive value of lying to oneself. In J. Masling (ed.), *Empirical Studies of Psychoanalytic Theory*, pp. 101–57. Hillsdale, NJ: Erlbaum.

Sackeim, H. A. and Wegner, A. Z. (1986). Attributional patterns in depression and euthymia. *Archives of General Psychiatry*, **43**, 553–60.

Sandifer, P. H. (1946). Anosognosia and disorders of body scheme. *Brain*, **69**, 122–37.

Sanz, M., Constable, G., Lopez-Ibor, I., Kemp, R. and David, A. (1998). A comparative study of insight scales and their relationship to psychopathological and clinical variables. *Psychological Medicine*, **28**, 437–46.

Schacter, D. L. (1989). On the relation between memory and consciousness. In H. Roediger and F. Craik (ed.), *Varieties of Memory and Consciousness.* Hillsdale, NJ: Erlbaum.

Searles, H. F. (1965). *Collected Papers on Schizophrenia and Related Subjects.* New York: New York International University Press.

Selten, J. P. C. J., Sijben, N. E.S., van den Bosch, R. J., Omloo-Visser, J. and Warmerdam, H. (1993). The subjective experience of negative symptoms: A self-rating scale. *Comprehensive Psychiatry*, **34**, 192–7.

Semrad, E. V. (1966). Long term therapy of schizophrenia. In G. Usdin, (ed.) *Psychoneuroses and Schizophrenia*, pp. 155–73. Philadelphia: Lippincott.

Schilder, P. (1935). *The Image and Appearance of the Human Body.* London: Kegan, Paul, Trench and Trubner.

Small, I. F., Small, J. G. and Gonzalez, R. (1965). The clinical correlates of attitudinal change during psychiatric treatment. *American Journal of Psychotherapy*, **19**, 66–74.

Smith, T. E., Hull, J. W., Israel, L. M. and Willson, D. F. (2000). Insight, symptoms, and neurocognition in schizophrenia and schizoaffective disorder. *Schizophrenia Bulletin*, **26**, 193–200.

Smith, T. E., Hull, J. W. and Santos, L. (1998). The relationship between symptoms and insight in schizophrenia: a longitudinal perspective. *Schizophrenia Research*, **33**, 63–7.

Stuss, D. T. and Benson, D. F. (1986). *The Frontal Lobes*. New York: Raven Press.

Takai, A., Uematsu, M., Ueki, H. and Sone, K. (1992). Insight and its related factors in chronic schizophrenic patients: A preliminary study. *European Journal of Psychiatry*, **6**, 159–70.

Swanson, C. L., Jr., Freudenreich, O., McEvoy, J. P., Nelson, L., Kamaraju, L. and Wilson, W. H. (1995). Insight in schizophrenia and mania. *The Journal of Nervous and Mental Disease*, **183**, 752–5.

Taylor, E. T. and Brown, J. D. (1988). Illusion and well-being. A social psychological perspective on mental health. *Psychological Bulletin*, **103**, 193–210.

Tremeau, F., Amador, X. F., Malaspina, D., Amodt, I., Goetz, R. and Gorman, J. (1997). Insight and anosognosia of tardive dyskinesia in schizphrenia. *Schizophrenia Research*, **24**(1–2), 273.

Vaman, M. (1962). *Behavioral Changes in Patients Following Strokes*. Springfield, IL: Charles C. Thomas.

Van Putten, T., Crumpton, E. and Yale, C. (1976). Drug refusal in schizophrenia and the wish to be crazy. *Archives of General Psychiatry*, **33**, 1443–6.

Vaz, F. J., Bejar, A. and Casado, M. (2002). Insight, psychopathology, and interpersonal relationships in schizophrenia. *Schizophrenia Bulletin*, **28**, 311–17.

Von Hagen, K. O. and Ives, E. R. (1939). Two autopsied cases of anosognosia. *Bulletin of the Los Angeles Neurological Society*, **4**, 41–4.

Warrington, E. K. (1962). The completion of visual forms across hemianopic defects. *Journal of Neurology, Neurosurgery, and Psychiatry*, **25**, 208–17.

Wciorka, J. (1988). A clinical typology of schizophrenic patients' attitudes towards their illness. *Psychopathology*, **21**, 259–66.

Whittman, J. R. and Duffey, R. F. (1961). The relationship between type of therapy received and a patient's perception of his illness. *Journal of Nervous and Mental Disease*, **133**, 288–92.

Wilson, W. H., Ban, T. A. and Guy, W. (1986). Flexible system criteria in chronic schizophrenia. *Comprehensive Psychiatry*, **27**, 259–65.

Wing, J. K., Monck, E., Brown, G. W. and Carstairs, G. M. (1964). Morbidity in the community of schizophrenic patients discharged from London mental hospitals in 1959. *British Journal of Psychiatry*, **110**, 10–21.

World Health Organization (WHO) (1973). *Report of the International Pilot Study of Schizophrenia*. Geneva: WHO Press.

Young, D. A., Davila, R. and Scher, H. (1993). Unawareness of illness and neuropsychological. performance in chronic schizophrenia. *Schizophrenia Research*, **10**, 117–24.

Young, D. A., Zakzanis, K. K., Bailey, C., Davilla, R., Griese, J., Sartory, G., *et al.* (1998). Further parameters of insight and neuropsychological deficit in schizophrenia and other chronic mental disease. *Journal of Nervous and Mental Diseases*, **186**, 44–50.

Chapter 2

Insight in the psychoses: a conceptual history

German E. Berrios and Ivana S. Marková

Attempting a history of insight (and of its clinical derivative, lack of insight or insight-lessness) illustrates the problem of chronicling the evolution of ambiguous notions. Should the historian use as a guiding object, or *invariant*, a narrow definition such as "correct attitude to being ill" (Lewis, 1934), or the equally narrow view implicit in most current empirical studies (Marková and Berrios, 1995) or in configurational learning (Hartmann, 1931; Sternberg and Davidson, 1994)? Or perhaps the historian should embrace the wider idea of insight as self-knowledge (Marková and Berrios, 1992; Gillett, 1995), mystical intellection (Lonergan, 1970, pp. 406–408), creative moment (Hutchinson, 1939, 1941), or psychoanalytic comprehension (Richfield, 1954). And how about the cognitive view that insight is a function of a putative mind reading system (Baron-Cohen, 1995)? The difficulty concerns not the history of any of these views in particular but the composition of a general history of insight. In other words, the problem is to determine whether such views are *conceptually cognate* (i.e., have a common ancestor) or whether their only link is the usage of the word insight.

The object of inquiry

It is important to specify what the main object of the inquiry is. Failure to distinguish between the history of the *term* "insight" (and its equivalents in other languages), and that of the pertinent *behaviours* (however termed) and *concepts* (however theoretically underpinned) can only lead to confusion. As in empirical work, choice in historical research is never objective; behaviour is not an atheoretical object but the result of overt or (often enough) covert conceptualization. This is because the behaviours corresponding to insight have even less ontological mass than other medical notions such as moles, murmurs, or hallucinations. This is not to say that insight has no neurobiological basis, but only that the capture of its behavioural core (ontology) depends on epistemological devices such as concepts. Hence, a history of insight must study the contextualized interaction of etymology, concepts and behaviours. In accordance with this rule and the theme of this book, we shall concentrate on the history of insight (and lack of insight) in relation to the psychoses. It should not be forgotten, however, that the history of insight in dementia, obsessional disorder, hysteria, and the like is still to be written.

Historical contexts

Insanity and awareness of illness

Until the early nineteenth century, the official view of insanity – as had been first put together by Hobbes and Locke during the nineteenth century (Berrios, 1994) – was based on the presence of delusions which were, in turn, definitionally embedded in an implicit "lack of insight". In other words, between the late seventeenth century and the early nineteenth century, the statement "he is aware of being deluded" would have involved a logical contradiction and been considered nonsensical. Insightlessness was thus not a variable but a parameter in the definition of insanity. This fact makes it difficult to find a writer from this period who may wish to discuss the importance of varying insightlessness in insanity. But there is also a second reason: subjective or introspective facts in general were not yet part of the definition of madness; indeed, they were added only during the middle of the nineteenth century.

The notion of "partial insanity", as it developed during the late eighteenth and early nineteenth century offered the first opportunity for the concepts of insight and insightlessness to be discussed as "variables". At the beginning of the nineteenth century, "partial" insanity meant both: *intermittent* (as in periods of madness interspersed with lucid intervals),[1] and *incomplete* (as in madness affecting only one region of the psyche, e.g. monomania[2]) (Kageyama, 1984). Because of the disparate sources contributing to the development of the concept of partial insanity, ensuing debates were complicated by intra-disciplinary issues. For example, one such issue pertained to legal medicine when there was much argument between alienists and lawyers on the relative implications of

[1] As late as 1875, Prosper Despine discussed in detail two senses of *lucidité*: "in the work of the alienists, the word *lucidity* has been used in two ways; one is a synonym of reason and refers to the moment when the mental faculties become normal . . . the other has been defined by Trélat as the sparing of the intellect in cases where the other mental faculties are diseased" (Despine, 1875, pp. 312–314). Ulysse Trélat (1795–1879) was a creative thinker whose busy political life prevented him from contributing further to psychiatry (Morel, 1988). The work quoted by Despine was *La Folie Lucide*, a rather old fashioned book, probably written much earlier, where Trélat studied a heterogeneous group of patients whose common denominator was that "in spite of their illness, they responded exactly to the questions and did not seem insane to the superficial observer" although their behaviour betrayed their condition (Trélat, 1861, p. xxx). A few years earlier, in a very popular forensic work, Legrand defined the lucid interval as: "an absolute albeit temporary suspension of the manifestations of insanity. It can be observed in about 25% of manics, less frequently in melancholia, rarely in monomania, never in dementia". (Legrand, 1864, pp. 109–110).

[2] We are using the term "partial insanity" in this latter sense in the broadest of ways. During the nineteenth century, many different terms were used to refer to insanity where different aspects or faculties of the mind were deranged whilst others were spared. Apart from the monomanias, other terms included Pinel's *manie sans délire*, Prichard's moral insanity, *folie raisonnante, folie lucide, partial délire*, etc. The terms are not equivalent in meaning as they have different origins and different conceptualizations underlying the divisions of mental faculties that define them. But they share the common feature of being conceived as insanities in which the whole mind is not disordered.

total and partial insanity (Goldstein, 1987) to criminal and civil responsibility. One central concern in these debates was the impact that having awareness of illness and/or awareness of the bad nature of the criminal acts had on the individual's responsibility.

The concept of partial insanity was also linked to the emergence of different forms of faculty psychology. In broad terms this referred to the view that the mind operates on the basis of individual, independent units or functions, and contrasted with the prevailing associationism of Locke and Condillac, according to which the mind was indivisible. Faculty psychology challenged the notion of total insanity from both theoretical and empirical perspectives. From the theoretical viewpoint, there was the phrenology movement which through the work of Gall and Spurzheim influenced the view of alienists in early nineteenth century France (Goldstein, 1987) and Britain (Cooter, 1979). Specifically, Gall proposed that innate, independent faculties were localizable to particular organs/regions in the brain and that these were responsible for individual mental qualities, constitutive of both mind and character (Spoerl, 1936). Another form of faculty psychology, viewing faculties more in functional terms (or powers) and consisting of different "content" (e.g., understanding, will, judgement, etc.), came from the eighteenth century Scottish philosophers, particularly Thomas Reid (1785/1863). This different trend was to influence the thinking of French philosophers and alienists during the early and middle of the nineteenth century (Boutroux, 1908).

The empirical challenge from faculty psychology was based on clinical observations by alienists during the early nineteenth century. Pinel, Prichard and Esquirol, among others, noted how patients could be affected in some areas of their psyche but not in others.[3] As a result, insanity could be defined in terms of faculties which in due course made possible the creation of new clinical categories such as the *emotional* and *volitional* insanities (Berrios and Gili, 1995). It was soon realized that the latter were not necessarily linked to "insightlessness" and observations were made of patients who although aware of their condition were unable to resist pathological impulses (Pinel, 1809). In other words, the concept of partial madness and of monomania allowed for the existence of an insanity that, to paraphrase Baillarger, was "aware of itself". This is the historical moment in which insightlessness ceased to be a substructure (or parameter or constant) in the conceptual lattice of insanity and became a variable in its own right.

Changes in views on the causes of insanity opened up yet more space for the possibility of studying insight into mental illness. As an anonymous historian put it in 1840: "all explanations of mental illness boil down to three options: they are localized in the brain. . . . or in the soul . . . or in both." (Fabre, 1840, p.118). The first two options had interesting implications. In general, notions of monomania and partial insanity (and hence insight) were more readily accepted by supporters of the anatomoclinical view

---

[3] For example, Pinel stated: ". . . the examples of manic patients with fury but without délire and without any incoherence in their ideas, are far from being rare in both women and men, and they go to show how much lesions of the will can be distinct from those of the understanding, even though they frequently occur together" (Pinel, 1809, p. 102).

of madness (Ackerknecht, 1967; López Piñero, 1983) than by those who believed that insanity was exclusively sited in the mind or soul (*l'âme*). In terms of the philosophical psychology of the period, it was difficult to accept that the soul was divisible and that its fragments could become independently diseased.

These categorical changes were made possible by a deeper shift in the notion of disease. Until the eighteenth century, total insanity was but a reflection of what has been called the ontological definition of disease – that is, being mad and losing one's reason was a sort of permanent state that affected the entire person. In a way, the problem at the time was to explain recovery. The notion of partial insanity, which took hold after the momentous changes brought about by the ideas of Bichat,[4] assumed a modular model for the mind and more or less specific cerebral localization.[5] This allowed for the coexistence of sanity and insanity in the human mind (Kageyama, 1984). Alienists during the 1830s were aware of the implications of this change, and a debate soon ensued on the legitimacy of such a mosaic-like model of the mind (SMP, 1866). For example, whilst believing that faculties represented useful psychological divisions, Falret did not think that they represented pathological divisions of the brain and argued against the view that mental faculties could be affected independently. Like Maudsley[6] some years later, Falret believed that even if predominantly disrupting specific faculties, madness had some effect on them all (Falret, 1866).[7] Opposing this view, Delasiauve (1866) argued that insanity could be faculty-specific and Fournet (1870) that the important task was to study the relationship between events occurring at the cellular level of the brain and events in the mind; but that the latter should be understood from a psychological perspective and not by reducing it to brain mechanisms.

Consciousness and insight

Yet more conceptual space was provided with the incorporation in the late nineteenth century of noble concepts such as *consciousness* (awareness), *introspection*

....

4 Xavier Bichat (1771–1802) developed a viable "tissue theory" that forced changes in the very concept of the localization of disease (see D'istra, 1926; Albury, 1977; Haigh, 1984).

5 Under the name of faculty psychology, the modular view had a distinguished career during the nineteenth century – for example, in relation to phrenology (Berrios, 1988); it was resuscitated by Marr and later Fodor (1983). For a criticism of the latter's view from a developmental perspective, see Karmiloff-Smith (1992).

6 Maudsley similarly believe that in the insane all regions of the mind were affected: "when an insane delusion exists in the mind, however circumscribed the range of its action may seem to be, the *rest of the mind is certainly not sound . . .*"(our italics) (Maudsley, 1885, p. 220).

7 Jules Falret wrote: "I firmly believe, both from a theoretical and practical point of view, that there is complete solidarity of the various faculties of the human mind both in the sane and the insane. In reasoning mania (*folie raisonnante*) clinical observation shows that although the moral faculties are predominantly involved there is also involvement of intellect." "The fundamental mistake in the work of alienists this century has been to import to the study of the mentally ill the divisions of the mind created by psychologists to study normal individuals" (Falret, 1866, pp. 384–385).

(Boring, 1953; Danziger, 1980), and *self* (Berrios, 1993) – without which the notion of insight would be difficult to understand.[8] The acceptance of these three notions was facilitated by contemporary efforts to incorporate *subjectivity* (i.e., descriptions of inner experiences) into the definition of insanity. Moreau de Tours (Bollotte, 1973) was important in articulating this need (Moreau de Tours, 1845). Encouraged by his work, alienists accepted the view that the way patients actually experienced their illness was essential for diagnosis and classification. This belief paved the way for development of a language of description and of interviewing techniques, and for the acceptance of the value and legitimacy of introspection (Lyons, 1986). During the nineteenth century, the psychological concept of consciousness was coached in terms of *perception* (an inner eye). Not surprisingly, the old English term *insight* was preferred to *inwit*, which could have been as useful but carried less visual connotations.

Insight and *Verstehen*

The final facilitator for a development of a science of insight was the arrival of the concept of *comprehension* (*Verstehen*), and later of self-consciousness (Marková, 1988). Important to the former were the ideas of Brentano (1874/1973) (Fancher, 1977), Dilthey (1976), Freud, Husserl and Jaspers (Martin Santos, 1955; Berrios, 1992). These grander concepts were more ambitious than the mere "looking into one's mind", as suggested by introspection: indeed, they attempted to grasp the totality of one's mental and existential state (including regions that were not conscious). Within this new conceptual frame, *full insight* needs more than a mere definition as the intellectual knowledge of being ill: it demands attitudinal processes involving emotions and volitions. However, the mechanisms that made such holistic insight possible varied according to their sponsors. In Brentano, it concerned intentionality and his mechanism of a "third consciousness".[9] In Dilthey, it pertained to grasping the totality, or *Verstehen* (Apel, 1987; McCarthy, 1972; Makkreel, 1975; López Moreno, 1990).[10] In the psychoanalytical movement, mechanisms varied according to model and region of the mind (Richfield, 1954).

---

[8] Unless a Rylean account is offered according to which to have insight is defined as "a disposition to behave in a particular way" (see Ryle, 1949, pp. 116–198).

[9] "Experience shows that there exist in us not only a presentation and a judgement, but frequently a third kind of consciousness of the mental act, namely a feeling which refers to this act, pleasure or displeasure which we feel towards this act" (Brentano, 1973, p. 143).

[10] *Verstehen* is not a transparent concept. Dilthey defined it in opposition to *explanation* and hence it is supposed to be more mediate and to involve more mental functions than the mere intellectual grasping provided by explanations. "Understanding presupposes experience and experience only becomes knowledge of life if understanding leads us from the narrowness and subjectivity of experience to the whole and the general" (Dilthey, 1976, pp. 187–188).

Insight: a convergence manqué?

We have now described three (no doubt there are more) conceptual spaces within which the history of insight could be explored. The question is, have the resulting views of insight converged into a unitary phenomenon? Current empirical studies seem to assume that this is the case: namely, that there is such a thing as "insightless behaviour", as an ontologically given. What has been said so far suggests that the various notions of insight developed *ab initio* never converged and that they have run parallel courses: for example, the so-called insightlessness of schizophrenia (even if the latter is the expression of organic disorganization) is in fact *concept-driven* – that is, it reflects the way in which this "disease" is portrayed in contemporary culture. This generates a mild form of relativism, and that will be the perspective used in this chapter.[11]

Another source for this conceptual relativism is the history of the process of symptom-construction itself. Like other mental phenomena, insight should have (ideally) resulted from the stable convergence of a *term* (insight, *Einsicht, conciencia de enfermedad*, etc.), a *concept* ("looking into", *Verstehen*, etc.) and a *behaviour* (which is partly dependent on the existence of deeper conceptual frames). Historical evidence shows that in contrast to symptoms such as hallucination or anxiety (where the convergence was firm and lasting), the one underlying insightlessness has been partial and unstable; i.e., it has been a convergence *manqué*. This status has important implications for the definition, study and capture of the phenomenon in question.

History of words

The history of the word *insight* and equivalents is informative. The term exists only in the North and West Germanic families of languages. The Latin family (French, Spanish, Italian, Portuguese, etc.) does not have a corresponding unitary term, and so translation of *insight* into any of these languages is according to verbal function; for example, a well-known nineteenth century German-French dictionary translates *Einsicht* as: *inspection, examen, connaissance de cause, bon sens, judgement* (Rose, 1878). This linguistic fact would be of little import were it not that it seems to correspond with a more marked interest in insight in the Germanic sphere. More research is needed to determine to what extent having a unitary term (*insight* or *Einsicht*) causes a referential or ontological mirage – that is, the belief that the term refers to *one* rather than to a family of objects.

For the German term *Einsicht*, Grimm and Grimm (1862) propose as equivalents the Latin terms *intelligentia* and *judicium*, and suggest that the term gained wider usage in the work of Goethe and Kant (Pauleikhoff and Mester, 1973). Adelung, at the very beginning of the nineteenth century, defined it as *Das sinneinsehen in eine*

---

[11] For a recent analysis of a contextualized approach that does not fall into a damaging, relativism see Warnke (1987).

Sache (understanding the sense of something) (Adelung, 1811, vol. 1). Ritter adds that the Middle German term *insehen* is present in medieval mystical writings meaning *hineinsehen* ("looking into"). J.C. Günther, at the beginning of the eighteenth century, discarded the religious denotation to use *Einsicht* as equivalent to personal evidence (Ritter, 1972, vol. 2). This writer also suggests that the psychological meaning introduced by Köhler (see below) was a departure, in that it simply meant "intelligence" and hence approached the old Aristotelian meaning of φρόνησις ("thought or understanding").[12]

As far as English is concerned, the *New Oxford English Dictionary* provides a set of definitions governed by the same metaphor: internal sight, with the eyes of the mind, mental vision, perception discernment or the fact of penetrating with the eyes of the understanding into the inner character or hidden nature of things; a glimpse or view beneath the surface; the faculty or power of thus seeing.

On the other hand, the earliest clinical usage of the term insightlessness we have been able to identify dates back to Krafft-Ebing: "in the later stages of insanity, where delusions have become organized or mental disintegration has ensued, the patient is completely insightless about his disease state" (Krafft-Ebing, 1893, p. 102).[13]

History of concepts

The history of the concept of insight is also illuminating, particularly in relation to the evolution of the notions of reason, consciousness, and self-knowledge. In this section we shall only deal with its psychiatric aspects. Because of the special nature of the behaviours corresponding to insight (i.e., they can be only accessed via concepts), their history will be dealt with together with the history of concepts.

French views

A debate specifically concerned with awareness of mental illness ("la discussion sur les aliénés avec conscience de leur état", SMP, 1870) was held by the Société Médico-Psychologique in 1869/1870, and again to a lesser extent, in 1875. These discussions were held in the context of medico-legal concerns in relation to determining responsibility for criminal and civil acts. There had been recognition many years earlier that some insane patients retained awareness of their pathological state. Pinel (1809) and Esquirol (1838) had both made clinical observations to that effect and the Belgian

---

[12] This noble Greek term is already present in Heraclitus: τοῦ λόγου δ ἐόντος ξυνοῦ ζώουσιν οἱ πολλοὶ ὡς ἰδίαν ἔχοντες φρόνησιν ("though reason is common to all, men live as though they had a *private understanding*"). (Heraclitus, Fr. 2; Kirk and Raven, 1966). On the inconsistent Aristotelian usage of *phronêsis* see Urmson (1990).

[13] "*In den späteren Stadien des Irreseins, da wo systematische Wahn-ideen oder ein geistiger Zerfall eingetreten sind, ist der Kranke absolut einsichtslos für seinen krankhaften Zustand . . .*" (Krafft-Ebing, 1893, p. 102).

alienist Guislain (1852) had also noted this specifically.[14] Similarly, Delasiauve (1866) had commented on the presence of awareness in some insane patients and had specifically designated the term "pseudo-monomanie" for patients with monomania who had awareness of their morbid condition. Falret (1866) had also pointed out that some patients with delusions and hallucinations knew that they were ill.[15] On the basis of this, he argued against allowing loss of awareness to be a criterion distinguishing between reason and insanity. It was thus accepted in the debates that followed that some patients with mental illness had awareness of their conditions. Discussion therefore focused first on the significance of such awareness, particularly in the area of legal responsibility, and second, on attempts at defining the criteria and limits of insanity itself.

Concerning the question of legal responsibility, most alienists (Delasiauve, 1866, 1870; Falret, 1866, 1870; Morel, 1870) argued that patients could have awareness of their mental illness and nevertheless be powerless to prevent the behaviours that arose as the result of their madness, and thus should not be held legally responsible for their acts. Morel (1870), emphasizing the importance of distinguishing between reason and awareness of illness, observed that some patients could continue to reason even when deluded but still remained unaware of their illness. Other patients, in contrast, might have poor ability to reason, but were nevertheless aware of their mental illness ("aliénés irréponsables mais non des aliénés inconscients", p. 116). On the other hand, Fournet (1870) argued that awareness of illness on the part of the patient implied some degree of reason which would mean partial responsibility for his acts, the degree of responsibility being proportionate to the amount of reason held. Fournet's arguments, based on the ability of the soul to resist "insane" impulses, were not generally upheld.

Awareness of illness was also discussed in relation to the nature of mental illness itself. For example, it was felt that terms such as "intelligence", "reason", "judgement", "understanding", etc. first needed to be clarified in the context of both brain physiology and mental or psychological processes (SMP, 1870). The question of whether patients with awareness into their illness could rightly be called insane, was also raised. In this regard, Billod (1870) reported that awareness of illness was more common in patients whose madness followed alcohol excesses and that if these were excluded, women showed greater awareness into their insanity than men. He presented data showing that of 378 men admitted to the asylum in that year, 61 showed awareness of their mental condition and in 53 of these patients, their mental illness followed alcohol excesses. Of the 61 patients with awareness of illness, 49 had complete awareness and 12 showed

---

[14] Guislain observed how some patients, particularly at the beginning of their illness, would tell others that they felt unwell, ill or that their illness was at the point of exacerbation. In his clinical descriptions of mental illnesses Guislain further pointed out that "awareness could remain intact and the patient is able to say to himself: I am mad" (Guislain, 1852, p. 62).

[15] Falret noted that many insane patients "have perfect awareness of their states, who struggle with energy against the pathological tendencies, against impulses or delusional ideas which are imposed on them . . ." (Falret, 1866, p. 387).

incomplete awareness. Similarly, of 350 women patients admitted in the same year, 19 (12 with complete and 7 with incomplete awareness) showed awareness of their condition and in 5 of these patients, their mental illness followed alcohol excesses. He did not state explicitly how the division between complete and incomplete awareness was decided. Interestingly, Billod distinguished between two types of awareness. There were those aware of being insane who nevertheless believed in the reality of their delusions. Billod held that this contradiction between their awareness and their belief in their delusional ideas signified a lesion of judgement and consequently this group were to be considered as truly insane. The second group, Billod labelled as "pseudo-insane" (pseudo-aliénés). In this group, patients showed awareness of being insane, but in contrast to the first group, they also recognized the falseness or unreality of their morbid experiences – even though they remained distressed by them. Because Billod believed that their judgement was thus relatively preserved, he argued that these patients were not truly insane.

One of the problems in examining the concept of awareness or insight in nineteenth century French psychiatry is that the term "conscience" refers to two different concepts. Prosper Despine (1875) pointed out that this was a source of confusion since psychologists and philosophers tended to use the concepts interchangeably. He suggested that the term "conscience morale" should be used to refer to the English equivalent of "conscience" (i.e. knowledge of right and wrong), whilst the term "conscience personelle" should refer to the English term "consciousness". For Despine, "conscience personelle" meant knowledge of one's mental faculties, i.e. knowledge of what is perceived, remembered, reflected, felt, feared, etc. and he did not separate this from the activities themselves. Thus, he stated that the conscience personelle "is not a special faculty . . . doing and knowing that one is doing, is the same thing" (Despine, 1875, p. 14). This knowledge, however, does not include further knowledge and judgements concerning the nature and cause of mental pathology. In fact, the concept of insight in this wider sense is not really possible for Despine because of his conception of insanity (folie). First, he links this awareness of thoughts/feelings intrinsically to the intellectual faculties themselves. Second, he views madness as a disturbance of the moral (affective/volitional) faculties resulting specifically in (moral) blindness to overwhelming passions. The intellectual faculties may be weakened but continue to work, albeit under the influence of the abnormal passions. He explicitly disagrees with Victor Cousin[16] and argues that "man always has conscience personelle of acts that he carries out, even when blinded by passion, he always knows what he is doing and can, subsequently recall it" (Despine, 1875, pp. 266–267). On the other hand, knowledge of the mental pathology itself is not possible, "the one afflicted by madness cannot judge it as madness because it is his own

---

[16] Despine cites Cousin as stating ". . . frequently the passions, removing our liberty, remove at the same time the consciousness of our actions and ourselves. Thus to use common parlance, one doesn't know what one does' (Despine, 1875, p. 266).

blindness that constitutes it" (Despine, 1875, p.271). Others followed Despine's position conceptualizing madness as inherently insightless, e.g. Sérieux and Capgras already during the early twentieth century described approximately 19 cases with circumscribed delusional disorder, none of whom had any insight into their condition. Indeed, when exploring the natural history of their delusions, the authors do not consider the question of insight (Sérieux and Capgras, 1909).

In a classic paper, "Conscience et alienation mentale", Dagonet (1881) directly addressed the concept of consciousness or awareness in relation to mental illness. He believed that in order better to comprehend mental illness and thus any relationship to anatomical change, it was essential to examine the mental symptoms in themselves. Foremost among these, he argued, should be the study of anomalies of consciousness. He based his concept of consciousness on the ideas of Littré and Despine. The former had defined consciousness as "the constant, intimate feeling of the activity of the self, that is within each phenomenon of moral and intellectual life" (Dagonet, 1881, p. 369). Dagonet himself defined consciousness as "the intimate knowledge of ourselves, or the moral and intellectual processes going on within us" (Dagonet, 1881, p. 370). Elaborating further, he conceived of consciousness as "capturing all the phenomena of our internal life, and committing them to memory". This knowledge included the "feeling of totality of the person which was subject to the transformations experienced by the latter under the influence of illness" (Dagonet, 1881, p. 370). In other words, Dagonet was suggesting a deeper notion of self-understanding and knowledge than Despine. At the same time, this consciousness was as vulnerable to pathology or disease as the rest of the psyche.

Dagonet observed that in relation to mental disorders there existed a wide range of anomalies of consciousness. In most cases of mental illnesses, the disorders of consciousness were related to the disorders affecting other faculties. For example, in most cases of hallucinated patients, the hallucination "removes the consciousness of self from the individual and renders him passive to its force . . . such that he will commit all sorts of unreasonable actions under its influence" (Dagonet, 1881, p. 392). Nevertheless, Dagonet pointed out, there are other cases where patients appear to retain awareness of the hallucination as an abnormal phenomenon and search for explanations but at the same time be unable to understand their passivity in the face of their illness. Dagonet believed that the awareness of illness shown by some patients could be explained on the basis of Luys' hypothesis of pathological asymmetry of the cerebral hemispheres.[17]

Seven years after Dagonet, Parant[18] offered a full analysis of the problem. *La Raison dans La Folie* is an important book for it directly tackles the issue of legal responsibility

---

[17] Thus Dagonet cites: "the coexistence of lucidity and délire can be rationally explained by the integrity of one cerebral hemisphere and pathological hypertrophy of the other" (Dagonet, 1881, p. 20).

[18] Victor Parant was one of the great clinicians of the second half of the century. He also did important work in neuropsychiatry, particularly the mental symptoms of Parkinson's disease (Parant 1883, 1892).

in insanity. Following Falret and Morel, he made it clear that awareness should not be confused with reason and defined the former as a "state [in mental illness] in which the patient can take account of his impressions, his actions, his internal experiences and their resultant effects". In other words, awareness, "implies not just knowledge of the mental state but also the capacity, in varying degrees to judge this" (Parant, 1888, p. 174). Concurring with Dagonet that patients could show a range of awareness and judgements with respect to the mental illness, he also pointed out that this varied according to the stage of illness. He then classified patients during an episode of illness into 5 groups on the basis of different types of awareness (Parant, 1888, pp. 177–179)[19]

1   Those who were aware of the goodness or badness of their acts but were unaware of their morbid state;

2   Those who were aware of being in an abnormal state but who did not understand or admit that this was insanity;

3   Those who were aware that their abnormal experiences were the result of insanity but who nevertheless behaved as if they did not realize this, i.e. not fully accepting that they had a mental illness;

4   Those who were aware of their morbid states and understood that these were due to insanity, but who were powerless to do anything about it; and

5   Those who were aware of their morbid states and understood that these were due to insanity, but who committed or were pushed into doing serious, dangerous acts.

Parant's concept of awareness incorporated awareness of thoughts, perceptions and actions together with the judgement of these as being morbid or the result of mental illness. He emphasized that whichever category patients fell into, the presence of awareness implied a persistence of the faculty of judgement. He further emphasized the dissociation between such judgement and the manifest behaviours (particularly in regard to categories 3–5). Patients "are like helpless spectators of the breaking down of what is most precious in themselves, that is their freedom as well as their intellectual faculties" (Parant, 1888, p. 223). Like Dagonet, he stated that preservation of awareness did not entail the preservation of free will and hence did not entail legal responsibility for criminal acts.

British views

The concept of consciousness in mental illness was also a subject of debate in nineteenth century England. However, interest focused on the notion of awareness of mental operations and on examining the nature of conscious and unconscious mental processes from the physiological and philosophical perspectives (Davies, 1873; Ireland, 1875).

---

[19] Echoes of Parant's classification can be found in twentieth century French psychiatry, in a recent tripartite classification of *la reaction consciente du malade à l'égard de son état morbide* (Deshaies, 1967, pp. 85–88).

There was less interest on the wider concept of awareness of or insight into mental illness and the effects of this on mental faculties. Occasional reference to insight is made by alienists when describing the various forms of insanities. For example, agreeing with Georget, Prichard (1835) commented that insane persons were fully convinced of their perfect sanity:

> yet, as the same author observes [Georget (1795–1828)], there are some patients who are well aware of the disorder of their thoughts or of their affections, and who are deeply affected at not having sufficient strength of will to repress it.

> (Prichard, 1835, p. 121)

Maudsley (1895) expressed considerable scepticism towards the importance and role placed on consciousness in relation to mental function. He stated:

> It has been very difficult to persuade speculative psychologists who elaborate webs of philosophy out of their own consciousnesses that consciousness has nothing to do with the actual work of mental function; that it is the adjunct not the energy at work; not the agent in the process, but the light which lightens a small part of it . . . we may put consciousness aside then when we are considering the nature of the mechanism and the manner of its work . . .

> (Maudsley, 1895, p. 8)

Years later he iterated this view: "consciousness is the dependent phenomenon or so-called epiphenomenona . . ." (Maudsley, 1916, p. 7). Maudsley's conception of insanity precluded the possibility of insight or proper judgement concerning the nature of the mental derangement on the part of the patient. The insane patient, whose mental functions were deranged, became alienated from himself, and, "he is now so self-regarding a self as to be incapable of right regard to the not self . . ." (Maudsley, 1895, p. 1). Whilst clinically the line between sanity and insanity could not be well demarcated in functional terms, Maudsley drew a strict line between the sane and the insane aspects of the mind, with no real communication or exchange between them. Thus, in the same way that the sane man was incapable of judging precisely the behaviours and experiences of an insane man (and hence carrying implications for determining legal responsibility) (Maudsley, 1885), then similarly patients with partial insanity could not judge with their sane mental functions the phenomena produced by their insane mental functions:

> Each self thinks its own *thinks* or *things* – that is, thinks its own world; the true self, or what remains of it, perceives the world as it looks to sane persons, and the morbid self or double perceives it as a strange and hostile world.

> (Maudsley, 1895, p. 304)

In other words, echoing Despine (1875) and antedating Lewis (1934), Maudsley did not believe it was possible for an insane mind to make a rational judgement concerning its derangement.

The question of the role and state of consciousness in insanity continued to trouble writers well into the twentieth century. For example, Claye Shaw (1909) inquired whether there was a disturbance of consciousness during the acute episode, and whether it could explain the lack of memory shown by psychotic patients of symptoms experienced during the attack. Linking consciousness to emotional tone, he went on to postulate that one way of recognizing altered consciousness in mental illness was by the dissonance or incongruence between patients' thoughts and their apparent emotional state:

> There is evidence that both in dream states and in insanity the emotional side of the idea may be wanting, and this must have great effect on both memory and consciousness . . . I have over and over again noticed that people with delusions of a very depressed type do not show the emotional tone which should co-exist with the delusions.

> (Shaw, 1909, pp. 406–407)

Once again, the implication behind Shaw's views is that the disordered mind, unable to attend to either internal or external events, and hence unable to subsequently recall them, is unlikely to be capable of forming "correct" or sane judgements concerning the nature of morbid pathology.

German views

A young Gustav Störring (1907) defined delusions as not susceptible to correction and as insightless, regardless of whether or not the function of judgement was affected (p. 210). Mendel (1907) agreed with this view; when discussing the issue of patterns of improvement from the psychoses, he wrote:

> The dictum of Willis, that "no one can be regarded as cured till he voluntarily confesses his insanity" cannot be accepted in this categorical form. There are sporadic cases which, in spite of a limited residual insanity, may undoubtedly be considered as cured.

> (Mendel, 1907, p. 147)

The nature, diagnostic and predictive significance of insight did not seem to have interested Kraepelin or Bleuler. The former referred to the notion under "judgement": "what always surprises the observer anew is the quiet complacency with which the most nonsensical ideas can be uttered by them and the most incomprehensive actions carried out" (Kraepelin, 1913/1919, p. 25). He observed that some patients showed awareness of the morbidity of their state early in the disease, but that this left them as the disease progressed:

> The patients often have a distinct feeling of the profound change which has taken place in them. They complain that they are "dark in the head", not free, often in confusion, no longer clear, and that they have "cloud thoughts" [but ultimately] understanding of the disease disappears fairly rapidly as the maladie progresses in an overwhelming majority of the cases even where in the beginning it was more or less clearly present.

> (Kraepelin, 1919, p. 25–26)

Beyond subsequently commenting that "a certain insight into their diseased state is frequently present" in patients with the catatonic form of dementia praecox (Kraepelin,

1919, p. 150), and that patients with manic-depressive psychosis had "more tendency to, and ability for, the *observation of self*, to painful dissection of their psychic state" in contrast to patients with dementia praecox (Kraepelin, 1919, p. 264), Kraepelin did not further elaborate on the concept. Bleuler likewise did not elaborate on views concerning awareness of illness.

Jaspers

Continuing in the tradition of Parant, Karl Jaspers (1948) wrote:

> Patients' *self-observation* is one of the most important sources of knowledge in regard to morbid psychic life; so is their *attentiveness* to their abnormal experience and the *elaboration* of their observations in the form of a psychological judgement so that they can communicate to us something of their inner life
>
> (Jaspers, 1948, p. 350 our italics)

Jaspers observed that in the early stage of their illness patients became perplexed, and he explained this as an understandable reaction. As the illness progressed, patients tried to make sense of their experiences – for example, by elaborating delusional systems. Thereafter, Jaspers described how, when the illness produced change in personality, a patient's attitude to the illness became less understandable to others as he/she could appear indifferent or passive to the most frightening delusions. As seen above, Shaw believed that this lack of reaction was due to lack of emotions.

Jaspers also observed that transient insight may occur during acute psychoses, but that this soon disappeared. He believed that where insight persisted, the patient was more likely to be suffering from a personality disorder than a psychosis. In patients who recovered from the psychotic state, Jaspers made a distinction between psychoses such as mania and alcoholic hallucinosis, where patients were able to look back on their experiences with complete insight; and a psychosis such as schizophrenia, where they did not show full insight. He described the latter patients as unable to talk freely about their experiences, becoming overtly affected when pressed to do so and occasionally maintaining some features of their illnesses. For chronic psychotic states, he described patients who, from their verbal contents, often appeared to have full insight, yet in fact these verbal contents would turn out to be learned phrases, meaningless to the patients themselves.

Jaspers' concept of insight was defined in terms of the patient's ability to judge what was happening to him or her during the development of psychosis, and the reasons why it was happening. He made a distinction between awareness of illness ("Krankheitsbewußtsein") – that is, experiences of feeling ill or changed – and insight proper ("Krankheitseinsicht") – where a correct estimate could be made of the type and severity of the illness. These judgements, however, depended on the intelligence and education of the individual; indeed, because judgements of this nature are inherently a part of the personality make-up, with patients of intelligence below a certain level (e.g., idiocy), it would be more appropriate to think of loss of personality rather than loss of awareness as the feature of their lack of self-knowledge.

Jaspers was aware of the difficulty involved in theorizing about insight, and of the extent to which the outsider can hope to understand a patient's attitudes toward his or her illness. In other words, it was easier to assess objective knowledge – that is, the ability of a patient to understand and apply medical knowledge to him or herself – than what Jaspers called the *comprehending appropriation* of it. This latter function, Jaspers stated, is intrinsically linked to the patient's self, and cannot be divorced from knowledge of self-existence itself.

The aftermath

Hartmann, Ogden and Lewis

Between the two World Wars, insight gained currency but usage became blurred. George Hartmann (1931), the German psychologist, expressed this neatly:

> Terminological difficulties are a notorious source of confused thinking . . . the notion of insight as elaborated by the Gestalt psychologists during the last decade is a case in point . . . examination of recent usage reveals at least three important meanings of insight . . . insight as general comprehension[20] . . . insight as a personality trait . . . and insight as configurational learning.[21]
>
> (Hartmann, 1931, pp. 242–243)

The second of these meanings concerns the theme of this book (namely, insight in the psychoses):

> Psychiatrists have long sought to discriminate between the functional disorders in psychotic and neurotic cases on the basis of awareness of one's condition. The sufferer from neurosis is maladjusted and knows it; the frankly insane person is said to be relatively oblivious to his abnormality. . . . Insight in this case has fundamentally an egocentric reference.
>
> (Hartmann, 1931, p. 243)

In 1932, R. M. Ogden replied to Hartmann and criticized his introspective stance. He also called into question the plausibility of trying to use insight as "a clear and simple idea", for questions about insight could not be answered in general. In a claim that fully applies to current empirical work on insight, Ogden (1932) wrote: "the point is that such questions cannot properly be asked outside the framework of a definite set of postulates; and when they are asked the framework will suggest most of the answers as

---

[20] Here Hartmann made an obscure reference to "the semi-technical employment of the term in the writings of the *Geisteswissenchaften* school (e.g. Erismann)". It is likely that he was referring to a great book by Theodor Erismann (1924).

[21] This third meaning referred to Kurt Köhler's usage in the context of Gestalt psychology; see Petermann (1932, p. 33). Elizabeth Bulbrook (1932) wrote on this: "to psychologists familiar with current and recent discussions, it will be unnecessary to dwell upon the revival in periodical and textbook of the term "insight". . . some of these meanings are perceptive apprehension, acute observation, understanding, foresight and forethought, rapid learning, an intuitive flash, sudden grasp or illumination, intelligence, sophisticated skill, cognized relations, the felt basis of an attitude, experienced determination, a new perception of a goal, and a new configuration' (p. 410).

a necessary consequence of the postulates" (p. 356). The same year, Hartmann (1932) retorted, defending the experiential aspects of insight: "my fourth question asked: 'is insight necessarily accompanied by ideas?'". Ogden rejects this phrasing as implying a "needless loyalty to an outworn creed, but I see no reason why a catholic psychologist of today should hesitate to avail himself of introspective data in the interests of a richer description of the event" (pp. 577–578).

These important exchanges contain the kernel of the views to be expressed by Lewis (1934) three years later. In an unreferenced paper, Lewis offered etymological disquisition, gave a summary of gestalt views, and explored views on the definition of normality. Only half way through the paper is the question asked: "what is complete insight? – a correct attitude towards a morbid change in oneself" (p. 340). After exploring physical causes ("there are numerous instances of grossly defective insight in physical disorder"), Lewis makes the pertinent observation (lost to later researchers) that

> In any mental disorder, whether mild or severe, continued or brief, alien or comprehensible, it is with his whole disordered mind that the patient contemplates his state or his individual symptoms, and in this disorder there are disturbances which are different from the healthy function either in degree, combination or kind.
>
> (Lewis, 1934, p. 343)

Lewis believed that during the earlier stage of schizophrenia patients often showed a considerable amount of insight that was "associated with a struggle against the illness that is tragic" (Lewis, 1934, p. 345). Lewis believed that changes in the level of insight had prognostic value, as did the gaining of retrospective insight. He mentioned in this context Targowla's study of Wernicke's autochthonous ideas.[22]

Conrad

Conrad (1958) carried out long-term observations on schizophrenic patients and described the development and progression of the psychotic state. Although he did not use the term, his conceptualization of awareness of change in the self and the environment owing to mental illness is related to what Jaspers called insight. Conrad named the early stage of the schizophrenic illness the *trema*. During this stage patients found it difficult to express their feelings and experiences; some would talk about fear, tension, anxiety, and anticipation, while others would describe feelings of guilt and helplessness. Conrad believed that the common theme was a feeling of oppression, an awareness that something was not right, and a sense of restriction of one's freedom. During the next stage of the illness, the *apophany*, patients attributed meaning to feelings and experiences; for example, when in the state of *anastrophe*, patients believed themselves to be the centre of the world.

---

[22] Lewis is referring here to a book by Targowla and Dublineau (1931). These authors, however, make no mention to Wernicke's work, and the book is on the role of intuition in the formation of delusions in various conditions (Fuentenebro and Berrios, 1995).

Conrad described further stages during which destructive processes were followed by partial resolution as residual schizophrenic effects persisted, and he postulated that schizophrenia was an illness affecting the higher mental functions that differentiate humans from animals. Thus, it affected the whole self-concept and, in particular, the ability of the individual to effect the normal transition from looking at oneself from within to looking at oneself from the outside – with the eyes of the world.

Conclusions

The following can be concluded: insight and its derivative insightlessness, including loss of awareness of illness or incapacity to gain it in the first place, are concepts sitting at the incomplete convergence between word, concept, and behaviour. This makes life hard for the historian. Before 1850, there is very little on insightlessness in the clinical literature. This is likely to be because questions concerning insight and awareness of illness were meaningless when insanity was defined as the presence of delusions. However, development of concepts such as partial, emotional, and volitional insanity during the second half of the nineteenth century led to early questioning of the clinical value of evaluating the attitude of patients vis-à-vis their insanity.

Equally important to the development of a concept of insight have been the psychological notions of consciousness, introspection, and self. Whether introduction of the notion of *Verstehen* has been equally useful remains to be seen. Additionally, it is difficult to map out the semantic structure of insight because of the uncertain origins of the concept.

The French and German psychiatric traditions have handled the problem of insight differently. Since there is no single French word to refer to all the mental states and actions pertaining to the German *Einsicht* (insight), the phenomenon has been paraphrased with references to the wider notion of *conscience*. This has, in general, kept French ideas broader. Having a specific term in English and German is likely to have caused an ontological mirage – that is, one resulting in the view that the clinical phenomenon of insight may be circumscribed, specific and self-subsistent. Further research is required to ascertain these hypotheses.

References

Ackerknecht, E. (1967). *Medicine at the Paris Hospital 1794–1848*. Baltimore: Johns Hopkins Press.

Adelung, T. (1811). *Grammatisch-Kritisches Wörterbuch der hohdeutschen Mundart*. Vienna: Bauer.

Albury, W. R. (1977). Experiment and explanation in the physiology of Bichat and Magendie. *Studies in the History of Biology*, **1**, 47–131.

Apel, K.-O. (1987). Dilthey's distinction between "explanation" and "understanding" and the possibility of its "mediation". *Journal of the History of Philosophy*, **25**, 131–49.

Baron-Cohen, S. (1995). *Mindblindness*. Cambridge, MA: MIT Press.

Berrios, G. E. (1988). Historical Background to Abnormal Psychology. In Miller E. and Cooper J. (ed.) *Adult Abnormal Psychology*, pp. 26–51. Edinburgh: Churchill Livingstone.

Berrios, G. E. (1992). Phenomenology, psychopathology and Jaspers: a conceptual history. *History of Psychiatry*, **3**, 303–27.

Berrios, G. E. (1993). European views on personality disorders: a conceptual history. *Comprehensive Psychiatry*, **34**, 14–30.

Berrios, G. E. (1994). Delusions: selected historical and clinical aspects. In E. M.R. Critchley (ed.) *The Neurological Boundaries of Reality*, pp. 251–68. London: Farrand Press.

Berrios, G. E. and Gili, M. (1995). The disorders of the will: a conceptual history. *History of Psychiatry*, **6**, 87–104.

Billod, E. (1870). Discussion sur les aliénés avec conscience. *Annales Médico-Psychologiques*, **3**, 264–81.

Bollote, G. (1973). Moreau de Tours 1804–1884. *Confrontations Psychiatriques*, **11**, 9–26.

Boring, E. G. (1953). A history of introspection. *Psychological Bulletin*, **50**, 169–89.

Boutroux, E. (1908). De l'influence de la philosophie Écossaise sur la philosophie Française. In *Études d'Histoire de la philosophie*, Paris: Felix Alcan.

Brentano, F. (1874/1973). *Psychology from an Empirical Standpoint* (A. C. Rancurello, D. B. Terrell and L. L. McAlister, trans.) London: Routledge and Kegan Paul.

Bulbrook, M. E. (1932). An experimental inquiry into the existence and nature of insight. *The American Journal of Psychology*, **44**, 409–53.

Conrad, K. (1958). *Die beginnende Schizophrenie*. Stuttgart: Thieme.

Cooter, R. J. (1979). Phrenology and British alienists c1825–1845, part I and part II. *Medical History*, **20**, 1–21; 135–51.

D'Istria, F. C. (1926). La psychologie de Bichat. *Revue de Metaphysique et de Morale*, **23**, 1–38.

Dagonet, M. H. (1881). Conscience et aliénation mentale. *Annales Médico-Psychologiques*, **5**, 368–97; **6**, 19–32.

Danziger, K. (1980). The history of introspection reconsidered. *Journal of the History of the Behavioral Sciences*, **16**, 241–62.

Davies, W. G. (1873). Consciousness and "unconscious cerebration". *Journal of Mental Science*, **19**, 202–17.

Delasiauve, L. J. F. (1866). Discussion sur la folie raisonnante. *Annales Médico-Psychologiques*, **7**, 426–31.

Delasiauve, L. J. F. (1870). Discussion sur les aliénés avec consciences. *Annales Médico-Psychologiques*, **3**, 103–9, 126–30, 290–1, 307–9.

Deshaies, G. (1967). *Psychopathologie Générale*. Paris: Presses Universitaires de France.

Despine, P. (1875). *De la folie au point de vue philosophique ou plus spécialement psychologique*. Paris: Savy.

Dilthey, W. (1976). *Selected Writings*, pp. 87–97. Cambridge: Cambridge University Press.

Erismann, T. (1924). *Die Eigenart des Geistigen; induktive und einsichtige Psychologie*. Leipzig: Quelle and Meyer.

Esquirol, E. (1838). *Des maladies mentales*. Paris: J. B. Ballière.

Fabre, Dr (ed.) (1840). *Dictionnaire des Dictionnaires de Medicine Français et Etrangers*. Paris: Béthune et Plon.

Falret, J. P. (1866). Discussion sur la folie raisonnante. *Annales Médico-Psychologiques*, **24**, 382–426.

Falret, J. P. (1870). Discussion sur les aliénés avec conscience, *Annales Médico-Psychologiques*, **3**, 120–1, 126.

Fancher, R. E. (1977). Brentano's psychology from an empirical standpoint and Freud's early metapsychology. *Journal of the History of the Behavioral Sciences*, **13**, 207–27.

Fodor, J. A. (1983). *The Modularity of the Mind*, Cambridge, MA: MIT Press.

Fournet, (1870). Discussion sur les aliénés avec conscience, *Annales Médico-Psychologiques*, **3**, 101–3, 121–5, 471–86.

Fuentenebro, F. and Berrios, G. E. (1995). The predelusional states. *Comprehensive Psychiatry*, **36**, 251–9.

Gillett, G. (1995). Insight, delusion and belief. *Philosophy, Psychiatry and Psychology* **1**, 227–36.

Goldstein, J. (1987). *Console and Classify. The French Psychiatric Profession in the Nineteenth Century.* Cambridge, UK: Cambridge University Press.

Grimm, J. and Grimm, W. (1862). *Deutsches Wörterbuch*, vol. 12. Leipzig: S. Hirzel.

Guislain, J. (1852). *Leçons Orales sur les Phrénopathies, ou Traité Théorique et Pratique des Maladies Mentales.* Gand: Hebbelynck.

Haigh, E. (1984). Xavier Bichat and the Medical Theory of the Eighteenth Century. *Medical History*, Suppl. 4, London: Wellcome Institute for the History of Medicine.

Hartmann, G. W. (1931). The concept and criteria of insight. *The Psychological Review*, **38**, 242–53.

Hartmann, G. W. (1932). Insight and the context of Gestalt theory. *American Journal of Psychology*, **44**, 576–8.

Hutchinson, E. D. (1939). Varieties of insight in humans. *Psychiatry*, **2**, 323–32.

Hutchinson, E. D. (1941). The nature of insight. *Psychiatry*, **4**, 31–43.

Ireland, W. W. (1875). Can unconscious cerebration be proved? *Journal of Mental Science*, **21**, 366–87.

Jaspers, K. (1948). *Allgemeine Psychopathologie*, 5th edn. Berlin: Springer.

Kageyama, J. (1984). Sur l'histoire de la monomanie. *L'Evolution Psychiatrique*, **49**, 155–62.

Karmiloff-Smith, A. (1992). *Beyond Modularity.* Cambridge, MA: MIT Press.

Kirk, G. S. and Raven, J. E. (1966). *The Presocratic Philosophers.* Cambridge: Cambridge University Press.

Kraepelin, E. (1913/1919). *Dementia Praecox and Paraphrenia* (B. M. Barclay, trans.). Edinburgh: E and S Livingstone.

Krafft-Ebing, R. (1893). *Lehrbuch der Psychiatrie*, 5th edn. Stuttgart: Enke.

Legrand du Saulle, H. (1864). *La Folie devant les Tribunaux.* Paris: Savy.

Lewis, A. (1934). The Psychopathology of Insight. *British Journal of Medical Psychology*, **14**, 332–48.

Lonergan, B. J. F. (1970). *Insight. A Study of Human Understanding*, 3rd edn. New York: Philosophical Library.

López Moreno, A. (1990). *Comprensión e interpretación en las ciencias del espíritu: Dilthey.* Murcia: El Taller.

López Piñero, J. M. (1983). *Historical Origins of the Concept of Neurosis* (D. Berrios, trans.). Cambridge: Cambridge University Press.

Lyons, W. (1986). *The Disappearance of Introspection.* Cambridge, MA: MIT Press.

Makkreel, R. A. (1975). *Dilthey.* Princeton: Princeton University Press.

Marková, I. (1988). The development of self-consciousness: Part I – Baldwin, Mead and Vygotsky. *History and Philosophy of Psychology*, British Psychological Society Newsletter 7 (November), 9–18.

Marková, I. S. and Berrios, G. E. (1992). The meaning of Insight in clinical psychiatry. *British Journal of Psychiatry*, **160**, 850–60.

Marková, I. S. and Berrios, G. E. (1995). Insight in clinical psychiatry revisited *Comprehensive Psychiatry*, **36**, 367–76.

Martin-Santos, L. (1955). *Dilthey, Jaspers y la Comprensión del Enfermo Mental.* Madrid: Paz Montalvo.

Maudsley, H. (1885). *Responsibility in Mental Disease.* London: Kegan Paul and Trench.

Maudsley, H. (1895). *The Pathology of Mind.* London: Macmillan and Co.

Maudsley, H. (1916). *Organic to Human Psychological and Sociological.* London: Macmillan and Co.

McCarthy, T. (1972). The operation called verstehen: towards a redefinition of the problem. In K. F. Schaffner and R. S. Cohen R. S. (ed.) *Boston Studies in the Philosophy of Science, vol. 20, Proceedings of the 1972 Philosophy of Science Section*, pp. 167–93. Dordrecht: Reidel.

Mendel, E. (1907). *Textbook of Psychiatry*, W. C. Krauss (trans.). Philadelphia: Davis.

Moreau de Tours, J. J. (1845). *Du Hachisch et de l'Aliénation Mentale*. Paris: Fortin, Masson et Cie.

Morel, B. A. (1870). Discussion sur les aliénés avec conscience. *Annales Médico-Psychologiques*, **3**, 110–19.

Morel, P. (1988). Ulysse Trélat: citoyen contestataire, aliéniste orthodoxe. In U. Trélat, *La Folie Lucide*, pp. V–XXI. Paris: Frénesie Editions.

Ogden, R. M. (1932). Insight. *American Journal of Psychology*, **44**, 350–5.

Parant, V. (1883). La paralysie agitante examinée comme cause de folie. *Annales Médico-Psychologiques*, **10**, 45–66.

Parant, V. (1888). *La Raison dans La Folie*. Paris: Doin.

Parant, V. (1892). Paralysis agitans. In D. H. Tuke (ed.), *Dictionary of Psychological Medicine*. London: Churchill.

Pauleikhoff, B. and Mester, H. (1973). Einsicht. In Müller, *Lexikon der Psychiatrie*, pp. 150–1. Heidelberg: Springer.

Petermann, B. (1932). *The Gestalt Theory*. London: Kegan Paul, Trench, Trubner.

Pinel, P. (1809). *Traité medico-philosophique sur l'aliénation mentale*, 2nd edn. Paris: Brosson.

Prichard, J. C. (1835). *A Treatise on Insanity and other Disorders Affecting the Mind*. London: Sherwood, Gilbert and Piper.

Reid, T. (1785). *The Works of Thomas Reid*. W. Hamilton (ed.) (1863), reprint 1994. Bristol: Thoemmes Press.

Richfield, J. (1954). An analysis of the concept of insight. *Psychoanalytical Quarterly*, **23**, 390–408.

Ritter, J. (1972). *Historiches Wörterbuch der Philosophie*. Darmstadt: Wissenschaftliche Buchgesellschaft.

Rose, G. (1878). *Neues Wörterbuch der Französischen und Deutschen Sprache*. Berlin: Schreiter.

Ryle, G. (1949). *The Concept of Mind*. London: Hutchinson.

Sérieux, P. and Capgras, J. (1909). *Les Folies Raisonnantes, Le Délire d'Interprétation*. Paris: Alcan.

Shaw, T. C. (1909). The clinical value of consciousness in disease. *Journal of Mental Science*, **55**, 401–10.

SMP (1866). Société Médico-Psychologique: Discussion sur la folie raisonnante, *Annales Médico-Psychologiques*, **7**, 382–431.

SMP (1870). Société Médico-Psychologique: discussion sur les aliénés avec conscience, *Annales Médico-Psychologiques*, **3**, 100–9; 110–30; 264–93; 304–10; 466–86.

Spoerl, H. D. (1936). Faculties versus traits: Gall's solution, *Personality and Character*, **4**, 216–31.

Sternberg, R. J. and Davidson, J. E. (ed.) (1994). *The Nature of Insight*. Cambridge, MA: MIT Press.

Störring, G. E. (1907). *Mental Pathology in its Relation to Normal Psychology*. London: Swan Sonnenschein.

Targowla, R. and Dublineau, J. (1931). *L'Intuition Délirante*. Paris: Malone.

Trélat, U. (1861). *La Folie lucide*. Paris: Adrien Delahaye.

Urmson, J. O. (1990). *The Greek Philosophical Vocabulary*. London: Duckworth.

Warnke, G. (1987). *Gadamer: Hermeneutics, Tradition and Reason*. Stanford: Stanford University Press.

Chapter 3

Insight and delusion: from Jaspers to Kraepelin and back again via Austin

Bill (K. W. M.) Fulford

Insight has a paradoxical place in late twentieth century psychiatry. As the central feature of key psychotic symptoms such as delusion and hallucination, loss of insight has proven peculiarly difficult to define, so much so that determined attempts have been made to eliminate the traditional psychotic/non-psychotic distinction from psychiatry. Yet, as we will see, notwithstanding the difficulties of definition, the distinction persists. Why, then, does the psychotic/non-psychotic distinction persist? Why, indeed, is insight so difficult to define? And what, after all, *does* insight mean?

In this article I explore these questions, not directly, by way of a further tilt at the problem of definition, but indirectly, by way of an examination of how the concept of insight is actually used. We owe this approach – examining the use of a concept as a guide to its meaning – to a former White's Professor of Moral Philosophy in Oxford, J. L. Austin (Warnock, 1989). The results of linguistic analysis, as Austin's method is called, are not definitions, in the sense of neat verbal formulae, but rather an enlarged or more complete understanding of the meanings of the concepts in question. In the case of the concept of insight, this more complete understanding turns out to be closer to the phenomenological psychopathology of Karl Jaspers than the descriptive psychopathology of Emil Kraepelin. And a Jaspersian rather than Kraepelinian psychopathology of insight, I will suggest in a brief concluding section, is better adapted to the contingencies of research and practice in the increasingly neuroscience-led psychiatry of twenty-first century medicine.

1.0 What is linguistic analysis?

Linguistic analysis starts from the observation that we are often better at using than at defining concepts. Psychiatry, we should be clear straight away, made considerable progress in the second half of the twentieth century by carefully defining many of its key psychopathological and diagnostic concepts. The development of standardized assessment instruments, such as the Present State Examination (PSE) (Wing, Cooper and Sartorius, 1974), and of clear descriptive criteria in classifications of mental disorder, such as the World Health Organization's ICD (WHO, 1992) and the American Psychiatric Association's DSM (American Psychiatric Association, 1994), all depended, in part but crucially, on careful definition of terms, including extensive field trials of reliability and clinical utility.

Important as twentieth-century psychiatry's successes with definition were, however, they were largely confined to what we might call, linguistic–analytically speaking, lower-level concepts. Thus, the higher-level concept of "delusion" turned out to be more difficult to define than such lower-level concepts as "delusion of guilt" or "delusional perception"; and, conversely, the still higher-level concepts of "insight" and "psychosis", not to mention the concept of "mental disorder" itself, all proved harder to define than "delusion".

Psychiatry has been criticized, by its friends (Phillips, 2000) as well as its enemies (Bentall, 1992), for its (perceived) failures of definition with higher-level psychopathological concepts. From the perspective of linguistic analysis, however, these are not failures at all but a reflection of a property that psychopathological concepts share with concepts in general. The concept of "time", to take a standard philosophical example, is (considerably) harder to define than, say, the lower-level "hour" or "wristwatch". And yet, to return to the starting point of linguistic analysis, we *use* the concept of time all the time (*sic*) effortlessly. In this respect, then, with higher-level concepts, whether medical or non-medical, there is a sense in which we know what they mean even though we are unable to define them. Indeed our ability to produce definitions of lower-level concepts actually trades on the fact that we already understand the meanings of the higher-level concepts in terms of which such definitions are framed.[1]

Why not, then, Austin and others argued, employ our enhanced ability to use higher-level concepts as a guide or probe to their meanings? Rather than philosophers sitting in an Oxford college and just thinking about the meanings of such concepts, this being a high-IQ counterpart of definition, philosophers should do what Austin called philosophical "field work" (Austin, 1956/7 p. 25). They should examine how the concepts with which they are concerned are actually used in relevant areas of discourse.

Linguistic analysis, so defined, has a range of applications in psychiatry (Fulford, 1990; Fulford, Thornton and Graham, forthcoming, Chapter 1); combined with empirical social science methods, it generates practically-relevant findings (Colombo *et al.*, 2003); and it is the basis of a powerful approach to skills-based training (Fulford, Williamson and Woodbridge, 2002). It has however a particular relevance to psychopathological and diagnostic concepts (Fulford, 1989, 1994, 2002). In the rest of this chapter, then, I will take a broadly Austinian approach to exploring the psychopathological concept of psychotic loss of insight, drawing on a series of brief clinical vignettes, and starting with a linguistic-analytic critique of early attempts at definition.

---

[1] Thus, a wristwatch is a small instrument for measuring time worn on the wrist.

1.1 Failure of early attempts to define insight

Loss of insight, as noted above, is peculiarly difficult to define. This is partly because the term has many meanings, non-medical as well as medical. The *Shorter Oxford English Dictionary* (3rd edition), includes "seeing *into* a thing or subject", "discernment", and "a mental looking *to* or *upon* something". In this broad sense of the term, we speak of people having mathematical insight, for example. In psychology, similarly, "insight" has been adopted as a term of art for the Gestalt "seeing as a whole". Even in medicine, insight has a wide range of meanings (David, 1990), including plain *awareness* of symptoms, recognition of them as symptoms of *illness*, understanding of their *causal* origins, appreciation of their *significance* (e.g., their seriousness), and compliance with *treatment*.

1.2 Aubrey Lewis' definition

An early and seminal attempt to distil from these many meanings of the term a definition specifically of *psychotic* loss of insight was made by Aubrey Lewis (1934). Insight, Lewis argued, means "a correct attitude to a morbid change in oneself". Loss of insight, so defined, is certainly a feature of conditions traditionally classified as psychotic.

CASE 1 Mr P D, age 48, Bank Manager [Diagnosis – psychotic depression] Brought to casualty by his wife. Showed headache, biological symptoms of depression, and the delusion that he had brain cancer. History of attempted suicide. Asking for something to "help him sleep". Refused to believe that he was suffering from depression.

CASE 2 Miss H M, age 25, Novice nun [Diagnosis – hypomania] Brought by superiors for urgent outpatient appointment as they were unable to contain her bizarre and sexually disinhibited behaviour. Showed pressure of speech, grandiose delusions (that she was Mary Magdalene; and that her reams of poetry were of inestimable aesthetic value), and auditory hallucinations.

CASE 3 Mr S, age 18, Student [Diagnosis – schizophrenia] Emergency psychiatric admission from his college. Behaving oddly. Showed thought insertion (Mike Yarwood, a TV presenter, "using his brain"). Complained that people were talking about him.

In each of these three cases, the patient had an "incorrect attitude" toward his or her illness. However, as Lewis pointed out, an incorrect attitude may also be seen in psychiatric disorders that are not traditionally thought of as psychotic.

CASE 4 Miss H, age 30, Secretary [Diagnosis – hysterical paralysis] Admitted to neurology ward and transferred to psychiatry under protest. Unable to use right hand (patient right-handed). Paralysis "nonanatomical". History of self-injury. Firmly rejected psychological diagnosis.

An "incorrect attitude to a morbid change in oneself", moreover, Lewis continued, may be seen even in patients with physical illness.

CASE 5 Dr A, age 60, Medical doctor [Diagnosis – acromegaly] Developed thickening of soft tissues (e.g., lips), skull enlargement, and other features of acromegaly over a period of years but refused to acknowledge that these changes were pathological, even when they were pointed out to him.

CASE 6   Mr V N, age 55, Schoolteacher [Diagnosis – visual neglect] Suffered left-sided stroke. Unable to recognize his paralysed arm as his own, even when it was placed within his intact visual field.

Loss of insight, then, Lewis argued, is very far from being confined to patients with conditions traditionally classified as psychotic. Such patients, indeed, and conversely, may sometimes have relatively well preserved insight.

CASE 7   Mr C S, age 27, Unemployed [Diagnosis – long term schizophrenia] Suffered a second episode of schizophrenia. Despite responding well to anti-psychotic medication, auditory hallucinations persisted – he heard two female voices talking about him. However, he described these as "his voices" and recognized them to be symptoms of his illness.

1.3 The attempt to eliminate the concept of insight

Aubrey Lewis described his definition of insight as "preliminary" and he went on to give a more detailed analysis of the concept (as described below). But his overall conclusion was that since some *non*-psychotic patients may *lack* insight, while some *psychotic* patients may show *good* insight, the psychotic *versus* non-psychotic distinction, important as it had been in traditional descriptive psychopathology, was a distinction without a difference and should be abandoned. This has since become the official line in psychiatric classifications. Thus the authors of ICD-9 indicated that they had retained the psychotic/non-psychotic distinction only because of its continued wide usage (WHO, 1978); it was (ostensibly) abandoned in DSM-III (APA, 1980); and it has remained (ostensibly) banned in DSM-IV (APA, 1994) and in ICD-10 (WHO, 1992).

1.4 Persistence of the concept of insight

Aubrey Lewis' conclusion, and the rejection of the psychotic/non-psychotic distinction by the authors of DSM-III and ICD-10, could have been right. Other distinctions have been dropped on similar grounds – the distinction between reactive and endogenous depression, for example.

However, unlike the reactive/endogenous distinction, the psychotic/non-psychotic distinction has persisted. It continues to be used in everyday psychiatric contexts and in academic journals, in expressions such as puerperal psychosis and anti-psychotic drug. More remarkably, perhaps, given official attempts to abandon the distinction, it persists, less visibly but essentially unchanged, even in our official classifications (Fulford, 1994).

Thus, in ICD-9 the psychotic/non-psychotic distinction was used, as it had been used in traditional psychopathology, as a primary division. In DSM-III and in ICD-10 this primary division, into psychotic and non-psychotic categories, was dropped in favour of a larger number of primary categories defined (mainly) by particular areas of symptomatology. Yet the psychotic/non-psychotic distinction reappears, implicitly or explicitly, in ICD-10 and DSM-III as a subdivision of most of these new primary categories: affective and organic disorders, for example, are both subdivided into psychotic and non-psychotic subcategories. To the extent of the psychotic/non-psychotic distinction, therefore, these two arrangements are strictly equivalent, ICD-10 and DSM-III having, in effect, the same essential structure as ICD-9 but turned upside-down!

1.5 The significance of the persistence of the concept of insight

From the perspective of linguistic analytic philosophy, continued use of the psychotic/non-psychotic distinction, even in our official classifications, is highly significant. It suggests that, contrary to Aubrey Lewis, the distinction is not only useful but *essential* to psychiatric usage. This can be seen in terms of the Austrian[2] philosopher Ludwig Wittgenstein's picture of words as tools (Wittgenstein, 1958). Tools are developed to do different jobs. With gardening tools, for example, we have forks, spades, hoes, rakes, and so forth. Someone trying to define a spade might notice that all garden spades have wooden handles and pick this as a definition. Applying this definition to spades and forks, then, would suggest that the fork-spade distinction is a distinction without a difference. But when we come to *use* these tools for real, it is of course their sharp ends that turn out to be essential.

By analogy, then, continued use of the psychotic/non-psychotic distinction, despite the difficulties of definition, and despite the best efforts of the authors of our classifications to suppress it, suggests that, like the sharp end of a garden tool, it has an essential role to play in the way we understand psychopathology. What is needed, correspondingly, is not, as Aubrey Lewis suggested, to abandon the distinction, but to develop a better understanding of the meaning of the concept of psychosis than that provided by Lewis' definition.

One way to do this is by moving directly to further attempts to define the concept. We will be returning to the further attempts of Lewis and others below. The approach of linguistic analytic philosophy, however, as noted above, is to start with some Austinian philosophical field work, i.e. to start with a careful look at how the concept of insight is actually *used*. Our aim in this will be to map out what another Oxford philosopher, Gilbert Ryle, called the "logical geography" of the concept (Ryle, 1980). Rather like the data of empirical research, the features of the logical geography of a concept are a constraint on theory, in the positive sense that they are features which any theory of the meaning of the concept in question must explain (Fulford, 1989, Chapter 1). In the case of the concept of insight, then, its logical geography, its given features in everyday psychiatric and lay usage, will provide a more informed basis both for a critique of further

---

[2] Although Austrian, Wittgenstein worked mostly in Cambridge.

attempts at definition (in section 3), and for my proposed move from a Kraepelinian to a Jaspersian account of the meaning of the concept (sections 4–8).

2.0 **A logical geography of insight**

First, then, the logical geography. The concept of psychotic loss of insight in everyday (psychiatric and lay) usage shows three key features: (1) *association with particular symptoms*, notably delusions, hallucinations and certain kinds of thought disorder; of these, (2) delusions are *central*, both (a) psychopathologically and (b) ethically, and (3) delusion, as the central symptom of psychotic disorders, can take a remarkable *range of logical forms*.

2.1 **Association with particular symptoms**

Psychotic loss of insight is associated paradigmatically with delusions, hallucinations and with certain forms of thought disorder, such as thought insertion, thought withdrawal and thought broadcasting. I will be looking at these symptoms in more detail later on. They are illustrated by cases 1–3 above: psychotic depression, hypomania and schizophrenia, respectively. Mr P D (Case 1), as just noted, had a hypochondriacal delusion (that he had brain cancer); Miss H M (Case 2) had grandiose delusions but also auditory hallucinations; while Mr S (Case 3) had delusions of reference (that people were talking about him) and thought insertion, i.e. Mr S experienced a TV presenter's thoughts being inserted into his mind (the TV presenter was "using his brain").[3]

Taken together, these symptoms (delusion, hallucination and certain forms of thought disorder) define the traditional category of (non-organic) psychotic disorder. A psychotic disorder, so defined, is one in which one or more of these psychotic symptoms typically occur. Particular psychotic disorders are then differentiated by particular psychotic symptoms (e.g. grandiose delusions in hypomania, Case 2) together with certain associated symptoms (e.g. elevation of mood in hypomania). Some of these associated symptoms may involve loss of insight of a non-psychotic kind – for example, the severe cognitive disturbances (of memory, attention, orientation, and so on), which are the defining characteristics of organic psychoses such as dementia, may involve non-psychotic (as well as psychotic) loss of insight.

CASE 8 Mrs D, age 65, Retired shopkeeper [Diagnosis – dementia] Brought to casualty by the police. Found wandering and unable to recall her address. Complained that she was being chased by cats. She could see these cats, especially at night; they moved very fast; some were huge, like a horse. Cognitive function testing showed marked impairment of short- and long-term memory and disorientation for time.

The phenomenological significance of psychotic loss of insight is well illustrated by depression, in which both obsessions (retained insight) and delusions (loss of insight) may occur.

---

[3] Some classify thought disorder of this kind with delusion; see Sims, 1988.

CASE 9 Mr O D, age 48, Bank Manager [Diagnosis – obsessional thoughts secondary to depression] Presented to his GP complaining of headaches, low mood, difficulty sleeping and repeated thoughts that he had brain cancer. He regarded these thoughts as irrational because he had had them before, when he got "run down". He tried to resist them but found himself unable to – they were like "a tune stuck in my head".

In this case, then, the patient's thoughts of brain cancer are perceived by the patient himself as a symptom of his depression. This is in contrast to Case 1 above, Mr P D, whose *belief* that he had brain cancer was not, from his perspective, the problem. The problem from Mr P D's perspective was that he actually *had* brain cancer. In some depressed patients an obsession (with retained insight) may switch over a period of a day or two to become a delusion (with loss of insight) as their condition worsens, and this may signal a dangerous increase in suicide risk (Gittleson, 1966). Here, again, the critical factor is loss of insight.

2.2 Centrality of delusions – psychopathological and ethical

Psychotic loss of insight, as Aubrey Lewis himself noted (Lewis, 1934), following a tradition stretching back at least to Jaspers (Musalek, 2003), is associated paradigmatically with delusion. The central status of delusions, in this respect, has both psychopathological and ethical aspects.

2.2.1 Delusions are psychopathologically central

Among psychotic symptoms in general, there is a sense in which, as Jaspers (1913/1963) emphasized, delusions are phenomenologically basic. Thus, hallucinations are often defined as perceptions in the absence of appropriate stimuli (Harre and Lamb, 1986). However, true or psychotic hallucinations are perceptions in the absence of appropriate stimuli that are *delusionally believed to be real*. Hallucinations as such may indeed be normal experiences – for example, hearing the telephone ring as you drop off to sleep. Even in pathological conditions, hallucinations may occur that are recognized to be hallucinatory; as in Case 7. Such hallucinations, contrary to Aubrey Lewis' claim that they provide counter-examples to the psychotic/non-psychotic distinction, are one form of *pseudo*-hallucination (Hare, 1973).[4] With true or psychotic hallucinations, by contrast, not only do the patients concerned believe their experiences to be real, they may even elaborate a complex argument to protect this belief, a process which is called *delusional elaboration* (Wing, Cooper, and Sartorius, 1974, p. 214 ff.).

CASE 10 Mr D E, age 50, Clerk [Diagnosis – delusional elaboration] Patient reported hearing voices coming from an adjacent room. When shown room to be empty, said the people concerned had jumped out of the window. When shown that they were on the fourth floor, suggested that a microphone had been used. On finding no microphone, he claimed they were invisible. And so on.

[4] I return to a non-psychotic example of thought insertion below, see Section 7, the subsection on Thought Insertion.

The central association of delusion with loss of insight is reflected in modern standardized mental state assessments. Thus, the glossary to the Present State Examination (see above) distinguishes partial delusions from full delusions according to whether there is "partial or full conviction" (Wing, Cooper and Sartorius, 1974, p. 167). Psychopathology textbooks take a similar line, distinguishing delusions proper from other kinds of abnormal beliefs, such as partial delusions and over-valued ideas, by relative preservation of insight. Thus, Leff and Isaacs (1990, p. 50) contrast "Patients who concede under questioning that their delusions might be mistaken, due to their imagination, or part of a psychiatric illness . . ." as suffering from "partial delusions", from "Patients whose false beliefs cannot be shaken by argument . . ." as suffering from "full delusions".[5] Sims (1988), similarly, defines a delusion (p. 84) as a belief which is "held with unusual conviction, (is) not amenable to logic, (and the) absurdity or erroneousness of (the) content (of which) is manifest to other people", and an over-valued idea (p. 82), by contrast, as "an acceptable, comprehensible idea pursued by the patient beyond the bounds of reason".

2.2.2 Delusions as ethically central

The centrality of delusions is evident also in respect to their ethical and medicolegal implications. "Insanity", defined paradigmatically by delusion, is the central case of mental illness as an excuse in law (Butler, 1975; Grubin, 1991; Fulford, 1993a). Similarly, although legally sanctioned for any mental disorder (at least in the United Kingdom), involuntary psychiatric treatment is in practice largely confined to people with psychotic disorders (Sensky, Hughes, and Hirsch, 1991).

Taken together, the psychopathological and ethical centrality of delusions has the consequence that psychotic disorders offer the best *prima facie* case for a genuine *mental* illness, i.e. for a specifically medical understanding of mental distress and disorder. Thus, broadly identifiable as these disorders are with the traditional "madness" or "insanity", psychotic disorders have been thought of as illnesses at least since classical times (Kenny, 1969; Robinson, 1996); they are cross-culturally stable (Wing, 1978) and individual psychotic symptoms are identifiable with a degree of reliability at least as good as that of many of the symptoms of physical illness (Clare 1979). It is for these reasons that Thomas Szasz, notoriously the author of *The Myth of Mental Illness* (1960), called schizophrenia, as the best case for a genuine *mental* illness, the "sacred symbol" of psychiatry (Szasz, 1976).

2.3 Logical range of delusions

Given the many textbook definitions of delusions as false beliefs (e.g. in Harré and Lamb, 1986; Hamilton, 1978; Sims, 1988), it is perhaps not surprising that philosophers have tended to assume that objective falsity is of the essence of delusion (e.g. Flew, 1973; Glover, 1970; Quinton, 1985). However, the actual *use* of the clinical

---

[5] The degree of conviction is on a continuum, therefore.

concept of delusion shows that this is very far from the case. In the first place, delusions, although indeed often obviously false, are not always so. Mr A B's belief in Case 1 that he had brain cancer, could have been true. Moreover, delusions are sometimes not *objectively* false at all; sometimes they turn out to be true. Sometimes, indeed, as in the Othello syndrome (Shepherd, 1961; Vauhkonen, 1968), they may be known to be true even at the time the diagnosis is made.

CASE 11   Mr O S, age 45, Publican [Diagnosis – Othello syndrome] Attended general practitioner's surgery with his wife who was suffering from depression. On questioning, delivered an angry diatribe about his wife being "a tart". Unable to talk about anything else. Offered unlikely evidence (e.g., pattern of cars parked in road). Psychiatric referral confirmed diagnosis of Othello syndrome even though the doctors concerned knew that Mrs O S was depressed following the break-up of an affair.

That delusions are not necessarily false factual beliefs is shown more dramatically still by the occasional delusion of mental illness.[6] A delusion of this kind would be logically impossible (i.e., a contradiction in terms) if delusions were by definition false beliefs. For if delusions were, essentially, false beliefs, then the delusion of mental illness would be a belief which if true is false and if false is true!

CASE 12   Mr M I, age 40 [Diagnosis – delusion of mental illness] Brought to casualty after an overdose. Had tried to kill himself because he believed he was mentally ill. Diagnosis of hypochondriacal delusion of mental illness.

Delusions, then, as judged by the clinical *use* of the concept, as opposed to standard textbook definitions, are not (always or essentially) false beliefs. To the contrary, they may take the form of true as well as of false beliefs. More remarkably still, though, from the perspective of standard textbook definitions of delusion, delusions may not be expressed as factual beliefs at all, but as *value judgements* (Fulford, 1991).

Thus, Case 2, Miss H M, the novice nun with hypomania, had a positive (aesthetic) evaluative delusion, that her rambling poetry was of "inestimable" literary merit. Positive evaluative delusions of this and other grandiose kinds are common in hypomania. Negative delusional evaluations, on the other hand, are common in depression. Depressed people, for example, often have delusions of guilt. Such delusions may be factual or evaluative in form. For example, someone may believe, as a matter of fact, that they have done something terrible. Equally, though, they may evaluate something trivial they have (actually) done in a delusionally negative way.

CASE 13   Mr E D, age 40, Postman [Diagnosis – evaluative delusion of guilt] Emergency admission with depressed affect, early morning waking and weight loss. Had forgotten to give his children their pocket money. He believed this to be the "worst sin in the world", himself "worthless as a father" and so on.

---

[6] Cases 12 and 13 below are taken from Fulford, 1989, Chapter 10. All cases are based on real cases with biographical information altered to protect confidentiality.

Delusions, it is worth adding, are not divided into factual and evaluative in the standard textbooks. This is because the two kinds of delusion, although logically quite distinct, have identical implications for practice – a delusion of guilt is just a delusion of guilt, whether factual or evaluative in form, when it comes, for example, to the indications for using antidepressant medication or for involuntary psychiatric treatment. This discontinuity, between logical separation and practical togetherness, is indeed yet another remarkable feature of the logical geography of delusion that any theory of the meaning of psychotic loss of insight must seek to explain (this is not covered here, but see Fulford, 1989, Chapter 10).

3.0 A second look at definition: impaired cognitive functioning and the logical geography of delusion

In denying the validity of the psychotic/non-psychotic distinction, Aubrey Lewis was of course denying neither the psychopathological significance of delusions and related psychotic symptoms, nor the reality of conditions such as schizophrenia and depression. He believed, indeed, that all these symptoms, and correspondingly all these conditions, could be defined, at least in principle, by disturbances of what he called elsewhere "part" functioning, disturbances that is to say in one or more parts of the cognitive machinery of the mind (Lewis, 1955). But can an account along these lines, in terms of cognitive functioning, explain the logical geography of delusions as just outlined?

An impaired cognitive functioning account is, on first inspection, consistent with at least the psychopathological centrality of delusions (2.2.1). Lewis indeed argued that the centrality of delusions was connected with what he took to be their evident falsity (Lewis, 1934). Other authors have sought to derive the ethically central nature of delusions (2.2.2) similarly, arguing that this feature is connected with the extreme degree of objective falsity of delusional beliefs – the belief that one is already dead, for example, or that one is in two places at once, or that one's body contains a nuclear reactor. Flew (1973) indeed, suggested that the objective falsity of delusions is the only secure defence against abusive misuses of the insanity defence (and, by implication, of involuntary psychiatric treatment).

Yet, as we have seen (feature 3 above), delusions are very far from being always, still less necessarily, false beliefs. Where this is recognized, the standard response has been to assume that there must be some (as yet to be discovered) disturbance of cognitive functioning underlying the formation of psychotic symptoms, a delusion, on this account, occasionally taking the form of a true belief just by accident. For example, in the *Oxford Textbook of Psychiatry*, delusion is defined not as a false but as an "unfounded belief" (Gelder, Gath, and Mayou, 1983). This, again, is initially persuasive. After all, some forms of loss of insight – as in dementia (Case 8, above) – do indeed involve impairments of cognitive functioning. In other psychotic disorders there may be more subtle deficits – distractibility in hypomania, for instance, or marked slowing of thought in depression. Moreover, cognitive deficits *do* excuse (feature 3b) – we do not hold the patient with dementia fully responsible. In bioethics, similarly, accounts of responsibility have been developed in terms of specific cognitive capacities

(Beauchamp and Childress, 1989). And in the UK, at least, attempts have been made to define a generic concept of legal incapacity, encompassing bodily as well as mental conditions, in cognitivist terms (Law Commission, 1995).

Closer inspection, however, shows that there are difficulties even with this more enlightened cognitivist approach. First, it says nothing substantive about feature 3, the remarkable logical range of delusions. This aspect of the logical geography of insight, if noted at all, is treated as being merely epiphenomenal. Second, precisely *because* cognitive impairment is the defining feature of *other* symptoms, the account must specify a *particular kind* of cognitive impairment, consistent with the psychopathological centrality of delusions (2.2.1), if it is to differentiate delusion from these other symptoms: and notwithstanding some initially promising findings (e.g. Hemsley and Garety, 1986), no such specific impairment has yet been demonstrated (Garety and Freeman, 1999). Third, and similarly, precisely because cognitive impairment forms the basis for the status of *other* conditions (such as dementia and mental deficiency) as legal excuses, a different and specific cognitive impairment would have to underlie the status of delusion as an excuse (2.2.2). The bioethical account of rationality, noted above, fails on just this point (Fulford and Hope, 1993). It works well for conditions like dementia but it fails to explain the irrationality of the functional psychotic disorders.[7] Consistently with this conclusion, indeed, the authors of the "MacCAT-T," one of the most widely used psychological measures of capacity, Thomas Grisso and Paul Appelbaum (1996), have repeatedly emphasized the importance of what they call "appreciation disorder", viz, an element of capacity, distinct from disturbances in cognitive functioning such as memory and reasoning ability, and which they explicitly identify as corresponding with "delusional or another belief that seriously distorts reality . . ." (p. 185).

The discovery of an impairment of cognitive functioning specific to delusion may be just around the corner. But there are reasons for believing it may not be. In the first place, cognitive impairments, when present, actually *impair* delusional belief formation just as they impair the formation of *normal* beliefs – the "best-quality" delusions (emotionally charged, elaborate, and well sustained) occur in the monosymptomatic paranoid psychoses, i.e., in psychotic conditions (like the Othello syndrome, Case 10 above) in which there are few if any symptoms other than a well-developed delusional system. In the second place, if an impaired cognitive functioning account were on the right lines, given the central place of delusions, we should expect the relevant cognitive impairment to be relatively transparent i.e., relatively *easy* to identify, rather than, as it has turned out to be, unexpectedly *difficult* to identify. It need not be; but we should expect it to be if an impaired cognitive functioning account were along the right lines. In the third place, as no less an advocate of impaired functioning accounts of disorder than the American

---

[7] Several of the vignettes in this paper, including cases 1 (psychotic depression), 2 (hypomania) and 3 (schizophrenia), were included in the study cited (by Fulford and Hope, 1993), showing the failure of purely cognitivist criteria for capacity in respect of functional, i.e. non-organic, psychotic disorders.

philosopher Christopher Boorse (1976) has pointed out, such accounts place other symptoms more naturally at the centre. This is because, as we will see in the next two sections, the concept of functioning is attached naturally to the parts and subsystems of people's bodies, whereas psychotic disorders, like schizophrenia, as Boorse and many others have noted, involve a more global disturbance of the person as a whole.

There is a *prima facie* failure of fit, then, between accounts of delusion that presuppose one or more underlying failures of cognitive functioning and the logical geography of insight. Again, this is not to say that an account of delusion, and other psychotic symptoms, along (purely) cognitivist lines may not eventually be forthcoming. There is a rich philosophical as well as empirical literature supporting the project of developing such an account (see e.g. Coltheart and Davies, 2000; Hoerl, 2001). Perhaps, though, given the *prima facie* failure of fit, it is worth trying a different approach, an approach that starts from and takes seriously the (remarkable) features of the logical geography of insight. It is to such an approach that I turn in the rest of this chapter, starting with feature 3 of the logical geography, the remarkable range of forms of delusion.

4.0 Feature three of the logical geography of insight: from cognitive functioning to practical reasoning accounts of delusion

Besides the somewhat negative reasons just given for believing that an impaired cognitive functioning account of delusions may not, after all, be just around the corner, there is also a positive reason. This positive reason is essentially that the logical geography of delusions themselves suggests that they may be, or reflect, impairment of a rather different kind of reasoning altogether, namely what Aristotle, no less, called *practical reasoning*. Cognitive functioning stands to practical reasoning broadly as the parts of the mind stand to the whole: viz cognitive functions, such as memory and attention, are the *parts* of the mental machinery, while practical reasons are the reasons that people, *whole* people as it were, give for their actions, for the things that they do. And in direct contrast with the *prima facie* failure of fit just noted between delusion and cognitive functioning, when we look carefully at the logical forms of reasons for action we find that these directly correlate with the logical forms of delusion.

The correlation between delusions and reasons for action is shown diagrammatically in Figure 3.1. In most contexts, facts and values, the two principle logical forms of delusion, are like chalk and cheese. Facts are objective, values subjective: facts are capable in principle of verification; values, as we say (as in the case of beauty) are in the eye of the beholder. Indeed there is a long debate in moral philosophy, going back at least to the eighteenth century British empiricist philosopher, David Hume, about whether facts and values can be connected logically at all (Hare, 1952). In the context of giving reasons, however, facts and values come together. *Reasons for doing* something, that is to say, may be expressed either in factual or evaluative terms: thus, if I am asked why am I writing this chapter, my reasons might include (1) because the editors invited me to (fact)

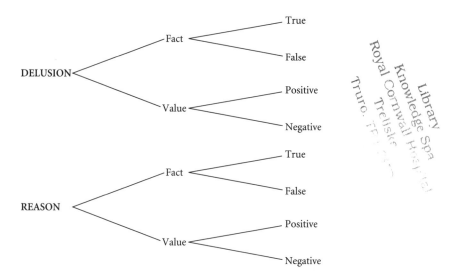

Fig. 3.1 Correlation between the logical forms of delusions and the logical forms of reasons for action. Although defined in most textbooks as false beliefs, and often objectively so, delusions may also take the form of true beliefs and of value judgements, either positive or negative. This remarkable logical range of forms of delusion is paralleled by that of reasons for action, i.e. the reasons we give for the things we do. This suggests that the irrationality of delusions may be better understood in terms of practical reasoning (reasons for action) rather than the (traditional) cognitive functioning.

or (2) because I enjoy writing (implicit positive value). Practical reasoning of this kind always involves some combination of facts and values (and other elements). Expressed as reasons for action, then, facts and values, far from being logical chalk and cheese, come, like factual and evaluative delusions, naturally together. Reasons, furthermore, in this sense, may, like delusions, take the form of false as well as of true factual beliefs, and/or of negative as well as positive value judgements (Fulford, 1989, Chapter 10, 1993).

The connection between delusions and practical reasoning suggested by the correlation between the logical forms of delusion and the logical forms of reasons (for action) is consistent with, and to this extent explains, feature 3 of the logical geography of delusions. It also opens up possible explanations for each of the other key features of the logical geography of insight outlined in Section 3, above. It is to these explanations, considered separately, that I turn below, in Sections 6 and 7. First, though, we need to consider briefly the wider relationship between function and action and how this connects with the relationship between medical knowledge of disease and patients' actual experiences of illness.

5.0 **From function to action, from disease to illness**

In everyday contexts, we tend to talk of the things people do in terms of actions rather than functions. Consider, for example, a very simple action – you wave your hand in the air. We would normally describe this as a (simple) *action* of yours, as something you are doing. This is how we generally talk about the things people do in everyday contexts, i.e. as their *actions*. It carries with it other everyday concepts, such as motive, intention, desire, purpose, willing, voluntariness, initiative, freedom and trying. If the circumstances were more medical, however, we might talk about your hand moving in terms not of action but of *function*. A doctor, for example, carrying out a neurological examination, might speak of the functioning of your hand and arm.

With simple actions of this kind, either the action way or the function way of talking is entirely appropriate, and we use one or the other depending on context (Fulford, 1989, Chapter 7). On a smaller scale, however, when we talk of the things that our bodies and minds do on the scale of nerves, synapses, speech centres, hearts, livers, and lungs, it is more natural to use function language. This smaller scale is, of course, the province of science and, hence, of disease theory. It is for this reason that in medicine, function language has become dominant. But, and this is a crucial "but", patients' experiences of illness arise in the *everyday* world, the world of agents and their *actions*. Hence there is a good *prima facie* case for believing that patients' experiences of illness, in so far as these are distinct from medical knowledge of disease (Fulford, 1989, Chapter 2), will be framed in the language of action rather than (or at any rate in addition to) that of function (Fulford, 1989, Chapter 5).

5.1 Action language and psychopathology

That action language is important at least in psychopathology, i.e., in patients' experiences of *mental* illness, can be seen, linguistic-analytically, by direct inspection of the language in which psychopathological concepts are defined even in medical-scientific classifications (Fulford, 1989, Chapters 7 and 8, 1994). This (further) exercise in Austinian philosophical "field work" indeed reveals many of the terms ordinarily associated with action rather than function. For example, in ICD-9, someone suffering from alcoholism is distinguished from the mere drunkard by the fact that he is not acting on his "own initiative" (WHO, 1978, p. 43). In ICD-10, similarly, a "central descriptive characteristic" of "alcohol dependence syndrome" is ". . . the desire (often strong, sometimes overpowering) . . ." to take alcohol (WHO, 1992, p. 75). Again, in ICD-9, a person with hysteria is unaware of his own "motives" (WHO, 1978, p. 35). In the American DSM-III, hysterical symptoms are said to be not under "voluntary control", as against those of the malingerer, which are, variously, "purposeful," "intentional," and "voluntary" (APA, 1980, pp. 331–2). The DSM-IV goes so far as to include "an important loss of freedom" in its over-arching definition of mental disorder (APA, 1994, p. xxi).

Once we start to think in terms of action as well as function, it comes as no surprise to find terms like voluntary and intentional in the language used of these conditions. For action language, as indicated a moment ago, is the language of everyday experience rather than of scientific disease theory; and, as also just noted, it is in everyday experience that patients' experiences of illness, including mental illness, arise. But how does all this explain the remaining two features of the logical geography of psychotic loss of insight? It is to this that we now turn, working backwards through feature 2 (the centrality of delusions) in the next section, to feature 1 (the paradigmatic association of psychotic loss of insight with particular symptoms) in section 7.

6.0 Feature two of the logical geography of insight: delusion as a constitutive failure of action

Feature 2 of the logical geography of insight, the centrality of delusions (psychopathological and ethical), drops directly out of the theory that delusions are, or are derived from, impaired practical reasoning.

6.1 Feature 2a: The psychopathological centrality of delusions

In section 3 above, we found that the psychopathological centrality of delusions poses a double problem for (exclusively) cognitivist theories. The first problem is that, despite much effort, and despite the success of cognitive functioning accounts of other symptoms (such as depression), no impairment of cognitive functioning specific to delusion has yet been identified. The second problem is that, given the contrality of delusions, a cognitive functioning account might be expected to be most, not least, readily available in respect of them. This is not a logical requirement. Contingently, though, if function language offered us a sufficient bag of conceptual tools (in Wittgenstein's metaphor, above) for talking about psychopathology, we should expect the central kind of psychopathology to yield first, not last, or not at all, to an account in terms of impaired cognitive functioning.

With action language, by contrast, the centrality of delusions follows naturally from the centrality of reasons themselves in what Austin (1956–7) called the "machinery of action".[8] Thus, other elements of this machinery (such as volition, control, and movement) are executive, i.e. they are necessary for successful *performance* of an action. But reasons are *constitutive* – that is to say, a given action is in part actually *defined by* the reasons for which it is done. You raise your hand in the air; this could be the action of hailing a taxi, signalling a bid, calling a waiter, swatting a mosquito, catching a ball, and so on. Which action it is depends not on the *movement* of raising your hand (which may be identical in each case) but on your *reasons* for raising your hand. It is, then, the constitutive nature of reasons that places delusions in a central place in the map of psychiatry. For if *reasons for action* have this central place in the structure of action, so a *failure* of reasons for action (i.e., delusion) will be a central kind of action failure (i.e., of psychopathology).

6.2 Feature 2b: The ethical centrality of delusions

This in turn explains feature 2b, viz the central medicolegal and ethical significance of delusions. Recall that psychotic disorders have traditionally been the central case for

---

8 Again, I set this argument out in full in *Moral Theory and Medical Practice* (Fulford, 1989), Chapter 10.

mental illness as a legal excuse (and correspondingly of involuntary treatment). Now, the essential feature of a legal excuse is a *failure of action* of one kind or another: the traditional list of excuses includes accident, inadvertence, duress, mistake, and so on (Hart, 1968). It has been something of a mystery, then, from the perspective of the standard medical model of delusion, why someone who is deluded should not be held responsible. Accident and inadvertence are not relevant. Some have argued, along cognitive functioning lines, that delusion involves a form of internal duress (Nordenfelt, 1992); but there is no compulsion as such; and *more* obviously compulsive symptoms (addictions, obsessions) are *less* central cases of mental illness as a legal excuse. Nor is the status of delusion as an excuse a question merely of mistake. The deluded person may be mistaken; but as the British social scientist, Baroness Wootton, was among the first to point out (Wootton, 1959), we would not excuse the man who has killed someone in the belief that he is being persecuted merely on the grounds that he was mistaken (though this might be raised in mitigation). As a *constitutive failure of action*, on the other hand, delusions fall automatically, along with other failures of action, within the traditional list of excuses (Fulford, 1989, Chapter 10, 1993).

The explanations now given of features 2 and 3 of the logical geography of insight, taken together, automatically accommodate the status of psychotic disorders as a central species of illness. The explanation of feature 3 linked psychotic loss of insight to patients' experiences of illness: and the explanation of feature 2 showed why delusion, understood as a defect of practical reasoning, is a central kind of illness experience. But psychotic disorders are defined by psychotic symptoms, to which, in turn, delusions are phenomenologically basic. Hence psychotic disorders, on this account, are, consistently with feature 2 of the logical geography of insight, a central species of illness.

7.0 Feature one of the logical geography of insight: "Illness-differential Diagnoses" of thought insertion, hallucination and delusion

If delusion is better understood in terms of the language of action rather than of function, and if action language is the language of patients' experiences of illness, this suggests that loss of insight generally might be analysed in terms of the experience of illness. The features of an experience that mark it out as an experience as illness, as something wrong with us, have been explored more by sociologists (e.g. Parsons, 1951; Lockyer, 1981) than by doctors or philosophers. A number of such features have been identified; for instance, intensity and duration – a mild, brief pain is unlikely to be experienced as "something wrong".

A further, and less well recognized, feature of the experience of illness, is that it is characterized (in part) by a two-way distinction. I describe the experiential basis of this two-way distinction in detail in *Moral Theory and Medical Practice* (Fulford, 1989, Chapters 6 and 7). Briefly, we experience "something wrong" as being different, both from things that are "*done by*" us, and from things that are "*done or happen to*" us. Most of our experiences are either "done by" experiences, i.e., things that we do, or "done/happens to" experiences, i.e., things that are done or happen to us. But if, say, I reach for my pencil and find, suddenly, that my hand will not move, this is experienced neither as something I am doing (i.e., just keeping my hand still), nor as something that is being done to me (e.g., someone or something restraining me). Similarly, pain, experienced as illness, is different both from deliberately hurting oneself (a "done by" experience) and from being hurt by someone or something (a "done/happens to" experience). Again, amnesia is different both from not remembering ("done by") and from being distracted ("done to").

This two-way distinction – "wrong with" being distinguished both from "done by" and "done/happens to" – can be shown to be a general feature of patients' primary experiences of illness (Fulford, 1989, Chapters 7 and 8). Once it is pointed out, the two-way distinction may seem self-evident, almost trivial. Yet it is sufficient not only to suggest a general account of specifically psychotic loss of insight but also, *contra* Aubrey Lewis, to generate detailed differential diagnostic tables discriminating psychotic from non-psychotic symptoms.

These differential diagnostic tables, which are illustrated below, are described in detail in *Moral Theory and Medical Practice* (1989, Chapter 10). They build on the idea that, if the (primary) experience of illness is distinct both from things that we do and from things that are done or happen to us, then psychotic loss of insight can be understood as a *misconstrual across this two-way distinction*. This is quite different from mere lack of awareness of symptoms (as in Cases 5, denial, and 6, visual neglect). It is also different from merely failing to accept the origins of acknowledged pathology in psychological rather than bodily causes (Case 7, hysterical paralysis). These are all negative accounts of loss of insight. The misconstrual account suggests, rather, a positive relocation of an experience across one or other limb of the two-way distinction by which the experience of illness, all illness, is characterized.

7.1 Thought insertion

Thought insertion (illustrated by Case 3, Mr S, the young man with a diagnosis of schizophrenia) provides a case in point (Fulford, 1989, Chapter 7, 1995). Thus, thinking is in many (though not all) respects like movement, something that we do. Like movement, it may be automatic rather than deliberative. But if thinking runs wholly out of control – as in, say, an obsessional disorder (Case 8) – it ceases to be experienced fully as something that we do and becomes something wrong with us. On the other hand, if we are merely preoccupied with some genuinely preoccupying experience (bereavement, say), this relative loss of control is experienced as something that happens to us. But thought insertion is odder than either of these. Thought insertion is neither our own thoughts running out of control nor our own thoughts being influenced by other people or by events. Thought insertion is the experience of other people

Thoughts in patient's mind	Attribution					
	By patient			By others		
	Done by	Wrong with	Done to	Done by	Wrong with	Done to
Normal	+			+		
Epileptic		+			+	
Obsessional		+			+	
Thought Insertion			⊕		+	

Fig. 3.2. An illness-differential diagnostic table for thought insertion. In this figure thought insertion is compared with other kinds of thought, normal and pathological, across the two-way distinction by which the (primary) experience of illness is (partly) defined. Thought insertion stands out as being the only kind of thought which is construed differently by the patient (left-hand side of the table) and everyone else (right-hand side of the table). Thought insertion, although understood by everyone else as something wrong with the patient, is experienced by the patient themselves as something that is being "done to" them.

actually using the patient's own mind for their thinking.[9] This is very difficult to characterize negatively. So much so, indeed, that with a non-psychotic equivalent of thought insertion, epileptic "forced thoughts", the patient readily accepts the doctor's explanation that this is "something wrong" (Lishman, 1987). But a patient experiencing thought insertion, like Mr S, far from accepting that there is something wrong with him, actively insists that something is being *done to* him. Mr S was angry that Mike Yarwood, a TV presenter, was "using his (Mr S's) brain".

This active relocation of the experience of thought insertion across the two-way distinction by which the experience of illness is (partly) defined, is illustrated by the differential diagnosis summarized in the table in Figure 3.3. I have called this elsewhere (Fulford, 1989, Chapter 10) an illness-differential diagnostic table to emphasize the fact that it draws only on the two-way distinction by which the experience of illness (all illness) is (partly) defined. Thus, thought insertion is analysed in this table along with other kinds of thought, normal and pathological, in terms of the "done by-wrong with-done to" distinction, first from the patient's perspective (left side of the table) and then from everyone else's perspective (right side). As can be seen, the psychotic symptom stands out. It is a "done to" experience for the patient whereas it is a "wrong with" experience for everyone else. The other phenomena listed in the table, by contrast, are the same from both perspectives.

[9] The remarkable separation of ownership of thought and first-personal thinking represented by thought insertion is attracting a growing philosophical literature: see e.g. Chadwick, R. F. (1994) and Stephens and Graham (1994). Also, Stephens and Graham (2000); and several articles in a special double issue of *Philosophy, Psychiatry, and Psychology* (Hoerl, 2001) June/September 2001 – 8/2 and 8/3) edited by the Warwick philosopher, Christoph Hoerl (2001), on philosophy and schizophrenia.

Perception	Attribution					
	By patient			By others		
	Done by	Wrong with	Done to	Done by	Wrong with	Done to
Normal	+		+	+		+
Illusion			++			++
Eye disease		++			++	
Psychotic hallucination	⊕		⊕		++	
"Normal" hallucination	++	+		++	+	
Imagery	++			++		

Fig. 3.3 An illness-differential diagnostic table for hallucination. The illness-differential diagnosis of hallucination is more complex than that for thought insertion but follows essentially the same lines. True (or psychotic) hallucinations thus stand out as the only form of perception which, in terms of the two-way distinction by which the experience of illness is defined, is construed differently by the patient (left-hand side of the figure) and by others (right-hand side of the figure).

7.2 Hallucination

A more complex illness-differential diagnostic table is needed for the more complex symptom of hallucination. This is because whereas thinking is normally something that we do, perception is partly something we do (it is active) and partly something that is done to us (by the environment). But the same principle applies. As can be seen from Figure 3.3 it is only for true or psychotic hallucinations that there is a discrepancy between the two sides of the table, between the patient's construction of the experience and the construction placed on it by everyone else.

7.3 Delusion

Delusion, again, requires a more complex treatment. We should expect this, delusion being phenomenologically basic, in the sense that it underpins all other psychotic symptoms (feature 1, above). As to content, as Figure 3.4 illustrates, most delusions can indeed be readily mapped across the two-way distinction by which the experience of illness is (in part) defined: with delusions of guilt, for instance, patients locate the problem as something they have *done*, whereas everyone else locates it as something *wrong with* them. With delusions of persecution, on the other hand, patients locate the problem as something that is being *done to* them. Even with hypochondriacal delusions (Case 1), the patient relocates the problem, not as something psychologically wrong with them, but as something that is *happening to* them in the form of a bodily disease.

With delusion, however, and hence, derivatively, with all other psychotic symptoms, form rather than content is the more important, psychopathologically. Translating this into the language of illness experience, this means that delusion involves not just a misconstrual across the "done by-wrong with-done to" distinction, but a *delusional*

Beliefs	Attribution					
	By Patient			By Others		
	Done by	Wrong with	Done to	Done by	Wrong with	Done to
Normal belief	+			+		
Obsession (e.g. Case 9)		+			+	
Partial delusion	±	±		±	±	
Overvalued idea	±	±		±	±	
Delusion of guilt (evaluative – e.g. Case 12)	+				+	
Delusion of guilt (factual)	+				+	
Delusion of reference (e.g. Case 3)			+		+	
Hypochondriacal delusion (e.g. Cases 1 and 10)			+		+	
Othello syndrome (e.g. Case 11)			+		+	
Grandiose delusion (e.g. Case 2)	+				+	
Delusional elaboration (e.g. Case 10)			+		+	

Fig. 3.4 An illness-differential diagnostic figure for delusion. To the extent that delusions are marked out from other kinds of belief, both normal and pathological, they can be mapped according to their content across illness-differential diagnostic figure similar to those for thought insertion (Figure 3.3) and hallucination figure.

misconstrual. As described in *Moral Theory and Medical Practice* (1989, Chapter 10), this implies that there is a sense in which psychotic forms of hallucination, thought insertion, and so forth, stand in much the same (logical) relation to the form of delusional beliefs as the content of delusional beliefs themselves. This in turn implies that illness-differential diagnostic tables of the kind illustrated in this section, while they do indeed differentiate psychotic from non-psychotic symptoms, nonetheless beg a whole series of questions about the precise sense in which delusions (and hence psychotic loss of insight) are (or involve) irrational thinking: what is the nature of the proposed defects in the structure of practical reasoning? How are these related to the misconstruals by which psychotic loss of insight are characterized experientially? How in turn is this related to the cognitive defects by which other forms of irrationality, as in dementia, are characterized? What is the relationship among all of these, as pathological forms of irrationality, and non-pathological forms of irrationality, such as self-deception and weakness of will?

8.0 **A more complete understanding**

That linguistic analysis should raise questions, as well as answer them, is a strength of the approach. The aim of linguistic analysis, as noted at the start of this chapter, is not to provide a "theory of everything", a neat formulaic definition summing up the full meaning and implications of a higher-level concept. Linguistic analysis aims, rather, to raise awareness, to give us a more complete understanding of the full meaning of the concepts with which we are concerned.

The ideas set out in this and the last three sections, linking delusion with practical reasoning, the centrality of delusions with the constitutive (hence central) kind of failure of action represented by failures of practical reasoning, and insight with the two-way distinction by which experiences of illness are (partly) defined, can be understood as falling within a more complete understanding of the medical concepts. This is illustrated diagrammatically by Figure 3.5. The account of insight offered by Aubrey Lewis and his successors draws on the elements of what has become widely known at the medical model. This term covers a variety of models, the common feature of which is a more or less tacit assumption that medicine is, at heart, exclusively an empirical science (Macklin, 1973; Fulford, 2003). The medical model thus focuses on what are assumed to be value-free disease theories, to which doctors in particular are expert, and which when well developed are cast in terms of disturbances in the functioning of bodily and mental parts and systems. Aubrey Lewis's account of insight (Section 1) is correspondingly all to do with, in his own words, viewing symptoms "objectively"; it is about "evidence" and "data"; a *morbid change* is one which ". . . interfere(s) with the integration of . . . part function . . ."; and, most telling of all, the *correct attitude* of his proposed definition of insight is one which "approximates to that of the clinician". The medical model is reflected, similarly, in those theories of delusion (examined in Section 3) that, derivatively on Aubrey Lewis' analysis, assume some underlying impairment of cognitive functioning. The present analysis, by contrast, involved a critical shift of focus, carried out over Sections 4 and 5, from medical disease theory and failures of cognitive functioning, to patients' experiences of illness and failures of practical reasoning. It was this shift, in the terms of Figure 3.5 a shift from the right to the left half-field, which gave us the expanded conceptual resources required to explain, in section 4 to 7 the key features of the logical geography of insight.

It is important to be clear that this approach, to the extent that it is successful, adds to rather than subtracting anything from, the traditional medical model. This is important, first, because the conceptual resources of the traditional medical model, if insufficient to explain the features of psychotic loss of insight, nonetheless remain necessary to the explanations of other forms of loss of insight (for example, as in the cognitive symptoms of organic psychoses, Case 8 above), not to mention other forms of psychopathology altogether. Function and action, anyway, as we saw in Section 5, and as Figure 3.5 illustrates diagrammatically, are not mutually exclusive but complementary ways of conceptualizing human agency.

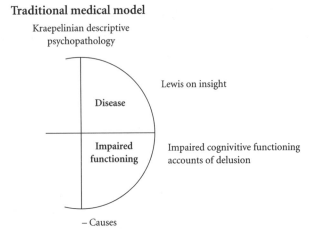

Traditional medical model

Kraepelinian descriptive
psychopathology

Lewis on insight

Disease

Impaired
functioning

Impaired cognivitive functioning
accounts of delusion

– Causes

A more complete model

Jaspersian phenomenological
psychopathology

Illness-differential
diagnostic tables
(Thought insertion;
hallucination; delusion)

Lewis on insight

Illness   Disease

Impaired
agency/
action

Impaired
functioning

Impaired
practical reasoning
accounts of delusion

Impaired cognivitive functioning
accounts of delusion

Meanings–Causes

Fig. 3.5 From a partial to a more complete understanding of the medical concepts. Linguistic analysis aims to give us a more complete understanding of the meanings of the concepts used in a given area. The analysis of insight outlined in this chapter draws on aspects of the meanings of the medical concepts (concerned with patients' experiences of illness) that are neglected in the traditional medical model (which focuses rather on medical knowledge of disease). This more complete understanding of the medical concepts stands to the medical model much as Jaspers' phenomenological psychopathology (encompassing meanings as well as causes) stands to Kraepelin's descriptive psychopathology.

The additive nature of linguistic analysis is important, second, because of the evident limitations even of the more complete view of the medical concepts outlined here, when it comes to understanding psychotic loss of insight itself. I have already noted (at the end of the last section), a whole series of questions about delusion and its relationship to insight, questions which are raised, and perhaps sharpened, but certainly not answered, by the analysis outlined in this chapter. The analysis, furthermore, in moving the focus from the parts of people (cognitive functions) to whole persons (practical reasoning), may have taken us a step towards a more complete understanding of the concept of insight. But it is clear that at least one further step is required, i.e., from persons, considered individually, to the inter-personal or collective space of social meanings.[10] Psychotic loss of insight, after all, is, among psychopathologies, uniquely defined *inter*-personally. The difference between obsession (Case 9) and delusion (Case 1) in depression, for example, is a difference between a problem *within* the person and a problem *between* persons: Mr O D, Case 9, had a problem with his *own* (obsessional) thoughts; the problem for Mr P D, Case 1, by contrast, was that he (delusionally) believed he had brain cancer while everyone else believed that he did not. The illness-differential diagnostic tables described in Section 7 help to define this shift from a problem within to a problem between people; the connection between delusion and impaired practical reasoning outlined in Sections 4 to 6 helps to show why the shift is so significant; but neither, in themselves, actually explain it.

9.0 **Conclusions: just getting started**

The broadly Austinian linguistic-analytic approach adopted in this chapter has generated at least partial answers to each of the three questions from which we began. We can summarize our findings thus:

Question 1: Why has the psychotic/non-psychotic distinction persisted in psychiatric (as well as lay) usage, despite the best efforts of Aubrey Lewis and his successors to eliminate it? *Answer*: because, like the sharp end of a garden fork, the distinction is essential to the conceptual tool-bag that we need in order to understand and talk about psychopathology.

Question 2: Why, then, is the concept of insight, by which the psychotic/non-psychotic distinction is characterized, so peculiarly resistant to definition? *Answer*: because insight, like the concept of time, is a higher-level concept and thus shares with higher-level concepts in general the property of being easier to use than to define.

Question 3: So, what *does* insight mean? *Answer*: while no definition of insight has been produced (none would be expected, linguistic-analytically), examination of the way the concept is actually used suggests that its meaning has to be understood within a picture of the conceptual structure of medicine which is more complete than that provided by the traditional medical-scientific model. The more complete picture outlined here adds, (1) patients' experiences of illness to medical knowledge of disease, and (2) an analysis of patients' experiences of illness in terms of failures of action to the medical-scientific analysis of disease in terms of failures of functioning.

---

[10] For work in this area of "discursive" psychology and philosophy, see e.g. Harré, 1997; and Harré and Gillett, 1994.

That word "adds" in the answer to question 3 is important. Linguistic analysis, as has several times been emphasized, adds to, rather than subtracting anything from, the traditional medical-scientific model. The additions noted in this chapter are important to the extent that they help to explain the key features of the logical geography of insight noted in Section 2: the addition of patients' experiences of illness to medical knowledge of disease helps to explain the association of insight with thought disorder, hallucination and delusion (feature 1 – see the illness-differential diagnostic tables, Section 7 above); the addition of an analysis of "illness experience" in terms of failure of agency to the medical-scientific analysis of disease in terms of failure of functioning, helps to explain the remarkable logical range of delusions (feature 3 – see the correlation between the forms of delusion and of reasons for action, Section 6 above); and this in turn helps to explain the central status of psychotic disorders, as defined particularly by delusions, both psychopathological and ethical (feature 2 – failure of reasons (for action) being a constitutive rather than merely executive failure of action, see Section 4 above). All the same, these additions, if amounting to a more complete understanding than that provided by the traditional medical model, are very far from amounting to a *complete* understanding. To the contrary, they open up a whole series of questions for further study, as signalled particularly at the ends of Sections 7 and 8.

Austin would have approved of the open-ended nature of this account of insight. Linguistic analysis, on the Austin model, is, at most, one way of getting started with some kinds of philosophical problem (Warnock, 1989, Chapter 1). In the present case, indeed, linguistic analysis should be understood, not so much as getting us started as getting us *back* where we started, i.e., with the psychopathology of Karl Jaspers at the start of the twentieth century. Jaspers, working as a philosopher as well as a psychiatrist, and during a period like our own of rapid advances in the neurosciences, argued for a phenomenological psychopathology (Jaspers, 1913a), a twin-track approach incorporating meaningful as well as causal-scientific accounts of psychosis (Jaspers, 1913b). For much of the twentieth century, psychiatry, through the work of Kraepelin and others, focused mainly on the scientific side of Jaspers' twin-track psychopathology. We have done well from this. As noted above, focusing in this way has given us a reliable descriptive psychopathology which in turn has been the basis of recently renewed progress in the neurosciences. Yet it is precisely this renewed progress in the neurosciences that has led many of those most directly concerned to recognize the need for a renewal of Jaspers' agenda for a twin-track, phenomenological rather than merely descriptive, psychopathology (Fulford *et al.*, 2003[11]).

---

[11] The renewed need for a phenomenological psychopathology, building on the successes of twentieth century descriptive psychopathology, arises partly from the requirements of the new neurosciences themselves for more sophisticated ways of understanding the structure of experience, partly from shifts in policy and practice towards more user-centred mental health services (DOH, 1999, 2000). These developments in turn tie in with a growing recognition of the ways in which values, alongside facts, help to structure psychopathological concepts (Fulford, 2003, 2004; Sadler, 2002). The importance of values in this respect is evident, for example, in cross-cultural diagnosis (Fulford, 1999), with implications, not least, for the assessment of insight (Perkins and Moodley, 1993).

It is as a contribution to the renewal of Jaspers' agenda for a phenomenological psychopathology, therefore, that the linguistic-analytic account of the clinical concepts of insight and delusion outlined in this chapter should be read.

Acknowledgements

I am grateful to the editors of this book for their helpful comments on an early draft of this chapter.

References

American Psychiatric Association (APA) (1980). *Diagnostic and Statistical Manual of Mental Disorders*, 3rd edn. Washington, DC: American Psychiatric Association.

American Psychiatric Association (1994). *Diagnostic and Statistical Manual of Mental Disorders*, 4th edn. Washington, DC: American Psychiatric Association.

Austin, J. L. (1956–7/1968). A plea for excuses, Proceedings of the Aristotelian Society, 57, 1–30. Reprinted in A. R. White, (ed.) *The Philosophy of Action*. Oxford: Oxford University Press.

Beauchamp, T. L. and Childress, J. F. (1989) (Year). *Principles of Biomedical Ethics*. Oxford: Oxford University Press.

Bentall R. (1992). A proposal to classify happiness disease as a psychiatric disorder. *Journal of Medical Ethics*, **18**, 94–8.

Boorse, C. (1976). What a theory of mental health should be. *Journal of Theory Social Behaviour*, **6**, 61–84.

Butler (Chairman). (1975). Report of the Committee on Mentally Abnormal Offenders. *Comd. 6244*. London: HMSO.

Chadwick, R. F. (1994). Kant, Thought insertion, and mental unity. *Philosophy, Psychiatry, and Psychology*, **1/2**, 105–14.

Clare, A. (1979). The disease concept in psychiatry. In P. Hill, R. Murray and A. Thorley, *Essentials of Postgraduate Psychiatry*. New York: Academic Press, Grune and Stratton.

Colombo, A., Bendelow, G., Fulford, K. W.M. and Williams, S. (2003). Evaluating the influence of implicit models of mental disorder on processes of shared decision making within community-based multi-disciplinary teams. *Social Science and Medicine*, **56**, 1557–70.

Coltheart, M. and Davies, M. (ed.) (2000). *Pathologies of Belief*. Oxford: Blackwell Publishers.

David, A. S. (1990). Insight and psychosis. *British Journal of Psychiatry*, **156**, 798–808.

DOH (1999). *National Service Framework for Mental Heath, Modern Standards and Service Models*. London: HMSO.

DOH (2000). *The NHS Plan, A Plan for Investment, A Plan for Reform*. London: HMSO.

Flew, A. (1973). *Crime or Disease?* New York: Barnes and Noble.

Fulford, K. W. M. (1989, reprinted 1995 and 1999; second edition forthcoming) *Moral Theory and Medical Practice*. Cambridge: Cambridge University Press.

Fulford, K. W. M. (1990). Philosophy and medicine: The Oxford connection. *British Journal of Psychiatry*, **157**, 111–15.

Fulford, K. W. M. (1991). Evaluative delusions; their significance for philosophy and psychiatry, *British Journal of Psychiatry*, **159**, supp. 14, 108–12.

Fulford K. W. M. (1993). Value, action, mental illness and the law. In K. Gardner, J. Horden. and S. Shute (ed.) *Criminals; Action, value and structure*. Oxford: Oxford University Press.

Fulford, K. W. M. (1994). Closet logics: hidden conceptual elements in the DSM and ICD classifications of mental disorders. In J. Z. Sadler, O. P. Wiggins and M. A. Schwartz (ed.) *Philosophical Perspectives on Psychiatric Diagnostic Classification*, pp. 211–32. Baltimore: Johns Hopkins University Press.

Fulford, K. W. M. (1995). Thought insertion and insight: Disease and illness paradigms of psychotic disorder. In M. Spitzer (ed.) *Phenomenology, Language and Schizophrenia*. Springer-Verlag.

Fulford, K. W. M. (1999). From culturally sensitive to culturally competent: a seminar in philosophy and practice skills. In K. Bhui and D. Olajide (ed.) *Mental Health Service Provision for a Multi-cultural Society*, pp. 21–42. London: W. B. Saunders Company Ltd.

Fulford, K. W. M. (2002). Values in psychiatric diagnosis: Executive summary of a report to the Chair of the ICD-12/DSM-VI Coordination Task Force (Dateline 2010). *Psychopathology*, **35**, 132–8.

Fulford, K. W. M. and Hope, R. A. (1993). Psychiatric ethics: A bioethical ugly duckling? In G. Raanon (ed.) *Principles of Health Care Ethics*. New York: John Wiley.

Fulford, K. W. M., Morris, K. J., Sadler, J. Z. and Stanghellini, G. (2003). Past improbable, future possible: the renaissance in philosophy and psychiatry. In K. W. M. Fulford, K. J. Morris, J. Z. Sadler and G. Stanghellini (ed.) *Nature and Narrative: an Introduction to the New Philosophy of Psychiatry*, pp. 1–41. Oxford: Oxford University Press.

Fulford, K. W. M., Williamson, T. and Woodbridge, K. (2002). Values-added practice (a values-awareness workshop). *Mental Health Today*, October, 25–7.

Fulford, K. W. M. (2003). Mental illness: definition, use and meaning. Long entry for Post, S. G. (ed.) *Encyclopedia of Bioethics*, 3rd edn. New York: Macmillan.

Fulford, K. W. M. (2004). Ten principles of values-based medicine. In J. Radden (ed.) *The Philosophy of Psychiatry: A Companion*. New York: Oxford University Press.

Fulford, K. W. M., Thornton, T. and Graham, G. (forthcoming). *The Concise Oxford Textbook of Philosophy and Psychiatry*. Oxford: Oxford University Press.

Garety, P. A. and Freeman, D. (1999). Cognitive approaches to delusions: A critical review of theories and evidence. *British Journal of Clinical Psychology*, **38**, 113–54.

Gelder, M. G., Gath, D. and Mayou, R. (1983). *Oxford Textbook of Psychiatry*. Oxford: Oxford University Press.

Gittleson, N. L. (1966). The relationship between obsessions and suicidal attempts in depressive psychosis. *British Journal of Psychiatry*, **112**, 889–90.

Glover, J. (1970). *Responsibility*. London: Routledge and Kegan Paul.

Grisso, T. and Appelbaum, P. S. (1998). *Assessing Competence to Consent to Treatment: A Guide for Physicians and other Health Professionals*. Oxford: Oxford University Press.

Grubin, D. H. (1991). Unfit to plead in England and Wales, 1967–88, a survey. *British Journal of Psychiatry*, **158**, 140–548.

Hare, E. H. (1973). A short note on pseudohallucination. *British Journal of Psychiatry*, **139**, 204–8.

Hare, R. M. (1952). *The Language of Morals*. Oxford: Oxford University Press.

Hamilton, M. (1978). *Fish's Outline of Psychiatry*, 3rd edn. Bristol: John Wright.

Harré, R. (1997). Pathological autobiographies. *Philosophy, Psychiatry, and Psychology*, **4/2**, 99–110.

Harré, R. and Gillett, G. (1994). *The Discursive Mind*. London: Sage.

Harre, R. and Lamb, R. (ed.) (1986). *The Dictionary of Physiological and Clinical Psychology*. Oxford: Basil Blackwell Ltd.

Hart, H. L. A. (1968). *Punishment and Responsibility: Essays in the philosophy of law*. Oxford: Oxford University Press.

Hemsley, D. R. and Garety, P. A. (1986). The formation and maintenance of delusions: A Bayesian analysis. *British Journal of Psychiatry*, **149**, 51–6.

Hoerl, C. (2001). Introduction: Understanding, explaining, and intersubjectivity in schizophrenia. *Philosophy, Psychiatry, and Psychology*, **8/2/3**, 83–8.

Jaspers, K. (1913). Causal and meaningful connexions between life history and psychosis. In S. R. Hirsch and M. Shepherd (ed.) (1974) *Themes and Variations in European Psychiatry*. Bristol: John Wright and Sons Ltd.

Jaspers, K. (1913/1963). *General psychopathology* (J. Hoenig and M. W. Hamilton, trans.). Manchester: Manchester University Press.

Jaspers, K. (1913b). The phenomenological approach in psychopathology. Zeitschrift fur die Gesamte Neurologie und Psychiatrie, 9, 391–408. Published in translation, (1968) (on the initiative of J. N. Curran), *British Journal of Psychiatry*, **114**, 1313–23.

Kenny, A. J. P. (1969). Mental health in Plato's republic. *Proceedings of the British Academy*, **5**, 229–53.

Law Commission (1995). *Mental Incapacity* (Law Commission Report No. 231). London: HMSO.

Leff, J. P. and Isaacs, A. D. (1978). (3rd edn, 1990) *Psychiatric Examination in Clinical Practice*. Oxford: Blackwell Scientific Publications.

Lewis, A. J. (1934). The psychopathology of insight. *British Journal of Medical Psychology*, **14**, 332–48.

Lewis, A. J. (1955). Health as a social concept. *British Journal of Sociology*, **4**, 109–24.

Lishman, W. A. (1987). Personal communication.

Lockyer, D. (1981). *Symptoms and Illness: The cognitive organisation of disorder*. London: Tavistock Publications.

Macklin, R. (1973). The medical model in psychoanalysis and psychotherapy. *Comprehensive Psychiatry*, **14** (1), 49–69.

Musalek, M. (2003). Meanings and causes of delusions. In K. W. M. Fulford, K. J. Morris, J. Z. Sadler and G. Stanghellini (ed.) *Nature and Narrative: An Introduction to the New Philosophy of Psychiatry*. Oxford: Oxford University Press.

Nordenfelt, L. (1992). *On Crime, Punishment and Psychiatric Care*. Stockholm: Almqvist and Wiksell International.

Parsons, T. (1951). *The Social System*. Glencoe, IL: Free Press.

Perkins, R. and Moodley, P. (1993). The arrogance of insight? *Psychiatric Bulletin*, **17**, 233–4.

Phillips, J. (2000). Conceptual Models for Psychiatry. *Current Opinion in Psychiatry*, **13**, 683–8.

Quinton, A. (1985). Madness. In A. P. Griffiths (ed.) *Philosophy and Practice*. Cambridge: Cambridge University Press.

Robinson, D. (1996). *Wild Beasts and Idle Humours*. Cambridge, Mass: Harvard University Press.

Ryle, G. (1980). *The Concept of Mind*. London: Penguin Books Ltd.

Sadler, J. Z. (ed.) (2002). *Descriptions and Prescriptions: Values, mental disorders, and the DSMs*. Baltimore: The Johns Hopkins University Press.

Sensky. T., Hughes. T. and Hirsch, S. (1991). Compulsory psychiatric treatment in the community. Part 1. A controlled study of compulsory community treatment with extended leave under the Mental Health Act: Special characteristics of patients treated and impact of treatment. *British Journal of Psychiatry*, **158**, 792–804.

Shepherd, M. (1961). Morbid jealousy: Some clinical and social aspects of a psychiatric syndrome. *Journal of Mental Science*, **107**, 687–704.

Sims, A (1988). *Symptoms in the Mind: An introduction to descriptive psychopathology*. London: Bailiere Tindall.

Stephens, G. Lynn, and Graham, G. (1994). Self-consciousness, mental agency, and the clinical psychopathology of thought insertion. *Philosophy, Psychiatry and Psychology*, **1**, 1–11.

Stephens, G. Lynn, and Graham, G. (1994). Commentary on "Kant, Thought Insertion, and Mental Unity". *Philosophy, Psychiatry, and Psychology*, **1/2**, 115–16.

Stephens, G. Lynn. and Graham, G. (2000). *When Self-Consciousness Breaks: Alien voices and inserted thoughts*. Cambridge, Mass: MIT Press.

Szasz, T. S. (1960). The myth of mental illness. *American Psychologist*, **15**, 113–18.

Szasz, T. S. (1976). *Schizophrenia: The Sacred Symbol of Psychiatry*. New York: Basic Books.

Vauhkonen, K. (1968). *On the Pathogenesis of Morbid Jealousy, with Special Reference to the Personality Traits of and Interaction between Jealous Patients and their Spouses*. Copenhagen: Munksgaard.

Warnock, G. J. (1989). *J L Austin*. London: Routledge.

Wing, J. K., Cooper, J. E. and Sartorius, N. (1974). *Measurement and Classification of Psychiatric Symptoms*. Cambridge: Cambridge University Press.

Wing, J. K. (1978). *Reasoning about Madness*. Oxford: Oxford University Press.

Wittgenstein, L. (1958). *Philosophical investigations*, 2nd edn, G. E. M. Anscombe, (trans.). Oxford: Basil Blackwell.

Wootton, B. (1959). *Social Science and Social Pathology*. London: George Allen and Unwin.

World Health Organization (WHO) (1978). *Mental Disorders: Glossary and guide to their classification in accordance with the ninth revision of the international classification of diseases*. Geneva: World Health Organization.

World Health Organization (1992). *Mental Disorders: Glossary and guide to their classification in accordance with the tenth revision of the international classification of diseases*. Geneva: World Health Organization.

World Health Organization (1992). *The ICD-10 Classification of Mental and Behavioural Disorders: Clinical Descriptions and Diagnostic Guidelines*. Geneva: World Health Organization.

Chapter 4

Cognitive insight: theory and assessment

Aaron T. Beck and Debbie M. Warman

The clinical concept of insight as evaluated by a variety of scales has been widely applied to determine the presence of mental illness and its prognosis, as well as prescribing appropriate treatment and management (Amador and David, 1998; Mintz, Dobson and Romney, 2003; Amador and Konengold Chapter 1). However, illness-oriented insight scales do not necessarily address the patients' limited capacity to evaluate their anomalous experiences and their cognitive distortions. This cognitive limitation contributes to the impairment in clinical insight and to the development of delusional beliefs and thinking. Moreover, the tenacity of a delusion does not reflect the capacity to correct specific misinterpretations or to respond to corrective feedback.

The lack of awareness of a mental illness requiring treatment may be designated as an impairment of "clinical insight". This form of insight focuses on those aspects of clinical phenomenology deemed essential for diagnosis and pharmacological treatment, whereas "cognitive insight" is concerned with distancing from and re-evaluating distorted beliefs and misinterpretations – ingredients of cognitive therapy. These secondary evaluations are derived from higher level cognitive processes (sometimes called metacognition), such as the patients' ability to assume perspective about their misinterpretations and to reappraise them.

Cognitive models of hallucinations (Beck and Rector, 2003) and delusions (Beck and Rector, 2002) ascribe a significant role to impaired insight in the development of psychotic phenomena. In the formation and maintenance of delusions, for example, the deviant beliefs become sufficiently intense to override the normal processes of reality testing, which are already attenuated in psychosis. Similarly, the patients' conviction of an external origin of their verbal hallucinations rests on their impaired recognition of the nature of the anomalous experience. What is important to the cognitive models is the degree to which the erroneous beliefs shape the interpretations (or, more precisely, misinterpretations) of ongoing experiences and interactions. Further, these models emphasize the importance of the salience of particular misinterpretations, their frequency, their degree of conviction, and their impermeability to corrective feedback. These characteristics of specific cognitive constructions of experience are viewed as more crucial to the patients' well-being and adjustment than a general paranoid or grandiose delusion per se. The emphasis is on the degree to which these delusional beliefs co-opt the patients' information processing and their capacity to view the resulting cognitive products (interpretations, predictions, doubts, etc.) objectively. Even though patients may accept an illness explanation for their symptoms and agree that it makes sense (intellectual insight), this may or may not produce any appreciable change in their underlying belief system (cognitive insight).

Some patients accept the explanation that they are mentally ill and that their unusual experiences are symptoms of a mental disorder – without being convinced of this. When questioned about the cause of their symptoms, these patients typically repeat what they have been told, namely that they have a mental illness and that their symptoms are caused by schizophrenia, or alternatively, by a chemical imbalance. Upon an in-depth clinical exploration of the content and characteristics of these experiences, however, it becomes apparent in many cases that this explanation does not reflect their strongly held beliefs. A hallucinating patient, for example, may acknowledge that the voices are caused by a mental illness. However, when questioned in greater depth, he or she may say that the voices are messages from Satan.

The crucial cognitive problem in patients with psychosis resides not only in their consistent distortions of their experiences, but also in their relative inability to distance themselves from these distortions and in their relative impermeability to corrective feedback. Some non-psychotic individuals, such as patients with depression or panic disorder, also misinterpret events: the depressed patient, for example, overinterprets interactions with others as a sign of rejection or personal inadequacy (Beck, Rush, Shaw and Emery, 1979), whereas the panic-prone patient misinterprets physical sensations as a sign of a serious ailment (Beck and Emery, 1985). In both disorders, the patients retain (but have difficulty accessing) the capacity to reflect on their experiences and to recognize that their conclusions were incorrect. In therapy, it is possible to prime this capacity and consequently enable the patients to reality-test their misinterpretations during the flare-up of their disorder. In contrast, this capacity is impoverished to varying degrees in patients with psychosis. The relevant components of this deficiency in psychosis are impairment of objectivity about the cognitive distortions, loss of ability to put these into perspective, resistance to corrective information from others, and overconfidence in conclusions.

The impairment in these processes of detecting and correcting misinterpretations is obviously related to the clinical phenomenon of impaired insight into the presence of symptoms and mental illness. If the patients with psychosis have impaired capacity to evaluate their cognitive processes they are compelled to regard their delusions as reality, their delusional interpretations as facts, and their thinking as rational. This problem is not absolute, however. The patients do have a limited capacity to distance themselves from their non-delusional beliefs and misinterpretations. A clue to the patients' potential for cognitive insight may be found in their ability to test and correct misinterpretations that are not related to delusional thinking, to accept the notion that their interpretations could be wrong, and to reflect on past anomalous experiences.

A feature of the mental functioning apparent in delusional thinking is the relationship of *reflective* and directed thinking on the one hand to automatic *reflexive* processing on the other (Hasher and Zacks, 1979). *Reflective processing* ordinarily serves as a check on reflexive processing. The higher level processing is immobilized, however, when the delusional beliefs capture the information-processing apparatus. Only when the patients' attention is diverted from the delusional concept does the higher mental functioning become operative once more. Cognitive therapy with delusions is directed in part at modifying the patients' automatic processing of information, but even more so at reinforcing the higher level of reflective thinking. This higher level of reflective thinking needs to be primed through questioning ("alternative explanations?") and prods ("What is the evidence?"). Even strictly psychoeducational strategies can help open the patients' minds to reflection and explanation of their automatic thoughts.

Of relevance to the understanding of cognitive insight is the finding that patients with schizophrenia who have some awareness of the possibility that they are mistaken show more improvement in Cognitive Behavioral Therapy (CBT) than patients without this "chink of insight" (Garety, Fowler and Kuipers, 2000). This kind of insight was assessed differently from the typical evaluation of beliefs about the presence (or absence) of mental illness (Amador, Strauss, Yale, Flaum, Endicott and Gorman, 1993). Rather than pretreatment questions of whether patients attributed their beliefs to schizophrenia, the investigators asked, "Is there any possibility you are mistaken about X?" (X referring to the patient's delusion). Patients who endorsed the possibility and subsequently received CBT had better outcomes than patients who did not endorse the possibility and received CBT. Furthermore, patients who demonstrated insight and received CBT had better outcomes than patients with and without insight who did not receive CBT. This assessment of insight points to another way of examining and conceptualizing insight – specifically evaluating the patients' ability to reflect on misinterpretations as opposed to their acknowledgement of an illness.

It is helpful to consider the literature on thinking styles associated with schizophrenia. Patients with delusions demonstrate a "jumping to conclusions" reasoning style, a form of reflexive thinking. This feature has been determined experimentally using emotionally neutral tasks (Huq, Garety and Hemsley, 1988) and emotionally salient material (Dudley, John, Young and Over, 1997; Young and Bentall, 1997). While jumping to conclusions is a common occurrence, it seems reasonable that such a dominant thinking style could contribute to delusional thinking. While the tasks just described assess a patient's actual tendency to jump to conclusions, they do not assess whether the patient has insight into this tendency. Thus, a measure of cognitive insight should assess a patient's awareness of this reasoning style.

Further, patients with delusions demonstrate overconfidence in the validity of their interpretations and explanations, even in the absence of information sufficient to make a judgment. For example, using a test of probabilistic judgments, individuals with delusions were asked to determine which jar a bead came from. They reported high confidence in their answers after receiving only minimal information (Huq *et al.*, 1998). Consistent with this finding, patients with delusions report extremely high conviction in their delusional beliefs, even when very limited evidence is available to support their convictions. In fact, when asked to provide evidence, numerous patients report that their evidence is their *belief*, rather than cite many forms of "hard" evidence to support it.

Development of the beck cognitive insight scale

The thinking styles and impairments described above were used to compose statements relevant to premature closure and overconfidence in interpretations of experiences in the construction of the Beck Cognitive Insight Scale (BCIS; Beck *et al.*, 2004). Items assessing these deviations included, "I have jumped to conclusions too fast," "Even though I feel strongly that I am right, I could be wrong," and "My interpretations of my experiences are definitely right." These items assessed premature closure, acknowledgement of fallibility, and overconfidence, respectively. The items also targeted flexibility, such as the recognition of having made mistakes.

We tested the Beck Cognitive Insight Scale with 150 inpatients in an acute hospital setting. All of the patients in the original sample were experiencing severe distress at the time of testing (Global Assessment of Functioning (GAF) < 30). Of the 150 patients, 91 had psychotic disorders – schizophrenia (n = 32), schizoaffective disorder (n = 43), or major depression with psychotic features (n = 16); the remaining patients (n = 59) were diagnosed with major depression, but were not psychotic. All patients were receiving psychiatric medication at the time of testing.

We determined (via varimax rotation) that the scale had two factors, which we labeled Self-Reflectiveness (9 items, which included a willingness to acknowledge fallibility, openness to external feedback, and recognition of dysfunctional reasoning styles) and Self-Certainty (6 items, which indicated overconfidence). Factor item loadings on the Self-Reflectiveness scale ranged from 0.33–0.66, and for the Self-Certainty scale ranged from 0.25–0.67. All but 1 of the 15 items loaded saliently (>0.30) on one factor as opposed to the other. Internal consistency was adequate; the coefficient αs were 0.68 for the Self-Reflectiveness scale and 0.60 for the Self-Certainty scale. Given that each scale had fewer than 10 items, these numbers were considered within the acceptable range.

There is evidence that the Beck Cognitive Insight Scale and the SUMD-A (Amador, Flaum, Andreasen, Strauss, Yale, Clark *et al.*, 1994) are related, providing support for the scale's concurrent validity. Higher self-reflectiveness was associated with higher awareness of delusions in a subsample (n = 15) of patients with schizophrenia and schizoaffective disorder who were administered both measures. All of the correlations of the SUMD-A with the Self-Reflectiveness scale were moderate to large, but lacked significance due to small sample size, and several correlations with the Self-Certainty scale also had moderate effect sizes.

Our results indicated that patients with psychotic disorders (schizophrenia, schizoaffective, and major depression with psychotic features) were significantly less self-reflective than patients without psychotic disorders ($P < 0.01$). In addition, patients with psychotic disorders demonstrated significantly more self-certainty than patients without psychotic disorders ($P < 0.05$). Finally, patients with psychotic disorders had lower Total Cognitive Insight (calculated by subtracting Self-Certainty subscale from the Self-Reflectiveness subscale) than patients without psychotic disorders ($P < 0.001$). These findings are consistent with previous studies that demonstrate that patients with delusions are more likely to jump to conclusions and to be overconfident in their decisions and suggest this scale may be useful in assessing such thinking deviations.

As the idea of cognitive insight is closely related to the insight demonstrated by patients with schizophrenia who benefited from cognitive behavioral therapy (Garety *et al.*, 1997; Garety and Jolley, Chapter 5), it is possible that patients who are highly self-reflective and not overly certain of their own judgments will have better clinical outcomes than patients with low cognitive insight. In addition, CBT interventions may serve to increase cognitive insight. This seems likely, as cognitive behavior therapy makes considerable use of cognitive insight (which was the case long before our measure was created). For example, CBT for schizophrenia aims at having patients recognize errors in their thinking and developing alternative explanations for their experiences. The CBT therapist is likely to point out to the patients that they may have drawn a quick and perhaps even understandable conclusion, though ultimately one that was faulty. In essence, the CBT therapist sets a primary goal to increase flexibility in thinking about experiences – increasing cognitive insight.

Consistent with the speculation above, Granholm and colleagues (2003), in the first study to utilize the Beck Cognitive Insight Scale in a treatment outcome study with schizophrenia, found that cognitive insight improves with group CBT treatment. Higher cognitive insight was associated with a decrease in positive symptoms for those who received CBT ($r = -0.38$, $P < 0.05$). While patients who received CBT demonstrated increased cognitive insight, patients who received treatment as usual (i.e., did not receive CBT) did not ($P < 0.05$). The authors suggest that cognitive insight may be a mediator of symptom change in CBT. It is worthy of note that although patients who evidenced increased cognitive insight had increased depression scores at mid-treatment ($r = 0.32$, $P < 0.05$), the relationship between depression and cognitive insight disappeared by the end of treatment ($r = -0.06$, $P > 0.05$). A separate analysis of the data in this study (J. McQuaid, 2003, Personal Communication) showed significant correlations of the BCIS with the Birchwood Insight Scale (Birchwood, Smith and Drury, 1994). The Granholm *et al.* results, taken together with Garety *et al.*'s (1997) findings suggest that those who have cognitive insight may fare best in CBT and that those who receive CBT may demonstrate improvements in cognitive insight. Further, patients who demonstrate increases in cognitive insight, while they may be distressed for a period of time, can be expected to recover from this distress while still in treatment.

Clinical applications

While the notion of cognitive insight is useful from an assessment perspective, it is also possible that using cognitive insight as a therapeutic strategy may be helpful. While educating the patient that he has schizophrenia may have considerable use, such as the opportunity to increase treatment adherence, it is possible that the patient's ability to think flexibly about his symptoms will be largely unchanged. Further, the patient may become depressed if he believes himself to be sick, psychotic, or "crazy". By targeting the thinking style, the patient's understanding of his experiences may shift, while also decreasing the depression. A case example will be presented briefly to highlight this point.

A patient in our clinic, Steven, reported 100% conviction that people were entering his home through a large window in his apartment. He was extremely distressed by this and reported he felt trapped in his home as a result. He was concerned people would slide through his window if he left the house, so he spent most of his time at home, protecting his belongings. His evidence included that his window was sometimes open and that things were often missing around his home. He made it clear he did not want to discuss this issue in therapy, as it was too distressing and people often told him he was "crazy" for thinking such things. At the start of therapy, his depression was in the severe range (BDI-II = 30). In order to respect his wishes, and with the expectation (or, perhaps, hope) that discussing thinking styles in general would ultimately generalize to his delusional thinking, the therapist spent the majority of time in session discussing thinking styles associated with depression. The thinking style of jumping to conclusions was highlighted, since the therapist hoped the patient would ultimately apply this to his delusional thinking. The patient completed thought records and determined that jumping to conclusions was an important issue for him. The patient then stated that he thought it might be important for him to consider many areas of his life where "jumping to conclusions" may have afforded his interpretations of situations. After only a few sessions, the patient presented a thought record that included his belief about someone entering his home through a window. This belief was treated in the same manner as all the other nondelusional thoughts and beliefs he had brought to prior meetings.

The patient responded well to examining this belief like any other that had been previously discussed, and he began to discuss the issue freely in session. He discussed numerous alternative explanations for his belief that people were breaking into his home and he engaged in behavioral experiments. He reported that he was more likely to jump to conclusions at times of stress and he linked the interpretations to his mood at the time. At the end of treatment, he reported 0% belief that anyone was sliding through his window and entering his apartment. In addition, his depression decreased dramatically, with a BDI-II score of zero at the end of treatment. Of note is that at no time did he (or the therapist) discuss this belief as one stemming from psychosis – rather he discussed his tendency to jump to conclusions, and he developed a plan to ensure he would not fall into such a thinking trap again. Thus, rather than treating his delusional belief as different from other beliefs he held, they used the same strategies of developing alternative explanations and engaging in behavioral experiments.

While alternative explanations for Steven's improvements are certainly possible, it is likely that use of the concept of cognitive insight played a role both in his receptivity to therapy and his response to it. While Steven's delusion might have responded to psychoeducation about schizophrenia, this seems unlikely, as he expressed full understanding of the illness and symptoms associated with schizophrenia (illness-oriented insight) at the start of treatment, yet showed limited understanding at that time of how his symptoms persisted and could be understood as part of the illness (cognitive insight).

Summary and conclusions

The construct of insight may be viewed in a variety of ways. Illness-oriented insight is focused on the patients' capacity and willingness to accept that their symptoms (delusions, hallucinations, thought disorder, and negative symptoms) are due to mental illness and require treatment. This construction of insight has historically been useful for purposes of diagnosis and prescription of treatment. A drawback of this narrow application of the term is that it excludes the broader aspect of insight, specifically the patients' awareness of their misinterpretations of their ongoing experiences and their ability to correct them.

Although delusional beliefs may shape a significant proportion of the misinterpretations of some patients, there are other patients who are able to maintain reasonably adaptive appraisals and reappraisals of their cognitive distortions in situations unrelated to their highly systematized delusional beliefs. In our clinical experiences the patients' ability to manage the distress caused by their delusions and hallucinations and to achieve reasonable personal and social adjustment is related, in part, to their reappraisal capacity. To distinguish this process of cognitive appraisal from clinical, or illness-oriented insight, we coined the term cognitive insight. This latter form of insight involves the patients' ability to "look into" their actual stream of consciousness, to distance themselves from specific dysfunctional cognitions, and to apply various techniques to evaluate and correct them. This form of insight is also facilitated by openness to corrective feedback from others but is impeded by premature closure ("jumping to conclusions") and overconfidence in the rightness of their inferences.

Cognitive insight has been an important aspect of cognitive approaches to psychopathology. It is the end product of the application of cognitive strategies such as examining the evidence, considering alternative explanations, and testing beliefs in real life situations. The attainment of such insight is generally judged by the therapist and is assumed to be related to clinical improvement. Some kind of pre-measurement of this insight seemed to be desirable both to assess the likelihood of a patient's response to cognitive therapy and also as our index of improvement. The pre-therapy score on such a measure might predict a positive outcome and within therapy scores would serve as a proxy mediator of improvement.

As an initial step in investigating this psychological process, we developed the Beck Cognitive Insight Scale (Beck *et al.*, in press). One subscale (self-reflectiveness) attempts to evaluate various facets such as the patients' ability to reflect on previous interpretations, determine that they may have been erroneous, and consider alternative explanations. Another independent subscale was labeled "self-certainty". Since these two subscales are scored in opposite directions, the cognitive index was obtained by subtracting the score on the self-certainty subscale from that of the self-reflectiveness subscale. The scale was found to have borderline internal consistency and adequate concurrent, discriminant, and predictive validity. A factor analysis yielded factors corresponding to the two subscales.

Of course, a self-report scale provides only a crude estimate of the patients' reappraisal capability. Specific exploration of the patients' erroneous cognitions and their efficiency in reframing them in a controlled experiment, for example, would provide more precise information. Further relevant data could be obtained by priming the patients' latent reappraisal cognitive strategies and determining their impact on erroneous interpretations.

A few speculative comments might provide the framework for future investigations. It is apparent that the patients' ability to review and modify their unrealistic interpretations depends on how well they can access the relevant cognitive strategies. The activation and application of these strategies, corresponding to the "reflective processing" described by Hasher and Zacks (1979), impose a significant demand on the patients' attenuated cognitive resources. During the onset or flare-up of their illness, or during stressful experiences, these resources are allocated, to a large extent, to their highly charged delusional thinking or hallucinations. Even so, such resources may become accessible when the delusional thinking and hallucinations are damped down by pharmacotherapy. The psychotherapist can then draw on them to train the patient in the application of the corrective cognitive strategies. In this way a more durable form of insight that will impact positively on illness-oriented insight and adherence to treatment can be achieved.

References

Amador, X. F., Flaum, M., Andreasen, N. C., Strauss, D. H., Yale, S. Z., Clark, S. C., *et al.* (1994). Awareness of illness in schizophrenia and schizoaffective and mood disorders. *Archives of General Psychiatry*, **51**, 826–36.

Amador, X. F., Strauss, D. H., Yale, S. A., Flaum, M. M., Endicott, J. and Gorman, J. M. (1993). Assessment of insight in psychosis. *American Journal of Psychiatry*, **150**, 873–9.

Amador, X. F. and David, A. S. (1998). *Insight and Psychosis*. London: Oxford University Press.

Beck, A. T., Baruch, E., Balter, J. M., Sterr, R. A. and Warman, D. M. (2004). A new instrument for measuring insight: The Beck Cognitive Insight Scale. *Schizophrenia Research*, **68**, 319–29.

Beck, A. T., Rush, A. J., Shaw, B. F. and Emery, G. (1979). *Cognitive Therapy of Depression.* New York: Guilford Press.

Beck, A. T. and Emery, G. (with Greenberg, R. L.) (1985). *Anxiety Disorders and Phobias: A cognitive perspective.* New York, NY: Basic Books.

Beck, A. T. and Rector, N. A. (2002). Delusions: A cognitive perspective. *Journal of Cognitive Psychotherapy,* **16**, 455–68.

Beck, A. T. and Rector, N. A. (2003). A cognitive model of hallucinations. *Cognitive Therapy and Research,* **27**, 19–51.

Birchwood, M., Smith, V. and Drury, V. (1994). A self-report insight scale for psychosis: Reliability, validity, and sensitivity to change. *Acta Psychiatr Scand,* **89**, 62–7.

Dudley, R. E. J., John, C. H., Young, A. W. and Over, D. E. (1997). The effect of self-referent material on the reasoning of people with delusions. *British Journal of Clinical Psychology,* **36**, 575–84.

Garety, P. A., Fowler, D. and Kuipers, E. (2000). Cognitive-behavioral therapy for medication-resistant symptoms. *Schizophrenia Bulletin. Special Issue: Psychosocial treatment for schizophrenia,* **26**, 73–86.

Garety, P., Fowler, D., Kuipers, E., Freeman, D., Dunn, G., Bebbington, P., *et al.* (1997). London–East Anglia randomized controlled trial of cognitive-behavioural therapy for psychosis. II: Predictors of outcome. *British Journal of Psychiatry,* **171**, 420–6.

Granholm, E., McQuiad, J. R., McClure, F. S. and Pedrelli, P. (2003). Changes in cognitive insight may mediate symptom changes in cognitive behavior therapy for older patients with schizophrenia. Paper presented at the 37th annual meeting of the Association for the Advancement of Behavior Therapy, Boston, MA.

Hasher, L. and Zacks, R. T. (1979). Automatic and effortful processes in memory. *Journal of Experimental Psychology: General,* **108**, 356–88.

Huq, S. F., Garety, P. A. and Hemsley, D. R. (1988). Probabilistic judgments in deluded and non-deluded subjects. *The Quarterly Journal of Experimental Psychology,* **40A**, 801–12.

Mintz, A. R., Dobson, K. S. and Romney, D. M. (2003). Insight in schizophrenia: A meta-analysis. *Schizophrenia Research,* **61**, 75–88.

Young, H. F. and Bentall, R. P. (1997). Probabilistic reasoning in deluded, depressed and normal subjects: Effects of task difficulty and meaningful versus non-meaningful material. *Psychological Medicine,* **27**, 455–65.

Chapter 5

Insight and delusions: a cognitive psychological approach

Suzanne Jolley and Philippa A. Garety

1.0 Introduction

1.1 Delusions

Delusion is a key concept in psychosis, representing for many the symptom that epitomizes madness. Early writers have emphasized the "un-understandability" of delusions – Jaspers (1913/1959) considered a true delusion to be "psychologically irreducible" and to represent a change in "the totality of understandable connections". Such views have had a strong influence on Anglo-American psychiatry where traditional definitions of delusions have emphasized fixity and incorrigibility in the face of "incontrovertible" evidence to the contrary (cf. DSM III, APA, 1980) and a comprehensive psychological understanding of delusion has until recently been notably absent.

However, with the advent of cognitive models of delusion, and of cognitive therapy for psychosis, delusional beliefs are increasingly being seen as multidimensional and both changing and changeable constructs; understandable within the context of a person's appraisal of their life and experiences and their cognitive and emotional processes, and perhaps not as different from normal beliefs as may have been previously thought (Garety and Hemsley, 1994).

This kind of understanding may have influenced psychiatric nosology: in the DSM IV definition of delusion, some reasoning processes are invoked as intermediaries between external events and internal belief, with delusions defined as "erroneous beliefs that usually involve a *misinterpretation of perceptions or experiences*"; and the idea of a continuum of belief is introduced, noting that the "distinction between a delusion and a strongly held idea is difficult to make and depends on the degree of conviction with which the belief is held despite clear evidence to the contrary" (APA, 1994, p. 783).

1.2 Insight

The notion of insight has long been seen as significant in the understanding of psychosis. One early use of the term implied only diagnostic relevance; the absence of insight being seen as a defining feature of psychotic illness (Berrios and Markova, 1998).

Later views reflected the possibility of variability in insight in psychosis, with prognostic significance attached to its presence, but with a unidimensonal, all-or-nothing conceptualisation of insight prevailing. Over the last 10 years, however, research into the area has burgeoned, with a recognition that the concept is potentially difficult to define comprehensively, and with an emerging consensus of a multidimensional model incorporating, broadly, awareness and labeling of change in oneself, appreciation of the implications of that change, and engaging in behaviours contingent on this appreciation – particularly, engagement with an appropriate treatment and/or management plan (Amador and David, 1998).

Such models have shown associations between insight and good outcome, probably mediated through medication compliance (Kemp and David, 1995); although findings of good outcome are not unequivocal (e.g. White, Bebbington, Pearson, Johnson and Ellis, 2000). David (1998) suggests that any negative impact of recognition of illness may result from realization of the multiple losses associated with severe and enduring mental health problems, rather than acknowledgement of an illness label per se, and that perhaps a "compromise" level of insight – sufficient to accept the need for treatment but not so much as to constantly dwell on the severity of one's illness, may be most adaptive (David, 1990).

1.3 Insight and delusion

Negotiating the meaning of insight into delusional belief within early definitions of both delusion and insight has left very little scope for manouevre – delusion and conventional psychiatric insight are inextricably linked – one cannot hold a delusional belief with conviction and have insight into its nature as a symptom.

This position is ameliorated by the development of multidimensional models such as that of David (1990). Only one of his components of insight – the relabeling of experience as the product of illness – is at odds with holding a delusional belief; thus a deluded person can be viewed as having partial insight within David's model.

However, David's model deals primarily with psychiatric insight, and assumes the view of psychotic experience as best understood within a "symptom" framework. Thus although a deluded person may have partial insight, improved insight requires that they understand their beliefs as a sign of illness. From a psychological perspective, and particularly from the standpoint of cognitive models of psychosis and of delusion, there is a great deal more in terms of life experiences, emotional reactions, thinking style, appraisals and so forth which one may wish to consider in understanding a person's beliefs, and wish to encourage the person themselves to appreciate in order to effect change through therapy.

Once delusional beliefs are viewed as potentially having more meaning than solely as a symptom of illness, or as a false belief, and as amenable to psychological treatment, the concept of insight into delusions is opened up to different interpretations. We might, for example, consider it "insightful" if a person could link experiences of being bullied at school with believing that others are laughing at them in adulthood, irrespective of his/her views on "illness".

1.4 Outline of chapter

In this chapter, we will present a recent integrated psychological model of the positive symptoms of psychosis, (and, therefore, of delusions) which emphasizes appraisal both of the symptoms of psychosis and of the implications of this as the key route to the development of a psychotic episode and as the main target of cognitive intervention.

We will consider the implications of this for a psychological understanding of insight, and the association between insight and adaptation to illness, making links with the developing field of illness perception in psychosis, and drawing on the relatively well-established body of research into the relationship between perceptions of physical health problems and health behaviour and outcome.

We will present some pilot data looking at the responses of a group of clients with early psychosis on an adapted version of the Illness Perception Questionnaire (IPQ), drawn from Leventhal's Self Regulation Model (SRM) of adjustment to physical health problems, tentatively linking findings with symptomatology and outcome, and moving towards the idea of developing an "adaptive profile" of attributions about psychotic experiences.

Our argument is that a psychological understanding of insight in psychosis should address the individual's appraisal of their experiences and the implications of those appraisals on a number of dimensions; with the idea in mind that we are encouraging insight with a view to improving outcome, and that this principle should guide any insight-oriented therapeutic intervention.

2.0 Developments in psychological views of psychosis

2.1 A new cognitive psychological model of psychosis

One of the authors, with colleagues, has recently put forward a new integrated model of the positive symptoms of psychosis (Garety, Kuipers, Fowler, Freeman and Bebbington, 2001). The model posits a bio-psychosocial vulnerability and an association with adverse life events and other stressors at onset, with factors such as isolation, adverse environment, and substance use as possible triggers for episodes. Two routes to psychosis are proposed. In the first route, triggering events in a vulnerable individual are argued to give rise to a "basic cognitive disturbance", underlying psychotic experience. In the second, less common pathway, emotional changes only are argued to lead to psychotic symptoms.

The main emphasis of the model is on the appraisal and interpretation of changed experiences, and the cognitive and emotional processes which influence these. Such appraisals then form the focus of cognitive therapy within the model. An illustrative case example is provided as Appendix I.

2.1.1 Vulnerability

Vulnerability within this framework is seen as associated not only with heredity and possible differences in nervous system organization, but also with early childhood emotional and social adversity, leading to the development of negative schematic beliefs about oneself, others and the world, which predispose to emotional disorder, and are likely to influence appraisal of psychotic experience. This is backed by a study of Van Os and colleagues in the Netherlands (Krabbendam *et al.*, 2002) demonstrating in a large prospective study that those who develop psychosis are more likely to have preexisting low self-esteem and depression. Similarly, Birchwood, Meaden, Trower, Gilbert and Plaistow (2000c), suggest that childhood social adversity may lead to the development of schemas relating to social humiliation and social subordination which are linked to voice hearing and paranoid beliefs.

2.1.2 Cognitive dysfunction

Different conceptualizations of a "basic cognitive disturbance" have been put forward, some general, some very specific. Hemsley (1993) suggests a "weakening of the influence of stored regularities on current perception", which leads to ambiguous and unstructured sensory input, and intrusion of material unrelated to current processing from memory. An alternative account is Frith's (1992) model suggesting a neurocognitive difficulty with labeling of actions, thoughts or intentions as one's own, leading to a perception of them as alien, which may be particularly relevant in passivity experiences. Ellis and Young (1990) have suggested that disruption of the "familiarity" pathway with preservation of the "identification" pathway in face recognition may underlie Capgras-type delusions. We would suggest that one or more types of "cognitive disturbance" may be most relevant for each individual, and the model allows for heterogeneity and individual tailoring in this.

2.1.3 Changed experience

It is argued that cognitive dysfunction gives rise to anomalous experience of some kind – for example: heightened perceptions, actions experienced as unintended, unconnected events appearing causally linked, an anomalous perception of significance, auditory hallucinations and other sensory modality hallucinatory experiences. In parallel with this, (or, in the second pathway, alone) emotional changes are taking place, in response to the triggering events and (in the first pathway) to the initial anomalous experiences. Increased arousal, anxiety, and low mood are themselves associated with cognitive changes (in perception, attention, and memory) and act to exacerbate dysfunctional experiences.

2.1.4 Appraisal

The stage above would be considered to be a prodromal phase of psychosis within the model. At this point, an initial appraisal of the experience is made. The experiences may be dismissed as something unusual but not worth bothering about; a sign of stress, and the need to take it easy for a while. It is argued that only appraisals of these experiences as personally significant, threatening and externally caused lead to psychosis. In support of this, Peters and colleagues have demonstrated in a number of studies examining beliefs in non-clinical groups compared to individuals considered to be deluded, that distress rather than content of belief or preoccupation with belief was the only variable to reliably discriminate the clinical group (e.g. Peters *et al.*, 1999). Similarly, Romme and Escher (1989) in their self-selected survey of Dutch voice-hearers found that many were not distressed by their experiences.

A number of factors are viewed as relevant in influencing this appraisal, in addition to pre-existing beliefs and earlier life experiences. First, there is the compelling nature of the experience itself, which may include anomalous feelings of personal significance and threat, and which often "feels" external. This will be accompanied by changes in information processing associated with emotional state, increased arousal, and, perhaps as a result of the "basic cognitive disturbance" itself. Second, pre-existing attributional style and reasoning biases may predispose to making a decision about an experience based on little evidence, and to explaining experiences in terms of other people rather than oneself (see Garety and Freeman, 1999). In addition to this, a tendency to need to explain, and poor tolerance of ambiguity (Need for closure – Colbert and Peters, 2002; Colbert, Garety and Peters, in prep.) has been noted in individuals holding delusional beliefs, and this may push an individual towards bizarre explanations, to try to understand material others may simply dismiss.

2.1.5 Maintenance

Once an appraisal has been made, this is subject to ordinary belief maintenance processes. Finding an explanation for a number of confusing and emotionally significant changes is hypothesized to be rewarding in itself, resulting in reduction of anxiety and termination of a "search for meaning" process (cf. Maher, 1974, 1988). Further, a number of studies have demonstrated that in non-clinical samples, confirmatory biases operate (selective attention to belief-congruent material), together with ignoring of non-occurrences, and even of contradictory evidence, in one study to the point of self-contradiction (see Garety and Hemsley, 1994). Freeman and colleagues have highlighted changes in attention and behaviour associated with anxiety, such as self-focus (Freeman *et al.*, 2000), use of safety behaviours preventing exposure to disconfirmatory evidence (Freeman, Garety and Kuipers, 2001), and metacognitive beliefs about the uncontrollability of one's thoughts (Freeman and Garety, 1999), as important factors in belief maintenance. It has been argued that some beliefs act to protect self-esteem (Bentall, Kinderman and Kaney, 1994), although this has been contested (Freeman *et al.*, 1998). Additionally, once a belief is in place, there is a certain amount of loss of "face" entailed in changing it – particularly if it has affected the way one has lived one's life for many years.

2.1.6 Secondary appraisal

The initial appraisal stage above concerns the labeling of and attribution of causes for the psychotic experiences and emotional changes occurring during the psychotic episode.

The model proposes that in addition to this, and in line with current insight models, appraisals are also made about the implications of those changes – what does it mean about oneself, other people, the world, the future; how long will it last; what can be done about it. While the last is covered to an extent in psychiatric models of insight in psychosis, by reference to medication compliance, the other implications of the changes, and indeed other behavioural reactions are more the domain of psychological models.

2.2 Implications of a cognitive model in terms of insight

We would argue, from this model, that in cognitive psychological terms, we might think of insight as an initial appraisal of the psychotic symptoms, and a further understanding of the implications of this appraisal. In our cognitive therapy, while the primary aim is to reduce distress rather than improve insight, it is often the case that a change in insight is necessary to effect reduction in distress.

The implications of appraisals are important targets of therapy – reducing hopelessness, increasing coping ability, reducing stigma and improving self-esteem. Changing these will often mean re-examination of appraisals for symptoms, and arrival at a new psychological understanding, which may or may not include ideas around illness. Often, the change in the new understanding revolves around the idea that something (achievable) can be done to help – if this is an illness then I can take medication and find other ways of coping; if I might be mistaken in my reasoning, then maybe there's a less worrying explanation; if this all relates to how I feel about myself then maybe if I feel better about myself, it will improve and so on. Even changes which remain delusional can be helpful, and construed as an improvement in insight – "if this is not the devil but my guardian angel, then maybe I'm not damned forever". In the London–East Anglia RCT of cognitive therapy for psychosis, cognitive flexibility, and acknowledging the possibility that one might be mistaken (i.e. that another view may be possible) were the only predictors of good outcome from a number of clinical variables (Garety *et al.*, 1997).

Within the framework of our model, where the meaning of an understanding or insight is emphasized, good psychiatric insight (the belief that one has a mental illness) will not necessarily be helpful if one also believes that this means a chronic and deteriorating course for the difficulties, stigmatization, inability to fulfil any life roles, inability to form relationships with others, and so on. We believe that this makes some sense of the apparently disparate results of studies looking at the relationship between psychiatric insight and outcome (see next section).

3.0 Developments in psychological approaches to understanding people's views of illness

3.1 Models drawn from health research

While the empirical study of individual, psychologically informed profiles of insight and illness appraisal in psychosis is in its infancy, such an approach has been established for some time in physical health research, where people's views of their physical health problems, including the severity of the condition, the impact of it on one's life, and the degree of control one has over outcome, have been systematically explored and the relationship of these to health behaviours and to outcome examined (Petrie *et al.*, 2002).

The Illness Perception Questionnaire (IPQ) was developed by Weinman *et al.* (1996) based on the Self Regulation Model (SRM) of Leventhal *et al.* (1984) who suggest that patients' representations of health problems may be represented within four dimensions – identity – what the illness is, causes, timeline (how long it will last) and consequences. Lau *et al.* (1989) also note the importance of patients' appraisals of the possibility of cure, and the controllability of their condition, and this fifth dimension is also included in the IPQ. The items assessing each component were generated from Leventhal's descriptions of the items, and from patient's own views elicited during interviews. The scale has good psychometric properties, and has shown associations between illness perceptions and adjustment, functioning and coping (see review by Lobban *et al.* 2003).

Lobban *et al.* (2003) suggest that the IPQ may be used as a framework to integrate research relating to appraisals and implications in psychotic illness. A number of studies have looked at acceptance of an illness label and perceived consequences, and the relationship between this and coping; together suggesting that labeling of difficulties as illness, while generally associated with good outcome (e.g. McEvoy *et al.*, 1984, 1989), if accompanied by negative appraisals of illness, can be unhelpful. Birchwood and Iqbal (1998) note the association between post-psychotic depression and experience of mental illness as humiliating and stigmatizing. Birchwood *et al.* (2000a,b) followed up a sample of 105 patients for 12 months after a psychotic episode. Over a third developed depression, and this depression was related to beliefs about illness, particularly the consequences of this, and an attribution of cause to oneself.

Jackson *et al.* (1998), with an early psychosis group, found that those whose adaptation style was to integrate their experiences showed more depression than those who sealed over (i.e. tried not think about their experience, get on with life, assume it won't happen again etc.) (McGlashan, 1987). They suggest this may arise through feeling overwhelmed by too acute an appreciation of the impact of a severe mental health problem on one's life and future, which although possibly realistic, may not, particularly at the onset of a psychotic illness, be helpful.

Lobban *et al.* also note other findings around label and cause and the impact of these on coping – Chadwick and Birchwood (1994) have shown that appraisal of voices influences coping – perceptions of voices as malevolent are associated with resistance and as benevolent with engagement. Junginger (1990) found that an appraisal of a voice as of a familiar person increased the likelihood of compliance.

Considering issues of control, Beck-Sander *et al.* (1997) found that perceptions of controllability influenced compliance with command hallucinations. Similarly, in Freeman and Garety's (1999) study of metacognition in psychosis, beliefs about the uncontrollability of one's own thoughts were associated with distress.

A modified version of the IPQ, adapted for use with carers of individuals with psychotic illness has also been used to assess the relationship between their perceptions of their relative's illness and adaptation to the carer role and quality of relationship with the identified patient (Barrowclough *et al.*, 2001).

3.2 A pilot study of the IPQ in psychosis

We have recently adapted the IPQ for use with a psychotic population, changing the identity components to incorporate psychotic symptomatology and, to increase the palatability of the items to a potentially sensitive group, adding a number of symptoms of general malaise, such as headaches and tiredness. The modified scale has been piloted with a small sample of people with psychosis to assess acceptability to this group, and to give an indication of psychometric quality with encouraging results (Bucher, unpub. BSc project). We have also used the measure on a pilot sample of 21 early psychosis participants in a cognitive therapy trial, and examined relationships with traditional insight measures, and with symptom profiles and outcome (Jolley *et al.*, in prep).

Overall some close relationships were found between the IPQ and psychiatric insight as measured by David's (1990) insight measure and insight into delusions from a multidimensional perspective as measured by the Maudsley Assessment of Delusions (MADS, Buchanan *et al.*, 1990). The MADS insight scale and David's insight measure correlate closely, and they both show positive relationships with endorsement of causes on the IPQ, particularly internal causes (more insight, more causes endorsed); and associations with the perceived timeline of the illness (more insight, longer timeline). Both also show correlations with ratings of delusional conviction (more insight, less conviction). David's insight measure, particularly the awareness of illness subscale, is related to perceived higher consequences of illness, which, together with perceived longer timeline is also correlated with depression at baseline, and with less change in symptomatology over the 6-month assessment period. Also interesting is an association between acceptance of treatment on David's scale and higher ratings on the cure-control component of the IPQ, which is associated with lower depression scores at 6 months, but not with symptom change. Longer timeline on the IPQ is also associated with greater preoccupation with delusional beliefs at baseline.

It should be noted that this data reflects multiple comparisons on a small group and findings are therefore suggestive only; however, our modified IPQ appears to compare adequately to two accepted measures of insight, and to pick up on some of the complex relationships between insight and adjustment raised by other researchers, particularly the potentially depressing impact in an early psychosis group of perceptions of psychotic illness as more enduring and disabling.

Conclusions

In summary, the cognitive psychological conceptualisation of delusional beliefs has developed considerably in recent years with a current widely accepted view of delusion as understandable within a multidimensional individualized formulation emphasizing biopsychosocial vulnerability factors, underlying schematic beliefs, a preponderance of traumatic and adverse life events, particularly around onset, changes in emotional and cognitive processes, and understanding of "normal" beliefs from the perspective of both information processing and phenomenology. In addition to this "primary" appraisal, "secondary" appraisals of the meaning of the changed experience are also relevant. Thus, from a psychological perspective, insight into delusional belief can be considered to be broader than the degree of acceptance of an illness model. Although such a model has been shown to have clinical utility in predicting medication compliance and outcome, data on the association of medical insight with good outcome is not unequivocal.

A number of studies of different appraisals of experience have been shown to be associated with adjustment, coping, distress, behavioural response to symptoms and outcome in cognitive therapy intervention. There is a need to integrate the various aspects of insight. Most recently, within psychological research, there has been a development of the concept of insight as a "shared model" construct towards a multidimensional appraisal of illness, borrowing from research into appraisals of physical health problems. It seems that measures are adaptable to a mental health sample, and that responses have some clinical utility. This represents one way of integrating aspects of insight; however, some important variables, such as cognitive flexibility, the possibility of being mistaken and perceived maleficence or beneficence of experiences are absent. These can be adequately captured by other measures and a small battery of insight-related measures comprising these, the IPQ and a psychiatric insight measure (such as David's) are capable of assessing all the variables apparently of interest from research to date.

We are currently using such a battery alongside a number of other measures of symptomatology and cognitive and emotional processes in psychosis in a large scale randomized controlled trial of cognitive therapy and family intervention for schizophrenia spectrum psychosis, permitting us to gather information in a large sample on the relationships between psychiatric insight, psychological measures of insight, the IPQ and symptomatology and outcome.

Appendix A: an illustrative case example

A young man who has just moved away to university is feeling isolated and lonely, insecure about his intellectual functioning, and socially anxious. Following a number of late nights drinking lots of coffee and worrying about an essay, he starts to notice an oddness about the faces of his fellow students, and a surreal feel to the whole campus. He starts to believe that the whole university experience is not in fact real, and that he has been placed there as part of some kind of experiment, and that people's interactions with him are designed to provoke some kind of experimental response. He starts to selectively pick out slight oddness in people's interactions, and to perceive things as odd that he would not ordinarily have noticed. He starts to try to deliberately subvert the perceived experimental process by doing or saying unusual things, to assess people's responses – the puzzled and avoidant reactions confirm that something strange is going on.

To deal with this, he starts increasingly to isolate himself, in order to minimize the experimentation. He does not discuss his experiences with anyone, thus limiting his exposure to any alternative explanations. A worry develops that he may be experimented upon while asleep, so he tries as much as possible to stay awake. He ruminates over past life events which seem consistent with the belief, which are likely to be more accessible in this state, and other events are reinterpreted in line with the belief.

Here, the individual has made an appraisal that his experiences are the result of experimentation, and this influences his perceptions of others and his behaviour with others, generating more confirmatory experiences. He goes on to think about why the experimentation may be occurring and reflects on a longstanding sense of difference, which suggests to him that he had always been set apart ready for this kind of experimentation, and that this is why it has always been difficult for him to get on with others. He thinks about early experiences of feeling bullied by step-sibs, and by peers at school, which he believes may have left him vulnerable to being manipulated by others. He realizes that this makes sense of why he has never had a girlfriend – because he has been set aside, rather than because he is unattractive, as he had worried previously, and that he must in fact be rather important because of these experiences. These reflections lead him to the idea that the experimentation may actually be malevolent rather than neutral as he had previously thought – designed to prevent him achieving happiness in life, and he starts to think that his stepmother, with whom he had a particularly stormy relationship, may be behind it. This is confirmed when he hears her voice commenting on what he is doing. He is aware that this only happens when he is stressed in some way, and thinks he suffers in such circumstances from heightened perception, allowing him to tune in to some kind of hidden communication.

References

Amador, X. F. and David, A. S. (1998). *Insight and Psychosis.* New York: Oxford University Press.

American Psychiatric Association (APA) (1980). *Diagnostic and Statistical Manual of Mental Disorders (DSM III).* Washington, DC: APA.

American Psychiatric Association (APA) (1994). *Diagnostic and Statistical Manual of Mental Disorders (DSM IV).* Washington, DC: APA

Barrowclough, C., Lobban, F., Hatton, C. and Quinn, J. (2001). Investigation of models of illness in carers of schizophrenic patients using the Illness Perception Questionnaire. *British Journal of Clinical Psychology,* **40**, 371–85.

Beck-Sander, A., Birchwood, M. and Chadwick, P. (1997). Acting on command hallucinations: a cognitive approach. *British Journal of Clinical Psychology,* **36**, 139–48.

Bentall, R. P., Kinderman, P. and Kaney, S. (1994). The self, attributional processes and abnormal beliefs: towards a model of persecutory delusions. *Behaviour Research and Therapy,* **32**, 331–41.

Berrios, G. E. and Markova, I. S. (1998). Insight in the psychoses: A conceptual history. In X. F. Amador and A. S. David (ed.) *Insight and Psychosis*, chapter 2. New York: Oxford University Press.

Birchwood, M. and Iqbal, Z. (1998). Depression and suicidal thinking in psychosis: a cognitive approach. In T. Wykes and N. Tarrier (ed.) *Outcome and Innovation in Psychological Treatment of Schizophrenia*. Wiley: Chichester.

Birchwood, M., Iqbal, Z., Chadwick, P. and Trower, P. (2000a). Cognitive approach to depression and suicidal thinking in psychosis. I. Ontogeny of post-psychotic depression. *British Journal of Psychiatry*, **177**, 516–21.

Birchwood, M., Iqbal, Z., Chadwick, P. and Trower, P. (2000b). Cognitive approach to depression and suicidal thinking in psychosis. II. Testing the validity of a social ranking model. *British Journal of Psychiatry*, **177**, 522–8.

Birchwood, M., Meaden, A., Trower, P., Gilbert, P. and Plaistow, J. (2000c). The power and omnipotence of voices: subordination and entrapment by voices and by significant others. *Psychological Medicine*, **30**, 337–44.

Buchanan, A., Garety, P., Grubin, D., Reed, A., Taylor, P. and Wessely, S. (1990). *The Maudsley Assessment of Delusions Schedule*.

Bucher, T. (1998). Unpublished BSc thesis. GKT Medical School, University of London.

Chadwick, P. and Birchwood, M. (1994). The omnipotence of voices. A cognitive approach to auditory hallucinations. *British Journal of Psychiatry*, **166**, 773–6.

Colbert, S. M. and Peters, E. R. (2002). Need for closure and jumping to conclusions in delusion-prone individuals. *Journal of Nervous and Mental Disease*, **190**, 27–31.

Colbert, S., Garety, P. A. and Peters, E. (in prep) Need for Closure, Anxiety and Delusions.

David, A. S. (1990). Insight and Psychosis. *British Journal of Psychiatry*, **156**, 798–808.

David, A. S. (1998). Commentary on: "Is insight into psychosis meaningful?". *Journal of Mental Health*, **7**, 579–83.

Ellis, H. D. and Young, A. W. (1990). Accounting for delusional misidentifications. *British Journal of Psychiatry*, **157**, 239–48.

Freeman, D., Garety, P., Fowler, D., Kuipers, E., Dunn, G., Bebbington, P., *et al.* (1998). The London–East Anglia randomised controlled trial of cognitive behaviour therapy for psychosis IV: Self-esteem and persecutory delusions. *British Journal of Clinical Psychology*, **37**, 4, 415–30.

Freeman, D. and Garety, P. A. (1999). Worry, worry processes and dimensions of delusions: An exploratory investigation of a role for anxiety processes in the maintenance of delusional distress. *Behavioural and Cognitive Psychotherapy*, **27**, 47–62.

Freeman, D., Garety, P. and Phillips, M. (2000). An examination of hypervigilance for external threat in individuals with generalised anxiety disorder and individuals with persecutory delusions using visual scan paths. *Quarterly Journal of Experimental Psychology*, **53** A(2), 549–67.

Freeman, D., Garety, P. A. and Kuipers, E. (2001). Persecutory delusions: developing the understanding of belief maintenance and emotional distress. *Psychological Medicine*, **31**, 1293–306.

Frith, C. D. (1992). *The Cognitive Neuropsychology of Schizophrenia*. LEA: Hove.

Garety, P. A. and Hemsley, D. R. (1994). *Delusions: Investigations into the Psychology of Delusional Reasoning*. Maudsley Monographs. Oxford: Oxford University Press.

Garety, P. A., Fowler, D., Kuipers, E., Freeman, D., Dunn, G., Bebbington, P., *et al.* (1997). The London–East Anglia randomised controlled trial of cognitive-behaviour therapy for psychosis II: Predictors of outcome. *British Journal of Psychiatry*, **171**, 420–6.

Garety, P. and Freeman, D. (1999). Cognitive approaches to delusions: A critical review of theories and evidence. *British Journal of Clinical Psychology*, **38**, 113–54.

Garety, P. A., Kuipers, E., Fowler, D., Freeman, D. and Bebbington, P. (2001). Theoretical paper: A cognitive model of the positive symptoms of psychosis. *Psychological Medicine*, **31**, 189–95.

Hemsley, D. R. (1993). A simple (or simplistic?) cognitive model for schizophrenia. *Behavioural Research and Therapy*, **31**, 633–45.

Jackson, H., McGorry, P., Edwards, J., Hulbert, C., Henry, L., Francey, S., *et al.* (1998). Cognitively-oriented psychotherapy for early psychosis (COPE). Preliminary results. *British Journal of Psychiatry*, **172** (suppl. 33) 93–100.

Jaspers, K. (1913/1959). *General Psychopathology*. (J. Hoenig and M. W. Hamilton, trans.). Manchester: Manchester University Press.

Jolley, S., Garety P. A. *et al.*, Illness perception and insight in early psychosis. Paper in preparation.

Junginger, J. (1990). Predicting compliance with command hallucinations. *American Journal of Psychiatry*, **147**, 245–7.

Kemp, R. A. and David, A. S. (1995). Insight and adherence to treatment in psychotic disorders. *British Journal of Hospital Medicine*, **54**, 222–7.

Krabbendam, L., Janssen, I., Bak, M., Bijl, R. V., de Graaf, R. and van Os, J. (2002). Neuroticism and low self-esteem as risk factors for psychosis. *Social Psychiatry and Epidemiology*, **37**, 1–6.

Lau, R., Bernard, J. M. and Hartman, K. A. (1989). Further explorations of common sense representations of common illness. *Health Psychology*, **8**, 195–219.

Leventhal, H., Nerenz, D. R. and Steele, D. F. (1984). Illness representations and coping with health threats. In A. Baum and J. Singer (ed.) *Handbook of Psychology and Health, volume IV*. Hillsdale, NJ: Erlbaum.

Lobban, F., Barrowclough, C. and Jones, S. (2003). A review of the role of illness models in severe mental illness. *Clinical Psychology Review*, **23**, 171–96.

McGlashan T. H. (1987). Recovery style from mental illness and long-term outcome. *Journal of Nervous and Mental Disease*, **175**, 681–5.

McEvoy, J. P., Howe, A. C. and Hogarty, G. E. (1984). Differences in the nature of relapse and subsequent inpatient course between medication-compliant and noncompliant schizophrenic patients. *Journal of Nervous and Mental Disease*, **172**, 412–16.

McEvoy, J. P., Apperson, L. J., Appelbaum, P. S., Ortlip, P., Breckosky, J. and Hammill, K. (1989). Insight in schizophrenia: its relationship to acute psychopathology. *Journal of Nervous and Mental Disease*, **177**, 42–7.

Maher, B. A. (1974). Delusional thinking and perceptual disorder. *Journal of Individual Psychology*, **30**, 98–113.

Maher, B. A. (1988). Anomalous experience and delusional thinking: the logic of explanation. In T. F. Oltmanns and B. A. Maher (ed.) *Delusional Beliefs*. New York: Wiley.

Peters, E., Joseph, S. and Garety, P. A. (1999). The assessment of delusions in the normal and psychotic populations – Introducing the PDI. *Schizophrenia Bulletin*, **25** (3), 553–76.

Petrie, K. J., Cameron, L., Ellis, C. J., Buick, D. and Weinman, J. (2002). Changing illness perceptions after myocardial infarction: An early intervention randomised controlled trial. *Psychosomatic Medicine*, **64**, 580–6.

Romme, M. A. J. and Escher, A. D. M. A.C. (1989). Hearing voices. *Schizophrenia Bulletin*, **15**, 209–16.

Weinman, J., Petrie, K., Moss-Morris, R. and Horne, R. (1996). The Illness Perception Questionnaire: a new method for asssessing the cognitive representation of illness. *Psychology and Health*, **11**, 431–45.

White, R., Bebbington, P., Pearson, J., Johnson, S. and Ellis, D. (2000). The social context of insight in schizophrenia. *Social Psychiatry and Epidemiology*, **35**, 500–7.

Chapter 6

Insight in mood disorders: an empirical and conceptual review

S. Nassir Ghaemi and Klara J. Rosenquist

Introduction

While it has long been recognized that insight is impaired in schizophrenia and other psychotic disorders, the topic of insight in mood disorders has been relatively neglected. In fact, insight can be quite impaired in mania, second only to schizophrenia, even in the absence of psychosis (Fig. 6.1; Amador *et al.*, 1994).

Given the importance of insight to diagnosis and prognosis of bipolar disorder, it is appropriate that more attention should be paid to this phenomenon. In the first part of this chapter, we review the available empirical evidence, including a meta-analysis of this literature. In the second part of this chapter, we conceptually analyze the topic of insight in mood disorders.

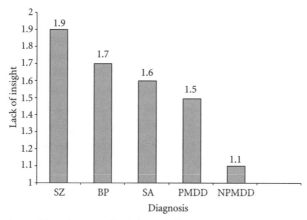

Fig. 6.1 Comparison of impairment of insight in different diagnostic groups in the DSM-IV field trials SZ = schizophrenia, BP = bipolar disorder, SA = schizoaffective disorder, PMDD = psychotic major depressive disorder, NPMDD = nonpsychotic major depressive disorder. A higher score indicates greater impairment of insight. A score of 1.0 indicates complete insight is present. A score of 5.0 indicates complete absence of insight (Amador, 1994, p. 1586).

Empirical studies

We conducted a MEDLINE literature search (1966 to 2003) of "insight, mania, bipolar disorder, awareness of illness, denial, depression, major depressive disorder", and supplemented those findings with hand-searches of major psychiatric journals for the past five years, as well as detailed bibliographic cross-referencing. We limited our search to studies which utilized standardized, validated insight rating scales, and to studies which separately analyzed and presented data on patients with mood disorders (with or without psychosis). Using these methods, we identified 11 original reports (Michalakeas *et al.*, 1994; Amador *et al.*, 1994; Ghaemi *et al.*, 1995; Swanson *et al.*, 1995; Peralta and Cuesta, 1998; McEvoy and Wilkinson, 2000; Dell'Osso *et al.*, 2002; Ghaemi *et al.*, 1997; Pallanti *et al.*, 1999; Ghaemi *et al.*, 2000; Cuesta *et al.*, 2000), nine of which presented data including patients with bipolar disorder (Michalakeas *et al.*, 1994; Amador *et al.*, 1994; Ghaemi *et al.*, 1995; Swanson *et al.*, 1995; Peralta and Cuesta, 1998; McEvoy and Wilkinson, 2000; Dell'Osso *et al.*, 2002; Pallanti *et al.*, 1999; Ghaemi *et al.*, 2000), and four of which presented data including patients with unipolar depression (Amador *et al.*, 1994; Peralta and Cuesta, 1998; Ghaemi *et al.*, 1997; Dell'Osso *et al.*, 2002) (Table 6.1). We conducted a meta-analysis of four longitudinal studies of acute mania (Michalakeas *et al.*, 1994; Ghaemi *et al.*, 1995; Swanson *et al.*, 1995; Peralta and Cuesta, 1998), after standardization of the absolute value scores of the insight rating scales used in those studies (see Table 6.1 for details on method of standardization). Meta-analysis was conducted using a random effects model with DerSimonian/Laird methods, due to evidence of statistically significant heterogeneity between studies (based on discordant sample sizes, variability of data distribution, and different insight scales used) (L'Abbe *et al.*, 1987).

Acute mania

Seven studies have assessed insight in mania and generally reported significant impairment of insight (Michalakeas *et al.*, 1994; Amador *et al.*, 1994; Ghaemi *et al.*, 1995; Swanson *et al.*, 1995; Peralta and Cuesta, 1998; McEvoy and Wilkinson 2000; Dell'Osso *et al.*, 2002). We will focus on four studies (Michalakeas *et al.*, 1994; Ghaemi *et al.*, 1995; Swanson *et al.*, 1995; Peralta and Cuesta, 1998), that compared insight before and after recovery from mania, and thus provide some data regarding potential state dependence of insight in bipolar disorder. Table 6.1 gives detailed information on all studies, including some studies not included in the meta-analysis due to being cross-sectional rather than longitudinal.

Despite some variability between studies, Figure 6.2 demonstrates that meta-analysis of these four studies found that insight is quite impaired in mania and appears to be state dependent with 20% improvement (95% confidence intervals: 7%, 34%) after recovery from mania ($P = 0.003$).[1] This finding to some extent conflicts with a number of studies in schizophrenia, in which insight appears more trait-like and less malleable

---

[1] This meta-analysis is currently in press at the *Journal of Nervous and Mental Disease*.

Table 6.1 Insight studies of mood disorders

Study	n	Insight scale used	Initial insight rating	Final insight rating	Initial standardized rating*	Final standardized rating*	Comments
Acute mania							
Michaelakas et al., 1994	13	ITAQ	11.6 ± 6.0	16.3 ± 3.9	0.47 ± 0.24	0.26 ± 0.06	Hospitalized mostly psychotic sample
Amador et al., 1994	40	SUMD	1.7 ± 0.82	–	–	–	Outpatient and inpatient sample
Ghaemi et al., 1995	28	ITAQ	12.0 ± 7.4	15.5 ± 7.4	0.45 ± 0.28	0.29 ± 0.14	Hospitalized half psychotic, half nonpsychotic sample
Swanson et al., 1995	20	Vignette	19.1 ± 1.5	17.8 ± 2.9	0.96 ± 0.08	0.89 ± 0.15	Hospitalized psychotic sample on admission
Peralta & Cuesta, 1998	21	AMDP	6.7 ± 3.2	2.7 ± 2.2	0.75 ± 0.36	0.30 ± 0.25	Hospitalized mostly psychotic sample
McEvoy & Wilkinson, 2000	17	ITAQ	15.1 ± 6.5	–	0.69 ± 0.30	–	Hospitalized mixed episode sample on admission
Dell'Osso et al., 2002	55	SUMD	–	3.5 ± 1.5	–	0.70 ± 0.30	Hospitalized pure mania sample at discharge
Dell'Osso et al., 2002	62	SUMD	–	2.9 ± 1.5	–	0.58 ± 0.30	Hospitalized mixed mania sample at discharge
Acute non-psychotic depression							
Michaelakas et al., 1994	22	ITAQ	16.9 ± 5.1	18.0 ± 5.3	0.23 ± 0.07	0.18 ± 0.05	Hospitalized bipolar sample
Amador et al., 1994	14	SUMD	1.1 ± 0.54	–	–	–	Outpatient and inpatient unipolar sample
Peralta & Cuesta, 1998	17	AMDP	1.3 ± 1.9	0.5 ± 0.8	0.14 ± 0.21	0.06 ± 0.09	Hospitalized unipolar and bipolar sample
Ghaemi et al., 1997	30	SUMD	2.5 ±–	2.8 ±–	0.5 ±–	0.56 ±–	Outpatient randomized clinical trial of seasonal affective disorder

Table 6.1 (continued)

Study	n	Insight scale used	Initial insight rating	Final insight rating	Initial standardized rating *	Final standardized rrating *	Comments
Acute psychotic depression							
Amador et al., 1994	24	SUMD	1.5 ± 0.80	–	–	–	Outpatient and inpatient, unipolar sample
Peralta & Cuesta, 1998	16	AMDP	3.9 ± 2.4	1.4 ± 1.6	0.43 ± 0.27	0.16 ± 0.18	Hospitalized unipolar and bipolar sample
Dell'Osso et al., 2002	30	SUMD	–	2.3 ± 1.3	–	0.46 ± 0.26	Hospitalized bipolar sample at discharge
Dell'Osso et al., 2002	30	SUMD	–	2.1 ± 1.5	–	0.42 ± 0.30	Hospitalized unipolar sample at discharge
Prophylaxis							
Pallanti et al., 1999	25	SUMD	–	2.3 ± 1.4	–	0.46 ± 0.28	Outpatient bipolar I sample in remission
Pallanti et al., 1999	32	SUMD	–	3.1 ± 1.1	–	0.62 ± 0.22	Outpatient bipolar II sample in remission
Ghaemi et al., 2000	45	SUMD	1.9 ± 1.0	1.6 ± 0.8	0.38 ± 0.20	0.33 ± 0.17	Outpatient non-psychotic bipolar sample
Cuesta & Peralta, 2000	27	SUMD	4.0 ± 1.5	4.3 ± 1.1	0.80 ± 0.29	0.86 ± 0.21	Hospitalized psychotic affective disorders sample

* Ratings were standardized to show a range of 0–1, with higher scores indicating more impaired insight, AMDP = Manual for the Assessment and Documentation in Psychopathology, range 0–9, high scores indicate more impaired insight, ITAQ = Insight and Treatment Attitudes Questionnaire, range 0–22, high scores indicate less impaired insight, SUMD = Scale to Assess Unawareness of Mental Disorder, range 1–5, high scores indicate more impaired insight. Vignette = 12 Brief vignettes designed by authors

Study	n	Initial insight mean (SD)	n	Final insight mean (SD)	WMD (95% CI Random)	Weight %	WMD (95% CI random)
Ghaemi *et al.*	28	0.45(0.28)	19	0.29(0.14)		25.8	0.16 (0.04,0.28)
Michaelakas *et al.*	13	0.47(0.24)	13	0.26(0.06)		24.6	0.21 (0.08,0.34)
Peralta and Cuesta	21	0.75(0.36)	21	0.30(0.25)		20.1	0.45 (0.26,0.64)
Swanson *et al.*	20	0.96(0.08)	20	0.89(0.15)		29.5	0.07 (0.00,0.14)
Total (95% CI)	82		73			100.0	0.20 (0.07,0.34)

Test for heterogeneity chi-square = 15.02 df = 3 P = 0.0018
Test for overall effect z = 2.93 P = 0.003

$$-1 \quad -0.5 \quad 0 \quad 0.5 \quad 1$$
Insight worsened   Insight improved

Fig. 6.2 Meta analysis of insight studies in mania. The figure demonstrates state dependence of insight in mania, with improvement in insight upon recovery from the acute manic episode. WMD = weighted mean difference, SD = standard deviation, CI = confidence interval.

to change. These acute mania studies also indicate that insight is about as impaired in non-psychotic as in psychotic mania, suggesting that psychosis is not the primary factor mediating impaired insight in mania.

Acute depression

There are four longitudinal studies of insight in the acute depressive episode (Michalakeas *et al.*, 1994; Amador *et al.*, 1994; Peralta and Cuesta, 1998; Ghaemi *et al.*, 1997), three of which involve subgroups from the above studies (Michalakeas *et al.*, 1994; Amador *et al.*, 1994; Peralta and Cuesta, 1998).

These studies suggest that insight is not very impaired in the acute non-psychotic depressive episode, and that insight in fact may increase as depression worsens. However, insight is moderately impaired in psychotic depression, though less so than in mania, a result also found in a large cross-sectional study (Amador *et al.*, 1994). Insight appears to improve markedly upon acute recovery from psychotic depression. Comparisons between unipolar and bipolar depression in acute episode studies have not been made.

Prophylaxis

There are two longitudinal studies of insight in mood disorders that met inclusion criteria for our review (Ghaemi *et al.*, 2000; Cuesta *et al.*, 2000). In the first study (Ghaemi *et al.*, 2000), 101 outpatients with psychiatric disorders (37 with bipolar disorder type I, 8 with bipolar disorder type II, 34 with non-psychotic unipolar depression, and the rest with anxiety or psychotic disorders) were followed for up to one year with insight ratings (Scale to assess Unawareness of Mental Disorder (SUMD), mean duration of follow-up 3.9 ± 3.5 months). In this medium-term outcome period, initiation of insight ratings was conducted primarily during periods of euthymia or at most mild symptoms (mean initial Clinical Global Impression (CGI) 3.5 ± 1.0, mean initial

Global Assessment of Functioning (GAF) 59.6 ± 9.3). Insight ratings in the bipolar group were also minimally impaired (initial SUMD 1.8) and not different from the unipolar group (initial SUMD 1.9). Improvement was also minimal given the already unimpaired levels at the start of follow-up (final SUMD 1.5 in the bipolar group and 1.6 in the unipolar group). Initial insight was not significantly correlated with improvement in clinical outcome (based on GAF and CGI ratings), but improvement in insight during the period of follow-up was associated with improvement in clinical outcome in the bipolar I group (r = 0.56 for GAF, r = 0.67 for CGI, P = 0.0005), though not in the unipolar group (r = 0.50 for GAF, P = 0.03; r = 0.36 for CGI, P = 0.14).

In the other study (Cuesta et al., 2000), 27 hospitalized patients with psychotic mood disorders (not subgrouped as bipolar versus unipolar, or as manic versus depressed) were assessed for insight during their acute episodes and at least six months after recovery (mean follow-up duration not provided). Again, baseline insight did not predict outcome, but there appeared to be a moderate association between improvement in insight and improvement in outcome (r = 0.48, P < 0.0005). Insight into current mood symptoms did not improve significantly over time (initial ITAQ 14.5 ± 7.3, final ITAQ 16.7 ± 5.8; initial SUMD 4.0 ± 1.5, final SUMD 4.3 ± 1.1)[2], as found in the above study. However, insight into past mood episodes improved over time. (The authors revised the scale in this analysis only, with higher scores indicating better insight: initial SUMD for awareness of illness 3.6 ± 1.5, final 4.3 ± 0.9; initial SUMD for awareness of medication effect 3.8 ± 1.3, final 4.7 ± 0.6; initial SUMD for awareness of social consequences 3.4 ± 1.6, final 4.5 ± 0.9). Overall, as a pooled absolute percentile summary, insight into past mood/psychotic episodes improved by 18%.

In a cross-sectional study of remitted patients with bipolar disorder, the SUMD was administered to 57 outpatients with bipolar I (N = 25) or bipolar II (N = 32) (Pallanti et al., 1999). All patients were being treated with mood stabilizers. Although general impairment of awareness was present in all bipolar patients, bipolar II patients had significantly less insight (3.1 ± 1.1) than bipolar I patients (2.3 ± 1.4; t = −2.42, df = 55, P = 0.02).

In another study, 189 inpatients (52 with bipolar disorder) were assessed for insight using the Hamilton Depression Rating scale before discharge and at a 6 month- follow-up visit (Fennig et al., 1996). Since this study did not use a specific insight rating scale, it did not meet the criteria for inclusion in the table but is applicable to the discussion on prophylaxis. Contrary to our data, this study reported that insight improved over time. Specifically, the study found a greater improvement of insight over time in the bipolar sample as compared to the schizophrenic sample. Eighty per cent of patients with psychotic depression had intact insight at baseline compared with 54% of patients with mania and 46.5% in the schizophrenic sample. At 6-month follow up, the original

---

[2] SUMD ratings here reflect item 1, current awareness of illness. Other items also showed no significant change.

mania sample showed the greatest improvement with 92% displaying intact insight. The schizophrenic sample and the originally psychotic depressed bipolar sample also showed a slight improvement (55% and 86% respectively). In conclusion, the study found the predictors of long-term insight to be: (1) baseline insight, (2) diagnosis of bipolar disorder (compared with schizophrenia) and (3) prior psychiatric treatment (vs. no prior treatment).

These studies differ in certain important ways. The first (Ghaemi *et al.*, 2000) and third (Pallanti *et al.*, 1999) studies were comprised of primarily non-psychotic patients, while the other two (Cuesta *et al.*, 2000; Fennig *et al.*, 1996) were comprised completely of psychotic patients. In the second study (Cuesta *et al.*, 2000), one cannot disentangle the possible effects of subtype of mood disorder (unipolar vs. bipolar) or type of mood episode (manic vs. mixed vs. depressed). Both the first two studies assessed patients during periods of relative euthymia (Ghaemi *et al.*, 2000; Cuesta *et al.*, 2000). They concur on the finding that initial impairment of insight does not predict poor outcome, and that improvement in insight is associated with improved outcome. This association is not necessarily causal: improvement of insight could lead to, or conversely be the product of, better clinical outcomes. As depicted in the fourth study (Fennig *et al.*, 1996), insight seems to be changeable, however, and not resistant to alterations in clinical state in mood disorders. The second study (Cuesta *et al.*, 2000) further suggests that there may be gradual improvement in insight in the euthymic state with mood disorders, but this improvement is largely limited to awareness of past mood episodes. Insight into current or prodromal symptoms of future mood symptoms did not improve. Unfortunately, it is just this kind of current insight that is most helpful for clinicians and patients.

Other empirical studies

Several other studies, though not meeting inclusion criteria for this literature review, provide some empirical data relevant to an understanding of insight in mood disorders. We review them here under their relevant categories.

Non-compliance

A major potential consequence of impaired insight is treatment noncompliance. In a Bayesian meta-analysis, the frequency of treatment noncompliance in bipolar disorder appears to be about 40%, with somewhat more noncompliance with medication than with psychotherapy (Basco and Rush, 1995). Another study found that of 140 bipolar patients, only 49% were compliant after a one-year follow up period. Denial of illness (lack of insight), reported by 63% of the patients, was the most common reason for noncompliance (Keck *et al.*, 1997). In another study of lithium prophylaxis in 38 patients with bipolar disorder, regression analysis found that negative attitudes towards lithium was the only significant predictor of noncompliance (Schumann *et al.*, 1999).

There are policy implications to the link between lack of insight and medication noncompliance, as suggested by Torrey (1997). If patients with severe mental illness lack insight, and if this is due (at least in part) to brain dysfunction, then a case could be made for involuntary outpatient treatment of such patients. While civil libertarians might object, the empirical evidence discussed in this paper suggests that these conclusions may not be unreasonable. Nor is such an approach incompatible with continued protection of a rather broad swath of civil liberties. In the United Kingdom, where the involuntary use of depot neuroleptic agents is more common than in the United States, civil liberties do not appear to have been materially harmed. In the United States, what is required is more empirical research and sustained public and professional education regarding the role of insight in serious mental illness.

Personality and insight

Another interesting issue is the relationship of personality traits to insight. This is an understudied topic. One study found that high neuroticism and low extraversion on the NEO personality scale predict enhanced insight into depression (Enns *et al.*, 2000).

Insight and suicidality

The relationship of insight to suicidality is complex, but there appears to be an association between intact insight and increased risk of suicide in some patients (Amador *et al.*, 1996; Schwartz and Petersen, 1999). Such data in mood disorders are lacking, but given the evidence of an association between intact insight and depression, it would not be surprising to find such a relationship with suicide in mood disorders also.

Clinically, these studies suggest that clinicians need to be attuned to possibly increased risk of depression and suicide in patients who are either highly insightful, or in those who, when recovering from a mood episode, may be gaining more insight.

Neuropsychology of insight in mood disorders

It has long been assumed that cognition is not impaired in mania, or that cognitive impairment in mood disorder was limited to active mood episodes but absent in periods of euthymia. Increasing evidence suggests, both in recurrent unipolar depression as well as in bipolar disorder, that cognitive impairment is present chronically in many patients. This impairment occurs even during euthymia, and appears to be associated with hippocampal atrophy related to hypercortisolemia occurring during repeated mood episodes (Tham *et al.*, 1997; van Gorp *et al.*, 1998; Martinez-Aran *et al.*, 2000; Gourovitch *et al.*, 1999).

Given that insight has been associated with some cognitive impairment in schizophrenia (particularly frontal) (McGlynn and Schacter 1997), and that there is cognitive impairment in many patients with recurrent mood disorders, it is logical to hypothesize that impairment of insight in mood disorders may be associated with cognitive impairment. There are very limited data on this topic, so far not finding evidence of such a link (Ghaemi *et al.*, 1996). But careful studies of frontal lobe function and insight in mood disorders have not been published. Since anosognosia in stroke patients is associated with parietal lobe impairment, it would also be logical to study parietal lobe function and insight in mood disorders. A proxy for such studies might be testing of facial recognition, which is parietally mediated. One study of 34 patients and controls found evidence of impairment of facial recognition during mania (Lembke and Ketter, 2002).

Bipolar subtypes

Another question of importance, unaddressed in our literature review of empirical studies, is the relationship of insight to bipolar subtypes, like mixed episodes or hypomania. One report (McEvoy and Wilkinson, 2000) of 17 hospitalized patients indicates that the mixed episode in bipolar disorder, where depressive mood predominates, is associated with more insight (ITAQ 15.1 ± 6.5) than pure euphoric mania (ITAQ 5.4 ± 6.3, 44.1% difference). Regarding hypomania, as mentioned previously, a study of 57 euthymic outpatients (Pallanti *et al.*, 1999) reported that bipolar disorder type II, where hypomania occurs rather than mania, was associated with more impairment of insight than bipolar disorder type I (SUMD 3.1 ± 1.1 vs. 2.3 ± 1.4, 16% difference, $P < 0.05$).

Misdiagnosis of bipolar disorder

Another often unnoticed aspect of insight in mood disorders is the issue of misdiagnosis. Since most patients possess insight into depression but many do not possess insight into mania, it would be logical to conclude that patients are more likely to complain of and seek treatment for depression than mania. This is a common clinical experience. In fact, an empirical study (Keitner *et al.*, 1996) found that families are twice as sensitive to behavioral symptoms of mania (47% of family members reported manic symptoms) than patients (22% of patients' self-reported manic symptoms); this finding held only for behavioral effects in mania, not in depression (10% of patients reported depressive symptoms vs. 13% of family members). As a consequence, impaired insight into mania likely predisposes patients and clinicians to misdiagnose bipolar disorder as unipolar depression. Numerous studies, which we have reviewed elsewhere, indicate that bipolar disorder is misdiagnosed as unipolar depression in about 40% of patients, with about 6–12 years elapsing from the initial misdiagnosis until the correct bipolar diagnosis is later made (Ghaemi *et al.*, 1999). There is no research yet directly linking this misdiagnosis to lack of insight in mania, as we are suggesting. Future research on this topic would be an advance in the literature.

Conceptual issues

In the first part of this chapter we focused on empirical studies, seeking to highlight gaps in knowledge as well as potential conclusions. We now seek to integrate these data with a conceptual understanding of the phenomenon of insight in mood disorders, dividing our discussion into depression and mania.

Depression: Depressive realism versus cognitive distortion

Two basic psychological models of depression may throw some light on the nature of insight in depression. In one model, cognitive distortion occurs. The depressive mood-state interferes with normal thinking, leading to the classic cognitive states of mind seen in depression: "all-or-nothing" thinking, self-blame, catastrophic reaction. This model is used to support cognitive-behavioral methods of therapy (Beck *et al.*, 1979). In the other model labeled depressive realism, depressed persons are seen to be more aware, compared to non-depressed persons, of their internal mood state and life circumstances. This increased awareness into the reality of the negative aspects of their circumstances leads to depressive symptoms (Alloy and Abramson, 1988).

For psychiatric clinicians, the cognitive distortion model is probably more popular and better known, perhaps because of the availability of its related cognitive behavioral form of therapy. In contrast, the depressive realism model is more prominent in the non-clinical academic psychology literature, perhaps partly due to the absence of a related form of psychotherapy. In fact, most of the evidence adduced to support the depressive realism model has come from non-clinical sources, such as college students, where subjects were given certain tests of cognitive functioning, in some of which their errors were due to their own decisions, and in others of which errors were introduced randomly outside of the subjects' control. Subjects were asked to describe to what extent they felt they were causing the errors produced. Those who had some depressive symptoms based on self-report rating scales were more accurate than those without depressive symptoms in correctly attributing error to themselves as opposed to random error beyond their control. Conversely, the "normal" non-depressed subjects had a sense of greater control than they really possessed. Hence researchers suggested that these mildly, but not necessarily clinically, depressed subjects were more realistic than their completely non-depressed counterparts.

In contrast to these non-clinical data, we would like to draw attention to the insight studies of depression reviewed here as supportive of the depressive realism model. Patients with clinically diagnosed non-psychotic major depression appear to have none to minimal impairment in insight.

If the depressive realism model is valid, then there are some potential implications for our understanding of insight and depression. Insight would not be viewed as inherently beneficial; it can be associated with more depression. Depressive realism suggests that having more insight into one's environment, feelings, and circumstances may correlate with dampened mood. Whether such heightened insight causes depression, or whether depression can lead to heightened insight is unclear. The direction of causality that underlies this association remains to be explored empirically. However, the possibility exists that in some cases depressive symptoms might be exacerbated by enhanced awareness of one's emotions and surroundings.

Further, there may be some benefits to a "normal" amount of denial, which keeps one from daily confronting what Karl Jaspers called the "limit-situations" of human existence

(Jaspers, 1998/1911), such as death, the tenuousness of human relationships, sickness and so on. Taken to an extreme, however, such denial could lead to a lack of authenticity in one's life, a lack of meaning in one's activities and relationships, a kind of "forgetfulness" in the details of daily living (Heidegger, 1962). Readers might note that we are alluding to a possible treatment implication of the depressive realism model: existential psychotherapy (Ghaemi, 2001). In this approach, depressed patients would be seen as overwhelmed by their awareness of their existential limit-situations. Therapy would consist of putting perspective on those existential circumstances, owning them and accepting them, while putting them in the context of the larger meaning of one's life (Havens, 1987).

Mania and cognition

The marked impairment of insight in non-psychotic mania is a clear clinical counter-example to the notion that impaired insight is part and parcel of psychosis. Empirical studies have now demonstrated that impaired insight is independent of psychosis (Ghaemi, 1997) but conceptually, the phenomenon of impaired insight in non-psychotic mania makes the same point. Yet while it is now generally recognized that impaired insight and psychotic states are not identical, the phenomenon of insight is most often associated with, studied in, and conceptualized in relation to psychotic states.

We wish to emphasize one point here: there is not necessarily any cognitive impairment in mania.[3] Unlike psychotic states of schizophrenia, manic states are not generally or even usually associated with illogicality or cognitive impairment. In schizophrenia, looseness of associations is common, with loss of logical connections between apposite thoughts. In mania, flight of ideas occurs, and it is distinguished from looseness of associations by the fact that logical connections between thoughts are maintained. The thoughts are simply faster than usual. One way of conceiving this phenomenon is to imagine one's usual thoughts as analogous to three cars racing down a highway in three lanes at the allowed maximum speed limit of 60 miles per hour. Flight of ideas consists of the same three cars racing down the highway in the same three separate lanes, but at 100 miles per hour. The cars do not veer into each other's lanes, or knock each other over. They simply go faster than usual. Hence one does not see in non-psychotic mania evidence of the same kind of impairment in logic as one sees in schizophrenia. Yet both conditions can be characterized by similar types and severity of impairment of insight. One possible conclusion is that conceptually, cognitive impairment, specifically illogical thinking, may not be closely related to impairment of insight. Further research is needed to elucidate the relationships of insight, cognitive impairment and mania.

---

[3] Exception: Bell's delirious mania.

Mania and the meaning of happiness

The topic of insight in bipolar disorder sometimes raises passions, partly, we think, because of the fact that most of us hold deeply felt (though not necessarily explicit) philosophical assumptions about the nature of happiness.

The problem of mild mania or hypomania highlights how the assessment of insight depends on the clinician's diagnostic certainty; if the clinician is not certain (or worse, is mistaken) about the patient's diagnosis, then there is no way to be certain whether the patient has insight into the diagnosis. In an important paper, Moore and colleagues (1995) relate the concept of insight in "mild" mania to ethical conceptions of well-being. They describe a manic patient who, when manic, does not wish to be married, leaves his family, spends money generously, and generally enjoys himself. When not manic, he regrets many of those behaviors, but he is not sure which "person" he is: the manic care-free person, or the not-manic responsible person. Thus, he vacillates between taking and not taking medication. The authors indicate that the perspective of the patient when manic may be as acceptable and deserving of respect as the perspective of the patient when not-manic; this is based on a desire-fulfillment theory of well-being, where the autonomous individual has the right to determine his/her well-being based on the satisfaction of whatever desires that person possesses. Other perspectives, such as hedonism (or simple pursuit of pleasure) might also be used to justify mania. Another viewpoint, which perhaps comes most naturally to clinicians, assumes that manic patients are not expressing their true desires due to a biological infirmity, and thus their perspective when manic is not representative of either their true wishes or their best interests. Moore and associates cast doubt on this clinical perspective as excessively paternalistic and disrespectful of patient autonomy.

At one level, the case presented above is not really a case of hypomania, nor even "mild" mania, but simply mania. The distinction between mania and hypomania rests largely on dysfunction, which if present leads to a diagnosis of mania. A diagnosis of hypomania (uniquely for major axis I DSM-IV mental disorders) requires the absence of significant social or occupational dysfunction. In the above case, the patient clearly has social dysfunction in relation to his marriage and his friendships, and this dysfunction is more than mild, since it is placing his marriage in serious jeopardy. At one level, the case can simply be conceptualized as with any case of mania, i.e. that the patient should take lithium to allow him to function well in his usual, average, "normal", "healthy" state. This average state is defined by how he is most of the time, outside of his brief manic or depressive episodes. Further, one could argue that he is not "himself" in the manic state, that his agency is impaired by his manic illness, and thus he is exercising his free will only in his non-manic state. All these considerations would argue for treatment with lithium.

However, the philosophical considerations raised by Moore and colleagues would indeed hold for a case of true hypomania. Imagine the same case without any significant dysfunction in the hypomanic state. The case would have to be rewritten, the spousal conflict would have to be minimal, but seen in that manner, it would be ethically less confusing. Many would agree that treatment for hypomania, in isolation, is not necessary.

While this dialectic of paternalism and autonomy is a common problem in medical ethics, it is important to recognize that making the diagnosis of mania itself is to some extent dependent on our conceptions, as physicians and as patients, of psychological well-being. And thus we need to be especially aware of our own conceptual assumptions or biases when we assess insight in mania.

Summary

In mania, impairment of insight is about as severe as in schizophrenia and probably is also associated with poor prognosis. The neuropsychological and/or psychosocial roots of lack of insight in these conditions are unclear. Lack of insight in mania appears to be a state phenomenon, unlike schizophrenia.

In depression, impairment of insight is less severe than in mania; psychotic depression is associated with less insight than non-psychotic depression, however. There is some evidence that insight in depression may be less impaired when depressive symptoms are more severe, possibly supporting the depressive realism hypothesis.

Finally, poor insight is associated with medication noncompliance in serious mental illness, with the policy implication that involuntary treatment may need to be utilized more frequently than it has been beforehand. Lack of insight may lead to underdiagnosis of bipolar disorder, since patients often will not report or be able to report symptoms of mood elevation.

It appears that our conceptual understanding of insight in mania is also influenced by our ethical theories regarding the concept of "well-being".

The following questions remain to be clarified by future research:

1 Are there neuropsychological correlates to lack of insight in mood disorders?

2 What cultural and social factors are relevant to the assessment of insight?

3 Is insight associated with medication noncompliance and poor prognosis in mood disorders?

4 Is there any drawback to excessive insight (as suggested by the depressive realism hypothesis)?

5 What is the relationship of insight to suicide in mood disorders?

6 Does poor insight lead to underdiagnosis of bipolar disorder?

7 Does involuntary treatment improve outcome in bipolar patients with poor insight?

References

Alloy, L. B. and Abramson, L. Y. (1988). Depressive realism: Four theoretical perspectives. In L. B. Alloy (ed.) *Cognitive Processes in Depression*. New York: Guilford Press.

Amador, X. A., Flaum, M., Andreasen, N. C., *et al*. (1994). Awareness of illness in schizophrenia and schizoaffective and mood disorders. *Archives of General Psychiatry*, **51**, 826–36.

Amador, X. F., Friedman, J. H., Kasapis, C., Yale, S. A., Flaum, M. and Gorman, J. M. (1996). Suicidal behavior in schizophrenia and its relationship to awareness of illness. *American Journal of Psychiatry*, **153**, 1185–8.

Basco, M. R. and Rush, A. J. (1995). Compliance with pharmacotherapy in mood disorders. *Psychiatric Annals*, **25**, 269–78.

Beck, A. T., Rush, A. J., Shaw, B. F. and Emery, G. (1979). *Cognitive Therapy of Depression*, New York: Guilford Press.

Cuesta, M., Peralta, V. and Zarzuela, A. (2000). Reappraising insight in psychosis. Multi-scale longitudinal study. *British Journal of Psychiatry*, **177**, 233–40.

Dell'Osso, L., Pini, S., Cassano, G. B., *et al.* (2002). Insight into illness in patients with mania, mixed mania, bipolar depression and major depression with psychotic features. *Bipolar Disorders*, **4**, 315–22.

Enns, M., Larsen, D. and Cox, B. (2000). Discrepancies between self and observer ratings of depression: The relationship to demographic, clinical and personality variables. *J Affect Disord*, **60**, 33–41.

Fennig, S., Everett, E., Bromet, E., *et al.* (1996). Insight in first-admission psychotic patients. *Schizophrenia Research*, **22**, 257–63.

Ghaemi, S. N. (1997). Insight and psychiatric disorders: a review of the literature, with a focus on its clinical relevance for bipolar disorder. *Psychiatric Annals*, **27**, 782–90.

Ghaemi, S. N. (2001). Rediscovering existential psychotherapy: The contribution of Ludwig Binswanger. *American Journal of Psychotherapy*, **55**, 51–64.

Ghaemi, S. N., Boiman, E. E. and Goodwin, F. K. (2000). Insight and outcome in bipolar, unipolar, and anxiety disorders. *Comprehensive Psychiatry*, **41**, 167–71.

Ghaemi, S. N., Hebben, N., Stoll, A. L. and Pope, H. G. (1996). Neuropsychological aspects of lack of insight in bipolar disorder: a preliminary report. *Psychiatry Research*, **65**, 113–20.

Ghaemi, S. N., Sachs, G. S., Baldassano, C. F. and Truman, C. J. (1997). Insight in seasonal affective disorder. *Comprehensive Psychiatry*, **38**, 345–8.

Ghaemi, S. N., Sachs, G. S., Chiou, A. M., Pandurangi, A. K. and Goodwin, F. K. (1999). Is bipolar disorder still underdiagnosed? Are antidepressants overutilized? *Journal of Affective Disorders*, **52**, 135–44.

Ghaemi, S. N., Stoll, A. L. and Pope, H. G. (1995). Lack of insight in bipolar disorder: The acute manic episode. *Journal of Nervous and Mental Disease*, **183**, 464–7.

Gourovitch, M. L., Torrey, E. F., Gold, J. M., Randolph, C., Weinberger, D. R. and Goldberg, T. E. (1999). Neuropsychological performance of monozygotic twins discordant for bipolar disorder. *Biological Psychiatry*, **45**, 639–46.

Havens, L. (1987). *Approaches to the Mind: Movement of the psychiatric schools from sects toward science*. Cambridge, Mass: Harvard University Press.

Heidegger, M. (1962). *Being and Time*. Harper and Row, New York.

Jaspers, K. (1998 (1911)). *General Psychopathology*. Baltimore: Johns Hopkins University Press.

Keck, P. E., McElroy, S. L., Strakowski, S. M., Bourne, M. L. and West, S. A. (1997). Compliance with maintenance treatment in bipolar disorder. *Psychopharmacology Bulletin*, **33**, 87–91.

Keitner, G. I., Solomon, D. A., Ryan, C. E., *et al.* (1996). Prodromal and residual symptoms in bipolar I disorder. *Comprehensive Psychiatry*, **37**, 362–7.

L'Abbe, K., Detsky, A. and O'Rourke, K. (1987). Meta analysis in clinical research. *Ann Intern Med*, **107**, 224–33.

Lembke, A. and Ketter, T. (2002). Impaired recognition of facial emotion in mania. *Am J Psychiatry*, **159**, 302–4.

Martinez-Aran, A., Vieta, E., Colom, F., *et al.* (2000). Cognitive dysfunctions in bipolar disorder: evidence of neuropsychological disturbances. *Psychother Psychosom*, **69**, 2–18.

McEvoy, J. and Wilkinson, M. (2000). The role of insight in the treatment and outcome of bipolar disorder. *Psychiatric Annals*, **30**, 495–8.

McGlynn, S. and Schacter, D. (1997). The neuropsychology of insight: Impaired awareness of deficits in a psychiatric context. *Psychiatric Annals*, **27**, 806–11.

Michalakeas, A., Skoutas, C., Charalambous, A., *et al.* (1994). Insight in schizophrenia and mood disorders and its relation to psychopathology. *Acta Psychiatrica Scandinavica*, **90**, 46–9.

Moore, A., Hope, T. and Fulford, K. W. M. (1995). Mild mania and well-being. *Philosophy, Psychology, and Psychiatry*, **1**, 166–91.

Pallanti, S., Quercioli, L., Pazzagli, A., Rossi, A., Dell'Osso, L., Pini, S., Cassano, G. B. (1999). Awareness of illness and subjective experience of cognitive complaints in patients with bipolar I and bipolar II disorder. *American Journal of Psychiatry*, **156**, 1094–6.

Peralta, V. and Cuesta, M. (1998). Lack of insight in mood disorders. *Journal of Affective Disorders*, **49**, 55–8.

Schumann, C., Lenz, G., Berghofer, A. and Muller-Oerlinghausen, B. (1999). Non-adherence with long-term prophylaxis: a 6-year naturalistic follow-up study of affectively ill patients. *Psychiatry Research*, **89**, 247–57.

Schwartz, R. and Petersen, S. (1999). The relationship between insight and suicidality among patients with schizophrenia. *The Journal of Nervous and Mental Disease*, **187**, 376–8.

Swanson, C. L., Freudenreich, O., McEvoy, J. P., Nelson, L., Kamaraju, L. and Wilson, W. H. (1995). Insight in schizophrenia and mania. *Journal of Nervous and Mental Disease*, **193**, 752–5.

Tham, A., Engelbrektson, K., Mathe, A. A., Johnson, L., Olsson, E. and Aberg-Wistedt, A. (1997). Impaired neuropsychological performance in euthymic patients with recurring mood disorders. *J Clin Psychiatry*, **58**, 26–9.

Torrey, E. F. (1997). *Out of the Shadows: Confronting America's mental illness crisis.* New York: John Wiley and Sons.

van Gorp, W., Altshuler, L. L., Theberge, D. C., Wilkins, J. and Dixon, W. (1998). Cognitive impairment in euthymic bipolar patients with and without prior alcohol dependence. *Arch Gen Psychiatry*, **55**, 41–6.

Part II

Neuropsychology

Chapter 7

The neuropsychology of insight in psychiatric and neurological disorders

Frank Larøi, William B. Barr, and
Richard S. E. Keefe

As the numerous contributions in this book clearly show, patients with schizophrenia often exhibit lack of awareness of their illness. More specifically, David (1990) has proposed that insight, in reference to psychosis, has three recognizable components: recognition that one has a disease, compliance with treatment, and the ability to categorize unusual mental events as pathological. Amador and colleagues make further distinctions and argue that deficits in awareness are of diagnostic significance and are useful in guiding treatment decisions (Amador, Strauss, Yale *et al.*, 1991). Although all are in agreement that the aetiology of unawareness in schizophrenia is poorly understood, the research literature points to a number of possible aetiological models for poor insight in schizophrenia, such as psychological defence, clinical, and neuropsychological causes (Amador *et al.*, 1991; Amador and Kronengold, 1998). In particular, the neuropsychological model draws a parallel between poor insight in psychotic patients and poor insight in those with demonstrable brain lesions (anosognosia), more specifically in those patients with frontal damage. The neuropsychological model suggesting frontal lobe dysfunction to be related to unawareness of illness in schizophrenia is particularly interesting as recent research from various disciplines has found that frontal and pre-frontal areas of the cortex are implicated as primary areas of dysfunction in schizophrenia (Devous *et al.*, 1985; Rubin *et al.*, 1991; Raine *et al.*, 1992; Seidman *et al.*, 1994). For these reasons, it has been proposed that models provided by neuropsychological studies of awareness phenomena may be useful for understanding the mechanisms underlying these disturbances in schizophrenia (David, 1990; Amador, Strauss, Yale *et al.*, 1991).

The following chapter comprises three parts. The first involves a description of impairments of awareness in neurobehavioural disorders. Then, a parallel between these impairments of awareness with those found in schizophrenia will be presented. The second part of the chapter involves the presentation of a form of awareness disorder that has recently been studied in schizophrenia, namely, an impairment in autonoetic awareness.

Finally, the third part will briefly present major theoretical approaches to disorders of awareness, in particular, neurobehavioural and neuropsychological theories.

Unawareness of illness may involve impaired awareness of the illness globally, or specific aspects of the illness such as symptoms or impairments. By unawareness, we refer to a lack of knowledge of symptoms, even when confronted with them. As mentioned briefly above, it is important to note that unawareness of illness or unawareness of impairments/symptoms may also be attributed to the emergence of psychological defence mechanisms aimed at blocking the presence of these symptoms from consciousness. This line of argument, however, will not be pursued in this chapter.

Disturbances of awareness in neurobehavioural disorders

Anosognosia

For over a century, neurologists have described patients with significant difficulties in motor abilities, vision, language, and various other cognitive functions who are totally unaware of their impairments. Over the years, these phenomena have been variably attributed to the direct effects of focal or diffuse brain dysfunction or to the emergence of psychological defence mechanisms aimed at blocking the presence of these symptoms from consciousness. There have been a number of excellent reviews on these phenomena (Fisher, 1970; McGlynn and Schacter, 1989; Prigatano and Schacter, 1991; Weinstein and Kahn, 1955). This section will briefly describe those syndromes characterized by altered awareness of a variety of primary motor or sensory disturbances. Disorders involving unawareness of aphasic or amnestic deficits will not be covered in this discussion, though the clinical and theoretical importance of these conditions is not denied.

Joseph Francois Félix Babinski is generally regarded as the author who first introduced anosognosia as a term to describe a denial of motor impairment (Babinski, 1914). Over the years, there has been some misunderstanding about whether anosognosia refers specifically to lack of awareness for distinct symptoms such as left hemiplegia or left hemianopsia or whether the term refers to a lack of knowledge or a failure to recognize one's disease in general. Today, the term is often used synonymously with the terms unawareness of deficits, lack of insight and imperception of disease to refer to a rather non-specific lack awareness of illness or neuropsychological impairment (McGlynn and Schacter, 1989). As with most neurobehavioural syndromes, it has been observed that unawareness deficits are rarely seen as "all-or-none" phenomena, but are rather observed on a continuum of severity. Most of these disorders are seen as the result of focal neurological impairment. The vast majority of awareness syndromes described in the classical neurological literature involve a disturbance of ability to detect an acute impairment in motor functions. Lhermitte (1939) separated anosognosia into two components. These include "classic" anosognosia (denial of the hemiplegia) and anosodiaphoria (indifference to the hemiplegia). It is well-known that symptoms of classic anosognosia are observed almost exclusively in response to left hemiplegia resulting from focal lesions in the right cerebral hemisphere. Babinski (1914) specified that the lack of awareness seen in these patients was observed without the loss of general intellectual capacities. It was also seen specifically for some symptoms and not others. For example, one patient denied the existence of her left-side weakness, though she admitted to having difficulties with backache and phlebitis. The clinician is typically unable to convince of the patient of the deficit, even where they are confronted with situations requiring use the hemiparetic limb. The patient may even accuse the clinician of attempting to fabricate the "so-called" impairment. The specificity of the symptoms, combined with the relative preservation of intellect, suggests that this syndrome is not the result of a generalized cognitive disturbance.

In addition to the disorders characterized by the patient's altered awareness of motor disability, there is a range of awareness syndromes that are the result of diminished ability to detect changes or abnormalities in sensory functions or receptive behaviour. One of the major features of these disorders is that they are often confined to a single sensory modality.

There are numerous descriptions of disorders affecting awareness of visual and auditory defects. Unawareness of visual field disturbances (hemianopia) has been described by numerous authors (Critchley, 1953; Teuber, Battersby, and Bender, 1960). Cortical blindness is a condition that is usually associated with bilateral occipital lesions (Bergman, 1957). Cortical deafness results from bilateral lesions in primary auditory regions (Goldstein, Brown, and Hollander, 1975; Mott, 1907). In most cases, patients are clearly aware of these acquired deficits (Aldrich, Alessi, Beck, and Gilman, 1987; Teuber, Battersby, and Bender, 1960). However, Anton's Syndrome is a variant of cortical blindness characterized by an unawareness of the deficit (Anton, 1898; David, Owen, and Förstl, 1993; Förstl, Owen, and David, 1993). Patients with this condition may behave as if they are blind, but deny the condition when queried. For example, we saw one man who failed to respond to visual stimuli in his environment but stated that his vision would be fine if somebody would turn on the overhead lights. Brockman and von Hagen (1946) have described patients who developed paranoid delusions and hallucinations in association with cortical blindness.

Disorders of body awareness

Anosognosic Behaviour Disorder   Frederiks made an important distinction between "verbal anosognosia" and "anosognosic behaviour disorder" (Frederiks, 1985a). While the first term refers to the patient's explicit denial of the symptom in response to the examiner's query, the second term refers to the patient's unusual reactions to the paralyzed half of the body. A listing of terms used to describe these disorders is provided in Table 7.1. Frederiks considers verbal anosognosia to be a perceptual disorder, while anosognosic behaviour disorders are considered to be "non-conscious" disturbances that solely affect behaviour (Frederiks, 1985a).

Table 7.1 Disorders of body awareness

Term	Description	Reference
1. Anososgnosic behaviour disorders:		Fredericks (1985a)
A. Misoplegia	A "hatred" of affected limb	Critchley (1953)
B. Personification	Tendency to refer to the limb with endearing terms or nicknames	Juba (1949)
C. Nosoagnosic overestimation	An overestimation of the strength of weakened limb	Anastasopoulis (1961)
D. Kinaesthetic hallucinations	A false belief that the limb is moving	Waldenstrom (1939)
2. Body schema disorders:		
A. Phantom limb	Perception of the presence of an amputated limb	Fredericks (1985a)
B. Phantom supernumerary limb	A sensation that another limb has evolved elsewhere	Critchley (1953)
C. Alien hand syndrome	Loss of volitional control of the contralateral hand	Bogen (1993)
D. Autotopagnosia	Loss of the ability to identify or name body parts	Pick (1908)
E. Macrosomatognosia	Experience body parts as abnormally large	Fredericks (1985a)
F. Microsomatognosia	Experience body parts as abnormally small	
G. Autoscopia	Experience of seeing oneself projected in external space	Lukianowicz (1958)

Anosognosic behavioural disorders may include rather bizarre reactions to the affected limb, characterized by beliefs that the affected body parts are no longer a part of the self. Some authors describe these conditions as having a "quasi-psychotic quality" (Bisiach, 1988). For example, some patients may develop paranoid delusions about the limb, whereas other patients may refer to their limbs by somewhat endearing terms or even give their limbs a nickname (Juba, 1949). One woman referred to her leg as "Fred" and her arm as "Little Fred" (Cutting, 1978). Some patients are known to confuse temporal elements by stating that their limb is not weak at the time of testing, though they will admit that its function may have been disturbed in the distant past (Weinstein and Kahn, 1955).

Body Schema Disorders   There are a range of other conditions involving alterations in body awareness that do not involve an explicit denial of disability. Many authors have combined these conditions with the syndromes described above and referred to them as "body-schema disorders" (Frederiks, 1985a). These are listed in the second half of Table 7.1. Some of these disorders are characterized by a misperception of sensory information regarding one half of one's own body (Lhermitte, 1939). The most striking of these conditions are the phenomena that may occur following the amputation of a limb or other body part. Patients experiencing a phantom limb may continue to perceive a presence of the missing limb, including pain, temperature, and all of the limb's spatial characteristics following the amputation (Frederiks, 1985b). Other conditions involve perceptual distortions about either the size or location of various parts of the body.

Another unusual condition is one where patients develop a condition where they feel do not have volitional control of one of their hands. This condition, known as the "alien hand syndrome" is usually observed in the hand contralateral to a lesion of the mesial frontal region (Bogen, 1993; Goldberg, Mayer, and Toglia, 1981). The limb often behaves as if it "has a mind of its own". For example, patients have described experiences where the hand begins to unbutton their clothing inappropriately and without their awareness. Some patients may react to this condition by slapping or attempting to restrain the hand. Others may refer to it in third person, in a manner similar to that which is seen in patients exhibiting personification of their hemiplegic limbs.

Brain lesions resulting in disorders of awareness

Most syndromes affecting awareness appear to be the result of right hemisphere lesions, though controversial cases of similar phenomena resulting from left hemisphere lesions have been reported (Denny-Brown and Banker, 1954; Olsen and Ruby, 1941; Paterson and Zangwill, 1944). Most authors agree that disorders affecting awareness of left hemiplegia are the result of lesions in the inferoparietal cortex of the right hemisphere (Gerstmann, 1942; Critchley, 1953). Others have emphasized the role of the thalamus and its disconnection from the frontal, temporal, and parietal cortices (Ives and Nielson, 1937; Spillane, 1942; Sandifer, 1946). Nielson proposed that syndromes characterized primarily by unawareness are the result of thalamic disconnection, while syndromes producing experiences of absent limbs are the result of lesions affecting the right thalamoparietal peduncle (Nielson, 1938). Feinberg and colleagues (1990) supported these findings and stressed the role of lesions in the right supramarginal gyrus and posterior corona radiata in the expression of verbal asomatognosia.

Lesions resulting in Anton's syndrome typically require damage to the primary sensory region and more extensive disruption of secondary sensory zones that may be responsible for awareness of sensory input (Goldberg and Barr, 1991). Cortical blindness is often the result of bilateral lesions involving the primary visual areas including the striate cortices and geniculocalcarine pathways (Bergman, 1957). However, the visual variant of Anton's Syndrome appears to be the result of more widespread lesions extending from primary visual areas to adjacent temporal and parietal association regions (Goldberg and Barr, 1991; Joynt, Honch, Rubin *et al.*, 1985; Redlich and

Dorsey, 1945; Von Monakow, 1905). Lesions resulting in the auditory variant of Anton's Syndrome usually involve combined damage to the primary auditory regions and adjacent association areas (Earnest, Monroe, and Yarnell, 1977; Goldberg and Barr, 1991; Mesulam, 1985).

Phantom limbs are usually the result of peripheral nerve alterations resulting from amputation, though it has been suggested that they occur more often in left than right-side amputees. These phenomena have also been reported following lesions in the parietal cortex (Head and Holmes, 1911; Hécaen, Penfield, Bertrand, and Malmo, 1956). It has been argued that no well-defined anatomical localization can be established for most other body schema disorders since large, bilateral, diffuse cerebral lesions are often present in these cases (Frederiks, 1985b).

Neurologically-based delusions and hallucinations

Delusional Misidentifications   A number of bizarre delusional syndromes resulting from central nervous system (CNS) disorders have been described in the literature (Marková and Berrios, 1994). The disorders reviewed in this section are characterized primarily by a derangement in the patient's insight. A number of disorders have been identified, all characterized by a rather specific tendency to confuse identities. The behaviours exhibited by these patients have been given previous labels such as "delusional misidentifications", "misidentification symptoms", "reduplicative phenomena", and "confabulation" (Förstl, Almeida, Owen *et al.*, 1991; Alexander, Stuss, and Benson, 1979; Stuss, Alexander, Lieberman *et al.*, 1978). Most of these conditions involve delusions about the identities of people, places, or body-parts. Weinstein and Kahn (1955) have also described a condition where patients exhibit a reduplication of time where they may insist that they are currently children though it is acknowledged that 60 years have passed since their childhood.

There are a number of conditions that involve striking delusions about the relation between self and other. In 1923, Capgras and Reboul-Lachaux described a case of a 53-year-old woman who exhibited a delusional belief that her family and friends had been replaced by identical doubles (Capgras and Reboul-Lachaux, 1923). What is now termed as Capgras syndrome has been linked to traditional psychiatric disorders (Berson, 1983), though there is ample evidence that many of the patients exhibit some form of brain abnormality (Alexander, Stuss, and Benson, 1979). Many cases of Capgras syndrome and its variants have been found to have confusional states resulting from toxic, metabolic, or post-traumatic causes (Morrison and Tarter, 1984; Weston and Whitlock, 1971).

A disorder characterized by fixed delusions about locations is commonly known as reduplicative paramnesia (Pick, 1903; Benson, Gardner, and Meadows, 1976). In this condition, patients are certain that a particular location has been duplicated. For example, they may admit that they are in a hospital, but insist that the hospital has been moved across the street from where they live. The prevalent confusion regarding the location of hospitals in this disorder indicates that some aspect of disorientation or memory impairment related to the patient's condition is a major factor in this syndrome.

Delusional syndromes are also known to occur for perception of one's own body parts. Critchley (1953) has described conditions where patients experience their hemiplegic limb as either peculiar or as not belonging to them. Others may exhibit conditions where they develop the delusion that their limb actually belongs to another person. Gerstmann (1942) gave this behaviour the label of "somatoparaphrenia". Patients with this disorder may insist that their arm belongs to somebody else who is in the bed with them. On some occasions, these patients may indicate that the limb belongs to themselves and others simultaneously.

There are numerous theories suggesting that delusional syndromes, especially Capgras syndrome, are the result of purely psychological factors (Berson, 1983). This was the result of many early reports suggesting that most of these patients had histories of psychosis and paranoid tendencies. More recently, the trend has been to describe the disorder in terms of a neurobehavioural syndrome. It has now been suggested that neurological disorders can be demonstrated in as many as 40% of the patients with Capgras syndrome (Signer, 1987). There have been many studies showing that Capgras syndrome is often the result of closed head injury or focal brain impairment (Silva, Leong, and Luong, 1989; Weston and Whitlock, 1971). It appears that many of these cases exhibit focal right hemisphere lesions. Others have emphasized the combination of posterior and frontal lesions of the right cerebral hemisphere (Alexander, Stuss, and Benson, 1979).

Brain lesions associated with reduplicative paramnesia are similar in location to those associated with Capgras syndrome (Kapur, Turner, and King, 1988). Like Capgras syndrome, there is evidence of reduplicative paramnesias resulting from head injuries (Hakim, Verma, and Greiffenstein, 1988). Again, many authors have stressed the combination of right-parietal and frontal lobe lesions (Benson, Gardner, and Meadows, 1976; Kapur, Turner, and King, 1988). As described previously, lesions causing perceptual alterations of body parts are located primarily in the right-parietal cortex. Nielson (1938) stressed the involvement of the right thalamoparietal peduncle in those disorders involving delusional symptoms. It appears that these conditions may also be the result of combined damage to the anterior and parietal systems of the right hemisphere.

Delusions and Hallucinations   Cummings (1985) has provided an extensive review of other delusional syndromes resulting from neurological illness. These may range from "simple" to "complex" delusional states. Simple delusions may involve objects that are merely present in the immediate environment, such as intravenous tubes or other medical equipment. They appear to be the result of conditions affecting cognitive abilities in a fairly global manner, such as the dementia resulting from Alzheimer's disease (for a recent review see Bassiony and Lyketsos, 2003). Levine and Grek (1984) have described similar phenomena in patients with right-hemisphere lesions superimposed on more generalized cerebral atrophy.

Complex delusions refer to those that are more common in psychiatric disorders, such as those involving Schneiderian first-rank symptoms or the grandiose delusions associated with manic episodes (Cummings, 1985). These delusions also frequently appear in neurological conditions affecting limbic structures and the basal ganglia (Cummings, 1985). More complex "neurologically-based" delusions have also been described in some patients with temporal lobe epilepsy. Here again, phenomenological similarities between schizophrenia and temporal lobe epilepsy have been described (Slater, Beard, and Gliteroe, 1963; Davison and Bagley, 1969).

Hallucinations have also been reported as part of numerous neurological syndromes (Hécaen and Albert, 1978; Brown, 1988; Brasić, 1998; Bassiony and Lyketsos, 2003). It is well known that elementary hallucinations such as visual phosphemes or "clicking" sounds may result from lesions of the primary visual and auditory cortices. More complex or "formed" hallucinations such as faces or voices are known to result from lesions of the secondary cortical zones (Penfield and Rasmussen, 1950). These may include the bizarre experience of seeing "little people" (Lilliputian Hallucinations) or the perception of animals, faces, or figures (Leroy, 1926; Lhermitte, 1951). Hécaen and colleagues have shown that complex visual hallucinations are equally likely to arise from either the right or left hemisphere, whereas auditory hallucinations are more likely to arise from the left hemisphere (Hécaen and Albert, 1978).

In contrast to the typical response to hallucinations resulting from psychotic disorders, patients with neurologically-based hallucinations often know that the images are not real and may respond to the images with amusement or wonder (Brown, 1988). Patients exhibiting acute confusional states with hallucinations have been described following right parietal lobe lesions (Mesulam, Waxman, Geschwind et al., 1976; Peroutka, Sohmer, Kumar et al., 1982). Lhermitte (1939) stressed upper brainstem pathology as the disturbance leading to peduncular hallucinations. Some authors have suggested that psychic phenomena resulting from brain tumours are not perceived as foreign to the patient. Instead, they appear to be more closely related to the patients' "wishes, anxieties, and neurotic complexes" (Mulder, Bickford, and Dodge, 1957).

Disorders of awareness and the frontal lobes

Although the majority of awareness disorders in neurological patients are the result of right hemisphere lesions, cases of anosognosia involving lesions in frontal regions of the brain, in particular in prefrontal regions, have been reported in the literature. Damage to the prefrontal cortex (both dorsolateral and orbitofrontal) is known to produce a massive, devastating cognitive disturbance, of which the patient may be completely oblivious. The lack of the patient's awareness of their impairment has been noted by numerous authors (Luria, 1980; Hecaen and Albert, 1978; Stuss and Benson, 1986; Goldberg et al., 1989). Evidence of an association between frontal-subcortical system circuitry and awareness deficits has also been found in studies including Alzheimer's disease patients – based on both imaging (Reed *et al.*, 1993; Starkstein *et al.*, 1995; Derouesné *et al.*, 1999) and neuropsychological data (Lopez *et al.*, 1994; Michon *et al.*, 1994; Ott *et al.*, 1996; Starkstein *et al.*, 1997; Gil *et al.*, 2001).

Patients with massive damage to prefrontal systems are notorious for their general lack of concern about their conditions and its implications for their lives (Luria, 1980; Blumer and Benson, 1975; Goldberg *et al.*, 1989). Such apathy and profound disregard for the severity of their situation sets "frontal lobe" patients apart from virtually every other category of brain-damaged population. This particular set of behaviours is often associated with the "orbitofrontal" syndrome, known for the generally euphoric, unconcerned, happy-go-lucky attitude, which is completely out of line with the severity of the patient's disability (Goldberg *et al.*, 1989). This implausible attitude is often combined with the patients' ability to describe details regarding the changes in their lives that have resulted from their acquired brain impairment.

The classical descriptions of frontal lobe syndromes have been based on descriptions of "productive" or "positive" in contrast to "deficit" or "negative" symptoms. Perseveration, stereotypic behaviour, imitative behaviour (echopraxia and echolalia), and field-dependent behaviour are all productive symptoms that have been described in patients with pre-frontal pathology (Luria, 1980; Stuss and Benson, 1984; Goldberg and Costa, 1986). "Local" error-monitoring is a phenomenon where the patient may exhibit one of these productive symptoms, and yet be totally unaware of its occurrence. Local error monitoring is also known to occur in situations where the patient actually knows the correct answer. For example, in the case of perseverations on classic tasks where patients are asked to draw simple geometric forms following a rapid sequence of verbal commands (Luria, 1980; Goldberg and Tucker, 1979), patients are able to draw the correct forms early in the sequence, yet may continue to perseverate as the sequence continues, completely unperturbed by their errors (Goldberg and Tucker, 1979). This indifference to errors cannot be attributed to the lack of knowledge of what the correct response should be, since earlier in the sequence the patients were drawing the same forms correctly. It can also be demonstrated that they can again continue to draw the forms correctly as soon as the intervals between the verbal instructions in the sequence are increased.

A similar dissociation between the preserved knowledge of correct responses, and the inability to use this knowledge to monitor one's own output, can be demonstrated in frontal lobe patients' field-dependent behaviour. Field-dependent motor behaviour can be elicited by the "competing-programmes" technique, first described by Luria (1980). In this technique, two hand postures are introduced (e.g., one finger or two fingers). Patients are instructed to watch the examiner and do the opposite hand posture ("When I raise one finger, you raise two; when I raise two fingers, you raise one"). Patients with frontal lobe dysfunction will often give correct responses initially, but will then slip into numerous "echopraxic" imitations of the examiner's postures. Their echopraxic imitation will often be accompanied by correct verbalizations, such that in response to the examiner's fist they will say, "I know I am supposed to raise only one finger" but they will in fact raise two fingers. Here too, the patient's indifference to his errors cannot be attributed to the lack of knowledge of the correct response, since he could do the task correctly early in the sequence, can verbalize the correct responses even as his actual motor output becomes echopraxic, and will be able to resume correct responses as soon as the intervals between instructions are increased. This appears to be a genuine instance of an error-monitoring breakdown, in spite of the relatively intact knowledge of the correct response. In Prigatano and Schacter's (1991) terminology, the patient would be described as having intact "objective" awareness, but disturbed "subjective" awareness.

Perseveration can be conceptualized as an impairment of behavioural plasticity, or the ability to switch from one cognitive element to another. Field-dependent behaviour, on the other hand, can be conceptualized as an impairment of behavioural stability, or the ability to maintain a stable cognitive set in the face of environmental distractors (Goldberg, 1990). These two types of impairment appear to be the two fundamental components of the so-called "executive syndrome" caused by prefrontal dysfunction. Both of them are characterized by the patient's impaired awareness of his own errors in on-line situations, even when the knowledge of correct responses can be elicited (Goldberg and Barr, 1991).

Anosognosia in schizophrenia

This section will outline some of the disorders of awareness that have been described in patients with schizophrenia. These disorders will be compared and contrasted with those seen in the neurological conditions described in this chapter. In many ways, the disorders of awareness seen in these two groups may seem very different, since it is clear that acute disturbances such as hemiplegia and cortical blindness are not seen in patients with schizophrenia. However, it will be demonstrated that there are a number of unusual conditions observed in schizophrenia that are analogous to the disorders of awareness observed in patients with focal brain impairment. It is argued that the disturbances of awareness observed in both groups may be the result of similar underlying neuropsychological mechanisms.

Types of disorders of awareness in schizophrenia

Neurologists at the turn of the century became interested in disturbances of awareness regardless of whether the aetiology was thought to be "psychiatric" or "neurological" in origin. Carl Wernicke, the German neurologist who remains famous for some of the earliest descriptions of sensory aphasia, made a distinction between disorders of awareness resulting from a patient's response to stimuli originating from the body and those resulting from a disturbed response to stimuli in the external world (Wernicke, 1900). He classified these disturbances as representing different forms of "psychosis". He used the term somatopsychosis to refer to the class of symptoms resulting from altered awareness of the body and interoceptive stimuli, and allopsychosis to refer to a disturbance of one's responses to exteroceptive stimuli. These terms receive little use in modern-day neurology and psychiatry, though they do provide a useful system for grouping the range of awareness disturbances seen in both neurological and psychiatric populations.

Karl Kleist, a student of Wernicke's, extended the use of his mentor's terms to describe similar phenomena in schizophrenic patients (Kleist, 1960). Kleist descriptions included a woman with "somatopsychosis" who reported that "her bowels were taken out, her blood burnt, her uterus completely filled, her breasts were as heavy as millstones, and her head had disappeared". These ideas were accompanied by abnormal bodily sensations. Kleist attributed the symptoms to a combination of misinterpreted somatosensory perceptions and a paralogical disturbance of thought. His descriptions also included a man who "felt himself mistaken for other men, thought he was given other names, and finally was in doubt of his own identity". He compares these symptoms of "allopsychosis" to those seen in neurological patients with focal lesions of the cingulate gyrus or insular cortex. We will review a body of literature describing additional forms of somatopsychoses and allopsychoses in patients with a diagnosis of schizophrenia.

SOMATOPSYCHOSES IN SCHIZOPHRENIA:

Altered Awareness of Motor and Sensory Functions   Although patients with schizophrenia do not exhibit severe neurological impairments such as hemiplegia, they do exhibit a number of unusual symptoms affecting motor functioning that are clearly similar to what is described among the somatopsychoses. A number of these conditions involve changes in awareness of voluntary and involuntary motor behaviours (Cutting, 1985). Some patients report that their movements seem somewhat "alien" to them, as if they are passive agents of some external force. McGhie and Chapman (1961) describe patients who perceive altered awareness of seemingly automatic movements such as sitting down. These authors have also described unusual conditions where patients automatically begin to imitate movements of others in their immediate environment (Chapman and McGhie, 1964). Arieti (1974) described a number of features of the "volitional" nature of movements and behaviour and argued that an understanding of the disturbance of these mechanisms may be important for understanding the schizophrenic process. Others have suggested that experiences of "involuntary" movements may be intrinsic to schizophrenia, whether or not the patients have been treated with neuroleptic medication (Owens *et al.*, 1982).

Most of the recent literature on motor behaviour in schizophrenia has focused on the development of abnormal involuntary movements associated with neuroleptic administration. Tardive dyskinesia (TD) is a syndrome characterized by involuntary choreoathetoid movements with occasional tics, grimaces, and dystonia. Prevalence studies have indicated that TD occurs in 20% of patients receiving chronic administration of neuroleptic medication (Kane, Woerner, Lieberman *et al.*, 1985). In spite of the socially debilitating nature of these obvious and unusual features, there are a number of studies indicating that schizophrenic patients are relatively unaware of these symptoms (Alexopoulos, 1979; Rosen, Mukherjee, Olarte et al., 1982; Myslobodsky, 1986; Caracci, Mukherjee, Roth et al., 1990; MacPherson and Collis, 1992).

Myslobodsky (1986) argued that the lack of awareness of TD was so striking that he proposed that it may be a result of an "anosognosia" stemming from right-hemisphere based cognitive deficits. Alexopoulos (1979) reported that outpatients with TD rarely complained about their abnormal movements. Others have demonstrated that awareness of these movements may vary depending on their location, with lack of awareness greater for orofacial than limb-kinetic movements (Rosen, Mukherjee, Olarte et al., 1982). Smith and colleagues (1979) found that patients were able to describe symptoms of TD in others, but not in themselves. Caracci and colleagues (1990) demonstrated that verbal and visual feedback resulted in an immediate increase in patients' awareness of the symptoms, though the patients were not able to sustain the increased level of awareness at follow-up testing two weeks later. Another study found unawareness of TD in association with cognitive impairment and negative symptoms characteristic of the "defect" state of schizophrenia (MacPherson and Collis, 1992).

As with hemiplegia, there is no evidence to suggest that patients with schizophrenia experience or deny acute disturbances in sensory functions. There is, however, ample evidence to suggest that patients with schizophrenia exhibit a number of unusual body sensations or "positive" symptoms that are more analogous to what is seen in conditions such as the phantom limb phenomena. Unusual sensory experiences, somatic distortions, and a loss of body image are well-known symptoms of schizophrenia (Bleuler, 1950). Experiences of bodily sensations induced by external forces are included among Schneider's "first-rank" symptoms.

Body image disturbances and somatic delusions are reported in 14–31% of the psychotic patients surveyed in various studies (Lukianowicz, 1967; Cutting, 1980). Lukianowicz (1967) classified these disturbances into those affecting a patient's perception of body shape, size, mass, or position in space. He reported that, in a sample of schizophrenic patients, 61% experienced changes in the shape of their body image, 17% experienced changes in size, and 22% experienced changes in their perceived position in space. He argued that these experiences are the result of a misinterpretation and elaboration of normal body sensations.

Some schizophrenic patients develop delusions that parts of their body are in the process of being mutilated or destroyed and some authors regard these symptoms as one of the earliest signs of the deterioration and poor outcome associated with the illness (Fenichel, 1945; Hamilton, 1976). It has been suggested that these distortions result from the patient's attempt to turn their interest from the outside world to the body (Fenichel, 1945; Szasz, 1957). Arieti (1974) found that somatic delusions most often involve the head, face, eyes, or hands, parts of the body that are often used as organs of communication. Bychowski (1943) recognized that disintegration of the body image in schizophrenia may be the result of combined psychological and somatic factors.

There have been numerous experimental studies examining features of body-image distortion in schizophrenic samples. In empirical studies, schizophrenic subjects have been shown to have impairments in body image boundaries and in estimation of the size of body parts (Cleveland *et al.*, 1962; Fisher and Cleveland, 1958; Weckowicz and Sommer, 1960). They have also demonstrated higher scores on measures of subjective "body distortion" (Fisher, 1970). Other investigators have obtained reports of unusual body experiences in schizophrenic patients with use of a questionnaire technique (Chapman, Chapman, and Raulin, 1978). In a summary of research using various experimental and questionnaire methods, it was reported that schizophrenic subjects were generally "more expansive" than nonpsychotic subjects in their judgements and measures of body image (Reitman and Cleveland, 1964). More recently, Priebe and Röhricht (2001) have reported significantly more abnormalities in body concept and body size perception in acute schizophrenics (paranoid schizophrenics and schizoaffective disorder patients) compared with patients with anxiety disorder, patients with depressive disorder and normal control subjects.

ALLOPSYCHOSES IN SCHIZOPHRENIA:

Delusions and Hallucinations   Delusions and hallucinations are well-known symptoms that form the core features of schizophrenia. Cutting (1980) reported that "abnormal beliefs" were observed in 90% of a sample of psychotic inpatients. An inability to recognize the erroneous nature and implausibility of the delusional belief is one of the key features of schizophrenia. Like patients with frontal-lobe dysfunction, it has been observed that schizophrenic patients are able to detect erroneous and implausible beliefs held by others, but not in themselves (Brown, 1973). Most theoretical approaches to the aetiology of delusions have considered these phenomena to be the result of primary disorders of attention, perception, or consciousness (Cutting, 1985). One view is that delusions are the result of a "normal" or "reasonable" interpretation of an abnormal sensory experience (Maher, 1974). Other theories have stressed the opposite, with "abnormal" logic used to interpret otherwise normal perceptual experiences (Arieti, 1974).

It was previously thought that complex delusional disorders such as Capgras syndrome were seen only in patients with "functional" psychotic disorders like schizophrenia (Berson, 1983). It had been suggested that the disturbance could be the result of a number of psychological mechanisms such as depersonalization, wish-fulfilment, inability to face ambivalent feelings, incestuous wishes, or homoeroticism (Todd, 1957; Berson, 1983). A weaker association exists between schizophrenia and other misidentification syndromes such as reduplicative paramnesia. Förstl and colleagues reported that, in a sample of 260 patients exhibiting misidentification syndromes, delusions regarding the self and others were associated with schizophrenia while reduplicative paramnesia was seen more frequently in patients with neurological disorders (Förstl, Almeida, Owen *et al.*, 1991). One of the primary features of the misidentification syndromes is that patients are able to accept and simultaneously maintain the duplicity of the "truth" and their delusions. A similar phenomenon, labelled the "double awareness phase", has been described in psychotic patients recovering from delusions (Sacks *et al.*, 1974).

Hallucinations are one of the major symptoms of schizophrenia. They were reported in 52% of the psychiatric patients studied in Cutting's (1985) sample. Thirty per cent of these patients experienced auditory hallucinations, while only 18% experienced visual hallucinations. The majority of these symptoms involve the perception of verbalizations in the form of a human voice. Most appear to be neutral in content and in the third person (e.g., "He is an idiot"). Schneider's symptoms of thought broadcasting and thought insertion are among the most common types of hallucinations (Mellor, 1970). Since these are subjective phenomena it is clear from patients' reports that they are aware of their existence. One study demonstrated that subjects can report on specific features of these symptoms in a very reliable manner (Junginger and Frame, 1985).

It is often suggested that hallucinations are more detailed and complex in schizophrenia than in those resulting from neurological causes. The major focus in the study of awareness of hallucinations is not in the patient's ability to detect them, but in their ability to interpret the "source" or "reality" of the experience. Amador and colleagues have developed a scale which evaluates precisely this aspect of awareness (Amador, Strauss, Yale, Gorman *et al.*, 1993). When used to study hallucinations, the patient's capacity to identify the source of the perception is assessed. More recently, they have reported that nearly 40% of a sample of 221 patients with DSM-III-R diagnoses of schizophrenia were unable to accomplish this (Amador, Flaum, Andreasen *et al.*, 1994). As with delusions, there are numerous theories suggesting that hallucinations are the result of a combination of faulty perceptual and interpretive processes.

Frontal lobe impairment in schizophrenia

Many authors have noted the similarities between symptoms observed in schizophrenia and those seen in neurological patients with frontal lobe dysfunction (Kraepelin, 1919; Kleist, 1960). Parallels between clusters of schizophrenic symptoms and their relations to the dorsolateral and orbital syndromes associated with frontal lobe dysfunction have been recognized by many authors (Levin, 1984; Muller, 1985; Goldberg and Costa, 1986). The frontal lobe model of schizophrenia has received support from studies using neuropsychological tests sensitive to frontal lobe dysfunction (Flor-Henry and Yeudall, 1979; Kolb and Whishaw, 1983; Malmo, 1974). The evidence for selective frontal lobe dysfunction comes from observations that the magnitude and pattern of performance decrements seen in schizophrenic groups is similar to the patterns observed in groups of patients with known frontal lobe pathology. It has not been adequately determined, however, whether these results reflect selective frontal lobe damage or may be secondary to generalized, non-specific structural and/or biochemical damage (Goldberg, 1986; Bilder and Goldberg, 1987).

Productive symptoms such as perseveration and field-dependent behaviour have been described in patients with schizophrenia (Goldberg and Costa, 1986). Most authors have noted that these symptoms are almost identical to those seen in patients with massive frontal lobe damage. As with what is seen in frontal lobe patients, schizophrenic patients appear to be relatively unaware of their impairments in executive functioning. This level of unawareness is similar to the defect in "local" error monitoring that is seen in patients with frontal lobe disturbance (Zaidel, 1987; Goldberg and Barr, 1991).

Bilder and Goldberg (1987) demonstrated that a variety of motor perseverations could be elicited in drawings from a sample of chronic schizophrenic patients. In many of these cases, patients would perseverate elements of previous drawings despite the fact that they could repeat the correct instructions. They appeared to be completely oblivious to the errors in their performance. Perseverations are also commonly observed in schizophrenic speech (Bleuler, 1950; Freeman and Gathercole, 1966; Chaika, 1982). It has been suggested that these symptoms are the result of a disturbance of language monitoring mechanisms resulting from frontal lobe disturbance (Barr, Bilder, Goldberg et al., 1989; McGrath, 1991). It is interesting to note that, in spite of these peculiarities, patients often fail to notice anything odd in their speech (Chaika, 1974; Amador, Flaum, Andreasen et al., 1994).

Echolalia, or the automatic repetition of others, is the most commonly discussed symptom of "field-dependence" in schizophrenia, though its existence is actually rare (Andreasen, 1982). Echopraxia is a condition where patients automatically imitate the actions of others. It is similar to the "imitative" behaviour that has been described in patients with frontal lobe impairments (Lhermitte, 1986). Echophraxia has been described in detail in schizophrenic subjects (Chapman and McGhie, 1964). One of the features of this behaviour is that the patients feel that the behaviour is not under their volition, even in cases where they are told not to do it. The symptom is not characterized by a lack of awareness but, rather, an acute awareness of the tendency or "pull" toward performing the act. This awareness may even precede the onset of manifest behaviour. One of their patients reported, "I was sitting with a friend, and suddenly he changed and I told him 'don't move or I'll have to move too' ". Patients are often critical of the behaviour, though they cannot refrain from doing it (Dromard, 1905).

It is clear that other forms of unawareness in schizophrenia are also similar to the impairments observed in frontal lobe patients. The fact that patients are able to detect delusional and symptoms of TD in others, but not in themselves, is comparable to the difficulties in error monitoring that have been described in frontal lobe patients (Konow and Pribram, 1970). David's (1990) dimension of "recognition of illness" and Amador and colleagues' (1991) concept of "incorrect attributions about illness" are both analogous to the apathy, lack of concern, and impairment in "global" error monitoring seen in frontal lobe patients (Zaidel, 1987; Goldberg and Barr, 1991). Furthermore, the "ability to re-label unusual events" and "unawareness of deficit" described by these authors is analogous to the "local" error monitoring deficits seen in frontal lobe patients. Recent studies examining the relationship between neuropsychological test performance and unawareness have found that patients' awareness of schizophrenic illness, as measured by a standardized questionnaire, is correlated with performance on tests of frontal lobe functions (Young, Davila and Scher, 1993; Young et al., 1998; Lysaker and Bell, 1994; Lysaker et al., 1997,

1998, 2002; McEvoy *et al.*, 1996; Mohamed *et al.*, 1999; Marks *et al.*, 2000; Larøi *et al.*, 2000; Rossell *et al.*, 2003; also see Morgan and David Chapter 9 for review). These findings suggest that at least some components of unawareness in schizophrenia may be related to frontal lobe dysfunction.

Interim summary

A variety of unusual conditions affecting patients' awareness of neurological deficits have been reviewed. These included unawareness of left-sided motor or sensory deficits, body schema disturbances, and syndromes characterized by delusions or hallucinations. Many past theories have explained these phenomena in terms of a combined impairment in perceptual and problem-solving mechanisms linked to right inferior parietal and frontal systems in the right cerebral hemisphere. A number of disorders in "self-awareness" or "error monitoring" have been described following focal damage to the frontal cortex. It has been proposed that these disorders are the result of an inability to monitor ongoing behaviour. More recent models have emphasized the role of "intention" and "self-monitoring" in a wider range of neurobehavioural disturbances affecting awareness. These models will be discussed in more detail at the end of the chapter.

There are many similarities between the disturbances of awareness seen in schizophrenia and those seen as a result of "known" neurological impairment. This is most apparent for the many disturbances of body awareness and delusional disorders resulting from right parietal lobe dysfunction. These have been described in the classical literature in neurology and psychiatry as either the somatopsychoses or allopsychoses. Other forms of unawareness in schizophrenia are similar to what is observed in patients with frontal lobe impairments or with seizures originating from the left temporal lobe. Recent theories have implicated the role of "willed action" and "self-monitoring" in disorders of awareness and many of the cognitive impairments and core symptoms of schizophrenia. It has been suggested that these symptoms are the result of a disturbance of a medial frontal system involving the anterior hippocampus, cingulate gyrus, supplementary motor area, and the dorsolateral prefrontal cortex.

It is clear that there are numerous advantages to using neurological models for understanding the symptoms associated with schizophrenia. The biggest advantage is that one is able to compare behaviours resulting from a "known" neurological basis to similar behaviours where the neurological basis is only inferred. This enables the development of speculations on the brain systems underlying various symptoms. For example, it may be possible to speculate that schizophrenic patients exhibiting disturbances of body awareness or somatic delusions may exhibit a different pattern of brain disturbance than those presenting with paranoid delusions. One may hypothesize that the patient with somatic delusions might exhibit a disturbance in brain systems involving the right parietal lobe, while the patient with paranoid delusions may have a disturbance involving the left mesiotemporal-limbic system. It is thus possible that the use of neurological models may provide a means for classifying various disorders of awareness. Further application of neurobehavioural models of awareness, emphasizing the roles of intention and self-monitoring functions, is recommended for future studies of awareness in schizophrenia.

Autonoetic awareness and schizophrenia

Many of the symptoms of schizophrenia suggest that the patient has difficulty in maintaining the distinction between mental events that originate within the limits of his own central nervous system, and those that occur outside of his body and are perceived through sensory awareness. These symptoms are referred to as manifestations of autonoetic agnosia, meaning literally "the inability to identify self-generated mental events" (Keefe, 1998).[1] These symptoms include poor insight, hallucinations, and various forms of delusions, such as thought insertion, thought withdrawal, thought broadcasting, delusions of control, and delusions of "made" actions, impulses, and feelings (Schneider, 1959), which are found in schizophrenia more frequently than in other major psychiatric disorders (Carpenter and Strauss, 1974). Examples of these symptoms that can be seen as deficits in autonoetic awareness will be provided. This will be followed by descriptions of empirical studies that have provided evidence of autonoetic agnosia in schizophrenia by means of experimental paradigms.

Hallucinations

Hallucinations are the result of the misinterpretation of an internally generated mental event which originated in the perceptual realm (Heilbrun, 1980; Bentall, 1990). Although the arguments in this paper could be applied to hallucinations in any of the five sensory modalities, auditory and visual hallucinations will receive the most attention, as these are the most common hallucinatory experiences of schizophrenic patients. The generation of auditory and visual images is a part of normal everyday cognitive experience. People without psychiatric disorders may vividly remember particular visual scenes from times long past, or recall words spoken to them, or music played, as though the event were occurring in the present moment. It is also within normal experience to generate visual images or auditory images that have never been directly experienced, through fantasy and imagination. There is a high degree of variability among normal individuals in the vividness of their images. However, it is not within normal experience to interpret these images, no matter how vivid, as having been perceived through external stimulation. This type of misinterpretation, which results in the experience of hallucination, has been found in 70% of patients with schizophrenia (Sartorius, Shapiro, and Jablensky, 1974).

---

[1] This definition differs somewhat from Tulving's notion of autonoetic awareness: "the ability to both mentally represent and become aware of ones subjective experiences in the past, present and future" (Wheeler, Stuss and Tulving, 1997).

Delusions

Many of the delusions found in patients with schizophrenia could be argued to involve a severe misunderstanding of the self. Grandiose delusions and religious delusions, for instance, may reflect a patient's severe absence of awareness of who he is, how he fits into society, and the general consensus of what is true. Here, however, the focus will be on a more specific disturbance of the self, that is, the firm belief of some patients with schizophrenia that self-generated, internally-mediated events are "physically" affected by forces outside of the self. The most notable of these delusions have been described as the "first-rank" symptoms of schizophrenia by Kurt Schneider (1959). Among these delusions are thought insertion, thought withdrawal, thought broadcasting, and delusion of control.

Lack of insight

Schizophrenic patients may not only have a lack of insight about the severity of their symptoms, but may lack the general ability to take an observer's perspective about themselves. Since insight involves the capacity of an individual to view himself accurately in the context of the external world, and to move without confusion between internal and external perspectives, lack of insight is considered as part of the manifestation of autonoetic agnosia in schizophrenia that will be proposed in this chapter. Patients with autonoetic agnosia may not be able to move flexibly between internal and external perspectives, due to an inability to maintain the distinction between externally generated mental events and internally generated events.

All of these symptoms – hallucinations, delusions, and lack of insight – involve a disruption of the normal mental flow of consciousness, resulting in a disturbance in the correct identification of internally generated events and externally generated events as such, ultimately affecting autonoetic awareness. In each symptom, there is a clear disturbance of consciousness – the misinterpretation of an internal event, generated and maintained by the nervous system of the experiencer, as having originated outside of the self. These mental events can be misinterpreted via the perceptual realm, as in hallucinations, or through the realm of cognition, as in thought insertion, delusions of control, and poor insight. We will now present studies that have examined autonoetic awareness functioning in schizophrenic patients. These studies have primarily utilized two major experimental paradigms, namely, source monitoring tasks (Johnson et al., 1993) and the Remember/Know procedure (Tulving, 1985).

Several studies have examined autonoetic awareness in schizophrenic patients with the help of source monitoring tasks (Johnson et al., 1993). Source monitoring refers to individuals' ability to remember the source of information that they have obtained. A number of studies suggest that source monitoring deficits in schizophrenic patients may be specifically related to reality monitoring, or the ability to discriminate between internally and externally generated source of information (Johnson and Raye, 1981). In particular, studies have repeatedly shown that schizophrenic patients have a tendency to show an external attribution bias for internal events (Heilbrun, 1980; Bentall and

Slade, 1985; Bentall *et al.*, 1991; Baker and Morrison, 1998; Blakemore *et al.*, 2000; Brébion *et al.*, 2000; Johns and McGuire, 1999; Johns *et al.*, 2001; Morrison and Haddock, 1997; Rankin and O'Carroll, 1995; Seal *et al.*, 1997). Findings of an externalizing bias have been more often observed in patients with hallucinations, although some studies have also provided evidence of an externalizing bias in patients with other symptoms such as delusions (Johns *et al.*, 2001; Brébion *et al.*, 2000) and disorganization (Brébion *et al.*, 2000).

Findings from these studies suggest that the source monitoring impairments observed in schizophrenic patients are only present when stimuli are self-generated. That is, when stimuli comes from an external source (i.e., heard or visually presented), patients with schizophrenia do not demonstrate source monitoring deficits (Bentall *et al.*, 1991; Mlakar *et al.*, 1994; Stirling *et al.*, 1998; Keefe *et al.*, 2002). For example, Keefe *et al.* (2002) administered a source monitoring task to three groups of subjects: a group of 18 schizophrenic patients with target symptoms (i.e., with at least one of the following symptoms: thought insertion, voices arguing, voices commenting, made feelings, made acts, made impulses), a group of 29 schizophrenic patients without any of the target symptoms, and a group of 19 controls. Participants were asked to remember word items. During the study phase, these items were identified by the participants from pictures (picture completion), generated by participants through word-stem completion (self-generated condition; e.g., B–S– as a type of fish), or read by the experimenter. During the test phase, participants were presented with the items from the study phase along with new items. Participants were asked to remember the item and the source of the item (i.e., picture, self-generated, heard or new). Results revealed that patients demonstrated significantly poorer old-new recognition, independent of the source of the information. Furthermore, patients with target symptoms demonstrated worse recognition of self-generated items than patients without the target symptoms. However, there was no difference between the two patient groups in terms of their ability to recognize externally generated stimuli. These results suggest that patients with symptoms such as thought insertion and passivity experiences may be attributable to a deficit in autonoetic awareness. Schizophrenic patients may exhibit a specific inability to identify the self as the source of self-generated information, leading the individual to search for alternative explanations. The result of this is that internally generated information is experienced as having originated from an external source in the form of symptoms such as hallucinations, thought insertion and delusions of control (Frith and Done, 1989; Frith, 1992; Keefe, 1998; Keefe *et al.*, 2002).

In light of this, it has been suggested that schizophrenic patients manifest a more general cognitive difficulty to combine all aspects of past events into a cohesive and memorable whole (Danion *et al.*, 1999), implicating a deficit in autonoetic awareness. One experimental paradigm used to test this hypothesis is the Remember/Know paradigm first developed by Tulving (1985), where autonoetic ("self-knowing") and noetic ("knowing") awareness are phenomenologically distinguished and dissociated from each other. Whereas noetic awareness refers to the subjective state that permits a mental retrieval of an event from the past, autonoetic awareness refers to the mental retrieval of the subjective state associated with the memorization of the event. The experimental paradigm consists of a recognition test where subjects are asked to indicate the subjective state that accompanied the recognition. The subject may choose between a "Remember" (representing an index of autonoetic awareness) and a "Know" (representing an index of noetic awareness) response. Subjects make a Remember response if recognition is accompanied by conscious recollection, that is, if recognition brings back to mind something they experienced when the item occurred in the study (e.g., the position of the item, a particular feeling or emotional reaction associated with the item, an image they formed, an association they thought of, a retrieval strategy, etc.). On the other hand, a Know response refers to recognition on the basis of familiarity in the absence of conscious recollection, that is, recognition of the item does not bring back to mind what they experienced when the item was presented during the encoding phase. A Remember response is thought to be influenced by consciously controlled or strategic memory processes, whereas Know responses are thought to be determined by automatic uses of memory (Huron and Danion, 2000).

Studies have shown that while noetic awareness seems preserved in schizophrenic patients, their autonoetic awareness seems to be specifically perturbed (Bacon et al., 2001; Huron et al., 1995, 2003; Kazès et al., 1999; Danion et al., 1999). Huron et al. (1995) tested the hypothesis that there is an association between memory deficit and impairments of awareness in schizophrenia by utilizing the Remember/Know procedure described above. Participants consisted of 30 chronic schizophrenic patients and 30 normal controls matched with the patients for sex, age and education level. Results revealed that the deficit of recognition memory observed in the schizophrenic patients was related to a lower number of Remember responses, but not with the number of Know responses to target words. Thus, schizophrenic patients exhibited a selective impairment of conscious recollection of the encoding phase, whereas recognition memory based on feelings of familiarity in the absence of conscious recollection was normal. These authors argue that these and other similar findings suggest that an important cognitive deficit in schizophrenia is related to autonoetic awareness.

Autonoetic awareness mediates an individual's awareness of his or her existence and identity in subjective time, both in terms of the past, present and future (Moscovitch, 1992). In that impairment in autonoetic awareness may result in events not being subjectively experienced, this is likely to induce an alteration of the sense of self and personal identity in schizophrenic patients. Furthermore, it has been suggested that a sense of self and personal identity is intrinsically associated with autobiographical memory (Conway and Pleydell-Pearce, 2000). It may therefore be postulated that particular impairments in autobiographical memory in schizophrenic patients (such as those involved in the impairment of conscious recollection) may negatively affect the construction and preservation of personal identity, resulting in an abnormal personal identity in patients with schizophrenia. However, few studies have been devoted to the investigation of autobiographical memory in schizophrenia. Nonetheless, Riutort *et al.* (2003) have recently provided evidence for an impairment of personal episodic and personal semantic memory in patients with schizophrenia. Also, results revealed that patients provided less specific autobiographical memories than normal controls. These findings provide support for the idea that abnormal personal identity may be related to impairment in autobiographical memory in schizophrenia.

Cognitive deficits related to disorders of autonoetic awareness

The process of distinguishing between internally and externally generated mental events is extraordinarily complex, and therefore is most certainly impaired by a variety of different cognitive deficits. A brief presentation of these deficits will follow including reduced perceptual input, memory, context, reasoning processes, working memory, executive functions, and motivation.

Reduced Perceptual Input   The first cognitive deficit to be considered as a possible contributor to autonoetic agnosia and the symptoms that may be produced as a result, is an impairment in the normal differences between the phenomenal qualities of perceived and imagined events. Disruptions in the normal flow of perceptual events could result in a relative weakening of the experience of perceptual stimuli compared to internally generated images. This weakening may render the process of making distinctions between internally and externally generated information more difficult. Thus, schizophrenic patients with autonoetic agnosia may misinterpret internally generated stimuli as having the richness of external stimuli. Such a misinterpretation could result in the perception of internally generated thoughts as hallucinations or "new" thoughts that are perceived as novel, and thus are determined to have originated from a non-internal source, as in thought insertion. Reduced perceptual input may also be a consequence of social isolation, lack of social skills, and deafness, all of which have been associated with the development of delusions (Swann, 1984; Maher and Spitzer, 1984). Not only are these states associated with a reduced capacity or opportunity to test ideas against the social consensus, but in addition, these are conditions in which the number of internally generated mental events increases relative to the number of externally derived mental events. Those who are restricted from social interaction and external stimulation may engage more frequently in self-generated processes. Thus, if they engage more in imagination than perception, the imagined processes may gain prominence over those that are based in the real world (Johnson, 1991a). The importance of social isolation in the development of the symptoms of autonoetic agnosia is supported by the documented relationship between premorbid social isolation and later schizophrenic delusions and hallucinations (Lewine, Watt, and Fryer, 1978; Watt, 1978).

Memory   Memory deficits, which are well documented in patients with schizophrenia (cf. Aleman *et al.*, 1999), may lead to autonoetic agnosia in at least two distinct ways. First, the effect of disrupted memory for perceptual events may have the effect of diluting the richness of the original perceptual event, which creates similarities in the phenomenal experiences of memories for actual experiences and self-generated imagined events. Second, memory deficits could result in an individual's inability to retrieve supporting information about the event whose source is under consideration. If this impairment persists over time, false beliefs about the principles on which reality is based could develop. More specifically, the repeated inability to establish an adequate context for memories and other internally generated mental events may result in the interpretation of mental events as coming into and out of awareness as if on their own accord. In the struggle to understand an internal world of contextless memories, thoughts, impulses and even motor movements, an individual may develop the belief that an external force is in control of the appearance of these mental events, resulting in delusions of thought insertion, thought withdrawal, and delusions of control. As noted by Johnson, Hashtroudi, and Lindsay (1993), delusional individuals are often vigilant about seeking supporting information about their delusions because normal supporting memories are not available. In patients with schizophrenia, delusions have been reported to be richer in perceptual content than real memories and fantasies (David and Howard, 1994). The authors of this study propose that the richness of delusional memories may be attributable to the great amount of attention they receive from the delusional individual, as evidenced by the increased rehearsal and affective tone associated with delusional memories compared with real memories.

Context   Autonoetic agnosia could also result from deficits in placing information in the proper context, independent of memory deficits. The deficits of schizophrenic patients on several attention- and language-related tasks have been explained in terms of a disturbance in the internal representation of contextual information (Cohen and Servan-Schreiber, 1992). If memories for internally and externally generated mental events are retrieved adequately, yet they are not adequately placed in the context of the relevant information available about reality, comparisons between internally generated events and external reality may be inaccurate. For example, after having visited his grandmother's grave site, a schizophrenic patient developed the belief that she was sending him thoughts about her painful death. Apparently, he was unable to connect his own memories about her death to the context of visiting her grave. The absence of a proper context for these memories, which were interpreted as having arrived in the patient's head completely out of context, resulted in the experience of thought insertion.

Reasoning Processes   Also, most symptoms that result from the cognitive deficit of autonoetic agnosia suggest a breakdown in the normal reasoning processes. Normal reasoning involves frequent comparisons between ideas and consensually derived reality. While the experiences that may result from autonoetic agnosia, such as the experience of thought withdrawal, are not likely to derive solely from an inability to place one's thoughts in the context of social reality, the maintenance of the belief that thoughts are actually regularly withdrawn from one's head by an outside force demands a certain degree of disconnection between internally generated beliefs and general consensus about the powers of the human brain. The delusions that may result from autonoetic agnosia may initially be borne from an inappropriately lax system for making the judgment whether a particular belief is implausible (Johnson, 1988). The criteria for plausibility are usually set by the context in which a belief is placed. As described by Johnson (1991a, b), people are more lax about detecting peaches in a tree than detecting enemy planes in the sky. Since schizophrenic patients have severe problems on tasks that require the establishment of a context for internal representations (Cohen and Servan-Schreiber, 1992), they may not be able to determine the plausibility of their beliefs because of chronic deficits in understanding the relationship between a belief and its context.

Working Memory   The inability to hold information "on-line" in working memory (Baddeley, 1986) may be a key aspect of a deficit in this system, as any comparison among mental events involves working memory, and an interruption in working memory processes interferes with the ability of the patient to keep a constant self in mind. Working memory has been shown to be impaired in patients with schizophrenia (Park and Holzman, 1992). Other aspects of a supervisory attentional system, such as abstraction and "executive functions", have also been demonstrated to be impaired in schizophrenia (Goldberg, Weinberger, Berman, Pliskin, and Podd, 1987). Deficits in the ability to keep different mental events, such as perceptions and internally generated notions, in mind at the same time may lead to confusion between them. Since perceptions are more stable, and are not under conscious control compared to images, which can be changed at will, a loss of control of internally generated images may make them seem more like externally generated events, even perceptual events (Johnson, 1988). A chronic deficit in maintaining the temporal connectedness among different mental events, as evidenced in some patients with schizophrenia, could be experienced as a loss of control of self-generated ideation. Consequently, these self-generated ideas could be perceived as having been generated externally.

Executive Functions   The access to information about one's own cognitive operations, an important part of executive functions (Stuss and Benson, 1986), is an essential component of identifying oneself as the origin of information (Johnson, 1991b). According to Frith (1987), corollary discharge is part of an internal monitoring system that enables an individual to distinguish between effects due to self-generated actions and events in the external world. Frith suggested that an internal monitor of actions and thoughts not only makes us aware that an action is about to occur, it also communicates information about the source of that action. Frith makes the distinction between stimulus driven actions ("stimulus intentions"), self-generated actions ("willed intention"), and actions currently being initiated. The monitor must be able to compare the information from these different sources and indicate mismatches, so that current goals, stimulus meanings, and actions, can be modified. According to Frith (1987), some of the psychotic symptoms of schizophrenia are experienced when self-generated acts occur, but information about willed intentions fails to reach the monitor. The occurrence of mismatches between intentions and actions could be reduced in two different ways. The signal to the monitor about willed intentions could be increased, or the signal that initiates self-generated acts could be reduced. The presence of a deficient "monitor" in schizophrenia and other psychotic disorders is supported by evoked potential studies. Self-generated tones (tones elicited by the subject's button press) in normals results in attenuated evoked potentials compared to randomly occurring tones. However, among schizophrenic patients, only 20% attenuate to the self-generated tones, while 40% of nonschizophrenic psychotic patients demonstrate attenuation (Frith and Done, 1988). The role of autonoetic agnosia in schizophrenia advanced in this chapter would suggest that patients with autonoetic agnosia may be the least likely psychotic patients to demonstrate attenuation to self-generated tones, since self-generated acts are frequently experienced as having been generated externally, and would thus be processed similarly to randomly occurring perceptual phenomena.

Shallice (1988) suggested that frontal cortical regions subserve a "supervisory attentional system" that is essential for the performance of novel tasks that require self-generated mental effort, but not for the performance of routine tasks in which actions are specified by the current situation. An impairment in supervisory attentional processes that causes the cognitive deficit of autonoetic agnosia may also lead to an impairment in the communication between conscious and unconscious awareness that normally results in insight. An important aspect of insight is the capacity of an individual to view him/herself (including her mental operations) accurately in the context of the external world, and to move without confusion between internal and external perspectives. The structure of cognition suggests that different aspects of cognitive functioning are differentially available to conscious awareness. For example, the brain systems necessary for computing particular visual stimulus properties such as facial identity or object shape are different from those necessary for conscious awareness of these aspects of a stimulus (Farah, 1992). Since the supervisory attentional system is responsible for keeping an individual aware of the information that he holds, and thus maintaining insight, a deficit in this system could result in a discrepancy between mental events and awareness of these events. Insight, in part, thus relies on the ability to be aware of what is part of the self, and distinguish it from what is not. Furthermore, in order to see oneself accurately from an external perspective, and thus have insight, one must be able to distinguish between one's internal perspective and one's estimate of an external perspective. If schizophrenic patients with autonoetic agnosia cannot distinguish between internally and externally generated mental events, they may have particular difficulty in distinguishing between observer and observed in the process of trying to gain insight about their symptoms, behaviours and circumstances. A schizophrenic patient with autonoetic agnosia may intend to move his arm, but this intention is not brought into awareness. The resultant experience may be that, since the arm moved, it was moved by an external force. It would be very difficult for a schizophrenic patient with autonoetic agnosia to gain "insight" into the fact that his belief in the powers of the "external force" is delusional. In terms of an individual's experience of self, he may be aware that, in general, his identity is different from that of other people, but some of his thoughts, feelings, and actions, may not be fully represented in conscious awareness, and may thus result in the "insightless" belief that they are alien to him. It is thus common for schizophrenic patients with autonoetic agnosia to believe that they are not ill, as they cannot take the perspective of the observer, which is necessary to establish the context, generally a social context, in which their symptoms are placed. For example, a patient with inappropriate affect can thus not recognize its inappropriateness, since that determination requires an understanding of how an individual's behaviour is viewed from the perspective of the (social) observer. Since the patient with autonoetic agnosia has difficulty distinguishing between internal and external perspectives, she cannot "view" her symptoms as an objective observer, and thus lacks insight about their pathological nature.

Motivation Lack of motivation, repeatedly observed in patients with schizophrenia, may also play an important role in disturbances of awareness in schizophrenia. For instance, lack of motivation may contribute to reducing the distinction between internally and externally generated events on many levels. Since the maintenance of this distinction is an effortful process that requires more motivation than the fusion of internally and externally generated events (Johnson, 1992), amotivation could blur the distinction through reducing an individual's ability to gather accurate data about real events, retrieve data about those events, make comparisons between real and imagined events, gather contextual support for real versus imagined memories, and finally, to observe one's own cognitive processes with enough vigilance to detect differences between real and imagined events.

From a more global viewpoint, certain authors suggest that a lack of emotional response to illness may be implicated in indifference reactions to illness (Amador, Flaum, Andreasen, Strauss *et al.*, 1994; Amador and Kronengold, 1998). Evidence for such a view comes from studies pointing to an association between poor awareness and primary negative symptoms in schizophrenia (Amador *et al.*, 1994; Kemp and Lambert, 1995; Collins, Remington, Coulter, and Birkett, 1997), suggesting that insight may be reflective of an individual's inability to experience emotion (Amador and Kronengold, 1998). Furthermore, since negative symptoms in schizophrenia are more often associated with cognitive deficits, it has been proposed that indifference reactions may have neuropsychological underpinnings (Amador *et al.*, 1994).

Interim summary

Several important symptoms of schizophrenia, including poor insight, hallucinations, and Schneiderian delusions can be understood as a function of autonoetic agnosia – the inability to distinguish between internally and externally generated mental events. Furthermore, findings from recent studies suggest that schizophrenic patients manifest a more general cognitive difficulty to combine all aspects of past events into a cohesive and memorable whole, implicating a deficit in autonoetic awareness. This disturbance may be the result of a variety of cognitive deficits reported in schizophrenia, including reduced perceptual input, memory deficits, the inability to place information in a relevant context, deficiencies in reasoning processes, and deficits in the ability of a "supervisory attentional system" to monitor cognitive and perceptual processes. The absence of normal motivation could also account for maintaining the effort required to distinguish internally and externally generated mental events. These deficits could be attributable to general brain dysfunction, as well as specific regional brain dysfunction in a number of areas. While dysfunction of the prefrontal cortex and the striatal connections to the prefrontal cortex are the most likely to be involved in autonoetic agnosia in schizophrenia, the dysfunction of other regions, such as the temporal cortex and the anterior cingulate, may also have an important role.

While this model of some of the symptoms of schizophrenia answers a few questions about the relationship between symptoms, cognitive deficits, and neuroanatomic dysfunction in schizophrenia, several questions are raised. The specific cognitive deficits that underlie autonoetic agnosia have not been determined, yet the patterns of cognitive deficit in schizophrenic patients with persistent poor insight, hallucinations or Schneiderian delusions could be investigated. As discussed above, it is likely that these relationships will not be revealed by cross-sectional data, since cognitive deficits and the symptoms of psychosis in schizophrenia appear to be uncorrelated. Questions about the brain regions or pathways that may be associated with autonoetic agnosia may be less difficult to address, as measures of brain structure and physiologic function tend to be more stable than measures of cognitive performance. However, since the development of the self and the monitoring of self-generated mental events is an extraordinarily complex process involving a multitude of brain regions, it is unlikely that any simple regional brain dysfunction will be associated with autonoetic agnosia.

Theoretical approaches to disorders of awareness

Neurobehavioural theories

A theoretical conception of the frontal lobe's role in awareness has been outlined by Stuss and Benson (1986). These authors provide a hierarchical model of frontal lobe functioning where a mechanism of "self-awareness" is considered the highest level of activity. In this model, the self-awareness mechanism is the means by which an individual monitors overall brain functioning and interacts with the environment. This mechanism is distinguished from other frontal executive functions involved in planning and sequencing complex behaviour. Stuss and Benson argue that frontal lobe functions provide the role of directing more basic fixed functional systems originating from more posterior/basal brain regions (Stuss and Benson, 1987). These operations include cognitive processes such as attention, memory, language, and perception. It can be argued that conditions such as anosognosia may be the result of a disturbance in the relationship between the self-awareness system and one or more of these posterior/basal operations. Likewise, the disorders of "local" error monitoring described earlier in this chapter may be a result of a disturbance of the relationship between the self-awareness system and more hierarchically-based executive systems.

Neuropsychological theories

Most neuropsychological theories of awareness disturbances have emphasized the role of a theoretical "error monitoring" system (Goldberg and Barr, 1991). In a very basic way, the process of error monitoring rests on three components. These are: (1) An internal representation of a desired output; (2) feedback regarding the output; and (3) a comparison between the desired output and feedback regarding the actual output. It can also be applied as the basis for understanding mechanisms underlying the awareness of neurological deficits. Breakdowns of different elements and their combinations of this three-stage mechanism may account for different types of awareness disturbances (Goldberg and Barr, 1991). Most neuropsychological theories of unawareness are examples of a disturbance in one or more components of this three-stage mechanism, either implicitly or explicitly.

McGlynn and Schacter (1989) have proposed a model of awareness that includes what they term a "conscious awareness system" (CAS). This system is responsible for detecting significant changes in certain output from various perceptual, memory, and knowledge modules. It is proposed that the anatomic location of the CAS is in the inferior parietal lobes. A disconnection of the CAS from these various modules thus leads to disorders of awareness for a particular cognitive or sensory domain. The CAS can also be disconnected from an executive system similar to those described in other models. Like other models, different disorders of awareness can result depending on whether the disturbance affects anterior or posterior brain systems. Shallice (1988) advances a similar model, stressing the role of a hypothetical "supervisory attentional system" in controlling lower level perceptual systems. As mentioned previously, a "self-awareness" system involving the frontal lobes is also crucial to the model proposed by Stuss and Benson (1987; Stuss, 1991).

It has been suggested that syndromes resulting from damage to awareness mechanisms themselves are seen following lesions of the prefrontal and related upper brain stem systems (Goldberg and Barr, 1991). "Frontal syndromes" are characterized not only by massive cognitive deficits, but also by a profound lack of awareness of and concern for these deficits. These authors believe that at least some disorders of awareness associated with the lesions of the right hemisphere, are best explained by the premorbid selectivity of the subject's awareness (and lack of awareness) of particular sensory or cognitive functions. A similar explanation for other examples of awareness disturbances has been provided by Levine (1990). Empirical support for this hypothesis has been provided more recently (Wagner and Cushman, 1994). Finally, Goldberg and

Barr (1991) argue that the lack of awareness associated with conditions such as cortical blindness or cortical deafness can be best understood in terms of the post-morbid disruption of the sensory basis of internal cognitive representations, a feedback or comparator mechanism, or both. According to this hypothesis, unawareness of impairment may be particularly frequent following combined damage to anterior and posterior right-hemisphere systems, since it may disrupt various stages of the neural cybernetic loop for functions in which awareness is already lacking.

Gary Goldberg (1987) has provided important contributions to the understanding of the neuroanatomic basis of "intentional" and "monitoring" functions. Using the cytoarchitectonic patterns described by Sanides (1969), he has made a distinction between "medial" and "lateral" premotor systems. The medial system is associated with the development of intentional states and a bias for receiving interoceptive information. The lateral system, in contrast, is associated with a "responsive" mode and a sensitivity to exteroceptive stimuli. Goldberg argues that the interplay between these two systems is critical to the organism's ongoing behaviour and response to the environment. He suggests that the alien hand syndrome is a result of purposeful action occurring independently of conscious volition. This behaviour is explained in terms of the lateral system operating in isolation from the medial system. It is clear that this conceptualization can also be used to explain the experiences associated with phantom phenomena. It also provides an "updated" and more specific anatomic basis for the numerous components of the intention and monitoring deficits seen in other disorders of awareness.

The cybernetic model, and its emphasis on "intention" and "monitoring" systems, has recently been applied to a number of the behavioural phenomena observed in schizophrenia. Frith (1992) has proposed that schizophrenia can be conceptualized as a disturbance in metarepresentation, which he argues plays a major role in awareness. In this model, self-awareness plays a central role in the manifestation of numerous symptoms associated with schizophrenia (see under Executive functions above).

Most neurobehavioural theories of hallucinations and delusions have stressed the role of a disturbance in perceptual input. The advantage of Frith's model is its reliance on the role of "output" rather than "input" mechanisms. In most theories, input mechanisms have been related to posterior brain systems including the parietal lobe, while output functions have been attributed to the role of more anterior systems including the frontal cortex. Frith argues that a disturbance of brain systems underlying "willed action", such as the dorsolateral prefrontal cortex, supplementary motor area, and anterior cingulate gyrus, are responsible for many of the positive symptoms observed in schizophrenia. The role of the "monitor" has been identified with the hippocampal system (Frith and Done, 1988). Goldberg (1985, 1987) has proposed that these structures form a medial frontal system responsible for mediation of volitional behaviours. It has been argued that a disruption of this medial system is responsible for many of the abnormal behavioural phenomena that are observed in schizophrenia (Frith, 1992). Gray and colleagues have proposed a similar model emphasizing subiculo-accumbens projections and their role in monitoring mechanisms (Gray, Feldon, Rawlins *et al.*, 1991). In this model, schizophrenia is characterized as a failure of monitoring mechanisms responsible for integrating representations of past input with ongoing motor or perceptual programmes.

Acknowledgements

F. Larøi is supported by a grant from the Government of the French Community of Belgium (Direction de la Recherche Scientifique – Actions de Recherche Concertées, Convention 99/04-246).

References

Aldrich, M. S., Alessi, A. G., Beck, R. W. and Gilman, S. (1987). Cortical blindness: Etiology, diagnosis and prognosis. *Annals of Neurology*, **21**, 149–58.

Aleman, A., Hijman, R., de Haan, E. H. and Kahn, R. S. (1999). Memory impairment in schizophrenia: A meta-analysis. *American Journal of Psychiatry*, **156**, 1358–66.

Alexander, M. P., Stuss, D. T. and Benson, D. F. (1979). Capgras syndrome: A reduplicative phenomenon. *Neurology*, **29**, 334–9.

Alexopoulos, G. (1979). Lack of complains in schizophrenics with tardive dyskinesia. *Journal of Nervous and Mental Disease*, **167**, 125–7.

Amador, X. F., Strauss, D. H., Yale, S. A. and Gorman, J. M. (1991). Awareness of illness in schizophrenia. *Schizophrenia Bulletin*, **17**, 113–32.

Amador, X. F., Strauss, D. H., Yale, S. A., Gorman, J. M. and Endicott, J. (1993). The assessment of insight in psychosis. *American Journal of Psychiatry*, **150**, 873–9.

Amador, X. F., Flaum, M., Andreasen, N. C., Strauss, D. H., Yale, S. A., Clark, S. C., *et al.* (1994). Awareness of illness in schizophrenia and schizoaffective and mood disorders. *Archives of General Psychiatry*, **51**, 826–36.

Amador, X. F. and Kronengold, H. (1998). The description and meaning of insight in psychosis. In X. F. Amador and A. S. David (ed.) *Insight and Psychosis*, pp. 15–32. Oxford: Oxford University Press.

Anastasopoulis, G. K. (1961). Die nosoagnositische Überschätzung. *Psychiatrie Neurologie*, **141**, 228–41.

Andreasen, N. C. (1982). The relationship between schizophrenic language and the aphasias. In F. A. Henn and H. A. Nasrallah (ed.) *Schizophrenia as a Brain Disease*. New York: Oxford University Press.

Anton, G. (1898). Ueber Herderkrankungen des Gehires, welche von Patienten selbst nicht wahrgenommen werden. *Wiener Klinische Wochenschrift*, **11**, 227–9.

Arieti, S. (1974). *Interpretation of Schizophrenia*, 2nd edn. New York: Basic Books.

Babinski, M. J. (1914). Contribution a l'étude des troubles mentaux dans l'hemiplegie organique cérébrale (Anosognosie). *Revue Neurologique*, **1**, 845–8.

Bacon, E., Danion, J.-M., Kauffmann-Muller, F. and Bruant, A. (2001). Consciousness in schizophrenia: A metacognitive approach to semantic memory. *Consciousness and Cognition*, **10**, 473–84.

Baddeley, A. (1986). *Working Memory*. Oxford: Clarendon Press.

Baker, C. A. and Morrison, A. P. (1998). Cognitive processes in auditory hallucinations: Attributional biases and metacognition. *Psychological Medicine*, **28**, 1199–208.

Barr, W. B., Bilder, R. M., Goldberg, E., Kaplan, E. and Mukherjee, S. (1989). The neuropsychology of schizophrenic speech. *Journal of Communication Disorders*, **22**, 327–49.

Bassiony, M. M. and Lyketsos, C. G. (2003). Delusions and hallucinations in Alzheimer's disease: Review of the brain decade. *Psychosomatics*, **44**, 388–401.

Benson, D. F., Gardner, H. and Meadows, J. C. (1976). Reduplicative paramnesia. *Neurology*, **26**, 147–51.

Bentall, R. P. (1990). The illusion of reality: A review and integration of psychological research on hallucination. *Psychological Bulletin*, **107**, 82–95.

Bentall, R. P. and Slade, P. D. (1985). Reality testing and auditory hallucinations: A signal detection analysis. *British Journal of Clinical Psychology*, **24**, 159–69.

Bentall, R. P., Baker, G. A. and Havers, S. (1991). Reality monitoring and psychotic hallucinations. *British Journal of Clinical Psychology*, **30**, 213–22.

Bergman, P. S. (1957). Cerebral blindness. *Archives of Neurological Psychiatry*, **78**, 569–84.

Berson, R. J. (1983). Capgras syndrome. *American Journal of Psychiatry*, **140**, 969–78.

Bilder, R. M. and Goldberg, E. (1987). Motor perseverations in schizophrenia. *Archives of Clinical Neuropsychology*, **2**, 195–214.

Bisiach, E. (1988). Language without thought. In L. Weiskrantz (ed.) *Thought without Language*. Oxford: Oxford University Press.

Blakemore, S. J., Smith, J., Steel, R., Johnstone, E. C. and Frith, C. D. (2000). The perception of self-produced sensory stimuli in patients with auditory hallucinations and passivity experiences: Evidence for a breakdown in self-monitoring. *Psychological Medicine*, **30**, 1131–9.

Bleuler, E. (1950). *Dementia Praecox or the Group of Schizophrenias*. New York: International Universities Press.

Blumer, D. and Benson, D. F. (1975). Personality changes with frontal and temporal lobe lesions. In D. F. Stuss and D. Blumer (ed.) *Psychiatric Aspects of Neurological Disease*, pp. 151–60. New York: Grune and Stratton.

Bogen, J. E. (1993). The callosal syndromes. In K. H. Heilman and E. Valenstein (ed.) *Clinical Neuropsychology*, 3rd edn, pp. 337–408. New York: Oxford University Press.

Brasić, J. R. (1998). Hallucinations. *Perceptual and Motor Skills*, **96**, 851–77.

Brébion, G., Amador, X., David, A., Malaspina, D., Sharif, Z. and Gorman, J. M. (2000). Positive symptomatology and source monitoring failure in schizophrenia: An analysis of symptom-specific effects. *Psychiatry Research*, **95**, 119–31.

Brockman, N. W. and von Hagen, K. O. (1946). Denial of blindness (Anton's syndrome). *Bulletin of the Los Angeles Neurological Society*, **11**, 178–80.

Brown, J. W. (1988). *The Life of the Mind: Selected papers*. Hillsdale, New Jersey: Erlbaum.

Brown, R. (1973). Schizophrenia, language, and reality. *American Psychologist*, **28**, 395–403.

Bychowski, G. (1943). Disorders of the body-image in the clinical picture of psychosis. *Journal of Nervous and Mental Disease*, **97**, 310–35.

Capgras, J. and Reboul-Lachaux, J. (1923). L'illusion des 'sosies' dans un délire systématisé chronique. *Bulletin de la Société Clinique de Médicine Mentale*, **11**, 6–16.

Caracci, G., Mukherjee, S., Roth, S. D. and Decina, P. (1990). Subjective awareness of abnormal involuntary movements in chronic schizophrenia patients. *American Journal of Psychiatry*, **147**, 295–8.

Carpenter, W. T. and Strauss, J. S. (1974). Cross-cultural evaluation of Schneider's first-rank symptoms of schizophrenia: A report from the International Pilot Study of Schizophrenia. *American Journal of Psychiatry*, **131**, 682–7.

Chaika, E. (1974). A linguist looks at "schizophrenic" language. *Brain and Language*, **1**, 257–76.

Chaika, E. (1982). A unified explanation for the diverse structural deviations reported for adult schizophrenics with disrupted speech. *Journal of Communication Diseases*, **15**, 167–89.

Chapman, J. and McGhie, A. (1964). Echopraxia in schizophrenia. *British Journal of Psychiatry*, **110**, 365–74.

Chapman, L. J., Chapman, J. P. and Raulin, M. L. (1978). Body-image aberration in schizophrenia. *Journal of Abnormal Psychology*, **85**, 374–82.

Cleveland, S. E., Fisher, S., Reitman, E. E. and Rothaus, P. (1962). Perception of body size in schizophrenia. *Archives of General Psychiatry*, **7**, 277–85.

Cohen, J. D. and Servan-Schreiber, D. (1992). Context, cortex, and dopamine: A connectionist approach to behavior and biology in schizophrenia. *Psychological Review*, **99**, 45–77.

Collins, A. A., Remington, G. J., Coulter, K. and Birkett, K. (1997). Insight, neurocognitive function and symptom clusters in chronic schizophrenia. *Schizophrenia Research*, **27**, 37–44.

Conway, M. A. and Pleydell-Pearce, C. W. (2000). The construction of autobiographical memories in the self-memory system. *Psychological Review*, **107**, 261–88.

Critchley, M. (1953). *The Parietal Lobes*. London: E. Arnold.

Cummings, J. L. (1985). Organic delusions: Phenomenology, anatomical correlations, and review. *British Journal of Psychiatry*, **146**, 184–97.

Cutting, J. (1978). Study of anosognosia. *Journal of Neurology, Neurosurgery, and Psychiatry*, **41**, 548–55.

Cutting, J. (1980). Physical illness and psychosis. *British Journal of Psychiatry*, **136**, 109–19.

Cutting, J. (1985). *The Psychology of Schizophrenia*. Edinburgh: Churchill Livingstone.

Danion, J.-M., Rizzo, L. and Bruant, A. (1999). Functional mechanisms underlying impaired recognition memory and conscious awareness in patients with schizophrenia. *Archives of General Psychiatry*, **56**, 639–44.

David, A. S. (1990). Insight and psychosis. *British Journal of Psychiatry*, **156**, 798–808.

David, A. S., Owen, A. M. and Förstl, H. (1993). An annotated summary and translation of "On the self-awareness of focal brain diseases by the patient in cortical blindness and cortical deafness" by Gabriel Anton (1899). *Cognitive Neuropsychology*, **10**, 263–72.

David, A. S. and Howard, R. (1994). An experimental phenomenological approach to delusional memory in schizophrenia and late paraphrenia. *Psychological Medicine*, **24**, 515–24.

Davison, K. and Bagley, C. R. (1969). Schizophrenia-like psychosis associated with organic disorders of the central nervous system: A review. In R. N. Hetherington (ed.) *Current Problems in Neuropsychiatry*, pp. 113–84. Kent, England: Headley Bros Ltd.

Denny-Brown, D. and Banker, B. Q. (1954). Amorphosynthesis from left parietal lesion. *Archives of Neurological Psychiatry*, **71**, 302–13.

Derouesné, C., Thibault, S., Lagha-Pierucci, S., Baudouin-Madec, V., Ancri, D. and Lacomblez, L. (1999). Decreased awareness of cognitive deficits in patients with mild dementia of the Alzheimer type. *International Journal of Geriatric Psychiatry*, **14**, 1019–30.

Devous, M. D., Raese, J. D., Herman, J. H., Stokely, E. M. and Bonte, F. J. (1985). Regional cerebral blood flow in schizophrenic patients at rest and during Wisconsin Card Sorting tasks. *Journal of Cerebral Blood Flow Metabolism*, **5**(suppl.), 201–2.

Dromard, G. (1905). Étude psychologique et clinique sur l'echopraxie. *Journal of Psychology* (Paris), **2**, 385–403.

Earnest, M. P., Monroe, P. A. and Yarnell, P. R. (1977). Cortical deafness: Demonstration of the pathologic anatomy by CT scan. *Neurology*, **27**, 1172–5.

Farah, M. J. (1992). Agnosia. *Current Opinion in Neurobiology*, **2**, 162–4.

Feinberg, T. E., Haber, L. D. and Leeds, N. E. (1990). Verbal asomatognosia. *Neurology*, **40**, 1391–4.

Fenichel, O. (1945). *The Psychoanalytic Theory of Neurosis*. New York: Norton.

Fisher, S. and Cleveland, S. E. (1958). *Body Image and Personality*. Princeton: Van Nostrand.

Fisher, S. (1970). *Body Experience in Fantasy and Behaviour*. New York: Appleton-Century-Crofts.

Flor-Henry, P. and Yeudall, L. T. (1979). Neuropsychological investigation of schizophrenia and manic-depressive psychoses. In J. Gruzelier and P. Flor-Henry (ed.) *Hemisphere Asymmetries of Function in Psychopathology*, pp. 341–62. New York: Elsevier.

Förstl, H., Almeida, O. P., Owen, A. M., Burn, A. and Howard, R. (1991). Psychiatric, neurological and medical aspects of misidentification syndromes: A review of 260 cases. *Psychological Medicine*, **21**, 905–10.

Förstl, H., Owen, A. M. and David, A. S. (1993). Gabriel Anton and "Anton's syndrome": On focal diseases of the brain which are not perceived by the patient. *Neuropsychiatry, Neuropsychology, and Behavioural Neurology*, **6**, 1–8.

Fredericks, J. A.M. (1985a). Disorders of the body schema. In J. A.M. Fredericks (ed.) *Handbook of Clinical Neurology*: **1** (45): Clinical neuropsychology, pp. 373–93. Amsterdam: Elsevier.

Frederiks, J. A.M. (1985b). Phantom limb and phantom limb pain. In J. A.M. Fredericks (ed.) *Handbook of Clinical Neurology*: **1** (45): Clinical neuropsychology, pp. 394–404. Amsterdam: Elsevier.

Freeman, T. and Gathercole, C. E. (1966). Perseveration - The clinical symptoms in chronic schizophrenia and organic dementia. *British Journal of Psychiatry*, **112**, 27–32.

Frith, C. D. (1987). The positive and negative symptoms of schizophrenia reflect impairments in the perception and initiation of action. *Psychological Medicine*, **17**, 631–48.

Frith, C. D. (1992). *The Cognitive Neuropsychology of Schizophrenia*. Hove, England: Lawrence Erlbaum Associates, Inc.

Frith, C. D. and Done, D. J. (1988). Towards a neuropsychology of schizophrenia. *British Journal of Psychiatry*, **153**, 437–43.

Frith, C. D. and Done, D. J. (1989). Experiences of alien control in schizophrenia reflect a disorder in the central monitoring of action. *Psychological Medicine*, **19**, 359–63.

Gerstmann, J. (1942). Problem of imperception of disease and of impaired body territories with organic lesions. *Archives of Neurology and Psychiatry*, **48**, 890–913.

Gil, R., Arroyo-Anllo, E. M., Ingrand, P., Gil, M., Neau, J. P., Ornon, C., *et al.* (2001). Self-consciousness and Alzheimer's disease. *Acta Neurologica Scandinavica*, **104**, 296–300.

Goldberg, E. (1986). Varieties of perseveration: A comparison of two taxonomies. *Journal of Clinical Experimental Neuropsychology*, **8**, 710–26.

Goldberg, E. (1990). Higher cortical functions in humans: The gradiental approach. In E. Goldberg (ed.) *Contemporary Neuropsychology and the Legacy of Luria*. Hillsdale, NJ: Erlbaum.

Goldberg, E. and Tucker, D. (1979). Motor perseveration and long-term memory for visual forms. *Journal of Clinical Neuropsychology*, **1**, 273–88.

Goldberg, E. and Costa, L. (1986). Qualitative indices in neuropsychological assessment: Executive deficit following prefrontal lesions. In K. Adams and I. Grant (ed.) *Neuropsychological Assessment of in Neuropsychiatric Disorders*. New York: Oxford University Press.

Goldberg, E., Antin, S. P., Bilder, R. M., Gerstman, L. J., Hughes, J. E.O., Antin, S. P., *et al.* (1989). A reticulo-frontal disconnection syndrome. *Cortex*, **25**, 687–95.

Goldberg, E. and Barr, W. B. (1991). Three possible mechanisms of unawareness of deficit. In G. P. Prigatano and D. L. Schacter (ed.) *Awareness of Deficit after Brain Injury: Clinical and theoretical issues*, pp. 152–75. New York: Oxford University Press.

Goldberg, G. (1985). Supplementary motor area structure and function: Review and hypotheses. *Behavioral and Brain Sciences*, **8**, 567–616.

Goldberg, G. (1987). From intent to action: Evolution and function of the premotor systems of the frontal lobe. In E. Perecman (ed.) *The Frontal Lobes Revisited*. New York: IRBN Press.

Goldberg, G., Mayer, N. H. and Toglia, J. U. (1981). Medial frontal cortex infarction and the alien hand sign. *Archives of Neurology*, **38**, 683–6.

Goldberg, T. E., Weinberger, D. R., Berman, K. F., Pliskin, N. H. and Podd, M. H. (1987). Further evidence for dementia of the prefrontal type in schizophrenia? *Archives of General Psychiatry*, **44**, 1008–14.

Goldstein, M. N., Brown, M. and Hollander, J. (1975). Auditory agnosia and cortical deafness: Analysis of a case with three-year follow-up. *Brain and Language*, **2**, 324–32.

Gray, J. A., Feldon, J., Rawlins, J. N.P., Hemsley, D. R. and Smith, A. D. (1991). The neuropsychology of schizophrenia. *Behavioral and Brain Sciences*, **14**, 1–84.

Hakim, H., Verma, N. P. and Greiffenstein, M. F. (1988). Pathogenesis of reduplicative paramnesia. *Journal of Neurology, Neurosurgery, and Psychiatry*, **51**, 839–41.

Hamilton, M. (ed.) (1976). *Fish's Schizophrenia*. Bristol: John Wright and Sons.

Head, H. and Holmes, G. (1911). Sensory disturbances from cerebral lesions. *Brain*, **34**, 102–254.

Hécaen, H., Penfield, W., Bertrand, C. and Malmo, R. (1956). The syndrome of apractognosia due to lesions of the minor cerebral hemisphere. *Archives of Neurological Psychiatry*, **75**, 400–34.

Hécaen, H. and Albert, M. L. (1978). *Human Neuropsychology*. New York: John Wiley.

Heilbrun, A. B. (1980). Impaired recognition of self-expressed thought in patients with auditory hallucinations. *Journal of Abnormal Psychology*, **89**, 728–36.

Huron, C., Danion, J.-M., Giacomoni, F., Grangé, D., Robert, P. and Rizzo, L. (1995). Impairment of recognition with, but not without, conscious recollection in schizophrenia. *American Journal of Psychiatry*, **152**, 1737–42.

Huron, C. and Danion, J.-M. (2000). Impairment of constructive memory in schizophrenia. *International Clinical Psychopharmacology*, **17**, 127–33.

Huron, C., Danion, J.-M., Rizzo, L., Killofer, V. and Damiens, A. (2003). Subjective qualities of memories associated with the picture superiority effect in schizophrenia. *Journal of Abnormal Psychology*, **112**, 152–8.

Ives, E. R. and Nielson, M. D. (1937). Disturbance of body scheme: Delusion of absence of part of body in two cases with autopsy verification of the lesions. *Bulletin of the Los Angeles Neurological Society*, **2**, 120–5.

Johns, L. C. and McGuire, P. K. (1999). Verbal self-monitoring and auditory hallucinations in schizophrenia. *The Lancet*, **353**, 469–70.

Johns, L. C., Rossel, S., Frith, C., Ahmad, F., Hemsley, D., Kuipers, E., *et al.* (2001). Verbal self-monitoring and auditory verbal hallucinations in patients with schizophrenia. *Psychological Medicine*, **31**, 705–15.

Johnson, M. K. (1988). Discriminating the origin of information. In T. F. Oltmanns and B. A. Maher (ed.) *Delusional Beliefs*, pp. 34–65. New York: John Wiley.

Johnson, M. K. (1991a). Reflection, reality monitoring, and the self. In R. Kunzendorf (ed.) *Mental Imagery*, pp. 3–16. New York: Plenum Press.

Johnson, M. K. (1991b). Reality monitoring: Evidence from confabulation in organic brain disease patients. In G. P. Prigatano and D. L. Schacter (ed.) *Awareness of Deficit after Brain Injury: Clinical and theoretical issues*, pp. 176–97. New York: Oxford University Press.

Johnson, M. K. (1992). MEM: Mechanisms of recollection. *Journal of Cognitive Neuroscience*, **4**, 268–80.

Johnson, M. K. and Raye, C. L. (1981). Reality monitoring. *Psychological Review*, **88**, 67–85.

Johnson, M. K., Hashtroudi, S. and Lindsay, D. S. (1993). Source monitoring. *Psychological Bulletin*, **114**, 3–28.

Joynt, R. J., Honch, G. W., Rubin, A. J. and Trudell, R. G. (1985). Occipital lobe syndromes. In J. A.M. Fredericks (ed.) *Handbook of Clinical Neurology*: **1** (45): Clinical neuropsychology, pp. 49–62. Amsterdam: Elsevier.

Juba, A. (1949). Beitrag zur Struktur der ein- und doppelseitiger Körperschemastörungen – Fingeragnosie, atypische Anosognosien. *Monatsschrift für Psychiatrie und Neurologie*, 118, 11–29.

Junginger, J. and Frame, C. L. (1985). Self-report of the frequency and phenomenology of verbal hallucinations. *Journal of Nervous and Mental Disease*, 173, 149–55.

Kane, J. M., Woerner, M., Lieberman, J., Weinhold, P., Florio, W., Rubinstein, M., *et al.* (1985). The prevalence of tardive dyskinesia. *Psychopharmacology Bulletin*, 21, 136–9.

Kapur, N., Turner, A. and King, C. (1988). Reduplicative paramnesia: Possible anatomical and neuropsychological mechanisms. *Journal of Neurology, Neurosurgery, and Psychiatry*, 51, 579–81.

Kazès, M., Berthet, L., Danion, J.-M., Amado, I., Willard, D., Robert, P., *et al.* (1999). Impairment of consciously controlled use of memory in schizophrenia. *Neuropsychology*, 13, 54–61.

Keefe, R.S. E. (1998). The neurobiology of disturbances of the self: Autonoetic agnosia in schizophrenia. In X. F. Amador and A. S. David (ed.) *Insight and Psychosis*, pp. 142–73. Oxford: Oxford University Press.

Keefe, R.S. E., Arnold, M. C., Bayen, U. J., McEnvoy, J. P. and Wilson, W. H. (2002). Source-monitoring deficits for self-generated stimuli in schizophrenia: Multinomial modeling of data from three sources. *Schizophrenia Research*, 57, 51–67.

Kemp, R. and Lambert, T. (1995). Insight in schizophrenia and its relationship to psychopathology. *Schizophrenia Research*, 18, 21–8.

Kleist, K. (1960). Schizophrenic symptoms and cerebral pathology. *Journal of Mental Science*, 106, 246–55.

Kolb, B. and Whishaw, I. Q. (1983). Performance of schizophrenic patients on tests sensitive to left or right frontal, temporal, and parietal function on neurological patients. *Journal of Nervous and Mental Disease*, 171, 435–43.

Konow, A. and Pribram, K. H. (1970). Error recognition and utilization produced by injury to the frontal cortex in man. *Neuropsychologia*, 8, 435–43.

Kraepelin, E. (1919). *Dementia Praecox and Paraphrenia*. Edinburgh: E. and S. Livingstone.

Larøi, F., Fannemel, M., Rønneberg, U., Flekkøy, K., Opjordsmoen, S., Dullerud, R., *et al.* (2000). Poor insight in schizophrenia and its relation to structural brain measures and neuropsychological tests. *Psychiatry Research: Neuroimaging*, 100, 49–58.

Leroy, E. (1926). *Les visions du demi sommeil*. Paris: Alcan.

Levin, S. (1984). Frontal lobe dysfunction in schizophrenia – II. Impairments of psychological and brain functions. *Journal of Psychiatric Research*, 18, 27–55.

Levine, D. N. (1990). Unawareness of visual and sensorimotor defects: A hypothesis. *Brain and Cognition*, 13, 233–81.

Levine, D. N. and Grek, A. (1984). The anatomic basis of delusions after right cerebral infarction. *Neurology*, 34, 577–82.

Lewine, R.R. J., Watt, N. F. and Fryer, J. H. (1978). A study of childhood social competence, adult premorbid competence, and psychiatric outcome in three schizophrenic subtypes. *Journal of Abnormal Psychology*, 87, 294–302.

Lhermitte, J. (1939). *L'image de notre corps*. Paris: Nouvelle Revue Critique.

Lhermitte, J. (1951). *Les hallucinations*. Paris: Doin.

Lhermitte, F. (1986). Human autonomy and the frontal lobes, I. Imitation and utilization behaviour: A neuropsychological study of 75 patients. *Annals of Neurology*, 19, 326–34.

Lopez, O. L., Becker, J. T., Somsak, D., Dew, M. A., *et al.* (1994). Awareness of cognitive deficits and anosognosia in probable Alzheimer's disease. *European Neurology*, 34, 277–82.

Lukianowicz, N. (1958). Autoscopic phenomena. *Archives of Neurological Psychiatry*, 80, 199–220.

Lukianowicz, N. (1967). "Body image" disturbances in psychiatric disorders. *British Journal of Psychiatry*, **113**, 31–47.

Luria, A. R. (1980). *Higher Cortical Functions in Man*, 2nd edn. New York: Basic Books.

Lysaker, P. and Bell, M. (1994). Insight and cognitive impairment in schizophrenia – Performance on repeated administrations of the Wisconsin Card Sorting Test. *Journal of Nervous and Mental Disease*, **182**, 656–60.

Lysaker, P., Bell, M. and Bryson, G. (1997). Impairment in insight: Evidence for an association with specific cognitive deficits in schizophrenia. *Schizophrenia Research*, **24**, 113–14.

Lysaker, P., Bell, M., Bryson, G. and Kaplan, E. (1998). Neurocognitive function and insight in schizophrenia: Support for an association with impairments in executive function but not with impairments in global function. *Acta Psychiatrica Scandinavica*, **97**, 297–301.

Lysaker, P. H., Bryson, G. J., Lancaster, R. S., Evans, J. D. and Bell, M. D. (2002). Insight in schizophrenia: Associations with executive function and coping style. *Schizophrenia Research*, **59**, 41–7.

MacPherson, R. and Collis, R. (1992). Tardive dyskinesia: Patients' lack of awareness of movement disorder. *British Journal of Psychiatry*, **160**, 110–12.

Maher, B. (1974). Delusional thinking and perceptual disorder. *Journal of Individual Psychology*, **30**, 98–113.

Maher, B. and Spitzer, M. (1984). Delusions. In H. E. Adams and P. B. Sutker (ed.) *Comprehensive Handbook of Psychopathology*. New York: Plenum Press.

Malmo, H. P. (1974). On frontal lobe functions: Psychiatric patient controls. *Cortex*, **10**, 231.

Marková, I. S. and Berrios, G. E. (1994). Delusional misidentifications: Facts and fantasies. *Psychopathology*, **27**, 136–43.

Marks, K. A., Fastenau, P. S., Lysaker, P. H. and Bond, G. R. (2000). Self-Appraisal of Illness Questionnaire (SAIQ): Relationship to researcher-rated insight and neuropsychological function in schizophrenia. *Schizophrenia Research*, **45**, 203–11.

McEvoy, J. P., Hartman, M., Gottlieb, D., Godwin, S., Apperson, L. J. and Wilson, W. (1996). Common sense, insight, and neuropsychological test performance in schizophrenic patients. *Schizophrenia Bulletin*, **22**, 635–40.

McGhie, A. and Chapman, J. (1961). Disorders of attention and perception in early schizophrenia. *British Journal of Medical Psychology*, **34**, 103–15.

McGlynn, S. M. and Schacter, D. L. (1989). Unawareness of deficits in neuropsychological syndromes. *Journal of Clinical and Experimental Neuropsychology*, **11**, 143–205.

McGrath, J. (1991). Ordering thoughts on thought disorder. *British Journal of Psychiatry*, **158**, 307–16.

Mellor, C. S. (1970). First rank symptoms of schizophrenia. *British Journal of Psychiatry*, **117**, 15–23.

Mesulam, M. (1985). Patterns in behavioral neuroanatomy: Association areas, the limbic system, and hemispheric specialization. In M. Mesulam (ed.) *Principles of Behavioral Neurology*. Philadelphia: F. A. Davis.

Mesulam, M., Waxman, S. G., Geschwind, N. and Sabin, T. D. (1976). Acute confusional states with right middle cerebral artery infarctions. *Journal of Neurology, Neurosurgery, and Psychiatry*, **39**, 84–9.

Michon, A., Deweer, B., Pillon, B., Agid, Y. and Dubois, B. (1994). Relation of anosognosia to frontal lobe dysfunction in Alzheimer's disease. *Journal of Neurology, Neurosurgery, and Psychiatry*, **57**, 805–9.

Mlakar, J., Jensterle, J. and Frith, C. D. (1994). Central monitoring deficiency and schizophrenia symptoms. *Psychological Medicine*, **24**, 557–64.

Mohamed, S., Fleming, S., Penn, D. L. and Spaulding, W. (1999). Insight in schizophrenia: Its relationship to measures of executive functions. *Journal of Nervous and Mental Disease*, **187**, 525–31.

Morgan, K. and David, A. S. (2004). Neuropsychological studies of insight in psychosis. In: *Insight and Psychosis*, 2nd edn. Oxford: Oxford University Press.

Morrison, A. P. and Haddock, G. (1997). Cognitive factors in source monitoring and auditory hallucinations. *Psychological Medicine*, **27**, 669–79.

Morrison, R. L. and Tarter, R. E. (1984). Neuropsychological findings relating to Capgras syndrome. *Biological Psychiatry*, **19**, 1119–28.

Moscovitch, M. (1992). Memory and working-with-memory: A component process model based on modules and central systems. *Journal of Cognitive Neuroscience*, **4**, 257–67.

Mott, F. W. (1907). Bilateral lesion of the auditory cortical centre: Complete deafness and aphasia. *British Medical Journal*, **2**, 310–15.

Mulder, D. W., Bickford, R. G. and Dodge, H. W. (1957). Hallucinatory epilepsy: Complex hallucinations as focal seizures. *American Journal of Psychiatry*, **113**, 1100.

Muller, H. F. (1985). Prefrontal cortex dysfunction as a common factor in psychosis. *Acta Psychiatrica Scandinavica*, **71**, 431–40.

Myslobodsky, M. S. (1986). Anosognosia in tardive dyskinesia: "Tardive dysmentia" or "Tardive dementia"? *Schizophrenia Bulletin*, **12**, 1–8.

Nielson, J. M. (1938). Disturbances of the body scheme. Their physiologic mechanism. *Bulletin of the Los Angeles Neurological Society*, **3**, 127–35.

Olsen, C. W. and Ruby, C. (1941). Anosognosia and autotopognosia. *Archives of Neurological Psychiatry*, **46**, 340–4.

Ott, B. R., Lafleche, G., Whelihan, W. M., Buongiorno, G. W., Albert, M. S. and Fogel, B. S. (1996). Impaired awareness of deficits in Alzheimer's disease. *Alzheimer Disease and Associated Disorders*, **10**, 68–76.

Owens, D. G. C., Johnstone, F. C. and Frith, C. D. (1982). Spontaneous involuntary disorders of movement. *Archives of General Psychiatry*, **39**, 452–61.

Park, S. and Holzman, P. S. (1992). Schizophrenics show spatial working memory deficits. *Archives of General Psychiatry*, **49**, 975–82.

Paterson, A. and Zangwill, O. L. (1944). Disorders of visual space perception associated with lesions of the right cerebral hemisphere. *Brain*, **67**, 331–58.

Penfield, W. and Rasmussen, T. (1950). *The Cerebral Cortex of Man*. New York: MacMillan.

Peroutka, S. J., Sohmer, B. H., Kumar, A. J., Folstein, L. and Robinson, R. G. (1982). Hallucinations and delusions following a right temporoparieto-occipital infarction. *Johns Hopkins Medical Journal*, **151**, 181–5.

Pick, A. (1903). Clinical studies: III. On reduplicative paramnesia. *Brain*, **26**, 260–7.

Pick, A. (1908). *Überstörungen der Orientierung am eigenen Körper*. Berlin: Karger.

Priebe, S. and Röhricht, F. (2001). Specific body image pathology in acute schizophrenia. *Psychiatry Research*, **101**, 289–301.

Prigatano, G. P. and Schacter, D. L. (ed.) (1991). *Awareness of Deficit after Brain Injury: Clinical and theoretical issues*. New York: Oxford University Press.

Raine, A., Lencz, T., Reynolds, G. P., Harrison, G., Sheard, C., Medley, I., *et al.* (1992). An evaluation of structural and functional prefrontal deficits in schizophrenia: MRI and neuropsychological measures. *Psychiatry Research*, **45**, 123–37.

Rankin, P. M. and O'Caroll, P. J. (1995). Reality discrimination, reality monitoring and disposition towards hallucination. *British Journal of Clinical Psychology*, **34**, 517–28.

Redlich, F. and Dorsey, J. F. (1945). Denial of blindness by patients with cerebral disease. *Archives of Neurological Psychiatry*, **53**, 407–17.

Reed, B. R., Jagust, W. J. and Coulter, L. (1993). Anosognosia in Alzheimer's disease: Relationships to depression, cognitive function, and cerebral perfusion. *Journal of Clinical and Experimental Neuropsychology*, **15**, 231–44.

Reitman, E. E. and Cleveland, S. E. (1964). Changes in body image following sensory deprivation in schizophrenia and control groups. *Journal of Abnormal Social Psychology*, **68**, 168–76.

Riutort, M., Cuervo, C., Danion, J.–M., Peretti, C. S. and Salamé, P. (2003). Reduced levels of specific autobiographical memories in schizophrenia. *Psychiatry Research*, **117**, 35–45.

Rosen, A. M., Mukherjee, S., Olarte, S., Vria, V. and Cardenas, C. (1982). Perception of tardive dyskinesia in outpatients receiving maintenance neuroleptics. *American Journal of Psychiatry*, **139**, 372–3.

Rossell, S. L., Coakes, J., Shapleske, J., Woodruff, P. W. R and Davis, A. S. (2003). Insight: Its relationship with cognitive function, brain volume and symptoms in schizophrenia. *Psychological Medicine*, **33**, 111–19.

Rubin, P., Holm, S., Friberg, L., Videbeck, P. and Andersen, K. S. (1991). Altered modulation of prefrontal and subcortical brain activity in newly diagnosed schizophrenia and schizophreniform disorder. *Archives of General Psychiatry*, **48**, 987–95.

Sacks, M. H., Carpenter, W. T. and Strauss, J. S. (1974). Recovery from delusions: Three phases documented by patients' interpretation of research procedures. *Archives of General Psychiatry*, **30**, 117–20.

Sandifer, P. H. (1946). Anosognosia and disorders of body scheme. *Brain*, **69**, 122–37.

Sanides, F. (1969). Comparative architectonics of the neocortex of mammals and their evolutionary significance. *Annals of NY Academy of Science*, **167**, 404–23.

Sartorius, N., Shapiro, R. and Jablensky, A. (1974). The international pilot study of schizophrenia. *Schizophrenia Bulletin*, **1**, 21–35.

Schneider, K. (1959). *Klinische Psychopathologie*, 5th edn. New York: Grune and Stratton.

Seal, M. L., Crowe, S. F. and Cheung, P. (1997). Deficits in source monitoring in subjects with auditory hallucinations may be due to differences in verbal intelligence and verbal memory. *Cognitive Neuropsychiatry*, **2**, 273–90.

Seidman, L. J., Yurgelun-Todd, D., Kremen, W. S., Woods, B. T., Goldstein, J. M., Faraone, S. V., *et al.* (1994). Relationship of prefrontal and temporal lobe MRI measures to neuropsychological performance in chronic schizophrenia. *Biological Psychiatry*, **35**, 235–46.

Shallice, T. (1988). *From Neuropsychology to Mental Structure*. Cambridge, England; New York: Cambridge University Press.

Signer, S. F. (1987). Capgras syndrome: The delusion of substitution. *Journal of Clinical Psychiatry*, **48**, 147–50.

Silva, J. A., Leong, G. B. and Luong, M. T. (1989). Split body and self: An unusual case of misidentification. *Canadian Journal of Psychiatry*, **34**, 728–30.

Slater, E., Beard, A. W. and Glitheroe, E. (1963). The schizophrenia-like psychoses of epilepsy. *British Journal of Psychiatry*, **109**, 95–150.

Smith, J. W., Kucharski, L. T., Oswald, W. T. and Waterman, L. J. (1979). A systematic investigation of tardive dyskinesia in inpatients. *American Journal of Psychiatry*, **136**, 918–22.

Spillane, J. D. (1942). Disturbances of the body scheme. Anosognosia and finger agnosia. *Lancet*, **1**, 42–4.

Starkstein, S. E., Vazquez, S., Migliorelli, R., Teson, A., Sabe, L. and Leiguarda, R. (1995). A single-photon emission computed tomographic study of anosognosia in Alzheimer's disease. *Archives of Neurology*, **52**, 415–20.

Starkstein, S. E., Sabe, L., Cuerva, A. G., Kuzis, G. and Leiguarda, R. (1997). Anosognosia and procedural learning in Alzheimer's disease. *Neuropsychiatry, Neuropsychology, and Behavioral Neurology*, **10**, 96–101.

Stirling, J. D., Hellewell, J. S. E. and Quraishi, N. (1998). Self-monitoring and schizophrenia symptoms of alien control. *Psychological Medicine*, **28**, 675–83.

Stuss, D. T. (1991). Disturbance of self-awareness after frontal system damage. In G. P. Prigatano and D. L. Schacter (ed.) *Awareness of Deficit after Brain Injury: Clinical and theoretical issues*, pp. 63–83. New York: Oxford University Press.

Stuss, D. T., Alexander, M. P., Lieberman, A. and Levine, H. (1978). An extraordinary form of confabulation. *Neurology*, **28**, 1166–72.

Stuss, D. T. and Benson, D. F. (1984). Neuropsychological studies of the frontal lobes. *Psychological Bulletin*, **95**, 3–28.

Stuss, D. T. and Benson, D. F. (1986). *The Frontal Lobes*. New York: Raven Press.

Stuss, D. T. and Benson, D. F. (1987). The frontal lobes and control of cognition and memory. In E. Perecman (ed.) *The Frontal Lobes Revisited*, pp. 141–58. New York: IRBN Press.

Swann, W. B. (1984). Quest for accuracy in person perception: A matter of pragmatics. *Psychological Review*, **91**, 457–77.

Szasz, T. (1957). The psychology of bodily feelings in schizophrenia. *Psychosomatic Medicine*, **19**, 11–16.

Teuber, H. L., Battersby, W. S. and Bender, M. B. (1960). *Visual Field Defects after Penetrating Missile Wounds of the Brain*. Cambridge, MA: Harvard University Press.

Todd, J. (1957). The syndrome of Capgras. *Psychiatric Quarterly*, 31, 250–65.

Tulving, E. (1985). Memory and consciousness. *Canadian Psychologist*, **26**, 1–12.

Von Monakow, C. (1905). *Gehirnpathologie*, 2nd edn. Vienna: Alfred Holder.

Wagner, M. T. and Cushman, L. A. (1994). Neuroanatomic and neuropsychological predictors of unawareness of cognitive deficit in the vascular population. *Archives of Clinical Neuropsychology*, **9**, 57–69.

Waldenstrom, J. (1939). On anosognosia. *Acta Psychiatrica*, **14**, 215–20.

Watt, N. F. (1978). Patterns of childhood social development in adult schizophrenics. *Archives of General Psychiatry*, **35**, 160–5.

Weckowicz, T. E. and Sommer, R. (1960). Body image and self-concept in schizophrenia. *Journal of Mental Science*, **106**, 17–39.

Weinstein, E. A. and Kahn, R. L. (1955). *Denial of Illness: Symbolic and physiological aspects*. Springfield, IL: Charles C. Thomas.

Wernicke, C. (1900). *Grundriss der Psychiatrie in Klinischen Vorlesungen*. Leipzig: Thieme.

Weston, M. J. and Whitlock, F. A. (1971). The Capgras syndrome following head injury. *British Journal of Psychiatry*, **119**, 25–31.

Wheeler, M. A., Stuss, D. T. and Tulving, E. (1997). Toward a theory of episodic memory: The frontal lobes and autonoetic consciousness. *Psychological Bulletin*, **121**, 331–54.

Young, D. A., Davila, R. and Sher, H. (1993). Unawareness of illness and neuropsychological performance in chronic schizophrenia. *Schizophrenia Research*, **10**, 117–24.

Young, D. A., Zakzanis, K. K., Bailey, C., Davila, R., Griese, J., Sartory, G., *et al.* (1998). Further parameters of insight and neuropsychological deficit in schizophrenia and other chronic mental disease. *Journal of Nervous and Mental Disease*, **186**, 44–50.

Zaidel, E. (1987). Hemispheric monitoring. In D. Ottoson (ed.) *Duality and Unity of the Brain*, pp. 247–81. London: Macmillan.

Chapter 8

Neural correlates of unawareness of illness in psychosis

Laura A. Flashman and Robert M. Roth

Introduction

Unawareness of illness, also commonly referred to as lack of insight, has received increasing empirical investigation in psychiatric disorders. It has been suggested that the majority of patients with schizophrenia demonstrate impaired awareness of their illness, including difficulty identifying their symptoms, recognizing that they have a mental disorder, and misattributing their symptoms to external causes (Amador et al., 1994). Unawareness of illness in patients with psychosis, such as schizophrenia, is of considerable clinical relevance as it has been reported to be associated with increased duration of untreated psychosis, treatment noncompliance, reduced work performance, and impaired social skills (Drake et al., 2000; Francis and Penn, 2001; Kampman et al., 2002; Lacro et al., 2002; Lysaker et al., 2002; Novak-Grubic and Tavcar, 2002).

There are several theories pertaining to the etiology of impaired awareness of illness in psychosis. Until relatively recently, most theories proposed that unawareness functions as an unconscious defense or coping mechanism that serves to preserve self-esteem and to minimize disability (Birchwood, 1993; Lally, 1989; Lysaker, 1998; McGlashan, et al., 1975; McGlashan and Carpenter, 1976; Mechanic et al., 1994; Warner et al., 1989; White et al., 2000). However, little empirical research has directly measured the relationship between unawareness of illness and defense, and what data is available has indicated that psychological or psychosocial etiologies account for only a small amount of the variance in unawareness (Kasapis, 1995; Nelson, 1997).

In contrast, over the last decade increasing attention has been paid to a possible neurobiological basis for unawareness of illness in patients with psychosis (Amador et al., 1993). The majority of such studies have investigated the relationship between insight and neuropsychological functioning (please see Chapters 7 and 9 for a comprehensive review). Several studies have reported that poorer awareness of illness is associated with lower overall intellectual ability (e.g., David et al., 1995; Lysaker and Bell, 1994; Young et al., 1993), raising the argument that unawareness is due to global cognitive dysfunction. However, research with a variety of populations has revealed that lower intellectual functioning is necessarily associated with greater global cognitive impairment (Cuesta and Peralta, 1994; McEvoy *et al.*, 1993). Other studies have specifically examined the hypothesis that frontal–subcortical circuitry-mediated executive dysfunction is related to unawareness of illness in psychosis. These studies have yielded inconsistent findings, with evidence both supporting (Buckley *et al.*, 2001; Mohamed *et al.*, 1999; Smith *et al.*, 2000; Young *et al.*, 1998) and failing to support (Amador *et al.*, 1994; Collins *et al.*, 1997; Cuesta *et al.*, 1995; Kemp and David 1996; McEvoy *et al.*, 1993) this hypothesis. In the very few studies that have reported data on other neuropsychological domains of functioning, a significant relationship has been noted between unawareness of illness and performance on tests sensitive to parietal lobe dysfunction (McEvoy *et al.*, 1996; Flashman, unpublished data). Despite the inconsistencies, neuropsychological studies clearly indicate that further investigation into the neurobiological basis of unawareness of illness in psychosis is warranted.

In the present chapter, studies using neuroimaging to investigate the neural basis of unawareness of illness in schizophrenia are reviewed. Given the relative dearth of such neuroimaging studies, studies of unawareness in neurological patients are reviewed as they point to brain systems that may be particularly promising for neuroimaging investigations of unawareness of illness in schizophrenia. We next present functional neuroimaging research on aspects of self-awareness in healthy controls and patients with schizophrenia, as they may provide clues to the cognitive and neural basis of unawareness. Finally, we present a novel cognitive neuroscience model for the etiology of unawareness of illness in schizophrenia. While the focus of the present chapter is largely on schizophrenia, the area in which most studies have been conducted, the data reviewed is also of relevance to understanding the relationship between brain anomalies and unawareness of illness in other psychiatric disorders that present with psychosis, such as bipolar I disorder and major depressive disorder with psychotic features (Ghaemi *et al.*, 2000; Pini *et al.*, 2001; Weiler *et al.*, 2000).

Neuroimaging of awareness of illness in psychotic disorders

Structural neuroimaging

The relationship between brain anatomy and unawareness of illness in patients with schizophrenia or other psychoses has received little empirical investigation to date (Table 8.1). David and colleagues (David *et al.*, 1995) used computerized tomography scans (CT) to obtain total volume of the lateral ventricles, calculated using the sum of area measurements for the body and frontal, anterior, and temporal horns of the lateral ventricle. Unawareness of illness was assessed using the Present State Examination insight item. Subjects included 150 inpatients with onset of psychosis within five years prior to scanning. No significant relationship between insight and ventricular volume was observed. More recently, Rossell *et al.* (2003) examined correlations between unawareness of illness and total volumes of grey matter, white matter, and cerebrospinal

Table 8.1 Neuroimaging correlates of unawareness in psychosis

Author	N	Patient sample	Method	Findings
Takai et al., 1992	22	Chronic schizophrenic inpatients	MRI	Increased VBR
David et al., 1995	128	Mixed, recent-onset (acute) mixed psychotic patients	CT	None
Larøi et al., 2000	20	In- and out-patients with schizophrenia	CT	7 showed frontal atrophy, 13 no frontal atrophy
Morgan et al., 2002	82	First-episode psychotic patients	MRI	Volume differences in cingulate gyrus and left insula grey matter
Flashman et al., 2000	30	Acute schizophrenia and schizoaffective disorder	MRI	Smaller whole brain volume
Flashman et al., 2001	16	Acute schizophrenia and schizoaffective disorder	MRI	Smaller bilateral middle frontal gyrus, right gyrus rectus, left cingulate
Rossell et al., 2003	72	Mixed psychotic patients	CT	No correlations between unawareness and grey, white or cerebrospinal fluid volumes

fluid on CT in 72 patients with psychotic disorders. Again, no significant relationship between unawareness of illness and volume was noted.

Larøi and colleagues (2000) examined 21 medicated inpatients and outpatients with schizophrenia using the Scale for Unawareness of Mental Disorders (SUMD), neuropsychological testing, psychiatric ratings, and CT. CT scans for 20 of the patients were blindly rated by two experienced neuroradiologists for degree of ventricular enlargement and cortical atrophy using a four point scale, as well as localization of any atrophy to frontal, parietal, temporal or occipital lobes. Overall, five patients (25%) were reported to have ventricular enlargement, and seven (35%) were identified as having cortical atrophy. Cortical atrophy was predominately localized to the frontal lobes in all patients, and greater degree cortical atrophy was related to lower current awareness of illness on the SUMD. Takai et al. (1992) measured the area of several brain structures on a midsagittal brain slice acquired using magnetic resonance imaging (MRI) in a sample of 22 male, chronic schizophrenic inpatients and outpatients. Results revealed that greater unawareness of illness was associated with ventricular enlargement, but not area of the cingulate gyrus, frontal, parietal or occipital lobes. Morgan et al. (2002) classified 82 first-presentation psychosis patients as having "low" or "high" awareness of illness, awareness of symptom recognition and total insight. Differences in grey and white matter volume between "low" and "high" insight groups were calculated, and statistically significant differences were observed in both grey and white matter in cingulate gyrus for low insight patients, grey matter in the cingulate gyrus and a region including insula and inferior frontal lobes bilaterally for the low symptom recognition patients, and both grey and white matter in the cingulate gyrus, and grey matter in left insula for low total insight patients. For the low total insight group, increased grey matter adjacent (superior) to left insula and increased white matter at left insula were also noted. Stepwise linear regression analyses controlling for age, sex, diagnosis, symptoms, social class, ethnicity, IQ, height and total tissue volume showed cingulate gyrus deficits were predictive of poorer illness awareness and poorer symptom recognition, while cingulate gyrus and left insula grey matter deficits were predictive of poorer total insight. The authors concluded that the cingulate gyrus and the insula may be part of a cortical system involved in self-appraisal of one's psychotic status.

Our group has also recently used MRI to investigate possible structural correlates of unawareness of illness in psychosis. In our initial study, we examined the relationship between lobar volumes and unawareness of illness in schizophrenia, using several measures of awareness from the SUMD (Flashman *et al.*, 2000). Based on the neuropsychological literature, we hypothesized that patients with unawareness of illness would show reduced frontal and parietal lobe volumes. Results revealed lower whole brain and bilateral frontal lobe volumes in the patients with impaired relative to those with intact awareness of illness (see Figure 8.1). However, the group difference for frontal lobe volume was no longer significant when intracranial volume was used as a covariate. Because global volumes of any given lobe may not be sensitive to subtle subregion differences, we subsequently measured the volume of eight frontal lobe subdivisions in

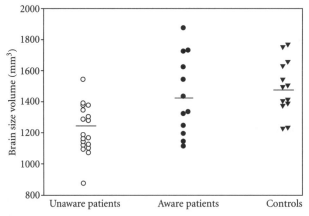

Fig. 8.1 Individual brain volumes for patients with schizophrenia who were unaware (N = 18) or aware (N = 12) of their symptoms and healthy controls (N = 13). Reprinted with permission from the *American Journal of Psychiatry.*

patients with schizophrenia to further evaluate structural correlates of unawareness (Flashman *et al.*, 2001). Findings indicated a significant relationship between lower SUMD awareness of symptoms and decreased bilateral middle frontal gyrus volume. Furthermore, the SUMD Misattribution of Current Symptoms subscale was significantly negatively correlated with bilateral superior frontal gyrus volume, indicating that patients with smaller superior frontal gyri were more likely to attribute their symptoms to reasons other than mental illness. These findings remained significant even when intracranial volume was used as a covariate.

Summary

Overall, the limited available structural neuroimaging evidence suggests that unawareness of illness in psychosis may be related in part to abnormality of the frontal lobes, including the cingulate gyrus and insula, and smaller brain size. Our observation of reduced middle and superior frontal lobe volume in relation to greater unawareness of illness is consistent with evidence of dorsolateral prefrontal cortex involvement in schizophrenia (Bertolino *et al.*, 2000; Carter *et al.*, 1998; Goldberg *et al.*, 1987; Manoach *et al.*, 1999; Park *et al.*, 1999; Goldman-Rakic, 1997, p. 160). No study to date has used functional neuroimaging to evaluate the neural correlates of unawareness of illness in schizophrenia or other psychoses. The structural neuroimaging literature suggests that functional studies focusing on frontal lobe circuitry-mediated cognitive functions may be particularly informative.

Unawareness of illness in neurological disorders

Unawareness of illness in patients with acquired brain lesions secondary to insults such as stroke or traumatic brain injury, as well as those with neurodegenerative disorders, provides indirect clues for understanding the neural basis of unawareness of illness in schizophrenia and other psychoses (Amador *et al.*, 1991). While the extension of this indirect evidence to the psychoses has been controversial, unawareness in psychiatric and neurological populations share several common clinical features, including being largely resistant to direct confrontation, providing delusional explanations to explain illness-related circumstances such as hospitalization, and the fact that unawareness appears to fall along a continuum of severity (Cuesta and Peralta, 1994).

Unawareness in acquired brain lesions

Unawareness of cognitive, motor or sensory impairment in patients with acquired brain lesions, also commonly referred to as anosognosia (Babinski, 1914; McGuire *et al.*, 1996), has generally been attributed to either diffuse brain damage or a focal brain lesion (McGuire *et al.*, 1996). Proponents of a diffuse brain damage explanation of unawareness have argued that this impairment results from an overall decline in cognitive functioning. However, a recent review by Lele and Joglekar (1998) indicated that unawareness may be observed in patients without general intellectual impairment, and unawareness may be observed for some aspects of illness but not others in the same patient. Proponents of a focal lesion view have pointed to evidence that unawareness tends to be more common in patients with focal lesions to right hemisphere areas, particularly those involving the frontal or parietal lobes and their connections (Stuss and Benson, 1986). More specifically, it has been hypothesized that unawareness of illness results from an interaction between frontal lobe circuitry impairment which compromises the ability to self-monitor, self-correct and draw proper inferences, and parietal lobe dysfunction which affects the complex integration of sensory input (Benson and Stuss, 1990; Ellis and Small, 1993).

Unawareness in neurodegenerative disorders

Unawareness of cognitive, motor, and/or psychiatric problems has also been observed in patients with neurodegenerative disorders. Alzheimer's disease has been the focus of most investigations, with a limited number of studies looking at other disorders such as Parkinson's disease, Huntington's disease, and frontotemporal dementia (Kertesz *et al.*, 2000; Seltzer *et al.*, 2001; Vitale *et al.*, 2001).

A number of studies have found an association between impaired awareness and general cognitive decline in patients with Alzheimer's disease (Lopez *et al.*, 1994; Migliorelli *et al.*, 1995; Reisberg *et al.*, 1985). Frontal–subcortical system circuitry dysfunction has been hypothesized to underlie unawareness in Alzheimer's disease (Ott *et al.*, 1996). In the limited number of studies to date, a significant relationship between unawareness and poorer performance on tests of executive functions has been reported in some (Lopez *et al.*, 1994; Michon *et al.*, 1994; Ott *et al.*, 1996; Starkstein *et al.*, 1997a; Starkstein *et al.*, 1997b), but not all (Auchus *et al.*, 1994; Mangone *et al.*, 1991; Starkstein *et al.*, 1996) studies. In patients with Parkinson's disease, impaired awareness of motor dysfunction and self-care deficits has been associated with overall cognitive decline, as well as lower scores on measures of attention, memory and visuoconstruction (Seltzer *et al.*, 2001).

The few published functional neuroimaging studies have shown a somewhat more consistent association between unawareness and brain anomaly in Alzheimer's disease. Using single photon emission computed tomography (SPECT), Reed *et al.* (1993) found blood flow hypometabolism in the dorsolateral frontal cortex of the right hemisphere in patients with AD who manifested unawareness. Starkstein *et al.* (1995) reported decreased perfusion in the inferior and dorsolateral frontal areas of the right hemisphere on SPECT scans in patients with impaired awareness. In a sample of 78 patients with mild AD, Derouesne *et al.* (1999) found that unawareness was most frequently related to SPECT perfusion deficits in parietotemporal regions, predominant in the right hemisphere.

Summary

As can be seen, very little work has directly examined neuroimaging correlates of unawareness of illness in psychosis. Structural neuroimaging studies of schizophrenia have suggested a relationship between unawareness of illness and ventricular enlargement, global brain atrophy, and frontal lobe abnormalities. Overall, research on unawareness in neurological patients has implicated right hemisphere dysfunction, particularly frontal and parietal regions. These findings are in general agreement with several theories that have implicated frontal lobe circuitry dysfunction in unawareness of illness in psychoses (e.g., Barr 1998; Frith *et al.*, 2000; Goldman-Rakic and Selemon 1997). These promising leads indicate that further structural and novel functional neuroimaging studies of unawareness of illness in psychosis are warranted.

Neuroimaging aspects of awareness in healthy controls and patients with schizophrenia

Several cognitive processes believed to reflect aspects of self-awareness have been studied using functional neuroimaging. These include self-evaluation, theory of mind (also called perspective taking), self-monitoring, and working memory. Much of this research has been conducted with healthy adults. Nonetheless, even healthy individuals can show variable awareness of their cognitive processes and behaviors, as well as demonstrate cognitive distortions such as attributing negative events to others (Sackeim and Wegner, 1986; Tournois *et al.*, 2000). Functional neuroimaging studies of such processes provide novel directions for research on the cognitive mechanisms and neurobiological substrates of unawareness of illness in psychosis.

Self-evaluation

Self-evaluation involves that ability to think about and make judgments regarding one's own cognitive, personality, physical, and emotional characteristics. Recent functional MRI (fMRI) studies have examined the neural correlates of self-evaluation in healthy control subjects. Johnson *et al.* (2002) had subjects listen to questions requiring either self-evaluation or general knowledge. Self-evaluation questions were in five domains: one's own physical body (e.g., "I am overweight"), cognitive abilities (e.g., "I forget things"), social functioning (e.g., "I have lots of friends"), emotional functioning (e.g., "I am usually happy"), and beliefs about the self (e.g., "I am a successful person"). The general knowledge questions included facts about quantities (e.g., "10 seconds is less than a minute") or other information (e.g., "The current president is Nixon"). Results revealed that self-evaluation was associated with a pattern of activation that included dorsal and ventral medial prefrontal areas and the posterior cingulate gyrus.

Fossati *et al.* (2001) presented healthy subjects with words reflecting positive and negative personality traits. In the SELF encoding condition, subjects judged whether or not each trait described them. During the OTHER condition, they judged whether or not each trait was generally positive. A control condition was also presented in which subjects decided whether or not each word contained a specific letter of the alphabet. No significant reaction time difference was noted between the three conditions. In addition, both the SELF and OTHER conditions activated the left medial frontal cortex, left frontal pole and insula; however, frontal activations were stronger on the SELF condition, and insula activation in the OTHER condition. In contrast, only the

SELF condition showed activation of the right medial prefrontal cortex, and only the OTHER condition showed bilateral activation of the medial orbital frontal cortex.

Similar to the Fossati *et al.* study, Kircher *et al.* (2002) also had healthy subjects make judgments as to whether personality traits were self-descriptive or not (Intentional task). Subjects also completed a task in which they categorized words according to whether they described physical or psychological attributes. However, unbeknown to subjects, the words presented in the latter task had been rated by them for self-descriptiveness six weeks prior to scanning (Incidental task). For both tasks, reaction times were faster for words rated as self-descriptive, and activation was observed in left superior parietal lobe and adjacent regions of the lateral prefrontal cortex. Differential signal changes were present in the left precuneus for the intentional task and right middle temporal gyrus for the incidental task.

Overall, functional neuroimaging studies indicate that self-evaluation is most closely associated with activation of frontal and parietal lobe regions. No study to date has used functional neuroimaging to evaluate the neural correlates of self-evaluation in patients with psychosis.

Theory of mind

Intact theory of mind, or the ability to correctly attribute feelings, knowledge, intentions, and goals to other people, is crucial for proper social interaction. Frith (1992) hypothesized that theory of mind skills in persons with persecutory delusions develop normally, but are impaired during an acute psychiatric episode. Several behavioral studies have reported abnormal theory of mind in schizophrenia (Corcoran *et al.*, 1995; Doody *et al.*, 1998; Drury *et al.*, 1998; Langdon *et al.*, 1997; Mazza *et al.*, 2001; Sarfati *et al.*, 1997a), although it has been observed more frequently in and associated with negative symptoms and thought disorder (Sarfati *et al.*, 1997a; Sarfati *et al.*, 1999; Sarfati *et al.*, 1997b). Impaired theory mind may contribute to unawareness of illness through inappropriate attribution of threatening thoughts, intentions or behaviors to others.

Various tasks have been employed to study theory of mind in healthy subjects. These have included processing of stories (Fletcher *et al.*, 1995; Happe, 1994) and cartoons, and object utilization among others, that vary in the degree to which the mental state or attribution of intent to others must be inferred to perform the tasks successfully. Several positron emission tomography (PET) and fMRI studies have been conducted with healthy subjects performing theory of mind tasks. In general, these studies have shown several areas of increased activation when theory of mind is required including medial and lateral inferior prefrontal cortex, temporal-parietal junction, bilateral temporal regions, and left amygdala and hippocampus (Baron-Cohen *et al.*, 1994, 1999; Brunet *et al.*, 2000; Castelli *et al.*, 2000; Fletcher *et al.*, 1995; Gallagher *et al.*, 2000; Goel *et al.*, 1995; Vogeley *et al.*, 2001). This circuitry has been associated with representations of the mental states of actions and goals of oneself and others (Frith and Frith, 1999; Hietanen and Perrett, 1993; Iacoboni *et al.*, 1999; Lane *et al.*, 1997).

To date, only one neuroimaging study has examined theory of mind in patients with schizophrenia (Russell *et al.*, 2000). In this task, subjects labeled the social/emotional expression of photographed eyes by choosing one of two words (e.g., "concerned" or "angry") that best described the mental state reflected by the photograph. In the control condition, subjects were asked to make a decision regarding the gender of the same pairs of eyes. Using fMRI, results revealed that patients made more errors in their attribution of mental state, along with decreased activation in the left inferior frontal gyrus and left middle and superior temporal lobe, than healthy controls.

Self-monitoring

The capacity to accurately monitor ones ongoing thoughts, emotions and behaviors is necessary to ensure accuracy of these, as well as to ensure that they are attributed to oneself and not to an external agent. It has been proposed that schizophrenia is related to impaired self-monitoring, resulting in symptoms such as hallucinations and delusions which are characterized by attribution to external agents (Frith *et al.*, 2000). In healthy subjects, PET and fMRI studies have shown that self-monitoring during various attention tasks is associated with prominent activation of the medial prefrontal cortex in the region of the anterior cingulate gyrus (Luks *et al.*, 2002; van Veen *et al.*, 2001).

Patients with schizophrenia demonstrate abnormal brain activation during response monitoring. Using a continuous performance test with degraded stimuli to increase the probability of errors, Carter *et al.* (2001) found that patients with schizophrenia showed lower error-related activity in the anterior cingulate cortex relative to healthy controls. Similarly, two studies reported reduced anterior cingulate activation during the incongruent condition of the Stroop task in both medicated and unmedicated patients with schizophrenia (Carter *et al.*, 1997; Nordahl *et al.*, 2001).

Several studies have employed a self-monitoring paradigm in which subjects perform a verbal task during which they can either hear their own voice with or without distortion, or another's voice with or without distortion. Subjects are required to report whether the voice they hear is their own or someone else's. Behavioral studies have shown that patients with schizophrenia are significantly more likely to misattribute their own distorted voice to someone else (Johns and McGuire, 1999; Johns *et al.*, 2001). Fu *et al.* (2001) applied this paradigm to healthy control subjects, acutely psychotic patients, and psychotic patients in remission. In healthy controls, reading with either distorted or alien feedback activated a network that included the insular, cingulate, temporal and cerebellar cortices. Specific components were differentially engaged by each condition. The hippocampus, cingulate gyrus, and cerebellum were particularly activated when healthy controls heard their own distorted voice, which they accurately identified. In contrast, acutely psychotic patients tended to attribute their own distorted voice to others and failed to engage these areas. The pattern of activation in patients in remission was intermediate between the control and acutely psychotic groups.

Abnormal brain activation attributed to self-monitoring impairment in schizophrenia has also been noted using other experimental paradigms. PET studies have revealed that patients with schizophrenia that have a strong history of auditory hallucinations show abnormal left middle temporal gyrus and rostral supplementary motor area when imagining sentences being spoken in another person's voice (McGuire *et al.*, 1996, 1995). Spence and colleagues (1997) reported overactivation of right inferior parietal lobe during random joystick movements in schizophrenics with prominent symptoms of passivity phenomenon (i.e., belief that one's actions or thoughts are being replaced or controlled by an external agent).

Overall, these studies suggest that abnormal self-monitoring in schizophrenia is associated with abnormal neural circuitry likely involving medial prefrontal, temporal and parietal cortices.

Working memory

Working memory (WM) refers to the ability to hold information in mind, or "online" while retrieving or processing other relevant information (Baddeley 1986; Baddeley and Hitch 1994). Impairments in this domain can contribute to the deficits found in a variety of other cognitive functions. One hypothesis that requires further corroboration is that the association between unawareness and smaller frontal subregions (Flashman *et al.*, 2001) may be mediated by deficits in working memory. The DLPFC and cingulate gyrus are important components of working memory circuitry (Goldman-Rakic and Selemon, 1997; McCarthy *et al.*, 1996; Smith *et al.*, 1998). The gyrus rectus has been conceptualized as an orbitofrontal extension of the cingulate complex (Morecraft *et al.*, 1992) that receives projections from the mediodorsal nucleus of the thalamus (the major thalamic relay to the prefrontal area). Partial resection of the gyrus rectus following anterior communicating artery aneurysm has been associated with problems in short-term memory (Hutter and Gilsbach, 1996). Patients with schizophrenia show impairment on many memory tasks, including those assessing working memory (e.g., WCST). In fact, working memory deficits may be a core component of the illness (Goldman-Rakic and Selemon, 1997). Working memory is important for comparing current and past experience, and for integrating this information to guide current and future behavior. Impairment in this domain might lead to problems in accurate interpretation of symptoms. The inability to hold symptom information online while comparing it to past experiences may make it difficult to successfully categorize the current symptom as aberrant, which might be manifested as unawareness of illness.

Numerous PET and fMRI studies of working memory have been conducted with healthy subjects. In general, the most prominent activations have been found in dorsolateral prefrontal cortex and parietal lobes bilaterally, with additional activation commonly observed in the basal ganglia, anterior cingulate, thalamus and cerebellum (Awh *et al.*, 1996; Baddeley and Hitch, 1994; D'Esposito *et al.*, 1998; Goldberg *et al.*, 1996; Goldman-Rakic 1995; Owen *et al.*, 1996; Paulesu *et al.*, 1993; Petrides *et al.*, 1993;

Smith and Jonides, 1998, 1999). PET and fMRI studies of working memory in patients with schizophrenia have generally shown abnormal activations in the regions normally recruited by healthy subjects (e.g., Bertolino *et al.*, 2000; Callicott *et al.*, 1998; Manoach *et al.*, 2000, 1999; Menon *et al.*, 2001; Meyer-Lindenberg *et al.*, 2001).

Inferential reasoning

Inferential reasoning involves the ability to take information from one's environment and make decisions or reach conclusions based on past and present personal experience. The judgments and attributions a person makes about him or herself fall within this purview, and this perspective relies on the ability to monitor and update information in light of changing circumstances or data. Decisions are often made with incomplete information. In healthy individuals, the ability to accommodate new information and reach logical conclusions as more data becomes available relies on inferential reasoning strategies and an accurate interpretation of information presented. In patients with psychosis, inferential reasoning has been shown to be impaired (e.g., Mujica-Parodi *et al.*, 2000). This impairment may contribute to unawareness of illness by interfering with the ability to accurately reinterpret circumstances as new data becomes available.

The neural substrates of hypothesis testing were examined in a PET study by Elliott *et al.* (1998), using a complex, insoluble, nonverbal task in which subjects attempted to determine a rule governing which of two checkerboard patterns was correct. Tasks were performed with and without a requirement to make a choice. Subjects were provided with inter-trial feedback to monitor and update their hypotheses; thus, in addition to generation and testing of hypotheses, this task involved working memory, response monitoring, and reasoning. Results indicated that cerebellum (bilaterally), left anterior cingulate, left inferior frontal gyrus, right precuneus, and right thalamus activated during hypothesis testing. When choosing a response was required, there was activation noted in the left anterior cingulate and right lateral orbitofrontal cortex. A significant modulation of activation associated with hypothesis testing was observed in the anterior cingulate that was also activated by making a choice.

To our knowledge, no neuroimaging studies have directly examined inferential reasoning ability in patients with schizophrenia or other psychosis. However, the involvement of frontal and parietal lobe circuitry shown in healthy individuals (Elliott and Dolan, 1998) appears consistent with other evidence for abnormality of this circuitry in unawareness of illness.

Summary

Functional neuroimaging studies on the neurobiological substrates of cognitive processes requiring self-awareness in healthy subjects have yielded important methodological and theoretical leads for studying unawareness of illness in psychosis. Relatively few functional neuroimaging studies have investigated whether these processes are abnormal in schizophrenia *per se*, and none have assessed patients with impaired awareness of illness as assessed using generally accepted measures such as the SUMD. Nonetheless, what evidence is available is consistent with other studies in suggesting prominent involvement of abnormal medial and dorsolateral prefrontal, temporal and parietal cortices in unawareness of illness in patients with schizophrenia.

A cognitive neuroscience model of awareness in psychosis

Over the past several years, a number of authors have reported that unawareness of illness is not a unitary concept, and there have been several attempts to identify distinct dimensions or components (Amador *et al.*, 1991; David 1990; Flashman *et al.*, 1998; Schwartz *et al.*, 2000). In general, multidimensional conceptualizations involve several parts, including (1) unawareness of symptoms or deficits; (2) impaired understanding the impact or consequences of symptoms or deficits (e.g., patient is aware of their illness and is concerned about it, but does not believe that it impacts on his/her ability to perform his/her job); and (3) misattribution of symptoms or deficits (e.g., "stress" or "tension" not mental illness) (Amador *et al.*, 1991; Flashman *et al.*, 1998). Most research to date has used simple categorical classification of patients with psychosis as either "aware" and "unaware", or as having "high" vs. "low" levels of unawareness. We hypothesize, based on the aspects defined above, that patients that are aware of their symptoms can be further classified into those who correctly attribute symptoms to mental illness ("aware, correct attributers") and those those who purport awareness of symptoms but incorrectly attribute them to nonpsychiatric reasons ("aware, misattributers"). An example of a patient in the latter group would be an individual who recognizes that he hears voices or has delusions of control, but believes he experiences these problems because of a government experiment where he has been implanted with a computer chip.

Given the evidence presented above that there appear to be multiple aspects involved in the awareness of ones' thoughts, emotions and behaviors, we have developed a cognitive neuroscience model of unawareness of illness in psychosis (see Table 8.2). This model was constructed to facilitate hypothesis testing of the relationship between the multidimensional conceptualization of unawareness of illness and cognitive processing abnormalities in psychosis. It is proposed that significant differences in the nature of cognitive processing abnormalities, and their relevant neurobiological substrates, may be found between three groups of patients described above (aware, correct attributers; aware, misattributers; unaware). It should be noted, however, that while a categorical grouping is presented to facilitate illustration of hypotheses, level of awareness within that group of patients that show at least some degree of awareness about their symptoms, and degree to which patients with psychosis misattribute their symptoms likely varies along a continuum.

The model identifies a number of meta-cognitive and sensory abilities that may contribute to unawareness of illness in both psychoses and neurological disorders. While sensory processing abnormalities have been noted in some patients with schizophrenia (e.g., Braus *et al.*, 2002; Salisbury *et al.*, 2002), it is hypothesized that these do

Table 8.2 Cognitive neuroscience model of correlates of aspects of unawareness of illness in psychosis

Domain	Aware, correct attributer	Aware, misattributer	Unaware
Sensory perception	+	+	+
Attribution style	+	+	−
Self-evaluation/reflection	+	−	−
Theory of mind	+/−	+/−	*
Self-monitoring	+	−	−
Working memory	+/−	−	*
Inferential reasoning	−	−	*

Note: + = Normal performance; +/− = Minimally impaired, if impaired at all; − = Impaired Performance; * = Very Impaired Performance

not contribute significantly to impaired awareness in patients with schizophrenia. This contrasts with the finding that some patients with Alzheimer's disease have delusional ideation that has been associated with abnormal auditory sensory processing (Bazargan *et al.*, 2001; Cooper *et al.*, 1974; Kay *et al.*, 1976). While the above functional neuroimaging literature review provides some possible clues to the neural underpinnings of these cognitive aspects of unawareness of illness, further research will be helpful.

Conclusions

At present, few studies have taken advantage of recent advances in structural and functional neuroimaging to further elucidate the neurobiological substrates of unawareness of illness in patients with psychosis. Nevertheless, these few studies, in the context of the body of literature pertaining to unawareness of illness in patients with acquired and neurodegenerative disorders, and functional neuroimaging studies of aspects of unawareness in healthy adults, provide promising avenues for future research. Overall, this body of evidence suggests that unawareness of illness in psychosis may be due to abnormality of prefrontal and parietal cortices and their associated cortical and subcortical neural pathways. Future research is likely to be further enhanced by taking into account the multidimensional nature of awareness of illness in psychosis. With this in mind, we have put forth a cognitive neuroscience model of unawareness of illness in psychosis that makes specific, testable predictions regarding the relationship between cognitive processing abnormalities and both unawareness of illness and misattribution of symptoms.

Acknowledgments

Some of the research presented in this chapter was supported by a Young Investigator Award from the National Alliance on Research on Schizophrenia and Depression (NARSAD), as well as by New Hampshire Hospital and the Ira DeCamp Foundation.

References

Amador, X. F., Flaum, M., Andreasen, N. C., Strauss, D. H., Yale, S. A., Clark, S. C., *et al.* (1994). Awareness of illness in schizophrenia and schizoaffective and mood disorders. *Archives of General Psychiatry*, **51**, 826–36.

Amador, X. F., Strauss, D. H., Yale, S. A. and Gorman, J. M. (1991). Awareness of illness in schizophrenia. *Schizophrenia Bulletin*, **17**, 113–32.

Amador, X. F., Strauss, D. H., Yale, S. A., Flaum, M., Endicott, J. and Gorman, J. M. (1993). Assessment of insight in psychosis. *American Journal of Psychiatry*, **150**, 873–9.

Auchus, A. P., Goldstein, F. C., Green, J. and Green, R. C. (1994). Unawareness of cognitive impairments in Alzheimer's disease. *Neuropsychiatry, Neuropsychology, and Behavioral Neurology*, **7**, 25–9.

Awh, E., Jonides, J., Smith, E. E., Schumacher, E. H., Koeppe, R. A. and Katz, S. (1996). Dissociation of storage and rehearsal in verbal working memory. *Psychological Science*, **7**, 25–31.

Babinski, J. (1914). Contribution a l'etude des troubles mentaux dans l'hemiplegie organique cerebrale (anosognosie). *Rev Neurol (Paris)*, **27**, 845–8.

Baddeley, A. D. (1986). *Working Memory*. Oxford University Press, Oxford.

Baddeley, A. D. and Hitch, G. J. (1994). Developments in the concept of working memory. *Neuropsychology*, **8**, 485–93.

Baron-Cohen, S., Ring, H., Moriarty, J., Schmitz, B., Costa, D. and Ell, P. (1994). Recognition of mental states terms: Clinical findings in children with autism and a functional neuroimaging study of normal adults. *British Journal of Psychiatry*, **165**, 640–9.

Baron-Cohen, S., Ring, H. A., Wheelwright, S., Bullmore, E. T., Brammer, M. J., Simmons, A., *et al.* (1999). Social intelligence in the normal and autistic brain: An fMRI study. *European Journal of Neuroscience*, **11**, 1891–9.

Barr, W. B. (1998). Neurobehavioral disorders of awareness and their relevance to schizophrenia. In X. F. Amador and A. S. David (ed.) *Insight and Psychosis*, pp. 107–41. New York: Oxford University Press.

Bazargan, M., Bazargan, S. and King, L. (2001). Paranoid ideation among elderly African American persons. *Gerontologist*, **41**, 366–73.

Benson, D. F. and Stuss, D. T. (1990). Frontal lobe influences on delusions: A clinical perspective. *Schizophrenia Bulletin*, **16**, 403–11.

Bertolino, A., Esposito, G., Callicott, J. H., Mattay, V. S., Van Horn, J. D., Frank, J. A., *et al.* (2000). Specific relationship between prefrontal neuronal n-acetylaspartate and activation of the working memory cortical network in schizophrenia. *American Journal of Psychiatry*, **157**, 26–33.

Birchwood, M., Mason, R., MacMillan, F. and Healy, J. (1993). Depression, demoralization and control over psychotic illness: A comparison of depressed and non-depressed patients with a chronic psychosis. *Psychological Medicine*, **23**, 387–95.

Braus, D. F., Weber-Fahr, W., Tost, H., Ruf, M. and Henn, F. A. (2002). Sensory information processing in neuroleptic-naive first-episode schizophrenic patients: A functional magnetic resonance imaging study. *Archives of General Psychiatry*, **59**, 696–701.

Brunet, E., Sarfati, Y., Hardy-Bayle, C. and Decety, J. (2000). A PET investigation of the attribution of intentions with a nonverbal task. *NeuroImage*, **11**, 157–66.

Buckley, P. F., Hasan, S., Fiedman, L. and Cerny, C. (2001). Insight and schizophrenia. *Comprehensive Psychiatry*, **42**, 39–41.

Callicott, J. H., Ramsey, N. F., Tallent, K., Bertolino, A., Knable, M. B., Coppola, R., *et al.* (1998). Functional magnetic resonance imaging brain mapping in psychiatry: Methodological issues illustrated in a study of working memory in schizophrenia. *Neuropsychopharmacology*, **18**, 186–96.

Carter, C. S., Braver, T. S., Barch, D. M., Botvinick, M. M., Noll, D. and Cohen, J. D. (1998). Anterior cingulate cortex, error detection, and the online monitoring of performance. *Science*, **280**, 747–9.

Carter, C. S., MacDonald, A. W., Ross, L. L. and Stenger, V. A. (2001). Anterior cingulate cortex activity and impaired self-monitoring of performance in patients with schizophrenia: An event-related fMRI study. *American Journal of Psychiatry*, **158**, 1423–8.

Carter, C. S., Mintun, M., Nichols, T. and Cohen, J. D. (1997). Anterior cingulate gyrus dysfunction and selective attention deficits in schizophrenia: an H₂O PET study during single-trial stroop task performance. *American Journal of Psychiatry*, **154**, 1670–5.

Castelli, F., Happe, F., Frith, U. and Frith, C. (2000). Movement and mind: A functional imaging study of perception and interpretation of complex intentional movement patterns. *NeuroImage*, **12**, 314–25.

Collins, A. A., Remington, G. J., Coulter, K. and Birkett, K. (1997). Insight, neurocognitive function and symptom clusters in chronic schizophrenia. *Schizophrenia Research*, **27**, 37–44.

Cooper, A. F., Curry, A. R., Kay, D. W., Garside, R. F. and Roth, M. (1974). Hearing loss in paranoid and affective psychoses of the elderly. *Lancet*, **2**, 851–4.

Corcoran, R., Mercer, G. and Frith, C. D. (1995). Schizophrenia, symptomatology and social inference: Investigating "theory of mind" in people with schizophrenia. *Schizophrenia Research*, **17**, 5–13.

Cuesta, M. J. and Peralta, V. (1994). Lack of insight in schizophrenia. *Schizophrenia Bulletin*, **20**, 359–66.

Cuesta, M. J., Peralta, V., Caro, F. and deLeon, J. (1995). Is poor insight in psychotic disorders associated with performance on the Wisconsin card sorting test? *American Journal of Psychiatry*, **152**, 1380–2.

David, A., Van Os, J., Jones, P., Harvey, I., Foerster, A. and Fahy, T. (1995). Insight and psychotic illness: Cross-sectional and longitudinal associations. *British Journal of Psychiatry*, **167**, 621–8.

David, A. S. (1990). Insight and psychosis. *British Journal of Psychiatry*, **156**, 798–808.

Derouesne, C., Thibault, S., Lagha-Pierucci, S., Baudouin-Madec, V., Ancri, D. and Lacomblez, L. (1999). Decreased awareness of cognitive deficits in patients with mild dementia of the Alzheimer type. *International Journal of Geriatric Psychiatry*, **14**, 1019–30.

D'Esposito, M., Aguirre, G. K., Zarahn, D., Ballard, R. K. and Shin, J. L. (1998). Functional MRI studies of spatial and nonspatial working memory. *Cognitive Brain Research*, **7**, 1–13.

Doody, G. A., Gotz, M., Johnstone, E. C., Frith, C. D. and Cunningham Owens, D. G. (1998). Theory of mind and psychoses. *Psychological Medicine*, **28**, 397–405.

Drake, R. J., Haley, C. J., Akhtar, S. and Lewis, S. W. (2000). Causes and consequences of duration of untreated psychosis in schizophrenia. *British Journal of Psychiatry*, **177**, 511–15.

Drury, V. M., Robinson, E. J. and Birchwood, M. (1998). 'Theory of mind' skills during an acute episode of psychosis and following recovery. *Psychological Medicine*, **28**, 1101–12.

Elliott, R. and Dolan, R. J. (1998). Activation of different anterior cingulate foci in association with hypothesis testing and response selection. *NeuroImage*, **8**, 17–29.

Ellis, S. J. and Small, M. (1993). Denial of illness in stroke. *Stroke*, **24**, 757–9.

Flashman, L. A., Amador, X. and McAllister, T. W. (1998). Lack of awareness of deficits in traumatic brain injury. *Seminars in Clinical Neuropsychiatry*, **3**, 201–10.

Flashman, L. A., McAllister, T. W., Andreasen, N. C. and Saykin, A. J. (2000). Smaller brain size associated with unawareness in patients with schizophrenia. *American Journal of Psychiatry*, **157**, 1167–9.

Flashman, L. A., McAllister, T. W., Saykin, A. J., Johnson, S. C., Rick, J. H. and Green, R. L. (2001). Specific frontal lobe regions correlated with unawareness of illness in schizophrenia. *Journal of Neuropsychiatry and Clinical Neurosciences*, **13**, 255–7.

Fletcher, P. C., Happe, F., Frith, U., Baker, S. C., Dolan, R. J., Frackowiak, R. S. J., *et al.* (1995). Other minds in the brain: A functional imaging study of "theory of mind" in story comprehension. *Cognition*, **57**, 109–28.

Fossati, P., Hevenor, S., Graham, S., Grady, C., Keightley, M., Craik, F., *et al.* (2001). *Self-evaluation during processing of emotional words: An fMRI study.* Presented at the Organization for Human Brain Mapping, Brighton, UK.

Francis, J. L. and Penn, D. L. (2001). The relationship between insight and social skill in persons with severe mental illness. *Journal of Nervous and Mental Disease*, **189**, 822–9.

Frith, C. D. (1992). *The Cognitive Neuropsychology of Schizophrenia.* Hove, UK: Lawrence Erlbaum Associates.

Frith, C. D., Blakemore, S. and Wolpert, D. M. (2000). Explaining the symptoms of schizophrenia: Abnormalities in the awareness of action. *Brain Research – Brain Research Reviews*, **31**, 357–63.

Frith, C. D. and Frith, U. (1999). Interacting minds – a biological basis. *Science*, **286**, 1692–5.

Fu, C. H. Y., Vythelingum, N., Andrew, C., Brammer, M. J., Amaro, E. Jr., Williams, S. C. R., *et al.* (2001). *Alien voices . . . who said that? Neural correlates of impaired verbal self-monitoring in schizophrenia.* Presented at the Organization for Human Brain Mapping, Brighton, UK.

Gallagher, H. L., Happé, F., Brunswick, N., Fletcher, P. C., Frith, U. and Frith, C. D. (2000). Reading the mind in cartoons and stories: An fMRI study of "theory of mind" in verbal and nonverbal tasks. *Neuropsychologia*, **38**, 11–21.

Ghaemi, S. N., Boiman, E. and Goodwin, F. K. (2000). Insight and outcome in bipolar, unipolar, and anxiety disorders. *Comprehensive Psychiatry*, **41**, 167–71.

Goel, V., Grafman, J., Sadato, N. and Hallet, M. (1995). Modeling other minds. *NeuroReport*, **6**, 1741–6.

Goldberg, T., Weinberger, D. R. and Berman, K. (1987). Further evidence for dementia of the prefrontal type in schizophrenia? A controlled study of teaching of the Wisconsin card sorting test. *Archives of General Psychiatry*, **44**, 1008–14.

Goldberg, T. E., Berman, K. F., Randolph, C., Gold, J. M. and Weinberger, D. R. (1996). Isolating the nmemonic component in spatial delayed response: A controlled PET ^{15}O-labeled water regional cerbral blood flow study in humans. *NeuroImage*, **3**, 69–78.

Goldman-Rakic, P. S. (1995). Cellular basis of working memory. *Neuron*, **14**, 477–85.

Goldman-Rakic, P. S. and Selemon, L. D. (1997). Functional and anatomical aspects of prefrontal pathology in schizophrenia. *Schizophrenia Bulletin*, **23**, 437–58.

Happe, F. (1994). An advanced test of theory of mind: Understanding of story of characters' thoughts and feelings by able autistic, mentally handicapped, and normal children and adults. *Journal of Autism and Developmental Disorders*, **24**, 129–54.

Hietanen, J. K. and Perrett, D. I. (1993). Motion sensitive cells in the macaque superior temporal polysensory area: I. Lack of response to the sight of the animal's own limb movement. *Brain Research – Brain Research Reviews*, **93**, 117–28.

Hutter, B. O. and Gilsbach, J. M. (1996). Early neuropsychological sequelae of aneurysm and subarachnoid haemorrhage. *Acta Neurochirurgica*, **138**, 1370–8.

Iacoboni, M., Woods, R. P., Brass, M., Bekkering, H., Mazziotta, J. C. and Rizzolatti, G. (1999). Cortical mechanisms of human imitation. *Science*, **286**, 2526–8.

Johns, L. C. and McGuire, P. K. (1999). Verbal self-monitoring and auditory hallucinations in schizophrenia. *The Lancet*, **353**, 469–70.

Johns, L. C., Rossell, S., Frith, C., Ahmad, F., Hemsley, D., Kuipers, E., *et al.* (2001). Verbal self-monitoring and auditory verbal hallucinations in patients with schizophrenia. *Psychological Medicine*, **31**, 705–15.

Johnson, S. C., Baxter, L. C., Wilder, L. S., Pipe, J. G., Heiserman, J. E. and Prigatano, G. P. (2002). Neural correlates of self-reflection. *Brain*, **125**, 1–7.

Kampman, O., Laippala, P., Vaananen, J., Koivisto, E., Kiviniemi, P., Kilkku, N., *et al.* (2002). Indicators of medication compliance in first-episode psychosis. *Psychiatry Research*, **110**, 39–48.

Kasapis, C. (1995). *Poor insight in schizophrenia: Neuropsychological and defensive aspects.* Unpublished doctoral dissertation. New York University, Department of Psychology.

Kay, D. W., Cooper, A. F., Garside, R. F. and Roth, M. (1976). The differentiation of paranoid from affective psychoses by patients' premorbid characteristics. *British Journal of Psychiatry*, **129**, 207–15.

Kemp, R. and David, A. (1996). Psychological predictors of insight and compliance in psychotic patients. *British Journal of Psychiatry*, **169**, 444–50.

Kertesz, A., Nadkarni, N., Davidson, W. and Thomas, A. W. (2000). The frontal behavioral inventory in the differential diagnosis of frontotemporal dementia. *Journal of the International Neuropsychological Society*, **6**, 460–8.

Kircher, T. T., Brammer, M., Bullmore, E., Simmons, A., Bartels, M. and David, A. S. (2002). The neural correlates of intentional and incidental self processing. *Neuropsychologia*, **40**, 683–92.

Lacro, J. P., Dunn, L. B., Dolder, C. R., Leckbland, S. G. and Jeste, D. V. (2002). Prevalence of and risk factors for medication nonadherence in patients with schizophrenia: A comprehensive review of recent literature. *Journal of Clinical Psychiatry*, **63**, 892–909.

Lally, S. J. (1989). Does being in here mean there is something wrong with me? *Schizophrenia Bulletin*, **15**, 253–65.

Lane, R. D., Fink, R. G., Chua, P. M. and Dolan, R. J. (1997). Neural activation during selective attention to subjective emotional responses. *Neuroreport*, **8**, 3969–72.

Langdon, R., Michie, P. T., Ward, P. B., McConaghy, N., Catts, S. V. and Coltehart, M. (1997). Defective self and/or other mentalising in schizophrenia: A cognitive neuropsychological approach. *Cognitive Neuropsychiatry*, **2**, 167–93.

Larøi, F., Fannemel, M., Ronneberg, U., Flekkoy, K., Opjordsmoen, S., Dullerud, R., *et al.* (2000). Unawareness of illness in chronic schizophrenia and its relationship to structural brain measures and neuropsychological tests. *Psychiatry Research*, **100**, 49–58.

Lele, M. V. and Joglekar, A. S. (1998). Poor insight in schizophrenia: Neurocognitive basis. *Journal of Postgraduate Medicine*, **44**, 50–5.

Lopez, O. L., Becker, J. T., Somsak, D., Dew, M. A. and DeKosky, S. T. (1994). Awareness of cognitive deficits and anosognosia in probable alzheimer's disease. *European Neurology*, **34**, 277–82.

Luks, T. L., Simpson, G. V., Feiwell, R. J. and Miller, W. L. (2002). Evidence for anterior cingulate cortex involvement in monitoring preparatory attentional set. *NeuroImage*, **17**, 792–802.

Lysaker, P. and Bell, M. (1994). Insight and cognitive impairment in schizophrenia: Performance on repeated administrations of the Wisconsin card sorting test. *Journal of Nervous and Mental Disease*, **182**, 656–60.

Lysaker, P. and Bell, M. (1998). *Impaired Insight in Schizophrenia: Advances from psychosocial treatment research.* Oxford, England: Oxford University Press.

Lysaker, P. H., Bryson, G. J. and Bell, M. D. (2002). Insight and work performance in schizophrenia. *Journal of Nervous and Mental Disease*, **190**, 142–6.

Mangone, C. A., Hier, D. B., Gorelick, P. B., Ganellen, R. J., Langenberg, P., Boarman, R., *et al.* (1991). Impaired insight in alzheimer's disease. *Journal of Geriatric Psychiatry and Neurology*, **4**, 189–93.

Manoach, D. S., Gollub, R. L., Benson, E. S., Searl, M. M., Goff, D. C., Halpern, E., *et al.* (2000). Schizophrenic subjects show aberrant fMRI activation of dorsolateral prefrontal cortex and basal ganglia during working memory performance. *Biological Psychiatry*, **48**, 99–109.

Manoach, D. S., Press, D. Z., Thangaraj, V., Searl, M. M., Goff, D. C., Halpern, E., *et al.* (1999). Schizophrenic subjects activate dorsolateral prefrontal cortex during a working memory task, as measured by fMRI. *Biological Psychiatry*, **45**, 1128–37.

Mazza, M., De Risio, A., Surian, L., Roncone, R. and Casacchia, M. (2001). Selective impairments of theory of mind in people with schizophrenia. *Schizophrenia Research*, **47**, 299–308.

McCarthy, G., Puce, A., Constable, R. T., Krystal, J. H., Gore, J. C. and Goldman-Rakic, P. (1996). Activation of human prefrontal cortex during spatial and nonspatial working memory tasks measured by functional MRI. *Cerebral Cortex*, **6**, 600–11.

McEvoy, J. P., Freter, S., Merritt, M. and Apperson, L. J. (1993). Insight about psychosis among outpatients with schizophrenia. *Hospital and Community Psychiatry*, **44**, 883–4.

McEvoy, J. P., Hartman, M., Gottlieb, D., Godwin, S., Apperson, L. J. and Wilson, W. (1996). Common sense, insight, and neuropsychological test performance in schizophrenia patients. *Schizophrenia Bulletin*, **22**, 635–41.

McGlashan, T. H. and Carpenter, W. T. J. (1976). Postpsychotic depression in schizophrenia. *Archives of General Psychiatry*, **33**, 231–9.

McGlashan, T. H., Levy, S. T. and Carpenter, W. T. J. (1975). Integration and sealing over: Clinically distinct recovery styles from schizophrenia. *Archives of General Psychiatry*, **32**, 1269–72.

McGuire, P. K., Silbersweig, D. A. and Frith, C. D. (1996). Functional neuroanatomy of verbal self-monitoring. *Brain*, **119**, 907–17.

McGuire, P. K., Silbersweig, D. A., Wright, I., Murray, R. M., David, A. S., Frackowiak, R. S., *et al.* (1995). Abnormal monitoring of inner speech: A physiological basis for auditory hallucinations. *The Lancet*, **346**, 596–600.

Mechanic, D., McAlpine, D., Rosenfield, S. and Davis, D. (1994). Effects of illness attribution and depression on the quality of life among persons with serious mental illness. *Society of Science and Medicine*, **39**, 155–64.

Menon, V., Anagnoson, R. T., Mathalon, D. H., Glover, G. H. and Pfefferbaum, A. (2001). Functional neuroanatomy of auditory working memory in schizophrenia: Relation to positive and negative symptoms. *NeuroImage*, **13**, 433–46.

Meyer-Lindenberg, A., Poline, J. B., Kohn, P. D., Holt, J. L., Egan, M. F., Weinberger, D. R., *et al.* (2001). Evidence for abnormal cortical functional connectivity during working memory in schizophrenia. *American Journal of Psychiatry*, **158**, 1809–17.

Michon, A., Deweer, B., Pillon, B., Agid, Y. and Dubois, B. (1994). Relation of anosognosia to frontal lobe dysfunction in alzheimer's disease. *Journal of Neurology, Neurosurgery and Psychiatry*, **57**, 805–9.

Migliorelli, R., Teson, A., Sabe, L., Petracca, G., Petracchi, M., Leiguarda, R., *et al.* (1995). Anosognosia in Alzheimer's disease: A study of associated factors. *Journal of Neuropsychiatry*, **7**, 338–44.

Mohamed, S., Fleming, S., Penn, D. L. and Spaulding, W. (1999). Insight in schizophrenia: Its relationship to measures of executive functions. *Journal of Nervous and Mental Disorders*, **187**, 525–31.

Morecraft, R. J., Geula, C. and Mesulam, M. M. (1992). Cytoarchitecture and neural afferents of orbitofrontal cortex in the brain of the monkey. *Journal of Comparative Neurology*, **323**, 341–58.

Morgan, K. D., Dazzan, P., et al. (2002). *Neuroanatomic correlates of poor insight: The aesop first-onset psychosis study*. Presented at the Biennial Winter Workshop on Schizophrenia, Davos.

Mujica-Parodi, L. R., Malaspina, D. and Sackeim, H. A. (2000). Logical processing, affect, and delusional thought in schizophrenia. *Harvard Review of Psychiatry*, **8**, 73–83.

Nelson, E. A. (1997). *'Poor insight' as a manifestation of psychological defensiveness in schizophrenia*. Unpublished doctoral dissertation. New York University, Department of Psychology.

Nordahl, T. E., Carter, C. S., Salo, R. E., Kraft, L., Baldo, J., Salamat, S., *et al.* (2001). Anterior cingulate metabolism correlates with stroop errors in paranoid schizophrenic patients. *Neuropsychopharmacology*, **25**, 139–48.

Novak-Grubic, V. and Tavcar, R. (2002). Predictors of noncompliance in males with first-episode schizophrenia, schizophreniform and schizoaffective disorder. *European Psychiatry: the Journal of the Association of European Psychiatrists*, **17**, 148–54.

Ott, B. R., Lafleche, G., Whelihan, W. M., Buongiorno, G. W., Albert, M. S. and Fogel, B. S. (1996). Impaired awareness of deficits in Alzheimer's disease. *Alzheimer Disease and Associated Disorders*, **10**, 68–76.

Owen, A. M., Evans, A. C. and Petrides, M. (1996). Evidence for a two-stage model of spatial working memory processing within the lateral frontal cortex: A positron emission tomography study. *Cerebral Cortex*, **6**, 31–8.

Park, S., Puschel, J., Sauter, B. H., Rentsch, M. and Hell, D. (1999). Spatial working memory deficits and clinical symptoms in schizophrenia: A 4-month follow-up study. *Biological Psychiatry*, **46**, 392–400.

Paulesu, E., Frith, C. D. and Frackowiak, R. S. (1993). The neural correlates of the verbal component of working memory. *Nature*, **362**, 342–5.

Petrides, M., Alivisatos, B., Evans, A. C. and Meyer, E. (1993). Functional activation of the human frontal cortex during the performance of verbal working memory tasks. *Proceedings of the National Academy of Sciences, USA*, **90**, 878–82.

Pini, S., Cassano, G. B., Dell'Osso, L. and Amador, X. F. (2001). Insight into illness in schizophrenia, schizoaffective disorder, and mood disorders with psychotic features. *American Journal of Psychiatry*, **158**, 122–5.

Reed, B. R., Jagust, W. J. and Coulter, L. (1993). Anosognosia in Alzheimer's disease: Relationships to depression, cognitive function, and cerebral perfusion. *Journal of Clinical and Experimental Neuropsychology*, **15**, 231–44.

Reisberg, B., Gordon, B. and McCarthy, M. (1985). Clinical symptoms accompanying progressive cognitive decline and Alzheimer's disease. In V. L. Melnick and N. N. Dubler (ed.) *Alzheimer's Dementia*. Clifton, NJ: Humana Press.

Rossell, S. L, Coakes, J., Shapeleske, J., Woodruff, P. W. R. and David, A. S. (2003). Insight: its relationship with cognitive function, brain volume and symptoms in schizophrenia. *Psychological Medicine*, **33**, 111–19.

Russell, T. A., Rubia, K., Bullmore, E. T., Soni, W., Suckling, J., Brammer, M. J., *et al.* (2000). Exploring the social brain in schizophrenia: Left prefrontal underactivation during mental state attribution. *American Journal of Psychiatry*, **157**, 2040–2.

Sackeim, H. A. and Wegner, A. Z. (1986). Attributional patterns in depression and euthymia. *Archives of General Psychiatry*, **43**, 553–60.

Salisbury, D. F., Shenton, M. E., Griggs, C. B., Bonner-Jackson, A. and McCarley, R. W. (2002). Mismatch negativity in chronic schizophrenia and first-episode schizophrenia. *Archives of General Psychiatry*, **59**, 686–94.

Sarfati, Y., Hardy-Baylé, M. C., Besche, C. and Wildlocher, D. (1997a). Attribution of intentions to others in people with schizophrenia: A non-verbal exploration with comic strips. *Schizophrenia Research*, **25**, 199–209.

Sarfati, Y., Hardy-Baylé, M.-C., Brunet, E. and Widlocher, D. (1999). Investigating theory of mind in schizophrenia: Influence of verbalization in disorganized and non-disorganized patients. *Schizophrenia Research*, **37**, 183–90.

Sarfati, Y., Hardy-Baylé, M.-C., Nadel, J., Chevalier, J.-F. and Widlocher, D. (1997b). Attribution of mental states to others by schizophrenic patients. *Cognitive Neuropsychiatry*, **2**, 1–17.

Schwartz, R. C., Skaggs, J. L. and Petersen, S. (2000). Critique of recent empirical research on insight and symptomatology in schizophrenia. *Psychological Reports*, **86**, 471–4.

Seltzer, B., Vasterling, J. J., Mathias, C. W. and Brennan, A. (2001). Clinical and neuropsychological correlates of impaired awareness of deficits in alzheimer disease and parkinson disease: A comparative study. *Neuropsychiatry, Neuropsychology, and Behavioral Neurology*, **14**, 122–9.

Smith, E. E. and Jonides, J. (1998). Neuroimaging analyses of human working memory. *Proceedings of the National Academy of Sciences USA*, **95**, 12061–8.

Smith, E. E. and Jonides, J. (1999). Storage and executive processes in the frontal lobes. *Science*, **283**, 1657–61.

Smith, E. E., Jonides, J., Marshuetz, C. and Koeppe, R. A. (1998). Components of verbal working memory: Evidence from neuroimaging. *Proceedings of the National Academy of Sciences USA*, **95**, 876–82.

Smith, T. E., Hull, J. W., Israel, L. M. and Willson, D. F. (2000). Insight, symptoms, and neurocognition in schizophrenia and schizoaffective disorder. *Schizophrenia Bulletin*, **6**, 193–200.

Spence, S. A., Brooks, D. J., Hirsch, S. R., Liddle, P. F., Meehan, J. and Grasby, P. M. (1997). A PET study of voluntary movement in schizophrenic patients experiencing passivity phenomena (delusions of alien control). *Brain*, **120**, 1997–2011.

Starkstein, S. E., Chemerinski, E., Sabe, L., Kuzis, G., Petracca, G., Teson, A., *et al.* (1997a). Prospective longitudinal study of depression and anosognosia in Alzheimer's disease. *British Journal of Psychiatry*, **171**, 47–52.

Starkstein, S. E., Sabe, L., Cuerva, A. G., Kuzis, G. and Leiguarda, R. (1997b). Anosognosia and procedural learning in Alzheimer's disease. *Neuropsychiatry, Neuropsychology, and Behavioral Neurology*, **10**, 96–101.

Starkstein, S. E., Sabe, L., Petracca, G., Chemerinski, E., Kuzis, G., Merello, M., *et al.* (1996). Neuropsychological and psychiatric differences between Alzheimer's disease and parkinson's disease with dementia. *Journal of Neurology, Neurosurgery and Psychiatry*, **61**, 381–7.

Starkstein, S. E., Vazquez, S., Migliorelli, R., Teson, A., Sabe, L. and Leiguarda, R. (1995). A single-photon emission computed tomographic study of anosognosia in Alzheimer's disease. *Archives of Neurology*, **52**, 415–20.

Stuss, D. T. and Benson, D. F. (1986). *The Frontal Lobes*. New York: Raven Press.

Takai, A., Uematsu, M., Ueki, H., Sone, K. and Kaiya, H. (1992). Insight and its related factors in chronic schizophrenic patients: A preliminary study. *European Journal of Psychiatry*, **6**, 159–70.

Tournois, J., Mesnil, F. and Kop, J.-L. (2000). Self-deception and other-deception: A social desirability questionnaire. *European Review of Applied Psychology*, **50**, 219–33.

van Veen, V., Cohen, J. D., Botvinick, M. M., Stenger, V. A. and Carter, C. S. (2001). Anterior cingulate cortex, conflict monitoring, and levels of processing. *NeuroImage*, **14**, 1302–8.

Vitale, C., Pellecchia, M. T., Grossi, D., Fragassi, N., Cuomo, T., Di Maio, L., *et al.* (2001). Unawareness of dyskinesias in Parkinson's and Huntington's diseases. *Neurological Sciences*, **22**, 105–6.

Vogeley, K., Bussfeld, P., Newen, A., Herrmann, S., Happé, F., Falkai, P., *et al.* (2001). Mind reading: Neural mechanisms of theory of mind and self perspective. *NeuroImage*, **14**, 170–81.

Warner, R., Taylor, D., Powers, M. and Hyman, J. (1989). Acceptance of the mental illness label by psychotic patients: Effects on functioning. *American Journal of Orthopsychiatry*, **59**, 398–409.

Weiler, M. A., Fleisher, M. H. and McArthur-Campbell, D. (2000). Insight and symptom change in schizophrenia and other disorders. *Schizophrenia Research*, **45**, 29–36.

White, R., Bebbington, P., Pearson, J., Johnson, S. and Ellis, D. (2000). The social context of insight in schizophrenia. *Society of Psychiatry and Psychiatric Epidemiology*, **35**, 500–7.

Young, D., Zakzanis, K. K., Bailey, C., Davila, R., Griese, J., Sartory, G., *et al.* (1998). Further parameters of insight and neuropsychological deficit in schizophrenia and other chronic mental disease. *Journal of Nervous and Mental Disease*, **186**, 44–50.

Young, D. A., Davila, R. and Scher, H. (1993). Unawareness of illness and neuropsychological performance in chronic schizophrenia. *Schizophrenia Research*, **10**, 117–24.

Chapter 9

Neuropsychological studies of insight in patients with psychotic disorders

Kevin D. Morgan and Anthony S. David

Introduction

In his 1934 paper "The Psychopathology of Insight", Aubrey Lewis advocated that poor illness awareness is rooted in neuropsychological dysfunction. Lewis argued that poor insight arose from ". . . a physiological disturbance of cerebral function, interfering with the integration of the contributory or part function" (Lewis, 1934). This somewhat speculative hypothesis was made in the absence of any empirical investigation. For the next 55 years the concept of an insight–cognition link eluded any concerted scientific enquiry and remained an essentially hypothetical construct. In the last 10 years however, the relationship between insight and cognitive function in the psychoses has become the focus of over 40 research investigations. While each of those studies has contributed to a growing body of data about the cognitive mechanisms that underlie poor insight, a clear understanding of the relationship between insight and cognition remains elusive. The lack of clarity arises from the inconsistent findings that frequently emerge from insight–cognition studies. Understanding why those inconsistencies occur will be crucial to identifying the neuropsychological architecture that underpins the capacity for illness awareness in the psychoses. In this review therefore, we first report on the main findings of insight–cognition investigations and then consider which factors might contribute to difficulties in their replication. Such factors may include: variations in the way insight is defined and measured; the particular aspects of neuropsychological function under investigation; and the clinical profile of study groups. The focus of the review will be on the behavioural aspect of neurocognition (i.e. the performance of subjects under test conditions). References from the literature were obtained by search of the electronic databases: Medline, PsychInfo, PubMed and Web of Science, using the keywords: insight, awareness, psychosis(es), psychotic disorder, schizophrenia, mania, neuropsychology, cognition, neurocognition, intelligence. Studies examining the possible neuroanatomical abnormalities underlying that behaviour are not included in this chapter as this subject area is described in detail elsewhere in this volume (Chapter 10).

Insight and IQ

Several studies have shown an association between reduced general intellectual functioning (usually measured by IQ) and poor insight (David *et al.*, 1992, 1995; Young *et al.*, 1993, 1998; Fennig *et al.*, 1996; MacPherson *et al.*, 1996; Startup, 1996; Marks *et al.*, 2000; Smith *et al.*, 2000; Lysaker *et al.*, 2002). The studies referred to have included patients with a range of clinical characteristics in terms of illness duration (recent onset and chronic), diagnostic classification (schizophrenia and affective psychoses) and illness severity (inpatients and outpatients). Both current IQ (e.g. Weschler Adult Intelligence Scale-Revised (WAIS-R)) and estimates of pre-morbid IQ (e.g. National Adult Reading Test (NART)) were used in those studies. Confirming an unequivocal association between lower intelligence and reduced insight has, however, proved to be difficult. Several investigations of insight in the psychoses have failed to find an insight–IQ association (Takai, 1992; McEvoy *et al.*, 1993; Almeida *et al.*, 1996; Ghaemi *et al.*, 1996; Kemp and David, 1996; Dickerson *et al.*, 1997; Sanz *et al.*, 1998; Carroll *et al.*, 1999; McCabe *et al.*, 2002). The same IQ tests (e.g. WAIS-R and NART) have been used in these studies.

This contradictory evidence could indicate that intellectual function is related to insight but that there is only a weak association. Higher levels of illness awareness may be partly dependent on higher levels of intellectual functioning, but other factors may also be implicated. It is, perhaps, unlikely that small variations in IQ levels could make a discernible difference in the conscious awareness of a psychotic episode experience per se. It might be the interpretation and attribution of anomalous mental experiences that is hampered by poor general cognition. It is also possible that insight questionnaires are no more than a form of IQ test and that low ratings on those schedules merely reflect a patient's current general intellectual functioning. According to this line of argument, educational levels could have an important influence in how patients respond to items on insight questionnaires. A poor or restricted education may limit the range of vocabulary and other linguistic skills necessary to understand and convey a perception of illness awareness. In other words, a major influence on insight levels may be one of information *availability* rather than one of information *processing*. Lewis (1934) commented on the manner in which psychotic patients communicate knowledge about changes in their mental (and somatic) function.

> It is our first ground for assessing his insight, or more correctly, his requisite for insight. Much of his difficulty in describing the change will be due to the inadequacy of words to cover such unfamiliar experiences.

This proposition suggests that ratings of insight are partly dependent on the ability of patients to articulate their abnormal psychological experiences. If the proficient use of language were to be a moderating factor, one would expect to find ratings of good insight occurring more often in patients who have a better educational background. The majority of findings from recent studies of insight do not support this notion. Several researchers have analysed the potential link between insight and years of education and have found no significant relationship between the two factors (Amador *et al.*, 1993; Young *et al.*, 1993; Cuesta and Peralta, 1994; Lysaker and Bell, 1994; Cuesta *et al.*, 1996; Dickerson *et al.*, 1997; Lysaker *et al.*, 1998a; Peralta and Cuesta, 1998; Larøi *et al.*, 2000; White *et al.*, 2000; Goldberg *et al.*, 2001; Pyne *et al.*, 2001). A small number of studies (e.g. Kemp and David, 1996; MacPherson *et al.*, 1996) have reported poor insight to be significantly correlated with less years of education, but findings such as these are uncommon. There is some evidence, however, that patients with psychosis and poor insight have retained the ability to apply knowledge of mental health situations to other psychiatric patients, but not to themselves. Startup (1997) studied a group of 28 patients with schizophrenia. The patients were presented with psychiatric case study vignettes and asked to indicate how likely it was that the individuals in the depicted scenarios had mental illnesses. Patients with low insight could distinguish between descriptions of psychotic symptoms and normal thoughts, and abnormal feelings and behaviours, as well as controls and health professionals. Thus it seems unlikely that insight is simply a reflection of one's educational background.

The association between insight and general intellectual functioning may indicate that more specific cognitive deficits than those of reduced IQ have a greater impact on insight. This perhaps would be more consistent with the intellectual functioning observed in neurological patients who show no or little awareness of their symptoms (a condition known as anosognosia). Babinski (1914) and Cutting (1978) have reported that patients with anosognosia do not demonstrate a loss of general intellectual capacities. Patients with the condition of anosognosia have, however, been observed to perform poorly on cognitive tasks that make demands on concept formation and flexibility of abstract thought (Starkstein *et al.*, 1993).

Insight and specific deficits of cognition

A range of cognitive tests have been employed to analyse insight in relation to several cognitive functions (e.g. executive function, set-shifting, verbal fluency, working memory, visual–spatial skills, attention, visual memory, verbal memory). The selection of particular neuropsychological tests has been based on studies of neurological patients with awareness deficits and on studies of the psychoses where cognition is most disrupted. In terms of neurological patients, locating the neuroanatomical site or network of cortical structures underlying disturbances to illness awareness has proved difficult. Some theories attribute the disorder to focal brain abnormalities, usually in the right hemisphere parietal area, while others suggest a more global cortical deficit underlies the condition. It has also been suggested that lesions to the frontal lobes may be implicated in deficits of awareness. In a presentation similar to the anosodiaphoria which is seen in stroke victims, people with frontal lobe damage commonly show a lack of concern about their condition and its impact on their lives and on those around them (Goldberg *et al.*, 1987). Stuss and Benson (1986) argue that the frontal lobes are an integral part of a neural mechanism that facilitates self-awareness, and that this mechanism is disrupted in patients with anosognosia.

The cognitive profile of many patients with schizophrenia is characterized by an inflexibility of thought that includes a tendency to perseverate in the use of mental and behavioural sets (Schultz and Searleman, 2002), and difficulties in the active processing and transient storage of information (working memory), abstract reasoning, concept formation and decision-making (Elvevag and Goldberg, 2000). All these aspects of cognitive function are thought to be dependent, at least to some degree, on the prefrontal cortex. Thus, many tests used in the analysis of insight are those thought to be dependent on prefrontal lobe function.

The Wisconsin Card Sorting Test (WCST) is the most commonly used test of frontal lobe function in insight–cognition studies. The WCST consists of a set of cards that vary according to the number, colour and shape of symbols displayed on the face of the cards (e.g. two blue stars or three red triangles). Participants are asked to sort the cards into sets according to a particular matching principle (number, colour or shape). The matching principle is not disclosed to the participants, who are only told whether they were correct or incorrect after each attempt to sort a card. Each time a set of 10 cards is successfully made, the matching principle changes. The two main scores derived from the test are "categories completed" (measured according to the number of sets made during the task) and "perseverative errors" (when the participant continues to sort according to the previous principle). Perseverative errors suggest problems in forming concepts, profiting from correction/feedback, and conceptual/mental flexibility.

The majority of insight studies (12/19) employing the WCST have reported a significant association between poor test performance and impaired insight (see Table 9.1).

Table 9.1 Studies of Insight and the Wisconsin Card Sorting Task

Insight associated with WCST Performance			
YES		**NO**	
Investigators	Patient group (n)	Investigators	Patient group (n)
Rossell et al. (2003)	Schizophrenia (78)		
Lysaker (2002)	Schizophrenia (121)		
Chen et al. (2001)	Mixed psychosis (80)		
Larøi et al. (2000)	Schizophrenia (21)		
Smith et al. (2000)	Schizophrenia (46)		
Marks et al. (1999)	Schizophrenia (59)	Simon et al. (2001)	Schizophrenia (38)
Young et al. (1998)	Schizophrenia (108)	Goldberg et al. (2001)	Schizophrenia (128)
Lysaker et al. (1998)	Schizophrenia (81)	Sanz et al. (1998)	Mixed psychosis (33)
Voruganti (1997)	Schizophrenia (52)	Dickerson et al. (1997)	Schizophrenia (87)
McEvoy et al. (1996)	Schizophrenia (32)	Collins et al. (1997)	Schizophrenia (58)
Lysaker & Bell (1994)	Schizophrenia (92)	Ghaemi et al. (1996)	Bipolar disorder (16)
Young et al. (1993)	Mixed psychosis (91)	Cuesta et al. (1995)	Mixed psychosis (49)

On the basis of such findings it has been suggested that impaired insight results, at least in part, from a compromise to frontal lobe and executive function (Lysaker *et al.*, 1998). It is of note that associations between insight and WCST test performance are found most frequently in relation to errors of perseveration. This type of error is made when participants are acting according to an established rule (e.g. where "red" denotes the set) and are unable to switch to a new rule. Thus, when confronted with a change of rule, and despite feedback to the contrary, they fail to conceptualize the new rule and continue instead with the previous (and now redundant) one. Analogies have been made between errors such as these in the WCST and an impaired ability to appraise psychotic events and illness. Larøi *et al.* (2000) have suggested, for example, that the cognitive processes underlying the inability to identify a change of rule (shift cognitive set) in the WCST may also underlie the apparent unawareness of the unreality of delusions regardless of evidence to the contrary. Similarly, Lysaker and Bell (1994) have argued that "psychotic patients with poor insight persevere in denial of illness despite every indication to the contrary".

The association between insight and set-shifting skills has also been examined with other neuropsychological test instruments. After the WCST, the most commonly used set-shifting assessment instrument in insight studies has been the Trail Making B Test (Reitan, 1958). In Trail Making B, participants draw lines to connect consecutively numbered and lettered (in alphabetical order) circles on a sheet of paper. The participants are required to alternate between the letter and number sequences. Scores for the task are based on completion time. Like the WCST, Trail Making B is thought to be dependent on prefrontal lobe function. It is of interest that an association between insight scores and Trail Making B completion times is found considerably less frequently than those relating to the WCST and insight. Only three studies (Kemp and David, 1996; Buckley *et al.*, 2001; Drake and Lewis, 2003) have reported a significant association between insight and Trail Making B times. (Drake and Lewis combined scores for Trail Making B and the Brixton Test into a composite measure of set-shifting). On the other hand, seven studies using the same test have failed to find such an association (Young *et al.*, 1993; Cuesta and Peralta, 1994; David *et al.*, 1995; Dickerson *et al.*, 1997; Sanz *et al.*, 1998; Larøi *et al.*, 2000; Simon *et al.*, 2001).

In respect of its relevance to the cognitive mechanisms of insight, Drake and Lewis (2003) hypothesize that an aspect of cognition that is related to both the mechanism of insight and the ability to change cognitive set is the capacity to "hold an abstract representation related to an actual situation, but different from it, at the same time as the more obvious immediate representation". The variance in findings relating to the WCST and trail making suggest there may be a high level of specificity in the cognitive resources for which insight is most dependent. That is to say, while it is likely that both tasks measure some aspect of executive function and set-shifting, there may be particular features of that function in the WCST that equate more closely with the cognitive demands of illness appraisal than those found in other tasks such as trail making. For example, the cognitive "set" in Trail Making B alternates with every single trial, thus limiting the chance of the particular rule (numerical or alphabetical order) becoming entrenched. This is in contrast to the WCST where a particular cognitive set such as "blue" or "stars" becomes an established routine over the course of 10 trials.

Verbal fluency is a classic neuropsychological test of language production. In the task, participants produce as many words as possible beginning with a nominated letter (without repeating previously vocalized words). Subjects monitor their word production and inhibit the tendency to perseverate. Like the WCST and Trail Making B, verbal fluency is thought to be a task dependent on frontal-executive function. It might be expected that a task of frontal lobe function that is combined with knowledge and production of language would show some association with poor insight. However, the ratio of positive to null findings is similar to those reported in studies of insight and trail making. Eight studies measuring insight and verbal fluency failed to find an association between the two factors (McEvoy, 1993; Young et al., 1993; Cuesta and Peralta, 1994; Almeida et al., 1996; Ghaemi et al., 1996; McEvoy et al., 1996; Dickerson et al., 1997; Smith et al., 2000). Only two studies, Kemp and David (1996) and Simon et al. (2001) reported a significant association between insight and verbal fluency.

Some theories relating to awareness deficits in neurological patients attribute their lack of awareness to right hemisphere parietal abnormalities (Von Hagen and Ives, 1939; Gerstman, 1942; Critchley, 1953; Warrington, 1962; Geschwind, 1965; cited in Amador and Kronegold, 1998, p. 26). Thus, in addition to tests measuring frontal-executive function, neuropsychological tests thought to be dependent on parietal lobe function (right and left) have also been utilized in the search for neuropsychological correlates of insight. In a study of 32 patients with schizophrenia, McEvoy et al. (1996) found that performance on the Right–Left orientation test (a test of left parietal function) correlated with insight ratings. In the same study other tests of parietal function e.g. judgement of line orientation (right parietal) and the finger localization test (left parietal) were not associated with measures of insight. Other investigations (e.g. Cuesta and Peralta, 1994; David et al., 1995; Dickerson et al., 1997; Smith et al., 2000) have been unable to find a correlation between tests of parietal lobe function and insight scores.

Links between insight and other aspects of cognition such as memory and attention have also been investigated, although less frequently than those relating to general intelligence and frontal lobe functioning. As with the findings relating to parietal lobe function, significant associations with insight are rarely found. Cuesta and Peralta (1994) observed that lack of insight was associated with better performance on both verbal and visual memory tasks and Marks et al. (2000) reported correlations between insight and tests of verbal memory. However, other studies investigating potential associations between insight and visual and verbal memory have failed to find such an association (McEvoy et al., 1993; Almeida et al., 1996; Lysaker et al., 1998). In terms of tasks of attention, Marks et al. (2000) assessed attention in 59 patients with schizophrenia using the Letter–Number sequencing and the symbol search subtests of the WAIS-lll and found no association with scores for insight. Almeida et al. (1996) and Smith et al.

(2000) also investigated the relationship between insight and attention and were unable to find an association between the two factors. Although uncommon, associations between insight and performance on tasks of attention have been reported. Voruganti *et al.* (1997), for example, found insight scores to correlate with Asarnow's Vigilance and span of apprehension task.

In terms of specific aspects of cognition, associations with insight have been found across a broad range of tests. However, most of the findings appear difficult to replicate and there is perhaps only some consistency with respect to studies using the WCST (and several null findings have been reported when this test is utilized). Nonetheless, it is perhaps noteworthy that the WCST, a task relatively free of language skills rather than one more directly concerned with verbal ability, such as verbal fluency, has the strongest link with insight. This suggests that insight has a closer association with non-verbal skills rather than language-based cognitive abilities. The notion that linguistically based aspects of cognition are less associated with insight is perhaps somewhat counterintuitive. Skills such as these are likely to have a significant impact on the capacity to understand and express ideas about a mental illness. It may be that important nonverbal aspects of cognition are crucially concerned with the self-evaluation of one's mental status.

The effect of IQ

In schizophrenia, the extent to which reduced global intelligence affects performance on tasks thought to be dependent on more specific aspects of cognition is unclear. In a number of cognition studies it has been observed that mental flexibility in schizophrenia is impaired irrespective of general intelligence levels (Iddon *et al.*, 1998; Elliott *et al.*, 2000; Elvevag and Goldberg, 2000). On the other hand, a meta-analysis of 29 studies examining WCST performance in schizophrenia found that the poor test performance reflected a generalized intellectual deficit (Laws, 2001). It might be possible, therefore, that the association between poor insight and impaired performance on tasks such as the WCST might also be mediated by reduced global intelligence. Twelve studies reporting a significant association between insight and a specific aspect of cognition have also examined the possible effect of IQ on the cognition – insight relationship (see Table 9.2). In those studies, the analyses took account of the patients' IQ scores so that an appraisal could be made as to whether the observed associations are relatively independent of general cognitive function. In 10 of those studies the insight – cognition associations appear to be independent of the effects of general intellectual functioning.

An appraisal of confounding factors

Some studies have pointed to a clear relationship between insight and cognition while others have found no such association. In this section we consider which factors may be most influential in the inconsistent insight–cognition findings.

Table 9.2 Insight and cognition: the effect of IQ

Studies where IQ was not independent of insight–cognition association			
Investigators	Patient group (n)	Insight associated with:	IQ measure
Rossell et al. (2003)	Schizophrenia (78)	WCST	NART
Lysaker et al. (2002)	Schizophrenia (121)	WCST	WAIS 111
Studies where IQ was independent of insight–cognition association			
Investigators	Patient group (n)	Insight associated with:	IQ measure
Drake & Lewis (2003)	Mixed psychosis (33)	Set shifting & perseveration	NART/Quick Test
McCabe et al. (2002)	Schizophrenia (78)	LNNB arithmetic function	LNNB Int. function
Smith et al. (2000)	Schizophrenia (46)	WCST	WAIS-R
Larøi et al. (2000)	Schizophrenia (21)	WCST	WAIS-R
Mohamed et al. (1999)	Schizophrenia (46)	Range of cognitive tests	WAIS-R
Marks et al. (1999)	Schizophrenia (59)	WCST	AMNART
Lysaker et al. (1998)	Schizophrenia (108)	WCST	WAIS-R
Startup (1996)	Schizophrenia (26)	Range of cognitive tests	Ravens/Spot-the-Word
Lysaker & Bell (1994)	Schizophrenia (92)	WCST	Slosson Int. Test
Young et al. (1993)	Schizophrenia (31)	WCST	WAIS-R

WCST = Wisconsin Card Sorting Task, NART = National Adult Reading Test, WAIS 111 = Weschler Adult Intelligence Scale Version Three, WAIS-R = Weschler Adult Intelligence Scale Revised, LNNB = Luria-Nebraska Neuropsychological Battery, AMNART = American NART, Ravens = Ravens Progressive Matrices

Instruments and components

The manner in which insight is assessed varies considerably across different studies. In some studies of insight and cognition (e.g. Lysaker et al., 1998; David et al., 1992) a single item from either the Positive and Negative Symptom Scales (PANSS) (Kay et al., 1987) or the Present State Examination (PSE) (Wing et al., 1974) is used as a gauge for insight. In other investigations, researchers have used more expansive rating scales such as the 11 item Schedule for the Assessment of Insight: Expanded version (SAI-E) (Kemp and David, 1997) or the 74 item Scale to assess Unawareness of Mental Disorder (SUMD, Amador et al., 1994). Furthermore, even when the same insight instrument is used there may be a considerable variation across researchers in terms of how the instrument's scores are used to operationalize insight.

When insight measures are based on a single or very limited number of items, those ratings will be confined to a single or global aspect of insight such as illness awareness. In contrast, multi-item scales are usually designed for the measurement of more than one component of insight (e.g. illness awareness, symptom relabelling and treatment compliance). Variation in the type of insight instruments used represents a substantial methodological problem when trying to make cross-study comparisons. First, the type of schedule used (e.g. brief or long) may, in itself, impose different cognitive demands on the respondent. A schedule with very few items can be completed quickly with little mental fatigue. Other instruments, such as the 74 item SUMD, a thorough but complex interview used to assess awareness across multiple domains and periods, may present difficulties for participants with slowed or abnormal cognition. Indeed, relationships between WCST performance and insight are predominately found in studies using the SUMD. The variation in which aspect of insight is being measured (i.e. unidimensional or multidimensional) is probably even more likely to confound cross-study analyses of insight and cognition. Are there specific aspects of insight that are more closely associated with neuropsychological function and are there specific aspects of cognition that are more closely related to insight? Illness awareness and treatment compliance, for example, are probably less subject to general cognitive demands and more subject to social and cultural factors when compared to the ability to identify and relabel symptom as pathological.

There appears to be clear evidence that the type of insight instrument used does indeed have an impact on the findings of insight–cognition studies. In an analysis of insight–cognition studies using either the PANSS, SUMD, ITAQ (Insight and Treatment Attitudes Questionnaire) or SAI (the four most commonly used instruments in insight–cognition studies) it is evident that associations between insight and cognition in studies using the SUMD are found more frequently than those using the other three measures of insight. This apparent "insight instrument bias" applies to both general intellectual functioning and more specific aspects of cognition, e.g. mental flexibility (see Figures 9.1 and 9.2).

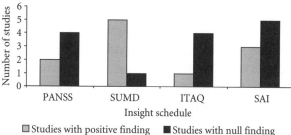

Fig. 9.1 Studies of insight and IQ: Do the findings vary according to insight scale?

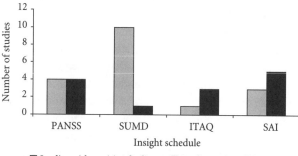

* Tests of mental flexibility include the WCST, Trail Making B & Verbal Fluency

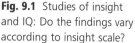

Fig. 9.2 Studies of insight and mental flexibility*: Do the findings vary according to insight scale used?

Associations between insight and cognition may be stronger in those processes of self-appraisal least affected by external influences such as social and cultural variations. The cognitive mechanisms that subserve the identification of individual psychotic symptoms as pathological may be more independent of those external influences than the processes that underlie the self-perception of being a psychiatric patient. Reduced symptom relabelling abilities may therefore be more closely related to deficits in cognitive functioning than other domains of insight such as illness awareness and treatment compliance. In this respect, it is of note that studies using the SUMD, an insight schedule with a focus on symptom awareness and attribution, demonstrate a considerably higher rate of insight–cognition associations than studies using other schedules. Thus, it is perhaps not surprising that associations between insight and cognition are rarely found in studies using the ITAQ, an insight schedule particularly sensitive to attitudes towards medication, hospitalization and follow-up treatment programs. With respect to the PANSS, insight ratings are based on a single item that reflects a combined measure of symptom recognition and attitudes to treatment. Like the ITAQ, the PANSS may also be less sensitive to the detection of insight–cognition associations. Separate ratings of illness awareness, symptom relabelling and treatment compliance are possible with the SAI. In SAI studies that have analysed those dimensions individually, associations of cognitive performance and symptom relabelling have been observed more frequently than those with illness awareness or treatment compliance (McCabe *et al.*, 2002; Drake and Lewis, 2003; Morgan *et al.*, 2001).

Clinical factors

A further potential confound for insight–cognition studies is cross-study variation in the clinical profile of the participant being assessed. Cognitive disruption to insight may vary according to a number of clinical factors including diagnostic category, illness severity, illness duration and medication regimen.

Diagnosis

Within the framework of a cognitive model of poor insight, it is perhaps not surprising that it is in schizophrenia, the psychotic disorder with most cognitive disruption, that there is most disruption to insight. The effect that variations in the patients' diagnostic status may have on studies of insight and cognition where there are mixed diagnostic samples is, however, unclear. It could be hypothesized, for example, that associations between insight and cognition in the psychoses are more likely to be found in "schizophrenia-only" patient samples. At the time of writing this review, data was available on five studies where analyses of insight–cognition associations in non-schizophrenic psychotic patients was made (Cuesta *et al.*, 1996; Almeida *et al.*, 1996; Ghaemi *et al.*, 1996; Young *et al.*, 1998; Morgan *et al.*, 2001). In all but one of those studies (Morgan *et al.*, 2001), no association was found between insight and cognition in patients without schizophrenia. However it should be noted that in the study by Cuesta *et al.* (1996) no association was found between insight and cognition in a corresponding sample of patients with schizophrenia. It is also of note that the sample in the study by Almeida *et al.* (1996) was comprised of patients with late-paraphrenia, a condition that many would consider to be a form of schizophrenia. A comparison of studies in which the samples are comprised of either patients with schizophrenia or patients with a range of psychotic disorders (including schizophrenia) is no more conclusive. In the studies reviewed in this chapter, 76% (19/25) of those examining groups with schizophrenia reported a positive finding (some of these studies included patients with schizoaffective disorder), compared with 70% (7/10) of studies with mixed diagnostic groups.

Illness duration and illness severity

There is little evidence that chronicity of illness is an important factor in the association between insight–cognition. Associations between insight and neuropsychological function are found in first-onset samples (David *et al.*, 1995; Fennig *et al.*, 1996; Morgan *et al.*, 2001) and chronic samples (Young *et al.*, 1993, 1998; Buckley *et al.*, 2001; McCabe *et al.*, 2002). Null findings are also reported in chronic samples and samples where the mean duration of illness is over nine years (Takai *et al.*, 1992; McEvoy *et al.*, 1993; Collins *et al.*, 1997). However, when making comparisons between groups of recent onset patients and chronic patients, some caution is needed before drawing conclusions based purely on the factor of illness duration. Recent onset patients with higher levels of insight and higher levels of cognitive functioning may be less likely to develop a chronic illness, i.e. in respect of insight and cognition, chronic patients may not be representative of patients with psychosis in general. It is also possible that chronic patients learn from the experience of long-term psychiatric care so that certain aspects of their insight, e.g. compliance and illness awareness, improve over the course of time. In terms of illness severity, the evidence available suggests that levels of psychopathology have little impact on the strength of insight–cognition associations. In a comparison of studies with either inpatient or outpatient samples there appears to be very little difference in the pattern of findings. In 13 studies where the samples were investigated exclusively as inpatients, eight (62%) reported a significant association between insight and cognition. In the 12 studies that investigated insight and cognition in outpatients only, six (50%) report a significant association.

Sample size

It may also be possible that the cognitive deficits that underlie poor insight occur in conjunction with other non-cognitive factors, so that their effects are relatively subtle. They may only become consistently evident when relatively large numbers of patients are tested. Forty studies of insight and cognition in the psychoses were reviewed as part of this chapter. An examination of the patient groups in those 40 studies reveals that sample size may be an important consideration. Only seven of the 40 studies had samples that exceeded 90 patients. Six of those seven larger sample studies reported a positive finding

Table 9.3 Summary of studies examining insight and cognition with samples >90

Investigators	Patient profile	n	Insight measure	Association
David et al. (1992)	Mixed Psychosis Mixed Chronicity	91	SAI	Pre-morbid IQ (NART)
Lysaker & Bell (1994)	Schizophrenia Mixed Chronicity	92	PANSS	Current IQ & WCST
David et al. (1995)	Mixed Psychosis Recent Onset	158	PSE & SAI	Pre-morbid IQ (NART)
Fennig et al. (1996)	Mixed Psychosis First Admission	189	HMD	IQ (The Quick Test)
Young et al. (1998)	Schiz. /Bipolar Chronic Illness	129	SUMD	Current IQ & WCST
Goldberg et al. (2001)	Sz. Spectrum Mixed Chronicity	128	PANSS	No association found*
Morgan et al. (2001)	Mixed Psychosis First Onset	94	SAI	Performance IQ and Trails A

SAI = Schedule for Assessment of Insight; PANSS = Positive & Negative Symptoms Scale; PSE = Present State Examination; HMD = Hamilton Depression Scale; SUMD = Scale for Unawareness of Mental Disorder.

* Levels of alcohol/substance misuse were very high in this sample. 75% of the patients had a lifetime diagnosis of substance misuse, 40% reported current use of alcohol or an illicit substance.

between insight and some aspect of cognitive function (see Table 9.3). In terms of their clinical profile, the patients in those investigations belonged to samples of mixed diagnosis and mixed illness duration. Of the remaining 33 studies 21 reported a positive finding and 12 a negative finding.

Medication

A potential confound to the findings is the factor of antipsychotic medication. Medication is a difficult variable to control for as different types of medication may have different effects on cognition. Typical antipsychotics may cause extra pyramidal side effects (e.g. tremors or muscular rigidity). Such effects could have influenced the performance of patients on tests of psychomotor speed (e.g. Trail Making A). Some atypical antipsychotics may enhance cognitive function. Risperidone, for example, may improve working memory, while clozapine may improve semantic memory (Meltzer et al., 1999). Pallanti et al. (1999) reported that during a six-month observation of 22 schizophrenic patients not only did clozapine enhance neurocognitive function, but it also increased awareness of illness. The majority of studies that have investigated possible relationships between insight and antipsychotic medication (Young et al., 1993; Cuesta and Peralta, 1994; Cuesta et al., 1996; Lysaker et al., 1998) have however, reported negative findings for any association between those factors. MacPherson et al. (1996) did find a correlation between insight (rated on the SAI) and both antipsychotic dose and duration of use.

However, the correlation was weak and neither the dose nor duration of use emerged as predictors for insight in a subsequent regression analysis.

Explanations for these disparate findings may lie with other factors not commonly associated with cognitive performance. Startup (1996) provides an illustration of how this may arise when he postulates that both intellectual capacity and a motivation to deny the presence of psychosis may combine to affect levels of insight. In a study of 26 schizophrenic patients, Startup found that very good and very poor insight was only evident in patients who had relatively slight cognitive deficits. Startup argues that patients with more serious cognitive deficits, while having difficulty recognizing the true extent of their illness, may not be able to meet the intellectual demands necessary for self-deception. This would result in intermediate levels of insight for those patients. Patients with only minimal cognitive deficits could vary between high and low levels of insight depending on their motivation. This interesting (although unreplicated) finding provides an indication of how complex an insight–cognition pathway is likely to be.

Conclusion

Variations in the insight concept, its components and its measurement, along with variations in the clinical profile of study samples, have made cross-study comparisons difficult and may have delayed the illumination of key insight–cognition pathways. Nonetheless, the studies conducted over the last ten years have pointed to some potentially important connections between insight and neuropsychological function. To date, the main findings can be summarized as follows:

- Educational background does not appear closely related to insight levels.

- There is a weak association between insight and general intellectual functioning.

- The association between insight and cognition is strongest with non-linguistic aspects of neuropsychological function.

- To date, there is little evidence linking areas of cognition thought to be associated with neurological deficits of awareness such as anosognosia (e.g. parietal lobe function), to insight in the psychoses.

- The most consistent findings of insight–cognition studies involve tasks of mental flexibility, (most notably the Wisconsin card sorting test), suggesting that good insight is at least partially dependent on intact frontal-executive functioning.

- The form of cognitive task used is only one important factor affecting the findings of insight–cognition studies. The instrument used to assess insight may also be crucial e.g. insight–cognition associations are most frequently found in studies using the SUMD.

- The identification of individual psychotic symptoms as pathological appears to be the aspect of insight most closely connected to neuropsychological function.

The association of poor insight with errors of perseveration and concept formation seen in the WCST studies currently provides the most promising avenue of enquiry in this field of research. In the next ten years, the accumulation of data from studies such as these, combined with the acquisition of data from neuroimaging investigations of illness and symptom awareness, is likely to bring a significant advancement to our understanding of the mechanisms underlying the insight that people have when experiencing a psychotic illness.

References

Almeida, O. P., Levy, R., Howard, R. J. and David, A. S. (1996). Insight and paranoid disorders in late life (late paraphrenia). *International Journal of Geriatric Psychiatry*, **11** (7), 653–8.

Amador, X. F., Flaum, M., Andreasen, N. C. and Strauss, D. H. (1994). Awareness of illness in schizophrenia and schizoaffective and mood disorders. *Archives of General Psychiatry*, **51** (10), 826–36.

Amador, X. F. and Kronegold, H. (1998). The description and meaning of insight in psychosis. In X. F. Amador and A. S. David (ed.) *Insight and Psychosis*, 1st edn, pp. 15–32. Oxford: Oxford University Press.

Amador, X. F., Strauss, D. H., Yale, S. A. and Flaum, M. M. (1993). Assessment of insight in psychosis. *American Journal of Psychiatry*, **150** (6), 873–9.

Babinski, J. (1914). Contribution a l'etude des troubles mentaux dans l'hemiplegie organique cerebrele (Anosognosie). *Revue Neurologique*, **27**, 845–8.

Buckley, P. F., Hasan, S., Friedman, L. and Cerny, C. (2001). Insight and schizophrenia. *Comprehensive Psychiatry*, **42** (1), 39–41.

Carroll, A., Fattah, S., Clyde, Z., Coffey, I., Owens, D. G. and Johnstone, E. C. (1999). Correlates of insight and insight change in schizophrenia. *Schizophrenia Research*, **35** (3), 247–53.

Chen, E. Y., Kwok, C. L., Chen, R. Y. and Kwong, P. P. (2001). Insight changes in acute psychotic episodes: a prospective study of Hong Kong Chinese patients. *Journal of Nervous and Mental Disease*, **189** (1), 24–30.

Collins, A. A., Remington, G. J., Coulter, K. and Birkett, K. (1997). Insight, neurocognitive function and symptom clusters in chronic schizophrenia. *Schizophrenia Research*, **27**, 37–44.

Critchley, M. (1953). *The Parietal Lobes*. New York: Hafner Publishing.

Cuesta, M. J. and Peralta, V. (1994). Lack of insight in schizophrenia. *Schizophrenia Bulletin*, **20** (2), 359–66.

Cuesta, M. J., Peralta, V., Caro, F. and de-Leon, J. (1996). Is poor sight in psychotic disorders associated with poor performance on the Wisconsin Card Sorting Test?: Correction. *American Journal of Psychiatry*, **153** (2), 270.

Cutting, J. (1978). Study of anosognosia. *Journal of Neurology Neurosurgery and Psychiatry*, **41** (6), 548–55.

David, A., van Os, J., Jones, P., Harvey, I., Foerster, A. and Fahy, T. (1995). Insight and psychotic illness. Cross-sectional and longitudinal associations. *British Journal of Psychiatry*, **167**, 621–8.

David, A., Buchanan, A., Reed, A. and Almeida, O. (1992). The assessment of insight in psychosis. *British Journal of Psychiatry*, **161**, 599–602.

Dickerson, F. B., Boronow, J. J., Ringel, N. and Parente, F. (1997). Lack of insight among outpatients with schizophrenia. *Psychiatric Services*, **48**, 195–9.

Drake, R. and Lewis, S. (2003). Insight and neurocognition in schizophrenia. *Schizophrenia Research*, **62** (1–2), 165–73.

Elliott, R., McKenna, P. J., Robbins, T. W. and Sahakian, B. I. (2000). Specific neuropsychological deficits in schizophrenia patients with preserved intellectual function. *Cognitive Neuropsychiatry*, **3** (1), 45–70.

Elvevag, B. and Goldberg, T. E. (2000). Cognitive impairment in schizophrenia is the core of the disorder. *Critical Reviews in Neurobiology*, **14** (1), 1–21.

Fennig, S., Everett, E., Bromet, E., *et al.* (1996). Insight in first-admission psychotic patients. *Schizophrenia Research*, **22**, 257–63.

Gerstmann, J. (1942). Problems of imperception of disease and of impaired body territories with organic lesions: Relation to body schema and its disorders. *Archives of Neurology and Psychiatry*, **48**, 890–913.

Geschwind, N. (1965). Disconnexion syndromes in animal and man. *Brain*, **88**, 237–94.

Ghaemi, S. N., Hebben, N., Stoll, A. L. and Pope-H. G. J. (1996). Neuropsychological aspects of lack of insight in bipolar disorder: a preliminary report. *Psychiatry Research*, **65** (2), 113–20.

Goldberg, E. and Bilder, R. M. (1987). The frontal lobes and hierarchical organization of cogntive control. In E. Perecman (ed.) *The Frontal Lobes Revisited*. New York: IRBN Press.

Goldberg, R. W., Green-Paden, L. D., Lehman, A. F. and Gold, J. M. (2001). Correlates of insight in serious mental illness. *Journal of Nervous and Mental Disease*, **189** (3), 137–45.

Iddon, J. L., McKenna, P. J., Sahakian, B. J. and Robbins, T. W. (1998). Impaired generation and use of strategy in schizophrenia: Evidence from visuospatial and verbal tasks. *Psychological Medicine*, **28** (5), 1049–62.

Kay, S. R., Fiszbein, A. and Opler, L. A. (1987). The positive and negative syndrome scale (PANSS) for schizophrenia. *Schizophrenia Bulletin*, **13** (2), 261–76.

Kemp, R. and David, A. (1996). Psychological predictors of insight and compliance in psychotic patients. *British Journal of Psychiatry*, **169**, 444–50.

Kemp, R. and David, A. (1997). Insight and compliance. In L. B. Blackwell (ed.) *Treatment Compliance and the Therapeutic Alliance*, 1st edn, pp. 61–84. Wisconsis: Harwood Academic Publishers.

Larøi, F., Fannemel, M., Ronneberg, U., *et al.* (2000). Unawareness of illness in chronic schizophrenia and its relationship to structural brain measures and neuropsychological tests. *Psychiatry Research*, **100** (1), 49–58.

Laws, K. R. (2001). A meta-analytic review of Wisconsin Card Sort studies in schizophrenia: General intellectual deficit in disguise? *Cognitive Neuropsychiatry*, **4**, 1–35.

Lewis, A. (1934). The psychopathology of insight. *British Journal of Medical Psychology*, **14**, 332–48.

Lysaker, P. and Bell, M. (1994). Insight and cognitive impairment in schizophrenia – performance on repeated administrations of the Wisconsin Card Sorting Test. *Journal of Nervous and Mental Disease*, **182**, 656–60.

Lysaker, P. H., Bell, M. D., Bryson, G. and Kaplan, E. (1998). Neurocognitive function and insight in schizophrenia: support for an association with impairments in executive function but not with impairments in global function. *Acta Psychiatrica Scandinavica*, **97**, 297–301.

Lysaker, P. H., Clements, C. A., Plascak-Hallberg, C. D., Knipscheer, S. J. and Wright, D. E. (2002). Insight and personal narratives of illness in schizophrenia. *Psychiatry, Interpersonal and Biological Processes*, **65** (3), 197–206.

MacPherson, R., Jerrom, B. and Hughes, A. (1996). Relationship between insight, educational background and cognition in schizophrenia. *British Journal of Psychiatry*, **168** (6), 718–22.

Marks, K. A., Fastenau, P. S., Lysaker, P. H. and Bond, G. R. (2000). Self-appraisal of illness questionnaire (SAIQ): relationship to researcher-rated insight and neuropsychological function in schizophrenia. *Schizophrenia Research*, **45** (3), 203–11.

Marks, K. M., Fastenau, P. S., Lysaker, P. and Bond, G. R. (1999). Insight and neuropsychological correlates in schizophrenia. *Schizophrenia Research*, **36** (1–3), 142.

McCabe, R., Quayle, E., Beirne, A. D. and Duane, M. M. A. (2002). Insight, global neuropsychological functioning and symptomatology in chronic schizophrenia. *Journal of Nervous and Mental Disease*, **190** (8), 519–25.

McEvoy, J. P., Freter, S., Merritt, M. and Apperson, L. J. (1993). Insight about psychosis among outpatients with schizophrenia. *Hospital and Community Psychiatry*, **44** (9), 883–4.

McEvoy, J., Hartman, M., Gottlieb, D., Godwin, S., Apperson, L. J. and Wilson, W. (1996). Common sense, insight and neuropsychological test performance in schizophrenia patients. *Schizophrenia Bulletin*, **22** (4), 635–41.

Meltzer, H. Y., Park, S. and Kessler, R. (1999). Cognition, schizophrenia and the atypical antipsychotic drugs. *Proceedings of the National Academy of Sciences of the United States of America*, **96** (24), 13591–3.

Mohamed, S., Fleming, S., Penn, D. L. and Spaulding, W. (1999). Insight in schizophrenia: its relationship to measures of executive functions. *Journal of Nervous and Mental Disease*, **187** (9), 525–31.

Morgan, K. D., Dazzan, P., Morgan, C., *et al.* (2001). Illness awareness and neuropsychological functioning in first onset psychosis. *Journal of Neurology, Neurosurgery and Psychiatry*, **71** (1), 140.

Pallanti, S., Quercioli, L. and Pazzagli, A. (1999). Effects of clozapine on awareness of illness and cognition in schizophrenia. *Psychiatry Research*, **86** (3), 239–49.

Peralta, V. and Cuesta, M. J. (1998). Lack of insight in mood disorders. *Journal of Affective Disorders*, **49**, 55–8.

Pyne, J. M., Bean, D. and Sullivan, G. (2001). Characteristics of patients with schizophrenia who do not believe they are mentally ill. *Journal of Nervous and Mental Disease*, **189** (3), 146–53.

Reitan, R. (1958). Validity of the Trail Making Test as an indicator of organic brain damage. *Perceptual and Motor Skills*, **8**, 271–6.

Sanz, M., Constable, G., Lopez-Ibor, I., Kemp, R. and David, A. (1998). A comparative study of insight scales and their relationship to psychopathological and clinical variables. *Psychological Medicine*, **28**, 437–46.

Schultz, P. W. and Searleman, A. (2002). Rigidity of thought and behavior: 100 years of research. *Genetic, Social and General Psychology Monographs*, **128** (2), 165–207.

Simon, A. E., Giacomini, V., Mohr, S., Bertschy, G. and Ferrero, F. (2001). Dysexecutive Syndrome and insight in schizophrenia. *Schizophrenia Research*, **49** (1–2), 121.

Smith, T. E., Hull, J. W., Israelm L,M, and Willson, D.F. (2000). Insight, symptoms and neurocognition in schizophrenia and schizoaffective disorder. *Schizophrenia Bulletin*, **26** (1), 193–200.

Starkstein, S. E., Fedoroff, J. P., Price, T. R., Leiguarda, R. and Robinson, R. G. (1993). Neuropsychological deficits in patients with anosognsia. *Neuropsychiatry, Neuropsychology and Behavioral Neurology*, **6**, 43–8.

Startup, M. (1996). Insight and cognitive deficits in schizophrenia – evidence for a curvilinear relationship. *Psychological Medicine*, **26**, 1277–81.

Startup, M. (1997). Awareness of own and others' schizophrenic illness. *Schizophrenia Research*, **26**, 203–11.

Stuss, D. T. and Benson, D. F. (1986). *The Frontal Lobes*. New York: Raven Press.

Takai, A., Uematsu, M., Ueki, H. and Sone, K. (1992). Insight and its related factors in chronic schizophrenic patients: A preliminary study. *European Journal of Psychiatry*, **6** (3), 159–70.

Von Hagen, K. O. and Ives, E. R. (1939). Two autopsied cases of anosognosia. *Bulletin of the Los Angeles Neurological Society*, **33**, 1443–6.

Voruganti, L. P., Heslegrave, R. J. and Awad, A. G. (1997). Neurocognitive correlates of positive and negative syndromes in schizophrenia. *Canadian Journal of Psychiatry-Revue Canadienne De Psychiatrie*, **42**, 1066–71.

Warrington, E. K. (1962). The completion of visual forms across hemianopic defects. *Neuropsychiatry, Neuropsychology and Psychiatry*, **25**, 208–17.

White, R., Bebbington, P., Pearson, J., Johnson, S. and Ellis, D. (2000). The social context of insight in schizophrenia. *Social Psychiatry and Psychiatric Epidemiology*, **35** (11), 500–7.

Wing, J. K., Cooper, J. E. and Sartorius, N. (1974). *The Measurement and Classification of Psychiatric Symptoms*, 1st edn. Cambridge: Cambridge University Press.

Young, D. A., Davila, R. and Scher, H. (1993). Unawareness of illness and neuropsychological performance in chronic schizophrenia. *Schizophrenia Research*, **10**, 117–24.

Young, D. A., Zakzanis, K. K., Bailey, C., *et al.* (1998). Further parameters of insight and neuropsychological deficit in schizophrenia and other chronic mental disease. *Journal of Nervous and Mental Disease*, **186**, 44–50.

Part III

Insight, culture, and society

Chapter 10

Inside knowledge: cultural constructions of insight in psychosis

Laurence J. Kirmayer, Ellen Corin, and G. Eric Jarvis

Introduction

Martin was a 30-year-old unmarried, unemployed man who presented to the emergency room with the certain knowledge that he was to be admitted to the psychiatric ward to be executed for crimes he did not commit. When asked how he came to this conviction, he reported that he had noticed a license plate on a passing car that read "K2DR" and immediately knew that this was a reference to the "K-2 Diaries", documents that had been forged by the FBI or some other malevolent agency to frame him for murder and thus precipitate his incarceration, trial and execution in a Kafkaesque nightmare.

Despite this terrifying predicament, Martin agreed to voluntary hospitalization on the psychiatric ward – not because he accepted that he was psychotic, but because he knew that events were unfolding in an inexorable way and nothing he could do would make any difference to the outcome.

Martin also reported other paranoid delusions, ideas of reference, and uncomfortable abdominal sensations which he believed were due to "subsonic beams" directed at him through the walls from unseen sources. Treated with neuroleptic medication, his ideas of reference, somatic hallucinations and delusions rapidly abated and he came to accept that he had experienced an exacerbation of his previously diagnosed schizophrenia.

The first author (LJK) followed Martin as an outpatient in weekly supportive psychotherapy sessions and, because he found it impaired his ability to think clearly, reduced Martin's neuroleptic medication. He continued to have occasional somatic hallucinations and paranoid delusions. He sometimes wore dark blue sunglasses "to block out the laser beams" and continued to complain of "the subsonics." He felt my occasional fidgeting indicated efforts to control him by special gestures. On one occasion, when he described a homeless person he knew as "crazy" because he believed that he had an atomic bomb inside him, I asked Martin how this was different from his own experiences of laser beams and subsonics. He was nonplussed and quickly replied, "Dr. K., I'm surprised at you – the laser beams are *real.*"

Martin was exceptionally intelligent – he had almost completed an honors degree in philosophy before falling sick in his early twenties – and brought his formidable intellect and extensive reading to bear on understanding his illness. He had been treated in twice-weekly psychoanalytically-oriented therapy intermittently for five years, but had left this therapy abruptly, for reasons he never made clear, some months before his emergency room admission.

Martin spoke at length about the knots and quandaries of his family life and offered critiques of R.D. Laing's writing on this theme. He said he planned to write down some of his own thoughts on schizophrenia, to set the record straight, but then added: "You know, my mind is dissolving. Someday I will have no choice but to kill myself." He left this therapy after eighteen months, as abruptly as he had left his earlier psychoanalysis, and was lost to follow-up. One year later, he jumped from a bridge to his death.

Martin's unusual experiences could be viewed as symptoms of schizophrenia, which itself is a result of disordered neurophysiology. Yet his struggle to understand and make sense of his predicament cannot be reduced to matters of brain chemistry, nor even to individual psychology. In this chapter, we will try to show how Martin's struggle for meaning, and the trade-offs it entailed, can only be understood in their social and cultural context. The ways in which Martin partitioned unusual experiences into symptoms of affliction and hard-won insights into the human condition reflected his active use of the cultural knowledge available to him to participate in a social world, preserve his self-esteem and make his often frightening and confusing experiences intelligible. Martin's quest for meaning, however, was largely a solitary activity; he received little support or confirmation from others. The psychiatric interpretation of his experience as schizophrenic delusions and hallucinations was of limited use in his efforts to integrate his psychotic experience.

Martin's story illustrates the paradoxes of insight: although he initially claimed not to be ill, he presented himself to the hospital for treatment; although he could recognize another person's delusions as absurd, he steadfastly held to his own; while continuing to experience hallucinations and delusions, he was able to describe his schizophrenic illness in psychologically sophisticated terms and had a clear concept of its prognosis. Clearly, insight is a complex phenomenon, with components that can evolve independently over time.

David (1990) identified three overlapping dimensions in clinicians' use of the term *insight*: (a) the recognition that one has a mental illness; (b) the ability to relabel unusual mental events as pathological; and (c) compliance with treatment. As Martin's case illustrates, these aspects of insight can occur independently and need not follow a fixed sequence or simple hierarchy. Thus, some patients may adhere to treatment, out of trust or coercion, despite disagreement with the clinician over their diagnosis or the meaning of specific symptoms.

Over the last ten years, efforts to develop measures of insight in patients with psychosis have adopted this essentially biomedical notion of insight as composed of three independent dimensions: awareness of illness, awareness that psychotic symptoms are abnormal, and acceptance of prescribed treatment (Sanz *et al.*, 1998; Peralta and Cuesta, 1998; Weiler *et al.*, 2000; Cuesta *et al.*, 2000). Some investigators have hoped that the reliable measurement of these insight dimensions would reveal neuropsychological deficits underpinning the loss of insight in psychosis and other disorders. Such correlations, however, have been elusive (Sanz *et al.*, 1998; see Morgan Chapter X).

Unfortunately, this line of research has tended to neglect the social determinants of insight. As a result, researchers have been reduced to measuring the degree to which patients with psychotic symptoms agree with their physicians' explanations of the origins of their experiences and behaviours. This produces a false dichotomy in which individuals who disagree with medical opinion, for whatever reason, are deemed to have less insight, while those who are able to convey a medical understanding of their symptoms are viewed as insightful. This approach ignores culture, ethnicity, religion, gender, education, and social class – all of which would seem to be obvious contributors to how one perceives and interprets psychotic symptoms and illness.

There is a small body of work assessing the impact of social factors, such as culture and ethnicity, on insight in psychosis. Johnson and Orrell (1995) have challenged the widely accepted position that insight reflects illness awareness and adherence to medical treatment. They suggest that because the stigma of mental illness is harsh in many societies, individuals with psychosis must deny the full extent of their symptoms in order to preserve their social status and relationships in the community. Viewed this way, an individual may reject a medical explanation not because they lack insight, but because they are giving priority to maintaining social relations and positions that otherwise might be damaged or lost.

Lay concepts of psychosis often differ fundamentally from traditional medical explanations (Kirmayer, 1989, 1994). Johnson and Orrell (1995) cite examples of Italian townsfolk who expressed representations of mental illness as a magical or morally based affliction, while simultaneously offering medical explanations for deviant behavior. French villagers feared contamination by mentally ill persons and consequently enforced taboos such as eating with separate cutlery and forbidding sexual contact. Along similar lines, Carter (2002) asserted that African-Americans frequently invoke religious or supernatural explanations for psychotic illness that may be at odds with medical theory and may discourage adherence to prescribed treatments. When patients or family members explain symptoms in this way they are frequently deemed to have poor insight. Along with the label of poor insight comes a devaluing of the patient's perspective. Interpreting cultural explanations of illness as indicators of poor insight may prevent accurate clinical assessment, undermine the working alliance, and impede successful negotiation of treatment.

Few individuals have one all-encompassing explanation of mental illness that they use consistently in all settings (Young, 1982; Good, 1994; Johnson and Orrell, 1995; Corin, 1998a; Corin *et al.*, 2004). On the contrary, patients and families usually have multiple systems of knowledge that they invoke depending on context and circumstances. Patients may be able to discuss medical explanations of psychosis, while privately maintaining alternate beliefs as to its origin and meaning. Often it is the clinician who insists on a single coherent biomedical explanation for psychotic symptoms.

Ethnoracial status may also lead to clinician bias in the assessment of insight in psychosis. Johnson and Orrell (1996) examined admission case notes for patients with a diagnosis of schizophrenia at a London hospital. The authors found that being Afro-Caribbean was significantly correlated with a rating of poor insight at the time of hospital admission. This may reflect more severe psychosis, or some other ethnocultural variation in the characteristics of British Afro-Caribbean patients with schizophrenia who come to medical attention. However, it is possible that white clinicians systematically mislabeled black patients with poor insight because of lack of familiarity with modes of expressing distress or subtle forms of racial bias (Jarvis, 1998). Some support for this hypothesis comes from the study by Kirov and Murray (1999), who found that Afro-Caribbean patients with bipolar disorder were rated by white clinicians as having more mood-incongruent psychotic symptoms than white Britons with the same diagnosis. These findings raise the possibility that cross-cultural ratings of insight depend on an interaction between clinician and patient rather than simply reflecting the patient's interpretation of symptoms, illness awareness and consequent help-seeking behavior.

Questions such as these prompted White and colleagues (2000) to prospectively examine the hypothesis that insight in psychosis would be less among ethnic minorities than the general population. A sample of 150 patients with schizophrenia was interviewed at length in order to gather demographic, quality of life and insight data. Insight was defined as the degree of endorsement of conventional (i.e., medical) illness beliefs and was quantified by asking questions about illness experience and assigning numeric scores to the answers. No differences emerged by ethnoracial category (Caucasian, Afro-Caribbean, African, Asian), although foreign-born respondents as a group rated significantly lower on insight measures than those born in Britain and Ireland. The authors concluded that their data did not strongly support the hypothesis that insight in psychosis varies by ethnicity. However, this study has important limitations. The comparisons lacked statistical power due to numbers in the ethnoracial groups (27 Afro-Caribbeans, 15 Africans, 14 Asians). The study design may have influenced the results by making clinicians alert to potential biases in their own practice. Finally, the insight measures used by White and colleagues reflect the classic concepts of insight and do not take into account possible cultural differences in illness explanation and clinician-patient interaction.

In our own research in Montreal, case record data on 517 emergency room admissions to psychiatry were retrospectively gathered and assessed with respect to insight ratings (poor versus good) (Jarvis, 2002). When all diagnostic categories were included in the statistical analysis, visible minorities were significantly more likely than other patients to be rated as having poor insight ($\chi^2 = 9.21$, df $= 1$, $p = 0.002$). Visible minorities in this patient population included Caribbean, African, South Asian, and Middle Eastern immigrants. The effect of minority status on ratings of poor insight among patients in general was maintained in logistic regression models controlling for age, gender, mode of admission (police versus self-referral), and the presence of bizarre symptoms at emergency evaluation. When the analysis was done only with patients who received an admission diagnoses of psychotic disorders, however, the results fell just short of significance ($\chi^2 = 3.74$, df $= 1$, $p = 0.053$), suggesting that patients with psychosis are more uniformly rated with respect to insight than persons with less severe psychopathology.

Of course, the clinical significance and judgment of insight in non-psychotic disorders differs in many ways from the construct of insight in psychosis. Nevertheless, taken together, these studies suggest that current clinical concepts and measures of insight may introduce biases when assessing patients who are culturally different from the clinician. Development of more complex insight models that attempt to understand patients' illness experience in cultural context is urgently needed, not only to address cultural difference but also to support a more socially informed approach for all patients.

Each of the three dimensions of insight identified by standard measures has many gradations. For example, recognition that one has a mental illness may range from superficial agreement that one is ill to detailed knowledge of the psychiatric model of one's condition. Similarly, the recognition and labeling of unusual mental events may range from interpretations of experience and behavior as "out-of-the-ordinary", as different from that of others or conventional norms, as indicating that something is wrong and, finally, as symptoms of an illness (which may be recognized and labeled or remain unspecified). Finally, treatment compliance may range from passive following of doctors' directions (owing to blind faith in medical authority or acquiescence to the more or less coercive demands of others), to active collaboration in a therapeutic relationship that involves trust in the clinician and creative use of the supportive relationship. This should make it clear that insight is not a fixed attainment but an evolving process of negotiating meanings of experience with clinicians and other significant actors in the patient's world.

As a folk psychological notion, the metaphor of insight implies that self-knowledge is acquired by direct observation of our mental processes and, as a corollary, that lack of insight in psychosis is a function of an impaired ability for self-observation. Social psychological studies call into question these connotations of the metaphor and suggest that much self-knowledge is based, not on direct observation of one's own mental functions or even of one's own behavior, but instead on cognitive schemata, collective representations and ongoing negotiations of meaning. Insight is inside knowledge then, but not in the sense that it involves accurate perception of mental processes: it is a context-sensitive construal of one's own behavior and situation that bears the impress of culture at every turn. We will illustrate the social and cultural construction of insight with an account of the psychotic experiences of the American science fiction writer Phillip K. Dick, who left a lengthy record of his struggle to explain his extraordinary experiences.

Much research indicates that the symptomatology, help-seeking, and course of schizophrenia, as well as other psychiatric disorders, are strongly influenced by cultural interpretations. If insight itself is such a culturally mediated interpretation, then we might expect that culture can act through insight to shape the "natural history" of these disorders. Indeed, we will argue that this is one possible contributor to the finding that schizophrenia has a better outcome in developing compared to developed countries.

Reflecting changes in the perspectives of cultural psychiatry, our focus in this chapter will move from a view of culture as cognitive representations carried by each individual, to culture as the evolving system of collective representations, social roles, and practices, to culture as local worlds of meaning that are negotiated and contested by patients, families, clinicians and other actors. Each more sophisticated view of culture suggests new ways of conceiving of insight in research and clinical practice.

Insight as metaphor

The metaphor of insight conveys the impression that we possess the ability to look into ourselves and see what is there. Patients who lack insight are simply unable to see what is evident to others: the fact of their own illness. The fact of illness provides a ready explanation for any unusual experiences or deviant behaviors, and mandates specific medical treatment. The insightful patient accepts the doctor's diagnosis, attributes deviant experiences and behaviors to illness and complies with treatment as prescribed (David, Buchanan, Reed and Almeida, 1992).

One implication of this notion of insight as direct perception is that, in the normal course of events, insight is unproblematic and what requires special explanation is *lack* of insight. Marková and Berrios (1992, p. 859) summarize three types of explanation for lack of insight: impaired awareness, self-deception and misattribution.

Impaired awareness implies that some psychotic patients are unable to have insight into their condition because the biological machinery executing "the algorithms for self-awareness" is disabled by disease. On this view, psychosis arises from disruptions of processes of self-awareness, perception, and cognition that leave people liable to hallucinations and delusions and, at the same time, unable to accurately observe and interpret their experiences in accord with feedback from their actions or information from others.[1] Lack of insight may then be treated as a symptom of an underlying disorder. This view is challenged, however, by the finding that level of insight is not substantially correlated with severity of psychosis (Amador, Strauss, Yale, Flaum, and Gorman, 1993).

....

[1] Indeed, the positive symptoms of schizophrenia (e.g., hallucinations and delusions), and the inability to notice that one is sick, could arise from a common underlying mechanism: for example, a disturbance in the feedback loops by which we ascertain the origin of our behavior could lead us to experience our own thoughts or subvocal speech as hallucinatory voices (Green and Kinsbourne, 1990).

The notion of *self-deception* is central to psychodynamic accounts of lack of insight as a form of defensive denial. In psychodynamic theory, insight refers to awareness of intrapsychic emotional conflict and of the connections between past events and current feelings, thoughts and behaviors. In the case of neurotic disorders, insight generally refers to the ability to give a psychological account of one's motivations and actions. Lack of insight then is a motivated response, a form of defensive self-protection against potentially painful or intolerable thoughts and feelings. It results from active efforts to cope with or adapt to distress. Self-deception refers to the defensive avoidance of clarifying and committing oneself to a particular view of reality and self because this is painful or disadvantageous. Of course, to the extent that the necessary faculties are intact, people coping with schizophrenia are likely to use all the same psychological resources marshaled by patients with anxiety, depression or dissociative disorders, so self-deception is equally relevant to efforts to cope with psychosis.

Finally, lack of insight may be viewed as *misattribution*, a form of cognitive error based on lack of information, systematic biases, or idiosyncratic beliefs. Misattribution implies there is a correct attribution for symptoms and experiences that is given by common accord or, in doubtful cases, by medical authority. We must consider the possibility, however, that what is called misattribution is really an interpretation of experience that is due neither to a deficit nor to purely defensive functions, but that reflects a genuine alternative construction of reality. While it may not accord with the dominant view of psychiatry, this alternative reality makes sense within the patient's local world of meaning and, hence, confers the benefits of coherence, order, and intelligibility on unusual, chaotic, or disturbing experience.

The transparency of illness experience implied by the metaphor of insight is misleading, in that a wealth of social psychological studies show that under ordinary circumstances, much self-knowledge is based not on objective self-awareness or direct perception (introspection) but on context-dependent interpretations of one's own behavior and experience based on multiple sources, including observations of others, acquisition of social norms and active construction of theories about the self (Neisser, 1988; Nisbett and Wilson, 1977; Ross and Nisbett, 1991).[2] These constructions are mediated and constrained by the different situations or social contexts that the individual lives in and through. Far from being a window into the self, insight is a half-silvered mirror held up between self and other.

---

[2] Ericcson and Simon (1984), however, have argued that under many circumstances we do have knowledge of our own mental processes based on our ability to report the contents of short-term or "working" memory. It is only when processes bypass short-term memory (STM), or when STM decays or is otherwise rendered inaccessible, that we completely lack introspective access to our mental processes. However, many forms of social learning occur without conscious awareness and result in procedural knowledge that, while it can be used, cannot be explicitly described (as can declarative knowledge). Emotionally charged or personally disagreeable information, such as a stigmatized medical diagnosis or a deflating interpretation of exalted psychotic experiences, is likely to be less accessible to conscious recall for all the defensive reasons adduced by psychodynamic theory.

Amador and colleagues (1993) suggest that insight involves both awareness and attribution. Awareness and attribution, though, are closely related. Clearly, attribution depends on awareness, since we must notice something to make it the object of explanations. In addition, the way in which we become aware of deviant experience itself carries information relevant to making causal attributions. Attributions or explanatory models also govern the deployment of attention and guide the search for sensations, experiences or events that fit a niche within the model or schema that may precede awareness. In practice, then, there can be no sharp distinction between awareness and attribution. Indeed, Dennett (1991) has argued against the notion of consciousness as an inner theater of representation implied by the primacy of awareness, and provides compelling evidence that awareness often occurs after the fact as a perceptual, cognitive or narrative construction in response to specific imperatives – questions, probes, actions.[3] As a corollary, the self is not a homunculus watching the inner theater of representations, but the narrative center of gravity of accounts about the individual's actions and life trajectory. Insight, like other forms of self-knowledge, must then be understood as a process of attribution or, more elaborately, as the construction of narratives about the self.

Insight involves a series of attributions: symptoms are attributed to affliction and the affliction is labeled as a mental disorder with specific causes, course, and outcome. But attributions do not occur in isolation; they are part and parcel of more extended networks of meaning. Such networks influence the perception of what constitutes a symptom or a sign of illness within a given culture (Corin, Bibeau and Uchôa, 1993; Good and Good, 1980; Kirmayer, 1989).

Accounts of the onset of psychosis reveal a situation of chaos and confusion, where the crucial question for the person and his or her entourage is what interpretations are at hand to organize experience (Bowers, 1974). Sensations that are initially inchoate can be labeled as symptoms of an illness only after an attributional search. In some cases, psychotic experiences themselves provide their own interpretations and these are typically religious or supernatural, or in modern societies, involve magical applications of technology like radio waves, lasers, and microelectronics. In other cases, explanations are found after the fact from some sympathetic or authoritative source – but in every case they represent cultural conceptions.

Kleinman (1980) introduced the notion of patients' explanatory models (EMs): information, beliefs, and expectations regarding the cause, symptomatology, course, appropriate treatment and probable outcome of illness based on a common fund of cultural knowledge, as well as personal experience. These EMs can be elicited by direct questions to patients in settings where medical authority does not inhibit their willingness to

---

[3] Sensory experiences that constitute the *qualia* of consciousness may occur on the basis of perceptual processes prior to narratization (Humphrey, 1992), and awareness of illness simply as pain, dysphoria, or malaise might be based on such preverbal qualia, but the type of awareness referred to as insight is clearly a form of narrative.

divulge alternative views. These models influence patients' perceptions of diagnosis and treatment, and hence can account for problems in communication and compliance.

However, the EM perspective imputes a greater degree of coherence and rationality to everyday thinking than it actually displays. Often people cannot give ready explanations for their symptoms or problems and when they do, they may offer multiple, fragmentary, and contradictory accounts. Young (1982) has tried to account for the manifest complexity, incompleteness and contradictions present in patients' illness narratives by positing at least three different forms of illness representation that coexist and that may conflict: explanatory models, prototypical cases or events, and *chain complexes* – a form of procedural knowledge derived from the sequence of lived experience. Faced with the fragmented and often contradictory character of illness narratives about epilepsy in Turkey, Good and Good (1993) understand them as *subjunctivizing tactics* aimed at preserving the indeterminacy of the future and the openness of the illness to change and cure. In addition, it is important to recognize that the semantic networks that confer meaning on experience are not simply lists of propositions; they include images, practices, and links to external situations that embody collective knowledge (Kirmayer, 1992). This knowledge is used to construct a story or narrative about the meaning of experiences.

Amador and colleagues (1993) found that insight about past and current episodes of psychosis were poorly correlated. Insight about past illness episodes involves the narrative reconstructions of memory; current insight may be more dependent on feedback from control mechanisms (intraspsychic and social feedback loops) that give evidence of dysfunction or lack of match of action with intention. But both forms of insight are highly context-dependent: past reconstruction and current self-perception must be seen as methods of positioning the self vis-à-vis others. Of course, it may be one feature of some forms of illness that individuals' capacity to respond to shifting contexts is impaired and hence, their self-presentation shows greater stereotypy than that of healthy individuals.

The notion of insight as a narrative construction has special significance for psychosis, because there is evidence that the ability to organize discourse at the level of narrative is impaired in schizophrenia (Hoffman, 1986). Narrative is particularly important in the construction of a coherent sense of self against which events are evaluated through the process of self-awareness (Bruner, 1990; Kirby, 1991; Ricoeur, 1992). If the stability and coherence of this narrative is interfered with, then the capacity for insight may be correspondingly impaired. Further, since the form of narratives varies cross-culturally (Ewing, 1990; Howard, 1991) – including those narratives that are about the self – culture may interact with psychotic impairment of insight at the level of what narratives of the self are available, socially coherent and credible. Detailed study of the narrative presentation and representation of self in psychotic patients may then offer a way to integrate psychological studies of the cognitive impairments in schizophrenia with the impact of social structure and cultural knowledge.

Deciding that we are sick, labeling particular sensations or behaviors as symptoms, and attributing them to a specific type of illness all depend on cognitively and socially mediated interpretations of experience (Kirmayer, 1989). The matrix of these interpretations of experience is the sum of shared beliefs and practices we call "culture". Insight then, is a culturally constructed version of experience that patients subscribe to, not simply because their cognitive machinery is intact, but by virtue of the way it fits with their social world. This cultural constructivist view of insight is at odds with a clinical perspective that measures patients' insight against the clinician's judgment as a gold standard, inasmuch as it insists that the clinician's view too is shaped by cultural concepts and values.

Insight as a sociocultural process

If insight is having "a correct attitude toward a morbid change in oneself" (Lewis, 1934, p. 333) then it is a value-laden concept that is likely to change with time and circumstance. "Correct" can only be judged with respect to some goal: cooperation with treatment, good outcome, ratification of professional judgment or social control. Since outcome is multidimensional, correct with respect to one dimension (e.g., willingness to accept medication) may conflict with correct with respect to other dimensions (e.g., sense of self-sufficiency, hopefulness, coherence of one's life). Further, the notion of correctness raises questions with respect to who or what authority (e.g., health professional, family, colleagues) establishes standards or criteria? The "correct" attitude toward an illness depends on changing medical concepts of illness as well as social norms for illness behavior, which may also conflict. Insight then is manifested by specific attitudes and attributions that are contingent on changing knowledge and practice.

Yet lack of insight in psychosis seems also to reflect some more general difficulty in maintaining a consensual view of reality. This more general or pervasive difficulty can be characterized by viewing insight as a process distinct from any specific interpretation or attribution. As a process, insight involves acquiring, stabilizing, and deploying consensual explanations for experience. This ability to conform in one's self-understanding and action does not preclude having strange or psychotic experiences. If the person enjoys a sufficient measure of flexibility, irony, playfulness and self-reflexive awareness, he or she may adopt a complex stance that allows idiosyncratic experiences to coexist with more conventional ones and still preserve a concern for – and ability to succeed in – making his or her experience intelligible to others.

In this regard, it is instructive to consider the response to psychotic experiences of a person without the persistent or recurrent thought disorder of schizophrenia. Consider, for example, the way the American science fiction writer Philip K. Dick generated alternative explanations for his own religious or psychotic experiences. Dick had a history of anxiety problems (probably panic disorder with agoraphobia) from adolescence, and was treated intermittently with amphetamines. However, he had no known episode of psychosis prior to the events to be recounted. He was a prolific and brilliantly inventive writer who gained a wide following, first in Europe and later in the United States. His stories were characterized by a pervasive sense of paranoia – of hidden connections between seemingly unrelated events and the growing intimation that things are not what they appear to be – which was typically confirmed in each story's denouement, when reality fell open to reveal alternate realities, like a series of Chinese boxes, so that the ultimate ground of experience was left in question. In one story, objects in the world dissolve, leaving slips of paper with their names written on them ("Soft-drink stand"); in another, the reader discovers the characters are programs inside a computer – but then, just as reality begins to settle down, the programmers of the computer are themselves revealed to be just programs in a still greater computer. In his stories, Dick made a virtue of paranoia's infinite regress (Kirmayer, 1983).

In 1974, following surgery for an impacted wisdom tooth, Dick answered the door to receive delivery of a prescription for a narcotic analgesic (propoxyphene, *Darvon*):

> There stood this girl with black, black hair and large eyes very lovely and intense; I stood staring at her, amazed, also confused and thinking I'd never seen such a beautiful girl, and why was she standing there. She handed me the package of medication, and I tried to think what to say to her; I noticed, then, a fascinating gold necklace around her neck and I said, "What is that? It certainly is beautiful," just, you see, to find something to say to hold her there. The girl indicated the major figure in it, which was a fish. "This is a sign used by the early Christians," she said, and then departed.
>
> (Sutin, 1989, p. 210)

At the time he felt only a sense of strangeness about this experience; although it felt significant, its meaning was uncertain. Over the next few days, probably intoxicated by medication, he had a series of visions: colorful patterns, abstract painting-like compositions and pink lights. While some appear to have been phosphenes, others were much more complex and constituted a veritable gallery of modern art. While the pink light had first appeared as a sort of prolonged after-image, he now felt it as beams fired into his brain that conveyed vast stores of esoteric information. With this came the increasing conviction that some god or alien intelligence was trying to contact him, that the world as we know it is an illusion, and finally, that we are all really living in the time of the early Christians and that our contemporary oppressors are Romans in disguise. The delivery girl's visit became a portent of this revelation.

Everyday experiences then took on dual significance: they had one meaning in the mundane world of illusion, and another, more profound sense in the realm that had been revealed to him. He actively participated in this alternate realm, performing rituals of purification and baptism with his young son. In addition to the new knowledge he seemed to have acquired, he felt his tastes, habits and attitudes had abruptly changed. After several weeks the unusual experiences became more sporadic and in a few months they stopped.

Dick spent years generating alternative explanations for these experiences, which he recorded in a lengthy colloquy with himself he called his "Exegesis" (Dick, 1991). In the process, he struggled to give them coherence. He was well aware of how they might appear to a clinician:

> I can see me telling my therapist this. "What's on your mind, Phil?" she'll say when I go in, and I'll say, "Asklepios is my tutor, from out of Pericleian Athens. I'm learning to talk in Attic Greek."

She'll say, "Oh really?" and I'll be on my way to the Blissful Groves, but it won't be after death; that'll be in the country where it's quiet and costs $100 a day. And you get all the apple juice you want to drink, along with Thorazine.

(Dick, 1991, p. 18)

He considered and rejected dozens of different theories drawn from psychology, religion and speculative fiction. He considered psychiatric explanations but found them inadequate to explain the details of his experience:

There is no known psychological process which could account for such fundamental changes in my character, in my habits, view of the world (I perceive it totally differently, now), my daily tastes, even the way I margin my typed pages. I've been transformed but not in any way I ever heard of.

(Dick, 1991, p. 6)

Note that it was not the hallucinations and delusions that Dick found hard to explain in psychological terms (as a toxic psychosis), but the more enduring changes in personality.[4] What Dick is calling his personality here is more accurately his sense of self- and personhood. Changes in sense of self and social personhood are extremely important for the person with chronic schizophrenia and crucial to understanding the process of constructing insight (Davidson and Strauss, 1992).

What sets Dick apart from the patient lacking insight, is his ability to generate, entertain and use multiple explanations, including those of psychiatric disorder.

I can entertain (hold) two normally contradictory beliefs – explanations – :

(1) I became totally psychotic and projected and imagined all that religious, supernatural stuff.

(2) The guide and savior, the figure of the beautiful woman who I met and whose voice I kept hearing, whose existence during my psychosis I imagined, was and is completely real – and I know when the need arises again, I will find her once more, or rather she will find me and again guide me.

(Dick, 1991, p. 38)

This ability to hold contradictory views is not a sign of disordered logic. It is the ordinary condition of us all, save that we usually are not so honest or adept at making our contradictory premises explicit (and when we do we usually try to elide their dissonance). As a common feature in the construction of meaning, it suggests that insight cannot be simply measured as the outcome of agreement with the clinician, but must be viewed as a process of giving due consideration to alternative explanations. Explanations will be adopted if they make sense and work in some region of the person's lifeworld. Psychiatric

---

4 In fact, Dick generated at least one hypothesis to take in these personality changes: he was the victim of a dissociative process, a shift to a dual personality that had arisen some years earlier at the time of a traumatic amnesia incurred during an automobile accident. He rejected this explanation as it could not account for the specific details of his personality. The recent vogue for diagnosing multiple personality disorder in the United States suggests that he was too quick to dismiss this hypothesis (Hacking, 1995).

explanations, along with many of the more outlandish science fiction explanations, were grist for Dick's creative mill. He wrote a trilogy of Gnostic science fiction novels in which a playful alter ego (named "Horselover Fat" in a multilingual pun) argued with him over the potential meaning of his experiences (Dick, 1990). Considering the psychiatric dimension of his experience did ultimately lead him to seek help for drug dependence, yet he felt strongly that what he had received in his visions were real insights into the human condition and that religion provided the only system to make them coherent in a positive way.

> You see a plan, you see a pattern of events, and if you have no transcendent viewpoint, no mystical view, no religious view, then the pattern must emanate from people. Where else can it come from, if that's all . . .? And you start sensing a kind of transcendent thing or mystical thing . . .
>
> I think . . . paranoia must be pulled inside out. Absolutely inside out. It's not that it should be destroyed. I mean, that the solution to paranoia is to convince the person there is no pattern to the universe, that everything is chaotic, chance, and that people have no intentions. And that he is unimportant . . . Turn it inside out, rather than just abolish it. That it's benign, and that it transcends our individualities, and so on. The way I feel is that the universe itself is actually alive, and we're in a part of it. And it is like a breathing creature, which explains the concept of Atman, you know, the breath, pneuma, the breath of God.
>
> (Williams, 1986, pp. 161–163)

Ultimately, Dick settled on a version of Gnosticism to account for his experiences, drawing heavily on the *Nag Hammadi Library* (Robinson, 1977). In striking illustration of the social embeddedness of even this most idiosyncratic of visionary experiences, the epilogue to a subsequent edition of the *Nag Hammadi Library* (Robinson, 1988) cites Dick as a contemporary rediscoverer of perennial Gnostic truths. This social legitimation might have served to stabilize Dick's own interpretation of his experience, had he survived to appreciate it.[5]

Certainly, Dick's experience was not typical. The flexibility, irony and humor with which he worked with his hallucinatory revelations – which resemble those of many patients with schizophrenia – were remarkable. No doubt, his vocation and social status as a writer, his lifelong creative play with the anxiety of paranoia, and his intelligence served him in good stead in making sense of his experience. He was able to stabilize and defend a particular interpretation of his experience due to these exceptional personal and social resources. The sense that he made was idiosyncratic in many respects yet deeply embedded in both popular culture and the esoteric tradition of Gnosticism. In religion he found a perspective to valorize and enrich his own sally into madness.

Dick's psychotic episode was prefigured by years of writing stories with a distinctly paranoid cast. His experience suggests that some people form tentative delusions or paranoid hypotheses much of the time as they seek connections between ambiguous or disturbing events (Lemert, 1962; Melges and Freeman, 1975). Ordinarily, people reappraise these hypotheses and dismiss them if they do not fit consensual reality, are

---

5 Dick died in 1982, a few months before the film *Blade Runner*, based on his novel *Do Androids Dream of Electric Sheep?*, was released.

unpleasant or interfere with adaptation. If the cognitive machinery of reappraisal is impaired, paranoid delusions may persist and strengthen. The effects of neuroleptic medication may be not so much to block delusion formation as to allow cognitive reappraisal (Hole, Rush and Beck, 1979). But the appraisal process itself is one of interpreting signs, symptoms, behaviors and events in terms of tacit social and cultural knowledge.

What distinguishes Dick from the prototypical psychotic patient lacking in insight is his ability to be self-reflexively aware of the process of constructing his own explanations and to adopt, if and when it is necessary, the perspective of the other (whether that other be a doctor, a fellow writer, or a theologian). Dick was insightful, no matter how thoroughly he rejected the pathological origins and nature of his experiences, because he was complexly aware of the nature of his own consciousness and his writing.[6]

In Dick's account, we can see the process of constructing insight. The experience of psychosis – which may be initially inchoate or consist of well-formed, vivid hallucinations that, nevertheless, rent the fabric of consensual reality – is woven into an integrated whole. Dick wove his compelling and evocative psychotic experiences into a life-affirming philosophy. What made this process possible for him was the time away from psychosis when nothing earth-shattering was happening. In this reflective space, Dick was able to construct a complex narrative with links to cultural traditions that legitimated his experience, gave it public anchor points, and supplied him with new metaphors and models to organize his experience. In memory, reconstructed through narrative, madness was made to cohere.

Insight emerges in Dick's exegetical diaries as partial, tentative, always awaiting confirmation and stabilization. In its tentativeness, his experience differs from that of some delusional patients for whom the sense of conviction that they have found the truth is present from the start. Some delusional experiences carry their own interpretations and are self-stabilizing.[7] In Dick's case this stabilization came partly from finding

---

[6] In his *Exegesis*, commenting on his science fiction writing, Dick noted: "I do seem attracted to trash, as if the clue – *the clue* – lies there. I'm always ferreting out elliptical points, odd angles. What I write doesn't make a whole lot of sense. There is fun and religion and psychotic horror strewn about like a bunch of hats. Also, there is a social or sociological drift – rather than toward the hard sciences. The overall impression is childish but interesting. This is not a sophisticated person writing. Everything is equally real, like junk jewels in the alley. A fertile creative mind seeing constantly shifting sets, the serious made funny, the ιunny sad, the horrific exactly that: utterly horrific as it is the touchstone of what is real: horror is real because it can injure . . . I certainly see the randomness in my work, and I also see how this fast shuffling of possibility after possibility might eventually, given enough time, juxtapose and disclose something important and automatically overlooked in more orderly thinking" (quoted in Sutin, 1989, pp. 154–155).

[7] This sense of conviction that accompanies delusions and some hallucinations may arise from several mechanisms: (1) the sensory-affective qualities of delusional thought and experience may be so vivid and compelling that they admit no doubt as to their significance (David and Howard, 1994); (2) cognitive appraisal mechanisms may be malfunctioning so that alternative explanations cannot be generated or tested; or (3) ordinary doubt itself may become emotionally threatening and aversive.

Gnostic religious texts that mirrored, organized and deepened his own experiences. It also came from his ability to authorize his own constructions, first as the writer's legitimate engagement with an imaginative world and then as published fictions with a playful yet hortatory style.

Although the process of constructing coherent narratives revealed in Dick's diaries is similar to what any person faced with psychotic experiences might engage in, it is distinctive in two important respects. First, Dick did not belong to a society or subculture with a single dominant tradition that offered him ready-made explanations for his experiences. He had to borrow and adapt a range of ideas; concepts drawn from great traditions were melded with themes from science fiction. Second, as we have noted, Dick had unique personal resources and a special social status that enabled him to authorize and stabilize his narrative constructions. This allowed him to experience some degree of satisfying resolution to his search and to use his insights to further his career.

Bateson (1972) called delusions "unlabeled metaphors" and held that in schizophrenia patients lost sight of the metaphorical status of utterances. Mistaking metaphors for reality, though, is a feature of everyday thinking: we live among unquestioned metaphors taken for natural categories and literal truths (Lakoff and Johnson, 1980). Analogical modes of reasoning and "magical thinking" (e.g., identity by resemblance, contagion by contact, misplaced concreteness) are ubiquitous and often not recognized as irrational (Rozin and Nemeroff, 1990). The crucial difference is whether metaphors are socially sanctioned and pass for literal truths or are idiosyncratic. For idiosyncratic metaphors, if we wish to avoid being labeled "odd" or "crazy", we had better have the rhetorical skills to defend them, and the irony and self-reflexive awareness to distance from them. What is characteristic of schizophrenia, then, is difficulty organizing tentative metaphoric constructions at the level of larger narrative structures that take into account the positions of speaker and listener. This overarching narrative structure determines which metaphors are interpreted as literal and which are just loose analogies, "figures of speech," or simply incoherent.

People with schizophrenia engage in the same sort of creative borrowing, adaptation and play with concepts, to explain their experience, a process that Corin (1990) has called 'bricolage' (borrowing the term from Lévi-Strauss). In Corin's study of people with schizophrenia in Montreal, she found that some gravitated toward marginal religious systems and ideas that they gleaned from books or from peripheral involvements with religious sects. Ideas borrowed from many places allowed them to develop a patchwork system of explanations that justified their withdrawal from conventional work and relationships; in some cases, informal and idiosyncratic religious practices also provided a degree of structure to both solitude and social contact. Their experience differs from Dick's, however, in several ways. The most important difference arises from the persistence and pervasiveness of psychotic experience. Given the tremendous amount of effort over years that Dick expended on explaining just a few weeks of intense experiences, we can only wonder at the information overload of someone enduring lengthy and repeated psychoses. The need to develop and adopt a system to filter, organize and make experience cohere is urgent. This may explain the rigidity with which some delusional systems are held – not so much as a primary feature of psychosis but as an effort to stabilize reality in the face of constant intrusions of the strange and ineffable. In many cases, the result is not a richly elaborated system but a sketchy or jury-rigged structure, anxiously defended against constant threats to its stability.

Then, too, most schizophrenic patients have neither the personal resources and talents nor the social status, as an accomplished writer, that Dick enjoyed. This means that it is harder for them to construct a coherent explanation, and, when they do, still more difficult to have others accept or ratify it. In consequence, they cannot stabilize their interpretation of the world except by withdrawing from others who challenge the picture they have constructed.

Finally, people with psychoses live in societies or subcultures that make different systems of belief available to them. Dick belonged to a liberal subculture in a pluralistic society that tolerates the sort of borrowing and informal adaptation of esoteric religion that he attempted. In urban, pluralistic societies, people with chronic psychoses may draw their explanatory concepts from marginal beliefs and practices because these allow greater freedom for idiosyncratic elaboration and are less likely to bring them into direct confrontation with authorities who destabilize or invalidate their tentative constructions (Corin, 1990). People in some traditional societies may engage in constructions of experience that draw from widely accepted beliefs that give religion or the supernatural a more prominent place in everyday life. Hence, authoritative meanings for psychotic experience may be more readily at hand. This may help with personal or collective efforts to make sense of psychotic experience and with the social integration of individuals with chronic psychoses. The greater availability in some cultures of meaning systems that allow people to positively reframe frightening or disturbing experiences should be reflected in an increased likelihood of reintegration following a psychotic episode and a correspondingly better prognosis.

Schizophrenia in cross-cultural perspective

While schizophrenia can be identified around the world, there are significant cultural and geographical differences in prevalence, symptomatology and course (Cooper and Sartorius, 1977; Kleinman, 1988; Leff, 1988; Murphy, 1982; Sartorius, *et al.*, 1986). A striking finding of cross-cultural studies of schizophrenia has been the repeated observation of a better long-term prognosis for individuals in some developing countries compared to patients in urban industrialized settings (Leff, Sartorius, Jablensky, Korten, and Ernberg, 1992; Murphy and Raman, 1971; Sartorius, Jablensky and Shapiro, 1978; WHO, 1979). Early studies, including the International Pilot Study of

Schizophrenia (IPSS), have been criticized because they included only patients presenting to westernized psychiatric health care services and used a limited range of outcome measures (Cohen, 1992).[8] More recently, the WHO Determinants of Outcome Study corrected many of the methodological limitations of the IPSS (Jablensky *et al.*, 1992; but see Edgerton and Cohen, 1994). Patients presenting with psychotic symptoms were accrued from many different types of helping agencies, including traditional healers. Again, the two-year follow-up indicated a better course for patients in developing countries compared to their counterparts in developed countries (Sartorius, 1992).

Lin and Kleinman (1988) reviewed speculations on the underlying mechanisms for better prognosis in developing countries. These hypotheses all have direct implications for the cultural construction of insight because of the reciprocity between patients' self-image and others' views of them.

First, they point to broad differences in the organization of society and the corresponding concepts of self and personhood. The industrialized urban societies of Europe and America foster an individualistic concept of the person and an egocentric sense of self. In this view, the individual is the prime locus of value, choice, and action and enters into relationships voluntarily with others (Bellah *et al.*, 1985). In contrast, the concept of the person in many developing countries is communalistic and sociocentric, emphasizing group membership as the core of identity so that individuals think of themselves predominately in terms of these larger affiliations, which are valued over and above the individual in many respects.

As Dumont (1986) points out, western individualism is paradoxical in that, at the same time as it claims to respect difference, it is linked to a fierce competitiveness and conformity that leave little room for real differences in behavior, values and life trajectory for individuals. Lin and Kleinman (1988) suggest that this "intensive individualism" of modern Western societies may interfere with recovery for many schizophrenic patients. The emphasis on self-reliance, competition and individual achievement as sources of self-esteem may contribute to despair in those less able to compete successfully. Schizophrenic individuals who find they cannot compete in conventional terms have no choice but to distance themselves from conventional sources of social status and self-esteem and to accept a position at the margins of society. The rapidity of social change, the frequency of dislocation, and a general sense of alienation undermine basic social solidarity or support and so may aggravate the course of illness. Where identity is drawn from group membership, supportive ties may be less likely to rupture with

---

[8] Acute psychoses with rapid resolution (brief reactive psychoses) appear to be more common in non-Western countries as well and may contribute to the better prognostic picture in studies that do not use a duration criterion for the diagnosis of schizophrenia (Guinness, 1992; Okasha, Dawla, and Saad, 1993; Stevens, 1987). These psychoses may be more closely related to affective and dissociative disorders than to schizophrenia.

chronic illness, and individuals who are able to conform minimally may still preserve their sense of identity, belonging, and importance.[9]

A second locus of the impact of culture on the prognosis of schizophrenia involves the family milieu. High levels of negative expressed emotion (EE) have been shown repeatedly to predict poor outcome in young male schizophrenics (Leff and Vaughn, 1985). At one-year follow-up, the WHO Determinants of Outcome Study found that high EE could be measured reliably cross-culturally and that it was related to poor outcome (Leff *et al.*, 1987). However, the global index of EE was no longer related to outcome at two-year follow-up (Leff *et al.*, 1990); only initial hostility remained significantly related to subsequent relapse. The actual prevalence of high EE families was found to be lower in some cultures (e.g., Indian). The authors conclude that in India, the tolerant and accepting attitudes of family members may contribute to the good prognosis of schizophrenia. Even more intriguing was the finding that the pattern of emotions associated with EE in India was quite different from that observed in Anglo-American families. This and related findings indicate the need to go beyond the EE construct to explore the nature of emotional relationships in specific cultures (Jenkins and Karno, 1992).

Jenkins's (1988) work with Mexican-Americans suggests that cultural beliefs and practices surrounding mental illness also interact with hostility in the family. In ethnographic research, she found that many schizophrenic patients were given the relatively benign label "*nervios*" (nerves) rather than "*loco*" (crazy) for their condition. The culturally appropriate response to an individual with *nervios* is to treat him or her gently and avoid conflict, arguments and confrontation. The cultural label for psychotic illness, and corresponding attitudes toward illness along with cultural differences in family communication of emotion, thus promote some of the same behaviors advocated in psychoeducational family treatment of schizophrenia. This may lead to a reduced prevalence of high EE families and hence, a better prognosis in the aggregate (Guarnaccia, Parra, Deschamps, Milstein and Argiles, 1992; Karno *et al.*, 1987).

The stigma of mental illness may differ across cultures (Fabrega, 1991; Kirmayer, 1989; Lin and Kleinman, 1988; Townsend, 1978). Waxler (1979) offered this as one explanation for the better prognosis for schizophrenia found in Sri Lanka. She argued that the cultural model for psychosis in Sri Lanka was similar to that for other acute illnesses in that it carried expectations for improvement or recovery and little implication that the individual's personhood was permanently damaged or invalidated. Consequently, individuals who did not display overtly bizarre behavior might be more

---

[9] One should, however, not fall into a stereotyped opposition between purely sociocentric selves in developing countries and purely egocentric selves in Western societies. Individual and social aspects of the person are important in all societies. It is more a matter of a differential emphasis on one of the two broad orientations based on the availability of collective symbols and rituals for valuing and working out each dimension of the person (Corin, 1998b). The sense of self varies along many other dimensions across cultures and also shows enormous intracultural variation.

readily re-integrated into the community following an acute episode and not suffer long-lasting stigmatization.

It is not possible, with current data, to determine which of many covarying factors contribute to the differential prognosis of schizophrenia across cultures (Edgerton and Cohen, 1994; Gupta, 1992). Although speculations have focused on the attitudes and actions of the patient's entourage, sociocultural factors may also exert their influence through the afflicted person's own interpretation of illness experience. In fact, lack of insight was the most frequent symptom of acute schizophrenia identified in the IPSS (WHO, 1973). Insight was assessed with item 104 of the Present State Examination: "Do you think there is anything the matter with you? What do you think it is? Could it be a nervous condition?" Clearly, this sequence of questions measures agreement with a psychiatric opinion rather than the functioning of underlying cognitive-interpretive processes. The high prevalence of lack of insight then may reflect not so much its status as a core symptom of schizophrenia, but the diversity of explanations tendered for psychotic experiences around the world.

Cultural concepts of mental disorder are closely related to insight both in terms of what images and explanations the individual has available to explain their symptoms and in terms of their personal and social costs in self-perceived stigma and self-blame. Sociological studies of labeling and stigmatization have dealt extensively with the consequences of attributing deviant behavior to mental illness (Link, 1987; Link, Cullen, Frank and Wozniak, 1987). These studies suggest that insight has its costs in reduced self-esteem and lower social status for the afflicted individual. Self-labeling also contributes to a sense of impaired efficacy and may maintain vicious circles of emotional distress (Corin and Lauzon, 1994; Thoits, 1985). At the same time, accepting an illness label may lead to treatment adherence and, if treatment is effective, to fewer symptoms and less basis for social stigmatization and rejection (Warner, Taylor, Powers, and Hyman, 1989). These costs and trade-offs must be figured into individuals' willingness and ability to entertain illness attributions for their own deviant experiences or behavior.

The tendency to apply illness labels to deviant behavior and to stigmatize mental illness may also be related to social structure. Raybeck (1988) has discussed how sociological labeling theory, developed in the context of large-scale urban pluralistic societies, must be modified to address the realities of small-scale societies. In smaller communities, he argues, there is an effort to avoid labeling deviant behavior or eccentricity in a way that would lead to ostracism. We have observed this in our work in small communities in the Arctic and in Africa, as illustrated in the following case:

A 25-year-old Inuit man living in a remote Arctic settlement became convinced that he had received religious revelations and pored over the Bible marking it with colored pens and memorizing extensive passages. He carried this Bible in a sling around his waist and responded to most questions about himself with lengthy quotations depicting the coming apocalypse. He began accosting others in the street and in their homes to exhort them to repent because the Day of Judgment was near. His enthusiasm was tolerated until he began to become visibly angry in his harangues. At the request of the settlement, he was then sent to the city for psychiatric evaluation. There he was found to have religious delusions but was otherwise lucid and appropriate. A provisional diagnosis of schizophreniform disorder was made and he was given neuroleptic medication. On returning to the community he continued to be active in the local church but tempered his attempts to convert others. He stopped taking medication after about a year. At five-year follow-up, he had become less religious, and recalled these experiences with some embarrassment, but did not think that he had been ill. He held a part-time wage-earning job and participated in group sports and other community activities, although he had no close friends and spent much time by himself. He was perceived by other community members as having been overly intense in his religious convictions but not as having any illness.

Both cultural values and social structure contributed to this man's reintegration into the community following his hospitalization. The tendency to avoid labeling individuals that is characteristic of small-scale societies, combined with community tolerance of enthusiastic religious expression and a cultural tendency among the Inuit to label behaviors or states rather than personalities, allowed him to escape disabling social stigma and to maintain a view of himself as not afflicted. This view of himself as not sick, in concert with others' acceptance, probably contributed to a relatively good outcome.

From individual to collective representation

While psychotic behavior is recognized as deviant across cultures (Murphy, 1976), the conceptual category of mental disorder itself is not universal (Kleinman, 1988; Kirmayer, 1993). In many cultures, deviant behavior is viewed first in terms of its interpersonal, social or moral significance (Kirmayer, 1989). These interpretations may be more salient and credible for both the sufferer and his social circle than accounts that focus on illness. This is so in part because psychotic experience is often uncanny and so prompts supernatural explanations. Religious explanations give more complete and satisfactory accounts of experience than illness attributions when the causes and mechanisms of disease remain shrouded from view and poorly worked out. Religious explanation provides a satisfying answer to psychosis not only because it ties up loose ends and gives an appropriate ontology for uncanny (supernatural) experiences, but also because it has esthetic, moral, and rhetorical force.[10]

Very commonly, then, psychotic experiences are viewed as religious, and individuals who are able to function well enough to parlay these experiences into work as a religious healer or ritual expert may continue to be symptomatic while enjoying an enhanced social role. Obeyesekere (1981) provided examples of this history in his

[10] Kirov and colleagues (1998) found that 61.2% of their sample of 52 schizophrenic patients actively used their religion for coping with their illness, and 30.4% of the sample reported increased religiousness after of the onset of psychotic illness. They found that religious practice was helpful to some subjects as a way to re-establish personal equilibrium following a psychotic episode or to find meaning for otherwise difficult-to-explain experiences. Many of those most likely to use religion as a coping style were also able to recognize that they had a mental health problem. Indeed, those using religion to cope were rated as having higher insight into their illness and were more likely to be compliant with antipsychotic medication than were the other sample subjects.

accounts of religious healers in Sri Lanka. However, the availability of cultural symbols does not suffice in itself. In a later recent work, Obeyesekere (1991) distinguished between two ways in which suffering individuals may use cultural symbols: a "progressive" mode that allows them to embed symptoms or conflicts within a larger shared universe of meaning, and a "regressive" mode which traps them in a symbolic realm of archaic fantasies and persistent anxiety. Both psychological and social factors influence the way in which cultural symbols are used.

Even if social functioning is impaired and the sufferer recognizes that something is wrong, the notion that it is an illness does not necessarily follow. Nor, if it is recognized as an illness, need it be a *mental* illness – i.e., one confined to specific faculties or aspects of the person (Kirmayer, 1988). Many of the great systems of medicine (e.g., traditional Chinese medicine, Ayurveda) do not have detailed theories of mental disorder as distinct from physical illness (Fabrega, 1991). Differences in disease classification are paralleled by ethnopsychological concepts that situate feelings and emotions not within the disembodied psyche of the individual but in the lived body or in social relationships, the environment, or a spirit world (Kirmayer, 1989; Shweder, 1991).

So far we have approached insight as an attainment of the individual that depends on self-perception and self-representation. Culture then impinges on insight through its effect on individual perception and representation. If we wish to characterize a group we can do so through the individual with a sort of "epidemiology" of cognitive representations (Sperber, 1985) – which might be differentially distributed across class, social status, education, occupation, and subcultural lines.

Culture, however, is a matter not only of individual representations but also of collective representations and actions that are embodied or enacted only through interactional processes that involve family, community and social institutions. Insight, then, is not simply the product and property of the individual – it is a social construction that many actors in the patient's world contribute to and which they, in turn, may use for differing ends.

The interpretation of a particular illness episode is made according to systems of meaning that belong to a culture through a process that involves negotiation among many actors. In a study in South India, Corin and colleagues (2004), found that the quest for a causal explanation among young schizophrenic patients was only part of a much larger set of questions about the meaning of life. Their search for meaning could be seen as an attempt to name a feeling of otherness, of the uncanny, in order to locate it in the field of culture and language. In interviews, patients tended to evoke less often the typical "cultural" etiologies (black magic or evil spirits) but instead scrutinized their own life to identify what might have contributed to their current problems. Problems were seen as a sign of something involving their fundamental identity (for example, a sense of a mission that might remain enigmatic, or a sign of their devotion to Lord Shiva) rather than as the outcome of a specific cause. An analogous quest for meaning also surfaced in the interest shown by a number of patients with psychosis (both in Montreal and in India) for the esoteric, evidenced by the reading of religious or pop-psychology books. The broad question of the meaning of life takes on particular importance in the context of psychosis because psychotic experience threatens the tacit order of common sense.

For family members in India, the evocation of causes involving evil spirits and black magic went on in parallel with diagnoses given by astrologists who explained the patient's problems by the position of auspicious and inauspicious planets. This allowed family members to inscribe the tragic drift of the patient's life within an ordered world, to assign it a place within a cosmic frame and to indicate an anticipated end to the problems. The same could be said of explanations evoking karma. These two etiological registers in the family's discourse respond to a desire to reintegrate the disorder manifested by psychosis within an ordered world.

For both patient and family, the evocation of evil spirits and black magic served to name a feeling of strangeness and alienation. The relative importance of a general quest for meaning and of astrological explanations among patients and family members may reflect their respective positions towards psychosis: for the patients', a desire to name strangeness and recover meaning; and for the families, a desire to reintegrate the patient within a shared sociocultural framework.

An analogous concern for integrating psychotic experience within a broader life framework is also evident in interviews done with psychotic patients met through alternative help groups in mental health in Montreal. These patients insisted on the importance of being listened to: to be able to express what they experience, to open the door to emotions, to find words for what remained unsaid, even beyond language – all of which helped to tame and control crises and allowed patients to work through their own life histories (Rodriguez, Corin, and Guay, 2000).

Corin's work with families of schizophrenic patients in India sheds light on the outcome of studies on expressed emotion and the course of schizophrenia (Corin *et al.*, 2004). It clarifies the broad notion of tolerance of psychotic experience within families by describing how it actually works: preserving a positive vision of the patient as he was in the past that is seen as reflecting his true being; adjusting to the patient's behaviors; and exercising restraint to avoid imposing too much pressure on him. This tolerance develops despite two major constraints: the enormous amount of grieving for lost hopes, dreams and expectations of a better life for the whole family that were invested in the patient; and the general stigmatization attached to mental health disorders in the larger society. Corin's work also shows the role played by broader cultural elements in helping to frame the attitude of tolerance, including: elaborating a general attitude of detachment towards the material world, in a way valued by the Hindu philosophy of life, through prayers, meditation and singing; the performance of rituals and prayers as a way to sustain hope; and a resort to karma theory, which relates current problems to events during past lives.

It is important to stress that culture itself is heterogeneous and polysemic, and different actors or one actor at different moments may mobilize different aspects of the cultural frame. Corin's work in India illustrates how patients and family members give a different weight to different aspects of the cultural frame – a weighting that reflects their particular position towards psychosis and the specific challenges that the problems entail for patients and family members. In the sphere of religion for example, patients seem to favour a strand of religious signifiers associated with a position of withdrawal and an ascetic pathway to spirituality, while family members favour ritual activities and inner detachment through prayer and confiding in God. This difference echoes broader tensions within Hinduism between ritual and worship on the one hand, and a more solitary path to spirituality associated with ascetic practices and a quest for enlightenment on the other.

Culture as contestation

Diagnosis is only one moment in a larger quest for meaning and therapy. In most societies, this quest is not an individual matter; it is the responsibility of the family group (what Janzen (1978) calls the *therapy management group*) to decide whom to consult, to evaluate the relevance of the diagnosis and to monitor the various treatments and their efficacy. Different members of the family may have their own hypotheses regarding the nature of the disease. Even in traditional societies, most belief systems are intrinsically pluralistic, allowing room for choice and confrontation. Different segments of the patient's social network bring to bear different systems of interpretation as a function of their own relationship to traditions. This diversity is intensified during periods of rapid culture change when members of the same family may rely on different strata of cultural meaning. For example, as described by Ortigues and Ortigues (1966) in Senegal, the generation of grandparents might favor an explanation in terms of *rab* (ancestral spirits) who have concluded an alliance with certain families and who may ask for ceremonial sacrifices. At the same time, parents may focus on malign magic, which entails a search for interpersonal conflicts. Young people may appeal to scientific explanations. Often, belief systems within a family are not so clearly demarcated along generational boundaries. Uchôa (1993) shows the multiple and conflicting interpretations employed by different family members in her detailed account of a woman in Mali with repeated psychiatric hospitalizations. Among the factors invoked to explain her difficulties are her status as a twin, raised by a childless stepmother, torn between her Western educational aspirations and her *griot* background, forced to marry against her will a husband who then takes a second wife. Each actor in her drama interprets her behavior from their position within the social and cultural field, thereby reproducing the familial and social contradictions that contribute to her distress.

Acknowledgment of the psychiatric nature of a problem or the decision to seek psychiatric help by an individual or by his or his entourage must be situated within such a context of pluralism and negotiation. Conventional Western psychiatric insight corresponds to the acceptance of one possible interpretation. However, in African societies, such insight may be accepted for a variety of reasons, not all of which are salutary. Far from always corresponding to an increased ability to understand the true nature of a disorder, acceptance of a conventional psychiatric diagnosis may be a sign that the family feels helpless to deal with the problem, has exhausted its resources, or cannot reach a consensus. Resort to Western psychiatry may also indicate that the patient has been socially marginalized or excluded from traditional cultural practices. Analogous dynamics can be observed in the context of immigration, where the presence of cultural differences between professional and patient can accentuate the perception that psychiatry is situated outside the patient's lifeworld. It seems clear then, that if the notion of insight is meant to characterize the patient's position toward the illness, other criteria than mere conformity to the biomedical view must be used.

This is well illustrated in the case from Senegal of a woman, called Animata, who was hospitalized for an acute episode of agitation (Ortigues, Martino and Collomb, 1967). This episode appeared abruptly, but she had faced many stresses over the previous two years: the deaths of her mother and her 18-month-old daughter; marital conflict; and a fire in her house. The authors described in detail the parallel evolution of her clinical course and her discourse regarding the potential causes of her affliction. An intelligent woman, she expressed herself with clarity, discussing the place of her family's ancestral spirits in her life, the fate of "exceptional" children regarded as reincarnated ancestors, and her expectations of the *marabouts* she consulted. The authors comment: "All has occurred as if she had organized her illness in front of us and this organization has appeared to us as the very moment of her recovery" (p. 121). They conclude that clinicians can benefit from close examination of patients' use of traditional illness beliefs, both to understand the patient herself, and also to shed light on diagnosis and prognosis. In his clinical work in Senegal, Henri Collomb (1965) also suggested that the deployment of these traditional interpretive systems allows patients to tame disturbing or frightening experiences and aids in their integration. This is one of the explanations Collomb offered for the apparent fact that in Africa the acute paranoid psychoses (*bouffées délirantes*) are less likely to evolve into chronic psychoses than in Western countries (Stevens, 1987; Okasha, Dawla and Saad, 1993).

In a study done in Montréal with people diagnosed as schizophrenic and their families, Corin observed a parallel quest for meaning (Corin, 1990; Corin and Lauzon, 1992). In this research, the interpretive principles applied to patients' discourse were not based on a grid of symptoms (e.g., simply assessing "is the discourse psychotic?") but on the type of experiential world that the discourse revealed. This is in line with the distinction made by the European phenomenological psychiatrists Binswanger (1970) and Blankenburg (1986), between a view of abnormal behaviors as *symptoms* of a hidden disease and as *phenomena* expressing a basic alteration of the experience of *being-in-the-world*. In the second perspective, behavior is considered a window on a lifeworld that comprises experience, action and the presentation of self. In her study, Corin took a phenomenological stance and collected two types of data relevant to the concept of insight. The first, considered the manner in which patients described their earlier experience and the way in which they sought to rebuild and give it meaning; the second type concerned patients' self-descriptions. In both cases, what emerged was the importance of recognizing individuals' fundamental suffering but, at the same time, its appropriation and "re-opening" by the play of symbolic meanings – particularly, the reintroduction of a gap, or a multiplicity of potential meanings, in the way in which they characterize themselves. Similarly, the distinction between negative symptoms and the position of *positive withdrawal* associated with a favorable course in Corin's study is to be sought at the level of the afflicted person's use of specific meaning systems.

In the urban North American context, however, we have been struck by the fragmented, solitary, and uncertain character of the explanations for illness offered by patients and their families. No encompassing framework is available to them through which they can explore and integrate the meaning of the illness. The therapeutic interaction tends to be restricted to a private colloquy between patient and clinician, and the meaning of symptoms is assimilated to the clinician's diagnostic grid rather than reflecting a dialogical understanding of the patient's lifeworld. As the diagnosis does not build on current understanding of patient and family, it is likely to remain external to the person and of little use in organizing the structure and meaning of everyday life. In this Western context, communicating the diagnosis and leading the patient to accept it, is a sort of pedagogical enterprise. The task assigned to patients is to accept the doctor's authoritative diagnosis and they have little freedom or encouragement to rework it in a personal and creative way (Kirmayer, 1994). While the mental illness label is not necessarily disabling in itself (cf. Warner, Taylor, Powers and Hyman, 1989), it is at least debatable whether the kind of insight that results from this approach is of greater clinical utility and healing efficacy that one supported by collective symbolic processes as found in other societies.

Davidson and Strauss (1992) suggest that the process of rediscovering and reconstructing a valued and functional sense of self is central to recovery from psychosis. The aspects of this process they observed in their longitudinal study of patients include: (1) discovering the possibility of a more active sense of self or agency; (2) taking stock of strengths and weaknesses and of possibilities for change; (3) putting into action some aspects of the self as a reflection of actual capabilities; (4) using an enhanced sense of self-identity as a refuge from illness and social stigma. They suggest that the self constitutes a fulcrum where both social factors and one's own efforts at self-definition exert comparable force in determining the course of illness.

To the extent that the self is a unitary construct, the multidimensionality of insight pointed out by David (1990) raises issues for dissonance theory centering on how people integrate discrepant information about the self. Do they keep it separate from information about the self (that is, as being about symptoms rather than about illness affecting the self) or add premises to their cognitive self-representation to neutralize, reframe or reinterpret the potentially dissonant information carried by recognition that they are ill?

In this regard, it is important to note that not all knowledge is directly related to the self and therefore does not demand the same level or type of coherence. Different cultural concepts of the self may allow different experiences and behaviors to be interpreted as either irrelevant to the self or support a view of the self as inherently less coherent and therefore tolerate higher degrees of inconsistency (Ewing, 1990). In fact, the whole notion of the self as a unitary construct may be misleading. Information relevant to the self may be acquired and organized in a variety of ways, resulting a series of "selves" that are held together by functional relationships and social requirements for coherence. (Neisser, 1988) distinguishes five types of self with corresponding forms of self-knowledge: (1) the *ecological self*, constructed through feedback from perception and action in the physical environment; (2) the *interpersonal self*, based on the felt significance of emotional attachments and relationships; (3) the *extended self*, developed through the narratives of autobiographical memory; (4) the *private self*, based on the experience of privileged access to one's own thoughts and feelings; (5) the *conceptual self*, comprising the network of assumptions, models and metaphors about oneself as a person, encompassing knowledge of social roles, ethnopsychology and the position of self in a moral universe. The conceptual self is the inward face of what anthropologists have studied as the cultural concept of the person (Carrithers, Collins, and Lukes, 1985; Markus and Kitayama, 1991; Marsella, DeVos and Hsu, 1985; Shweder, 1991). Although these different selves are woven together into a unitary conception of the self through their functional interactions, the process of acquiring knowledge about each of these selves can be quite distinct.

Indeed, it is possible for contradictions to exist between different versions of the self; these discrepanices need not be wilful, although it is possible for the person to intentionally maintain scotomata toward certain aspects of self-knowledge. As Markova and Berrios (1992) suggest, such self-deception may be considered a failure to spell out, or to commit oneself to, a version of reality. The term "self-deception", however, implies that a cold, clear, "accurate" vision of one's own status is best, when much work in social psychology suggests that healthy people enjoy many self-serving biases and distortions in their view of self (Greenwald, 1980; Kiersky, 1998; Taylor and Brown, 1988; for a critique of this literature see Shedler, Mayman and Manis, 1993). Both intrapsychic and interpersonal factors may lead an individual to adopt a stance of denial, self-deception or positive misconstrual. A social-cultural perspective would emphasize that this stance must be understood as a form of social positioning (or maintaining a fluid position) vis-à-vis others (Davies and Harré 1990).

Conclusion

We began this chapter with the case of Martin to emphasize that culture is not something "out there" – relevant only to exotic peoples in far away places. All experience is culturally embedded, and the personal and social significance of psychotic symptoms can be understood only with close attention to the history and practices of the sufferer and his milieu. The psychiatric concept of insight privileges the professional explanation of events in terms of disorder or disease over the patient's lived experience. But illness admits of many possible interpretations that serve different functions for the individual and his or her entourage. The notion that there is a single accurate or correct view of things given by neuroscience or psychology will not suffice when we face the more pressing clinical question of what to do to make chronic illness livable. Martin understood, better than most, the contemporary psychiatric view of his condition: it is no exaggeration to say that he was killed by insight.[11]

The metaphor of insight implies that self-awareness is based on introspection. Social psychological studies, however, suggest that self-knowledge is largely the product of social processes involving observation of others and acquisition of culture-specific modes of self-description. Insight, then, does not involve a transparent act of self-perception but a cognitive and social construction or construal of the self. As such, it is profoundly shaped by cultural beliefs and practices.

Recognition of the presence of a psychiatric problem is not simply an individual process that depends on the nature or degree of illness. It consists equally of social processes negotiated among patients, families and experts – who may belong to the patient's culture of origin or be situated outside that culture. If we conceptualize insight as defined in the psychiatric literature as a specific form of interpretation, contingent on a larger interpretive field, we can appreciate that the link to reality that allows one to gain insight can be through other things than simply the recognition of symptoms. The emphasis on the recognition of symptoms reflects the dominant orientation of the current psychiatric system or, more precisely, its naturalistic perspective toward mental illness.

Psychological explanations are based on a culturally distinctive construction of the self that emphasizes privacy, individualism, autonomy, and self-control. While this mode of self-depiction is highly valued in many Western societies, it is only one possible construal of the self. In recent years, much attention has been given to cultures with a more sociocentric notion of the self. This different concept of the self may influence the symptomatology, course, and treatment response of psychotic disorders.

Culture influences the psychotic person's insight into his condition in diverse ways: (1) developing habits of self-observation and self-description that allow the person to recognize and communicate alterations in private experience; (2) drawing attention to certain behaviors or experiences as deviant and hence as signs or symptoms of affliction; (3) offering specific accounts for deviant behavior and experience that lead the person to categorize his own condition as sickness, moral failing, divine visitation, etc.; (4) providing ways of assimilating psychotic experience into a social identity. This last

---

[11] Nor is this situation exceptional. Suicide among schizophrenics tends to occur within two years of a first episode and to affect mostly better-educated subjects; its occurrence cannot be predicted by traditional suicide risk scales nor does it appear to be modified by drug therapy. Becker (1988) describes it as a "syndrome of cognitive despair", which is a consequence of functional impairments, social disabilities, and a loss of realistic hope for recovery.

is particularly important, since most knowledge – including the sort of self-knowledge that is taken as insight – is not stored as abstract representations but remains implicit in modes of practice or a way of life (Kirmayer, 1992).

Cross-cultural studies of schizophrenia demonstrate the pervasive and profound effects of culture on insight in psychosis. Existing epidemiological studies, while limited by a focus on establishing cross-cultural similarities, have nevertheless indicated sub-stantial variation in the symptomatology, course and outcome of schizophrenia and other psychoses, with better outcomes reported in some less industrialized countries (Waxler, 1979; Jablensky *et al.*, 1992). Culturally determined modes of insight and explanation may account, in part, for these clinically important differences.

Unfortunately, there is as yet little empirical work on insight in psychosis from a cross-cultural perspective. However, there are studies of social labeling, experience, and social course and treatment of psychosis that have suggestive implications for future work on insight. A sociocultural perspective can do much to clarify issues in this area, in part by insisting that insight be understood as culturally constructed in at least three ways: through culturally informed cognitive schemata, through collective representa-tions and practices that are socially embodied (and hence, not to be found within the individual) and through an understanding of insight as a form of self-presentation or positioning in a local world where meanings and self-ascriptions are negotiated, col-laboratively constructed, and often, hotly contested. This adds another dimension to efforts to measure insight as some intrinsic property or capacity of the individual and insists that we attend equally to the social contexts in which insight is being measured and in which it is used.

Ultimately, insight serves not only self-regulatory functions but also social-rhetorical purposes. Consequently, insight and denial must be seen as facets of the afflicted per-son's stance or position in relationships with health care providers, in the family, and in wider social spheres. The nature and degree of insight is context dependent and must be understood by researchers and clinicians as a response to the cultural meaning of psychotic experience.

References

Amador, X. F., Strauss, D. H., Yale, S. A., Flaum, M. H. and Gorman, J. M. (1993). Assessment of insight in psychosis. *American Journal of Psychiatry*, **150**, 873–9.

Bateson, G. (1972). *Steps to an Ecology of Mind*. New York: Ballantine Books.

Becker, R. E. (1988). Depression in schizophrenia. *Hospital and Community Psychiatry*, **39** (12), 1269–75.

Bellah, R. N., Madsen, R., Sullivan, W. M., Swidler, A. and Tipton, S. M. (1985). *Habits of the Heart: Individualism and commitment in American life*. Berkeley: University of California Press.

Binswanger, L. (1970). *Analyse existentielle et psychanalyse freudienne*. Paris: Gallimard.

Blankenburg, W. (1986). Sur le rapport entre Pratique Psychiatrique et Phénoménologie. In P. Fédida (ed.) *Phénoménologie, Psychiatrie, Psychanalyse*, pp. 133–40. Paris: Edition G.R.E. U.P. P.

Bowers, M. B., Jr. (1974). *Retreat From Sanity: The Structure of Emerging Psychosis*. Baltimore: Penguin Books.

Bruner, J. (1990). *Acts of Meaning*. Cambridge: Harvard University Press.

Carrithers, M., Collins, S. and Lukes, S. (ed.) (1985). *The Category of the Person*. Cambridge: Cambridge University Press.

Carter, J. H. (2002). Religion/spirituality in African-American culture: An essential aspect of psychiatric care. *Journal of the National Medical Association*, **94**, 371–5.

Cohen, A. (1992). Prognosis for schizophrenia in the Third World: A reevaluation of cross-cultural research. *Culture, Medicine, and Psychiatry*, **16** (1), 53–77.

Collomb, H. (1965). Bouffées délirantes en psychiatrie africaine. *Psychopathologie Africaine*, 167–239.

Cooper, J. and Sartorius, N. (1977). Cultural and temporal variations in schizophrenia: A speculation on the importance of industrialization. *British Journal of Psychiatry*, **130**, 50–5.

Corin, E. (1990). Facts and meaning in psychiatry: An anthropological approach to the lifeworld of schizophrenics. *Culture, Medicine and Psychiatry*, **14**, 153–88.

Corin, E. (1998a). The thickness of being: Intentional worlds, strategies of identity and experience among schizophrenics. *Psychiatry*, **61** (2), 133–46.

Corin, E. (1998b). Refiguring the person: The dynamics of affects and symbols in an African spirit possession cult. In M. Lambek and A. Strathern (ed.) *Bodies and Persons, Comparative Perspectives from Africa and Melanesia*, pp. 80–102. Cambridge (UK): Cambridge University Press.

Corin, E., Bibeau, G. and Uchôa, E. (1993). Eléments d'une sémiologie anthropologique des troubles psychiques chez les Bambara, Soninké et Bwa du Mali. *Anthropologie et sociétés*, **17** (1–2), 125–56.

Corin, E. and Lauzon, G. (1992). Positive withdrawal and the quest for meaning: The reconstruction of experience among schizophrenics. *Psychiatry*, **55**, 266–78.

Corin, E. and Lauzon, G. (1994). From symptoms to phenomena: The articulation of experience in schizophrenia. *Journal of Phenomenological Psychology*, **25** (1).

Corin, E., Thara, R. and Padmavati, R. (2004). Living through a staggering world: The play of signifiers in early psychosis in South India. In J. Jenkins and R. Barrett (ed.) *Schizophrenia, Culture and Subjectivity: The Edge of Experience* (pp. 110–45). New York: Cambridge University Press.

Cuesta, M. J., Peralta, V. and Zarzuela, A. (2000). Reappraising insight in psychosis. *British Journal of Psychiatry*, **177**, 233–40.

David, A. S. (1990). Insight and psychosis. *British Journal of Psychiatry*, **156**, 798–808.

David, A. S. and Howard, R. (1994). An experimental phenomenological approach to delusional memory in schizophrenia and late paraphrenia. *Psychological Medicine*, **24** (2), 515–24.

David, A., Buchanan, A., Reed, A. and Almeida, O. (1992). The assessment of insight in psychosis. *British Journal of Psychiatry*, **161**.

Davidson, L. and Strauss, J. S. (1992). Sense of self in recovery from severe mental illness. *British Journal of Medical Psychology*, **65**, 131–45.

Davies, B. and Harré, R. (1990). Positioning: The discursive production of selves. *Journal for the Theory of Social Behavior*, **20** (1), 43–64.

Dennett, D. C. (1991). *Consciousness Explained*. Boston: Little, Brown and Company.

Dick, P. K. (1990). *The VALIS Trilogy*. New York: Book-of-the-Month Club.

Dick, P. K. (1991). *In Pursuit of Valis: Selections from the Exegesis*. Novato, CA: Underwood-Miller.

Dumont, L. (1986). *Essays on Individualism: Modern Ideology in Anthropological Perspective*. Chicago: University of Chicago Press.

Edgerton, R. B. and Cohen, A. (1994). Culture and schizophrenia: The DOSMD challenge. *British Journal of Psychiatry*, **164**, 222–31.

Ericsson, K. A. and Simon, H. A. (1984). *Protocol Analysis*. Cambridge: MIT Press.

Ewing, K. (1990). The illusion of wholeness: Culture, self, and the experience of inconsistency. *Ethos*, **18**, 251–78.

Fabrega, H., Jr. (1991). Psychiatric stigma in non-western societies. *Comprehensive Psychiatry*, **32** (6), 534–51.

Good, B. J. (1994). *Medicine, Rationality, and Experience: An anthropological perspective*. Cambridge: Cambridge University Press.

Good, B. and Good, M. J. D. (1980). The meaning of symptoms: A cultural hermeneutic model for clinical practice. In L. Eisenberg and A. Kleinman (ed.) *The Relevance of Social Science for Medicine*, pp. 165–96. Dordrecht: D. Reidel.

Good, B. J. and Good, M.-J. D. (1993). Au mode subjonctif. La construction narrative des crises d'épilepsie en Turquie. *Anthropologie et sociétés*, **17** (1–2), 31–42.

Green, M. F. and Kinsbourne, M. (1990). Subvocal activity and auditory hallucinations: Clues for behavioral treatments? *Schizophrenia Bulletin*, **16** (4), 617–25.

Greenwald, A. (1980). The totalitarian ego: Fabrication and revision of personal history. *American Psychologist*, **35** (7), 603–18.

Guarnaccia, P. J., Parra, P., Deschamps, A., Milstein, G. and Argiles, N. (1992). Si Dios quiere: Hispanic families' experiences of caring for a seriously mentally ill family member. *Culture, Medicine and Psychiatry*, **16** (2), 187–216.

Guinness, E. A. (1992). Brief reactive psychosis and the major functional psychoses: Descriptive case studies in Africa. *British Journal of Psychiatry*, **160** (suppl. 16), 24–41.

Gupta, S. (1992). Cross-national differences in the frequency and outcome of schizophrenia: A comparison of five hypotheses. *Social Psychiatry and Psychiatric Epidemiology*, **27**, 249–52.

Hacking, I. (1995). *Rewriting the Soul*. Princeton: Princeton University Press.

Hoffman, R. E. (1986). Verbal hallucinations and language production processes in schizophrenia. *Behavioral and Brain Sciences*, **9** (3), 503–48.

Hole, R. W., Rush, A. J. and Beck, A. T. (1979). A cognitive investigation of schizophrenic delusions. *Psychiatry*, **42**, 312–19.

Howard, G. S. (1991). Culture tales: A narrative approach to thinking, cross-cultural psychology, and psychotherapy. *American Psychologist*, **46** (3), 187–97.

Humphrey, N. (1992). *A History of the Mind: Evolution and the birth of consciousness*. New York: Simon and Schuster.

Jablensky, A., Sartorius, N., Ernberg, G., Anker, M., Korten, A., Cooper, J. E., *et al.* (1992). Schizophrenia: Manifestations, incidence and course in different cultures: A World Health Organization Ten-Country Study. *Psychological Medicine* (Monograph Supplement 20).

Janzen, J. M. (1978). *The Quest for Therapy in Lower Zaire*. Berkeley: University of California.

Jarvis, E. (1998). Schizophrenia in British immigrants: Recent findings, issues and implications. *Transcultural Psychiatry*, **35** (1), 39–74.

Jarvis, G. E. (2002). *Emergency psychiatric treatment of immigrants with psychosis*. Unpublished M.Sc., McGill University, Montreal.

Jenkins, J. H. (1988). Ethnopsychiatric interpretations of schizophrenic illness: The problem of nervios in Mexican-American families. *Culture, Medicine and Psychiatry*, **12**, 303–31.

Jenkins, J. H. and Karno, M. (1992). The meaning of expressed emotion: Theoretical issues raised by cross-cultural research. *American Journal of Psychiatry*, **149** (1), 9–21.

Johnson, S. K., and Orrell, M. (1995). Insight and psychosis: A social perspective. *Psychological Medicine*, **25**, 515–20.

Johnson, S. K., and Orrell, M. (1996). Insight, psychosis and ethnicity: A case-note study. *Psychological Medicine*, **26**, 1081–4.

Karno, M., Jenkins, J. H., de la Selva, A., Santana, F., Telles, C., Lopez, S., *et al.* (1987). Expressed emotion and schizophrenic outcome among Mexican-American families. *Journal of Nervous and Mental Disease*, **175** (3), 143–51.

Kiersky, J. E. (1998). Insight, self-deception, and psychosis in mood disorders. In X. F. Amador, and A. S. David (ed.) *Insight and Psychosis*, pp. 91–104. New York: Oxford University Press.

Kirby, A. P. (1991). *Narrative and the Self*. Bloomington: Indiana University Press.

Kirmayer, L. J. (1983). Paranoia and pronoia: The visionary and the banal. *Social Problems*, **31** (2), 170–9.

Kirmayer, L. J. (1988). Mind and body as metaphors: Hidden values in biomedicine. In M. Lock and D. Gordon (ed.) *Biomedicine Examined*, pp. 57–92. Dordrecht: Kluwer.

Kirmayer, L. J. (1989). Cultural variations in the response to psychiatric disorders and emotional distress. *Social Science and Medicine*, **29** (3), 327–39.

Kirmayer, L. J. (1992). The body's insistence on meaning: Metaphor as presentation and representation in illness experience. *Medical Anthropology Quarterly*, **6** (4), 323–46.

Kirmayer, L. J. (1993). Is the concept of mental disorder culturally relative? In S. A. Kirk and S. Einbinder (ed.) *Controversial Issues in Mental Health*, Boston: Appleton-Century-Croft.

Kirmayer, L. J. (1994). Improvisation and authority in illness meaning. *Culture, Medicine and Psychiatry*, **18** (2), 183–214. [Erratum **18** (4), 515]

Kirov, G., Kemp, R., Kirov, K. and David, A. S. (1998). Religious faith after psychotic illness. *Psychopathology*, **31** (5), 234–45.

Kirov, G., and Murray, R. M. (1999). Ethnic differences in the presentation of bipolar disorder. *European Psychiatry*, **14**, 199–204.

Kleinman, A. M. (1980). *Patients and Healers in the Context of Culture*. Berkeley: University of California Press.

Kleinman, A. (1988). *Rethinking Psychiatry*. New York: Free Press.

Lakoff, G. and Johnson, M. (1980). *Metaphors We Live By*. Chicago: University of Chicago Press.

Leff, J. (1988). *Psychiatry Around the Globe: A Transcultural View*. London: Gaskell.

Leff, J., Sartorius, N., Jablensky, A., Korten, A. and Ernberg, G. (1992). The International Pilot Study of Schizophrenia: five-year follow-up findings. *Psychological Medicine*, **22**, 131–45.

Leff, J. and Vaughn, C. (1985). *Expressed Emotion in Families*. New York: Guilford Press.

Leff, J., Wig, N. N., Bedi, H., Menon, D. K., *et al.* (1990). Relatives' expressed emotion and the course of schizophrenia in Chandigarh: A two year follow-up of a first contact sample. *British Journal of Psychiatry*, **156**, 351–6.

Leff, J., Wig, N. N., Ghosh, A., Bedi, H., Menon, D. K., Kuipers, L., *et al.* (1987). III. Influence of relatives' expression emotion on the course of schizophrenia in Chandigarh. *British Journal of Psychiatry*, **151**, 166–73.

Lemert, E. M. (1962). Paranoia and the dynamics of exclusion. *Sociometry*, **25**, 2–20.

Lewis, A. (1934). The psychopathology of insight. *British Journal of Medical Psychology*, **13**, 332–48.

Lin, K-M. and Kleinman, A. (1988). Psychopathology and clinical course of schizophrenia: A cross-cultural perspective. *Schizophrenia Bulletin*, **14** (4), 555–67.

Link, B. G. (1987). Understanding labeling effects in the area of mental disorders: An assessment of the effects of expectations of rejection. *American Sociological Review*, **52**, 96–112.

Link, B., Cullen, F. T., Frank, J. and Wozniak, J. F. (1987). The social rejection of former mental patients: Understanding why labels matter. *American Journal of Sociology*, **92** (6), 1461–500.

Markova, I. S. and Berrios, G. E. (1992). The meaning of insight in clinical psychiatry. *British Journal of Psychiatry*, **160**, 850–60.

Markus, H. R. and Kitayama, S. (1991). Culture and the self: Implications for cognition, emotion, and motivation. *Psychological Review*, **98** (2), 224–53.

Marsella, A. J., DeVos, G. and Hsu, F. L. K. (ed.) (1985). *Culture and Self: Asian and Western Perspectives*. New York: Tavistock.

Melges, F. T. and Freeman, A. M., III (1975). Persecutory delusions: A cybernetic model. *American Journal of Psychiatry*, **132** (10), 1038–44.

Murphy, H. B. M. (1982). *Comparative Psychiatry: The International and Intercultural Distribution of Mental Illness*. New York: Springer-Verlag.

Murphy, H. B. M. and Raman, A. C. (1971). The chronicity of schizophrenia in indigenous tropical people. Results of a twelve year follow-up survey in Mauritius. *British Journal of Psychiatry*, **118**, 489–97.

Murphy, J. M. (1976). Psychiatric labeling in cross-cultural perspective. *Science*, **191**, 1019–28.

Neisser, U. (1988). Five kinds of self-knowledge. *Philosophical Psychology*, **1**, 35–59.

Nisbett, R. E. and Wilson, T. D. (1977). Telling more than we can know: verbal reports on mental processes. *Psychological Review*, **84** (3), 231–59.

Obeyesekere, G. (1981). *Medusa's Hair: An Essay on Personal Symbols and Religious Experience*. Chicago: University of Chicago Press.

Obeyesekere, G. (1991). *The Work of Culture: Symbolic Transformation in Psychoanalysis and Anthropology*. Chicago: University of Chicago Press.

Okasha, A., El Dawla, S. and Saad, A. (1993). Presentation of acute psychosis in an Egyptian sample: A transcultural comparison. *Comprehensive Psychiatry*, **34** (1), 4–9.

Ortigues, M.-C., Martino, P. and Collomb, H. (1967). L'utilization des données culturelles dans un cas de bouffée délirante. *Psychopathologie Africaine*, 121–47.

Ortigues, M. C. and Ortigues, E. (1966). *Oedipe africain*. Paris: Plan.

Peralta, V. and Cuesta, M. J. (1998). Lack of insight in mood disorders. *Journal of Affective Disorders*, **49**, 55–8.

Raybeck, D. (1988). Anthropology and labeling theory: A constructive critique. *Ethos*, **16**, 371–97.

Ricoeur, P. (1992). *Oneself as Another*. Chicago: University of Chicago Press.

Robinson, J. M. (Ed.). (1977). *The Nag Hammadi Library*. New York: Harper and Row.

Robinson, J. M. (Ed.). (1988). *The Nag Hammadi Library in English* (3rd revised edn. Leiden: E. J. Brill.

Rodriguez, L., Corin, E. and Guay, L. (2000). La thérapie alternative: se (re)mettre en mouvement. In Y. Lecomte and J. Gagné (ed.) *Les Ressources Alternatives de Traitement*. Montreal: Regroupement des ressources alternatives en santé mentale du Québec and Santé Mentale au Québec.

Ross, L. and Nisbett, R. E. (1991). *The Person and the Situation: Perspectives of Social Psychology*. Philadelphia: Temple University Press.

Rozin, P. and Nemeroff, C. (1990). The laws of sympathetic magic: A psychological analysis of similarity and contagion. In J. W. Stigler, R. A. Shweder and G. Herdt (ed.) *Cultural Psychology*, pp. 205–32. Cambridge: Cambridge University Press.

Sanz, M., Constable, G., Lopez-Ibor, I., Kemp, R. and David, A. S. (1998). A comparative study of insight scales and their relationship to psychopathological and clinical variables. *Psychological Medicine*, **23**, 437–46.

Sartorius, N. (1992). Commentary on Prognosis for Schizophrenia in the Third World by Alex Cohen. *Culture, Medicine, and Psychiatry*, **16** (1), 81–4.

Sartorius, N., Jablensky, A., Korten, A., Ernberg, G., *et al.* (1986). Early manifestations and first contact incidence of schizophrenia in different cultures. *Psychological Medicine*, **16**, 909–28.

Sartorius, N., Jablensky, A. and Shapiro, R. (1978). Cross-cultural differences in the short term prognosis of schizophrenic psychoses. *Schizophrenia Bulletin*, **4** (1), 102–13.

Shedler, J., Mayman and Manis, M. (1993). The *illusion* of mental health. *American Psychologist*, **48** (11), 1117–31.

Shweder, R. A. (1991). *Thinking Through Culture: Expeditions in Cultural Psychology*. Cambridge: Harvard University Press.

Sperber, D. (1985). Anthropology and psychology: towards an epidemiology of representations. *Man*, **20** (1), 73–89.

Stevens, J. (1987). Brief psychoses: Do they contribute to the good prognosis and equal prevalence of schizophrenia in developing countries? *British Journal of Psychiatry*, **151**, 393–6.

Sutin, L. (1989). *Divine Invasions: A Life of Philip K. Dick*. New York: Harmony Books.

Taylor, S. E. and Brown, J. (1988). Illusion and well-being: A social psychological perspective on mental health. *Journal of Personality and Social Psychology*, **48**, 285–90.

Thoits, P. A. (1985). Self-labeling processes in mental illness: The role of emotional deviance. *American Journal of Sociology*, **91** (2), 221–47.

Townsend, J. M. (1978). *Cultural Conceptions and Mental Illness*. Chicago: University of Chicago Press.

Uchôa, E. (1993). Espace dévolu, espace désiré, espace revendiqué. Indifférenciation et folie d'Ajaratou. *Anthropologie et sociétés*, **17** (1–2), 157–72.

Warner, R., Taylor, D., Powers, M. and Hyman, J. (1989). Acceptance of the mental illness label by psychotic patients: Effects on functioning. *American Journal of Orthopsychiatry*, **59** (3), 398–409.

Waxler, N. E. (1979). Is outcome for schizophrenia better in nonindustrial societies? The case of Sri Lanka. *Journal of Nervous and Mental Disease*, **167** (3), 144–58.

Weiler, M. A., Feisher, M. H., and McArthur-Campbell, D. (2000). Insight and sympom change in schizophrenia and other disorders. *Schizophrenia Research*, **43**, 29–36.

White, R., Bebbington, P. E., Pearson, J., Johnson, S. and Ellis, D. (2000). The social context of insight in schizophrenia. *Social Psychiatry and Psychiatric Epidemiology*, **35**, 500–7.

Williams, P. (1986). *Only Apparently Real: The World of Philip K. Dick*. New York: Arbor House.

WHO (World Health Organization) (1973). *The International Pilot Study of Schizophrenia, volume 1.* Geneva: WHO.

WHO (World Health Organization) (1979). *Schizophrenia: An International Follow-up Study*, New York: John Wiley.

Young, A. (1982). Rational men and the explanatory model approach. *Culture, Medicine and Psychiatry*, **6**, 57–71.

Chapter 11

Japanese attitudes towards insight in schizophrenia

Yoshiharu Kim

Historical background

The development of modern Japanese psychiatry was inaugurated after the Meiji Reformation in 1867. Pre-Meiji Japan had few asylums or hospitals to segregate the mentally ill (such as as existed in Europe), and had only certain temples which offered treatment through water bathing. Through Japan's long history, officials had taken a fairly generous attitude toward the mentally ill: records show few incidents of political persecution against them, and in 701, it was already determined that the mentally ill should be treated medically. During the Edo era (1604–1867) the criminal law admitted insanity as a mitigating circumstance. Unlike the situation in Europe, where the stigmatization of the mentally ill aroused moral protest by Pinel and Esquirol, there had been only a weak social and political tendency to alienate them in Japan. Moreover, the modern scientific urge to classify natural phenomena, promoted in Europe by Linne and Darwin, had no basis in traditional Japanese culture, which consequently experienced little systematic discussion of how to define and classify mental illness. Little interest was paid to the subject of insight in the mentally disordered, a feature whose lack was regarded in late nineteenth-century Europe as a kind of agnosia which was sometimes claimed to be the definition of mental illness (Pick, 1882, Dagonet, 1881; see Berrios and Markova, Chapter 2).

During the late Edo period, with the development of industry, incidents of discrimination against the mentally disordered, including deportation from their villages and the confinement to private prisons, increased. After the Meiji Reformation a number of psychiatric asylums were founded in the naive belief that it was more humane to treat the mentally disordered in hospitals than to leave them in their home or village. Since then, Japanese psychiatric practice has been largely based upon such inpatient treatment, borrowing its methodology mainly from German, and to a lesser degree French and English psychiatry. The school of psychopathology that was methodologically founded by Jaspers (1913), especially his assertion of the un-understandability of psychoses and the lack of insight in schizophrenia, became so influential in Japan as to determine the view of the majority of psychiatrists.

After the Second World War, the influence of American psychiatry reached Japan in the form of a more flexible view of the possibility of recovery from schizophrenia. Klerman (1991) stated that this American optimism was originally derived from experience with soldiers who suffered from reactive psychosis during wartime and recovered afterwards. Despite the fact that reactive psychosis was not always included in a narrower definition of schizophrenia used in Japan at that time, this new attitude stimulated the interest of a number of Japanese psychiatrists in the social rehabilitation of schizophrenics. After the introduction of anti-psychotic drugs in 1955, Japanese psychiatric treatment started to change toward outpatient management, social rehabilitation and day care treatment. In 1958, Utena and his colleagues at Gunma University instituted the *Seikatsu-rinshou*, a long-term programme for the social rehabilitation of schizophrenics that still continues today.

Under these circumstances, in 1963 a symposium on insight in schizophrenia was held by the Japanese Conference of Psychopathology with the aim of re-evaluating the definition of insight promoted by Jaspers, which divided sense of illness from insight, regarding the former as a vague feeling of sickness without precise awareness of its nature and extent, and the latter as an exact consciousness of the illness including its type, severity and symptoms. The criticisms made by Japanese psychiatrists at that time arose because ongoing changes in the clinical practice of treatmenr of schizophrenia came to require more positive and flexible views of schizophrenics' attitudes toward their illness.

In 1964 the then-American Ambassador to Japan, Edward Reischauer, was attacked and nearly assassinated by a young Japanese schizophrenic. Because the Japanese government wanted to avoid diplomatic conflict with the United States, it decided to revise the Mental Hygiene Law toward the seclusion and confinement of psychiatric patients, in order to demonstrate that Japan was determined not to let such an incident happen again. The construction of psychiatric hospitals was accelerated with the result that the number of psychiatric inpatients increased from 100,000 in 1960 to 300,000 in 1970. Regrettably, these additional inpatients were sometimes managed by an insufficient number of staff and by doctors who lacked psychiatric training and knowledge. In this climate, Jaspers' notion of lack of insight was superficially popularized and sometimes used as an excuse for involuntary admission, a situation that was subsequently deplored by a number of psychiatrists including Kumakura (cited below). At the time some untrained psychiatrists actually said that there was no use persuading schizophrenics to accept inpatient treatment because their condition was, by definition, un-understandable and they lacked insight. One of the most unfortunate consequences of such a distorted view of insight in schizophrenia was the Utsunomiya Hospital case, where a number of involuntarily admitted psychiatric patients suffered from humiliating, sometimes even violent treatment. Eventually, in 1984, the hospital had to undergo inspection by a committee of the International Congress of Jurists (ICJ). The case resulted in considerable social interest in inhumane treatment in several Japanese psychiatric hospitals, and in 1987 the current Mental Health Act, which is oriented towards the legal assurance of the patient's human rights, was introduced.

The anti-psychiatric movement of the 1960s, joining forces with the student movement, became so influential in Japan as to temporarily occupy the Japanese Society of Psychiatry and Neurology. Psychopathological study was criticized as being practically useless, as serving nothing but to stigmatize the mentally disordered, so that at times it was difficult even to hold an open meeting for psychopathological discussions. During this period, efforts to challenge the pessimistic view of schizophrenia as characterized by poor insight were rarely broadened by psychopathologists, but rather were maintained by clinicians (discussed below) who were interested in psychotherapeutic approaches. As they were not strongly bound by the methodology of German academic psychiatry, it appears that they felt relatively free from Jaspers' narrow concept of insight.

In the 1980s, the movement towards open-door psychiatric treatment was again accelerated. In 1987, the year of the enactment of the new socially-oriented Mental Health Law, a Japanese forensic psychiatrist came out strongly against the notion of lack of insight on the grounds that it had come to be used as an excuse for the involuntary admission of schizophrenics into hospitals. In a symposium held in 1988 upon the topic, several outstanding Japanese psychopathologists argued this issue, not only criticizing the traditional concept, but also proposing their own alternatives (see the section on debates in the 1980s).

Today, as the questionnaire study cited in the last section of this chapter shows, many Japanese psychiatrists believe clinical interventions can improve various aspects of insight in schizophrenia. In the coming decade it is expected that this problem will be discussed more concretely using empirical data, to which end several Japanese investigations have already been initiated.

Insight as an issue for psychopathology

Japanese psychopathological discussion of insight in schizophrenia has struggled to overcome the strict definition made by Jaspers, which had become so influential it almost dominated the psychopathological background of Japanese psychiatry. The notion of insight in Jaspers' sense has been accepted, criticized and challenged by Japanese psychopathologists.

Debates in the 1960s

It was not until 1963 that some Japanese psychopathologists began to criticize Jaspers' restricted notion of insight in schizophrenia. Nishizono (1963) compared Jaspers' notion of insight with insight into illness derived from psychoanalysis, claiming that the latter concerns not only an intellectual but also a profound emotional understanding of the illness, associated with a deep change of psychodynamics. Thus, he held, schizophrenics could sometimes learn about their illness but lacked this psychological insight. Doi (1961) interpreted this phenomenon as a kind of resistance against confronting their psychotic experiences, based particularly in Japan upon the sentiment inherent in Japanese culture called *ama'e*, reliance and dependence, whose most typical example can be observed in the relationship between infant and mother. In Japan, *ama'e* is not something that grown-ups should strictly overcome or avoid, but constitutes the backbone of the basic human trust among healthy individuals. Japanese schizophrenics who are not willing to confront their psychotic experience sometimes assume this attitude of *ama'e* in front of psychiatrists, and may seem as if they are children at the mother's breast, not caring to think about the problems of real life. Contrary to Freud, Nishizono contended that this defense mechanism is related to the intact self of the schizophrenic person and could be a target of psychotherapy to increase insight into their psychotic experience.

Ohashi (1963) discussed the denial of illness seen in anosognosia as defined by Babinski, and maintained that this denial concerned not only focal neurological symptoms such as paralysis, but also the total mental state of the patient, and thus could not be regarded as a disturbance of any single sensorial pathway. Kajitani (1963) argued that insight is not a solid attribute of the disease and that the information obtained from schizophrenics about insight in Jaspers' sense would be dependent on the relationship between the doctor and the patient, because an admission of psychosis would necessarily evoke a deep sense of *haji*, harassment and shame, which must be strictly avoided according to Japanese ethical code.

Shimazaki and Abe (1963) followed the argument of Mayer-Gross (1920) maintaining that although schizophrenics were incapable of insight in the narrow sense defined by Jaspers, they were able to have a "Stellungsnahme," an attitude toward their illness. Shimazaki examined 35 first-episode schizophrenics in complete or incomplete remission and classified them into six groups according to their attitudes toward their illness. The first group remembered the psychotic episode as something like a natural disaster, which is transitory and leaves no pathological wake. Patients of this group were ready to admit that they had been ill, but would not reconsider the details of their illness. The second group considered their illness to be a precious experience in terms of their mental maturation, although these explanations were delusional in some cases. The third group was in some despair. They could not find any explanation of their psychosis, which they perceived as something vague and horrible. In the fourth group the memory of the psychosis was still so vivid that the patients were at a loss as to how to express their feelings or opinions about it. In the fifth, the patients had a rather childish and optimistic attitude, stating that they were quite relieved and relaxed after their illness. They did not seem to have any conflicts or any desire for a productive future and seemed to be totally indifferent to their disastrous experience.

Shimazaki suggested that these different attitudes toward the psychotic experience should be included in the term insight in clinical use, which, as a consequence, would not be something that ranges linearly from null to full, but would be composed of several dimensions of different qualities. He criticized those clinicians who would consider only the patients' direct statements and tended to discuss the presence or absence of insight in schizophrenics, emphasizing instead the importance of a clinical knowledge of how schizophrenics tried to incorporate their illness into their actual lives.

Ishikawa (1963) pointed out that insight in Shimazaki's sense was already preferred in clinical practice and that he would evaluate not the lack, but the presence of insight in schizophrenics in terms of a positive attitude toward the future, notwithstanding its being a delusional explanation of psychotic experience.

Debates in the 1980s

In the mid-1980s, debates concerning insight in schizophrenia were resurrected in response to social criticism of the involuntary admission of schizophrenics and the new movement towards outpatient management and social rehabilitation.

Kondoh *et al.* (1985) surveyed 60 schizophrenic inpatients, asking "why are you coming to (staying in) hospital?", "what is worrying you most?," "in what sense do you think you are ill?," "is something wrong with your body?," "what is mental illness?" "do you have some hope in your treatment with your doctor?," etc. Kondoh concluded that all the subjects possessed awareness to some extent that they had something wrong in them. Interestingly, only four of them were judged by their clinicians to have insight into their illness, 42 to have a sense of illness (incomplete insight) and 14 to have no insight at all. Although the definition of insight used in this study was not clear, it seemed that 22 years after the work of Shimazaki, the doctors included in this study were still influenced by some narrow definition of insight and tended to dismiss various aspects of the patients' attitudes towards schizophrenia.

The debates were especially stimulated by Kumakura (1987), a forensic psychiatrist, who tried to reconsider the notion of lack of insight in schizophrenia in light of the medical paternalism characteristic of Japanese psychiatry. His work must be considered against the background of the fact that during the 1960s most of the increased number of psychiatric beds were occupied by patients who were, under the name of paternalism, involuntarily admitted without being sufficiently informed about their treatment and rights. In part such a crude paternalism was the inevitable consequence of the hastened increase of psychiatric beds, whose main aim was more often the protection of society than the treatment of patients. Psychiatrists, especially those engaged in the anti-psychiatric movement, made this attitude a target of protest in the 1970s. Kumakura argued that the opposition between paternalism and antipaternalism is inherent to psychiatric practice, and that in Japan the former had been sustained naively by the assumption that the psychiatric patients are incapable of any judgment at all, with the notion of the lack of insight in schizophrenia being used as a kind of excuse for this assumption. This is evidently too broad an interpretation of Jaspers' original discussion, which applied this concept only to an awareness of psychotic experiences.

Several psychopathologists made their own contributions to Kumakura's contention. Their arguments generally emphasized the distinction between insight as a subjective experience and insight as objective recognition. They claimed the former to be particularly important, for schizophrenics do have a certain understanding of their psychotic experience, a fact which had been partly demonstrated by Shimazaki. They further maintained that there was no use in discussing whether this type of insight was true or false, because it constituted a perceived reality for the patients. The attempt to criticize this subjective insight in the light of objective medical knowledge would be, in this way of thinking, akin to the old Marxists who blamed ordinary citizens for not having knowledge of dialectical materialism. Even since the 1960s, many psychiatrists had paid scant attention to their patients' cognitive efforts to incorporate their catastrophic experience into their intact healthy self. Jaspers' narrow notion of insight was not aimed at describing this integrative aspect of subjective insight; its central purpose was rather to define the lack of objective insight that was presumed to be an essential feature of psychoses like schizophrenia. Jaspers himself admitted that psychopathology, as a branch of science, could not touch the subjective aspects of insight, which he regarded as an existential matter. Matsumoto (1988) criticized this attitude as too rigid, and asserted that there was room in clinical practice for the clinician to deal with patients' subjective perceptions of their illness. Nakayasu (1988) pointed out that the Jasperian notion of "lack of insight" in schizophrenia could not be regarded as a symptom experienced by patients, but as a sort of sign that is measured by an observer through a certain method or a frame of reference, which is in this case a standard medical knowledge of mental illness. He also noted that the symptoms used to define the notion of schizophrenia, such as delusion and hallucination, are also mainly observed phenomena and would be better regarded as signs rather than symptoms. A similar view was expressed later in Europe by Bitter *et al.* (1989), who stated that delusions and hallucinations should be regarded as objective rather than subjective symptoms. Nakayasu regarded lack of insight as one of those objective signs that define schizophrenia from the viewpoint of medical science.

Yasunaga (1988) describes the "awareness of deportment" that reflects insight as a subjective perception. By this term he implied the sense of self which is projected onto one's perception of the position and movement of one's body and mind. This sense is different from any static knowledge, and concerns integrated physical as well as mental activities. It is a sense of the whole activity itself and does not necessarily concern a precise knowledge of every part of an action. To understand this explanation, we could think of a golf swing. Good golfers are aware of their swing and may explain it like this: "I swing as if I am throwing my club away to the green." This type of awareness does not need to coincide with an observation of their actual body movement, and it is often helpful wise to advise them to swing as if they were throwing the club away rather than tell them to keep the left elbow three inches above eye level, etc. According to Yasunaga we all have this type of awareness of every physical and mental activity, the awareness of deportment, which becomes altered in schizophrenia and other mental disorders.

The core of Yasunaga's discussion is that we should synchronize our minds with the patient's, and use our own awareness of deportment to understand the patient's experience so that we can give them appropriate advice. To that end, we should try to incorporate the patient's physical and mental activities into our own self and maintain an awareness of the whole therapeutic situation. To illustrate the latter, Yasunaga cites a saying of Ze'ami, a famous fifteenth-century Japanese Nou actor, that a performer should be aware of the whole stage, even that part that is behind him. However, a similar experience of intermingled self boundaries between the doctor and the patient is also described in the theory of empathy by Kohut (1959), in the works of Sullivan (1953) and Schwing (1940). Many Japanese psychiatrists balance a meditative way of understanding patients with a modern scientific knowledge of mental disorders.

Contemporary research on insight in Japan

In recent years, clinical concern about the insight in schizophrenia has been increasing in Japan. First, Kim *et al.* (1994, 1997a) demonstrated the two dimensions of the subjective experience in schizophrenia, namely, sense of incoherence and sense of opacity. They respectively correlated with objectively measured negative and positive symptoms and thus can be regarded to reflect an awareness of the robust disease phenomena. The works by Amador *et al.* (1991) and David *et al.* (1990) have been introduced to Japan and their scales have been standardized into Japanese (Sakai *et al.*, 2000, 2002). The correlation of insight and subjective symptoms has been also detected (Kim, 1997b).

On the other hand, less than 20% of the patients with schizophrenia have been informed of their diagnosis in Japan. In this situation it is absurd to ask that patients gain and develop sound insight into their illness. What is crucial is to provide sufficient knowledge and information so that the patients can approach the modern concept of consent-based treatment. The main obstacle is that the term schizophrenia has been translated into Japanese as the *Sei-shin-bun-retsu-byo*, the disease of split and catastrophic mind. In addition, this translation is expressed in colloquial words so that lay people can grasp the meaning, so that a sort of iatrogenic stigmatization can be easily spread. The efforts to rename the translation involved a heated discussion on the very nature of schizophrenia and it took nearly a decade to accomplish (Ono *et al.*, 1999, Kim *et al.*, 2001, Kim, 2002a). Still the result was fruitful in that the renaming was incorporated into the anti-stigma program supported by the World Psychiatric Association, whose core is to promote insight on the part of the patients, family members and society, based on accurate knowledge and information. The authors are now struggling to develop standardized psychoeducation, including the promotion of insight and to making it a clinical routine authorized by the National Insurance System.

British and Japanese views on insight

Kim and David conducted a comparative study of Japanese and British clinicians' view of insight (cited in Kim, 2002b). They mailed a questionnaire on views of insight to a random selection of 200 Japanese and 310 British psychiatrists and obtained 52% and

35.8% response rates, respectively. The results revealed that the Japanese responders interpreted the concept of insight so broadly as to include the awareness of subjective and social suffering, while the British held a narrower view which limited insight to the awareness of being mentally ill, treatment need and psychotic experience. Also, the Japanese responders estimated the possibility of improving insight when appropriate treatments are provided as higher than their British counterparts. So Japanese psychiatrists seem to have a more flexible and optimistic view of insight in schizophrenia, an attitude that was perhaps cultivated through continuous interest and concern in this issue in recent decades.

In total, approximately 95% of the responders in the groups included to a varying degree some type of insight disturbance into the definition of schizophrenia. Interestingly, most responders answered that they preferred the use of the DSM and ICD, which do not include the loss of insight in the definition of schizophrenia. This signifies that they hold dual diagnostic concepts of schizophrenia, one that is a DSM-like system and the other, based on the traditionally constructed understanding of the nature of psychotic disorders.

Such a dual system of diagnosis is not very new and has been inherited from Kurt Schneider, who provided the background of the DSM-III criteria of schizophrenia. He first defined the category of psychosis as a state lacking a meaningful definition, and then proposed first-rank symptoms in order to define schizophrenic psychosis as separate from manic-depressive psychosis. He apparently referred to the notion of psychosis as defined by Jaspers as an incomprehensible state in which the patient lacks insight. The DSM-III version of schizophrenia adopted Schneider's first rank symptoms as an aid to differential diagnosis, but not as fundamental to the concept of psychosis and the nature of schizophrenia. Presumably, the idea of loss of insight is still held up by clinicians, because it supplements the category of psychosis that in turn informs our model of what schizophrenia is.

Summary and conclusion

Like other fields of science, modern Japanese psychiatry was founded upon imported knowledge from Europe, which reached this country during the late nineteenth century. Considerable efforts were made to understand a new perspective brought by the then European psychiatry and to incorporate it into Japanese culture. The issue of insight came to be known to Japanese psychiatrists through the assertion of Jaspers that schizophrenics lacked insight into illness, which was very strictly defined by him to include the precise and reasonable understanding of the disease. Gradually some Japanese psychiatrists started to criticize this view through their own clinical experiences, because such a strict definition of insight would miss various important attitudes that schizophrenics actually assumed towards their illness. A number of Japanese psychiatrists came to struggle for the promotion of various aspects of insight in schizophrenia, challenging an old pessimistic view of this illness.

It is a regrettable fact that the rapid construction of psychiatric hospitals urged by the government in the 1960s resulted in the superficial popularization of the notion of lack of insight, which was used by some psychiatrists as a quasi definition of schizophrenia or as an excuse for involuntary admission of schizophrenic patients. In response to the severe criticism against this issue, the current Mental Health Act orders more open and socially-oriented treatments of psychiatric patients as well as a supervisory system for the guarantee of their basic human rights. In this stream of change, the issue of insight has attracted broad attention from contemporary psychopathologists and clinicians. Thus we may be allowed to say that insight in schizophrenia, which is dependent upon the relationship between patient and doctor as Kajitani stated, also reflects the extent to which psychiatrists are concerned about the community treatment and basic human rights of schizophrenics.

Different aspects of insight have been pointed out by several Japanese psychiatrists, especially by those who were engaged in clinical psychotherapy of schizophrenia using a particular sensitivity to other people's feelings inherent to Japanese culture – see for example Yasunaga's argument about the sense of deportment derives from fifttenth-century Japanese literature of Nou acting. This sense signifies insight into the loss of the balance of one's mental and physical activities as a whole and may include the awareness of the total therapeutic situation, which can be promoted through metaphorical rather than analytical suggestion. Shinkai (1988) focuses upon a subtle micropsychotic change during clinical interviews and tries to help schizophrenics become aware of that change so that they can develop insight in their past psychotic experiences. Utena (1965) deconstructed several social codes such as shame, self-esteem or competency, which are closely related to the social conflicts of Japanese schizophrenics, in the recovery process from psychosis. This argument concerns a kind of social insight in the sense of the awareness of dysfunction in social adaptation, whose improvement can be expected through practical advice and discussion on how to overcome actual social conflicts.

Although most of these practices have been conducted separately, not under a single rubric of insight, they seem to have some common characteristics in that they do not view schizophrenia as an autonomic disease process but as a mixture of social and interpersonal transactions. These practitioners do not deny the biological basis of schizophrenia and use antipsychotic medication, nor do they, in general, hesitate to regard schizophrenia as a result of a disease process. However, the plausible assumption that there is some biological underpinning for schizophrenia does not mean that the clinical manifestation of this illness affecting complicated mental functions is a result of some neural disease in the same sense that paralysis is caused by a cerebral lesion. There may exist a number of modifiers between basic biological findings and the manifestation of schizophrenia as a disorder of human transaction. It is possible that in some cases several modifiers have even stronger determinative power for the clinical appearance of schizophrenia than a biological disturbance postulated to initiate the disease process. In the author's eyes such a view is held by a number, if not the majority, of Japanese psychiatrists, who conduct their treatment of schizophrenics not only by assessing symptoms and selecting drugs, but also through focusing on the *patients'* motivation for treatment and awareness of illness, interpersonal conflicts, social handicaps etc. Insight, or self-monitoring and the regulatory function of self, could be one of these strong modifiers, although some schizophrenics seem to lack it not because of a kind of agnosia caused by the illness, but because of some psychological defenses. Why, then, do they hesitate to use this precious mental function? Is it because of the psychological trauma during psychosis, the social handicap and stigma due to the illness, or because they are overwhelmed by the power and authority of medical staff? The answer could be closely related to the cultural codes of each patient and, in most cases in Japan, to the preference of the clinicians for the kinds of methods used and goals set.

Such an ambiguity highlights the importance of clinical studies of insight in Japan, where the promotion of insight will play a significant role in therapeutic settings in favor of more open treatment for schizophrenia. Some preliminary studies ongoing in this country have revealed that insight in schizophrenia is composed of several *independent* dimensions, such as the motivation for treatment, the awareness of delusions and hallucinations, the awareness of subjective suffering, etc. Some of the confusion found in the previous Japanese discussions of insight can be explained as a result of confounding some of these different dimensions: for example, the absence of differentiation between the awareness of psychosis and that of treatment need, resulting in the superficial use of the Jaspers' notion of lack of insight as an excuse for involuntary admission. It is hoped that through further clarification of robust components of insight in schizophrenia we will be able to evaluate this useful phenomenon more precisely and integrate various clinical attempts for its promotion mentioned in this chapter. It is a precious opportunity in this connection that a diversity of interests in insight has been aggregated in this book to encourage us towards the investigation of more effective interventions for schizophrenia from this stimulating perspective.

References

Amador, X. F., Strauss, D. H., Yale, S. A. and Gorman, J. M. (1991). Awareness of illness in schizophrenia. *Schizophrenia Bulletin*, **17**, 113–32.

Bitter, I., Jaeger, J., Agdeppa, J. and Volavka, J. (1989). Subjective symptoms: part of the negative syndrome of schizophrenia? *Psychopharmacology Bulletin*, **25**, 180–4.

Dagonet, H. (1881). Conscience et alienation mentale. *Annal Médico Psychologique*, **39**, 368–97.

David, A. S. (1990). Insight and psychosis. *British Journal of Psychiatry*, **156**, 798–808.

Doi, T. (1961). The insight into illness. *Psychiatria et Neurologia Japonica*, **63**, 403–11.

Ishikawa, K. (1963). (In Japanese) Über Krankheitseinsicht der schizophrenien und Neurose. *Seishin-igaku*, **6**, 105–10.

Jaspers, K. (1913). *Allgemeine Psychopathologie*. Springer-Verlag, Berlin.

Kajitani, T. (1963). (In Japanese) Zum Wesen und Erfassungen der Krankheitseinsicht. *Seishin-igaku* **5**, 131–40.

Kim, Y. (2002a). Renaming the term schizophrenia in Japan. *Lancet*, **360**, 879.

Kim Y (2002b). The psychological foundation of insight in schizophrenia. In H. Kashima, I. Falloon, M. Mizuno, M. Asai (ed.) *Comprehensive Treatment of Schizophrenia*, pp. 109–18. Heidelberg: Springer Verlag.

Kim, Y. and Berrios, G. (2001). Impact of the term schizophrenia in the culture of ideograph. *Schizophrenia Bulletin*, **27**, 181–5.

Kim, Y., Sakamoto, K., Kamo, T., Sakamura, Y. and Kotorii, N. (1997a). Subjective experience and related symptoms in schizophrenia. *Comprehensive Psychiatry*, **38**, 49–55.

Kim, Y., Sakamoto, K., Kamo, T., Sakamura, Y. and Miyaoka, H. (1997b). Insight and clinical correlates in schizophrenia. *Comprehensive Psychiatry*, **38**, 117–23.

Kim, Y., Takemoto, K., Mayahara, K., Sumida, K. and Shiba, S. (1994). An analysis of the subjective experience of schizophrenia. *Comprehensive Psychiatry*, **35**, 430–6.

Klerman, G. (1991). An American perspective on the conceptual approaches to psychopathology. In A. Kerr and H. McCleiland (ed.) *Concepts of mental disorder* pp. 74–83. London: Gaskell.

Kohut, H. (1959). Introspection, empathy, and psychoanalysis. *Journal of American Psychoanalytic Association*, **7**, 459–83.

Kondoh, H., Iwadate, T., Onizawa, T., Musha, M. and Ohira, T. (1985). (In Japanese) Byoushiki-ron'no shuhen (on insight in schizophrenia). *Psychiatria et Neurologia Japonica*, **87**, 114.

Kumakura, N. (1987). (In Japanese) Some considerations on "paternalism" and "self-determination" in psychosis. *Psychiatria et Neurologia Japonica*, **89**, 593–614.

Matsumoto, M. (1988). (In Japanese) Eine Kritische Überlegung zum Begriff der Krankheitseinsicht. *Seishinka-chiryogaku*, **3**, 25–31.

Mayer-Gross, W. (1920). Über die Stellungnahme zur abgelaufenen akuten Psychose. *Zeitschrift für die Gesamte Neurologie und Psychiatrie*, **60**, 160–212,

Nakayasu, N. (1988). (In Japanese) "Loss of insight into disease" as a method of descriptive phenomenology. *Seishinka-chiryogaku*, **3**, 33–42.

Nishizono, M. (1963). (In Japanese) Psychodynamics of "Krankheitseinsicht". *Seishin-igaku*, **5**, 111–19.

Ohashi, H. (1963). (In Japanese) Anosognosia: denial of illness. *Seishin-igaku*, **5**, 123–30.

Ono, Y., Satsumi, Y. and Kim, Y. (1999). Schizophrenia. Is it time to replace the term? *Psychiatry Clin Neurosci*, **53**, 335–41.

Pick, A. (1882). Über Krankheitsbewußtsein in psychischen Krankheiten: Eine historisch-klinische Studie. *Archiv für Psychiatrie und Nervenkrankheiten*, **13**, 518–81.

Sakai, Y., Kim, Y., Akiyama, T., Tachimori, H. and Kurita, H. (2000). (In Japanese) Reliability and validity of the Japanese version of the SAI. *Rinsho-Seishin-Igaku*, **29**, 177–83.

Sakai, Y., Kim, Y., Akiyama, T. and Tachimori, H. (2002). (In Japanese) Reliability and validity of the Japanese version of the SUMD. *Seishin-Igaku*, **44**, 491–502.

Schwing, G. (1940). *Ein Weg zur Seele des Geisteskranken*. Zurich: Rascher-Verlag.

Shimazaki, T. and Abe, T. (1963). (In Japanese) Ein Aspekt der "Krankheitseinsicht" in der Schizophrenie. *Seishin-igaku*, **5**, 97–103.

Shinkai, Y. (1988). (In Japanese) About the attitude of schizophrenics to their illness from the viewpoint of SOYEGI. *Seishinka-chiryogaku*, **3**, 51–60.

Sullivan, H. S. (1953). *The Interpersonal Theory of Psychiatry*. W. W. Norton and Company, New York.

Utena, H. (1965). (In Japanese) Tenkanki ni tatsu bunretsubyo no chiryou (New perspective of the treatment of schizophrenia). *Kitakanto-igaku*, **15**, 327–31.

Yasunaga, H. (1988). (In Japanese) From "self-judgment of illness" to "awareness of deportment". *Seishinka-chiryogaku*, **3**, 43–50.

Chapter 12

The relationship of insight to violent behavior and stigma

E. Fuller Torrey

That proves you mad because you know it not.
Thomas Dekker, *The Honest Whore*, 1604

The problem of insight in individuals with severe psychiatric disorders is the problem of damage to a self-measuring ruler. The part of the brain that is responsible for assessing the needs of the person is often impaired and thus cannot perform its function. This may occur in individuals with schizophrenia, bipolar disorder, or severe depression. Percy Knauth, in *A Season in Hell*, expressed the dilemma as follows:

> More realistically, I understood that the only tool I could fight with – my mind – was the very part of me that was affected. Can a legless man get up and walk even if he knows that only walking will save his life? My mind was going; how could I use it to extricate myself from my despair?

(Knauth 1975)

Two of the most important consequences of impaired insight are increased violent behavior by some individuals with severe psychiatric disorders and its inevitable sequel, increased stigma against all individuals with psychiatric illness. In undertaking a review of this literature, it was the hypothesis of the author that impaired insight leads to increased violent behavior in a direct linear fashion, with medication noncompliance being the mediating factor. Expressed as an equation, the hypothesis can be expressed as follows:

Thus, individuals with impaired insight are less likely to take their medication, because they do not believe they are sick. Failure to take medication leads to an increase in symptoms, including paranoid delusions, command hallucinations, and mania, which in turn increases the chances that the affected individual will behave violently toward others.

The case of Russell Weston

The relationship of insight to violent behavior and stigma can be illustrated by the tragic case of Russell Weston. In July 1998, Mr Weston entered the US Capitol and allegedly killed two Capitol police officers. At the time, he was attempting to reach a safe in the building that he believed contained the "ruby satellite", which, among other things, could be used to make time go backwards. Mr Weston wished to combat a government conspiracy of "theft, murder and cannibalism" that was "selling one-inch pieces of human flesh for about $300 apiece". He believed that then President Clinton was part of this conspiracy and that Clinton had killed his daughter, Chelsea. He also believed that Clinton had participated in the assassination of President Kennedy because Kennedy had cut off Clinton's cocaine supply.

Also among Mr Weston's beliefs were that he was a clone; that FBI and CIA agents had planted atomic bombs in Montana (the location of which Weston sent to CNN television); that a radioactive chip had been implanted in his jaw, allowing him to communicate with "the Ambassador of Russia"; that the government was spying on him via TV satellite dishes and bombarding him with lethal rays, so that he slept under a blanket of tinfoil; and that he was a CIA agent and received instructions via coded messages on the radio and television.

Mr Weston had been diagnosed with paranoid schizophrenia in 1984 and received SSI disability payments thereafter. He was well known to the local police in Montana and Illinois, the county sheriff in Montana, mental health professionals in both states, SSI officials, the CIA (which he visited in Washington), and the Secret Service. In April 1996, he threatened President Clinton and, at the request of the Secret Service, was evaluated at a mental health center in Illinois, where it was determined that he had schizophrenia but did not meet criteria for involuntary commitment. In May 1996, he sought admission to a general hospital in Montana to be screened for poisons he believed had been given him; however, he refused to accept treatment and left after one day.

In October 1996, he threatened the life of a laboratory technician and was involuntarily committed to the Montana State Hospital for 90 days. A hospital admission note said that Weston "reminds people of the Unabomber". Mr Weston punched a female employee in the face shortly after admission. His condition significantly improved on low dose antipsychotic medication (loxapine 10–20 mg.). He was discharged after 52 days, told to take his medication, and an appointment was made for him at the mental health center near his home in Illinois, where he said he was going. Because he believed that the courts had ordered him to do so, he continued to take his medication for 11 days, until he went to the mental health center. At that time, he was told that there was no court order and that he was free to take his medication or not as he wished. The mental health center noted that "he was very bizarre, paranoid" and that "he taped the entire session". They also noted that in the past he had been "noncompliant with meds". Mr Weston stopped taking his medication at that time and never returned to the mental health center.

At no time during his illness did Mr Weston demonstrate any insight into his illness. He really believed, for example, that a safe in the US Capitol contained a "ruby satellite" that could make time go backwards. His violent entry into the Capitol building, resulting in the deaths of two police officers, was Mr Weston's attempt to obtain the "satellite" which he apparently intended to use to save the world.

Since he had no insight, he refused to take medication that, during his one treatment trial while involuntarily hospitalized, had significantly improved his symptoms. His untreated symptoms directly led him to commit violent acts, acts that seemed logical within the framework of his psychotic symptoms. And Mr Weston's violent acts, massively publicized because he breached the security of the US Capitol, almost certainly produced a significant increase in stigma against individuals with psychiatric disorders.

Impaired insight and medication noncompliance

Many studies have established a relationship between impaired insight and medication noncompliance. Older studies describing this linkage have been thoroughly reviewed by McEvoy in this volume and also by Amador and Strauss (1993), Ghaemi and Pope (1994), and Kemp and David (1995).

Recent studies of insight and medication compliance also suggest a causal association. For example, a 1997 American study of 33 patients with schizophrenia reported that "the participants who were more aware of their mental illnesses and of the beneficial effects of medication were more likely to be compliant with their prescribed medication" (Smith *et al.*, 1997). A 2000 Australian study of 218 outpatients, "the great majority of whom are seriously mentally ill" reported a strong correlation ($P < 0.007$) between measures of awareness of illness and compliance with medication (Trauer and Sacks, 2000). And a 2001 study of 87 patients with schizophrenia or schizoaffective disorder in Ireland reported a significant correlation ($P < 0.003$) between insight and medication compliance but only when those patients who were substance abusers were omitted from the analysis (Kamali *et al.*, 2001).

It is, in fact, surprising that so many studies have found a statistical correlation between insight and medication compliance, since insight is only one of several factors that determine compliance. Substance abuse plays a major role as well, as the Irish study cited above illustrates. Thus, an individual may have good insight but, because of chronic alcohol or drug abuse, fail to take medication. Medication side-effects are another major reason for noncompliance with medication, and such side-effects may occur in patients with or without insight.

Conversely, many patients may take their medication regularly despite having very little insight. This is especially true in inpatient settings and in cultures in which physicians are highly regarded. However, despite the fact that insight does not necessarily lead to medication compliance, and that medication compliance does not necessarily require patient insight, almost all studies of this relationship have reported a statistically significant association. This suggests that insight and medication compliance are, indeed, closely connected, even if other factors confound the relationship.

Impaired insight and increased violent behavior

Three recent studies have examined the direct effect of insight on violent behavior. In Spain, Arango *et al.* (1999) prospectively studied 63 newly admitted inpatients diagnosed with schizophrenia or schizoaffective disorder. Nurses rated all violent acts on a 1 to 5 scale, and the insight of the patients was measured by the Scale of Unawareness of Mental Disorder (SUMD). The authors reported a significant association between impaired insight and increased violent acts, and in a logistic regression "the single variable that best predicted violence was [impaired] insight into psychotic symptoms". Since the patients were receiving medications on the inpatient unit, impaired insight appeared to be a risk factor for increased violence, even with medication.

A second recent study examining insight and violent behavior was carried out in Ohio (Buckley *et al.*, 2002; Friedman *et al.*, 2003). They compared 122 patients with schizophrenia or schizoaffective disorder who had committed violent acts and 111 patients with the same diagnoses who had not been violent. The violent patients had more symptoms ($P < 0.0001$) and also had less insight into their illness ($P < 0.0001$).

The most detailed study on insight and gradations of severity of violent behavior was carried out in New York by Alia-Klein *et al.* (2004a,b) on 60 male inpatients with psychoses who had been charged with serious crimes. Their violent behavior was retrospectively quantified on the Violence Assessment Scale (Alia-Klein *et al.*, 2001). Multiple variables were examined, including age, history of abuse in childhood, substance abuse, repeated psychiatric hospitalizations, medication compliance, and insight into illness. In a multiple regression analysis, impaired insight was found to be the fourth most important factor in increasing violent behavior but clearly was separate from any effect of medication compliance. As the author summarized it, "compliance and insight play independent roles by each providing a separate contribution to the severity of violence".

Medication noncompliance and increased violent behavior

Anecdotally, there is much evidence linking the failure to take medication by individuals with severe psychiatric disorders to their subsequent violent behavior. News stories of these tragedies often include such phrases as "he had gone a long time without his medication" ("Baltimore man" 1990) and "his daughter was not taking her medication at the time of the slaying" ("Crofton woman" 1990).

Multiple studies have supported this anecdotal impression. Individuals with severe psychiatric disorders who are arrested are significantly more likely to have been noncompliant with their medications (McFarland *et al.*, 1989). Psychiatric inpatients who are unmedicated or undermedicated have been shown in several studies to be more violent (Yesavage, 1982; Weaver, 1983; Smith, 1989; Kasper *et al.*, 1997; Steinert *et al.*, 2000). And individuals with severe psychiatric disorders who have active psychotic symptoms, a frequent indicator of medication noncompliance, are also significantly more violent (Taylor, 1985; Kunjukrishnan and Bradford, 1988). For example, in a 1992 study by Link *et al.* of psychiatric patients living in the community, psychotic symptoms were highly correlated with fighting ($P < 0.001$) and with hitting others ($P < 0.01$) and were "the only variable that accounts for differences in levels of violent/illegal behavior between patients and never-treated community residents" (Link *et al.*, 1992).

Other studies have directly linked medication noncompliance with violent behavior. For example, in a 1991 study of psychiatric outpatients, "71% of the violent patients . . . had problems with medication compliance, compared with only 17% of those without hostile behaviors," and the correlation was statistically significant ($P < 0.001$) (Bartels *et al.*, 1991). Similarly, a study of inmates in a state forensic hospital reported a significant correlation ($P < 0.001$) between the failure to take medication and having committed violent acts in the community (Smith, 1989).

Other studies provide additional support for linking medication noncompliance to violent behavior. One study, being carried out in Spain, is prospectively following for one year individuals with schizophrenia who have a history of violent behavior (Arango *et al.*, 2002). Relatives of the patients are interviewed each month to ascertain medication compliance and violent behavior. Partway through the study, the researchers reported that

> a significant correlation (Pearson's χ^2: $P = 0.004$) was found between therapeutic adherence and presence of violent behavior. . . . From preliminary results, it seems that violent behavior is more frequent in those patients who have not been consistently compliant with medication.

Another study is the Ohio study, referred to above, where 122 individuals with schizophrenia or schizoaffective disorder who had a history of violent behavior were being compared to 111 individuals with the same diagnoses but no history of violent behavior. Violent behavior in this study was defined as "direct physical aggression against person or property (not merely the threat of violence) for which legal charges were or would have been incurred". Three-quarters of the acts of violence were assault, 34% of which were against a law enforcement officer and 18% of which were against a family member. The other one-fourth of the acts of violence included attempted murder, arson, robbery, and vandalism.

The most striking difference between the two groups was treatment noncompliance, which was said to be "ubiquitous among violent patients" (Hrouda *et al.*, 2003). Among those who had been violent, 76% (93 out of 122) had been noncompliant with the medication. By contrast, among those individuals who had not been violent, only 1% (1 out of 111) had been noncompliant. The use of alcohol and/or street drugs also differentiated the two groups. Among those who had been violent, 69% had abused alcohol and/or drugs, whereas among those who had not been violent, only 20% had abused alcohol and/or drugs.

The other ongoing study is that by Alia-Klein (2004b), described above. In that study, "those noncompliant with their medications are 1.7 times more violent than those who are compliant". The author concludes that "compliance with medications plays an important role in the severity of violence" and, in fact, is the single most important factor of all variables in the study.

Violent behavior and increased stigma

Stigma and negative stereotypes are major problems for both individuals with severe psychiatric disorders and their families. They limit the availability of housing, jobs, social programs, and even psychiatric care; indeed, some affected individuals say the stigma is worse than the disease itself. For this reason, anti-stigma campaigns were undertaken by the White House under President Clinton and by organizations such as NAMI.

The major cause of stigma against individuals with psychiatric disorders is the perceived relationship between psychiatric illness and violence. This was demonstrated by Link *et al.*, who, after reviewing several studies, concluded that

> When a measure of perceived dangerousness of mental patients is introduced, strong labeling [stigma] effects emerge. The interaction between labeling and perceived dangerousness is highly significant . . . Such individuals find former patients threatening and prefer to maintain a safe distance from them.

(Link *et al.*, 1987)

Examples of such studies include a 1984 survey in California that reported that the majority of adults believed that individuals with schizophrenia were more likely than other people to commit violent crimes (Field Institute, 1984). A 1987 study reported that 43% of students and 47% of police officers associated individuals with schizophrenia with "aggression, hostility, violence" (Wahl, 1987). A 1993 survey reported that more than half of the people interviewed agreed with the statement that "those with mental disorders are more likely to commit acts of violence" (Clements, 1993). A 1994 survey of Utah residents reported that 38% agreed that "people with mental illness are more dangerous than the rest of society" (Fraser, 1994). And a 1996 survey reported that 61% of adults believed that an individual with schizophrenia was "very likely" (13%) or "somewhat likely" (48%) to do "something violent to others" (Pescosolido *et al.*, 1999).

The cause-and-effect relationship between perceived dangerousness and stigma against psychiatrically ill individuals has also been demonstrated by naturalistic studies. A study in Germany reported that, following two attempts on the lives of prominent politicians by psychiatrically ill individuals in 1990, "there occurred a marked increase in social distance towards the mentally ill among the German public". Although this social distance slowly decreased over the following two years, "it had not yet completely returned to its initial level by the end of 1992" (Angermeyer and Matschinger, 1995). An American study of university students similarly reported that reading a newspaper article reporting a violent crime committed by a psychiatric patient led to increased "negative attitudes toward people with mental illness" (Thornton and Wahl, 1996).

Most disturbing, the association of psychiatric illness with violence is apparently increasing and, therefore, stigma is increasing. One of the most remarkable findings to emerge from the 1999 Surgeon General's Report on Mental Health was the fact that "the perception of people with psychosis as being dangerous is stronger today than in the past. . . . People with mental illness, especially those with psychosis, are perceived to be more violent than in the past" (US Department of Health and Human Services, 1999). This finding was based on a study that compared public opinion concerning psychiatric illness and violence in 1950 and again in 1996 using the same survey instrument. The study found that "the proportion [of respondents] who described a mentally ill person as being violent increased by nearly 2½ times between 1950 and 1996" (Phelan *et al.*, 2000). In 1950, only 13% of interviewees believed that psychiatrically ill individuals were dangerous, but in 1996, 31% believed that was true.

The authors of the Surgeon General's report noted that they had expected to find a significant *decrease* in stigma. During the 46-year period, there had been a marked increase in knowledge of psychiatric illness among the general public, an increased number of people who themselves utilized mental health professionals, and self-revelations by many public figures, such as William Styron and Mike Wallace, about their own psychiatric illnesses. However, the Surgeon General's report concluded:

> Stigma was expected to abate with increased knowledge of mental illness, but just the opposite occurred: stigma in some ways intensified over the past 40 years even though understanding improved.

> (US Department of Health and Human Services, 1999)

It seems highly likely that the reason stigma against individuals with psychiatric disorders is increasing is because violent acts committed by such individuals are increasing. There have always, of course, been occasional high-profile violent acts by individuals with psychiatric disorders. In 1857, for example, prominent American psychiatrist John Gray published an analysis of 49 cases of attempted or completed homicide committed by seriously psychiatrically ill patients he had treated (Gray, 1857). Ironically, Gray himself was murdered by one of his own patients 24 years later.

Since approximately 1980, however, reports of violent acts committed by psychiatric patients appear to have increased. The beginning of the increase was the 1980 murder of ex-Congressman Allard Lowenstein by Dennis Sweeney, one of Lowenstein's protégés in the Civil Rights movement who had subsequently developed schizophrenia. This was followed in 1981 by the attempted assassination of President Reagan by John Hinckley; both Sweeney and Hinckley had schizophrenia and were not being treated.

Since the early 1980s, there has been a continuing series of high-profile violent acts committed by individuals with severe psychiatric disorders. The increase has been noted anecdotally (Torrey, 1997) as well as by recent studies. A study in New York (Tardiff *et al.*, 1997), for example, assessed all psychiatric admissions to a university hospital over an 18-month period in 1991–1992, regarding whether they had "physically attacked another person in the month before admission"; these results were compared with an identical survey done at this hospital in 1981–1982. The frequency of such assaults had increased over the decade among male patients from 10% to 14% and among female

patients from 6% to 15%. In both studies, all admissions were voluntary and the diagnoses of the patients were similar. The authors attributed the increasing violence to an
increased availability of cocaine and other illegal drugs.

Furthermore, on 9–12 April 2000, the *New York Times* published the results of a
study of 100 "rampage killings" (Fessenden, 2000), defined as "multiple-victim killings
that were not primarily domestic or connected to a robbery or gang" committed during the preceding 50 years. As part of their research, the *Times* staff examined "nearly
25 years of homicide data from the Federal Bureau of Investigation" and concluded
that "the incidence of these rampage killings appears to have increased". Most of the
increase was noted to have taken place in the late 1980s and 1990s (Fessenden, personal
communication, 26 April 2000). Among the 100 killers examined by the *Times*, "more
than half had histories of serious mental health problems" and 48 of them had "some
kind of formal diagnosis, often schizophrenia". Although the *Times* attempted to
identify cases across 50 years, 90 of the 100 "rampage killings" they examined occurred
during the 1980s and 1990s, which was said to be due at least partially to the availability of more recent information on electronic databases.

In reviewing these acts of violence by individuals with severe psychiatric disorders,
two aspects stand out. In almost every instance, the person committing the crime was
not taking medication for his or her disorder at the time of the crime. And, in many
instances, the individual was also abusing alcohol and/or drugs. Medication compliance thus appears to be a crucial link in the chain connecting insight to violent behavior and stigma.

Discussion

Accumulating evidence clearly indicates that impaired insight and medication noncompliance are important contributors to violent behavior committed by individuals
with severe psychiatric disorders. However, rather than being a simple linear relationship, as hypothesized, from impaired insight to medication noncompliance to violent
behavior, the relationships are more complex. Based on the recent research of Alia-
Klein and other studies, it appears that impaired insight alone increased violent behavior, even without being mediated through medication noncompliance. Thus, the linear
equation proposed earlier in this chapter should be corrected as follows:

It is important to stress that impaired insight is not merely denial of illness. Denial is a psychological mechanism that everyone uses to avoid facing unpleasant truths. Impaired insight, by contrast, is a biological deficit with neuropsychological and neuroanatomical correlates, as explained in the chapters by Barr, Flashman, and David and Morgan. Recent studies of individuals with schizophrenia suggest that impaired insight correlates with smaller brain volume (Flashman *et al.*, 2000) and frontal lobe atrophy (Larøi *et al.*, 2000; Sahni *et al.*, 2002). Similarly, studies of individuals with bipolar disorder also suggest that impaired insight correlates with cortical atrophy (Varga *et al.*, 2002). Antonio Damasio, in his book *Descartes' Error*, provides a lucid description of biological aspects of awareness of illness as seen in some neurological patients with strokes or brain tumors. Damasio suggests that awareness of illness is primarily a function of the right hemisphere and that the specific brain areas involved include the inferior parietal lobule and insula and their connections to the prefrontal cortex, thalamus, and basal ganglia (Damasio, 1994).

If there truly is a direct causal relationship from severe psychiatric disorders to impaired insight and medication noncompliance to violent behavior, then one would expect individuals with severe psychiatric disorders to have a higher rate of violent behavior than the general population. This has been examined in many studies and has been found to be true (Torrey, 1994). For example, "27% of released male and female [psychiatric] patients report at least one violent act within a mean of four months after discharge" (Monahan, 1992); 8.6% of individuals with schizophrenia living in the community had used a weapon in a fight within the preceding year (Swanson *et al.*, 1990); and 10.6% of individuals with severe psychiatric illnesses had physically harmed another person within the preceding year (Steinwachs *et al.*, 1992). As summarized by Dr. John Monahan after his review of such studies: "The data that have recently become available, fairly read, suggest the one conclusion I did not want to reach . . . there appears to be a relationship between mental disorder and violent behavior" (Monahan, 1992). Since there are by conservative estimates approximately 4 million individuals with schizophrenia and bipolar disorder in the United States, the total number of violent acts being committed by these individuals should be of great concern.

At the same time, it is important to stress that most individuals with severe psychiatric disorders are not more dangerous than the general population, especially if those individuals are taking medication to control their symptoms. Further, it should be noted that America is a violent society; of the 19 million crime victimizations reported in 1990, nearly one-third of them involved violence (Reiss and Roth, 1993). Within this broad landscape of violence, the contribution of seriously psychiatrically ill individuals to the total picture is not large. This stands in contrast to less violent societies such as Iceland, in which only 47 homicides were committed over 80 years, but individuals with serious psychiatric illnesses were responsible for 13 (28%) of them (Petersson and Gudjonsson, 1981). Alcohol and drug abusers in the United States are, as a group, much more violent than are individuals with serious psychiatric illnesses.

It should also be remembered that violent behavior by individuals with severe psychiatric illnesses is merely one aspect of a larger problem: the failure of public psychiatric services and deinstitutionalization. Other aspects of this problem include the large number of seriously psychiatrically ill individuals among the homeless (Torrey, 1988), the large number of seriously psychiatrically ill individuals in jails and prisons (Torrey *et al.*, 1992; Jemelka *et al.*, 1989), and the revolving door of psychiatric hospital readmissions through which 30% of discharged patients are readmitted to the hospital within 30 days following discharge (Davidson, 1991), with some individual patients accumulating over 100 readmissions (Geller, 1992).

Finally, it should be noted that psychiatric recidivism is strongly related to an increase in the severity of violence by those with psychotic disorders (Alia-Klein *et al.*, 2004b). One would think that receiving more care would decrease these rates. However, the disjointed intermittent process of multiple hospital readmissions appears to be contributing to an increase in violence. The relationship between nonadherence with medications, poor insight, and psychiatric recidivism should be further investigated to test whether readmissions have an impact on the effect of poor insight leading to non-adherence and to increased violence (Alia-Klein, personal communication, 2003).

The fact that some severely psychiatrically ill individuals, especially those who have impaired insight and are not taking prescribed medications, are more prone to acts of violence has important implications for psychiatric services. Many such acts are theoretically preventable with good medication compliance and assertive case management; under such conditions, one Canadian study reported a comparatively low incidence of violent acts by discharged patients with serious psychiatric illnesses (Lafave *et al.*, 1993). These data suggest that, if medication compliance can be increased, then the risk of violent acts can be reduced. The use of outpatient commitment, conditional release, and other forms of assisted treatment have been found to be effective in increasing medication compliance and in ultimately reducing violence (Torrey and Zdanowicz, 2001). A study in North Carolina, for example, demonstrated that extended outpatient commitment lasting longer than six months decreased violent behavior among the patients by 40% (Swanson *et al.*, 2000). Similarly, a study in New Hampshire demonstrated that using conditional release for patients being released from the state hospital increased medication compliance by more than threefold and reduced episodes of violence to less than one-third the rate prior to the use of conditional release (O'Keefe *et al.*, 1997).

There have also been attempts to improve insight in individuals with severe psychiatric disorders in an attempt to improve medication compliance. These efforts have included cognitive behavior therapy (David *et al.*, 1998), video self-observation (Davidoff *et al.*, 1998), and use of specific antipsychotics claimed to be especially effective in improving insight (Pallanti *et al.*, 1999). It is not yet clear whether any of these methods will effectively improve insight and lead to behavioral changes such as increased medication compliance.

What is clear, however, is that any significant decrease in violent behavior by individuals with severe psychiatric disorders, and the consequent stigma that affects all individuals with psychiatric illnesses, must come through improved insight and/or medication compliance. Trying to decrease stigma without addressing its root cause is a waste of time and resources, similar to trying to decrease the waves in a harbor while ignoring the passing ships causing the waves.

Current attempts to decrease stigma without acknowledging the role played by violent behavior will fail. Lagos, Perlmutter, and Saexinger (1977) noted this fact as early as 1977, in an article entitled "Fear of the Mentally Ill: Empirical Support for the Common Man's Response." In 1981, Steadman similarly observed that:

> Recent research data on contemporary populations of ex-mental patients supports these public fears [of dangerousness] to an extent rarely acknowledged by mental health professionals . . . It is [therefore] futile and inappropriate to badger the news and entertainment media with appeals to help destigmatize the mentally ill.

> (Steadman 1981)

In a similar vein, Monahan recently added:

> The data suggest that public education programs by advocates for the mentally disordered along the lines of "people with mental illness are no more violent than the rest of us" may be doomed to failure. . . . And they should: the claim, it turns out, may well be untrue.

> (Monahan, 1992)

Currently, then, the average citizen may ride to work on a bus with a poster proclaiming that psychiatrically ill individuals are not dangerous while simultaneously reading that day's newspaper headline that says in effect that some of them are dangerous.

If we are unable to learn the lessons that the Russell Weston's of the world are demonstrating, then we will continue to perpetuate this sad cycle.

Acknowledgment

Dr. Nelly Alia-Klein reviewed the manuscript and provided helpful comments.

References

Alia-Klein, N., O'Rourke, T., Yale, S., Mahony, A. and Amador, X. F. (2001). Violence Assessment Scale (VAS): A study of validity and reliability and suggestions for future use. Poster session presented at the International Congress of Schizophrenia Research, Whistler, British Columbia, May 2001.

Alia-Klein, N., O'Rourke, T. M., Goldstein, R. Z. and Malaspina, D. (2004a). The Violence Assessment Scale (VAS): Psychometric properties and sensitivity to gradations of severity. Submitted for publication.

Alia-Klein, N., O'Rourke, T. M., Goldstein, R. Z. and Malaspina, D. (2004b). Insight into illness and adherence to psychotropic medications predict violence severity in a forensic sample. Submitted for publication.

Amador, X.F. and Strauss, D. H. (1993). Poor insight in schizophrenia. *Psychiatric Quarterly*, **64**, 305–318.

Angermeyer, M. C. and Matschinger, H. (1995). Violent attacks on public figures by persons suffering from psychiatric disorders: Their effect on the social distance towards the mentally ill. *European Archives of Psychiatry and Clinical Neuroscience*, **245**, 159–64.

Arango, C., Calcedo Barba, A., González-Salvador, T. and Calcedo Ordóñez, A. (1999). Violence in inpatients with schizophrenia: a prospective study. *Schizophrenia Bulletin*, **25**, 493–503.

Arango, C., Bombín, I., González-Salvador, M. T., García-Cabeza, I. and Bobes, J. (2002). Prediction and prevention of violence in schizophrenia outpatients: Preliminary report. Abstract, *Schizophrenia Research*, **53**, 233.

"Baltimore man charged in mother's slaying" (1990). *Washington Post*, 27 December, p. D3.

Bartels, J., Drake, R. E., Wallach, M. A. and Freeman, D. H. (1991). Characteristic hostility in schizophrenic outpatients. *Schizophrenia Bulletin*, **17**, 163–71.

Buckley, P. F., Hrouda, D. R., Resnick, P. J., Aronoff, M., Caso, M., Friedman, L., *et al.* (2002). Violence and schizophrenia: implications for continuity of care. Abstract, *Schizophrenia Research*, **53**, 233.

Clements, M. (1993). "What we say about mental illness." *Parade Magazine*, 31 October, pp. 3–6.

"Crofton woman found guilty in mother's slaying" (1990). *Washington Post*, 28 September, p. D3.

Damasio, A.R. (1994). *Descartes' Error*. New York: Avon Books.

David, A. S., Kemp, R., Kirov, G., Everitt, B. and Hayward, P. (1998). Improving insight and compliance: Predictions and consequences. Abstract, *Schizophrenia Research*, **29**, 34.

Davidoff, S. A., Forester, B. P., Ghaemi, S. N. and Bodkin, J. A. (1998). Effect of video self-observation on development of insight in psychotic disorders. *Journal of Nervous and Mental Disease*, **186**, 697–700.

Davidson, R. (1991). A mental health crisis in Illinois. *Chicago Tribune*, 9 December, p. 18.

Fessenden, F. (2000). They threaten, seethe and unhinge, then kill in quantity. *New York Times*, 9 April, p. A1.

Field Institute, The (1984). *In Pursuit of Wellness, vol. 4: A survey of California adults regarding their health practices and interest in health promotion programs*. San Francisco: California Department of Mental Health, Mental Health Promotion Branch.

Flashman, L. A., McAllister, T. W., Andreasen, N. C. and Saykin, A. J. (2000). Smaller brain size associated with unawareness of illness in patients with schizophrenia. *American Journal of Psychiatry*, **157**, 1167–69.

Fraser, M. E. (1994). Educating the public about mental illness: What will it take to get the job done? *Innovations and Research*, **3**, 29–31.

Friedman, L., Hrouda, D., Noffsinger, S., Resnick, P. and Buckley, P. F. (2003). Psychometric relationship of insight in patients with schizophrenia who commit violent acts. Abstract. *Schizophrenia Research*, **60**, 81.

Geller, J.L. (1992). A report on the "worst" state hospital recidivists in the US. *Hospital and Community Psychiatry*, **43**, 904–8.

Ghaemi, S. N. and Pope, H. G. (1994). Lack of insight in psychotic and affective disorders: A review of empirical studies. *Harvard Review of Psychiatry*, **2**, 22–33.

Gray, J. P. (1857). Homicide in insanity. *American Journal of Insanity*, **14**, 119–43.

Hrouda, D., Resnick, P. J., Friedman, L., Noffsinger, S. G. and Buckley, P. F. (2003). Violence and schizophrenia: further observations on standards of care. Abstract. *Schizophrenia Research*, **60**, 40.

Jemelka, R., Trupin, E. and Chiles, J. A. (1989). The mentally ill in prisons. *Hospital and Community Psychiatry*, **40**, 481–5.

Kamali, M., Kelly, L., Gervin, M., Browne, S., Larkin, C. and O'Callaghan, E. (2001) Insight and comorbid substance misuse and medication compliance among patients with schizophrenia. *Psychiatric Services*, **52**, 161–3, 166.

Kasper, J. A., Hoge, S. K., Feucht-Haviar, T., Cortina, J. and Cohen, B. (1997). Prospective study of patients' refusal of antipsychotic medication under a physician discretion review procedure. *American Journal of Psychiatry*, **154**, 483–9.

Kemp, R. A. and David, A. S. (1995). Insight and adherence to treatment in psychotic disorders. *British Journal of Hospital Medicine*, **54**, 222–7.

Knauth, P. (1975). *A Season in Hell*. New York: Harper and Row.

Kunjukrishnan, R. and Bradford, J. M. W. (1988). Schizophrenia and major affective disorder: Forensic psychiatric issues. *Canadian Journal of Psychiatry*, **33**, 723–33.

Lafave, H. G., Pinkney, A. A. and Gerber, G. J. (1993). Criminal activity by psychiatric clients after hospital discharge. *Hospital and Community Psychiatry*, **44**, 180–1.

Lagos, J. M., Perlmutter, K. and Saexinger, H. (1977). Fear of the mentally ill: Empirical support for the common man's response. *American Journal of Psychiatry*, **134**, 1134–7.

Larøi, F., Fannemel, M., Rønneberg, U., *et al.* (2000). Unawareness of illness in chronic schizophrenia and its relationship to structural brain measures and neuropsychological tests. *Psychiatry Research: Neuroimaging Section*, **100**, 49–58.

Link, B. G., Andrews, H. and Cullen, F. T. (1992). The violent and illegal behavior of mental patients reconsidered. *American Sociological Review*, **57**, 275–92.

Link, B. G., Cullen, F. T., Frank, J. and Wozniak, J. (1987). The social rejection of former mental patients: Understanding why labels matter. *American Journal of Sociology*, **92**, 1461–500.

McFarland, B. H., Faulkner, L. R., Bloom, J. D., Hallaux, R. and Bray, J. D. (1989). Chronic mental illness and the criminal justice system. *Hospital and Community Psychiatry*, **40**, 718–23.

Monahan, J. (1992). Mental disorder and violent behavior. *American Psychologist*, **47**, 511–21.

O'Keefe, C., Potenza, D. P. and Mueser, K. T. (1997). Treatment outcomes for severely mentally ill patients on conditional discharge to community-based treatment. *Journal of Nervous and Mental Disease*, **185**, 409–11.

Pallanti, S., Quercioli, L. and Pazzagli, A. (1999). Effects of clozapine on awareness of illness and cognition in schizophrenia. *Psychiatry Research*, **86**, 239–49.

Pescosolido, B. A., Monahan, J., Link, B. G., Stueve, A. and Kikuzawa, S. (1999). The public's view of the competence, dangerousness, and need for legal coercion of persons with mental health problems. *American Journal of Public Health*, **89**, 1339–45.

Petersson, H. and Gudjonsson, G. H. (1981). Psychiatric aspects of homicide. *Acta Psychiatrica Scandinavica*, **64**, 363–72.

Phelan, J. C., Link, B. G., Stueve, A. and Pescosolido, B. A. (2000). Public conceptions of mental illness in 1950 and 1996: What is mental illness and is it to be feared? *Journal of Health and Social Behavior*, **41**, 188–207.

Reiss, A. J. and Roth, J. A. (1993). *Understanding and Preventing Violence*. Washington, DC: National Academy Press.

Sahni, S. D., Mankowski, I., Patel, A. R., Muddasani, S., Diwadkar, V. R. and Keshavan, M. S. (2002). Insight and the prefrontal cortex in psychotic disorders. Abstract, *Biological Psychiatry*, **51**, 62S.

Smith, C. M., Barzman, D. and Pristach, C. A. (1997). Effect of patient and family insight on compliance of schizophrenic patients. *Journal of Clinical Pharmacology*, **37**, 147–54.

Smith, L. D. (1989). Medication refusal and the rehospitalized mentally ill inmate. *Hospital and Community Psychiatry*, **40**, 491–6.

Steadman, H. J. (1981). Critically reassessing the accuracy of public perceptions of the dangerousness of the mentally ill. *Journal of Health and Social Behavior*, **22**, 310–16.

Steinert, T., Sippach, T. and Gebhardt, R. P. (2000). How common is violence in schizophrenia despite neuroleptic treatment? *Pharmacopsychiatry*, **33**, 98–102.

Steinwachs, D. M., Kasper, J. D. and Skinner, E. A. (1992). *Family Perspectives on Meeting the Needs for Care of Severely Mentally Ill Relatives: A national survey*. Arlington, VA: National Alliance for the Mentally Ill.

Swanson, J. W., Holzer, C. E., Ganju, V. K. and Jono, R. T. (1990). Violence and psychiatric disorder in the community: Evidence from the epidemiologic catchment area surveys. *Hospital and Community Psychiatry*, **41**, 761–70.

Swanson, J. W., Swartz, M. S., Borum, R., Hiday, V. A., Wagner, H. R. and Burns, B. J. (2000). Involuntary out-patient commitment and reduction of violent behaviour in persons with severe mental illness. *British Journal of Psychiatry*, **176**, 224–31.

Tardiff, K., Marzuk, P. M., Leon, A. C., Portera, L. and Weiner, C. (1997). Violence by patients admitted to a private psychiatric hospital. *American Journal of Psychiatry*, **154**, 88–93.

Taylor, P. (1985). Motives for offending amongst violent and psychotic men. *British Journal of Psychiatry*, **147**, 491–8.

Thornton, J. A. and Wahl, O. F. (1996). Impact of a newspaper article on attitudes toward mental illness. *Journal of Community Psychology*, **24**, 17–24.

Torrey, E. F. (1988). *Nowhere to go: The tragic odyssey of the homeless mentally ill*. Harper and Row, New York.

Torrey, E. F. (1994). Violent behavior by individuals with serious mental illness. *Hospital and Community Psychiatry*, **45**, 653–62.

Torrey, E. F. (1997). *Out of the Shadows: Confronting America's mental illness crisis*. John Wiley and Sons, New York.

Torrey, E. F. and Zdanowicz, M. (2001). Outpatient commitment: What, why, and for whom. *Psychiatric Services*, **52**, 337–41.

Torrey, E. F., Stieber, J., Ezekiel, J., Wolfe, S. M., Sharfstein, J., Noble, J. H., *et al.* (1992). *Criminalizing the Seriously Mentally Ill: The abuse of jails as mental hospitals*. Washington, DC: National Alliance for the Mentally Ill and Public Citizen's Health Research Group.

Trauer, T. and Sacks, T. (2000). The relationship between insight and medication adherence in severely mentally ill clients treated in the community. *Acta Psychiatrica Scandinavica*, **102**, 211–16.

US Department of Health and Human Services. (1999). *Mental health: A report of the Surgeon General*. Rockville, MD: US Department of Health and Human Services, Substance Abuse and Mental Health Services Administration, Center for Mental Health Services, National Institutes of Health, National Institute of Mental Health.

Varga, M., Rønneberg, U., Flekkoy, K., Opjordsmoen, S., Babovic, A. and Haakonsen, M. (2002). Unawareness of illness and its relation to functional and structural brain measures in patients with bipolar disorder. Abstract, *Journal of Affective Disorders*, **68**, 139.

Wahl, O. F. (1987). Public vs. professional conceptions of schizophrenia. *Journal of Community Psychology*, **15**, 285–91.

Weaver, K. E. (1983). Increasing the dose of antipsychotic medication to control violence. Letter, *American Journal of Psychiatry*, **140**, 1274.

Yesavage, J. A. (1982). Inpatient violence and the schizophrenic patient: An inverse correlation between danger-related events and neuroleptic levels. *Biological Psychiatry*, **17**, 1331–7.

Chapter 13

Why lack of insight should have a central place in mental health law

Ken J. Kress

Insight as a mental health law concept

Introduction

Recent advances in our understanding of and ability to measure insight raise the question whether insight could, or should, play a more significant role in mental health law, particularly in coerced treatment, civil commitment, and criminal law. This chapter examines insight and coerced treatment.

Improvements in interrater reliability in determining degrees of insight engender surprisingly extensive and powerful consequentialist arguments in favor of deploying insight as a central concept in mental health law. Deployment of lack of insight is further supported by autonomy and equality rights. Although this chapter focuses on insight and coerced treatment, much of the discussion of coerced treatment applies to commitment with the necessary changes. Civil commitment can be understood as a form of coerced treatment because isolation from society, enhanced observation, and confinement in the less stimulating and more serene environment of a hospital is a (drug-free) treatment designed to reduce risk, as well as marginally treat the illness.

With a few notable exceptions, the literature on justifications for coerced treatment (and civil commitment) is regrettably discouraging. While this chapter only sketches a theory of conditions when coerced treatment by the state is morally justified, it is intended to develop those justifications. Moreover, it develops novel ways of understanding, and arguing about, coerced treatment that will support fruitful investigations in the future.

A unique feature of this theory is its natural application to lack of insight, rather than incompetence. I shall demonstrate that lack of insight should play a heightened role in legal doctrine in justifying coerced treatment. In this chapter, I shall not urge that incompetence should play a diminished role. There are arguments that recommend that conclusion, but whether those arguments outweigh considerations supporting a prominent place for incompetence will not be examined here.

Although competence is traditionally divided into four aspects: ability to communicate a choice, understanding, appreciation, and ability to rationally weigh and balance alternatives, I will deploy competence in this chapter to refer to ability to weigh and balance. I do so in order that the discussion fit within the parameters of this medium, and because weighing and balancing appears to be the most important aspect of competence in theoretical scholarship. Most of the treatment decision-making process is categorized under rational weighing and balancing. By contrast, understanding appears to be an ability that is, in most cases, necessary to rational decision-making, but as a prerequisite that allows one to know what to weigh and balance. Similarly, in many cases, being able to communicate a choice is essential to others being able to respect that choice. But it is not clear that the ability to communicate a decision is part of the ability to make the decision. Inability to sustain a choice can be problematic when changes in desire are unrelated to new information or reevaluating the relevant considerations. But that means that problematic instability can be understood in terms of a failure of rational weighing and balancing.

Insight

Although insight could apply to any proposition, in the mental health context it is traditionally understood as insight respecting the existence of mental illness and insight respecting the need for treatment. Thoughtful accounts frequently add insight respecting obvious (or non-obvious) symptoms, as well as, in some versions, awareness that the symptoms are pathological. Less frequently, accounts explicitly include awareness of the value of treatment, and of the social consequences of having the disorder, concepts that are at least implicit in most need for treatment determinations.

Rarely stated, however, is a crucial point: insight cannot be understood without exploring the reasons for a belief respecting mental illness, need for treatment, symptoms, value of treatment, or the social consequences of having the psychiatric disorder. For example, a patient who appears hypomanic could rationally reject the bipolar denomination because poor decision-making resulting from diabetic high blood sugar is inducing impulsive behavior, manifesting poor judgment that is being mistaken for hypomania. This diabetes example also demonstrates that whether one rationally believes one has a need for treatment depends upon what beliefs one has about alternative explanations of symptoms, alternative treatments, and individual values respecting side-effects.

If one can rationally believe both that one has a need for treatment and that one has no need for treatment, depending upon what other beliefs one has, then it follows as a matter of logic that determinations based solely upon surface beliefs, and not also upon the reasons or grounds for those beliefs, will sometimes be incorrect. Many of these cases will be garden variety situations. Consider a previously depressed patient in remission requiring no treatment who contacts his psychiatrist reporting the return of modest symptoms, which the patient rationally believes indicates a need for treatment. The psychiatrist, however, after hearing of the symptoms, informs the patient that these symptoms do not warrant any action, but that the patient should call back if symptoms increase significantly. At this point, based upon the same symptoms, the patient now rationally believes that there is no need for treatment, as does his doctor. Later, the patient attends a lecture on new approaches to depression by a highly respected researcher who indicates that symptom *A*, which the patient has, almost invariably requires anti-depressant therapy, the earlier the better. Now, the patient rationally believes that there is a need for treatment, and his psychiatrist agrees after reviewing this new research. Based upon the same symptoms, both the patient and the psychiatrist can rationally believe at times that there is a need for treatment and, at other times, that there is not a need for treatment, as their beliefs about what is the best treatment change. Similarly, while symptoms remain constant, changes in (beliefs about) the patient's goals and values, changes in (beliefs about) how risk averse the patient is, and changes in (beliefs about) how to weigh and balance danger to others against the patient's liberty rights and other values can engender changes in whether it is rational to believe that there is a need for treatment.

But if acquisition of new information (possibly refuting prior beliefs) can rationally and justifiably engender changes in belief as to whether there is a need for treatment, then powerful results follow. Two individuals with different beliefs, for example, doctor and patient, may rationally and justifiably come to different beliefs about the need for treatment (Kress, 1990). Indeed, even two individuals with the same evidence can rationally believe different propositions because data underdetermines theory. That is, any finite set of data is consistent with multiple – if not infinite – sets of more universal, theoretical beliefs that explain the data (Quine, 1960).

Another way of understanding the relativity or contextualized nature of the concept "need" is to note that need is always relative to some purpose, and to what one owns or in some sense has. Imelda Marcos may "need" a new pair of shoes given her obsession for them, given her desire to get into the *Guinness Book of World Records*, or in order to attend the Ambassador's dinner in a new pair of shoes. By contrast, having one thousand – or several thousand – shoes, as she allegedly already has now, would probably be enough for the rest of us.

Similarly, two patients diagnosed with schizophrenia report hallucinations and difficulty sleeping. As it turns out, the hallucinations greatly disturb the first patient but the sleeping disorder does not, whereas the second patient has just the opposite reaction. One way to put this would be that the first patient has a great need for relief from the hallucinations, and a mild need for relief of the sleep disorder, whereas the second patient has the opposite desires. It could easily turn out that the patients should be treated with different medications whose action best targets the symptom most complained about by each patient. In this way, the individual patient's needs, wants, and values are an essential part of the treatment decision. Alternatively, rather than conceiving of the patient under the rubric schizophrenia, the psychiatrist could conceive of herself as treating symptoms, especially those most complained about. In so doing, the treating professional would be taking account of the patient's values at the beginning, in deciding what should be treated. In either event, even at this elementary level, patients' values are relevant to treatment decisions.

Although it will not matter in the current context, I prefer not to employ the concept of insight respecting the existence of mental illness in order to avoid stigma, and deploy insight only to mean awareness of need for treatment and symptoms. Any information lost with the banning of the term "mental illness" or its subcategories, respecting insight (or mental health generally) I would urge, is substantially outweighed in a normative account of insight by the reduction in stigma. Regrettably, the argument for this position cannot be developed here. The main significant information lost will be about prognosis, and much of that information may be available from past history. Indeed, past history frequently provides better evidence of prognosis than bare categorization under a major mental illness. Moreover, from a clinical and therapeutic perspective, it matters little if a patient denies that he has mental illness, if he believes that he has a need for treatment.

I should add some cautionary notes: that an individual believes that he has no need for treatment, or at least asserts he has no need, does not mean that he will not accept treatment if offered. Conversely, many individuals who believe or assert that they have a need for treatment do not accept it when offered, or are treatment noncompliant. This chapter does not endorse the view that coerced treatment is appropriate for all persons with serious mental illness who lack insight; rather, it supposes that coerced treatment is appropriate only for a small minority of those lacking insight. Moreover, nothing in this chapter demonstrates that only individuals lacking in insight should be coercively treated.

Some scholars understand lack of insight as a continuum, that is, as a single property that can manifest itself in a person in varying degrees (Grisso and Applebaum, 1998). This model is, unfortunately, too crude. A more complex understanding interprets insight not as a continuum, but rather as a number of, or infinity of, continua, that is, a multidimensional property, N-space or Hilbert-space. The generalization of the two-dimensional Cartesian coordinate system, taught in high school, to n dimensions is a multidimensional property, N-space or Hilbert-space.

Suppose that you are considering purchasing a new residence. At first, you look at a new development of identical tract houses that differ, surprisingly, only in price. The desirability of these houses can be mapped as a continuum along the property of price. Each house is equally, more, or less desirable than each other house. This comparability of houses along the parameter of price is what mathematicians mean when they say that a set is totally ordered. None of those houses turns out to be your cup of tea.

As a result, you begin looking at used houses. You narrow your preferences down to two. One is larger, and has a nicer frontage. The other has been kept up better, and is cheaper, but it is in a less safe and otherwise less desirable neighborhood. Without denying that you will make a choice, it is nevertheless unclear whether it is always accurate to say, under these circumstances, that one house is better overall than the other. It may not be possible to sum up size, frontage, condition, price, safety and location so as to determine, for any two houses, which is better overall. Put differently, the concept of better used housing may not be totally ordered, but only partially ordered.

Similarly, it is not always possible to say that one person has more insight than another because the first may be stronger on some aspects of insight, yet weaker on others. For example, Jones may be able to recite that he has schizophrenia, and be able to describe that he hears things that other people don't, and believes things that other people don't and that they regard him as having no evidence for believing; sometimes he accepts treatment, and sometimes he doesn't. By contrast, Smith denies he has mental illness, admits that his hallucinations and delusions and flattened affect are pathological, and create substantial negative social consequences for him, but he nevertheless vehemently denies that he needs treatment and rejects it if offered. Finally, Brown denies that he is ill, or has symptoms, but believes he needs treatment, and faithfully follows his treatment plan. Jones has the most insight into the fact that he is ill; Smith has the best insight into his symptoms and their consequences; Brown perhaps has the best insight into his need for treatment. It is controversial which of the three has the best insight overall. Insight can be understood as a continuum only under the problematic supposition that its many properties can be reduced to one property that can be assessed along a single scale.

An important question is the relationship between insight and appreciation, an aspect of incompetence described by the McArthur Mental Health Network's Competence Project. As appreciation refers to a patient's understanding that descriptions of the illness and alternative treatments apply to the patient, the notion overlaps with insight's inquiry into the patient's understanding that he has the illness, and that its profundity gives rise to a need for treatment. I suspect that these terms are frequently enough employed differently by alternative scholars, that it would be difficult to determine to what extent insight and appreciation overlap.

I shall distinguish lack of appreciation from lack of insight by not deeming a cognitive deficit lack of insight unless that lack of insight is a biologically based case of true anosogonosia. By contrast, lack of appreciation may be anosogonosia, or based in psychological denial or fear of stigma not grounded in neurobiology. Under this definition, lack of appreciation includes behavior and cognitive deficits not properly deemed lack of insight because they are not biologically based cases of anosogonosia. (There are other differences, but they are not significant for our current purposes.) There is no reason why some could not lack insight and also manifest psychological denial.

Conditions for determining whether a disability justifies state intervention, and that allow comparative determinations among disabilities that allegedly justify state intervention

This section briefly introduces four factors for determining whether a proposed disability justifies liberty-reducing state intervention. The more of each factor that a disability has, other things equal, the more state intervention is justified. The four factors will be briefly described, and then examined in more detail thereafter. First, the disability must be *objectively discernible* (objectivity). Second, the disability must have a *material basis* (materiality). Third, the proof of objective discernability and material basis must be *substantially independent of the allegedly bad outcome* (independence), but not independent of the process of reasoning employed to arrive at the purported bad outcome. Finally, and most important, *the disability must be ethically significant and justify the proposed state intervention* (justificatory), presumably by demonstrating an ethically significant deficit in the autonomousness of action by the consumer.

If the disability exceeds a certain threshold of the four factors, then the state may be morally justified in intervening in the treatment decision, largely on the ground that the consumer's decision-making process lacks qualities necessary for informed, autonomous action. However, although the disability may undercut the autonomous or informed quality of the consumer's decision, that will not always be the case. In the section "The justification of the four criteria", I shall compare insight and competence on the four factors, and conclude that insight does better than incompetence on each of the factors, suggesting that intervening on the basis of lack of insight is even more justified than intervening on the basis of incompetence.

In addition to the four factors, the state must also show causation: that the disability caused the allegedly bad decision and outcome. This involves showing two things. First, it must be demonstrated that the decision does have a bad outcome. Second, it must be shown that the disability caused that bad outcome. Alternatively, we might say the problematic inferential process leading to the decision must exemplify the disability, or, better yet, that the fallacious decision-making process, in conjunction with other problematic inferences, constitutes – in part – the disability. If the disability is irrelevant to the process leading to the bad outcome, it does not justify liberty-restricting intervention. Moreover, even if the state has a moral or constitutional power to intervene and make the decision for a non-autonomous agent, sound policy recommends that the power should not always be exercised. There are two main circumstances where a disability that can justify state intervention should nevertheless not support such intervention. The first, as just noted, is where the disability does not cause the bad outcome, or, more accurately, where the flawed decision-making process and outcome do not exemplify or manifest the disability. The second circumstance is where the outcome the consumer prefers is reasonably good. If the patient makes a decision likely to have good consequences based upon a non-autonomous or irrational process, the better part of wisdom would be not to intervene. After all, there are negative consequences to patients from having been coerced: loss of self esteem and respect; learned helplessness (Goffman, 1961); incompetency labeling effects (Winick, 1995); and feelings of being forced/coerced into treatment (Gardner *et al.*, 1999; Greenberg *et al.*, 1996). If the patient's outcome is reasonably good, then presumably the corresponding treatment could have been prescribed under appropriate practices and ethical standards by a psychiatrist or mental health professional. Even according to the principles supporting rational weighing and balancing as cost–benefit analysis, a subject should not be coerced unless the additional value of the coerced treatment exceeds the negative consequences of coercion.

The claim that an outcome is bad requires clarification. My own view is that the meaning of "bad" is inherently controversial, just as the concepts of morality and normativity are. Nevertheless, some possible candidates for the best interpretation of something being a bad outcome should be mentioned. First, an outcome could be considered bad if it is bad according to conventional morality, that is, the moral beliefs of some group. Here, promising candidates include: the views of society, patients, mental health professionals, or lawyers. Second, an outcome could be considered bad if it is bad according to the particular patient's own values, or according to the patient's views when competent. This perspective parallels the substituted judgment requirement on interventions. Third, an outcome could be considered bad if it is bad according to critical morality, what might here be called objective or absolute morality. The two main contenders for critical morality are consequentialism and rights-based theories. An outcome is bad according to consequentialism if it has bad consequences. On a rights-based view, an outcome is bad if it violates rights. A theory of coerced treatment supported by lack of insight need not choose among these prospects: each reader can use her favored moral theory. On the other hand, a legal system must choose, or risk developing an incoherent doctrine.

Objectivity

The disability must be objectively discernible (epistemic requirement). For current purposes, this requirement can be understood to require interrater reliability, or interrater reliability among clinicians for determinations that an individual has a disability, and for determinations of the particular realization of the disability. (For other purposes, or to other audiences, the objectivity requirement might be understood to require that sound arguments about disability deploy public criteria, available to most citizens. In other contexts, objectivity could be a statement about the existence of a physical condition that causes, in the proper way, beliefs about disability [Greenawalt, 1992].)

Materiality

There must be a real material basis (or medically demonstrable syndrome) for the disability (constitutive or ontological criterion). In the current context, that means that the disability can be seen as residing in the brain and neurological system. In non-psychiatric cases, of course, a disability may be lodged elsewhere in the body. This criterion does not mean that one must be able to demonstrate in each circumstance the existence of a material basis. All one needs is good reason to believe that a material basis exists, even if that material basis has not been established for this disability, or for this particular individual. This requirement protects consumers from unjustified interventions, based upon disabilities of dubious existence.

But materiality also requires that disabilities have an origin or realization in the brain, which can be the basis for stigmatizing remarks, attitudes, and behavior. Some might urge that if persons with severe mental illness differ neurologically from the chronically mentally healthy, that difference supports an ideology of inferiority, incompetence, and discrimination. Why not maintain that the difference supports an ideology of superiority? Or superiority in some respects, inferiority in others?

Independence

The constitutive and epistemic criteria for the existence and proof of the disability must be substantially independent of the 'bad' outcome: decisions are to be judged in terms of their processes of justification, that is, in terms of the reasons given and inferences taken in support of the outcome, and not in terms of the outcome itself.

Put differently, a decision is good or bad based upon the quality of its reasoning rather than the desirability of its outcome. Of course, a bad outcome puts one on notice that investigation of the reasoning that led to the outcome might provide evidence of disability. Indeed, a bad outcome *is* evidence of disability; but we must remember that it is weak evidence, easily overcome by contrary information.

Part of the reason for this criterion is that even the best (non-deductive) reasoning sometimes results in false or bad conclusions. Indeed, the chronically mentally healthy not infrequently manifest errors in reasoning leading to false or absurd conclusions. Tversky and Kahneman have created a cottage industry arguing that most people, including probability theorists, Bayesian statisticians, empirical researchers, and psychiatrists, frequently make errors in statistical and probabilistic reasoning (Tversky and Kahneman, 1982).

The independence requirement is also intended to guard against differences in treatment philosophy between treatment provider and patient being interpreted as lack of insight or incapacity. Otherwise, consumers are not being treated equally with mentally healthy persons, which constitutes discrimination. Courts have held that a treatment decision differing from the doctor's recommendation, or even medically inadvisable, is nevertheless rational if it is supported by reasons:

> In determining whether a decision is responsible [that is, reasonable], the focus must be on whether the grounds for the decision are rational or reasonable not what conclusion is reached. A decision, although medically inadvisable, may be rationally reached, and if so, it is not the court's place to second guess the decision.

In the Interest of J.P., 574 N.W. 2d 340, 343 (Iowa 1998) The MacArthur Mental Health Network's Project on Capacity also accepts the claim that reasons and inferences must be understood before concluding that someone lacks insight or is incompetent: a bad outcome, by itself, proves little (Grisso *et al.*, 1995). It cannot be determined whether the decision is the result of lack of insight (or incompetence) until the reasons and inferences of the patient have been examined from the perspective of the patient's goals, attitudes, and moral views.

The MacArthur Capacity Project looks at reasons/inferences and outcome, but not premises or values. Some might justify this on the ground that the liberal state may not impose its values or beliefs on citizens. Not examining premises or values, however, is problematic, at least if the non-examined belief or value is itself a product of the disability, lack of insight or incompetence, and is problematically false or skewed. Because the decision-making process can often be construed either as an inference from belief 1 to decision/outcome, or as a process from belief 2 to belief 1 to decision/outcome, or as a process from belief 3 to belief 2 to belief 1 to decision/outcome, or . . . . When belief 1 is plausible (even if possibly false) and the outcome is bad, the inference from belief 1 to outcome may well be an instance of, or indistinguishable from, the kind of mistaken inference chronically mentally healthy people make every day, and therefore cannot justify intervention. However, if belief 2 or belief 3 cannot be understood as a garden-variety mistake, but only, or almost only, the result of disability, then the state may well be justified in intervening.

Regrettably, the position that incompetence is responsive to the consumer's justification of underlying beliefs, such as beliefs 2 and 3, is also problematic, at least in practice. It is difficult enough to ascertain one step of anyone's inferences, let alone several, or all the way back to the individual's first relevant belief. Indeed, the position avoids an infinite regress only because humans are finite creatures. Moreover, many persons, including patients, have difficulty articulating their reasoning. Finally, because we are not infinite beings with infinite memory space, we often remember conclusions but not the reasons supporting those conclusions. Thus, earlier beliefs and inferences may be inaccessible.

Whether competence doctrine takes cognizance of premises and values or not, it is seriously problematic. This profound critique has the potential to devastate competence theory and practice. Competence's importance recommends further thought on this problem.

Many psychiatrists have commented to me that they are frequently called on to consult respecting medical patients' competence. Upon examination, the psychiatrist finds that the medical doctor claims that the patient is incompetent solely on the basis that the patient rejects the medical doctor's treatment recommendation, and without investigating the patient's reasoning. I regret to report that some psychiatrists engage in the same fallacious reasoning with their own patients.

Ethical significance

Most important, the disability or disabled inference or decision must have ethical significance: it must justify the envisioned intervention by the state (justificatory). Current doctrine and theory justify coerced treatment on the primary ground of incompetence to make rational treatment decisions. That is, they justify coerced treatment on the basis of an inability to reason from goals and principles (good mental health, avoidance of certain side-effects, facts about consequences of alternative treatments, and public safety) to good ways to satisfy those concerns. This is the realm of technocrats, who will take any goal and find the best means to achieve it. This is a form of what Aristotle, Kant, and other philosophers call "practical reason". But it is hard to see why a substantial deficit in practical reasoning ability justifies intervention, other than the bald assertion that better decisions have better outcomes. Even so able a philosopher as Michael Moore provides a conclusory argument that a significant deficit in practical reasoning ability means that one is not autonomous, and therefore not a (moral) person, so that intervention is justified (Moore, 1985). After all, we permit autonomous agents to do silly and self-destructive things all the time without intervening. By contrast, lack of autonomous action has been thought to justify paternalistic intervention because it is the possession of autonomous abilities that underpins the right to be treated with equal concern and respect, the foundation of Western ethics since Immanuel Kant. Lack of insight justifies intervention on the ground that the individual's disability results in the individual not being capable of free and informed action because conditions necessary for free, informed action are defeated or eliminated by the individual's particular form of disability.

The justification of the four criteria, and their application to lack of insight and incompetence

We shall now probe deeper into why these four criteria provide justification for state intervention. We shall discuss each prerequisite in turn. For each criterion in turn, after we have understood how it helps to justify intervention in the abstract, we will examine how well each of lack of insight and incompetence do in justifying state intervention on that criterion. Finally, we will compare how well lack of insight and incompetence fare on the four criteria overall. We shall find that insight fares better than incompetence as rational weighing and balancing on each of the four criteria. It follows that insight justifies intervention better than incompetence. On the plausible assumption that incompetence is properly a part of coerced treatment doctrine, it would appear that insight should also have a place in coerced treatment doctrine.

Although it would be nice to be able to develop a theory demonstrating that possession of the above four conditions to degrees A, B, C, and D justifies paternalistic state intervention, it would be unduly optimistic to expect such a result. Nor should we expect a theory of necessary and sufficient conditions for justified intervention. Rather, we should aim no higher than a theory that demonstrates that certain conditions are sufficient to justify coerced treatment, and that indicates that those circumstances with more of the four conditions overall can better justify intervention. We will soon assess and apply the four criteria.

Before providing a deeper examination of the first two criteria, and of the argument from reliability and certainty, it will prove useful to explore why legal systems aspire to reasonable certainty, generally a consequence of good interrater reliability. Bentham, perhaps the greatest legal philosopher in the history of Western civilization, thought that the purpose of law was to create certainty (Postema, 1986). Other major legal scholars, for example, Austin and Hart, also embrace certainty as a virtue. When law is uncertain, it is difficult for persons and businesses to plan their behavior so as to avoid undesirable entanglements with the legal system, creating wasteful and unintended costs and losses. By contrast, a reasonably certain set of laws provides notice to citizens and businesses, thereby allowing more efficient behavior[1] than is possible under greater uncertainty. Because the applicable laws are more certain, it is easier to ascertain whether University of Michigan President Mary Sue Coleman's driving has exceeded the speed law than whether Michigan's various affirmative action programs have violated the constitution. By minimizing waste, efficient behavior increases societal wealth. The argument from efficiency is a consequentialist argument maintaining that reliability, one version of certainty, allows people to plan so as to avoid undesirable consequences, thereby minimizing undesirable costs and losses, resulting in increased societal wealth and happiness.

Consequentialist arguments never before deployed in this context demonstrate that certainty also enhances liberty and equality, the two rights most deeply embedded in Anglo-American culture. This may surprise many, because most moral thinkers describe consequentialism and rights-based theories as bitter opponents, recommending conflicting actions. Certainty enhances liberty because greater certainty allows you to walk closer to the line where the government will intervene without crossing that line. For example, a "bright line" rule regarding which speech is protected by the First Amendment generates more liberty than a jagged or eroded rule that leaves unclear which speech is protected, because people have more freedom to express themselves if they know the exact point at which that freedom ends. Certainty also minimizes discretion and the ensuing risk of improper exercise of that discretion. Biased exercise of discretion risks arbitrariness, idiosyncrasy, prejudice, and self-dealing. The rule of law, however, insists that we are a nation of laws, not men. The rule of law is generally understood as requiring that those applying the law should follow existing law, not create new law.

Finally, intersubjective reliability that increases certainty will also, in general, increase the number of individuals reaching the same conclusion. Thus, reliability inducing certainty increases equality: the chance that courts and government actors will show all citizens equal concern and respect, and treat like cases alike. Every modern regime claims to respect and promote liberty and equality. Indeed, liberty and equality are so important that even regimes that egregiously violate these rights find it necessary to pretend to respect them. In summary, increases in interrater reliability respecting insight raise the prospect that deploying lack of insight as a main factor in coerced treatment determinations may have benefits for social wealth, liberty, and equality.

---

[1] The concept of efficiency used here is Kaldor-Hicks efficiency. A change in the state of the world is Kaldor-Hicks superior if, after the implementation of the change, the winners could pay off the losers, so that nobody is worse off, and some are better off. A state of the world is Kaldor-Hicks-efficient if no further exchange of goods that is Kaldor-Hicks superior is possible. See Coleman (1988).

There is a second, and more important, reason for augmenting the role of insight in mental health law, particularly in coerced treatment and civil commitment hearings. Because lack of insight negates central knowledge essential to an informed, autonomous decision, intervention by government may well be justified on the ground that non-autonomous behavior does not deserve the same rights and protections as autonomous action, or, more respectfully, that those rights and protections should be exercised by autonomous agents on behalf of those behaving non-autonomously (Kress, 2000).

The disability must be objectively discernible (epistemic requirement)

The justification for objectivity

The objectivity requirement is justified by two or three foundational principles, depending upon how you count. The first principle is a duty upon government actors, such as police and courts, to treat citizens with equal concern and respect. In order that government actors treat citizens with equal concern and respect, they are required to act on the basis of principles that can be articulated to foster public debate, criticism, and to minimize various risks of bias and unequal treatment that would be harder to detect in the absence of articulated principles.

The other principle(s) that support the first principle for justifying state intervention, the objectivity criteria, is the void-for-vagueness doctrine in American constitutional law, and its moral counterpart that it is improper for the state to deprive an individual of life, liberty, or property unless the individual knew what behavior might lead to the state intervening in these ways. Thus, the state may not intervene unless it provides sufficiently definite notice of the areas where citizens may be subject to state intervention so that citizens can plan their conduct accordingly.

We turn first to the principle of articulate consistency that constrains government actors to treat like cases alike. The principle of treating all citizens as equal under the law requires, in the case of public officials, such as judges, and psychiatrists in their official roles within the commitment process, to act not merely in a manner that can be described as equal towards all, but more strongly, on the basis of a theory of just state intervention that can be stated explicitly in a general theory of justice. Such a theory constrains public actors (1) to consistency, in the deep sense that they must consistently apply the same principles in relevantly similar situations (and consistently apply the same methods for resolving conflicts between principles in like situations of conflict); (2) to coherence, so that conflicts among principles are resolved by meta-principles of weight, or priority, or the like, in a way that reflects a coherent and plausible theory of justice, such as a theory of when state paternalism and intervention is justified (Kress, 1999); (3) to provide a public standard for debating and predicting their behavior; and (4) to discredit appeals to unique (idiosyncratic) intuitions that could: (5) mask prejudice, (6) self-interest, or (7) risk-biased decision-making.

Objectivity is also necessary because vague terms generate vague laws that cannot justly be applied to individuals to restrict their liberty because (8) vague laws do not sufficiently convey definite warning as to proscribed conduct when measured by common understanding or practice, (Giaccio v. Pennsylvania, 382 U.S. 399, 402–03 (1966)), (9) thereby leading to inefficient responses; (10) vague laws do not let respondent or attorney know what evidence is admissible (Bezanson, 1975); (11) and in effect deny respondent the right to present a defense (ibid.); (12) vague language fails to confine the discretion of the decision-maker, and thereby delegates policy matters to policemen, judges, and juries for ad hoc, subjective resolution (Grayned v. City of Rockford, 408 U.S. 104, 108–9, 92 S.Ct. 2294, 2299, 33 L.Ed.2d 222, 227 (1972)). In the case of civil commitment and coerced treatment hearings, vagueness delegates decisions to police, mental health professionals, juries, and judges (Papachristou v. City of Jacksonville, 405 U.S. 156, 170, 92 S.Ct. 839, 847, 31 L.Ed.2d 110, 120 (1970); Bezanson, 1975); (13) moreover, overly broad vague language may curtail conduct that a statute was not intended to curtail (ibid.), (14) thereby unnecessarily restricting liberty.

In short, vague laws restrict liberty unnecessarily, risk government violating equality, and induce inefficient responses compared to those possible with more precise language.

Comparing the reliability of insight and rational competence

Applying these principles to insight, we find that recent tests for insight enjoy reasonably good reliability. For example, (McEvoy et al., 1989), report an interrater reliability on the Insight and Treatment Attitudes Questionnaire (ITAQ) between interviewer and psychiatrist of r = 0.82, $P < 0.001$. The MacArthur competence study reached similar levels of reliability for both rational weighing and balancing (TRAT), and for understanding (UTD). (Grisso et al., 1995).

Although insight and competence both do well on interrater reliability, ultimately that is not the correct test. Although perhaps they should be, few lack of insight or incompetence determinations are significantly based upon such instruments. In practice, whether inside or outside of court, most judgments of lack of insight and incompetence are based upon clinical judgments.

In general, lack of insight is substantially easier to determine than ability to rationally weigh and balance, and perhaps simpler than other aspects of the standard subfactors of competence. In general, determinations of lack of insight require fewer items and easier items to ascertain than evaluations of inability to rationally weigh and balance. Frequently, one can determine that an individual lacks insight simply by asking her if she needs treatment, is exhibiting obvious symptoms, or is mentally ill. Indeed, many individuals who lack insight will link these concepts, maintaining that they do not need treatment because they are not ill. Asking the above questions as well as engaging in modest inquiries into the reasons for the individual's beliefs can determine many other cases of lack of insight.

By contrast, determining whether someone can weigh and balance will usually require a deeper inquiry into the individual's reasoning process, beliefs and inferences.

Moreover, as I shall argue later, the concept of weighing and balancing is yet more indeterminate, because the best notion of weighing and balancing is itself in dispute. I shall urge that there are rational and competent methods of resolving disputes that do not engage methods of weighing and balancing that attempt to maximize expected value or utility. For example, Rawls's maximin procedure attempts to minimize the worse case scenario, so as to avoid being destitute, a slave, or the victim of terrorists. An individual might deploy that method to minimize the chance of dying from neurolep-tic malignant syndrome, or other side effects. Alternatively, one might rely upon an expert rather than doing the calculation oneself. The existence of incompatible modes of rational balancing is an embarrassment to competence doctrine.

Since lack of insight is a simpler concept than incompetence, and one that might be more determinately and precisely measurable, it is plausible that in legal applications lack of insight will command more intersubjective agreement than competence. There is a logical possibility that the vagueness of various aspects of complex concepts of incompe-tence will be in harmony, or even partially cancel out each other's vagueness, but in prac-tice the chance of that happening is miniscule. Although it is plausible that clinical applications of insight would command greater intersubjective agreement than compe-tence, empirical research would be helpful in determining whether the plausible is actual.

There must be a real material basis (or medically demonstrable syndrome) for the disability (constitutive or ontological criterion).

Disabilities with material bases better justify intervention

The existence of a material basis for a disability, such as a neurobiological basis, con-strains decision-makers to disabilities that are consistent with the neurobiological facts. Conversely, the requirement of a material basis constrains potential intervention justifying disabilities to those that are – or could – reasonably be seen as seated in the brain. Both of these consequences of the material basis requirement minimize decision-maker discretion, thereby reducing the risk of bias, prejudice, self-interest, and the importation of subjective values. At the same time, these consequences increase the prospect that government will treat citizens with equal concern and respect, and treat like cases alike. Thus we see that, in practice, the requirements of objectivity and materiality both serve equality by constraining the discretion of actors in the system, although in different ways.

Without a material basis for the disability (or a medically demonstrable syndrome), it is perhaps mysterious in what the disability consists. Without a material basis, there is a risk that the alleged disability consists solely in behavior that is disapproved. For example, if a patient habitually engages in sophisticated conversation with particularly intelligent yellow dogs, a claim of disability appears implausible, despite recurrent behav-ior, because the behavior does not appear to be grounded in the neurological system. Moreover, if the behavior is grounded in the neurological system in some sense, it would not be grounded in the appropriate sense because speaking to yellow dogs is not the sort of basic or central (dis)ability that is relevant to coerced treatment. Moreover, the behavior would lack the necessary material, hierarchical structure and organization that justifies, based upon current scientific knowledge, the view that the behavior meets standards for being understood neurologically.

Additionally, if there were no material basis, there would be a risk that any behavior found sufficient for intervention would not amount to a deficit justifying overriding the individual's autonomy. Without a material basis, or a reasonable belief that an underlying material basis exists, it is hard to see how one could demonstrate the existence of a disability, as opposed to a frequent poor exercise of an ability. Without a material basis, there is a risk that the finding of disability constitutes bias on the part of the testifying psychiatrist or factfinder. Without a material basis, there is a risk that a finding of disability results from prejudice. Without a material basis, there is a risk that a finding of disability reflects self-interest, for example, on the part of the testifying mental health professional. Without a material basis, there is a risk that a finding of disability reflects sympathy for emotionally distraught family members and friends.

There is evidence that lack of insight has a material basis

As I have defined lack of insight, by definition it has a neurobiological and therefore material basis. However, mounting evidence suggests that even a more intuitive notion of lack of insight, that is not defined as grounded in neurobiology, nevertheless has a material basis. Amador and colleagues suggest that when persons who are mentally ill deny they are ill, that denial is the result of the illness, rather than merely an attempt to deny their condition or guard against stigma. (Amador *et al.*, 1993, 1994; Amador and Johanson, 2000; Schwartz and Amador, 1994).

Significant negative correlations between all realms of awareness and neuropsychological dysfunction suggested to one group of researchers that persons with schizophrenia may be more influenced by physical defects than mistaken self-evaluations. (Young *et al.*, 1998). Other researchers agree: "[P]oor insight into illness and refusal of treatment stem from neuropsychological defects rather than denial, defensiveness, or informed choice" (Kasapis *et al.*, 1996).

There is significant evidence that lack of insight has a material base, but I am aware of no comparable research supporting the claim that incompetence, or specifically weighing and balancing, has a material base. On constitutive and ontological grounds, our confidence level that lack of insight is a real defect that is located in the brain should perhaps exceed our confidence level that incompetence is located as matter in the brain. We should therefore be cautious with claims that incompetence is a real defect that justifies coerced treatment (with other properties), because of the risk that incompetence is a socially, or psychiatrically, created concept that reflects the creators' values and beliefs more than it describes an actual defect. Because of the stronger evidence that lack of insight is a neurophysiological phenomenon, coerced treatment based upon it is more likely to be responsive to its neurobiological basis, and constrained by that basis, and less likely to reflect the values of the inventors and appliers of lack of insight. In this, and other ways, lack of insight is arguably a more legitimate basis for coerced treatment than incompetence.

Independence: Evidence for disability and for its material basis is largely independent of bad outcomes (independence)

The need for independence

If the evidence for the existence of a disability, and for its material basis, depended upon the bad outcome(s), then state intervention is not justified, but would merely reflect a difference in values between the individual and the state. Still, a bad outcome, especially a very bad outcome, will often suggest that an examination of whether there is a disability is in order, particularly if the individual's initial explanation or justification for the decision and outcome is unsatisfying. A bad decision also provides minor evidence of the existence of a disability, on the assumption (definition?) that persons with disabilities are less likely to make good decisions than those without disabilities. So we may wish to inquire whether the bad outcome resulted from lack of insight. Similarly, on the view that competence is rational weighing and balancing, a bad outcome raises the issue of whether the bad outcome arose from reasoning that is sufficiently deficient to rise to the level of incompetence, or whether the reasoning results from unusual goals, desires, and beliefs.

In making these inquiries, evidence of disability must derive primarily from evidence other than the bad outcome. If not, the determination that the individual has a disability justifying intervention will be based largely upon the "bad" decision alone. But if a bad decision alone justified State intervention, smokers and heavy consumers of fat would be subject to the law's paternalistic power. Indeed, one illuminating way of describing the question of the limits of justified State intervention is to ask the question, "Why isn't a bad decision sufficient to justify intervention?" The reasons why bad decisions are insufficient by themselves should point to additional conditions required for just interventions.

A major purpose of competence doctrine is to allow individuals to make their own decisions when they are competent to do so. If the only evidence for incompetence were the allegedly bad decisions, then competence doctrine is not playing a part in the outcome, and we might as well scrap the whole doctrine. The same could be said of lack of insight doctrine, as articulated in this chapter. Any disability doctrine that purports to justify coerced treatment is doing little or no work if the proof of disability is the bad outcomes themselves. In such cases, it would be more honest to have a theory of bad outcomes that support intervention. It would be difficult to justify a theory of bad outcomes that applied, not merely to the very worst outcomes, but also to many outcomes not among the worst, as incompetence doctrine currently does.

If the existence and proof of a disability were dependent almost entirely upon the bad outcome, then the State would be intervening essentially on the basis of its disagreement with the individual's values (although not necessarily moral values). However, proponents of the recovery model (Anthony, 1993; Beale and Lambric 1995; Jacobson and Greenley, 2001) will urge that persons with severe mental illness should be provided opportunities to exercise, and therefore improve, their autonomous capacities on the ground that, due to their illnesses, many persons with severe mental illness have not exercised their free will sufficiently to significantly enhance those abilities. Hence, there is a special need to provide these individuals with opportunities to learn from their mistakes, and enhance their autonomous capacities. Thus, as Mill argued in *On Liberty*, one consequentialist virtue of autonomy rights is that when they are exercised, the individual becomes better at making choices and exercising autonomy. Moreover, it has been argued that persons who consent to treatment are likely to better adhere to it and therefore achieve better results (Winick, 1997).

Almost every commentator who has addressed the issue maintains that bad decisions are not, by themselves, sufficient to prove a disability to make rational treatment decisions (Grisso and Applebaum, 1998). Case law supports the necessity for independent proof: *In the Interest of J.P.*, 574 N. W. 2d 340, 343 (Iowa 1998); United States v. Charters, 849 F.2d 479 (4th Cir. 1987).

Insight is more likely to support independence than incompetence is

Lack of insight is frequently determinable by asking simple questions, questions that are independent of the outcome chosen, or the support for it. One can ask whether the patient believes he needs treatment, what symptoms she has, or, for those including this proposition, whether the patient has a mental illness, and if so, which one. Sometimes a determination of the need for treatment requires a complicated analysis taking into account the efficacies and side effects of multiple treatments as applied to the consumer's goals and attitudes, such as risk-averseness, and explicit moral consideration of the proper balance, in a particular case, between safety and the patient's liberty. In general, however, the determination will be straightforward. Moreover, in many cases, lack of insight can be determined without first knowing the outcome (or the reasoning that led to it), and independently of that outcome when it is known in advance.

Although incompetence is determinable without resort to outcomes, the chance that outcomes will be the primary determinant in practice likely exceeds the corresponding probability for lack of insight. Frequently, ability to rationally weigh and balance will involve an evaluation of the outcome. Investigating weighing and balancing involves applications of the patient's values, risk-averseness, and moral values. This will much less frequently be the case in judging lack of insight. Incompetence determinations are more likely to be improperly affected by the treatment provider's or other values. Lack of insight is a more legitimate ground for coerced treatment because it is less likely to be corrupted by improper considerations.

Although in theory outcomes should not be relevant to determinations of either insight or ability to weigh and balance, in practice this will not be so. Outcomes will be more likely to be centrally relevant to determinations of ability to weigh and balance than to determinations of lack of insight. Whether an outcome is good or bad, however, should largely be a reflection of the patient's values, not the psychiatrist's. Even if the individual is incompetent or lacks insight, the test of a good outcome is the individual's: we may, however, disagree as to whether it should be the patient's current values or a hypothetical construction of the patient's values if competent and insightful. Because insight determinations are less likely to import the treatment provider's values than competence determinations are, lack of insight is a more legitimate ground for state intervention.

The disability or disabled inference or decision must have ethical significance

Most importantly, the disability must, in conjunction with the other criteria, and no doubt some additional factors, justify the envisioned paternalistic intervention (justificatory).

Informed, free action

The state must apply a principled theory of when paternalism is justified, and apply that theory to the particular disability of the individual. In general, serious interventions require demonstrating a sufficient deficit in informed, autonomous action. For example, we act paternalistically towards children, persons with serious brain trauma, persons with dementia, and some disabled persons because of deficits in knowledge or autonomous abilities, or both. Each of these persons lacks some autonomous capacities. What magnitude of disability is required to justify intervention is likely to be controversial.

Disability justifies coerced treatment as an ethically significant reduction in free, informed action

Lack of insight is a cognitive disability that justifies intervention by the state in those circumstances where lack of insight substantially interferes with free, informed decision-making. By contrast, incompetence, or failure to be able to rationally weigh and balance, operates on the absence of a practical ability, namely, given goal G, what is the best route R to achieve G? In order for incompetence to justify coerced treatment, it must be demonstrated that the deficit in practical reasoning ability justifies paternalistic intervention. This is difficult to accomplish, in large part because we know almost nothing about how practical reasoning occurs, and because we allow chronically mentally healthy people to make incredibly self-destructive decisions resulting from bad reasoning without intervening. On the other hand, *lack of insight proceeds by asserting that a central piece of information, necessary to motivate treatment decision-making, is missing. It thus avoids a straightforward determination of whether the disability results in a loss in autonomous abilities. Rather, it asks the question whether the autonomous decision, if any, is sufficiently* informed *to be recognized as a valid act by a member of the community, or whether the lack of informed choice undercuts informed, autonomous decision-making sufficiently to justify paternalism.* The new theory of disability justifying paternalistic intervention, as applied to lack of insight, therefore locates the justification in the right place. Philosophers nearly uniformly justify paternalistic interventions by deficits in informed, autonomous action. If only for this one central advantage, the thesis that lack of insight justifies intervention deserves to be further developed and explored.

Lack of insight operates on a central piece of knowledge, not on autonomous abilities or practical abilities, and is therefore better justified and less ambiguous in its application than inability to weigh and balance. Lack of practical reasoning ability does not justify paternalistic state action as a general matter.

We are now in a position to understand how the four criteria for being a disability capable of justifying state intervention work together as a unit so that the whole is superior to the sum of its parts. The requirement of proof of disability independent of bad outcomes constrains the state to proving the existence of a disability by means other than differences in values between the state and the individual. The requirement of intersubjective objectivity, understood in this context as reliability, increases the chance that mental health professionals and courts will agree about the existence of the disability, and whether that disability (with other legal requirements) justifies intervention. It thus increases the chances that persons in like circumstances will be treated equally. The requirement of a material basis also enhances the prospect for equality. Additionally, these requirements increase certainty, and therefore efficiency and social wealth. Moreover, greater equality and certainty increase liberty by identifying those behaviors that do not risk state intervention. However, equality alone may not be a virtue. As Vince Lombardi was reputed to have said, "I treat all my players equally. Like dogs." The requirement that the disability justify state intervention attempts to make sure that individuals are treated with the equal concern and respect due to persons, not that owed to dogs. A principled state outlook requires both equality and justice.

I have argued that insight does better than competence as rational weighing and balancing on each of the four criteria, and that it does substantially better on the fourth and most important criterion, justification. For this reason, insight deserves to be provided an important role in coerced treatment, and other aspects of mental health law. I will provide some final reasons supporting insight as a legal concept.

Incompetence theory as rational weighing and balancing appears to presuppose that employing standard (Bayesian) probability theory to support cost–benefit analysis is the only rational decision procedure. If advocates of weighing and balancing do not intend it to be limited to mathematized or intuitive cost–benefit analysis, then they owe us an explanation of, and complete list of, the forms of reasoning that are permissible. If the list is presented as complete, then an obscure or brilliant inference will be mistakenly evaluated irrational. I suspect that human beings will never have a complete list of all valid inferences, nor of all valid inferences in making mental health treatment decisions. This is one plausible inference from Gödel's Incompleteness Theorem and Tarshi's Truth Theorem. Especially if natural languages like English are a version of second or higher order logic. Thus, the claim that rational weighing and balancing explains all mental health treatment decisions appears vulnerable. Mathematicians, economists, and political philosophers have rejected that claim for decades. For one thing, Bayesian theory cannot deal well with small probability events, such as death from neuroleptic malignant syndrome, or with pervasive uncertainty.

Incompetence doctrine, psychiatrists, law and social science analysis, conventional scientific thought, Bayesian probability theory, classical utilitarianism, and the law and economics movement all would recommend a cost–benefit analysis – weighing the anticipated harm ($P \times L$) against the anticipated benefits – in decision-making, including about mental health treatment. Under these approaches, personal decision rules should be formulated to maximize anticipated personal benefits less harms, thereby maximizing efficient behavior, and expected utility.

Several objections to cost–benefit analysis will now be briefly stated. First, the utilitarian theory underlying cost–benefit analysis presupposes that individual losses and gains are balanced off against one another in the *long run*. It presupposes a sufficient number of outcomes for the benefits of desirable activities to outweigh the costs. Yet some losses, such as death, are so large – or final – that they cannot be balanced off against later gains. For example, when playing Russian Roulette, maximizing anticipated Bayesian costs and benefits does not appear to be the best strategy. Alternative strategies are more "competent" (that is, rational). Consider a rational refusal of an invitation to play Russian Roulette with a five-chamber revolver. Even if the offer included a great reward if one were to win, it may still be rational to refuse to play. Now a further offer is made to play with a six-chamber revolver. The damage resulting from a self-inflicted gunshot wound to the head is so severe that the significant improvement in safety in moving from a five- to a six-chamber revolver is irrelevant to the decision of whether to play (Shrader-Frechette, 1991; Waldron, 1993). The harm, not the probability of injury, is the crucial factor: "if this is reasonable for Russian Roulette, it is hard to say that imperviousness to probabilities must be dismissed out of hand as irrational hysteria in [other] cases" (Waldron, 1993). Consumers may rationally resist treatments that risk death.

Relatedly, it is unclear what it means to apply *small probabilities to individual* (and not multiple) *decisions*. If there is a one in twenty-five thousand chance that a child brought up near high-voltage electrical lines will acquire cancer from that exposure, a family with two children who own a home near such electrical lines will have difficulty determining the implications for them of that fact. By contrast, a teeming metropolis with one-hundred thousand children so exposed can predict that four, plus or minus, will acquire high-voltage-induced cancer.

The city can then place some value on the deaths, and on the steps that would be required to reduce, or eliminate the risk. For the parents it is different. Although they could calculate the cost of a cancer death and the one out of twenty-five thousand chance that each child will die, that concept is less meaningful to them because, for each child, either he will or he won't die. Indeed, what we tend to find is that families either completely ignore the risk, or else move at substantial expense. No matter how thoughtfully arrived at, either decision appears to outsiders as somewhat extreme. This may explain some disagreements between psychiatrists and their patients about treatment risks, particularly treatment risks engendered by ingestion of antipsychotic medications. To the psychiatrist, who treats two-thousand patients a year, a risk of one in a thousand of death from a particular medication appears acceptable. Yet, if the high-voltage example applies, we would expect some patients to ignore the risk, and others to decide that they are not willing to risk death from this medication. Both decisions may look somewhat extreme to the psychiatrists or others. To enhance understanding, psychiatrists and patients should imagine themselves in the position of the other and reconstruct the reasoning leading to the other's position.

Bayesian decision-making[2] is on comparatively solid ground when probabilities and losses are known. Its application is problematic when these numbers are uncertain. Additionally, Bayesian theory, like classical utilitarianism, is indifferent to distributional issues – who gains and who loses. *It fails to take seriously the distinction among individuals.* Moreover, when (1) the probabilities of various alternatives occurring are uncertain, (2) the worst-case scenario is unacceptable, and (3) improvements above a baseline are not highly valued, then decision-making that maximizes the minimum prospect is preferable to expected-utility maximization, as Rawls has made famous. Possibly, these conditions hold respecting mental health treatment. Bayesian decision-making is acceptable when the risks involved are *consented to,* but it appears problematic when the risks are *involuntarily imposed.* Coerced treatment imposes involuntary risks.

Finally, there are hypothetical situations that demonstrate for each aspect of competence, that a person's failure to have that aspect alone is insufficient to ensure that the person is incompetent. Although I cannot describe them all here, a few examples will suffice. A person incompetent to weigh and balance, or to understand what is said when alternative treatments are described, can nevertheless make a rational and competent decision by consulting an expert. For example, the patient may consult his cousin Sally, who is a psychiatrist, first, because he trusts her. Second, he follows her suggestion because she is an expert relative to him at making such decisions in the sense that if he follows her suggestions he will achieve his goals more often than if he tries to choose among the treatment options by himself. Second, a recherché counterexample: one of the foremost researchers on mania and its treatments is injured in a serious accident that causes him to be unable to hear, read, or otherwise absorb complicated communications. The accident also causes a post-traumatic mania. He is aware that he has manic symptoms. Although he cannot understand what is said to him, his former and still existing knowledge of the possible treatments allows him to competently choose the treatment he prefers, and to communicate it to others.

---

[2] Following modern usage in political and economic theory, in this essay the term 'Bayesian decision-making' refers to expected-utility maximization, not merely to the theory of the conditionalization of subjective degrees of belief upon presentation of new evidence (Hasanyi, 1975).

Because incompetence doctrine is problematic in many circumstances, this strengthens the motivation for deploying insight to underpin coerced treatment, particularly where incompetence is problematic. Because insight equals or exceeds incompetence on each of the four criteria, intervention based upon lack of insight is more legitimate and justified than intervention based upon incompetence. Moreover, difficulties in the application of incompetence, particularly rational weighing and balancing, raise concerns that intervention based upon incompetence might be less justified than previously believed, particularly in the areas where incompetence is problematic. These considerations combine to recommend that courts and legislatures take greater advantage of insight in developing and declaring mental health law.

Although this chapter has been framed as a comparison between lack of insight and incompetence, though presented in muted terms, the choice between the two is not the winner take all form of "weighing and balancing" (Kress, 1999). The proper way to respond to the difficulties arising for those who have serious mental illness and for society is not to consider potential social programs, forms of organization, and laws one by one, determining, for each one, whether we are better off with or without it. Regrettably, such bipolar, on/off thinking is too simplistic to provide best solutions. A more nuanced approach requires us to search for that overall combination of responses that works best, or comes closest to satisfying our goals and doing justice. This subtler methodology need not recommend that insight replace competence, even if the arguments in this chapter are sound. Quite possibly, lack of insight alone will work better under certain circumstances, competence alone will work better under others, and the two might work best in concert in yet other areas. I conjecture that those with better insight will find this latter approach more competent.

References

Amador, X. F., Strauss, D. H., Yale, S. A., Flaum, M. M., Endicott, J., *et al.* (1993). Assessment of insight in psychosis. *American Journal of Psychiatry*, **150**, 873–9.

Amador, X. F., Flaum, M., Andreasen, N. C., Strauss, D. H., Yale, S. A., *et al.* (1994). Awareness of Illness in Schizophrenia and Schizoaffective and Mood Disorder. *Archives of General Psychiatry* **51**, 826–36.

Amador, X. F. and Johanson, A. (2000). *I'm Not Sick, I Don't Need Help!*. New York: Vida Press.

Anthony, W. (1993). Recovery from mental illness: the guiding vision of the mental health service system in the 1990s. *Psychological Rehabilitation Journal*, **16** (4), 11–23.

Beale, V. and Lambric, T. (1995). *The Recovery Concept: Implementation in the Mental Health System: A Report by the Community Support Program Advisory Committee*. Columbus, Ohio, Ohio Department of Mental Health.

Bezanson, R. P. (1975). Involuntary treatment of the mentally ill in Iowa: the 1975 legislation, *Iowa Law Review*, **61**, 261–324.

Coleman, J. (1988). Efficiency, utility and wealth maximization. In J. Coleman (ed.) *Markets, Morals and the Law*, pp. 98–105. Cambidge: Cambridge University Press.

Gardner, W., Lidz, C., Hoge, S., Monahan, J., Eisenberg, M., *et al.* (1999). Patients' revisions of their beliefs about the need for hospitalization, *American Journal of Psychiatry*, **156**, 1385–91.

Giaccio v. Pennsylvania, 382 U. S. 399, 402–3 (1966).

Goffman, E. (1961). *Asylums: essays on the social situation of mental patients and other inmates.* New York City: Anchor Books.

Grayned v. City of Rockford, 408 U. S. 104, 108–9, 92 S.Ct. 2294, 2299, 33 L.Ed.2d 222, 227 (1972).

Greenawalt, K. (1992). *Law and Objectivity.* New York: Oxford University Press.

Greenberg, W. M., Moore-Duncan, L. and Herron, R. (1996). Patients' attitudes toward having been forcibly medicated. *Bulletin of the American Academy of Psychiatry and the Law*, 24 (4), 513–24.

Grisso, T., Appelbaum, P., Mulvey, E. and Fletcher, K. (1995). The MacArthur treatment competence study. II: measures of abilities related to competence to consent totreatment, *Law and Human Behavior*, 19 (2), 127–48.

Grisso, T. and Appelbaum, P. (1998). *Assessing Competence to Consent to Treatment.* New York: Oxford University Press.

Hasanyi, J. C. (1975). Can the maximin principle serve as a basis for morality? A critique of John Rawls's theory. *American Political Science Review*, 69, 594–606.

In the Interest of J. P., 574 N. W. 2d 340, 343 (Iowa 1998).

Jacobson. N. and Greenley, D. (2001). What is recovery? A conceptual model and explication. *Psychiatric Services*, 52, 482–5.

Kasapis, C., Amador, X. F., Yale, S. A., Strauss, D. and Gorman, J. M. (1996). Poor insight inschizophrenia: neuropsychological and defensive aspects. *Schizophrenia Research*, 20, 123.

Kress, K. (1990). A preface to epistemological indeterminacy. *Northwestern University Law Review*, 85, 134–47.

Kress, K. (1999). Therapeutic jurisprudence and the resolution of value conflicts: What we can realistically expect, in practice, from theory. *Behavioral Science and Law* 17, 555–8.

Kress, K. (2000). An argument for assisted outpatient treatment for persons with serious mental illness illustrated with reference to a proposed statute for Iowa. *Iowa Law Review*, 85, 1269–345.

McEvoy, J., Apperson, J., Appelbaum, P., Ortlip, P., Brecosky, J., *et al.* (1989). Insight in schizophrenia: its relationship to acute psychopathology. *Journal of Nervous and Mental Disease*, 177, 43–7.

Moore, M. (1985). *Law and Psychiatry: Rethinking the relationship.* Cambridge: Cambridge University Press.

Papachristou v. City of Jacksonville, 405 U. S. 156, 170, 92 S.Ct. 839, 847, 31 L.Ed.2d 110, 120 (1970).

Postema, G. J. (1986). *Bentham and the Common Law Tradition.* New York: Oxford University Press.

Quine, W. V.O. (1960). *Word and Object.* Cambridge: MIT Press.

Schwartz, C. E. and Amador, X. F. (1994). Insight in psychosis: state or trait. *American Journal of Psychiatry*, 151 (5), 788–9.

Shrader-Frechette, K. S. (1991). *Risk and Rationality: Philosophical foundations for populist reforms.* Berkeley: University of California Press.

Tversky, A. and Kahneman, D. (1982). *Judgment Under Uncertainty.* Cambridge; New York: Cambridge University Press.

Waldron, J. (1993). Risk and rationality: philosophical foundations for populist reforms (book review). *Ecology Law Quarterly*, 20, 347–69.

Winick, B. J. (1995). The side effects of incompetency labeling and the implications for mental health law. *Psychology Public Policy and Law*, 1, 30–3.

Winick, B. (1997). Coercion and mental health treatment. *Denver Law Review*, 74, 1145–68.

Young, D. A., Zakzanis, K. K., Baily, C., Davila, R., Griese, J., *et al.* (1998). Further parameters of insight and neuropsychological deficit in schizophrenia and other chronic mental disease. *Journal of Nervous and Mental Disease*, 186, 44–50.

Part IV

Clinical and personal implications of poor insight

Chapter 14

Delusions, action, and insight

Alec Buchanan and Simon C. Wessely

Introduction

Do psychotic patients act on their delusions? Not in the opinion of Bleuler: "They really do nothing to attain their goal; the emperor and the pope help to manure the fields; the queen of heaven irons the patients' shirts or besmears herself and the table with saliva" (1924, p. 392).

Bleuler's contemporaries shared his view (Kant, 1927; Jaspers, 1963). Since then those writers who have not ignored the issue have argued that delusional action is rare (Anderson and Trethowan, 1973; Fish, 1974; Merskey, 1980; Slater and Roth, 1969). We are unaware of any major text or paper suggesting that acting on delusions is a common occurrence.

There are few data to support this conclusion, however, and some suggestions that it may not be correct. In a study of pre-trial prisoners Taylor (1985) noted associations between delusions and violent offending and between violent behaviour and the presence of passivity experiences. In Gibbens' (1958) review of 115 cases of homicide admitted to New Jersey State Hospital one-third of insane murderers had well structured delusional motives for their crimes. Lanzkron (1963) reported that 40% of insane homicide occurred "as offspring of a delusional system". And delusions are amongst the symptoms to which Fuller Torrey has attributed violence by the mentally ill (see Chapter 12 of this volume).

The studies of Taylor, Gibbens and Lanzkron concerned prisoners, in many ways an atypical group. In the 1990s a group at the Institute of Psychiatry undertook a study of acting on delusions in a general psychiatric population. The study investigated the prevalence and phenomenological correlates of acting on delusional beliefs and has been described in detail elsewhere (Buchanan *et al.*, 1993; Wessely *et al.*, 1993; Taylor *et al.*, 1994). The purpose of this chapter is to discuss some theoretical aspects of acting on delusions, to review the results of the study and to discuss the relationship between delusional action and insight.

What form might this relationship take? One possibility is that the level of delusional action falls as the degree of insight increases. If I have a suspicion that my persecutory ideas are the result of illness I may be less likely to defend myself. On the other hand, it may be that some delusional actions have the effect of challenging the veracity of the delusion itself, as when a jealous man rifles through his wife's handbag and finds nothing incriminating. In such cases delusional action might be expected to be associated with increased levels of insight. Our group's research sheds some light on these issues which will be discussed later in the chapter. First, however, an attempt will be made to outline some theoretical aspects of the relationship between abnormal beliefs, action and insight.

Theoretical considerations

This section of the chapter will first discuss the role of normal beliefs in determining behaviour. While essential to the discussion which follows, this is not an area which has been extensively examined by psychiatric researchers; debate has focused principally on information drawn from the fields of psychology and philosophy. The second part of this section will review the various types of delusional belief which have been implicated in action. Among the many factors which may affect the likelihood of a psychotic patient acting on a delusional belief, personality and previous experience, will be elements of the psychosis distinct from the belief itself. One of these is insight and perceptual changes, motor symptoms and cognitive functioning are others. These elements will be reviewed in the third part of the section.

Mention must also be made of what will not be discussed in this review of the theoretical aspects of delusional action. A considerable literature now exists pertaining to the nature of delusions, much of which is discussed elsewhere in this volume. Principal components analyses by workers such as Kendler *et al.* (1983) and Garety and Hemsley (1987) have identified dimensions such as conviction and preoccupation. These dimensions bear some similarity to the criteria for delusional beliefs described by reviewers such as Kraupl Taylor (1983). It might be expected that each of these dimensions would affect substantially the likelihood of a belief being acted upon but, to the authors' knowledge, little research was conducted in this area prior to that described in the next section. For the purposes of this paper, the definition of delusion will follow the criteria suggested by reviewers such as Kraupl Taylor and Mullen (1979), namely, that they are false beliefs, held with conviction and regarded by the subject as self-evident, which are not amenable to reason and inherently unlikely in content.

Beliefs and behaviour

A review of the link between abnormal belief and behaviour demands some discussion of the role of normal beliefs in the genesis of action. In the 1940s and 1950s early behaviourists (e.g. Hull, 1943; Guthrie, 1952) opposed the then widespread notion that action must be explained in terms of purpose. They argued that human behaviour could be better explained in terms of "receptor impulses" and "movements". The elucidation of these "primary principles" would in turn allow a rigorous definition of terms such as "purpose" and "intention". In the words of Hull:

> The present approach does not deny the motor reality of purposive acts (as opposed to movements), of intelligence, of insight, of goals, of intents, of stirrings or of value; on the contrary, we insist upon the genuineness of these forms of behaviour. We hope ultimately to show the logical

right to the use of such concepts by deducting them as secondary principles from more elementary objective primary principles.

(Hull, 1943, pp. 25–26)

While beliefs are clearly important if behaviour is to be explained in terms of purpose, their role is less clear when this behaviour is explained in terms of "primary principles". Hull was clear that purposive behaviour could be derived from postulates involving only "stimulus" and "movement".

The role of goal-directed thought was similarly dismissed by Guthrie (1952) who suggested that thinking, like action, was a product of conditioning and tended to occur when action was blocked. These authors aspired to a science which was more rigorous and quantitative. As Hull wrote in 1951 "the continuous quantitative use of relevant postulates and corollaries will hasten the elimination of errors and the day when mammalian behaviour will take its place among the recognized quantitative systematic sciences" (p. 2).

But it was not the advocacy of a rigorous scientific method which concerned other authors, rather the theory which lay behind the writings of Guthrie and Hull. Keith Campbell (1970) noted that behaviourists had placed "the mind" not behind an action but in the behaviour itself and hence, worryingly for a philosopher, omitted the causal element in mental concepts. In the second half of the twentieth century philosophers' arguments have followed two related themes, both of which allow a pivotal role for belief in the explanation of action.

The first has been expanded by Papineau (1978) who argues that the reasons behind an action involve, first, a desire and, second, a belief that the action will contribute to the satisfaction of that desire. He acknowledges that everyday explanations of action commonly invoke only a desire or a belief but argues that both are in fact required; we mention only that part of the cause which is most surprising, least generally known or most morally significant. The second theme has been described by Charles Taylor. Taylor (1964) explains behaviour in terms of Aristotelian teleology, that is, he argues that our present use of the terms "action" and "behaviour" do not allow them to be broken down into units of stimulus and response but require an explanation of behaviour in terms of its purpose. Thus he differs from Papineau in regarding behaviour as "pulled" into existence by its purpose, as opposed to "pushed" into existence by the belief and desire of its agent. Taylor's teleological explanation of human behaviour clearly implies certain knowledge or beliefs on the part of the subject as well as a desire to act. The author refers to the "Canute view" of those who reject purposive explanations of action and is graphic in his description of the logical consequences of behaviourist theory:

The area in which we can attribute responsibility, deal out praise or blame, or mete out reward or punishment, will steadily diminish until in the limiting case, nothing will be left; the courts will be closed or become institutes of human engineering, moral discourse will be relegated to the lumber-room of history.

(Taylor, 1964, pp. 42–43)

The emotive quality of Taylor's plea is not a new feature of the debate. In the sixteenth century the use of teleological arguments to demonstrate the existence of a deity led Francis Bacon to compare teleological explanations to vestal virgins: "They are dedicated to God, and are barren" (quoted by Papineau, 1990).

Even as they were written the views of Hull and Guthrie were not universally held. William Hunter (1930) referred to the importance of "symbolic processes" in influencing man's instinctive behaviour, invoking a model more cognitive than that allowed by some behaviourists. In 1932 Krechevsky published his claim to have found empirical evidence that rats running mazes formed hypotheses to assist them in solving problems. In the second half of the twentieth century writers in medicine and psychology have been more prepared to entertain a cognitive view of behaviour where a subject's knowledge and beliefs assume a greater role. Austin (1956–7) described some of the elements in his "machinery of action" as consciousness, voluntariness, self-control, knowledge and foresight.

Fulford (1989, p. 112) developed this theme in *Moral Theory and Medical Practice*, writing "in the case of raising my arm, what has to be specified, in addition to the state of motion of my arm, is my purpose in raising it." Psychologists such as Spence (1956) and Mowrer (1960) still draw heavily on a view of learning based on Pavlovian conditioning, but Mowrer's references to subjects "learning to be afraid" and "learning what to do" make it clear that he gives greater weight to the cognitive processes of his subjects than did his predecessors. McGinn (1979), developing the work of Davidson (1971), divides bodily movements into active and passive. Action is based on reasons and reasons for actions are based on a combination of desires and beliefs; in McGinn's words, "desire without belief is blind, belief without desire is purposeless". He adds several qualifications to this description of action. First he argues that desires and beliefs exist in a dynamic state in the conscious mind and that interaction occurs between them; beliefs must be reckoned in the light of the pattern of desires. Second he argues that no general law of action can be derived from this framework; "what was sufficient to make me cross the road on a certain occasion will almost certainly not be repeated". Finally, he considers that belief and desire are not in themselves sufficient to produce the will to act and that this will is dependent on what he calls "noticings", internal or external cues which precipitate action.

In the second half of the twentieth century the influence of purely behaviourist explanations of human action has diminished. Recent medical and psychological writing has focused more on the influence of belief on human action and this reflects the tenor of philosophical writing on the subject. The role of beliefs in behaviourist theory is vague and this may go some way to explaining the lack of research in the psychological literature into actions based on delusions.

Delusions implicated in action

The literature pertaining to the behavioural consequences of delusional beliefs will now be reviewed. Ideally, such a review would be informed by epidemiological data providing information as to the likelihood of a particular type of delusion being acted upon. Unfortunately most reports in this area are anecdotal and allow no such estimate of risk. In the absence of such data reference will be made, where the original literature allows, to descriptions of phenomenology to illuminate the link between abnormal belief and behaviour.

Delusions of persecution

Reports of actions based on delusional beliefs most frequently concern persecutory delusions; often these reports focus on violence inflicted on others. On 20 January 1843 Daniel McNaghten, apparently under the impression that he was attacking the Prime Minister, Sir Robert Peel, fired at and mortally wounded Edward Drummond who was Sir Robert's Private Secretary. At his trial it emerged that McNaghten believed he was the victim of a conspiracy and that he was being followed by spies sent by Catholic priests with the aid of the Tories, of whom Peel was the leader. At his trial he stated:

> The Tories in my native city have compelled me to do this . . . They have accused me of crimes of which I am not guilty; they do everything in their power to harass and persecute me; in fact, they wish to murder me.

> (Rollin, 1977, p. 92)

McNaghten was found not guilty and the "McNaghten Rules", which govern the use of an insanity defence in English courts, were the direct outcome of his case. In this century many authors have recorded persecutory delusions in mentally ill offenders but often make only vague reference to the motive for the crime. Bach-y-rita (1974) and Bach-y-rita and Veno (1974), examining 62 violent prisoners, found 13 who demonstrated "subtle delusional systems" and who "warranted a diagnosis of paranoid schizophrenia". Green (1981), looking at 58 male homicidal patients in Broadmoor Hospital reported that in 27 cases the act of killing "appeared to be a response" to the patients' persecutory beliefs. Shore *et al.* (1988, 1989) examined the subsequent criminal records of mentally ill people arrested near the White House, in many cases trying to see the President. They found that amongst those with no record of violent behaviour persecutory delusions were significantly associated with future violence. They gave no further details as to the nature of the delusions.

Other authors give fuller descriptions. Maas *et al.* (1984) describe the case of a man who killed both parents claiming that they had tried to kill his children by drowning them in battery acid. Reviewing the records of ten men charged with patricide, Cravens *et al.* (1985) found four cases where the father was considered by the patient to pose threats of "physical of psychological annihilation". Mawson (1985) found 14 patients with delusions of poisoning in a case note study at Broadmoor Hospital and "in all but one the symptom seemed an important antecedent factor to serious violence". In a study of 15 matricidal men Campion *et al.* (1985) refer to a schizophrenic patient who killed his mother because he was convinced that she was a sadist who tortured him.

Other authors have reported actions based on persecutory beliefs in association with Capgras delusions (Crane, 1976; Weinstock, 1976; Christodoulou, 1978; Romanik and Snow, 1984; Tomison and Donovan, 1988); De Pauw and Szulecka (1988) report that a patient attacked her mother believing that every time her mother put on her glasses she changed into a local woman whom she disliked intensely. Hafner and Boker (1973) found that eight percent of their sample of 263 violent schizophrenics exhibited "paranoid feelings of malaise" and felt that these patients were especially likely to act on their delusions when they perceived an immediate threat to their lives or when persecutory beliefs were accompanied by bodily hallucinations or delusions of bodily harm.

Persecutory delusions have also been described in cases of self harm but here again the degree to which the delusional belief motivates the act is often unclear. In some cases, such as that described by Mintz (1964) where a cook on board ship cooked and ate his index finger in attempt to "rise above his persecutors in the way that Christ had", it is difficult to see any logical link. In other cases, such as those of ocular self-mutilation described by Shore *et al.* (1978), Shore (1979) and Yang *et al.* (1981) or of auto-castration described by Mendez *et al.* (1972), the link between persecutory belief and action seems vague. Blacker and Wong (1963) are more specific, describing the case of a man who castrated himself believing that evil spirits were using his body to perform unnatural acts. Standage *et al.* (1974) describe a case of genital self-mutilation in a female schizophrenic who believed that the men in her community were going to sexually molest her. Fire-setting, eating and hospital attendance have also been claimed to be influenced by persecutory delusions. Virkkunen (1974) found that three out of 30 cases of arson committed by schizophrenics represented an attempt to escape persecutors. In 1911 Bleuler had described the case of a woman refusing to drink milk because she believed it was poisoned and Lyketsos *et al.* (1985) have described cases where the eating habits of chronic schizophrenics have been influenced by similar fears. Hutchesson and Volans (1989) have described patients whose persecutory delusions led them to attend hospitals with unsubstantiated complaints of being poisoned.

Delusions of jealousy and grandiose delusions

The propensity of jealous delusions to be acted upon in a manner dangerous to others has been described by Shepherd (1961) and Mowat (1966). Gillies (1965) described the case of a schizophrenic who murdered his wife, telling his psychiatrist, "a mysterious power told me she was being unfaithful". More recently, Hafner and Boker (1973) noted delusions of love and jealousy in 11.2% of their sample of violent schizophrenics as against 1.4% of non-violent schizophrenic controls. Of the 14 patients at Broadmoor with delusions of poisoning described by Mawson (1985), six also had delusions of jealousy.

Actions based upon grandiose delusions were described in 1823 by John Haslam. Shortly after the New Bethlem Hospital was built in St George's Fields in London Haslam described the case of Thomas Lloyd, whose confidence in his madrigal and linguistic abilities led him to dance and sing in public and address foreign visitors in miserable

French. In the presence of a hypomanic affect, however, it becomes debatable whether such phenomena should be attributed to the mood state or to the delusional belief. Kraines (1957) wrote that

> The manic patient who says that he is the son of God is not expressing a delusion of symbolic significance as would be true in schizophrenic thinking, but has merely left unsaid the feelings that he is superior, that he is capable of undertaking any enterprise, that he is superior enough to be as powerful as the poetic concept of "Son of God".

(pp. 280–281)

Should such a patient attempt to walk on water it is not clear whether this would occur as a consequence of his belief or his mood. This point will be returned to in the discussion of drive, motivation and affect.

Delusions of passivity, ill health or bodily change

The influence of delusions of passivity on behaviour was alluded to by Tomison and Donovan (1988) in their description of a 23 year old man who attacked two others with a Stanley knife but no details were given. Two studies of matricidal men (Campion et al., 1985; Green, 1981) have also mentioned passivity but in association with command hallucinations. Planansky and Johnston (1977) are more explicit. Looking at 59 male schizophrenics who had attacked others or made verbal threats to kill, they identified nine cases where the subject "had to attack against their will, as if directed by others or by an impersonal force". Delusions of passivity have also been described in cases of self-mutilation (Rosen and Hoffman, 1972; Sweeney and Zamecnik, 1981); Shore et al. (1978) describe the case of a man who enucleated both of his eyes believing that "a force" had overpowered him and had taken control of his actions.

Delusions of ill health or bodily change have been described by Green (1981) in matricidal men and by d'Orban and O'Connor (1989) in women who kill their parents. Jones (1965) studied 13 chronic schizophrenic patients with stereotypies. One of his cases touched his car repeatedly, explaining that it controlled the pumping of his blood. Hafner and Boker (1973) considered that delusions of bodily harm, when linked with persecutory delusions, were associated with violence in schizophrenics. Delusions of bodily change leading to self harm were described in 1928 by Lewis while Beilin (1953) reported the case of a Polish labourer who amputated his penis claiming that there had been a change in his body contour and that he was assuming the form of a woman. Sweeney and Zamecnik (1981), reviewing predictors of self-mutilation in patients with schizophrenia, described instance of patients acting on beliefs that their blood needed to be cleansed or that a limb required surgical investigation.

De Clerambault's syndrome and Capgras; delusions of guilt

De Clerambault (1942), quoted by Goldstein (1987), included a description of a man who repeatedly struck his ex-wife in public in his original description of the eponymous syndrome. Goldstein reviewed seven cases of erotomania and found that all had acted on their delusions, several to the extent of making physical assaults.

Enoch *et al.* (1967) and Taylor *et al.* (1983) both emphasized the possibility of physical assaults consequent upon the imagined infatuation but a recent review referring to the "spectre of dangerousness" in de Clerambault's syndrome has concluded that "the evidence that it usually represents anything more than an apparition remains unconvincing" (Bowden, 1990). Capgras syndrome has been linked with violent behaviour in several case reports (Weinstock, 1976; Crane, 1976; Christodoulou, 1978; Shubsacks and Young, 1988; De Pauw and Szulecka, 1988; Tomison and Donovan, 1988; Silva *et al.*, 1989); Romanik and Snow (1984) described the case of a 57-year-old woman who pointed a loaded gun at two meter readers believing that one of them was a homosexual who had been impersonating her by wearing a mask since he was eight. He had acted like a prostitute and sullied her reputation. Fishbain (1987) attempted to quantify the frequency of Capgras delusions but his paper highlights the methodological problem that Capgras delusions are usually reported only when attention is drawn to them by violent behaviour.

Reports of delusions of guilt associated with behaviour usually involve self harm. Numerous examples exist in the literature of such an association in depression (e.g. Albert *et al.*, 1965) and even mania (Hartmann, 1925) and in depression the frequency of suicide attempts has been shown to correlate with delusional ideation (Miller and Chabrier, 1988). In schizophrenia, MacLean and Robertson (1976) described the case of a man who enucleated his own eye when preoccupied with his "sins". Numerous reports exist of self-inflicted eye injuries (Westmeyer and Serpass, 1972; Shore *et al.*, 1978; Crowder *et al.*, 1979) and genital self-mutilation (Beilin and Gruenberg, 1948; Greilsheimer and Groves, 1979; Waugh, 1986) in the presence of delusions of guilt which do not appear to be mood congruent.

Religious and sexual delusions

Delusions with religious or sexual themes are common in psychiatry and similar themes are evident amongst those delusions which are acted upon. Witherspoon *et al.* (1989), reviewing the literature on self-inflicted eye injuries, found that 34 out of 85 patients gave religious reasons for their action. Often these were associated with delusions of guilt. Waugh (1986) describes a schizophrenic man who severed his testicles with a razor blade stating that he felt evil and that self-castration was the only way to gain forgiveness. In other cases religious beliefs in themselves seem to have motivated an act of self harm. Kushner (1967) quotes a schizophrenic who was "sure that he had castrated himself in search of purification and not because of feelings of guilt". In many cases the religious motivation is described in very general terms (Gorin, 1964; Anaclerio and Wicker, 1970; Tapper *et al.*, 1979; Crowder *et al.*, 1979; Sweeney and Zamecnik, 1981); Tenzer and Orozco (1970) describe the case of a woman who removed her own tongue after receiving a message from God that "duty demanded it". In other cases the motivation seems more specific. Shore (1979) describes a patient who was found with a pencil lodged in his right eye who quoted Mathew 5: 29, "And if they right eye offend thee, pluck it out, and cast it from thee, for it is profitable for thee that one of thy members should perish, and not that thy whole body should be cast into hell." Greilsheimer and Groves (1979) describes a case of genital self-mutilation invoking a similar passage at Mathew 18: 7–9. Waugh (1986) describes a man who castrated himself in response to a later passage at Mathew 19: 12, "There are eunuchs made so by men and there are eunuchs who have made themselves that way for the sake of the Kingdom of Heaven." A religious component is frequently present in delusionally based acts which arm others (Maas *et al.*, 1984); Campion *et al.* (1985) report the case of a 23-year-old man who killed his mother believing she was the devil. Sexual ideation was present in the motivation of 21 out of 85 cases of ocular self-mutilation reviewed by Witherspoon *et al.* (1989). Frequently associated with guilt in such cases (e.g. MacLean and Robertson, 1976; Crowder *et al.*, 1979), such ideation may also be implicated when the harm is directed at others. Cravens *et al.* (1985) described homosexual delusions focused on the father in three out of their ten cases of patricide.

Other psychotic phenomena affecting action

In the cases described a delusional belief is an important contributor to the psychotic individual's course of action. In many cases, however, the belief in question was held for a considerable period before being acted upon. And many patients hold similar beliefs without doing anything about them. As mentioned in the discussion of theoretical considerations, McGinn (1979) has argued that in addition to a belief itself, "desire" and "noticings" are required to explain an action. Is it possible to find equivalents for these terms in psychiatric phenomenology and hence use McGinn's model as a framework to investigate delusional action? This section will consider those elements of psychosis which affect the likelihood of a belief influencing a patient's behaviour.

Insight

As discussed in the introduction, insight might be expected to influence the likelihood of a patient acting on his or her delusions. A persecuted man might be less likely to take defensive measures if he had a suspicion that his persecutory beliefs were part of a psychiatric illness. Arango *et al.* (1999) demonstrated in a prospective study that reduced levels of insight were associated with violence among inpatients with schizophrenia. Roback and Abramowitz (1979) studied the behaviour of schizophrenics in hospital and found that patients with a greater level of insight were rated as better adjusted behaviourally on nine out of twelve measures. Van Putten *et al.* (1976), Lin *et al.* (1979) and Bartko *et al.* (1988) all found that compliance with treatment was improved in patients who were rated as exhibiting more insight.

The principal methodological problem with all four studies is that decreased insight and behavioural disturbance could both be indicators of the severity of a patient's illness. The patients of Roback and Abramowitz who were insightful and behaviourally adjusted may have been less ill and the subjects in the other three studies may have possessed insight and complied with medication for the same reason. In any case, influencing behaviour in general is not the same as influencing actions based on delusions. The problem was addressed by Arango *et al.* (1999) whose conclusion, that their violent and non-violent groups were discriminated better by insight into delusions than by other dimensions of insight, does suggest that insight exerts an effect independent of general levels of psychopathology.

Perceptual changes

Foremost amongst these elements may be the perceptual changes associated with schizophrenia. These will be examined with regard to two areas, namely, the perception of form and the perception of emotion. Cutting (1985) considers that although basic visual processes are probably normal in schizophrenia a deficit exists in the appreciation of visual form. He quotes Levin and Benton (1977) who demonstrated that chronic schizophrenics were worse than neurotics in their ability to recognize faces. Auditory perception may also be affected and, reviewing other modes of perception, Cutting concludes that there is evidence for a disorder of body image perception in some patients (Weckowicz and Sommer, 1960; Cleveland *et al.*, 1962). Examples given by the authors make clear the threatening nature of these perceptual changes: Weckowicz and Sommer quote the case of a man whose eyes were being pulled out so that in the mirror they appeared to be completely out of their sockets. Several workers have commented on the propensity of perceived threat to lead to violent action in psychosis (e.g. Mullen, 1988).

Perception of emotion has been found by several authors to be abnormal in schizophrenia. Dougherty *et al.* (1974) showed photographs of facial expressions to schizophrenic and control subjects and found that schizophrenics were significantly worse at identifying the emotion shown. Iscoe and Veldman (1963) found that schizophrenics did worse than controls when asked to arrange nine drawings in order from "happy" to "sad" and argued that they had difficulty in perceiving "subtle emotional graduations". Spiegel *et al.* (1962) found schizophrenics "normally sensitive to the nuances of facial expression" but found that, while they were able to arrange facial expressions in order from angry to happy, they were unable to derive the criteria they were using. Similar findings have been described with reference to emotion in speech. Turner (1964) tested the ability of 60 schizophrenics and 30 controls to identify the emotional flavour of a taped nonsense sentence and found that the performance of schizophrenics was impaired. Studying 24 acute schizophrenics Jonsson and Sjostedt (1973) found that they did worse than controls when asked to identify the emotional intonation of spoken single words. Perceptual changes such as these may correspond to the "noticings" described by McGinn (1979) as triggers for action based on belief. The abnormal sensitivity of schizophrenics to certain emotional themes (Brodsky, 1963; Cutting, 1985) may also affect the likelihood of their acting on their delusions. Finally it is possible that the decreased empathic ability of schizophrenics described by Milgram (1960) allows them to act in ways which cause harm to others.

The importance of these perceptual changes has been alluded to by several authors. MacLean and Robertson (1976) considered that a perception that an alarming change was occurring in one's body contributed to self-mutilation in psychotic patients. Mowat (1966) found that many of his sample of morbidly jealous murderers described, as grounds for their delusional beliefs and subsequent action, a change in their wives' emotional attitudes. In their review of homicidal aggression in schizophrenic men Planansky and Johnston (1977) conclude that "transient misperception of danger to life, very frightening and potentially ominous, was distinctly revealed by some men". Of relevance here may be the work of Bemporad (1967) and Reich and Cutting (1982) showing that schizophrenics faced with visual problems were more likely to approach them by concentrating on details rather than on any overall view. In the works of Shakow (1950): "If there is any creature who can be accused of not seeing the forest for the trees, it is the schizophrenic." It may be that schizophrenia renders sufferers prone to concentrate on one or two threatening aspects of a situation which would be innocuous if viewed in overall perspective.

Motor changes

In depression, psychomotor retardation inhibits all types of action and the increased risk of suicide attendant on the lifting of this retardation with treatment has long been recognized. In schizophrenia, the catatonic symptoms have been reviewed by Abrams and Taylor (1976). Of these, the possibility of explaining stereotypies in delusional terms has already been mentioned (Jones, 1965). As pointed out by Mayer Gross *et al.* (1960), however, this is very different from establishing a psychological cause and in any case the behaviours described by Jones are invariably of little consequence. Other catatonic symptoms such as negativism and stupor will influence actions based on delusions in the same nonspecific and inhibitory way in which they influence all behaviour.

Drive, motivation and affect

Perhaps more important influences on motor behaviour in psychosis are such factors as drive, inclination and motivation. These concepts are very close to that of "desire" as described by McGinn (1979), who considered it a prerequisite for action based on belief. They also bear comparison with the concept of "affectivity" described by Eugene Bleuler in 1924:

> Action is for the most part influenced by affectivity, if one at least agrees with us when we designate the force and direction of the impulses, or of the "will" as partial manifestations of the affects. He who is happy, sad or furious will react accordingly.

(p. 143)

In normal subjects the drive and inclination to act are closely linked to the affective and emotional aspects of a belief, and it seems likely that the likelihood of a delusional belief being acted upon will be influenced by similar factors. In depression the link between a delusional belief and its affective component is so close that it becomes impossible to distinguish the two: the fact that psychiatrists use the term "mood congruent" to describe certain delusions reflects the fact that these delusions are regarded as having an emotional quality which is inseparable from the belief itself. Any discussion of whether a psychotically depressed patient kills himself because of what he believes or because of what he feels rapidly becomes one of semantics. Similarly in mania it is difficult to differentiate between grandiose delusions and hypomanic affect as the cause of a patient's extravagant behaviour.

In chronic schizophrenia a reduction in the capacity to experience pleasure has been described by several authors (Harrow *et al.*, 1977; Watson *et al.*, 1979; Cook and Simukonda, 1981). It is unclear whether a similar reduction occurs in the capacity to experience other emotions although work previously mentioned, describing schizophrenics' difficulties in perceiving such emotions as anger (Spiegel *et al.*, 1962) provides some circumstantial evidence that this is the case. If this is so it might be expected that the delusional beliefs of schizophrenics, charged with less emotion than those of others, should be acted upon less often. Other workers, however, have reached different conclusions. Feffer (1961) presented neutral and emotionally charged words to schizophrenic subjects and normal controls and found that schizophrenics avoided words with an affective connotation. Garety and Hemsley (1987) found that a high proportion of deluded subjects found their delusions distressing. The work of Vaughn and Leff (1976), showing that schizophrenics living with high "expressed emotion" (EE) relatives were more prone to relapse, and later work (Leff *et al.*, 1982), showing that relapse rates fell when EE was reduced would suggest that, in some cases, schizophrenics are over-sensitive to emotion. It seems likely that the emotional responsiveness of schizophrenics is not simply reduced but altered in quality. It may be that schizophrenics may attach emotion inappropriately to certain beliefs, including delusional ones, and are then more likely to act upon them.

Cognitive factors

In this connection mention must be made of cognitive factors which may influence delusional behaviour. With regard to depression the effect of psychomotor retardation has already been discussed. With regard to schizophrenia several mechanisms have been proposed while little confirmatory evidence has emerged. An impaired ability to make probabilistic judgements has been described (Huq *et al.*, 1988). Frith (1987) described a model for first rank symptoms and "negative signs" in schizophrenia. First rank symptoms, he argued, are consequent upon defective monitoring of action while negative signs result from an imbalance between "willed intentions" and "stimulus-based intentions". A later paper (Frith and Done, 1989) provided some experimental evidence for the first of these proposals, but not for the second relating to negative symptoms and the implications for delusional behaviour are unclear. Robertson and Taylor (1985) tested a group of men held in prison or maximum security hospital on criminal charges and found that their deluded group showed a deficit of "immediate memory". It is possible that such memory deficits are the result of the impaired use of mnemonic strategies: Bauman (1971) showed that schizophrenics' memory for three letter sequences failed to improve even when it was pointed out to them that the sequences began with consecutive letters of the alphabet. Robertson and Taylor argued that, as a consequence of their memory deficits, deluded patients were likely to misinterpret external stimuli. Other specific cognitive deficits have been invoked with regard to perception and have already been discussed. In more general terms it has been argued that the relatively intact cognitive function of chronic paranoid patients is associated with a greater propensity for planned violence than is the impaired cognitive function of patients with an acute psychosis (Krakowski *et al.*, 1986; Wessely, 1993). It is not clear that this association represents a causative link, however, or what form such a link might take.

Although a distinct thread has yet to emerge from the investigation of cognitive function in schizophrenia, this area of research does offer some correspondence with theoretical writing on the subject. The views of Fulford (1989) with regard to the importance of belief in the genesis of action have already been mentioned. The work of the same author offers the tantalising suggestion that the link between a delusional belief and an ensuing action may be impaired in a way which is inseparable from the genesis of the belief itself. Fulford rejects the conventional definitions of delusion pointing out, inter alia, that many delusions are not beliefs at all but value judgements. He suggests that delusions could better be described as "defective reasons for action". Could these defective reasons be the products of defective reasoning of a type not previously described? Fulford argues that the nature of the deficit is unclear and that considerable clinical and philosophical work is required even to clarify the issues involved.

Other factors

Several other aspects of the mental states of psychotic patients have been implicated in delusional action. Shore (1979) reported that flattening of affect allowed the schizophrenic patient to severely injure himself as a consequence of his delusion. Other authors (Greilsheimer and Groves, 1979; Waugh, 1986) have also reported flattening of affect in association with self harm based on delusions and Mullen (1988) has argued that "emotional blunting" is associated with violence in schizophrenia. Hafner and Boker (1973), however, in their large study of mentally abnormal offenders, found that "only a small proportion of schizophrenic offenders have flatness of affect". Some of the issues involved have been discussed in the section covering drive, motivation and affect. The degree of systemization of delusional beliefs was found by Hafner and Boker to be related to violent behaviour and several less methodologically sound studies, reviewed by Krakowski *et al.* (1986), have reached similar conclusions. Recent work suggests that the link is not simply with violent action, but on violent action based on delusions (Oulis *et al.*, 1996).

The presence of hallucinations or perceptual changes in cases where delusions of jealousy and poisoning are associated with violence has been referred to by

Shepherd (1961), Mowat (1966) and Varsamis *et al.* (1972). In mania, Schipkowensky (1968) has invoked the "pathologically increased social connection of the manic" to explain what he regards as a very low incidence of violence in these patients (quoted by Krakowski *et al.*, 1986). Psychodynamic factors are important concomitants of delusionally motivated self harm according to Maclean and Robertson (1976) who state that "castration fears, failure to resolve oedipal conflicts, repressed homosexual impulses, severe guilt and self punishment are ubiquitous in such cases". Other authors describe such theories as "unwarranted generalization" (Tapper *et al.*, 1979) or "subjective" (Sweeney and Zamecnik, 1981); the debate here has echoes of a more general one concerning the relevance of psychodynamic theory to psychiatry.

Conclusions regarding the literature

This section of the chapter has reviewed the theoretical basis for action, pointing to the reappearance of beliefs as important causes of action after a period during which more behaviourist explanations held sway. Recent explanations have been described in which action is seen as being caused by a combination of belief and desire and triggered by factors such as "noticings". It has been argued that these concepts correspond to some of the findings of psychiatric research. "Desire" may well correspond to psychiatric concepts of motivation, drive and inclination and "noticing" find likely equivalents in the field of perceptual changes, perhaps influenced by other cognitive aspects of psychosis. The correspondence is far from exact, however, while the details of how desires and beliefs are triggered by "noticings" to form the intention to act have not been clarified for healthy subjects, let alone for patients suffering from psychosis. As Fulford (1989) has pointed out, avenues of research in this area are legion and underexplored.

An improved understanding of the likelihood of delusional beliefs being acted upon would help psychiatrists to assess the risk to the psychotic patient and to others. To this end it would be advantageous to be able to attribute risk either to the belief itself or to other features of the patient's psychosis. Unfortunately most of the studies quoted here rely on a violent or otherwise spectacular act for their case ascertainment: there is a clear need for more broadly based studies of delusional action if this understanding of the risk of delusional action is to be approached.

In 1941 Aubrey Lewis wrote:

> Patients often do not act in accordance with their delusional beliefs, especially when these are fleeting or chronic . . . But this is, on the whole, unusual in the early or acute stages of the illness: a patient will then act on his beliefs violently or in terror; he may go to the police or be driven to suicide.

> (p. 1189)

Lewis alludes to two factors which have been discussed here, namely the chronicity of delusions and their emotional context. It seems that research could also usefully measure such aspects of delusional beliefs as conviction and preoccupation and quantify the behavioural correlates of these components. Measurement of the behavioural correlates of other aspects of psychosis such as insight and affective incongruity and also seems likely to be of value. It was in the light of these considerations that the research described in the next section was designed.

Investigation of acting on delusions using the Maudsley Assessment of Delusions Schedule

The method

We screened all psychotic patients admitted to a general psychiatric hospital in South London and identified 98 who were suffering from at least one non-mood congruent delusion. Fifteen either refused to participate in the study or were too thought disordered to do so, leaving us with a study population of 83. Using a reliable instrument, the Present State Examination (PSE) (Wing *et al.*, 1974), we obtained a description of their psychiatric phenemenology. Some suffered from more than one delusion; these subjects were asked which was most important to them. The next stage involved the detailed measurement of the phenomenology of this delusion, henceforth referred to as the "Principle Belief". This was done using the Maudsley Assessment of Delusions Schedule (MADS), a standardized interview covering various aspects of phenomenology. These were seven: the degree of conviction with which the belief was held, the evidence which supported the belief, the associated affect, the actions which (in the subject's own view) resulted, the degrees of preoccupation and systematization and the level of insight present. The inter-rater reliability of the MADS is satisfactory (Wessely *et al.*, 1993) and the development of the scale has been described in detail elsewhere (Taylor *et al.*, 1994). Finally, a description of the subject's behaviour was obtained from informants; this description was obtained blind to the results of the interview with the patient.

There were three stages to the analysis of our data. First, we estimated the frequency with which actions based on delusions occurred. This was done both for actions as described by the subjects themselves and for actions described by informants. When subjects described their own actions we allowed them to assess the link with a delusion themselves, asking whether the principle belief led them to do anything. When informants rated action we used the consensus judgement panel of experts to judge whether that action was or was not the result of a delusion. Second, we tried to establish whether any of the various categories of delusion mentioned in the previous section were particularly associated with action. Third, we tried to establish whether any of the more subtle elements of phenomenology, measured using the MADS, were similarly associated with action. Of particular interest in the context of this book was the assessment of the role if insight. David (1990) identified three elements to the phenomenon, each of which was addressed by our methodology. An awareness of being ill is covered by items such as, "Are you psychologically unwell in any way . . . is there anything wrong with your nerves?" and "Do you think that seeing a psychiatrist might help you?". A willingness to accept treatment was being examined for by such items as, "Do you think that medication would help you in any way?" And an ability to re-label abnormal experiences was tested in the same way that David has suggested, namely, by rating the subject's response to a contradiction of their belief, a contradiction couched in hypothetical terms.

The quantity and quality of acting on delusions

Self- and Informant-reported delusional action

The prevalences of self reported delusional action are listed in Table 14.1. Sixty per cent of the sample reported at least one delusional action and 20% claimed three or more.

Latent class analysis (see Everitt, 1986) was used to study the underlying distribution of these actions. Table 14.2 gives the final parameter values for the three classes generated; each value represents the probability of a positive response on a given action for each of the three classes.

The first class gave high probabilities on combinations involving either no action at all or any single action, with the exception of protect and escape. It also included responses involving two behaviours, of which one was writing. This class we have labelled "none or single action". All the combinations with high probabilities of membership of class 2 contained various combinations of hitting and breaking objects, together with any other action. This we have labelled "aggressive action". The third class

Table 14.1 Prevalence of specific self-reported delusional actions

	Yes	**(%)**
Have you written to anyone?	10	(13)
Have you tried to stop X happening?	27	(35)
Have you tried to protect yourself in any way?	19	(25)
Have you ever tried to escape what is happening?	13	(17)
Have you ever broken anything because of this?	15	(19)
Have you hit anyone because of this?	14	(18)
Have you tried to harm yourself because of X?	11	(14)
Have you tried to move or leave your house (area) because of X?	9	(12)
Has X stopped you from meeting friends?	28	(36)
Has X stopped you from watching TV or	22	(29)
listening to the radio?	28	(33)
Has X stopped you from eating or drinking anything?	15	(19)
Has X stopped you from using transport?	14	(18)
Has X stopped you from going to work?	12	(15)
Has X stopped you from taking medication?	6	(8)
Has X stopped you from going to the hospital or your doctor on an outpatient basis?	4	(5)

Table 14.2 Latent class analysis of self-reported delusional action

	Class 3 (Defensive)	Class 1 (None or single action)	Class 2 (Aggressive and/or self-harm)
Action			
Write	0.14	0.12	0.08
Stop	0.13	0.45	0.59
Protect	0.05	0.74	0.56
Escape	0.00	0.23	0.63
Break	0.17	0.70	0.00
Hit	0.10	1.00	0.00
Self-harm	0.07	0.54	0.14
Move	0.04	0.46	0.18
Number	13	61	9
Percentage	15.7%	73.5%	10.8%

consisted largely of combinations of behaviour involving stopping, protecting, escaping and moving. A single response of escaping, and to a lesser extent protecting, had high probabilities of belonging to this class, which we have labelled "defensive action". Frequencies of each category are listed in Table 14.2.

On the basis of information given to us by informants, half of our subjects were rated as having either definitely or probably acted on their Principle Belief in the month prior to admission. This figure rose to 77% when behaviour based on any delusion was rated from the same information. No association was found between self- and informant-reported delusional action. Two examples of lack of congruence will be given. A 22-year-old woman believed that people were trying to harm her using occult powers but denied doing anything as a result. Her parents, on the other hand, reported that she had assaulted her sister, climbed out of a window to escape her persecutors and gone to the police station to complain about her parents' use of diabolic powers. An opposite example was a 30-year-old lady who believed people in her neighbourhood were impostors. She described asking them who they really were and also visits to other neighbourhoods looking for new accommodation. However, her sister had not observed any unusual behaviour concerning the neighbours, or any attempts to leave the area. Instead the sister said that the subject would only buy food in certain shops and only ate food for diabetics, although she was not a diabetic. She was classified as a non actor by informant report because none of the informant observed actions could be linked to her mental state as revealed by the PSE.

Categories of delusion associated with action

Attempts were made to link the content of delusion with both self-reported and observer-reported action. For this purpose only those delusions reported by more than

10% of the sample were studied further. Thus excluded were delusions of depersonalization, subcultural delusions, delusions of jealousy and delusions concerning physical appearance. Looking first at the latent class-derived classification of self-reported acting on delusions, the presence of delusions of catastrophe was significantly associated with the subject being classified as an aggressive actor. There was a similar but weak trend for passivity experiences. There was no association between membership of any of the three classes of self-reported delusional action and the presence of delusions of reference, delusional memories, religious delusions, delusions of jealousy, persecutory delusions, grandiose delusions, delusions of guilt or sexual delusions.

Turning to the consensus derived judgements based on informant reported action, delusions of catastrophe were significantly associated with lack of action on the principle belief. Furthermore, there was a strong association between delusions of catastrophe and lack of action on any belief. There was a suggestion that delusions of guilt are negatively associated with delusional action and a similar negative association was obtained if grandiose delusions were present. There was no relationship, either positive or negative, between passivity delusions and action and IQ had no apparent effect. The presence of persecutory delusions, on the other hand, was associated with probable and definite delusional action.

Certain cautions are necessary when interpreting these findings. Although significant statistical associations were found between the presence of delusions of catastrophe and passivity delusions, on the one hand and lack of action on the other, the proportion of the sample with each delusion was small. Seventeen percent had delusions of catastrophe and 19% passivity delusions. Nevertheless, we have identified a class of abnormal beliefs which seem to inhibit acting on delusions. It is important to differentiate, however, between the presence of a delusion being associated with delusional action in general and action based on that delusion in particular. The results described above show that the presence of certain delusions inhibit delusional action in general, not that certain delusions are more likely to be directly acted upon. To address this issue we analysed specific associations between the type of principal belief and action. Only persecutory and passivity delusions occurred with sufficient frequency for this to be done. Using the consensus ratings, persecutory delusions were significantly more likely to be acted upon than all other principal beliefs but passivity delusions were no more likely to be acted upon than all other delusions.

Phenomenology of delusions which are acted upon

When behaviour was rated by informants no association was found between aspects of delusional phenomenology and action. In assessing the phenomenological correlates of action when that action was defined by the patient, the sample was divided using the latent class analysis described above. Patients who failed to act on their delusions or who acted very little ("non-actors") were compared with those who acted in an aggressive or defensive manner ("actors"). Action based on delusions was associated with delusional phenomenology in two areas. First, acting was associated with being aware of evidence which supported the belief and with having actively sought out such evidence; it was also associated with a tendency to reduce the conviction with which a belief was held when that belief was challenged using a hypothetical contradiction. Second, acting was associated with feeling sad, frightened or anxious as a consequence of the delusion. None of the other elements of phenomenology examined, namely the degree of conviction with which a belief was held, its systematization or the degree of preoccupation which it provoked, were associated with action. Non-significant trends towards an association with action were noted for some items relating to insight ("Are you psychologically unwell . . . ?", "Do you think that medication might help you?") but not for others ("Do you think that seeing a psychiatrist might help you . . . ?", "How far do you think others share your belief?").

As part of the testing of the MADS all subjects were re-interviewed three to five days after the collection of the data presented above. The same questions were asked concerning the phenomenology of the principal belief. The data from this second interview was analysed to test for associations with delusional action. The associations with action were maintained for the affective features. With regard to the ability to identify information supporting the delusional belief, actively seeking such information and the response to a hypothetical contradiction of the delusion, the associations with acting were not maintained. An attempt was also made to compare the two groups of "actors" identified by latent class analysis, namely, those who acted predominantly aggressively and those whose actions were generally defensive. The numbers were small (14 and nine) and no significant differences were noted between the two groups.

Our results in the light of previous work

The methods we chose had a number of limitations. First, with regard to the material collected from informants, it is reasonable to assume that informants were unaware of at least some delusional action. Other possible causes of false negatives were that informants might only describe actions they considered relevant to the subject's illness, although this was reduced by using a standardized interview containing a checklist of actions. False positives were also possible. With the occasional exception, informants were not trained observers of unusual behaviours. They may have reported some that did not occur, perhaps to precipitate admission. All interviews took place after admission, however, and it was emphasized that the information obtained would not be communicated to the clinical team or recorded in the notes. Second, with regard to the information obtained from the subject, it is possible that some behaviour was not admitted to, either because it was considered too trivial or too embarrassing. The reverse is equally possible – that the subject was more likely to reveal both beliefs and actions to a neutral observer than a member of his or her family. Indeed, one of the most robust findings of the study was the lack of congruence between the subjects' assessment of action and that of the informants.

Methodological problems are also apparent in the manner in which abnormal beliefs were linked to abnormal behaviour. Some delusions were by their nature almost impossible to link with actions. For example, the principal belief identified for one subject was "thoughts are put into my mind from spaces in the air". It is difficult to think of any behaviour which could logically be linked to this belief, so although the subject had shown a number of unusual behaviours, which may have been linked in the subject's mind to his beliefs, as these links were not accessible to an outside observer, the subject was classified as a non actor. These problems notwithstanding, we have described delusional action in a general psychiatric population. We have investigated which categories of delusion are more likely to be associated with action and identified some of the phenomenological correlates of that action. What are the implications?

The previous finding of an association between violent behaviour in the mentally disordered and passivity experiences (Taylor, 1985) led us to hypothesize a relationship between passivity experiences and self-reported delusional action. This was not confirmed, however; nor was an association found for informant observed actions. This may reflect sample differences between the studies, since violent behaviour was considerably less frequent in the current study than in that conducted by Taylor. We had also reasoned that the perceptual abnormalities associated with passivity experiences give additional "proof" of the correctness of the delusional intuition. This may be correct but was not a risk factor for delusional action. Again, however, it is possible that passivity delusions are not risk factors for the non-violent behaviour typical of our sample but are associated with serious violence.

The finding of an association between delusions of catastrophe and self-report of aggressive action was surprising and unexpected. Furthermore, delusions of catastrophe were significantly negatively related to informant-observed delusional action. We cannot explain why delusions of catastrophe should have apparently opposite effects on self- and informant-reported behaviour and, unless replicated, cannot exclude a Type 1 error. Turning to the consensus judgements made on the basis of informant reported action, we report that persecutory delusions were the sole phenomenological feature associated with delusional action in general. Although this is intuitively comprehensible, we were surprised that the association did not extend to passivity delusions and we also did not predict that certain delusions (catastrophe and, perhaps, guilt) would protect against action. Observable delusional action is more likely in the presence of persecutory delusions and less likely in the presence of delusions of guilt and grandiose delusions. It should be emphasized that these results do not mean that acting upon grandiose or delusions of guilt is unlikely, but that delusional action as a consequence of any belief becomes less likely if the subject experiences either grandiose or delusions of guilt. We are only able to conclude that persecutory delusions per se are more likely to be acted on than other types of delusion.

The discrepancy between self-report and information from informants was maintained with regard to the phenomenological correlates of a delusion being acted upon.

Thus, when the testimony of informants was used to define action, there was no association between aspects of delusional phenomenology and the likelihood of that delusion being acted upon. This contrasts with the positive findings noted when action is defined by the subject himself. Action is a more likely consequence of a delusional belief if the subject can identify evidence in support of that belief; this finding, as we have seen, is not simply a reflection of intellectual function. It is consistent with the view of McGinn (1979), discussed earlier, that action is based on a combination of desires and beliefs and triggered by "noticings", internal or external cues which precipitate action. The findings of the study suggest that these "noticings" are a far from passive experience; action is rendered much more likely where a subject actively seeks evidence to confirm or refute his belief. The findings also raise the possibility that some acting on delusional beliefs may be the result of the subject testing his beliefs in an attempt to confirm or refute them. This interpretation would in turn be supported by the finding that acting on a delusion is more likely when the subject is able to countenance evidence which contradicts that belief.

The finding that emotions such as unhappiness, fear and anxiety, when found as a consequence of a delusion, are associated with action is consistent with Bleuler's (1924) view, discussed in the second section, that action is largely a consequence of affectivity. The willingness of patients who act on their delusions to countenance hypothetical contradiction of their delusional beliefs is perhaps surprising; it might have been expected that patients who ignored contradiction would be more likely to act. It is consistent, however, with the findings that conviction and systematization are not associated with action and with the suggestion that action is more likely when beliefs are questioned and evidence is sought to confirm or refute them.

Previous studies have found an association between the ability to countenance a hypothetical contradiction and recovery from delusions. Brett-Jones *et al.* (1987) found this in subjects being treated with psychotropic medication; Chadwick and Lowe (1990) found that drug resistant subjects who were able to countenance a contradiction to their delusional beliefs responded better to cognitive behavioural therapy than those who were not so able. They also found that noticing actual evidence contradictory to the belief was associated with recovery. We have found that a positive response to a hypothetical contradiction is associated with acting on delusional beliefs. These findings raise the possibility that acting on delusional beliefs, particularly where that action is designed to test out the validity of the belief, is itself related to recovery; this issue is worthy of further investigation.

That the associations between the ability to identify information supporting a delusional belief and acting on that belief were not maintained when the subjects were re-interviewed three to five days later may suggest that the questions used to elicit this information were unreliable. The inter-rater reliability was good, however, and the findings are consistent with each other. It is more likely that the ability to identify information supporting a delusional belief is a genuine but transient element of the phenomenology of delusional action. The affective connotations of a belief, on the other hand, would seem to be more stable over time. It is possible that an affect-laden delusional belief is acted upon only when the subject perceives certain information which seems to bear out that belief; again, this is consistent with the theoretical work of McGinn (1979). There remains the question of the degree to which these associations are independent of phenomenological categories based on content of the delusion. When the presence of persecutory content was controlled for, the associations described above were maintained. The results suggest that the associations we have described are independent of phenomenological categories based on content. One exception may concern feeling frightened as a result of a delusion, which is associated with action for delusions of persecution but not for other delusions.

Of the negative findings relating to the phenomenological correlates of acting on delusions, the effect of conviction on self-reported action has since been investigated by Sharp *et al.* (1996) and similarly found not to be significant. The lack of an association between action and elation may shed some light on the apparent low incidence of violence in manic patients (see Schipkowensky, 1968). Our finding of a lack of association between action and systematization is at odds with the findings of others (Hafner and Boker, 1973; Oulis *et al.*, 1996). Our sample contained few violent actors. It may be that systematization is more strongly correlated with violent acts than with the mundane.

We found only non-significant trends in favour of an association between insight into one's being unwell and need for treatment, on the one hand, and action, on the other. Others have found significant associations between insight and behaviour (Roback and Abramowitz, 1979) and between insight and violence in psychosis (Arango *et al.*, 1999). It may be that that insight influences behaviour through different processes than by inhibiting acting on delusions. It may also be that two processes are taking place simultaneously. One may be a general inhibitory effect on inappropriate behaviour as a result of an awareness that one is unwell and in need of treatment. The other may be the inhibition of delusional action as a result of insight. Arango *et al.* found that an appreciation of the pathological nature of delusions was the aspect of insight which best discriminated their violent and non-violent groups. And we have shown the ability to alter one's degree of conviction in a delusion in response to a hypothetical contradiction to be associated with a reduced likelihood of acting on that delusion.

Summary

Research in the 1990s showed that delusions are acted upon more commonly than had previously been recognized. This is the case whether action is measured using self-report or information from informants. Half of the sample described here reported that they had acted at least once in accordance with their delusions. We have also identified some phenomenological correlates of acting on delusions. Acting, we now know, is more likely when the subject is aware of evidence which supports his belief and with affect-laden delusions. One challenge for the first decades of the twenty-first century is to test these associations in prospective studies. Research on larger patient populations may also be able to identify phenomenological differences in the delusional beliefs of aggressive and defensive actors. Violent behaviour in response to delusions is uncommon and may have different phenomenological correlates.

Acknowledgements

The team was led by Dr Pamela Taylor and included Drs John Cutting, Graham Dunn, Philippa Garety, Don Grubin, Mrs Katarzyna Ray, Dr Alison Reed and Dr Simon Wessely. The project was funded by a grant from the John D. and Catherine T. MacArthur Foundation and Dr Wessely was a recipient of a Research Fellowship from the Wellcome Foundation. At the time this chapter was written Dr Buchanan was the recipient of a Research Fellowship from the Special Hospitals Service Authority. That part of the chapter which reviews some theoretical considerations has been published previously (Buchanan, 1993).

References

Abrams, R. and Taylor, M. A. (1976). Catatonia. *Archives of General Psychiatry, 33*, 579–81.

Albert, D. M., Burns, W. P. and Scheie, H. G. (1965). Severe orbitocranial foreign-body injury. *American Journal of Opthalmology, 60*, 1109–111.

Anaclerio, A. M. and Wicker, H. S. (1970). Self induced solar retinopathy by patients in a psychiatric hospital. *American Journal of Opthalmology, 69*, 731–6.

Anderson, E. and Trethowan, W. (1973). *Psychiatry*, 3rd edn. London: Bailliere, Tindall.

Arango, C., Barba, A., González-Salvador, T. and Ordóñez, A. (1999). Violence in inpatients with schizophrenia: a prospective study. *Schizophrenia Bulletin, 25*, 493–503.

Austin, J. L. (1956–7). A plea for excuses. *Proceedings of the Aristotelian Society, 57*, 1–30. Reprinted in A. R. White (ed.) *The Philosophy of Action*, pp. 19–42. Oxford: Oxford University Press.

Bach-y-Rita, G. (1974). Habitual violence and self mutilation. *American Journal of Psychiatry, 131*, 1018–20.

Bach-y-Rita, G. and Veno, A. (1974). Habitual violence: a profile of 62 men. *American Journal of Psychiatry, 131*, 1015–17.

Bartko, G., Herczeg, I. and Zador, G. (1988). Clinical symptomatology and drug compliance in schizophrenic patients. *Acta Psychiatrica Scandinavica, 77*, 74–6.

Bauman, E. (1971). Schizophrenic short-term memory: a deficit in subjective organisation. *Canadian Journal of Behavioural Science, 3*, 55–65.

Beilin, L. M. (1953). Genital self-mutilation by mental patients. *Journal of Urology, 70*, 648–55.

Beilin, L. M. and Gruenberg, J. (1948). Genital self mutilation by mental patients. *Journal of Urology, 59*, 635–41.

Bemporad, J. R. (1967). Perceptual disorders in schizophrenia. *American Journal of Psychiatry, 123*, 971–6.

Blacker, K. and Wong, N. (1963). Four cases of autocastration. *Archives of General Psychiatry, 8*, 169–76.

Bleuler, E. (1911). *Dementia praecox oder die Gruppe der Schisophrenien* (trans. J. Zinkin 1950). New York: International University Press.

Bleuler, E. (1924). *Textbook of Psychiatry* (trans. A. A. Brill). New York: Macmillan.

Bowden, P. (1990). de Clerambault syndrome. In R. Bluglass and P. Bowden (ed.) *Principles and Practice of Forensic Psychiatry*, pp. 821–2. Edinburgh: Churchill Livingstone.

Brett-Jones, J., Garety, P. A. and Hemsley, D. (1987). Measuring delusional experiences: a method and its application. *British Journal of Clinical Psychology*, **26**, 257–65.

Brodsky, M. (1963). Interpersonal stimuli as interference in a sorting task. *Journal of Personality*, **31**, 517–33.

Buchanan, A. (1993). Acting on delusion: a review. *Psychological Medicine*, **23**, 123–34.

Buchanan, A., Reed, A., Wessely, S., Garety, P., Taylor, P., Grubin, D., *et al.* (1993). Acting on delusions. II: The phenomenological correlates of acting on delusions. *British Journal of Psychiatry*, **163**, 77–81.

Campbell, K. (1970). *Body and Mind*. New York: MacMillan.

Campion, J., Cravens, J. M., Rotholc, A., Weinstein, H. C., Covan, F. and Alpert, M. (1985). A study of 15 matricidal men. *American Journal of Psychiatry*, **142**, 312–17.

Chadwick, P. and Lowe, C. (1990). The measurement and modification of delusional beliefs, *Journal of Consulting and Clinical Psychology*, **58**, 225–32.

Christodoulou, G. N. (1978). Syndrome of subjective doubles. *American Journal of Psychiatry*, **135**, 249–51.

Cleveland, S. E., Fisher, S., Reitman, E. E. and Rothaus, P. (1962). Perception of body size in schizophrenia. *Archives of General Psychiatry*, **7**, 277–85.

Cook, M. and Simukonda, F. (1981). Anhedonia and schizophrenia. *British Journal of Psychiatry*, **139**, 523–5.

Crane, D. L. (1976). More violent Capgras. *American Journal of Psychiatry*, **133**, 1350.

Cravens, J. M., Campion, J., Rotholc, A., Covan, F. and Cravens, R. A. (1985). A study of 10 men charged with patricide. *American Journal of Psychiatry*, **142** (9), 1089–92.

Crowder, J. E., Gross, C. A., Heiser, J. F. and Crowder, A. M. (1979). Self-mutilation of the eye. *Journal of Clinical Psychiatry*, **40**, 420–3.

Cutting, J. (1985). *The Psychology of Schizophrenia*. Edinburgh: Churchill Livingstone.

David, A. (1990). Insight and psychosis. *British Journal of Psychiatry*, **156**, 798–808.

Davidson, D. (1971). Mental events. In L. Foster and J. W. Swanson (ed.) *Experience and Theory*, pp. 79–101. London: Duckworth.

De Clerambault, C. G. (1942). Les psychoses passionelles. In *oeuvres psychiatriques*, pp. 315–22. Paris: Presses Universitaires de France.

De Pauw, K. W. and Szulecka, T. K. (1988). Dangerous delusions. *British Journal of Psychiatry*, **152**, 91–6.

D'orban, P. T. and O'connor, A. (1989). Women who kill their parents. *British Journal of Psychiatry*, **154**, 27–33.

Dougherty, F. E., Bartlett, E. S. and Izard, C. E. (1974). Responses of schizophrenics to expressions of the fundamental emotions. *Journal of Clinical Psychology*, **30**, 243–6.

Enoch, M. D., Trethowan, W. H. and Barker, J. C. (1967). *Some Uncommon Psychiatric Syndromes*. Bristol: John Wright and Sons.

Everitt, B. (1986). Finite mixture distributions as models for group structure. In A. Lovie (ed.) *New Developments in Statistics for Psychology and the Social Sciences*, pp. 113–28. London: Methuen.

Feffer, M. H. (1961). The influence of affective factors on conceptualization in schizophrenia. *Journal of Abnormal and Social Psychology*, **63**, 588–96.

Fish, F. (1974). *Fish's Clinical Psychopathology* M. Hamilton (ed.). Bristol: Wright.

Fishbain, D. A. (1987). The frequency of Capgras delusions in a psychiatric emergency service. *Psychopathology*, **20**, 42–7.

Frith, C. D. (1987). The positive and negative symptoms of schizophrenia reflect impairments in the perception and initiation of action. *Psychological Medicine*, **17**, 631–48.

Frith, C. D. and Done, D. J. (1989). Experiences of alien control in schizophrenia reflect a disorder in the central monitoring of action. *Psychological Medicine*, **19**, 359–63.

Fulford, K. W. M. (1989). *Moral Theory and Medical Practice*. Cambridge: Cambridge University Press.

Garety, P. A. and Helmsley, D. R. (1987). Characteristics of delusional experience. *Archives of Psychiatry and Neurological Sciences*, **236**, 294–8.

Gibbens, T. C. N. (1958). Sane and insane homicide. *The Journal of Criminal Law, Criminology and Police Science*, **49**, 110–15.

Gillies, H. (1965). Murder in the West of Scotland. *British Journal of Psychiatry*, **111**, 1087–94.

Goldstein, R. L. (1987). More forensic romances: de Clerambault's syndrome in men. *Bulletin of the American Academy of Psychiatry and the Law*, **15** (3), 267–74.

Gorin, M. (1964). Self-inflicted bilateral enucleation. *Archives of Opthalmology*, **72**, 225–6.

Green, C. M. (1981). Matricide by sons. *Medicine, Science and the Law*, **21**, 207–14.

Greilsheimer, H. and Groves, J. C. (1979). Male genital self-mutilation. *Archives of General Psychiatry*, **36**, 441–6.

Guthrie, E. R. (1952). *The Psychology of Learning*. New York: Harper.

Hafner, H. and Boker, W. (1973). *Crimes of Violence by Mentally Abnormal Offenders*. Cambridge: Cambridge University Press.

Harrow, M., Grinker, R. R., Holzman, P. S. and Kayton, L. (1977). Anhedonia and schizophrenia. *American Journal of Psychiatry*, **134**, 794–7.

Hartmann, H. (1925). Self-mutilation. *Jahrbuch fur Psychiatrie und Neurologie*, **44**, 31. Abstracted in *Archives of Neurology and Psychiatry*, **15**, 384–6.

Haslam, J. (1823). *Sketches in Bedlam*. London: Sherwood, Jones and Co.

Hull, C. L. (1943). *Principles of Behaviour*. New York: Appleton-Century-Crofts.

Hull, C. L. (1951). *Essentials of Behaviour*. New Haven: Yale University Press.

Hunter, W. J. (1930). *Human Behaviour*. Chicago: University of Chicago Press.

Hutchesson, E. A. and Volans, G. N. (1989). Unsubstantiated complaints of being poisoned. *British Journal of Psychiatry*, **154**, 34–40.

Huq, S. F., Garety, P. A. and Hemsley, D. R. (1988). Probabilistic judgements in deluded and non deluded subjects. *Quarterly Journal of Experimental Psychology*, **40A** (4), 801–12.

Iscoe, I. and Veldman, D. J. (1963). Perception of an emotional continuum by schizophrenics, normal adults and children. *Journal of Clinical Psychology*, **19**, 272–6.

Jaspers, K. (1963). *General Psychopathology* (trans. J. Hoenig, M. Hamilton). Manchester: Manchester University Press.

Jones, I. H. (1965). Observations on schizophrenic stereotypies. *Comprehensive Psychiatry*, **6**, 323–5.

Jonsson, C-O. and Sjostedt, A. (1973). Auditory perception in schizophrenia: a second study of the intonation test. *Acta Psychiatrica Scaninavica*, **49**, 588–600.

Kant, O. (1927). Beitrage zur Paranoiaforschung. 1. Die objektive Realitatsbedentung des Wahns. *Zeitschrift fur die gesamte Neurologie und Psychiatrie*, **108**, 625–44.

Kendler, K. S., Glazer, W. M. and Morgenstern, H. (1983). Dimensions of delusional experience. *American Journal of Psychiatry*, **140**, 466–9.

Kraines, S. H. (1957). *Mental Depressions and Their Treatment*. New York: Macmillan.

Krakowski, M., Volavka, J. and Brizer, D. (1986). Psychopathology and violence: a review of literature. *Comprehensive Psychiatry*, **27** (2), 131–48.

Kraupl Taylor, F. (1983). Descriptive and developmental phenomena. In M. Shepherd and O. L. Zangwill (ed.) *Handbook of Psychiatry vol. 1*, pp. 59–94. Cambridge: Cambridge University Press.

Krechevsky, I. (1932). "Hypotheses" in rats. *Psychological Review*, **39**, 516–32.

Kushner, A. W. (1967). Two cases of autocastration due to religious delusions. *British Journal of Medical Psychology*, **40**, 293–8.

Lanzkron, J. (1963). Murder and insanity: a survey. *Americal Journal of Psychiatry*, **119**, 754–8.

Leff, J., Kuipers, L., Berkowitz, R., Everlein-Vries, R. and Sturgeon, D. (1982). A controlled trial of social intervention in the families of schizophrenic patients. *British Journal of Psychiatry*, **141**, 121–34.

Levin, H. S. and Benton, A. L. (1977). Facial recognition in "pseudoneurological" patients. *Journal of Nervous and Mental Diseases*, **164**, 135–8.

Lewis, A. J. (1941). Psychological medicine. In F. W. Price (ed.) *A Textbook of the Practice of Medicine*, 6th edn, pp. 1804–93. London: Oxford University Press.

Lewis, N. D. C. (1928). The psychobiology of the castration reaction. *Psychoanalytic Review*, **15**, 174–209, 304–23.

Lin, I. F., Spiga, R. and Fortsch, W. (1979). Insight and adherence to medication in chronic schizophrenics. *Journal of Clinical Psychiatry*, **40**, 430–2.

Lyketsos, G. C., Paterakis, P., Beis, A. and Lyketsos, C. G. (1985). Eating disorders in schizophrenia. *British Journal of Psychiatry*, **146**, 255–61.

McGinn, C. (1979). Action and its explanation. In N. Bolton (ed.) *Philosophical Problems in Psychology*, pp. 20–42. London: Methuen.

Maclean, G. and Robertson, B. (1976). Self enucleation and psychosis. *Archives of General Psychiatry*, **33**, 242–9.

Maas, R. L., Prakash, R., Hollender, M. H. and Regan, W. (1984). Double parricide – matricide and patricide: a comparison with other schizophrenic murders. *Psychiatric Quarterly*, **56** (4), 286–90.

Mawson, D. (1985). Delusions of poisoning. *Medicine, Science and the Law*, **25** (4), 279–87.

Mayer-Gross, W., Slater, E. and Roth, M. (1960). *Clinical Psychiatry*. London: Cassell.

Mendez, R., Keily, W. F. and Morrow, J. W. (1972). Self emasculation. *Journal of Urology*, **107**, 981–5.

Merskey, H. (1980). *Psychiatric Illness*, 3rd edn. London: Balliere, Tindall.

Milgram, N. A. (1960). Cognitive and empathic factors in role-taking by schizophrenic and brain-damaged patients. *Journal of Abnormal Psychology*, **60**, 219–24.

Miller, F. T. and Chabrier, L. A. (1988). Suicide attempts correlate with delusional content in major depression. *Psychopathology*, **21**, 34–7.

Mintz, I. L. (1964). Autocannibalism: a case study. *American Journal of Psychiatry*, **120**, 1017.

Mowat, R. (1966). *Morbid Jealousy and Murder*. London: Tavistock Press.

Mowrer, O. H. (1960). *Learning Theory and Behaviour*. New York: Wiley.

Mullen, P. E. (1979). The mental state and states of mind. In P. Hill, R. Murray and A. Thorley (ed.) *Essentials of Postgraduate Psychiatry*, pp. 3–36. London: Grune and Stratton.

Mullen, P. E. (1988). Violence and mental disorder. *British Journal of Hospital Medicine*, **40**, 460–3.

Oulis, P., Mavreas, V., Mamounas, J. and Stefanis, C. (1996). Formal clinical characteristics of delusional beliefs. *Psychopathology*, **29**, 201–8.

Papineau, D. (1978). *For Science in the Social Sciences*. London: MacMillan.

Papineau, D. (1990). To every purpose under heaven. *The Sunday Correspondent* May 6.

Planansky, K. and Johnston, R. (1977). Homicidal aggression in schizophrenic men. *Acta Psychiatrica Scandinavica*, **55**, 65–73.

Reich, S. S. and Cutting, J. (1982). Picture perception and abstract thought in schizophrenia. *Psychological Medicine*, **12**, 91–6.

Roback, H. B. and Abramowitz, S. I. (1979). Insight and hospital adjustment. *Canadian Journal of Psychiatry*, **24**, 233–6.

Robertson, G. and Taylor, P. J. (1985). Some cognitive correlates of schizophrenic illness. *Psychological Medicine*, **15**, 81–98.

Rollin, H. R. (1977). McNaughton's madness. In D. J. West and A. Walk (ed.) *Daniel McNaughton: His Trial and the Aftermath*, pp. 91–9. Ashford: Gaskell.

Romanik, R. L. and Snow, S. (1984). Two cases of Capgras' syndrome. *American Journal of Psychiatry*, **141**, 720.

Rosen, D. H. and Hoffman, A. M. (1972). Focal suicide: self-enucleation by two young psychotic individuals. *American Journal of Psychiatry*, **128**, 1009–12.

Schipkowensky, N. (1968). Affective disorders: cyclophrenia and murder. *International Psychiatry Clinics*, **5**, 59–75.

Sharp, H., Fear, C., Williams, M., Healy, D., Lowe, C., Yeadon, H., *et al.* (1996). Delusional phenomenology – dimensions of change. *Behaviour Research and Therapy*, **34**, 123–42.

Shakow, D. (1950). Some psychological features of schizophrenias. In M. L. Reymert (ed.) *Feelings and Emotions*, pp. 383–90. New York: McGraw Hill.

Shepherd, H. (1961). Morbid jealousy: a psychiatric symptom. *Journal of Mental Science*, **107**, 687–753.

Shore, D. (1979). Self-mutilation and schizophrenia. *Comprehensive Psychiatry*, **20** (4), 384–7.

Shore, D., Anderson, D. J. and Cutler, N. R. (1978). Prediction of self-mutilation in hospitalized schisophrenics. *American Journal of Psychiatry*, **135**, 1406–7.

Shore, D., Filson, C. R. and Johnson, W. E. (1988). Violent crime arrests and paranoid schizophrenia: the White House case studies. *Schizophrenia Bulletin*, **14** (2), 279–81.

Shore, D., Filson, C. R., Johnson, W. E., Rae, D. S., Muehrer, P., Kelley, D. J., *et al.* (1989). Murder and assault arrests of White House cases: clinical and demographic correlates of violence subsequent to civil commitment. *American Journal of Psychiatry*, **146** (5), 645–51.

Silva, J. A., Leong, G. B., Weinstock, R. and Boyer, C. L. (1989). Capgras syndrome and dangerousness. *Bulletin of the American Academy of Psychiatry and the Law*, **17**, 5–14.

Slater, E. and Roth, M. (1969). *Clinical Psychiatry*, 3rd edn. London: Bailliere.

Spence, K. W. (1956). *Behaviour Theory and Conditioning*. New Haven: Yale University Press.

Spiegel, D. E., Gerard, R. M., Grayson, H. M. and Gengerelli, J. A. (1962). Reactions of chronic schizophrenic patients and college students to facial expressions and geometric forms. *Journal of Clinical Psychology*, **18**, 396–402.

Standage, K. F., Moore, J. A. and Cole, M. G. (1974). Self-mutilation of the genitalia by a female schizophrenic. *Canadian Psychiatric Association Journal*, **19**, 17–20.

Sweeney, S. and Zamecnik, K. (1981). Predictors of self-mutilation in patients with schizophrenia. *American Journal of Psychiatry*, **138** (8), 1086–9.

Tapper, C. M., Bland, R. C. and Danyluk, L. (1979). Self inflicted eye injuries and self-inflicted blindness. *The Journal of Nervous and Mental Disease*, **167** (5), 311–14.

Taylor, C. (1964). *The Explanation of Behaviour*. London: Routledge.

Taylor, P. J. (1985). Motives for offending among violent and psychotic men. *British Journal of Psychiatry*, **147**, 491–8.

Taylor, P., Garety, P., Buchanan, A., Reed, A., Wessely, S., Ray, K., *et al.* (1994). Delusions and violence. In J. Monahan and H. Steadman (ed.) *Violence and Mental Disorder*, pp. 161–82. Chicago: University of Chicago Press.

Taylor, P., Mahendra, B. and Gunn, J. (1983). Erotomania in males. *Psychological Medicine*, **13**, 645–50.

Tomison, A. R. and Donovan, W. M. (1988). Dangerous delusions: the "Hollywood phenomenon". *British Journal of Psychiatry*, **153**, 404–5.

Tenzer, J. A. and Orozco, H. (1970). Traumatic glossectomy. *Oral Surgery*, **30**, 182–4.

Turner, J. B. (1964). Schizophrenics as judges of vocal expressions of emotional meaning. In J. R. Davitz (ed.) *The Communication of Emotional Meaning*, pp. 129–42. New York: McGraw Hill.

Van Putten, T., Crumpton, E. and Yale, C. (1976). Drug refusal in schizophrenia and the wish to be crazy. *Archives of General Psychiatry*, **33**, 1443–6.

Varsamis, J., Adamson, J. D. and Sigurdson, W. F. (1972). Schizophrenics with delusions of poisoning. *British Journal of Psychiatry*, **121**, 673–5.

Vaughn, C. E. and Leff, J. P. (1976). The influence of family and social factors on the course of psychiatric illness. *British Journal of Psychiatry*, **129**, 125–37.

Virkkunen, M. (1974). On arson committed by schizophrenics. *Acta Psychiatrica Scandinavica*, **50**, 152–60.

Watson, C. G., Jacobs, L. and Kucala, T. (1979). A note on the pathology of anhedonia. *Journal of Clinical Psychology*, **35**, 740–3.

Waugh, A. C. (1986). Autocastration and biblical delusions in schizophrenia. *British Journal of Psychiatry*, **149**, 656–9.

Weckowicz, T. E. and Sommer, R. (1960). Body image and self concept in schizophrenia. *Journal of Mental Science*, **106**, 17–39.

Weinstock, R. (1976). Capgras syndrome: a case involving violence. *American Journal of Psychiatry*, **133**, 855.

Wessely, S. (1993). Violence and psychosis. In C. Thompson, P. Cowen (ed.) *Violence: Basic and Clinical Science*, pp. 119–34. London: Butterworth-Heinemann.

Wessely, S., Buchanan, A., Reed, A., Cutting, J., Everitt, B., Garety, P., *et al.* (1993). Acting on delusions. I: Prevalence. *British Journal of Psychiatry*, **163**, 69–76.

Westmermyer, J. and Serpass, A. (1972). A third case of self-enucleation. *American Journal of Psychiatry*, **129**, 484.

Wing, J. K., Cooper, J. E. and Sartorius, N. (1974). *Measurement and Classification of Psychiatric Symptoms*. Cambridge: Cambridge University Press.

Witherspoon, C., Feist, F., Morris, R. and Feist, R. (1989). Ocular self-mutilation. *Annals of Opthalmology*, **21**, 255–9.

Yang, H., Brown, G. and Magargal, L. (1981). Self-inflicted ocular mutilation. *American Journal of Opthalmology*, **91**, 658–63.

Chapter 15

The relationship between insight into psychosis and compliance with medications

Joseph P. McEvoy

It appears that the psychiatric patients who would benefit most by systematic medication are often seriously remiss.
Klein *et al.*, 1974

Schizophrenia is a terrible illness. It most commonly strikes people at a young age. It severely limits their potential to work and support themselves, to marry and have satisfying relationships. If untreated, it pushes its victims to the sidelines of existence, where they may expend their lives attending to hallucinatory perceptions or preoccupied with mistaken beliefs. Acute exacerbations of schizophrenia bring immediate dangers to afflicted patients themselves, pain and hardship to their families, and steep financial costs to society. It is a chronic disease, and, especially if untreated, may follow a deteriorating course (Wyatt, 1991).

Effective treatments are available for schizophrenia. Classical antipsychotic drugs resolve exacerbations and forestall relapse. New therapeutic agents (e.g., clozapine, risperidone, aripiprazole, and others) appear to offer greater therapeutic efficacy and more benign side-effect profiles. With early (i.e., as soon as possible after the initial psychopathology appears) treatment of first psychotic episodes, the likelihood of good recovery approaches 80% (Lieberman *et al.*, 1992). However, half of those patients treated for a first psychotic episode discontinue their prescribed treatment within 6 months (Weiden and Olfson, 1995).

Clinicians almost never see patients with schizophrenia who complain of having a terrible illness, or who actively seek treatment for its ravages. Rather, "among chronic schizophrenics, failure to comply with prescribed drug schedules is the most common reason for hospital readmission" (Caton, 1984, p. 76).

In this chapter, we will present evidence that lack of insight in psychosis is associated with noncompliance with medication. First, we will review the studies that provide valid estimates of the prevalence of medication noncompliance among patients with schizophrenia. Second, we will examine the often flawed conceptual frameworks within which patients consider their need for medications, and determine how these flawed frameworks relate to noncompliance. Third, we will examine the effects of substance use disorders and cognitive impairment on insight and compliance. Finally, we will review the interventions that have been tried to improve compliance in patients with psychosis.

Do patients with schizophrenia take their medications?

Only studies that include an external validating measure of compliance – i.e., urine colorimetric tests, receipt of long acting injectable drugs, or microelectronic devices that record the date and time of each opening of a medication bottle – are examined.

Studies that utilize urine colorimetric tests

The Forrests (1961) developed colorimetric tests which could detect the presence of the original phenothiazine antipsychotic drugs and their metabolic products in the urines of patients who had recently been taking these drugs. Although the tests have limitations (they can only detect very recent noncompliance), they offer advantages over patient self-report or pill counts. Only completely negative urine tests will be utilized as indicators of noncompliance in this review.

On the basis of extensive work with these urine tests, the Forrests (1961, p. 301) conclude that, "spot checks as well as systematic testing of hospital populations show that at least 5 percent to 15 percent of patients in institutions successfully 'cheek' their drugs". This 5–15% noncompliance rate among inpatients is confirmed by reports from other authors who have studied the problem. Hare and Willcox (1967) found negative urines in 6% of inpatients and in 15% of less well-supervised day hospital patients for whom chlorpromazine or imipramine was prescribed. Wilson and Enoch (1967) found negative urines in 16% of 50 inpatients with schizophrenia supposedly taking chlorpromazine tablets; these patients' urines all converted to positive when the medication orders were switched from tablets to liquid concentrate. Irwin *et al.* (1971) found that 7% of closed ward patients, but 32% of less supervised open ward patients, had negative urines despite prescribed chlorpromazine or thioridazine. These authors also note:

> Another interesting group consisted of 27 inpatients who were permitted to leave the hospital during the Christmas holiday for two to four weeks. Urine specimens were obtained when these patients returned to the hospital. Urinary testing indicated that 13 of 23 patients (57%) had not taken chlorpromazine as prescribed.
>
> (Irwin *et al.*, 1971, p. 1633)

We may expect that outpatients, who are largely without medical supervision, will have even higher rates of noncompliance. Indeed, Willcox, *et al.* (1965) found negative urines in 32% of 22 outpatients with schizophrenia for whom chlorpromazine was prescribed. Irwin *et al.* (1971) report that 35% of outpatients had negative urines despite prescribed phenothiazines.

Table 15.1 The Relationships between Level of Supervision of Compliance (Urine Colorimetric Tests)

Study	Number (%) with Negative Urines
Hare and Willcox (1967)	
Inpatients	7/120 (6%)
Day patients	4/27 (15%)
Outpatients	42/125 (33%)
Irwin et al. (1971)	
Locked ward	5/67 (7%)
Open ward	6/19 (32%)
Outpatients	14/40 (35%)

When the rates of negative urines are compared across patient groups at a single institution (see Table 15.1), "the principal factor governing patient intake of medication appeared to be the amount of direct patient supervision" (Irwin et al., 1971, p. 1631).

Studies utilizing long-acting intramuscular preparations

Whether or not a patient comes to clinic to receive his or her injection of long-acting antipsychotic is another objective measure of compliance. Johnson and Freeman (1972) twice surveyed the attendance registers at four outpatient clinics in their geographical region to determine the percentages of patients who had failed to appear for recently scheduled injections of long-acting antipsychotic medication. Noncompliance rates ranged from 7–27% with a mean of 17%.

Carney and Sheffield (1976) reported on 418 patients treated with long-acting injectable antipsychotic medications (fluphenazine enanthate, fluphenazine decanoate, or flupenthixiol decanoate) for, on average, 2–3 years. The rates at which patients were withdrawn from treatment with these drugs ranged from 23–43%. Only 5–7% of patients were listed as uncooperative. The remainder were withdrawn primarily because of extrapyramidal side-effects. It is possible that the willingness of these clinicians to discontinue injectable medications when extrapyramidal side-effects became distressing kept "uncooperativeness" to a minimum.

Even in highly selected populations of patients who agree to participate in long-term follow-up studies of treatment with long-acting injectable antipsychotic medications, substantial rates of noncompliance are present. Sixteen of 44 (36%) patients missed at least one injection during the one year study of Falloon et al. (1978), despite regular visits in the patients' homes by community nurses. Given the high level of support and supervision in this trial, only 2 (5%) of these patients persisted in their refusal of medications to the point of relapse.

Quitkin *et al.* (1978) also listed noncompliance as a reason for withdrawal from study in 8 of 30 (27%) chronic schizophrenic patients treated with fluphenazine decanoate and followed prospectively for one year.

Studies in which patients control their own pharmacotherapy

Two studies in which matched groups of patients were randomly assigned to either receive their medications in a standard, supervised manner or to be in charge of taking their own medications are available. Both include external validating measures of compliance.

Klein *et al.* (1974) studied 40 inpatients for whom chlorpromazine and/or imipramine was prescribed. Twenty of these patients were randomly assigned to open wards where they were responsible for taking their own medications. The other 20 remained on a locked ward where their medications were administered by a nurse. Urine tests were negative in only 7.5% of the patients who received their medications from nurses, but were negative in 40% of those patients responsible for taking their own medications. It is noteworthy that half of the patients in both groups received instruction from Nursing Staff as to the nature, uses, dosage, and side effects of their medications. This instruction did not increase compliance.

Chien (1975) studied 47 chronically ill patients with schizophrenia who resided in cooperative apartments in the community. All were stabilized on injections of fluphenazine enanthate 37.5 mg IM every two weeks. These patients were randomly assigned to one of three treatment strategies: the first group continued to receive fluphenazine enanthate 37.5 mg IM Q 2 wks as originally prescribed by the physician; the second group selected the frequency of injections themselves; the third group received placebo injections Q 2 wks. At the end of one year, 13 of 15 patients (87%) who were switched to placebo had deteriorated sufficiently to be removed from the study, i.e., failed. Only 2 of 16 patients (12%) receiving the physician-regulated fluphenazine injections failed. In contrast, 6 of 16 (37%) of the self-regulated patients failed. However, 5 of the 6 failures in the self-regulated group (i.e., 32% of that group) stated during the first week of the study that they did not need any medication, they rapidly deteriorated to the point of removal from the study within the first 6 months. The remaining patients in the self-regulated group took, on average, about half the originally prescribed number of injections (i.e., extended their dosing interval to Q 4 wks). Perhaps because of the high dose originally prescribed, these patients did well.

Electronic monitoring of compliance

The use of electronic devices such as the MEMS® (Medication Event Monitoring System; APREX, Union City, California) cap has been shown to be feasible in patients with schizophrenia (Cramer and Rosenheck, 1999). Diaz *et al.* (2001) used MEMS® caps as a measure of compliance in 14 socially disadvantaged patients with schizophrenia or schizoaffective disorder. Compliance data were available from 10 of the 14 patients for the first month, from 7 for the second month and from 5 through

6 months. The mean dose-compliance rates for the first month was 63% (range 18% to 92%), and over the next 5 months it ranged from 56 % to 45%. First month compliance rates were significantly lower for those patients who were rehospitalized during the 6 months than for those who were not.

Byerly *et al.* (2002) found that, as measured by MEMS® caps, 13/21 patients took <70% of their prescribed antipsychotics over a 3 month period, including 7/21 who took <50%, 4/21 who took <30%, and 3/21 who took <10%. Clinicians ratings of these patients' drug-taking greatly underestimated the high levels of noncompliance found. The authors note that "Patients were frequently non-adherent despite consistently obtaining prescription fills and regularly attending monthly research study visits."

Summary of compliance studies

When patients with schizophrenia are responsible for taking their own *pills* (e.g., when they are outpatients), one-third to one half of them will be noncompliant at any given time. This medication noncompliance may be temporary or fluctuating in individual patients. Weiden *et al.*(1991) report that although 48% of their patients became noncompliant for at least one week over a year of follow-up, only 30–40% were noncompliant at any given assessment interval.

The rates at which patients fail to take *injections* of long-acting antipsychotic medications are slightly lower (15–35%). The use of long-acting injectable preparations may facilitate supervision (see section on ways to increase compliance), thereby limiting noncompliance. However, the samples studied in programs of treatment with long-acting injectable preparations may be biased by the refusal of highly noncompliant patients to participate.

Rates of medication compliance appear to be powerfully influenced by the level of supervision in differing treatment situations. However, there also appear to be differences intrinsic to patients that may determine whether or not they comply. Approximately 50% of patients will take their medications as prescribed with little or no support required. An additional 35% of patients will comply if provided with supervision and support. The remaining 15% of patients will do anything they can to avoid taking medications under any circumstances, and may require coercion to remain compliant.

Patients' conceptual frameworks regarding medication

What are the conceptual frameworks within which patients with schizophrenia consider their need for medications?

General populations of patients with schizophrenia

Parkes *et al.* (1962) followed a group of 68 patients with schizophrenia for whom antipsychotics were prescribed at index discharge. Twenty-seven of the 68 (40%) stopped their medications within two months of leaving hospital. When asked why, all claimed that they did not need drugs.

Serban and Thomas (1974) surveyed 516 patients with chronic schizophrenia at the time of their discharge from an index hospitalization. Although 69% of these patients stated they believed regular use of medications would be helpful in treating their illness, only 29% stated that they took their medications regularly when outpatients.

Soskis (1978) compared 25 inpatients with schizophrenia who were receiving antipsychotics with 15 medical inpatients receiving medication for a variety of serious medical illnesses. Only 4% of the schizophrenic patients acknowledged a diagnosis of schizophrenia, and only 32% included any concepts related to mental illness in their explanation as to why they were receiving medications. In contrast, 40% of the medical patients knew their diagnoses, and 87% included accurate concepts as to what was wrong in explaining their need for medications. Although both schizophrenic and medical patients gave generally positive assessments of how helpful the medications had been for them, 44% of the schizophrenic patients (in contrast to only 7% of the medical patients) said they would stop medications if they had the choice. Both groups were more likely to say they would take medications the more they reported that medications helped them ($r = 0.54$, $P < 0.01$ for schizophrenic patients; $r = 0.57$, $P < 0.05$ for medical patients). The patients with schizophrenia were also less likely to say they would take medications the more they reported awareness of side effects ($r = 0.42$, $P < 0.05$).

McEvoy *et al.* (1981) studied 45 chronically hospitalized schizophrenic patients. Although 98% of these patients were aware they were taking medications, only 47% reported any present need for medications, and only 44% believed they would need medication in the future. A small but significant positive correlation ($r = 0.32$, $P < 0.05$) existed between the patients' beliefs that they had a mental illness and their reported need for medications.

Thompson (1988) studied a group of 65 young adult chronic psychiatric patients, "nearly all" of whom had diagnoses of schizophrenia. These patients were asked to characterize "the typical adult in the community", "the typical hospitalized mental patient", and themselves on a 20 item semantic differential. Two thirds ($n = 43$) of these patients described themselves as much more like a typical member of the community than like a mental patient. Although this subgroup reported less psychological distress than the subgroup who described themselves as mental patients, they also reported less compliance with medications and they more frequently required hospitalization.

Adams and Howe (1993) administered a questionnaire addressing side-effects, difficulties obtaining medication, reinforcement for not taking medication, symptom relief, and indirect benefits of medication to 42 patients admitted to a local inpatient unit for treatment of a psychotic exacerbation. Only indirect benefits (keeps me out of the hospital; something bad will happen if I don't take my medicine; it allows me to make friends) accounted for a significant portion of the variance (18%) in self-reported compliance level.

Adams and Scott (2000) administered six rating instruments to assess components of the health belief model in 39 newly admitted patients with chronic and disabling affective or schizophrenic disorders. Medication compliance was associated with patients' perceived severity of illness and perceived benefits of treatment (particularly prevention of hospitalization).

Medication refusers

A small proportion of patients with schizophrenia actively refuse treatment. Reporting on a mixed diagnostic group of patients assigned to one of several classes of pharmacotherapy, Raskin (1961) found that refusers had little faith in their clinicians and readily acknowledged their hostility to treatment.

Serban and Thomas (1974) noted that, at the time of discharge, 19% of their chronic schizophrenic patients stated that they would not take medications as outpatients under any circumstances.

Van Putten (1974) reported that 12% of the chronic schizophrenic patients he followed in an outpatient clinic adamantly refused to take medication at all, and equated the drugs with poison. Discomforting extrapyramidal side-effects (EPS), in particular, akathisia, were significantly associated with reluctance to take medications. This author stated that, " . . . even mild EPS is difficult to bear on a maintenance basis".

In a later study, Van Putten, Crumpton, and Yale (1976) acknowledged that extrapyramidal side-effects were not a complete explanation. They contrasted 29 habitual drug refusers with 30 drug compliers at the end of hospitalizations during which "medication was adjusted so that each patient experienced either none or minimal extrapyramidal side-effects". At the time of discharge, after all patients had been treated, albeit involuntarily if necessary, with antipsychotic medications, the initial medication refusers were *still* rated as significantly more ill and less cooperative then the medication compliant patients.

Appelbaum and Guthiel (1980) examined occurrences of medication refusal on a 40-bed inpatient ward which had 56 admissions over the three months of study. Refusal, as defined in this study, "required an affirmative act beyond mere nonappearance at the medication room door, i.e., either explicit verbal rejection of the medications or a failure to respond to a direct approach by a member of the ward staff". Most of these episodes of refusal were brief and quickly resolved by clarifications about the medications. However, in 10 patients (18% of all admissions) refusals were recurrent or persistent, and refusals interfered with treatment in 5 patients. Eight of these 10 patients were schizophrenic, with either " . . . prominent paranoid elements in their illnesses which appeared to motivate their refusal", or " . . . deep-seated delusional beliefs about their medications". The authors argued that these delusion-based refusals must be conceptualized as manifestations of the illness, rather than as an exercising of civil rights, or else these patients would not receive needed care.

When new regulations in California required that all patients must sign informed consent prior to treatment with antipsychotic medications, Marder *et al.* (1983) studied 15 schizophrenic patients admitted on a *voluntary* basis who subsequently refused to sign consent for treatment, and compared these patients to 15 non-refusing patients. The refusers were rated as significantly more ill on the Brief Psychiatric Rating Scale (BPRS) (Overall and Gorham, 1962). They were rated as having less insight into their illness, less confidence in staff, and a more impaired understandings of the rationale for treatment. The authors note that many of the refusing patients appeared bewildered and confused by the consent form, and they were often unable to explain their refusal. They often refused to participate in other ward activities as well, and this negativism and perplexity seemed to be intrinsic components of their psychopathology.

This same group (Marder, Swann *et al.*, 1984) reported that 15 of 31 (48%) *involuntarily* committed patients would refuse medication if they had the choice. Refusers had higher psychosis ratings on the BPRS, and higher ratings for mood elevation. They had significantly less confidence in the staff, less acknowledgment of their illness, less understanding of the rationale for treatment, and were less likely to believe that medications helped them, relative to non-refusers. After treatment was administered to these patients, despite their objections, their psychopathology diminished. Significant improvements occurred in their confidence in the ward staff and their understanding of the rationale for treatment, but not in their acknowledgment of illness. Six of the 12 initial refusers who were still available for interview at the end of two weeks no longer wished to refuse medication.

Irwin *et al.* (1985) interviewed 33 sequentially admitted patients with schizophrenia, and found that only 5 (15%) would prefer to refuse treatment. Neither acknowledgment of illness, factual understanding about the medications, nor prior experience of extrapyramidal side-effects predicted consent vs. refusal. Rather, patients' perceived benefits from prior antipsychotic treatment most powerfully predicted willingness to consent.

Hoge *et al.* (1990) found that 103 (7.2%) of the 1434 psychiatric patients admitted to four acute inpatient units in state-operated mental health facilities in Massachusetts over a 6-month period refused treatment with antipsychotic medication. On admission, refusers had significantly higher psychosis ratings than compliant patients, and significantly less acknowledgement of illness and need for treatment. Refusers were significantly more likely to have refused medications in the past as well. During the index hospitalization, refusers were more likely to require seclusion or restraint and had longer hospitalizations than treatment acceptors.

Macpherson *et al.* (1996) assessed insight and compliance in 64 outpatients with schizophrenia, 15 of whom had "actively refused" antipsychotic treatment over the preceding two weeks. Patients who "actively refused" treatment had significantly lower insight scores than those who actively pursued treatment.

Fennig *et al.* (1999) obtained data on all 9,081 patients in Israel who had a nonforensic first admission between 1978 and 1992 and a diagnosis of schizophrenia. The 12.9% of these cases whose first admission was involuntary, were significantly more likely to later require additional involuntary hospitalizations than were the patients who initially came voluntarily to hospital.

Patients with coexisting organic impairment

Geller (1982) surveyed 281 very chronic patients at a state psychiatric hospital. Only 8% of these patients could correctly name at least one medication they were taking *and* accurately report its dosing schedule and its intended effect. Of the patients who could give understandable verbal responses to the questions, fewer than 50% opined that the medications they were taking helped them in any way. Not surprisingly, longer length of stay, and diagnoses of dementia or mental retardation each independently contributed to the likelihood that patients would have no understanding of their medications.

Macpherson *et al.* (1993) reported on a similar chronically institutionalized group of 100 patients randomly selected from the population of a long stay hospital. The mean age of these patients was 63 years, with a range from 24 to 89 years. Only 23 of these patients could correctly name at least one of their medications. Ten patients showed some understanding of the intended therapeutic action of the medication, with 5 of these 10 also being among those who could name a medication. Thus, a total of 28 of the 100 patients could *either* name a medication they were taking *or* tell something about its method of therapeutic action. Of note, only 36 of these 100 patients could accurately give their age to within one year. Patients who knew their age were significantly more likely to understand the therapeutic action of their medications.

Over the past decade, the majority of studies assessing neurocognitive function and insight have reported a positive relationship (for example, Young *et al.*, 1998; Smith *et al.*, 1999) although some have failed to show a significant association (for example, Takei *et al.*, 1992; Cuesta and Peralta, 1994).

Three of four neuroimaging studies reported significant associations between brain atrophy and lack of insight (Takai *et al.*, 1992; Flashman *et al.*, 2000; Larøi *et al.*, 2000), although the largest study (David *et al.*, 1995) did not find a relationship.

Substance use disorder (SUD) and compliance

Swartz *et al.* (2003) used radioimmunoassay of hair to detect the use of amphetamines, cocaine, marijuana, opiates, and phencyclidine over the preceding 3 months among outpatients with schizophrenia. Thirty-one percent had a positive hair assay.

Hunt *et al.* (2002) examined the effects of medication noncompliance and/or a comorbid SUD on 4-year outcomes in 99 patients following index relapses of schizophrenia. Over the 4 years of follow-up, the median survival (the time until a rehospitalization for psychopathology) for compliant patients without a SUD was 37 months. The median survival for patients who were either noncompliant or had a SUD was 10 months, and the median survival for patients who were noncompliant and had a SUD was 5 months. The n = 28 patients (28%) who were noncompliant and had a SUD accounted for 57% of all hospital readmissions and averaged 1.5 admissions per year. Patients with a current or previous SUD were more likely to be male, younger, and to have a forensic history.

Kamali *et al.* (2001) studied 87 patients readmitted to hospital with exacerbations of schizophrenia or schizo-affective disorder. Twelve of the 21 (57%) patients for whom a depot antipsychotic was prescribed, but only 22 of the 65 (33%) patients for whom an oral antipsychotic was prescribed, had been regularly compliant prior to admission. Fifteen of the 66 patients for whom an oral antipsychotic was prescribed (23%) had a SUD, and 14 of these 15 had been noncompliant prior to admission. Among the entire group of 66 patients for whom an oral antipsychotic was prescribed, insight scores did not differ between those who were compliant and those who were noncompliant. However, when the 15 patients with a comorbid SUD were excluded from the analysis, the 21 compliant patients had significantly higher insight scores than the 30 noncompliant patients. In a logistic regression analysis, comorbid SUD and insight independently predicted compliance.

Summary of patients' views

When we query general populations of patients with schizophrenia about their need for treatment, 30–50% of them report that they do not need medications or would stop taking them if that option was readily available (Parkes *et al.*, 1962; Soskis, 1978; McEvoy *et al.*, 1981; Thompson 1988). Fewer than half acknowledge that they have a mental illness (Soskis, 1978; McEvoy *et al.*, 1981; Thompson, 1988). Those patients who do not see themselves as ill, or who report no need for medications, are less likely to report compliance with medications (Soskis, 1978; McEvoy, 1981; Thompson, 1988).

Up to 20% of patients with schizophrenia may openly and clearly refuse to take medications; as expected, among the "enriched" population of newly-involuntarily-committed patients the portion of refusers approaches 50%. It is almost tautologic to note that refusers are more hostile and have less confidence in the staff caring for them. It is important to understand that the decision process leading to refusal takes place in a mind altered by psychopathology. Certainly at the time of refusal, and perhaps even after treatment (Van Putten *et al.*, 1976), refusers evidence higher levels of psychopathology than patients who agree to medications.

Among chronically hospitalized patients in whom there is clear evidence of cognitive compromise (e.g., age disorientation), understanding of medications is markedly limited, and we cannot expect compliance in such patients unless they are completely supervised. Even in the community, it appears that cognitive impairment will have some deleterious effects on insight and compliance.

Having a comorbid substance use disorder is addative to impaired insight in predicting poor compliance.

Insight as predictor of compliance

Does acknowledgment of illness and need for medication predict that patients will take their medications?

The available studies

The studies reviewed in this section reflect wide variations in how acknowledgment of illness and need for medication were rated, and in how compliance was determined. Nonetheless consistent themes emerge.

Lin, Spiga, and Fortsch (1979) studied a group of 100 patients with schizophrenia shortly after their release from index hospitalizations. Patients were scored as having insight (I+) if they answered "yes" to *any* of the following three questions which referred back to their recent inpatient stay: "Do you think you had to be in the hospital?", "Do you think you had to see a psychiatrist?", "Do you think you had to see a doctor?" (Only 31 patients were I+, and 69 I−.) Patients were scored as perceiving benefit from treatment (B+) if they responded affirmatively to the question, "While you were in the hospital, did the medication do you any good?" (Forty-nine patients were B+, and 51 B−). Patients whose claims to have faithfully taken their medications could be corroborated by family or aftercare staff were judged as adherent to medications (M+, n = 26). The other 74 patients were considered M−. Fourteen of 31 patients (45%) who had insight were medication adherent, in contrast to 12 of 69 (17%) patients without insight (chi square = 7.19, P < 0.01). Eighteen of 49 (36%) patients who perceived benefit from treatment were medication adherent, in contrast to 8 of 51 (15%) who did not perceive benefit (chi square = 4.71, P < 0.05).

Bartko *et al.* (1988) developed two 4-point scales for assessing "lack of feeling of illness (the patient denies being ill either spontaneously or when interviewed)", and "lack of insight into illness (the patient fails to acknowledge his/her emotional state and behavior assessed as pathologic by the physician, and does not perceive the necessity of treatment)". Fifty-eight patients with schizophrenia were rated on these scales at the time of their discharge from an index hospitalization. All of these patients were treated with long-acting depot antipsychotics, and followed over one year of aftercare. Thirty-two of the 58 patients (55%) became noncompliant over the follow-up, as evidenced by missed appointments or deliberate discontinuation of medications. Baseline ratings of "lack of feeling of illness" and "lack of insight into illness" were significantly higher in those patients who noncomplied than in compliant patients.

McEvoy, Apperson *et al.* (1989) administered an 11-item Insight and Treatment Attitudes Questionnaire (ITAQ) to 46 patients with schizophrenia at index discharge. Two to three years after these patients were discharged, two research associates independently reviewed these patients' aftercare records and interviewed all available clinicians who were familiar with these patients' course and outcome. At 30 day follow-up, 75% of patients were compliant, but only 53% remained compliant over the total duration of follow-up; and 61% of patients were rehospitalized at least once. Multivariate tests revealed that the presence of an assertive individual in the patient's aftercare environment who supported the patient's continuation in treatment was significantly associated with outcome. In particular, patients with such an individual supporting their involvement in aftercare were significantly more likely to be compliant with treatment 30 days after discharge and over the long-term follow up. The association between insight and outcome approached statistical significance (F = 1.95; 10, 66 df; $P = 0.053$). In particular, patients with more insight were significantly less likely to be readmitted over the course of follow-up, and there was a trend for patients with more insight to be compliant with treatment 30 days after discharge. The contributions to outcome of an assertive individual in the aftercare environment and the patient's level of insight appeared to be independent.

The finding by McEvoy, Apperson *et al.* (1989) that lack of insight is associated with rehospitalization supports the earlier reports of Heinrichs (1985) that early insight, defined as "a patient's ability, during the early phase of a decompensation, to recognize that he or she is beginning to suffer a relapse of his or her psychotic illness", predicts that a decompensation can be successfully resolved on an outpatient basis, without need for rehospitalization.

Weiden *et al.* (1991) followed 72 patients, 85% of whom had schizophrenia, after an index hospitalization. Forty-eight percent of these patients became noncompliant with medications for at least one week over a year of follow-up. Baseline features of patients which were significantly associated with noncompliance included denial of illness, perceived coercion, and perceived stigma. In contrast, baseline features significantly associated with compliance included perceived good relationship with the physician, perceived benefit from medications, and fear of future relapse.

Buchanan (1992) measured insight in 61 patients with schizophrenia prior to their discharge from an index hospitalization by asking six questions:

1 Do you think that you have been unwell during this admission?

2 Do you think that you will become ill again?

3 Did treatment help?

4 Will you take treatment after you discharge?

5 Will you ever get back to your old self?

6 Why were you in the hospital?

Compliance over the ensuing two years of follow-up was assessed by inspection of records and by analysis of urine. Fifty-nine percent of patients were compliant at the end of one year, and 51% at the end of two years. Affirmative responses to question 3 (a belief that medication had helped during the admission) and question 4 (a stated willingness to take treatment after discharge) were significantly positively associated with compliance over the follow-up. A history of compliance with treatment prior to the index hospitalization, and voluntary status during the index hospitalization, were also significantly associated with compliance over follow-up.

McEvoy *et al.* (1993) prospectively followed 24 outpatients with schizophrenia over a year of follow-up. These patients, as a group, were relatively insightful and were engaged in highly active aftercare programmes. Only three of these patients required rehospitalization over the year of follow-up, precluding comparison between rehospitalized and not rehospitalized patients using standard statistical tests. However, the mean scores of the three rehospitalized patients were outside the 95% confidence limits for the 21 not rehospitalized patients on two of the baseline measures: rehospitalized patients had lower baseline insight scores (15.3 vs. 19.2 SEM 1.4) and fewer years since their first hospitalization (1.3 vs. 9.7, SEM 1.4).

Kemp and David (1996) administered insight assessments to 74 patients during an index hospitalization. Better insight predicted better compliance after discharge, independently of whether compliance therapy was given.

Smith *et al.* (1999) assessed insight in 46 individuals with schizophrenia or schizoaffective disorder at the time of discharge from an inpatient unit. Patients who were insightless regarding the psychopathologic features that led to their recent hospitalizations showed poorer treatment compliance after discharge.

Insight predicts compliance

The percentages of patients remaining compliant with treatment in these studies ranged from a low of 26% over one year (Lin *et al.*, 1979) to a high of 51% over two years (Buchanan, 1992). Acknowledgment of illness (Lin *et al.*, 1979; Weiden *et al.*, 1991; Heinrichs *et al.*, 1985; Bartko *et al.*, 1988; Kemp and David 1996; Smith *et al.*, 1999) and/or benefit from medications (Lin *et al.*, 1979; McEvoy, Apperson *et al.*, 1989, McEvoy *et al.*, 1993; Buchanan, 1992) was significantly associated with compliance and avoidance of rehospitalization across all the available studies.

Approximately one-third to one half of patients with schizophrenia will noncomply with medications if given the opportunity. Approximately one-third to one half of patients with schizophrenia deny they are ill or need treatment. Those patients who deny their illness or need for treatment are significantly more likely to be among the group who noncomply.

Ways to increase compliance

What can be done to increase the likelihood that patients with schizophrenia will take their medications?

Practical issues

For general medical patients, longer times between referral and actual appointment (Haynes, 1979a, b), and longer waiting times at clinic before actually being seen (Blackwell, 1976) are associated with diminished likelihood of continuation in treatment. We may expect that delays in service delivery will similarly reduce compliance in patients with mental illness. In fact, immediate responsiveness may be required to adequately address the needs of patients with serious mental illness (Cohen, 1993). When released into the community after brief hospitalizations for psychotic excerbations, patients are often still confused about their medications (Velligan *et al.*, 2003).

Cost can limit access to treatment among the poor (Haynes, 1976). Davis (1977) have reported significantly higher drop-out rates among self-pay patients with schizophrenia, relative to those on public support.

Pharmacologic issues

More complex pharmacologic treatments, both in terms of the number of drugs prescribed and the frequencies at which they must be taken, are associated with diminished compliance (Haynes, 1979a,b). Fortunately, the most commonly prescribed antipsychotic and antiparkinson agents can be taken once daily.

It is very likely that distressing extrapyramidal side effects contribute to noncompliance (Falloon et al., 1978; Hogan et al., 1983; Seltzer, Roncari, and Garfinkel, 1988). In many (Marder, Van Putten et al., 1984; Van Putten et al., 1990; McEvoy, et al., 1991) but not all (Rifkin 1990) acute treatment studies prospectively comparing different doses of antipsychotics, significantly more patients dropped out of study in the higher dose groups complaining of distressing side effects. In outpatient maintenance studies comparing long-acting injectable medications (the blood and brain levels of which cannot be altered by the patients who receive them) with oral medications (the levels of which patients may surreptitiously lower by partial noncompliance), significantly higher rates of termination due to "toxicity" are reported with the injectable preparations (Rifkin et al., 1977; Falloon et al., 1978). We may recall that among the patients reported by Chien (1975) who could self-regulate their fluphenazine enanthate injections, the 10 of 16 who remained on treatment halved their doses. Side effects of medication were the most common reasons (35%) for refusal of medications in the study of Hoge et al. (1990).

Weiden et al. (1991) made the important point that old extrapyramidal side effects (EPSE) that were very distressing may, although now remote in time, have left a lingering distaste for medications.

Dolder et al. (2002) compared prescription refill records for 117 patients receiving conventional neuroleptics and 171 patients receiving atypical antipsychotics over the course of a year. Cumulative mean gap ratios (the number of days when medication was unavailable in relation to the total number of days) were 23.2% for conventional neuroleptics and 14.1% for atypical antipsychotics. Patients receiving conventional neuroleptics were without medication for an average of 7 days per month; patients receiving atypical antipsychotics were without medication for an average of 4 days per month. Compliant fill rates (the number of correct prescription fills) were 50.1% for conventional neuroleptics and 54.9% for atypical antipsychotics.

Other studies confirm that, if there is better compliance with the atypical antipsychotics, the advantages are small (Sajatovic et al., 2002; Velligan et al., 2003).

As noted earlier, rates of documented noncompliance appear to be lower in patients treated with long-acting injectable antipsychotic medications than in patients receiving pills (see also Kane and Borenstein, 1985). Perhaps the most important way in which long-acting injectable preparations support compliance is by making noncompliance openly apparent when it occurs (Johnson and Freeman, 1972). Clinicians do not observe patients taking or not taking pills at home, however, they do know when patients fail to appear for their injections. The information that a patient has not taken an injection is useful, however, only if family, friends, or clinical staff go out and attempt to re-engage the patient in treatment.

Support, supervision, coercion

The studies reviewed earlier in this chapter document that compliance with medication can be progressively increased to levels greater than 90% by progressively increasing supervision by staff, but that compliance falls to levels approaching 50% in unsupervised outpatients for whom pills are prescribed.

Supervision of outpatients by family members or friends can enhance compliance (Willcox *et al.*, 1965; Reilly, Wilson, and McClinton, 1969; McEvoy, Apperson *et al.*, 1989; Buchanan, 1992). Parkes *et al.* (1962) reported that it made a great difference whether the taking of the drug was supervised: 14 (82%) of the 17 patients whose drug administration was supervised by a relative or a friend took their drugs as ordered, compared with 26 (46%) of the 56 nonsupervised patients. (p. 975).

Supervision need not be unpleasant. In an inpatient study (McEvoy *et al.*, 1981), we were impressed by the many patients who consistently responded "no" when asked if they were ill or needed treatment, but who expressed a clear willingness to take medications in the hospital. When we asked them to explain this pattern of response, they generally noted how pleasant the nurses were, and that it was a routine and not a bother. Others have reported improved compliance when they offered free lunches at clinic on the days that injections were given (Cassino *et al.*, 1987).

All too often, coercive (as opposed to supportive) forms of supervision must be brought to bear after patients have failed to comply with medications, have become actively psychotic, and have become dangerous to themselves or others. The available evidence suggests that the patients who most resist treatment, and require coercion, show little or no improvement in acknowledgment of illness and need for treatment even when they are forcibly treated, despite the fact that their psychopathology diminishes significantly (Marder, Swann *et al.*, 1984; McEvoy, Applebaum *et al.*, 1989). Therefore, it seems foolish to expect that after discharge these patients will continue on treatment when the choice is again theirs in the outpatient setting. Unfortunately, the outpatient commitment laws in many states, and the procedures for enduring outpatient follow-up of resistant patients in many mental health centers, are not adequate at the present time to assure that such patients take their prescribed medications outside of hospital.

A randomized trial of involuntary outpatient commitment (OPC) among severely mentally ill patients in North Carolina found that OPC, especially if sustained for 6 months or more and combined with frequent outpatient services, reduced hospital readmission and length-of-stay, violent behavior, and victimization and improved treatment adherence (Swartz *et al.*, 2001). Subjects in the trial had low levels of insight (mean ITAQ scores of 5.1 and 4.5 in the experimental and treatment groups respectively). Individuals with lower levels of insight were significantly more likely to see OPC as unwanted and coercive. However, subjects with lower levels of insight were no less likely to benefit from the procedure (Swartz *et al.*, 2002).

Can insight be improved?

This question requires much more study. Methods for directly improving insight through psychoeducation and cognitive rehabilitation are currently under investigation (described in detail elsewhere in this book), with the hope that improvements in insight will translate into improvements in treatment compliance. However, given the limited improvements in insight and treatment compliance produced by stark learning experiences such as repeated involuntary commitments and hospitalizations, it may be that these techniques will prove only partially successful.

Interestingly, in the general medical literature, "there appears to be no relationship between patients' knowledge of their disease or its therapy and their compliance with the associated treatment regimen" (Haynes, 1976), nor is there a correlation between patients' intelligence or educational achievement and compliance (Haynes, 1976). Most authors (Soskis, 1978; Hogan *et al.*, 1983; Irwin *et al.*, 1985) report no relationship between schizophrenic patients' abstract knowledge about the illness and compliance. Klein *et al.* (1974) and Boczkowski *et al.* (1985) reported no improvement in compliance among patients given education about the illness.

On a more optimistic note, Boczkowski *et al.* (1985) found a behavioral tailoring (BT) approach to result in significantly higher levels of compliance than psychoeducation. The BT approach is described as follows:

> The investigator helped each participant tailor his prescribed regimen so that it was better adapted to his personal habits and routines. This involved identifying a highly visible location for placement of medications and pairing the daily medication intake with specific routine behavior of the participant. Each participant was given a self-monitoring spiral calendar, which feature a dated slip of paper for each dose of the neuroleptic. The participant was instructed to keep the calendar near his medications and to tear off a slip each time he took a pill.

Seltzer, Roncari, and Garfinkel (1980) combined didactic information about the nature of schizophrenia and its pharmacological treatment with a behavioral component that reinforced drug-taking behavior. The latter intervention may have been the more important component in producing improved compliance in the treated group.

(Kemp, Haywood *et al.*, 1996; Kemp *et al.*, 1998) report a study of 74 patients with psychotic disorders randomly assigned to 4–6 sessions of compliance therapy or non-specific counseling. Compliance therapy is based upon motivational interviewing, and is described by the authors as follows:

> In the first two sessions of compliance therapy patients were invited to review their history of illness and conceptualize the problem. In the next two sessions, discussion became more specific,

focusing on symptoms and the side effects of treatment. The benefits and drawbacks of drug treatment were considered, the patient's ambivalence was explored, and the therapist highlighted discrepancy between the patient's actions and beliefs, focussing on adaptive behaviors. In the last two sessions the stigma of drug treatment was tackled by considering that drugs are a freely chosen strategy to enhance the quality of life. Self efficacy was encouraged and the value of staying well and thus the need for prophylactic or maintenance treatment was emphasized. The therapist encouraged the use of metaphors such as "protective layer" and "insurance policy".

At 18 month follow-up, the patients who received compliance therapy had greater insight and more favorable attitudes towards treatment. They were rated by clinicians as more compliant with treatment, and survived longer in the community without readmission.

Zygmunt *et al.* (2002) summarize the results of their review of interventions to improve compliance with medication among patients with schizophrenia as follows:

> Psychoeducation interventions without accompanying behavioral components and supportive services are not likely to be effective in improving medication adherence in schizophrenia. Models of community care such as assertive community treatment and interventions based on principles of motivational interviewing are promising. Providing patients with concrete instructions and problem-solving strategies, such as reminders, self-monitoring tools, cues, and reinforcements, is useful. Problems in adherence are recurring, and booster sessions are needed to reinforce and consolidate gains.

Ways to increase compliance

A number of simple, common-sense procedures appear capable of improving compliance in patients with serious mental illness. (It is striking how rarely they are applied). These include seeing patients quickly when they need to be seen, avoiding complicated medication schedules, protecting patients from having to pay the full costs of expensive medications, and avoiding distressing side effects.

There is no evidence that abstract understanding about schizophrenia or the pharmacological mechanisms of antipsychotic medications is associated with greater compliance, and those studies which attempted to improve patients' understanding of their illness and its treatment showed no improvement in compliance (Klein *et al.*, 1974; Boczkowski *et al.*, 1985).

There is compelling evidence that patients who state that they personally are ill and/or need treatment are more compliant. I am not aware of studies which have tested an approach which strives to directly change patients' self-images to one more acknowledging of illness and need for treatment. It appears that greater acknowledgment of illness is associated with higher levels of depression, and such an approach should be taken cautiously.

It appears that behavioral compliance may be achievable independently of expressed insight, through behavioral programs which incorporate medication compliance into patients' daily routines and provide consistent rewards for taking medications.

Conclusions

The degree to which a patient with schizophrenia acknowledges that he or she has a serious mental illness and needs treatment (insight) has consistently been found to predict how readily that individual will seek, or at least cooperate with treatment. Patients with low levels of insight, whether measured at discharge from an index hospitalization or in the outpatient setting, are less likely to comply with treatment and more likely to require hospitalization during follow-up care. Low levels of insight are common in schizophrenia and, as Weiden *et al.* (1991) state, "it seems that public health planning for the outpatient treatment of schizophrenia should *assume* that most patients become noncompliant to their maintenance neuroleptic regiment" (p. 294).

Methods for directly improving insight through motivational interviewing and cognitive rehabilitation are currently under investigation (described in detail elsewhere in this book), with the hope that improvements in insight will translate into improvements in treatment compliance. However, until such techniques are demonstrated to be successful, clinicians must expect the continued necessity to bring treatment to a substantial percentage of schizophrenic patients who do not believe they need it, and who certainly do not actively seek it. We need to follow up the positive studies (e.g., Boczkowski, 1985) which suggest that we bypass the provision of abstract knowledge, to instead directly incorporate simple medication taking behaviors into patients' daily routines and reward patients for compliance.

Many schizophrenic patients will, despite having little insight, "go along with" treatment that is brought to them. The presence of an effective individual (family member, rest home supervisor, outreach worker, etc.) in the patient's aftercare environment who urges the patient to stay in treatment will assist in compliance. Research is needed to determine how to educate and assist such individuals in the patient's aftercare environment so that they can most effectively support compliance.

In contrast to their limited acknowledgment of the benefits of treatment, patients with schizophrenia are well aware of the distressing side-effects (extrapyramidal side-effects, weight gain, sexual dysfunction, etc.) associated with antipsychotic medications. Studies to determine whether pharmacologic strategies that produce fewer side-effects result in improved compliance have yet to be done. Long-acting intramuscular forms of antipyschotic (e.g., fluphenazine decanoate or haloperidol decanoate) permit closer monitoring of compliance than oral forms.

A small percentage of patients actively resist treatment. Presently available evidence suggests that such patterns of deficient insight and noncompliance are fairly stable over time. If repeatedly noncompliant patients become dangerous when actively ill, caregivers may attempt to enforce treatment through prolonged inpatient commitment or through outpatient commitment.

Thus, those who wish to care for patients with schizophrenia must realize that, in many cases, treatment cannot simply be offered. Rather all too often, we must *influence* our patients to accept treatment. Much research is needed to determine how we can most effectively, and least intrusively, exert this influence to enhance compliance and preempt relapse.

References

Adams, J. and Scott, J. (2000). Predicting medication adherence in severe mentl disorders. *Acta Psyhiatrica Scandinavica*, **101**, 119–24.

Adams, S. G. and Howe, J. T. (1993). Predicting medication compliance in a psychotic population. *Journal of Nervous and Mental Disease*, **181**, 558–60.

Appelbaum, P. S. and Gutheil, T. G. (1980). Drug refusal: A study of psychiatric inpatients. *American Journal of Psychiatry*, **137** (3), 340–6.

Bartko, G., Herczeg, I., and Zador, G. (1988). Clinical symptomatology and drug compliance in schizophrenic patients. *Acta Psychiatrica Scandinavica*, **77**, 74–6.

Blackwell, B. (1976). Treatment adherence. *British Journal of Psychiatry*, 129, 513–31.

Boczkowski, J. A., Zeichner, A. and DeSanto, N. (1985). Neuroleptic compliance among chronic schizophrenic outpatients: An intervention outcome report. *Journal of Consulting and Clinical Psychology*, **53** (5), 666–71.

Buchanan, A. (1992). A two-year prospective study of treatment compliance in patients with schizophrenia. *Psychological Medicine*, **22**, 787–97.

Byerly, M., Fisher, R., Rush, A. J., Holland, R. and Varghese, F. (2002). Comparison of clinician vs electronic monitoring of antipsychotic adherence in schizophrenia. Presented at the American College of Neuropsychopharmacology (ACNP) Meeting, San Juan, Puerto Rico, December 10, 2002.

Carney, M. W. P. and Sheffield, B. F. (1976). Comparison of antipsychotic depot injections in the maintenance treatment of schizophrenia. *British Journal of Psychiatry*, **129**, 476–81.

Cassino, T., Spellman, N., Heiman, J., Shupe, J. and Sklebar, H. J. (1987). Invitation to compliance: The Prolixin brunch. *Journal of Psychosocial Nursing and Mental Health Services*, **25**, 15–19.

Caton, C. (1984). *Management of Chronic Schizophrenia*. New York: Oxford University Press.

Chien, C. P. (1975). Drugs and rehabilitation in schizophrenia. In M. Greenblatt (ed.) *Drugs in Combination with Other Therapies*, pp. 13–34. New York: Grune and Stratton.

Cohen, N. L. (1993). Stigmatization and the "noncompliant" recidivist. *Hospital and Community Psychiatry*, **44** (11), 1029.

Cramer, J. A. and Roseheck, R. (1999). Enhancing medication compliance for people with serious mental illness. *Journal of Nervous and Mental Disease*, **187**, 53–5.

Cuesta, M. J. and Peralta, V. (1994). Lack of insight in schizophrenia. *Schizophrenia Bulletin*, **20**, 359–66.

David, A., van Os, J. V., Jones, P., Harvey, I., Foerster, A. and Fahy, T. (1995). Insight and psychotic illness: cross-sectional and longitudinal analyses. *British Journal of Psychiatry*, **167**, 621–8.

Davis, K. L., Estess, F. M., Simonton, S. C. and Gonda, T. A. (1977). Effects of payment mode on clinic attendance and rehospitalization. *American Journal of Psychiatry*, **134** (5), 576–8.

Diaz, E., Levine, H. B., Sullivan, M. C., Sernyak, M. J., Hawkins, K. A., Cramer, J. A., *et al.* (2001). Use of the Medication Event Monitoring System to estimate medication compliance in patients with schizophrenia *Journal of Psychiatry and Neuroscience*, **26**, 325–9.

Doller, C. R., Lacro, J. P., Dun, L. B. and Jeste, D. V. (2002). Antipsychotic medication adherence: is there a difference between typical and atypical agents? *American Journal of Psychiatry*, **159**, 103–8.

Falloon, I., Watt, D. C. and Shepherd, M. (1978). A comparative controlled trial of pimozide and fluphenazine decanoate in the continuation therapy of schizophrenia. *Psychological Medicine*, 8, 59–70.

Fennig, S., Robinowitz, J. and Fennig, S. (1999). Involuntary first admissions of patients with schizophrenia as a predictor of future admissions. *Psychiatric Services*, 50, 1049–52.

Flashman, L. A., McAllister, T. W., Andreasen, N. C. and Saykin, A. J. (2000). Smaller brain size associated with unawareness of illness in patients with schizophrenia. *American Journal of Psychiatry*, 157, 1167–9.

Forrest, F. M., Forrest I. S. and Mason, A. S. (1961). Review of rapid urine tests for phenothiazine and related drugs. *American Journal of Psychiatry*, 118, 300–7.

Geller, J. L. (1982). State hospital patients and their medication: Do they know what they take? *American Journal of Psychiatry*, 139 (5), 611–15.

Hare, E. H. and Willcox, D. R. C. (1967). Do psychiatry inpatients take their pills? *British Journal of Psychiatry*, 113, 1435–9.

Haynes, R. B. (1976). A critical review of the "determinants" of patient compliance with therapeutic regimens. In R. B. Haynes and D. L. Sackett (ed.) *Compliance with Therapeutic Regimens*, pp. 27–39. Baltimore: Johns Hopkins University Press.

Haynes, R. B. (1979a). Determinants of compliance: The disease and the mechanics of treatment. In R. B. Haynes, D. W. Taylor and D. L. Sackett (ed.) *Compliance in Health Care*, pp. 49–63. Baltimore: Johns Hopkins University Press.

Haynes, R. B. (1979b). Strategies for improving compliance: A methodological analysis and review. In R. B. Haynes, D. W. Taylor and D. L. Sackett (ed.) *Compliance in Health Care*, pp. 121–43. Baltimore: Johns Hopkins University Press.

Heinrichs, D. W., Cohen, B. P. and Carpenter, W. T. (1985). Early insight and the management of schizophrenic decompensation. *Journal of Nervous and mental Disease*, 173, 133–8.

Hogan, T. P., Awad, A. G. and Eastwood, R. (1983). A self-report scale predictive of drug compliance in schizophrenics: Reliability and discriminative validity. *Psychological Medicine*, 13, 177–83.

Hoge, S. K., Appelbaum, P. S., Lawlor, T., Beck, J. C., Litman, R., Greer, A., et al. (1990). A prospective, multi-center study of patients' refusal of antipsychotic medication. *Archives of General Psychiatry*, 47, 949–56.

Hunt, G. E., Bergen, J. and Bashir, M. (2002). Medication compliance and comorbid substance abuse in schizophrenia: impact on community survival 4 years after a relapse. *Schizophrenia Research*, 54, 253–64.

Irwin, D. S., Weitzel, W. D. and Morgan, D. W. (1971). Phenothiazine intake and staff attitudes. *American Journal of Psychiatry*, 127 (12), 1631–5.

Irwin, M., Lovitz, A., Marder, S. R., Mintz, J., Van Putten, T. and Mills, J. J. (1985). Psychotic patients' understanding of informed consent. *American Journal of Psychiatry*, 142 (11), 1351–4.

Johnson, D. A. W. and Freeman, H. (1972). Long acting tranquilizers. *The Practitioner*, 208, 295–400.

Kamali, M., Kelly, L., Gervin, M., Browne, S., Larkin, C. and O'Callahan, E. (2001). Insight and comorbid substance misuse and medication compliance among patients with schizophrenia. *Psychiatric Services*, 52, 161–6.

Kane, J. M. and Borenstein, M. (1985). Compliance in the long-term treatment of schizophrenia, *Psychopharmacology Bulletin*, 21 (1), 23–7.

Kemp, R. and David, A. (1996). Psychological predictors of insight and compliance in psychotic patients. *British Journal of Psychiatry*, 169, 444–50.

Kemp, R., Haywood, P., Applewhaite, G., Everitt, B. and David, A. (1996). Compliance therapy in psychotic patients: randomized controlled trial. *British Medical Journal*, **312**, 345–9.

Kemp, R., Kirov, G., Everitt, B., Haywood, P. and David, A. (1998). Randomized controlled trial of compliance therapy: 18 month follow-up. *British Journal of Psychiatry*, **172**, 413–19.

Klein, R. H., Lynn, E. J., Axelrod, H. and Dluhy, J. (1974). Self-administration of medication by psychiatric inpatients. *Journal of Nervous and Mental Disease*, **158** (6), 450–5.

Larøi, F., Fannemel, M., Ronneberg, U., Flekkoy, K., Opjoursman, S., *et al.* (2000). Unawareness of illness in chronic schizophrenia and its relationships to structural brain measures and neuropsychological tests. *Psychiatry Research*, **20**, 49–58.

Lieberman, J. A., Alvir, J. M. J., Woerner, M., Degreef, G., Bilder, R. M., Ashtari, M., *et al.* (1992). Prospective psychobiology in first-episode schizophrenia at Hillside Hospital. *Schizophrenia Bulletin*, **18** (3), 351–71.

Lin, I. F., Spiga, R. and Fortsch, W. (1979). Insight and adherence to medication in chronic schizophrenics. *Journal of Clinical Psychiatry*, **40**, 430–2.

MacPherson, R., Jerrom, B. and Hughes, A. (1996) Relationship between insight, educational background and cognition in schizophrenia. *British Journal Psychiatry*, **168**, 718–22.

MacPherson, R., Double, D. B., Rowlands, R. P. and Harrison, D. M. (1993). Long-term psychiatric patients' understanding of neuroleptic medication. *Hospital and Community Psychiatry*, **44** (1), 71–3.

Marder, S. R. Swann, E. Winslade, W. J., Van Putten, T., Chien, C. P. and Wilkins, J. N. (1984). A study of medication refusal by involuntary patients. *Hospital and General Psychiatry*, **35** (7), 724–6.

Marder, S. R., Mebane, A., Chien, C. P., Winslade, W. J., Swann, E. and Van Putten, T. (1983). A comparison of patients who refuse and consent to neuroleptic treatment. *American Journal of Psychiatry*, **140** (4), 470–2.

Marder, S. R., Van Putten, T., Mintz, J., McKenzie, J., Lebell, M., Faltico, G., *et al.* (1984). Costs and benefits of two doses of fluphenazine. *Archives of General Psychiatry*, **41**, 1025–9.

McEvoy, J. P., Aland, J., Wilson, W. H., Guy, W. and Hawkins, L. (1981). Measuring chronic schizophrenic patient's attitudes towards their illness and treatment. *Hospital and Community Psychiatry*, **32** (12), 586–8.

McEvoy, J. P., Appelbaum, P. S., Apperson, L. J., Geller, J. L. and Freter, S. (1989). Why must some schizophrenic patients be involuntarily committed? The role of insight. *Comprehensive Psychiatry*, **30** (1), 13–17.

McEvoy, J. P., Apperson, L. J., Appelbaum, P. S., Ortlip, P., Brecosky, J., Hamill K., *et al.* (1989). Insight in schizophrenia: Its relationship to acute psychopathology. *Journal of Nervous and Mental Disease*. **188** (1), 43–7.

McEvoy, J. P., Freter, S., Everett, G., Geller, J. L., Appelbaum, P., Apperson, L. J., *et al.* (1993). Insight and the clinical outcome of schizophrenic patients. *Journal of Nervous and Mental Disease*, **177** (1), 48–51.

McEvoy, J. P., Hogarty, G. E. and Steingard, S. (1991). Optimal dose of neuroleptic in acute schizophrenia. *Archives of general Psychiatry*, **48**, 739–45.

Overall, J. E. and Gorham, D. R. (1962) BPRS: The Brief Psychiatric Rating Scale. In W. Guy (ed.), *ECDEU Assessment Manual for Psychopharmacology*, revised edn, pp. 157–69. Rockville, MD: National Institute of Mental Health.

Parkes, C. M., Brown, G. W. and Monck, E. M. (1962). The general practitioner and the schizophrenic patient. *British Medical Journal*, *i*, 972–6.

Quitkin, F., Rifkin, A., Kane, J., Ramos-Lorenzi, J. R. and Klein, D. F. (1978) Long-acting oral vs. injectable antipsychotic drugs in schizophrenics. *Archives of General Psychology*, **35**, 889–92.

Raskin, A. (1961). A comparison of acceptors and resistors of drug treatment as an adjunct to psychotherapy. *Journal of Consulting Psychology*, **25** (4), 366.

Rifkin, A., Doddi, S., Karajgi, B., Borenstein, M. and Wachspress, M. (1991). Dosage of haloperidol for schizophrenia. *Archives of General Psychiatry*, **48**, 166–70.

Rifkin, A., Quitkin, F. and Rabiner, C. J. (1977). Fluphenazine decanoate, oral fluphenazine and placebo in remitted schizophrenics. *Archives of General Psychiatry*, **34**, 43–7.

Sajatovic, M., Rosch, D. S., Sivec, J. H., Sultana, D., Smith, D. A., Alamic, S., *et al.* (2002). Insight into illness and attitudes towards medications among inpatients with schizophrenia. *Psychiatric Services*, **53**, 1319–21.

Seltzer, A., Roncari, I. and Garfinkel, P. (1980). Effect of patient education on medication compliance. *American Journal of Psychiatry*, **25**, 638–45.

Serban, G. and Thomas, A. (1974). Attitudes and behaviors of acute and chronic schizophrenic patients regarding ambulatory treatment. *American Journal of Psychiatry*, **131** (9), 991–5.

Smith, T. E., Hull, J. W., Goodman, M., Hedeyat-Harris, A., Wilson, D. G., Israel, L. M., *et al.* (1999) The relative influences of symptoms, insight and neurocognition on social adjustment in schizophrenia and schizoaffective disorder. *Journal of Nervous and Mental Disease*, **187**, 102–8.

Soskis, D. A. (1978). Schizophrenic and medical inpatients as informed drug consumers. *Archives of General Psychiatry*, **35**, 645–7.

Swartz, M. S., Swanson, J. W., Hannon, M. J. (2003). Detection of illicit substance use among persons with schizophrenia by radioimmunoassay of hair. *Psychiatric Services*, **54**, 891–5.

Swartz, M. S., Swanson, J. W., Hiday, V. A., Wagner, H. R., Burns, B. J. and Borum, R. (2001). A randomized controlled trial of outpatients commitment in North Carolina. *Psychiatric Services*, **52** (3), 325–9.

Swartz, M. S., Wagner, H. R., Swanson, J. W., Hiday, V. A. and Burns, B. J. (2002). The perceived coerciveness of involuntary outpatient commitment; Findings from an experimental study journal of the *American Academy of Psychiatry and the Law*, **30** (2). 207–17.

Takai, A., Nematsu, M., Neki, H., Sone, K. and Kaiya, H. (1992). Insight and its related factors in chronic schizophrenic patients, a preliminary study. *European Journal of Psychiatry*, **6**, 159–170.

Thompson, E. H., Jr. (1988). Variation in the self-concept of young adult chronic patients: Chronicity reconsidered. *Hospital and Community Psychiatry*, **39** (7), 771–5.

Van Putten, T. (1974). Why do schizophrenic patients refuse to take their drugs? *Archives of General Psychiatry*, **31**, 67–72.

Van Putten, T., Crumpton, E. and Yale, C. (1976). Drug refusal in schizophrenia and the wish to be crazy. *Archives of General Psychiatry*, **33**, 1443–6.

Van Putten, T., Marder, S. R. and Mintz, J. (1990). A controlled dose comparison of haloperidol in newly admitted schizophrenic patients. *Archives of General Psychiatry*, **47**, 754–8.

Velligan, D. I., Lam, F., Ereshefsky, L. and Miller, A. L. (2003). Perspectives on medication adherence and atypical antipsychotic medications. *Psychiatric Services*, **54**, 665–7.

Weiden, P. J. and Olfson, M. (1995) Cost of relapse in schizophrenia. *Schizophrenia Bulletin*, **21**, 419–29.

Weiden, P. J., Dixon, L., Frances, A., Appelbaum, P., Haas, G. and Rapkin, B. (1991). Neuroleptic noncompliance in schizophrenia. In C. A. Tamminga and S. C. Schulz (ed.) *Advances in Neuropsychiatry and Psychopharmacology*, pp. 285–96. New York: Raven Press.

Willcox, D. R., Gillan, R. and Hare, E. H. (1965). Do psychiatric outpatients take their drugs? *British Medical Journal*, **ii**, 790–2.

Wilson, J. D. and Enoch, M. D. (1967). Estimation of drug rejection by schizophrenic inpatients, with analysis of clinical factors. *British Medical Journal*, **113**, 209–11.

Wyatt, R. J. (1991). Neuroleptics and the natural cause of schizophrenia. *Schizophrenia Bulletin*, **17** (2), 325–50.

Young, D. A., Zakzanis, K. K., Bailey, C., Davila, R., Griese, J., *et al.* (1998). Further parameters of insight and neuropsychological deficit in schizophrenia and other chronic mental disease. *Journal of Nervous and Mental Disease*, **186**, 44–50.

Zygmunt, A., Olfson, M., Boyer, C. A. and Mechanic, D. (2002). Interventions to improve medication adherence in schizophrenia. *Am J Psychiatry*, **159**, 1653–64.

Chapter 16

Awareness of illness in schizophrenia: advances from psychosocial rehabilitation research

Paul H. Lysaker and Morris D. Bell

Persons with schizophrenia, relative to those suffering with other psychiatric conditions are often unaware of their symptoms, psychosocial deficits and/or need for assistance (Amador *et al.*, 1991, 1995; David, 1990). While aware of much in their environment, persons with schizophrenia may deny or appear oblivious to what others readily perceive as evidence that something has gone seriously wrong in their lives. They may appreciate their own financial woes, follow the story line of a movie or offer an insightful political opinion. Yet they seem unable to generate a plausible story of why they have not worked for years or account for why they have beliefs and experiences which are so disparate from those common in their community (Lysaker, *et al.*, 2003c).

Such deficits in self-awareness have long been of interest because of their links with poorer treatment compliance (Bartko *et al.*, 1988; Cuffel *et al.*, 1996; Smith *et al.*, 1999), poorer clinical outcome (Schwartz, 1998), and deficits in function (Francis and Penn, 2001; Lysaker *et al.*, 1998a). This research has found that the less aware that a person with schizophrenia is of being ill, the more likely he or she may be to decline treatment and to experience interpersonal difficulties. Yet, what do we know about what specific aspects of function are and are not linked to awareness of illness, and what are the possible causes of unawareness?

In the current chapter we will present three studies that address these questions. In the first study we focus on correlations between unawareness of illness and social and vocational function in a vocational rehabilitation setting. Then in the second and third studies, we will consider how psychological factors and neurocognitive impairments may contribute to unawareness of illness. Finally we will discuss our ongoing attempts to understand unawareness of illness as a phenomenon embedded within personal narrative.

Study 1: The association of awareness of illness with social and vocational function

It seems commonsensical that deficits in awareness of illness should impact upon psychosocial function, beyond their influence through psychopharmacological treatment adherence. Without a story of "what is" and "is not wrong", and without knowledge of personal deficits, it seems unlikely that a person could readily correct social or vocational weaknesses or determine what help they might need. Yet, while several studies indicate that that global function is impeded by unawareness of illness (Francis and Penn, 2001; Lysaker *et al.*, 1998a, 1995), less clear is whether unawareness affects some domains of behavior more than others.

To examine the effects of lack of awareness of illness on function, our first study examined correlations between global awareness of insight and social and vocational function at a rehabilitation program (Lysaker *et al.*, 2002). In particular, we were interested in whether participants who were relatively aware vs. unaware would show a different pattern of deficits in the five domains of work performance measured by the Work Behavior Inventory (WBI) (Bryson *et al.*, 1997): Social skills, Cooperativeness, Work Habits, Work Quality and Personal Presentation.

Methods   Participants were 22 female and 99 males with Structured Clinical Interview for DSM IV (SCID) (Spitzer *et al.*, 1994) confirmed DSM IV diagnoses of schizophrenia (n = 76) or schizoaffective disorder (n = 45), recruited from a VA Medical Center Psychiatry Service or community mental health center. All were receiving outpatient treatment and were in a post acute or stable phase of their disorder as defined by no hospitalizations, or changes in psychiatric medication or housing 30 days prior to screening. Participants with developmental disabilities, known neurological disorder or physical disabilities precluding work were excluded. Participants had a mean age of 42, a mean education level of 13 years and a mean of 9 lifetime hospitalizations.

Following informed consent, participants first were administered a series of assessments of neurocognitive function and awareness of illness. To assess global intellectual function the Information, Picture Completion, Digit Span, Block Design, Similarities and Digit Symbol subtests of the Wechsler Adult Intelligence Scale III were administered (Wechsler, 1997). To assess flexibility of abstract thought we administered the Wisconsin Card Sorting Test (WCST; Heaton *et al.*, 1993). To assess awareness of illness we employed the abbreviated Scale to Assess Unawareness of Mental Disorder (SUMD) (Amador *et al.*, 1995). The SUMD provides separate scores for (a) awareness of mental disorder; (b) awareness of the consequences of mental disorder; and (c) awareness of the need for treatment. Each of these items is rated on a three point scale: "1": aware; "2": somewhat aware/unaware; and "3": severely unaware. All three items can be combined to provide a global index.

Next, participants were offered a paid job placement at a VA medical center. Available job placements included the escort service, purchasing office, pharmacy and medical administration. Job duties were equivalent to entry-level positions, and supervision was provided by regular job-site supervisors. Finally, participants were expected to work between 10 and 20 hours per week at their job placement, and their social and work behavior was assessed bi-weekly using the Work Behavior Inventory (WBI) (Bryson *et al.*, 1997). The WBI is a reliable and valid inventory developed specifically to assess work behavior among persons with severe mental illness and yields five scores: social skills, cooperativeness, work habits, work quality, and personal presentation.

Analyses and Results To determine the relationship of awareness of illness to function, participants were categorized as being generally "aware" or "unaware" based on the their SUMD total score. Following a procedure previously reported (Lysaker *et al.*, 1998a) participants with either full awareness of all three dimensions (total score = 3) or full awareness on two dimensions and partial awareness on one (total score = 4) were classified as "aware" and all others as "unaware". Accordingly 65 participants (53%) met criteria for "aware" and 56 (47%) for "unaware". T-tests and chi-square analyses comparing background variables including medication status did not detect any significant differences between groups. T-tests examining performance on neuro-cognitive testing indicated that the impaired insight group demonstrated poorer performance on the WCST ($t = 2.21, P = 0.03$).

To obtain an overall measure of work performance on each WBI category, we averaged the WBI scores for the third, fifth and seventh weeks. We chose this range since we reasoned that by the third week, subjects would have settled into stable work patterns and by the seventh week underlying strengths and weaknesses should have become fully apparent. Research has suggested that work behavior in the third week of work is a considerably more reliable indicator of future performance than work in the first week (Lysaker *et al.*, 1993). Of the initial 121 participants 85 worked in the third, fifth and seventh weeks, with statistically equivalent proportions in the unaware (n = 41, 73%) and aware groups (n = 45, 69%; $X^2 = 0.82, P = $ ns).

A multivariate analysis of variance (MANOVA) was conducted comparing the five WBI scores of participants in the aware and unaware groups. This revealed a significant group difference (Wilks' Lambda = 0.85; $F(5,79) = 2.88, P = 0.02$). As summarized in Table 16.1, subsequent analyses of variance (ANOVA) indicated that the unaware group had poorer cooperativeness, work habits, work quality, and personal presentation. No differences were found for social skills. Since function in schizophrenia has been closely linked to neurocognition (cf. Green, 1996) and neurocognition to insight,

Table 16.1. Work performance on the Work Behavior Inventory

Work behavior inventory domain	Intact insight (n = 65)	Impaired insight (n = 56)	F	P =
Social skills[a]	22.2 ± 4.0	20.8 ± 3.9	2.7	ns
Cooperativeness[a]	25.2 ± 3.8	23.0 ± 4.0	7.7	.009
Work habits[a]	24.9 ± 4.5	22.5 ± 5.0	5.1	.03
Work quality[a]	24.0 ± 4.5	21.4 ± 4.7	6.6	.01
Personal presentation[a]	25.6 ± 3.8	22.7 ± 3.7	12.9	.001

[a] mean ± 1 standard deviation

we repeated these analyses as analyses of covariance (ANCOVA) covarying for WCST categories correct score and IQ scores. In these analyses the unaware group again demonstrated poorer performance on cooperativeness ($F(1,81) = 4.6$, $P = 0.035$) and personal presentation ($F(1,81) = 9.6$, $P = 0.003$). Groups, however, differed only at the trend level on work habits ($F(1,81) = 3.5$, $P = 0.06$) and work quality ($F(1,81) = 3.9$, $P = 0.05$). In these analyses poorer performance on the WCST was significantly related to poorer social skills ($F(1,81) = 4.7$, $P = 0.03$) and to work quality at the trend level ($F(1,81) = 4.6$, $P = 0.08$). No links between IQ and work function were found.

Summary and discussion

In this sample, participants less aware of illness had greater difficulties cooperating with coworkers, demonstrated poorer work habits, tended to produce poorer quality work and presented to others in a less workmanlike manner. No evidence was found linking awareness of illness to poorer social skills. Difficulties in cooperativeness and personal presentation persisted when global intellectual and executive functions were controlled for statistically. One interpretation of these results is that unawareness of illness specifically impacts on adaptation to the worker role. The two scores most closely linked to awareness – personal presentation and cooperativeness – reflect interpersonal behavior as a worker (e.g. as conforming to the work role in terms of dress, appropriateness of language and behavior, or comfort working in tandem with others). Work habits and work quality, by contrast, reflect how well a job is done, (e.g. are jobs done on time). Thus, impaired insight may protect some from understanding themselves as "sick" in the sense of permanently broken or spoiled (e.g. Warner *et al.*, 1989) but it paradoxically seems to be linked with difficulties in the functional problem of fulfilling the worker role. We speculate that the work role requires a socially validated appraisal of personal strengths and weaknesses and that the doing so is profoundly affected by unawareness of illness.

The fact that the significant relationships to work habits and work quality were reduced to trends when cognitive function was accounted for suggests that unawareness of illness is more likely to affect these features of work when combined with executive function impairments such as cognitive inflexibility. The fact that social skills were unrelated to awareness of illness suggests that persons with schizophrenia are likely to reach out to others and be sociable regardless of whether they see themselves as ill or not.

Study 2: The associations of neurocognition and coping style with unawareness of illness

While there is agreement about the importance of unawareness of illness, there are at least two ways of thinking about its antecedents. First, paralleling observations about anosognosia (unawareness of deficits in neurological disorders), persons with schizophrenia may fail to recognize their illness because they cannot process information about themselves in a manner that allows them to grasp their own mental state in its totality (e.g. Amador *et al.*, 1991). Empirical studies supporting this view include reports that insight is correlated with concurrent and prospective assessments of executive function (David *et al.*, 1995; Lysaker and Bell, 1994; Lysaker *et al.*, 1998b; Marks *et al.*, 2000; Mohamed *et al.*, 1999; Young *et al.*, 1993, 1998), and that severity of impairments in executive function predict the persistence of deficits in awareness (Lysaker and Bell, 1995).

A second theory, however, is that unawareness of illness may result from a style of coping. If a person copes with mental illness by denying it or by minimizing or avoiding stressful events or recasting them as positive events, others will likely view the person as unaware. Yet refusing to accept the stigmatizing social role associated with chronic mental illness (Link, 1987; Wahl and Harman, 1989; Warner *et al.*, 1989) by denying the illness itself may reflect a desire to preserve personal autonomy and dignity that admission of mental illness may compromise. Evidence supporting this view includes findings that embracing beliefs about oneself as "mentally ill" is linked with a pattern of more recalcitrant psychosocial deficits (Taylor and Perkins, 1991; Thompson, 1988) and possibly increased dysphoria and hopelessness (Schwartz, 2001).

While the neurocognitive and coping approaches are not necessary mutually exclusive, it is unclear how we should consider them in light of one another. Are neurocognitive impairments and coping styles equally and linearly related to different facets of awareness of illness? Thus, in our second study we examined whether three different domains of unawareness of illness – unawareness of the disorder, unawareness of treatment need and unawareness of the consequences of disorder – were associated with three different types of coping style and two measures of impairments in executive function (Lysaker *et al.*, 2003a).

Methods Participants were 114 male and 8 females with SCID (Spitzer *et al.*, 1994) confirmed DSM IV diagnoses of schizophrenia or schizoaffective disorders who were recruited from the Psychiatry Service of a VA Medical Center and a community mental health center. All participants were outpatients and were in a post acute or stable phase of disorder as defined by no hospitalizations, or changes in psychiatric medication or housing 30 days prior to screening. Exclusion criteria were as described in the first study. Participants had a mean age of 43, a mean education level of 13 years and had been hospitalized an average of 8 times during adulthood.

In the realm of neurocognitive function we chose to focus exclusively on executive function, and administered the WCST (Heaton *et al.*, 1993) and the Letter Number Sequencing Subtest of the WAIS III (LNS) (Wechsler, 1997). The LNS presents participants with increasingly long strings of letters and number, which they are to repeat back first saying the numbers in ascending order and then the letters in alphabetical order. From the WCST, described above, we utilized the total number of perseverative errors, the score most closely linked with impairments in frontal lobe function. To assess coping styles potentially related to insight, we used the distancing, escape-avoidance and positive reappraisal scales of the Ways of Coping Questionnaire (WCQ) (Folkman and Lazarus, 1988), an instrument used successfully with other schizophrenia samples (Rollins *et al.*, 1999). On the WCQ distancing describes efforts to passively detach oneself and to minimize or deny the significance of a stressor and includes items such as: "I went on as if nothing had happened." Escape-avoidance describes wishful thinking and behavioral efforts to actively escape or avoid a problem and includes items such as: "I wished the situation would go away or be over with." Positive reappraisal describes efforts to create positive meaning by focusing on personal growth and includes items such as: "I changed or grew as a person in a good way." For the purposes of this study we utilized the relative score for each scale. According to this procedure the mean score for each scale is divided by the total mean to create an index of relative preference for the coping strategy of interest. To assess awareness of illness, need for treatment and awareness of consequences we chose again to use the abbreviated Scale to Assess Unawareness of Mental Disorder (Amador, 1995), as described above. Ratings of awareness of illness were performed blind to performance on the WCST, LNS and WCQ.

Analyses and Results   On Unawareness of disorder, 64 participants (48%) were rated as "fully aware", 45 (34%) as "partially aware" and 23 (18%) as "unaware". Second, on Unawareness of treatment need, 74 (56%) were rated as "fully aware", 34 (26%) as "partially aware", and 24 (18%) as "unaware." Lastly on Unawareness of consequences of illness, 61 (46%) were rated as "fully aware", 43 (33%) as "partially aware", and 28 (21%) as "unaware".

Three ANCOVA's (one per dimension of SUMD) were performed comparing the three levels of awareness groups on WCQ, WCST and LN S scores using age and education as covariates. As summarized in Table 16.2, the SUMD Unawareness of disorder groups differed on the WCST ($F(2,128) = 5.17$, $P = 0.007$), LNS ($F(2,128 = 5.18$, $P = 0.007$), and WCQ positive reappraisal ($F(2,128) = 4.73,$; $P = 0.01$). On SUMD Unawareness of need for treatment groups differed only on the LNS ($F(2,128) = 6.07$, $P = 0.003$). On SUMD Unawareness of consequences groups differed on the WCST ($F(2,128) = 3.89$; $P = 0.02$); LNS ($F(2,128) = 4.03$), $P = 0.02$; and WCQ escape-avoidance ($F(2,128) = 3.42$; $P = 0.03$).

Multiple comparisons using Fishers LSD method found that on SUMD unawareness of disorder, the unaware group had a significantly ($P < 0.05$) greater preference for positive reappraisal, and poorer performance on the LNS and WCST than the aware group. The unaware group also had a greater preference for positive reappraisal than the partially unaware group, while the partially unaware group had poorer performance on the WCST than the aware group. On the SUMD unawareness of need for treatment, the partially aware group performed more poorly on the LNS than the aware group. On SUMD unawareness of consequences, the unaware group performed more

Table 16.2 Neurocognitive and coping scores per Insight domain (n = 132)

SUMD scale	Test Score	SUMD category Aware 1	Partially Unaware 2	Unaware 3	Significant group differences
Awareness of symptoms	WCST PE[ab]	23.0 ± 2.7	35.2 ± 3.3	35.8 ± 4.5	3 > 1[d], 2 > 1[e]
	LNS [ac]	9.0 ± 0.3	8.1 ± 0.4	6.6 ± 0.6	3 < 1[e]
	Positive reappraisal[a]	0.9 ± 0.1	0.9 ± 0.1	1.3 ± 0.1	3 > 1[d], 3 > 2[e]
	Escape-avoidance				ns
	Distancing				ns
Awareness of treatment need	WCST PE				ns
	LNS[ac]	9.0 ± 0.3	8.1 ± 0.5	6.6 ± 0.6	3 < 1[e]
	Positive reappraisal				ns
	Escape-avoidance				ns
	Distancing				ns
Awareness of consequences	WCST PE[ab]	24.6 ± 2.8	30.6 ± 2.3	37.7 ± 4.1	3 > 1[d]
	LNS[ac]	9.0 ± 0.3	7.6 ± 0.5	7.5 ± 0.6	1 > 3[d], 1 > 2[d]
	Positive reappraisal				ns
	Escape-avoidance[a]	1.1 ± 0.1	0.9 ± 0.1	1.2 ± 0.1	3 > 2[d]
	Distancing				ns

[a] mean ± 1 standard deviation
[b] greater scores indicate greater impairment
[c] lesser scores indicate greater impairment

[d] $P < .05$;
[e] $P < .01$

poorly on LNS and WCST than the aware group. The partially unaware group also performed more poorly on the LNS. The unaware of consequences group reported more reliance on escape-avoidance than the partially unaware group. Groups did not differ on their preference for distancing as a coping strategy.

Summary and discussion

Results of this study suggest persons grossly unaware of their disorder experience greater impairments in executive function than do fully aware persons. Results are also consistent with the hypotheses that unawareness in schizophrenia is associated with coping style, though here the picture seems more complex. It is possible that different types of coping strategies are related to deficits in different domains of insight. Perhaps positive reappraisal affects how people interpret their symptoms, while actively avoiding stressors is preferred by those who are trying to escape facing the consequences of their illness.

We were surprised that we did not find that the partially unaware group consistently differed from the aware or unaware groups on executive function. This may suggest that the phenomenon of partial unawareness (which represented between a quarter and third of our population) is a more complex, mixed mental state. It may be that partial recognition of schizophrenia is qualitatively different from complete unaware-ness of schizophrenia and that it may result less from executive function deficits and more from other, perhaps unmeasured, determinants. We were also surprised that there were few differences found among groups on unawareness of treatment need. Perhaps unawareness of treatment needs differs from unawareness of symptoms and consequences because it involves deciding upon a course of action based on interpreta-tions of experience. In this interpretative process, a wider variety of influences, includ-ing sociocultural and familial ones, come into play. It is also possible that our sample represents a subset of those with unawareness of need for treatment who nonetheless have chosen to participate in rehabilitation. It may be that those with greater convic-tion about their treatment refusal would have a distinctive neurocognitive or coping style that would differ from the other two types of unawareness.

Study 3: Unawareness, coping and neurocognition: a cluster analytic approach

In our first and second studies we looked for differences on measures of function, cop-ing and neurocognition between groups who were more vs. less aware of their mental illness. One limitation of this approach is that it groups together persons in the unaware group who may be unaware of illness for very different reasons and thus have different kinds of deficits. Consistent with this possibility, Startup (1996) has suggested that neuro-cognition and coping may contribute to unawareness of illness in generally separate ways. He theorized in particular that there might be two distinct groups of persons who lack awareness of illness: those who lack awareness because of neurocognitive deficits and those that are denying illness as a way of coping. He further suggested that these two "unaware" groups might differ in terms of the extent of their unawareness. Persons unaware because of neurocognitive impairments, he argued, might be able to grasp some of the facts of their illness and thus have moderately impaired insight. By contrast, those who deny that they are ill in order to cope with a painful reality may deny all aspects of their condition and thus appear as severely unaware.

Our third study (Lysaker et al., 2003b) thus seeks to determine if two distinct groups with unawareness of their schizophrenia can be found: one with average neurocogni-tion and a greater preference for avoidant forms of coping and one with poor levels of neurocognition. To that end, we performed a cluster analysis of a new sample of persons with schizophrenia spectrum disorders on the basis of two measures: global insight as assessed by the insight and judgment item of the Positive and Negative Syndrome Scale (PANSS; Kay et al., 1987) and the WCST Perseverative Errors score (PE). A priori we planned to label any cluster as having poor vs. average neurocognition if their PE score was below one standard deviation of the general population mean. Following criteria used in earlier studies (Lysaker *et al.*, 1998b) an average PANSS insight score of 3 or less was predetermined to indicate awareness while a score of 4 or more was to be considered to reflect unawareness.

Methods Sixty-three male and one female participant with SCID (Spitzer *et al.*, 1994) confirmed DSM-IV diagnoses of schizophrenia or schizoaffective disorder were recruited from the Psychiatry Service of a VA Medical Center. As in the other two studies all participants were outpatients and were in a post acute or stable phase of their disorder. Participants had a mean age of 43, a mean education level of 13 years and had been hospitalized an average of 8 times during adulthood. Following written informed consent, symptoms were assessed using the Bell *et al.* (1994) 5-component model of the PANSS. Neurocognition was assessed using WCST and coping using the WCQ. All PANSS ratings were performed blind to performance on the WCST and WCQ.

Analysis and Results PANSS insight and WCST PE scores were standardized into z-scores and a K-means cluster analysis was performed to identify relatively homogenous participant groups. Cluster analysis as a method classified people into groups by determining clusters of participants that display small within-cluster variation relative to the between-cluster variation (Carpenter *et al.*, 1976; Dillon and Goldstein, 1984; SPSS, 1999a). In cluster analysis each participant is assigned to a cluster, and participants are moved from one cluster to another until terminating conditions are met. Cluster analysis is thus similar to factor analysis, differing only in that its end is the determination of orthogonal groups of participants rather than orthogonal groups of variables.

K-means cluster analyses were performed specifying as few as two groups to as many as six and a three-cluster solution was chosen as optimal. As presented in Table 16.3, cluster A had 28 participants, cluster B had 13 participants, and cluster C had 23 participants. The A cluster was labeled aware–average executive function because its mean insight impairment was rated as between "none" or "minimal" impairment (1 or 2 on the PANSS 7 point item) and a WCST score within one standard deviation of populations norms. The B cluster was labeled unaware–average executive function because its mean insight ratings was between "moderately severe" and "severe" (5 and 6) and its WCST score was within one standard deviation of populations norms. The C cluster, was labeled unaware–poor executive function because it's mean insight scores was between "moderately" and "moderately severely" impaired (4 and 5) and its WCST PE score was two standard deviations below the population norm.

ANOVA comparing insight and neurocognition of the three groups confirmed our interpretations of the clusters. The unaware–average executive function group had significantly poorer insight than the unaware–poor executive function group. Both had significantly poorer insight than the aware–average executive function group. The unaware–poor executive function cluster had significantly poorer WCST PE scores than either average executive function group. The WCST PE scores of the two average executive function clusters did not differ significantly from one another. No differences

Table 16.3 Symptoms and coping style across three awareness clusters[a]

	Cluster 1 aware average executive function (n = 28)	Cluster 2 unaware average executive function (n = 13)	Cluster 3 unaware poor executive function (n = 23)	Group differences using ANOVA	Differences using ANCOVA controlling for WCST PE
Age	45.4 ± 10.0	45.2 ± 12.53	45.3 ± 7.6	NS	–
Education	12.6 ± 2.1	12.9 ± 1.41	12.4 ± 1.5	NS	–
PANSS insight item[1]	1.8 ± 0.8	5.5 ± 1.1	4.6 ± 0.7	F = 111.8, P < .0001[1]	–
WCST PE	48.6 ± 14.9	48.6 ± 11.6	27.4 ± 7.2	F = 20.6, P < .0001[2]	–
PANSS components					
Positive	17.7 ± 4.5	17.2 ± 6.3	19.0 ± 6.4	NS	–
Negative	16.3 ± 6.4	17.6 ± 5.1	18.4 ± 7.7	NS	–
Cognitive[b]	10.2 ± 3.1	14.4 ± 3.8	16.7 ± 4.2	F = 19.6, P < .0001[3]	–
Ways of coping Scores					
Distancing	1.2 ± 0.5	1.4 ± 0.3	1.0 ± 0.5	F = 3.9, P < .05[4]	F = 3.3, P < .05[4]
Positive reappraisal	1.1 ± 0.5	0.8 ± 0.6	1.6 ± 0.6	F = 1.5, P < .10	NS
Escape-avoidance	1.5 ± 0.5	1.5 ± 0.4	1.5 ± 0.7	NS	NS
Lifetime psychiatric hospitalizations	6.71 ± 6.6	4.4 ± 3.8	12.1 ± 9.6	F = 5.1, P < .01[5]	F = 4.6, P < .05[6]

a mean ± standard deviation;
b Cognitive component calculated without including the insight and judgment item

1 2 > 3 > 1   4 2 > 3
2 3 < 1, 3 < 2   5 3 < 2
3 1 < 2, 1 < 3   6 3 > 2

were found in the mean age, education, or level of positive or negative symptoms between the three groups. Both unaware clusters had significantly higher levels of cognitive symptoms than the aware cluster.

As summarized in Table 16.3, ANOVA also revealed differences in preference for distancing as a coping strategy. Post hoc tests found that the unaware–average executive function cluster had a greater preference for distancing than the unaware–poor executive function cluster. ANOVA also indicated differences in history of hospitalization. Here Fisher's LSD tests revealed that the unaware–poor executive function cluster had more hospitalizations than the unaware–average executive function group. No differences were found for distancing or hospitalizations between the aware group and unaware cluster. No overall differences were found for escape avoidance or positive reappraisal scores.

Lastly, given that group differences in executive function might contribute to the observed differences in distancing and hospitalization, we repeated our group comparisons this time using the WCST PE score as a covariate in ANCOVA. As summarized in Table 16.3, these ANCOVA and post hoc tests continued to find the same pattern of significant group differences.

Summary and Discussion

Results are consistent with the hypothesis that among persons with schizophrenia, there is a group unaware of their illness that has poor executive function and another unaware of their illness with better executive function. Our cluster analyses produced three groups of participants: one aware and two unaware. As predicted, the aware group had average executive function scores, while one of the unaware groups had average executive function and the other one poor executive function. Comparisons of group characteristics suggest the unaware–average executive function group had a greater preference for distancing but their coping score differed significantly only from the unaware–poor executive function group. Similarly, the unaware–poor executive function group had significantly more lifetime hospitalizations but also only differed statistically from the unaware–average executive function group.

These findings provide support for Startup's (1996) belief that among persons with schizophrenia spectrum disorders who are unaware of their disorder (55% of our sample) there are at least two very different subgroups. One group may only partially grasp the realities of their illness because of concurrent deficits in executive function (36% of our sample) while the other, with intact executive function (19% of our sample), may acknowledge little to nothing about their illness, due in part to a tendency to ignore or deny unpleasant realities. With regard to the specific coping strategy associated with unawareness of illness, the data point to a passive dismissal rather than active avoidance of stressors or the recasting of stressors as positive events.

Interestingly, the finding that the unaware–poor executive function group had nearly two-thirds fewer lifetime hospitalizations than the aware–average executive function group suggests that denial of illness may sometimes be adaptive in schizophrenia (Warner *et al.*, 1989), or it may merely indicate that such people will avoid all but involuntary hospitalizations despite severe symptoms. The higher scores on cognitive symptoms for the two unaware groups reinforces the relationship between impaired cognition and unawareness. This finding suggests that thought disorder, poor attention and other cognitive symptoms increase the likelihood of unawareness of illness, even when executive function is relatively preserved as was the case with the unaware group with average executive function.

Conclusions, limitations and future directions

In this chapter we have reported three related studies. In the first, unawareness of illness in schizophrenia was linked to particularly grave difficulties embracing the worker role in a rehabilitation program. In the second and third we found that many with limited awareness tend to have deficits in executive function, while a subgroup exists which has relatively intact executive function but other cognitive symptoms. They also show a greater preference for distancing as a coping strategy. Some evidence also emerged that complete unawareness of symptoms is linked to preference to positive reappraisal as a coping strategy.

There are limitations to these studies. All were correlational and causality cannot be determined. While results are consistent with the theoretical models discussed, each represents at best a "piece" of the larger picture and was exploratory in nature. Generalizability is limited by the fact that participants were generally males in their 40s, enrolled in treatment. Further research is thus needed with more diverse samples including women, persons in an earlier phase of illness, and those who refuse treatment. Since these and many other studies essentially measure function and beliefs during relatively brief intervals, longitudinal studies are also necessary to better understand variation in unawareness over time.

Lastly, we are beginning to ask what is happening within the narratives of persons with schizophrenia that they fail to capture the essential aspects of disorder commonly perceived by others. As noted elsewhere in more detail (Kleinman, 1988; Kirmayer and Corin, 1998; Lysaker *et al.*, 2003b) awareness of any type of illness is not merely an isolated cognition but an element of a larger personal and narrative understanding of one's life. Awareness or denial of illness is a collection of beliefs shared and remembered in a narratized form that is itself embedded in a larger life story. Do deficits in executive function result in accounts that are just too implausible? Does a preference for avoidant coping lead to the omission of key details, or does concrete thinking impede a person's ability to see themselves as part of a larger abstract group such as those with mental illness?

Answer to these questions about unawareness of illness may thus be especially important to a richer theoretical understanding of the whole recovery process for mental health consumers. Many believe that in schizophrenia, as for other disabilities, enhanced personal agency and wellness can involve a narrative transformation including the acknowledgment of illness, and the rejection of any attached stigmatizing beliefs. Perhaps then future research on these questions will assist professionals to better help persons with schizophrenia to convert unbearable aspects of their lives and symptoms into healing narratives, underscoring the humanity and transformational possibilities of every person.

Acknowledgment

Research funded by the Department of Veteran Affairs, Rehabilitation, Research, and Development Service, USA.

References

Amador, X. F., Strauss, D. H., Yale, S. A. and Gorman, J. M. (1991). Awareness of illness in schizophrenia. *Schizophr Bull*, **17**, 113–32.

Amador, X. F., Flaum, M., Andreasen, N., Strauss, D. H., Yale, S. A., Clark, S. C., *et al.* (1995). Awareness of illness in schizophrenia and mood disorders. *Archives of General Psychiatry*, **51**, 826–36.

Bartko, G., Herczeg, I. and Zador, G. (1988). Clinical symptomatology and drug compliance in schizophrenia. *Acta Psychiatric Scand*, 77, 74–6.

Bell, M. D., Lysaker, P. H., Goulet, J. G., Milstein, R. M. and Lindenmayer, J. P. (1994). Five component model of schizophrenia: Factorial invariance of the Positive and Negative Syndrome Scale. *Psychiatry Res*, 52, 295–303.

Bell, M. D., Bryson, G. J., Greig, T., Corcon, C. and Wexler, B. B. (2001). Neurocognitive enhancement therapy with work therapy: Effects on neuropsychological test performance. *Archives of General Psychiatry*, 58, 763–8.

Bryson, G. J., Bell, M. D., Lysaker, P. H. and Zito, W. X. (1997). The Work Behavior Inventory: A scale for the assessment of work behavior for clients with schizophrenia. *Psychiatric Rehabil J*, **20**, 47–55.

Carpenter, W. T., Bartko, J. J., Carpenter, C. L. and Strauss, J. S. (1976). Another view of schizophrenia subtypes: A report from the international pilot study of schizophrenia. *Archives of General Psychiatry*, 33, 508–16.

Corrigan, P. W., Nugent-Hirschbeck, J. and Wolf, M. (1995). Memory and vigilance training to improve social perception in schizophrenia. *Schizophr Res*, **17**, 257–65.

Cuffel, B. J., Alford, J., Fischer, E. P. and Owen, R. R. (1996). Awareness of illness in schizophrenia and outpatient treatment compliance. *Journal of Nervous and Mental Diseases*, **184**, 653–9.

David, A. S. (1990). Insight and psychosis. *British Journal of Psychiatry*, **156**, 798–805.

David, A. S., van Os, J., Harvey, I., Foerster, A. and Fahey, T. (1995). Insight and psychotic illness: Cross sectional and longitudinal associations. *British Journal of Psychiatry*, **176**, 621–8.

Davidson, L. and Strauss, J. S. (1995). Beyond the biopsychosocial model: Integrating disorder, health and recovery. *Psychiatry*, **58**, 44–55.

Dillon, W. R. and Goldstein, M. (1984). *Multivariate Analysis: Methods and applications.* New York: John Wiley and Sons.

Folkman, S. and Lazarus, R. S. (1988). *Ways of Coping Questionnaire Manual.* Palo Alto CA: Consulting Psychologists Press.

Francis, J. L. and Penn, D. L. (2001). The relationship between insight and social skill in persons with severe mental illness. *Journal of Nervous and Mental Diseases*, **189**, 822–9.

Green, M. F. (1996). What are the functional consequences of neurocognitive deficits in schizophrenia? *Am J Psychiatry*, **153** (3), 321–30.

Heaton, R. K., Chelune, G. J., Talley, J. L., Kay, G. G. and Curtiss, G. (1993). *Wisconsin Card Sorting Test manual: Revised and expanded*. Odessa: Psychological Assessment Resources, Inc.

Kay, S. R., Fizszbein, A. and Opler, L. A. (1987). The positive and negative syndrome scale for schizophrenia. *Schizophr Bull*, **13**, 261–76.

Kirmayer, L. J. and Corin, E. (1998). Inside knowledge: Cultural constructions of insight in psychosis. In X. F. Amador and A. S. David (ed.) *Insight and Psychosis*. New York: Oxford University Press.

Kleinman, A. (1988). *The Illness Narratives: Suffering, healing and the human condition*. New York: Basic Books.

Link, B. G. (1987). Understanding labeling effects in the area of mental disorders: An assessment of the effects of expectations of rejections. *American Sociological Review*, **52**, 96–112.

Lysaker, P. H., Bell, M. D., Milstein, R. M., Goulet, J. G. and Bryson, G. J. (1993). Work capacity in schizophrenia. *Hosp Comm Psychiatry*, **44**, 278–80.

Lysaker, P. H. and Bell, M. D. (1995). Work rehabilitation and improvements in insight in schizophrenia. *Journal of Nervous and Mental Diseases*, **183**, 103–7.

Lysaker, P. H. and Bell, M. D. (1994). Insight and cognitive impairment in schizophrenia: Performance on repeated administrations of the Wisconsin Card Sorting Test. *Journal of Nervous and Mental Diseases*, **182**, 656–60.

Lysaker, P. H., Bell, M. D. and Goulet, J. B. (1995). The Wisconsin Card Sorting Test and work performance in schizophrenia. *Psychiatry Res*, **56**, 45–51.

Lysaker, P. H, Bell, M. D., Bryson, G. J. and Kaplan ,E. (1998a). Psychosocial function and insight in schizophrenia. *Journal of Nervous and Mental Diseases*, **186**, 432–6.

Lysaker, P. H., Bell, M. D., Bryson, G. J. and Kaplan, E. (1998b). Neurocognitive Function and Insight in schizophrenia: Support for an Association with Impairments in Executive Function but not with Impairments in Global Function. *Acta Psychiatrica Scand*, **97**, 297–301.

Lysaker, P. H., Bell, M. D., Milstein, R. M., Bryson, G. J. and Goulet, J. (1994). Insight and psychosocial treatment compliance in schizophrenia. *Psychiatry*, **57**, 307–15.

Lysaker, P. H., Bryson, G. J. and Bell, M. D. (2002). Insight and work function in schizophrenia. *Journal of Nervous and Mental Diseases*, **190**, 142–6.

Lysaker, P. H., Bryson, G. J., Lancaster, R., Evans, J. D. and Bell, M. D. (2003a). Insight in schizophrenia: Associations with executive function and coping style. *Schizophrenia Research*, **59** (1), 41–7.

Lysaker, P. H., Lancaster, R. S., Davis, L. and Clements, C. A. (2003b). Patterns of neurocognitive deficits and unawareness of illness in schizophrenia. *Journal of Nervous and Mental Disease*, **1**, 38–45.

Lysaker, P. H., Wickett, A. M., Wilke, N. and Lysaker, J. T. (2003c). Narrative incoherence in schizophrenia: The absent agent-protagonist and the collapse of internal dialogue. *American Journal of Psychotherapy*, **57**, 153–66.

Marks, K. A., Fastenau, P. S., Lysaker, P. H. and Bond, G. R. (2000). Self-appraisal of illness questionnaire: Relationship to researcher-rated insight and neuropsychological validation. *Schizophr Res*. **45**, 203–11.

Mohamed, S., Fleming, S., Penn, P. and Spaulding, W. (1999). Insight in schizophrenia: Its relationship to measures of executive function. *Journal of Nervous and Mental Diseases*, **187**, 525–31.

Rollins, A,L., Bond, G. R. and Lysaker, P. H. (1999). Characteristics of coping with the symptoms of schizophrenia. *Schizophr Res*, **36**, 30.

Schwartz, R. C. (1998). The relationship between insight, illness and treatment outcome in schizophrenia. *Psychiatric Q*, **69**, 1–22.

Schwartz, R. C. (2001). Self-awareness in schizophrenia: Its relationship to depressive symptomatology and broad psychiatric impairments. *Journal of Nervous and Mental Diseases,* **189**, 401–3.

Smith, T. E., Hull, J. W., Goodman, M., Hedayat-Harris, A., Wilson, D. F., Isreal, L. M., *et al.* (1999). The relative influences of symptoms, insight and neurocognition on social adjustment in schizophrenia and schizoaffective disorder. *Journal of Nervous and Mental Diseases,* **187**, 102–8.

Spitzer, R., Williams, J., Gibbon, M. and First, M. (1994). *Structured Clinical Interview for DSM IV.* Biometrics Research: New York.

SPSS (1999a). *SPSS Base 10.0 Applications Guide.* SPSS, Inc.: Chicago.

SPSS (1999b). *SPSS Base 10.0 User's Guide.* SPSS, Inc.: Chicago

Startup, M. E. (1996). Insight and cognitive deficits in schizophrenia: evidence for a curvilinear relationship. *Psychological Medicine,* **26**, 1277–81.

Taylor, K. T. and Perkins, R. E. (1991). Identity and coping with mental illness in long-stay psychiatric rehabilitation. *Br J Clin Psychology,* **30**, 73–851.

Thompson, E. H. (1988). Variations in the self-concept of young adult chronic patients: Chronicity reconsidered. *Hosp Comm Psychiatry,* **39**, 771–5.

Wahl, O. F. and Harman, C. R. (1989). Family views of stigma. *Schizophr Bull,* **15**,131–4.

Warner, R., Taylor, D., Powers, M. and Hyman, R. (1989) Acceptance of the mental illness label by psychotic patients: effects on functioning. *American Journal of Orthopsychiatry,* **59**, 389–409.

Wechsler, D. (1997). *Wechsler Adult Intelligence Scale – III.* San Antonio, TX: Psychology Corporation.

Young, D. A., Davila, R. and Scher, H. (1993). Unawareness of illness and neuropsychological performance in schizophrenia. *Schizophr Res,* **10**, 117–24.

Young, D. A., Zakzanis, K. K. and Bailey, C. (1998) Further parameters of insight and neuropsychological deficit in schizophrenia and other chronic mental diseases. *Journal of Nervous and Mental Diseases,* **186**, 44–50.

Chapter 17

Inside "Insight" – a personal perspective on insight in psychosis

Frederick J. Frese III

As will be amplified in this chapter, it is my current belief that I have been living with a condition called schizophrenia for almost four decades now. I also believe that for me this condition is accompanied by tendencies toward aspects of paranoia. Because of these tendencies that I occasionally observe in myself, and the fact that I have been repeatedly diagnosed as having this disorder, some time ago I came to the conclusion that, all things considered, it is probably not inappropriate for me to think of myself as a paranoid schizophrenic, albeit one who is fortunate enough to spend lengthy periods in partial, and sometimes even in full, remission.

During the time that I have been living with this condition I have developed certain strategies so that I might better conduct myself in a manner that does not tend to upset my chronically normal friends and neighbors. I have previously produced a published list of aspects of coping with this schizophrenia in general (Frese, 1994, 1997). I would now like to take this opportunity to mention a few things about my strategy for living with the paranoid aspect of this condition.

As I see myself, I think that I am probably a bit more suspicious concerning some situations than is true for most others. One result of this tendency is that I tend to become relatively careful and somewhat circumspective whenever I feel that I, or my thoughts, might be viewed or examined by others.

In that this is a discussion of insight in psychosis, I feel that some further clarification of how I will be using this term is in order. This is because the meaning of the term, insight, varies from rather general – "knowledge of, or skill in (a particular subject or area)" – to more specialized uses of the term in psychology such as a "sudden perception of the solution to a problem or difficulty", and the even more specialized psychoanalytic use of the term, where it is defined as "perception of one's repressed drives and their origin".

Consonant with my tendency for circumspection, I suppose I can also point out that the term, insight, can be viewed as being phonologically isomorphic with "incite", as well as being viewed as a semantic intermediary between "foresight" and "hindsight". But these observations, while perhaps interesting, are obviously tangential to the primarily focus of this thesis.

Part I–A

My interpretation of the word "insight" for the purpose of this thesis will be restricted to the more common sense use of the term. That is, I am addressing the question, "Does a person who has 'schizophrenia', or other form of psychosis, understand that he has the condition, and what is the nature of that understanding?"

In order to address this question, I will draw primarily from the experience of the one person that I know best who has been repeatedly diagnosed with, and treated for this condition during the past four decades – namely myself.

To be more succinct, I will be addressing not only (1) the question of whether I have insight, but also, if one considers that I might have some insight, (2) to what degree do I have such insight, and (3) whether my description of insight as I see it has any relevance for others?

First to the question, "Do I have insight?"

My response to being faced with such a question is probably what one would expect from a person diagnosed with paranoid schizophrenia, that being, "exactly what are you asking me?" Are you asking whether I understand that my cognitive functioning will at times be different from that of other, more normal people?

"Yes, I understand and agree that I am different, but then all people are different to some degree, aren't they?"

You may then ask, "Do you understand that you have schizophrenia?"

I would respond that I know that in March of 1966, while I was in the U.S. Marine Corps, I was hospitalized and given the diagnosis of schizophrenia, which was followed by five months inpatient treatment for this condition.

I also know that about a year after my release from that military hospital, I was involuntarily hospitalized, after I had the experience of "breaking the code of the universe" during a Catholic mass service one Sunday morning in Milwaukee.

I also know that after my release from the public psychiatric hospital in Wisconsin, I spent the following year, without paid employment, residing in several states, being re-hospitalized for a time, and eventually being picked up by the police near Ohio State University in Columbus, for handing out money to passers by and proclaiming that people should remember that we are all in that same human family and that we should not focus so much on chasing after money.

At that point I was placed in an isolation room in a back ward of a very large state hospital. Eventually, I was taken to a courtroom in that hospital where I was told I had schizophrenia, which was explained to me as being degenerative disease from which people do not recover. I was also declared to be "insane" by the presiding magistrate and officially "committed" indefinitely to the care of the Ohio state psychiatric hospital system.

Following my release from Columbus State Hospital, I was hospitalized in one Veterans' Administration Hospital (in Chillicothe, Ohio) and later in private psychiatric facilities, in Cleveland, Ohio, and in Brevard County, Florida.

To this day I continue to receive treatment from the Veterans Administration. I notice that on the folder that I am regularly given to take to the pharmacy for my medications, after my scheduled interviews with my psychiatrist, I am identified as "Frederick J. Frese III – Paranoid Schizophrenic".

I would also mention that the medications that I have been prescribed during these years by various psychiatrists have consistently been anti-psychotics and drugs to help with their side-effects, with two or three brief periods where I was also prescribed medication for affective episodes.

All of the above would appear to indicate to me that I have a condition called schizophrenia, paranoid type.

Part I–B

However, I also acknowledge there are some in the mental health community who take exception to me identifying myself as having schizophrenia.

One obvious factor is that most of the time I function well enough to "pass for normal". Subsequent to my first being diagnosed I have managed to earn three additional academic degrees (one in management, two, including a doctorate, in psychology), and I managed to maintain full-time employment as a psychologist and administrator in Ohio's State mental health system until my retirement in 1995. Additionally, I have managed to maintain part-time employment with the Summit County Mental Health Board (three days per week), and academic appointments at the local medical schools, since leaving my full-time civil service position with the State. And I have been married for 27 years now during which my wife and I have managed to raise four children to adulthood.

As a result of my "normal-type appearance" and activities I am occasionally told by respected psychiatrists and others that "I cannot be schizophrenic. I must have been misdiagnosed."

I am aware that the diagnostic criteria for schizophrenia have changed since I was originally diagnosed. I also know that American psychiatrists were found to be diagnosing schizophrenia at three times the rate of British psychiatrists and as a consequence altered their practice in this regard subsequent to my first being diagnosed (Valenstein, 1988). I also am aware that the diagnosis "schizo-affective disorder" was not in the psychiatrist's diagnostic manual until the publication of the DSM-III in 1980, well after my initial diagnosis. In this regard, an excellent expanded discussion concerning organized psychiatry's evolving approaches to defining schizophrenia, has been laid out by the late Lasker Award Recipient, Seymour Solomon Kety (1985).

In the light of the above, I therefore respect the fact that arguments can be made that if I were being diagnosed today, I might be diagnosed with something other than schizophrenia. Nevertheless, my view is that, as much as I might like to be reclassified (promoted) to being a person with schizoaffective disorder, or bipolar illness, or some other, less stigmatizing condition, the weight of the historical evidence suggests to me that I have had a condition for almost four decades now that a reasonable person might characterize as schizophrenia.

I find that those who communicate to me that I am not schizophrenic because the rules have changed since my original diagnosis are usually younger psychiatrists or other mental health professionals. They suggest, that because the diagnostic criteria for schizophrenia have been revised since my initial diagnosis, I cannot currently be schizophrenic and properly should have another diagnosis. They have claimed that I have been misdiagnosed.

While I respect the opinions of these professionals, I do not feel that I should have to change my view of myself because organized psychiatry has decided to change its diagnostic system. I tend to view the well-meaning professionals who insist that I change how I characterize my condition because there has been a change in wording in the latest iteration of the DSM as being revisionistic. Although I can understand the arguments of my revisionistic friends, I (1) believe that I probably continue to meet even the revised criteria for schizophrenia and (2) in that my "official" diagnosis continues to be schizophrenia, or a form thereof, I really do not want to go to the trouble of having to mount an official challenge to that segment of the psychiatric profession that has had me classified as schizophrenic during all these years.

On the other side of the psychiatric coin, I also occasionally run into professionals, usually somewhat more senior, who tend to be influenced by the Kraepelinian tradition. Dr. Emil Kraepelin (1902), of course, referred to what we now call schizophrenia as dementia praecox and believed that this disorder was essentially a degenerating brain disease from which one did not recover. Professionals of this viewpoint also occasionally offer the opinion that I have been misdiagnosed, but the justification for their opinion rests on a quite different assumption about the nature of schizophrenia than does that of our revisionistic colleagues. I fondly view those who contribute opinions based on the belief that schizophrenics cannot recover as venerable, but perhaps a little antediluvian in their outlook.

Still another group in the mental health field who take exception to me identifying myself as schizophrenic is a subgroup of consumer activists who generally identify themselves as "survivors". These, often high-profile, activists with whom I am fairly frequently in contact and whose membership continues to include a surprising number of psychiatrists and psychologists, will often be most insistent that I cannot possibly be schizophrenic because they are quite certain that there is no such thing as schizophrenia or any other mental illness. Interestingly they are able to find substantive support for their beliefs in this regard from highly credentialed, well-published professionals such as Drs. Szasz (1961), Breggin (1991), and Bassman (1997).

Yet another group who are not comfortable with my characterizing myself as being schizophrenic are the good-hearted reformers, many of whom have for some reason decided that the world will be a better place for persons like myself if we are referred to only with "person first" language. These well-meaning individuals, often mental health advocates or administrators, frequently insist that I cannot be "schizophrenic" because if I were, I must dutifully identify myself as "a person with schizophrenia". My repeated response to these "person first word-police", is that if an alcoholic does not have to be a "person with alcoholism" and a diabetic does not have to be a "person with diabetes" those of us with schizophrenia should also be afforded the dignity of being able to choose whether we are comfortable with this particular "person first" vehicle for political correctness.

So, regarding insight into my condition, if I acknowledge that I have schizophrenia, I must recognize that there are at lease four influential segments of the mental health community who will view this characterization of my condition as a lack of understanding, and presumably a lack of insight (from their perspective). This being the case, I nevertheless maintain that my contention that I have schizophrenia is an indication of at least some modicum of insight into this condition that I believe I have.

Part II

I understand, however, that simply because a person recognizes that he carries the diagnosis of schizophrenia, that does not necessarily mean he has insight as to the nature of this condition. Real insight would seem to require that the person with the condition be able to describe that he understands how he is affected by this condition. He should be able to describe how this condition causes him to think, feel, perceive, or act in a manner that is unusual enough to be considered "not normal".

In order to communicate how I see my cognitive processes appear to be different, let me reflect on the circumstances which accompanied my early manifestations of this condition.

First, I initially came to believe that high-ranking officials had been "hypnotized by the enemy" and were engaging in untoward behaviors that could be harmful to our country. My original belief was that the enemy had developed a new psychological weapon and was influencing the thoughts and behaviors of our leaders. Subsequently I have come to realize that all people engage in untoward behaviors from time to time, but this is not necessarily evidence that some human enemy has hypnotized them. I am still of the belief that high-ranking officials (and others) engage in unfortunate behavior from time to time, but I no longer assume that this behavior is a function of an enemy's newly developed weapon system.

Second, concerning my subsequent breakdowns, I notice in retrospect that each time I began to experience an episode, my mind would begin to behave in a particular manner. As I would go into psychosis I would begin to make connections that would lead my thought processes to come to conclusions that in retrospect were very strange. Since those early days I have come to understand that every few months my mind will start over-connecting concepts and ideas. At first this activity can be very interesting, but I have learned that if I allow this process to continue, I will soon be talking and acting in a manner that other persons may view as being problematic.

Because of these experiences, in recent years I have come to appreciate the statement in DSM-IV-TR (American Psychiatric Association, 2000) that "disorganized thinking ("formal thought disorder") has been argued by some to be the single most important feature of schizophrenia." Although the DSM-IV-TR goes on to operationalize thought disorder primarily in terms of observable speech, it has been my observation that the same sort of descriptions in the DSM of the articulated indications of thought disorder – "slip(ping) off the track", "derailment", "loose associations", "tangentiality", etc. – are indeed good descriptions of what happens with my thought processes, even when unspoken, as I begin to edge toward and experience an episode of psychosis.

When I begin to have these experiences, I have learned that it is best to withdraw from highly stimulating situations, and usually increase the dose of my medication. Sometimes I will not recognize that my mind is beginning to over-connect as these episodes begin until after others bring to my attention that I may be speaking or acting in a strange or even bizarre manner. But fortunately, during the past few decades, I have always been able to catch myself before I have had to be hospitalized.

I have been told that I tend to rebound from these episodes much faster than most persons diagnosed with schizophrenia. For this ability I am most grateful, in that I am able to limit my time away from work and other productive activity to fairly short periods.

Although I feel I have fairly good insight overall concerning the fact that I have this condition, I do want to stress that as one begins to enter a state of "over-connecting" it is very difficult to realize that you are entering this state as you are in the process of experiencing it. Therefore, regarding the matter of insight, even after I have come to the realization that I have this condition, it does not necessarily follow that I have insight as to what is transpiring at the time my mind begins a journey toward the state of psychosis.

Part III

First, one's development of insight can to a large degree be related to one's experience with the condition. When I initially came down with this condition four decades ago, my over-connecting thought process led me to conclusions that were most terrifying for me. I was filled with the fear that "the enemy" was planning to eliminate me because I had discovered their new weapon.

As I experienced additional psychotic breaks, I have come to realize that my "discoveries" in the world of having an expanded horizon of meaningfulness need not be terrifying. More importantly, recognition that I have a brain that is subject to more lability in neurochemical reactivity than are the brains of my more normal friends has been a great help in my development of what insight I may be seen to have.

I am stressing that for me the insight that I may have developed seems to be in large part a function of learning from my experience with my own breakdowns. I am fully aware that many others who have had numerous breakdowns still do not accept that they have a psychotic condition, however. Therefore for some persons with this condition, repeated episodes, in and of themselves, do not necessarily lead to insight. It has been my experience that a person's acceptance that they have such a condition seems to be related to how well they understand how the functioning of the brain is related to cognitive and perceptual processes, but there are many exceptions to this observation.

Second, there continue to be many divergent views as to the causes and correlates of schizophrenia and other forms of psychosis. These conditions are still not well understood. As a result, we continue to have strong opinions concerning these disorders held by various segments in the mental health community. Although I feel I have developed some degree of insight regarding the way my mind works, I fully recognize that others may have very different approaches to viewing this condition. I respect all those views, particularly if they are held by persons who have personal experience with these phenomena. Indeed, I feel that it is quite possible for persons to make progress toward recovery independent of their having insight or understanding with respect to the disorder. Certainly one does not have to subscribe to my admittedly rather biological perspective of the condition in order to be seen as having insight or making recovery.

Conclusion

In conclusion, let me summarize the points I have with respect to my personal experiences as they relate to this condition of schizophrenia.

First, insight is not necessarily related to how others view your condition, because others often do not agree among themselves concerning their own views.

Second, insight involves more than accepting that you have a condition that others view as mental illness. Insight also entails development of an understanding of how such a condition affects you and hopefully learning how best to live with such a condition.

Third, I have come to understand that I have a condition that I must constantly learn to live with. I am most comfortable in viewing this as a brain-based condition where my thoughts, feelings and perceptions tend to be affected by brain activity. However, just because I am comfortable with this perspective on this disorder, that does not mean that I necessarily feel that this is the only way anyone can develop insight. Others may have more philosophical, mystical or even religious interpretations of their experiences and may also see themselves as having developed insight.

Finally, let me say that, regardless of our personal interpretations of our adventures, I am so very pleased with how we, on the whole, view these disorders compared to the world I found myself in the spring of 1966. Today we catch these disorders much earlier. I am so pleased when I meet youngsters who have been recently diagnosed and are doing well on their medication. I am also so pleased when I meet older, more experienced consumers who readily identify themselves as being schizophrenic or schizoaffective, who frequently show no obvious signs of disability.

Insight is hard earned and difficult to come by when you have a disorder that can so readily induce you into developing firm beliefs that seem so real to you, even when others so readily recognize that you may no longer be in good contact with reality. It is my hope those who are struck with these conditions in the future will increasingly be able to develop adequate insight as to how their minds are functioning compared to what has been the case for so many of us in the past.

References

American Psychiatric Association (2000). *Diagnostic and Statistical Manual of Mental Disorders*, fourth edition, text revision. Washington DC: American Psychiatric Association.

Bassman, R. (1997). The mental health system: Experiences from both sides of the locked doors. *Professional Psychology: Research and Practice*, **28** (3), 238–42.

Breggin, P. R. (1991). *Toxic Psychiatry*. New York: St. Martin's Press.

Frese, F. J. (1994). Twelve aspects of coping for persons with schizophrenia. *Innovations and Research*, **2** (3), 39–46.

Frese, F. J. (1997). Twelve aspects of coping for persons with serious mental illness. In L. Spaniel, C. Gagne, and M. Koehler (ed.) *Psychological and Social Aspects of Psychiatric Disability*, pp. 145–55. Boston: Center for Psychiatric Rehabilitation.

Kety, S. S. (1985). The concept of schizophrenia. In M. Alpert (ed.) *Controversies in Schizophrenia*, pp. 3–11. New York: Guilford Press.

Kraepelin, E. (1902). *Clinical Psychiatry: A textbook for students and physicians*, 6th edn, (trans. A. R. Diefendorf). New York: Macmillan.

Szasz, T. S. (1961). *The Myth of Mental Illness*. New York: Harper and Row.

Valenstein, E. S. (1988). *Blaming the Brain*. New York: The Free Press.

Chapter 18

The clinical importance of insight: An overview

Anthony S. David

The publication of *Insight and Psychosis* (Amador and David, 1998) in 1998 and this subsequent edition, attests to the revival in interest in the concept of insight in psychosis since Aubrey Lewis' first foray into this area in 1934 (David, 1999). A number of reviews paved its way (see, for example, David, 1990; Amador, Strauss, Yale and Gorman, 1991; Ghaemi and Pope, 1994). One might cite the clutch of studies published by Joe McEvoy and his colleagues in 1989 as being the harbinger of this modern revival. Since then there has been a steady and growing output of publications on insight sufficient for systematic review (see Kampman and Lehtinen, 1999; Mintz *et al.*, 2003a).

Assessing insight has always been seen as an important part of phenomenology and psychopathology and is defined in most textbooks of psychiatry and abnormal psychology, although usage and definitions of the term vary (Markova and Berrios, 1992; Berrios and Markova, Chapter 2 this volume). There are now a wide range of psychometrically tested instruments for assessing insight and related constructs (see Amador and Seckinger, 1997; Sanz *et al.*, 1998; Amador, Chapter 1 this volume). In the last edition of *Insight and Psychosis* I stated that "the clinical importance of insight is now being studied" and that "certain themes have been addressed". These included, the relationship between insight and treatment compliance (McEvoy, Apperson *et al.*, 1989a; Buchanan, 1992; McEvoy, Chapter 15 this volume; McFarlane and Lukens 1998); acting upon hallucinations (Rogers, Gillis, Turner and Frise-Smith, 1990) and delusions (Buchanan *et al.*, 1993; Buchanan and Wessely, Chapter 14; Torrey, Chapter 12 this volume) and the nature of delusions (Garety, Chapter 5 this volume); the specificity of poor insight for the diagnosis of schizophrenia (Amador *et al.*, 1994; Wing, Cooper and Sartorius, 1974; Amador and Kronengold, Chapter 1 this volume 4); the relationship of insight with depression (Kiersky, 1998; Ghaemi *et al.*, Chapter 6 this volume) and positive and negative symptoms of schizophrenia (Cuesta and Peralta, 1994; Kemp and Lambert, 1995; Selten *et al.*, 1998); the value of insight as a predictor of outcome (McGlashan, 1981; McEvoy, Appelbaum, Apperson, Geller and Freter, 1989). At that time work had also begun to look at insight in anorexia nervosa (Greenfield *et al.*, 1991); the relationship of insight to cognitive impairment (Young, Davila and Scher, 1993; McEvoy, Freter, Merritt and Apperson, 1993; Cuesta and Peralta, 1994; Lysaker and Bell, 1994 Chapter 16 this volume; Morgan and David, Chapter 9 this volume) and cerebral volumetric changes (Takai, Uematsu, Hirofumi, Sone and Kaiya, 1992, see Flashman and Roth, Chapter 8 this volume); much of the data were based on relatively small samples with measures taken at a single point in time.

It is now possible to review the relationship between insight and these variables plus many others with reference to several published papers and to observe the tendency for the methodology to improve as time passes. Furthermore, other topics have become linked to insight, such as assessment of needs (Carter, 2003), premorbid personality (Debowska *et al.*, 1998; Lysaker *et al.*, 1999) interpersonal relationships and social context (Startup, 1998; Francis and Penn, 2001; Vaz *et al.*, 2002; White *et al.*, 2000), suicidal thoughts and behaviour (Kim *et al.*, 2003; Yen *et al.*, 2002; see Ghaemi, Chapter 6 this volume), recovery style (Tait *et al.*, 2003) coping style (Lysaker *et al.*, 2003) including religious belief (Kirov *et al.*, 1998); quality of life (Ritsner, 2003; Doyle *et al.*, 1999), duration of untreated psychosis (Drake *et al.*, 2000) family attitudes (Main *et al.*, 1993; Smith *et al.*, 1997; Chen *et al.*, 2001) work performance (see Lysaker *et al.*, 2002 and Chapter 16 this volume), child care ability (Mullick *et al.*, 2001) differential effects of atypical versus typical antipsychotic drugs (Pallanti *et al.*, 1999; Aguglia *et al.*, 2002; Sajatovic *et al.*, 2002; Buckley *et al.*, 2001) and competency (Neumann *et al.*, 1996). That is not to say that each of these issues has been dealt with once and for all, on the contrary, often such studies succeed most in revealing unanticipated complexity.

Fractionation of insight

One way of trying to justify insight as important clinically and beginning the task of constructing cognitive models, involves fractionation. By this I mean showing first that insight is not entirely reducible to psychopathology (that is, it adds something to talk about insight, having already established the presence of delusions, hallucinations, etc.) and second that within insight there are separable components. A third level of fractionation is the demonstration of some independence in the application of such components of insight in different domains. In 1990 I proposed that insight be viewed as three overlapping dimensions, embodied in a brief Schedule for the Assessment of Insight (SAI) (David, 1990):

1   The awareness that one is suffering from a mental illness or condition;

2   The ability to relabel mental events such as hallucinations and delusions as pathological;

3   Acceptance of the need for treatment.

A possible fourth element has been called *hypothetical contradiction* by Brett-Jones, Garety and Hemsley (1987) and seems to entail a test of perspective taking. Further fractionation of the basic insight concept is possible: Kemp and David (1997) suggested that awareness of illness should also encompass awareness of change. It is readily understandable that a person may note a change in him or herself without taking the additional step of illness attribution. This led us to expand the original insight schedule (SAI-E) and this has since been validated against the old measure and found to have good utility (Sanz *et al.*, 1998).

Similarly, a patient may be able to label certain mental events but not others – analogous to the extreme specificity seen in some neurological cases (see Kinsbourne, 1998; Jehkonen *et al.*, 2000). For example, the patient may recognize memory impairment but not blindness, the paradoxical combination first noted by Gabriel Anton at the end of the nineteenth century (David, Owen and Forstl, 1993) and extended more recently by Young, De Haan and Newcombe (1990). The latter studied a woman who, after a stroke, was aware of her rather mild memory loss but not a much more profound facial recognition deficit (see also Barr, 1998; Keefe, 1998 ; Laroi *et al.*, Chapter 7 this volume). Detailed study of awareness of deficits is a growing area of interest in neuropsychiatry, especially Alzheimer's disease (Mullen *et al.*, 1995; Clare, 2003a and b). A striking example of the lack of correspondence between awareness in different domains is that between the abnormal movements of tardive dyskinesia (Sandyk *et al.*, 1993) and of mental disorder in the same people (Arango *et al.*, 1999; see Amador and Kronengold; Chapter 1 this volume).

Markova and Berrios (2001 and Chapter 2 this volume) have questioned the analogy between insight in psychiatric disorders (however defined) and lack of awareness in neurological disorders; in particular the "content" of the awareness. Building on their observations we might expect that awareness of motor paralysis – which is visible to the outside observer – may require a different set of cognitive operations than awareness of cognitive deficits (e.g., memory), which though demonstrable objectively and relatively easily quantified, are different again from awareness of behaviours which are abnormal by virtue of violation of social rules, or indeed, purely subjective experiences or mental states (beliefs, perceptions, hallucinations etc.), some of which we chose to label rightly or wrongly as signs and symptoms of mental disorder. There are then several additional steps from awareness, through attribution to action (e.g., help-seeking or violence (see Buchanan and Wessely, Chapter 14 this volume).

Finally, acceptance of treatment may include acceptance of *the need for treatment* without actual compliance. There are also instances where behavioral acceptance dissociates from verbalized acceptance and indeed this verbal–behavior discordance may apply to all of the proposed dimensions of insight and itself may fluctuate markedly over time. The expanded schedule includes further rating of compliance to take this into account. Although this fractionation has some face validity and arguments may be advanced in its support, does it have (a) empirical support and (b) is it of heuristic value?

Empirical support

Is insight separable from psychopathology?

Using principal components analysis (PCA), David, Buchanan, Reed and Almeida (1992), Peralta and Cuesta (1994) and Aga, Agarwal and Gupta (1995) each found that the different elements of insight all loaded on a single factor. However, all of these studies emphasize the relatively weak correlation with overall psychopathology as rated by scales such as the Brief Psychiatric Rating Scale (BPRS) (Overall and Gorham, 1962). David *et al.* (1992) found a correlation of r = −0.31 (n = 91, P < 0.005) between the Present State Examination (PSE) (Wing *et al.*, 1974) total symptom score and the SAI total score. Peralta and Cuesta (1994) used PCA to examine insight and psychopathology using the Scale for the Assessment of Positive Symptoms (SAPS) (Andreasen, 1984) and found that while insight produced a factor explaining 19.6% of the variance, negative symptoms, thought disorder and delusions and hallucinations each loaded on separate factors.

McEvoy, Apperson *et al.* (1989a) were the first to propose an insight scale (as a single dimension) called the Insight and Treatment Attitudes Questionnaire (ITAQ). In a study of 52 acute or acute-on-chronic schizophrenic patients, they found a variable correspondence between BPRS scores and ITAQ at various time points, including acute admission and follow-up, reaching a maximum of r = −0.35 (P = 0.006) at 14 days post admission. Michalakeas *et al.* (1994) also used the ITAQ to examine insight and psychopathology using the BPRS in 77 patients with schizophrenia and mood disorders. They found that ITAQ and BPRS correlated poorly in the schizophrenic group at various points during admission, but reached r = −0.4 (P < 0.007) at discharge. However, the correlations were consistently stronger in the manic group and weaker in the depressives.

Birchwood *et al.* (1994) adapted the SAI for use as a self-report measure. Again PCA derived a single factor from the three subscales and found that the scale had the sensitivity to detect change in psychopathology in 31 acute patients undergoing treatment. However, the intercorrelation between components was moderate (r = 0.42 on average). David *et al.* (1992), found that the items intercorrelated at r between 0.51 and 0.26. Kulhara, Basu *et al.* (1992) followed 22 inpatients in Chandigarh, India and calculated correlation coefficients with the BPRS on admission and after one and two weeks as well as intercorrelations among the three dimensions from the SAI. Like David *et al.* they found that compliance and relabeling showed the weakest, and compliance and illness awareness the strongest, intercorrelation. The (negative) relationship with symptom severity, as measured by the BPRS, was significant only after the second week: r between 0.47 and 0.26, again, remarkably similar to David's figures in spite of the different populations under study. Kulhara, Chakrabarti and Basu (1992) then compared a small group of schizophrenic and affective disorder patients and found that the latter group had better insight. The overall correlation between SAI-E and BPRS total score found by Sanz *et al.* (1998) in 33 psychosis patients was again of this order (r = −0.53).

Single or multiple dimensions?

Cuesta and Peralta (1994) reported correlations between compliance and both relabelling and awareness of 0.5 but a correlation of 0.87 was found between awareness and relabelling (n = 40). A similar pattern but with lower and marginally significant results was found by McCabe *et al.* (2000) in a study of 78 chronic outpatients (r's = 0.15, 0.09 and 0.32, respectively) and with an intermediate level of strength of association by Morgan *et al.* (in preparation; David *et al.*, 2003) in 116 first episode mixed psychotic patients (compliance and: awareness; r = 0.56, relabelling r = 0.41; awareness and relabelling, r = 0.54). A principal components analysis of the SAI-E was also carried out (David *et al.*, 2003) which this time yielded a three-factor solution mirroring the proposed three dimensions, which accounted for 66.5% of the variance with hypothetical contradiction loading on the first relabelling factor. Trauer and Sacks (2000) used the Birchwood scale in a large sample of 218 community patients with severe mental illness. Using a confirmatory factor analytic technique they were able to extract three latent variables, which fit with the three insight dimensions in the scale.

In summary, correlations between "total insight scores" and "psychopathology scores" – each rated on standardized scales are consistently weak to moderate supporting a prima facie case for regarding insight as being more than "just psychopathology". Longitudinal studies (see later) confirm this view. The particular subdivision of insight proposed in 1990 seems to have some support using factor analytic methods in sample sizes >100. Correlational analyses show moderate intercorrelation between components, of an order that suggests both common variance an independence.

Insight and individual symptoms/symptom clusters

The study by Amador *et al.* (1994), the largest study of its kind to date involving 412 patients with psychotic or severe mood disorders from a variety of centers, used the Scale to Assess Unawareness of Mental Disorder (SUMD) to examine the diagnostic specificity of insight. Unawareness of mental disorder in general, its consequences and the efficacy of medication, plus six specific symptoms, were inquired about and rated on a 0–3 scale. Overall, the DSM-111R schizophrenia group (n = 221) showed the poorest insight even though some 41% of them were aware that they suffered from a mental disorder. Of interest is the proportion of schizophrenia patients who were completely unaware of individual symptoms. This ranged from 28% for asociality to 58% for delusions. Severity of positive symptoms measured by the SAPS, e.g., delusions, correlated with SUMD items with coefficients ranging from 0.14 to 0.23 (worse symptoms, less awareness).

The relationship between insight and hallucinations is another area that has been addressed, although David *et al.* (1992) found no relation between these in any modality and insight. Fulford (1989, Chapter 3 this volume) has argued that hallucinations are false beliefs about possible perceptions and thus a subset of delusions; Garety and colleagues have concentrated on delusions themselves and have shown that the dimensions of delusional beliefs, such as strength of conviction, preoccupation and so on, are also dissociable (see Garety and Hemsley, 1987; Kendler, Glazer and Morgenstern, 1983; Garety, Chapter 5 this volume). Sanz *et al.* (1988) reported that the item of the

BPRS with which total insight scores correlated most strongly (negatively) was that for delusions (n = 33; r = −0.54) and remained so even after controlling for other symptoms.

In the Amador *et al.* study (1994), hallucinations were regarded as real in 39.5% of schizophrenics (the proportions in the other diagnostic groups were not significantly different). Such awareness did not appear to relate to current or past functioning (as measured by the Global Assessment Scale) (GAS) (Endicott, Spitzer and Fleiss, 1976), unlike other positive and negative symptoms. This concurs with data from a phenomenological survey of 100 psychotic hallucinators (Nayani and David, 1996) with a variety of diagnoses. The belief that the hallucination "came from outside" did not seem to covary with insight into illness more broadly defined. Insight was, however, positively correlated with the number of coping mechanisms employed by the subject (r = 0.26, *P* = 0.001). Hence, insight does not appear to be enmeshed in the process whereby perceptions, even those derived from internal cognitive processes such as those underlying auditory–verbal hallucinations (David, 1994), are apprehended, but occurs in some sense after the fact. Nevertheless, there did seem to be a link between bizarre delusions and lack of awareness of the unreal nature of hallucinations in Amador *et al.*'s survey.

Positive vs. negative symptoms

Insight as currently defined is conceptually related more to positive symptoms – hallucinations, delusions and productive thought disorder – than to negative or deficit symptoms. Indeed, this accords with lay views of what constitutes mental illness as McEvoy, Schooler, Friedman, Steingard and Allen (1993) demonstrated by recording judgments of case vignettes. Amador *et al.* (1994) hint that patients with deficit symptoms have poorer insight in general, although the actual awareness of such symptoms was not greatly different and if anything slightly better than their positive counterparts. Taking a broad overview, lack of insight has been linked to both positive and negative symptoms in different patient groups (David *et al.*, 1992; Amador *et al.*, 1993, 1994; Kemp and Lambert, 1995; Collins *et al.*, 1997; Carroll *et al.*, 1999; Smith *et al.*, 1998; Goldberg *et al.*, 2001; Buckley *et al.*, 2001; Vaz *et al.*, 2002; Rossell *et al.*, 2003). Patients undergoing acute relapse (Sanz *et al.*, 1998) as well as those with chronic conditions (Schwartz, 1998; Collins *et al.*, 1997) show significant correlations between positive rather than negative symptoms and poor insight, whereas Cuesta and Zarzuela (1998) found a significant relationship in acute schizophrenics between poor insight and negative symptoms. Selten *et al.* (Selten, van den Bosch and Sijben, 1998) discussed insight in relation to negative symptoms in the previous edition of *Insight and Psychosis* (1998). They have also shown that subjective distress with negative symptoms was explained in part by insight into positive symptoms (Selten, Wiersma and van den Bosch, 2000).

The mechanisms underlying insight into positive and negative symptoms may be different. Mohamed *et al.* (1999) found that deficits in executive function correlated with insight into negative, but not positive, symptoms which they speculate is dependant on other intra- and inter-personal processes (see Morgan and David, Chapter 9 this volume). The fundamentally different nature of positive and negative symptoms, as well as their different status in the eyes of lay people, implies that different processes are required to register them (see below).

Relationships have also been found between insight and a disorganized dimension (Amador et al., 1994; Cuesta and Zarzuela, 1998; Kim et al., 1997a; Lysaker and Bell, 1994; Smith et al., 1998, 1999) and grandiosity (Kemp and Lambert, 1995; David and Kemp, 1998; David et al., 1995). Smith et al. (1998) showed that in the course of treatment, insight and symptoms (particularly disorganization) tended to improve in tandem, more so in inpatients than outpatients. Also, as depression worsened so awareness increased.

Cuesta et al. (1996) investigated the relationships between those subjective experiences in schizophrenia which conform to neither positive nor negative symptoms and neuropsychological performance. As in Kim et al. (1997b), subjective experiences did not correlate with insight but scores were highly correlated to neuropsychological performance. This rules out a global deficit in detection of impairment and again emphasizes that awareness is separable from attribution. Data from a study of late paraphrenia, a condition characterized by florid positive symptomatology, illustrates the positive–negative distinction. Almeida, Howard, Levy and David (1996) plotted SAPS scores and scores on the High Royds Evaluation of Negativity Scale (HENS) (Mortimer, McKenna, Lund and Mannuzza, 1989) against the SAI total score and found the now expected modest correlation with positive symptoms (n = 40; r = -0.48, $P < 0.001$). However, HENS scores showed no discernable relationship (r = -0.1).

Reviewing these questions systematically and using meta-analytic techniques, Mintz et al. (2003a) concluded that there was a "small negative relationship between insight and global, positive and negative symptoms. There was also a small positive relationship between insight and depressive symptoms in schizophrenia". However, these associations seemed to be moderated by such variables as acute vs. chronic illness and age of onset. In the acute phase, relationships with insight tend to be stronger.

Heuristic interest

If the dissociability or relative independence of insight components can be established, this opens up various possibilities for understanding and even management. If treatment compliance can be separated – to a degree – from delusions and hallucinations or awareness of illness, then it may be possible to improve compliance without the symptoms having first to abate or without the requirement that the individual accepts the illness label. It is possible that compliance may be a facet of personality and stable across a number of situations, but that it evolves across the individual's life span. Similarly, it could be hypothesized that recognizing that one has an illness is tightly culture bound and will be aligned with other illness beliefs and models. Hence, this aspect of insight should vary according to culture and perhaps ethnicity (as suggested by Johnson and Orrell, 1995; see also Perkins and Moodley, 1993a; Goldberg et al., 2001; Saravanan et al., 2004). On the other hand, the neurological analogy with anosognosia may be more applicable to the relabelling of abnormal phenomena or "self-monitoring" (Blakemore and Frith, 2003; Kircher and David, 2003), and so would be predicted to be relatively hard-wired and universal.

Whether or not our multidimensional view of insight is correct, it seems to have sufficient face validity and adaptability to have been taken up in a variety of settings and countries (see Tables 18.1a and 18.1b). Reviewing published studies that have used multidimensional insight measures in clinical populations both in the UK,

Table 18.1a Summary of studies from countries other than UK and USA that used multidimensional insight scales developed in the Europe and North American countries

Authors/ Study Site	Subjects	Insight scale	Total mean scores	Sub-items score
Kulhara et al. (1992) India	22 Mixed psychosis	SAI	Admission – 1.75 Discharge – 4.75	NA
Aga et al. (1995) India	59 ICD-10/SZ	SAI (Hindi translation)	4.9	NA
Kim et al. (1997) Japan	63 ICD-10/SZ	SAI	7.8	Awareness – 3.49 Relabeling – 1.26 Compliance – 3.04
Collins et al. (1997) Canada	58 DSM III-R/SZ	SAI	8.5	NA
Tharyan and Saravanan (2000) India	67 ICD-10/SZ	SUMD		Awareness – 2.2 Medication – 1.8 Consequence – 2.3
Cuesta et al. (2000) Spain	75 DSM IV/SZ, SA and PMD	SUMD		Awareness – 2.6 Medication – 2.8 Consequence – 2.7 Symptoms – 2.9
Chen et al. (2001) Hong Kong	80 psychotic inpatients	SUMD (Chinese translation)	9.4+	NA
Hayashi et al. (2001 Japan	118 DSM-IV/SZ	SUMD		Awareness – 2.6 Medication – 2.4 Consequence – 2.6)
Thompson et al. (2001) Australia	456 SSD	SUMD		
Yen et al. (2002) Taiwan	74 DSM IV SZ	SAI	7.4	Awareness – 3.1 Relabeling – 1.6 Compliance – 2.7

Table 18.1b Summary of studies from the UK and USA that used multidimensional insight scales

Authors/ Study Site	Subjects	Insight scale	Total mean scores	Sub-items score
David et al. (1992) UK	91 Mixed psychosis	SAI	7.7 (9.5)#	NA
Amador et al. (1994), USA	412 Psychotic and mood disorder patients	SUMD		Awareness – 1.9 Medication – 1.7 Consequence – 1.9 Symptoms – 2.1
Kemp et al. (1996) UK	22 ICD-10/SZ	SAI-E	5.8	Awareness – 2.1 Relabeling – 0.8 Compliance – 1.7
Almeida et al. (1996) UK	40 ICD-10/ Paraphrenia	SAI	4.3	NA
Sanz et al. (1998) UK	33 Mixed psychosis	SAI SAI-E	7.0 12.1	NA
Garavan et al. (1998) Ireland	82 DSM III-R/SZ	SAI	8.4	NA
Smith et al. (1999) USA	46 DSM-IV/SZ and SA	SUMD		Awareness* Medication* Consequence* Symptoms – 2.1
Pini et al. (2001) USA	236 DSM-IV/SZ, SA and PMD	SUMD		Awareness – 2.0 Medication – 2.5 Consequence – 2.3 Symptoms – 2.9
McCabe et al. (2002) UK	89 DSM III-R/SZ	SAI	7.5	Awareness – 2.7 Relabeling – 1.9 Compliance – 2.7

SAI, Schedule for the Assessment of Insight; SAI-E, Schedule for the Assessment of Insight-Expanded version; SUMD, Scale to Assess Unawareness of Mental Disorder; BPRS, Brief Psychiatric Rating Scale; RDC, Research Diagnostic Criteria (Spitzer et al., 1978); WCST, Wisconsin Card Sorting Test; NA, Not Available for Comparison

+ Total SUMD score used   * Skewed distribution of the data

Grand total sore

North America and the rest of the world, there is a certain consistency around the ratings – depending mostly on the acuteness of the clinical disorder being assessed. There is also some impression of a pattern in that the item with the most consistency appears to be the ability to "relabel" psychotic symptoms, which was generally scored lower than other dimensions. This may be because poor insight is at least in part a form of neuro-psychological deficit somewhat independent of cultural influences, as posited above.

Can unawareness of illness be caused merely by lack of knowledge, i.e. patients cannot re-label their experiences as pathological, because they do not know the criteria of mental disorder (see Lam *et al.*, 1996; Chung *et al.*, 1997)? However plausible this explanation may seem, supporting evidence is lacking. Startup (1997) discovered a close to normal ability of patients to recognize the symptoms of mental illness in others (as tested using case vignettes), but this was in stark contrast to their impaired awareness of illness in themselves (as inferred from ITAQ scores). McEvoy *et al.* (1993b) had earlier shown that schizophrenia patients admitted to (or were more aware of) negative symptoms than positive ones (see also Amador *et al.*, 1994). At the same time, patients considered negative features as least typical of mental illness (cf. positive symptoms). Moreover, the study revealed selectivity of (un)awareness towards those negative symptoms which could be construed as most pejorative (e.g., loss of motivation). This is in line work by Swanson *et al.* (1995), where patients with schizophrenia and mania were shown the vignettes describing the examples of positive, negative and manic psychopathology. On admission, schizophrenia patients rated themselves as significantly less similar to the positive symptom vignettes than psychiatrists' rated them, although the patients correctly labelled the presented signs as pathological. Patients with mania did not differ from the psychiatrists' rating of their similarity to the vignettes, but they strongly denied that the vignettes reflected mental illness. It is likely that in at least some cases apparent lack of insight might be determined by the reluctance of the patients to admit having socially undesirable characteristics.

The vignette study mentioned above also raised another dissociation, that between self and other perception. Those symptoms that patients rated as indicating mental illness, correctly in the view of the psychiatrists involved, were generally regarded as less applicable to themselves than to others (McEvoy, Schooler *et al.*, 1993). This need not apply just to psychotic symptoms. Social inappropriateness was correctly identified in videotaped role-plays by schizophrenic patients, but they rated their own, at times inappropriate behaviour as higher in social appropriateness than judges (Carni and Nevid, 1992). In considering such work, we must not forget that, like many aspects of insight, the perfect self-knowledge that we seem to demand of our patients is an unattainable ideal. To assume that those of us who are not psychotic have the gift to "see ourselves as others see us"[1], especially in complex social situations, would be to display a profound lack of insight.

Against insight

It is curious to observe the strength of feeling among professionals when the topic of insight is considered. The first of two editorials for the *Lancet* (1990) medical journal belittled academic exploration of the concept, arguing that this was pretentious or "hifalutin" – "academically nourishing but clinically sterile". The second (Joyce, 1993) discarded the cloak of anonymity and seemed to be in favour of preserving the mystery

---

[1] Robert Burns, Scots poet (1759–1796).

of insight as though it was beyond scientific explanation. More cogent criticism has come from mental health professionals worried about the judgment of insight, framed by Perkins and Moodley (1993b) as a kind of political coercion of the disenfranchised (the mentally ill) by a powerful "Eurocentric" body, better known as psychiatrists.

Ignoring the antipsychiatry rhetoric, these critics do highlight the sociocultural influences on illness beliefs that, as mentioned above, must surely be relevant to insight or elements of it (see Kirmayer and Corin, Chapter 10 this volume; Kim, Chapter 11 this volume; Saravanan *et al.*, 2004). Similarly, considering compliance, there may be many reasons, some of them perfectly reasonable – not the least of which is unpleasant side effects – why some patients refuse medication. It would be disingenuous to ascribe all of these to a psychopathological symptom we choose to call poor insight.[2] However, while Van Putten (1974) drew attention to the adverse influence extrapyramidal side effects (EPS) have on such adherence, he later showed (Van Putten *et al.*, 1976) that, when these were abolished or minimized, some patients continue to refuse medication on account of their denial of illness (or, in some cases, enjoyment of it). It has also been shown that neither EPS (Pan and Tantum, 1989) nor a history of adverse effects (Marder *et al.*, 1983) reliably discriminates between medication compliance and non-compliance in depot clinics and open inpatient units, respectively. Moreover, Marder's group went on to show that the belief that medication was beneficial exerted a strong influence on consent to treatment (see McEvoy, Chapter 15 this volume). This is dealt with at length by McEvoy and in recent reviews (Lacro *et al.*, 2002; Perkins, 2002); it appears that insight, or more generally illness beliefs tend to emerge as the decisive factors governing adherence rather than the nature of the experience of medication. Such attitudes persist in patients despite switching from typical to atypical antipsychotics (Loffler *et al.*, 2003). Lastly, the general public appears to have ambivalent attitudes to medication. The US General Social Survey carried out in 1998 showed that while 77% agreed that "medications help people control their [psychiatric] symptoms", only 30–40% would take them for stresses they could no longer cope with or symptoms of depression (Croghan *et al.*, 2003).

Another criticism related to compliance is the perceived tautology between insight, comprising, in part, compliance yet being used to predict compliance (Beck-Sandler, 1998; Budd *et al.*, 1997; but see David, 1998b). This is a potential pitfall for those investigating insight and compliance but is generally well recognized and guarded against (David 1999). The multidimensional concept of insight allows the investigator to omit the compliance dimension when examining treatment adherence (Trauer and Sacks, 2000; McCabe *et al.*, 2000).

A more "moral" objection levelled at insight and by implication insight researchers is that by in some sense promoting insight, one exposes a ". . . *risk to the self-identity of individuals with psychosis from engulfment into the devalued patient role*" (Beck-Sandler, 1998).

---

[2] Indeed, the term *treatment compliance*, entomologically reducible to "bending with," is too passive, less attractive than and perhaps ethically inferior to treatment adherence or "sticking to" (Holm, 1993).

Others have raised similar concerns in more or less conciliatory language (McCabe and Quayle, 2002). Much of this concern is related to the conundrum regarding the inverse relationship between insight and depression. Conventional psychiatric dogma has it that there is a clear causal sequence: a person develops insight into their illness, sees the bleak future ahead and becomes depressed (see e.g., Carroll *et al.*, 1999). Lack of insight is seen as "protective". As one commentator put it, it is bad enough being told you have a mental illness but why add "insight to injury"? The truth may be more complex. Iqbal *et al.* (2000) in a detailed longitudinal study of "post psychotic depression" in which patients recovering from psychosis were interviewed five times over one year found that increases in insight did not predate increasing low mood: they tended to change together so that, at the very least, it is conceivable that lowered mood engenders a more self-critical attitude which may foster insight, rather than *vice versa* (see Ghaemi, Chapter 6 this volume). Qualitative research has made a significant contribution to this debate. Roe and Kravetz (2003) weigh up the pros and cons from the consumer and professional points of view and cite the avoidance of "self-stigmatization" as one problem of gaining insight, which is to be avoided.

There is scant evidence that accepting the mental illness label worsens prognosis or increases perceived stigma. On the contrary, outcome may be improved. External attributions lead to poor outcome (Warner *et al.*, 1989). The hypothetical paranoid patient who makes external attributions to protect his self esteem or regain control over his life at the expense of complying with treatment, is headed for relapse, readmission and social decline and all the stigma and loss of esteem that goes with it. It has been argued that even in the extreme circumstance where treatment is enforced and control is temporarily taken away by the clinical team, the benefits to the individual greatly outweigh the costs (Kane *et al.*, 1983; Kjellin *et al.*, 1997). Indeed in ongoing work, colleagues and I have found that such "hindsight approval" or retrospective insight occurs in a significant minority of patients who have undergone involuntary admission and treatment and this correlates with insight formally assessed at discharge (Hubbeling *et al.*, 2001).

Few people advocate insight into schizophrenia as a necessary end in itself from a theoretical point of view and certainly not on an individual therapeutic level. However, if clinicians avoid the issue they may be guilty of a form of collusion or self-deception, which mirrors the problem itself. As an enterprise, research into insight is, in my view, not a matter of pressurizing people with psychotic disorders to conform in some totalitarian way – far from it. It is about recognizing the awareness that does exist about problems and contradictions in one's "personal narrative" (Lysaker *et al.*, 2002). In short it is more about insight than lack of insight (David, 1998).

Insight and outcome

State or trait?

In order to convince the sceptic of the clinical importance of insight over and above the other features of psychosis, which may wax and wane with treatment and recovery, it must be shown to be predictive and somewhat enduring. Since the first edition of Insight and Psychosis was published evidence has accumulated on what happens to insight, however broadly defined, over time within an episode (Cuesta *et al.*, 2000; Weiler *et al.*, 2000), although tracking insight in general or its dimensions over successive illness episodes remains under-researched. There is some evidence on compliance (Hoge *et al.*, 1990; Buchanan, 1992) that suggests that patterns of non-compliance repeat themselves in successive relapses of psychosis. McEvoy, Freter and Merritt *et al.* (1993) followed a small group of outpatients and found that initial ITAQ scores in 22 subjects correlated with those one year later at $r = 0.7$, the mean difference being 0.6 points (SD = 4.5). In an earlier study of inpatients, McEvoy, Apperson and colleagues (1989a) found that while psychopathology improves with treatment (see also Carroll *et al.*, 1999; Smith *et al.*, 1998), insight might be slower to change. Some authors have found an inverse association between insight and the number of previous hospitalizations when studied at a single time point. The scenario is of a person who may recover from an illness, yet deny that he or she was ill and refuse or discontinue maintenance therapy and contact with his or her carer, only to relapse and repeat the cycle. However, clinical experience suggests that such a negative cycle need not be inevitable. Some individuals appear to learn from experience and develop insight. When calculating a simple correlation between insight and number of hospitalizations, such individual variation may be obscured (David *et al.*, 1992).

Data from a longitudinal cohort study of a large representative sample of first episode psychotic patients admitted to hospital in south east London (van Os *et al.*, 1996) have been analysed further to explore the correlates and associations of insight (David *et al.*, 1995; see later). One hundred and fifty only had full data sets including a simple insight measure derived from the PSE (item 104). The observation frames were: (1) at recruitment of the cohort, a within-episode comparison; and (2) follow-up of cohort (those cases who were psychotic, n = 94) after four years: the insight measures showed some correlation over time (Pearson's $r = 0.23$, $P = 0.039$). Not surprisingly, insight measured by the SAI and PSE correlated very highly ($r = -0.85$). Twenty-six subjects were psychotic and in hospital at the time of the second assessment, four years after the first. Their mean PSE insight score was 2.27 (SD = 0.78) on the first occasion and 1.92 (SD = 0.98) on the second, a trend toward improvement; the two scores were moderately correlated ($r = 0.344$, $P = 0.085$). It should be noted that the patients might not have been at equivalent phases of their illness on both occasions.

An interesting prospective study by Chen and colleagues (2001) sheds light on the stability of insight. Eighty consecutive patients in Hong Kong with psychosis were assessed at weekly intervals over their admission, which was on average around four weeks. Symptoms and insight as assessed by the SUMD improved – the moderate correlation between insight and positive symptom change was in line with previous work (see above). However, the authors found that a minority of patients showed a deterioration in their insight despite symptomatic improvement. Part of the explanation for this seemed to be changes in executive function. Improvements on Wisconsin card sorting test performance (fewer perseverative errors) correlated more strongly with improvements in insight (partial correlation coefficient – controlling for education – was 0.39, $P = 0.015$). Younger patients showed greater insight changes, in both directions, than older patients.

Cuesta and colleagues (2000) examined 75 psychotic patients first, after remission of an acute episode and again after 6 months. They used three different insight measures, including the ITAQ and SUMD. All the scales showed a pattern of rather weak correlations with psychopathological dimensions at both time points although all three showed similar, significant improvements. Additionally, each measure showed strong correlations with itself across time, for example ITAQ: $r = 0.62$ and SUMD awareness of mental disorder (current), $r = 0.64$ – in essence a demonstration of test–retest reliability. Weiler et al. (2000) in a large study across acute patients with schizophrenia, bipolar disorder and other related disorders found that *change* (i.e., improvement) in insight as assessed with the ITAQ correlated with symptomatic improvements on the BPRS over the course of hospital treatment. A recent study from Canada (Mintz et al., 2003b) followed 180 with early psychosis and found that insight (assessed from the Positive and Negative Syndrome Scale for Schizophrenia [PANSS] [Kay et al., 1987]) improved at 3, 6 and 12 month assessments, along with improvements in positive and negative symptoms (range of Pearson's r values: 0.27–0.47). The largest change was in the first three months.

To summarize the results of studies that have looked at insight scores at more than one point in time, there are consistent indications that insight varies to some extent with psychopathology – the association being modest and variable across studies (a "state" effect). The strength of association between insight scores measured at two or more time points with the same instrument is somewhat stronger and could be interpreted as demonstrating a trait-like quality.

Insight and outcome: the effect of medication adherence

The relationship between treatment adherence or compliance and other facets of insight has already been mentioned above and covered in detail (McEvoy, Chapter 15 this volume). Since treatment with neuroleptic agents undoubtedly confers a better outcome on psychosis, at least in the short and probably medium term (Valenstein et al., 2002) and since insight *has something to do with* compliance (although the two terms are far from synonymous), it follows that insight and outcome *ought* to be related. As stated earlier, beliefs about illness and the origin of symptoms and about the effects of medication on the illness and symptoms, predict medication compliance to a moderate degree (Bartko, Herczeg and Zador, 1988; Van Putten, 1974; Pan and Tantum, 1989; Lin, Spiga and Fortsch, 1979; Marder et al., 1983; Adams and Howe, 1993; Cuffel et al., 1996; Kampman et al., 2002; Corrigan, 2002), leaving a stubborn proportion of the variance unexplained.

Can insight be improved?

Traditional psycho-educational methods do not necessarily improve illness awareness and adherence to medication (Streicker *et al.*, 1986). Seltzer *et al.* (1980) studied the effects of six sessions of didactic education providing mainly medication information. Knowledge about medication was enhanced but actual compliance was not improved. Eckman and colleagues (1990, 1992) used an intensive behaviourally orientated group programme aimed at improving compliance and medication management skills in out-patients with schizophrenia. The study showed that medication management skills could be learned and utilised over a three month follow-up. Compliance as independently assessed improved significantly from about 60% to 80%. Therefore, this was a group with relatively good baseline compliance. MacPherson *et al.* (1996) examined the effectiveness of a single and a three-session psychoeducational intervention in a group of 64 schizophrenia patients. Insight and knowledge about medication improved, most of all in the three-session group, but compliance as rated on the SAI did not. Carroll and colleagues (1999) carried out a randomized controlled trial with 100 schizophrenia patients, of an educational package said to be designed to improve insight. It consisted of a video and booklet which, "explained the biomedical model of mental illness . . . and emphasized the value of maintenance medication". The intervention had no effect.

Two studies (Kemp *et al.*, 1996; Lecompte and Pelc, 1996) have shown that insight and outcome can both be changed for the better in tandem with compliance. "Compliance Therapy" (CT) (Kemp *et al.*, 1996, 1998) draws inspiration from a number of sources, e.g., the approaches of motivational interviewing (Miller and Rollnick, 1991) and cognitive–behavioural therapy of schizophrenia (Garety *et al.*, 1994). The intervention used in the Kemp *et al.*, studies was deliberately kept simple and consisted of 4–6 sessions during hospital admission, each lasting less than 1 hour, with a view to it being easy to teach and disseminate (Surguladze *et al.*, 2001). The results of the study showed improvements, compared with a control group who had "non-specific counselling" in addition to their routine clinical care, in attitudes to medication, insight (as measured by the SAI-E) and global functioning (see Figure 18.1). Survival curves over 18-months

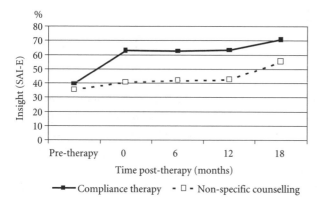

Fig. 18.1 Randomized controlled trial of compliance therapy vs non-specific counselling: Insight (SAI-E) [data from Kemp *et al.* (1998)].

or more follow-up (Kemp *et al.*, 1998) showed a significant increase in the time before readmission in the intervention group while the controls had approximately two-times the risk of readmission. Finally, Turkington and colleagues (2002) tested the effectiveness of a broad cognitive behavioural intervention in a large pragmatic trial of over 400 community patients with schizophrenia in the UK and showed improvements in general symptomatology and insight scores.

Such work has now been subjected to a number of systematic reviews (Pekkala and Merinder, 2000; Cormac *et al.*, 2000; Zygmunt *et al.*, 2002; Nosé *et al.*, 2003). The unanimous conclusion is that treatment adherence can be improved with the right kind of targeted cognitive behavioural intervention.

Insight and prognosis

Historical perspective

Ever since Emil Kraepelin's attempt to delineate dementia praecox (schizophrenia) from manic depressive insanity at the end of the last century, psychiatrists have looked toward prognosis as the most powerful arbiter of validity of any psychopathological construct. Seminal work by Strauss and Carpenter in the mid 1970s (1974) and more recently by Warner (1985) raised a weakness in this method if only illness-related factors were considered, since the premorbid adjustment and the prevailing socioeconomic climate both exert substantial influences on the outcome of psychosis. The extent to which insight into psychosis is determined premorbidly or is intrinsic to the morbid process, or the result of the interface between illness and culture, are all questions for research. As stated, a working hypothesis could be proffered to the effect that illness beliefs are especially malleable by culture; that compliance might be somewhat more of a premorbid characteristic distributed differently among individuals in a population (yet still influenced by learning and experience); and that the ability to relabel psychotic phenomena as symptoms of a disorder is more a cognitive ability vulnerable to disruption by the disorder itself. Since the same array of influences may act differentially upon the presence of delusions, negative symptoms, age of onset and so on, insight is no more or less worthy of consideration as a prognostic indicator as any other traditional predictor.

It is hard to imagine a modern, naturalistic study of the relationship of insight to prognosis that was not confounded, to some extent, by adherence to medication or other treatments. Historical cohort studies, such as those undertaken by Kraepelin, Bleuler and Langfeldt in the early twentieth century, did not isolate insight as a possible explanatory variable. Poor compliance was clearly not the same source of despair for clinicians then as it is today. This may be because the treatments available were not effective (although many were believed to be so at the time), or perhaps because patients were *submitted* to treatment by their relatives or on the instruction of the psychiatrist, with little regard for their own views. Another reason why insight was not examined as a predictor of outcome may have been because absence of insight was seen as the *sine qua non* for psychosis (see Berrios and Markova, Chapter 2 this volume). In his textbook *Dementia Praecox and Paraphrenia* (1919), Kraepelin discussed aspects of what we might term insight under the heading of "judgment": "the faculty of judgment .. suffers without exception severe injury .. [in] the judgment of circumstances not hitherto experienced and in *particular of their own state* .. they not infrequently commit the grossest blunders" (italics added; p. 25).

Later, when discussing course, Kraepelin writes that the initial episode may quickly resolve: "He [the patient] knows time and place and the people round him, remembers all that has happened, even his own nonsensical actions, *admits he is ill . . .*" but, he goes on: "a lack of clear understanding of morbid phenomena as a whole will always be found on more accurate examination" (p. 182).

Later still, Kraepelin discusses the "observation of self" and notes that in patients with dementia praecox, unlike those with manic depressive illness,

> it is only with difficulty that a glance is gained into the occurrences of their inner life, even when the patients are able to give utterance without difficulty to their thoughts, they are taciturn, repellent, evade questions, give indefinite information that tells nothing.

(p. 264)

Psychiatrists from the Johns Hopkins Hospital, Baltimore (Stephens *et al.*, 2000) have been able to go back over records of patients diagnosed and hospitalised with "a paranoid state" during 1913 to 1940. They found that poor insight, as judged by modern standards, did indeed predict a poorer outcome over the subsequent 5 years post-discharge (2/31 in the unimproved group "showed insight" compared with 11/28 of those who recovered or were improved). Even the classic follow-up studies in the immediate pre- and peri-neuroleptic era (e.g., Valliant, 1964; Stephens, Astrup and Mangrum, 1966) failed to examine the prognostic implications of insight – or if they did, it clearly did not emerge as a significant finding (see Carpenter, Bartko, Strauss and Hawk, 1978).

Modern studies of insight and level of functioning

Cross-sectional studies are able to show a relationship of insight or awareness to current functioning and previous course. One of the first to do so (Roback and Abramowitz, 1979) was atypical, since the author's concept of insight was more akin to that used in psychoanalysis, which includes viewing symptoms as a reflection of intrapsychic conflicts rather than attributing them to illness (see Reid and Finesinger, 1952). Perhaps this explains why individuals in that study, though rated as better adjusted, felt themselves to be less so and were generally more troubled. Taylor and Perkins (1991) interviewed 30 residents of a rehabilitation unit for chronic psychiatric disabilities. They found that those who denied mental health problems had a longer history of contact with services, but higher self-esteem and less subjective distress. Takai and colleagues (1992) from Gifu, Japan, investigated 57 chronic schizophrenic patients (mean duration of illness, 16 years; age 39). As well as being the first group to show an association between poor insight and cerebral ventricular enlargement using MRI, Takai *et al.* also demonstrated an association with number of prior hospitalizations ($r = 0.23$), which remained significant after a multiple regression analysis that controlled for other clinical variables. Work from Australia by O'Connor and Herrman (1993) was aimed primarily at identifying factors related to successful rehabilitation. The SAI was used in 41 schizophrenic patients and the 21 with low insight scores (<9) spent more than six months in the programme and 8 of them spent more than two years. Other factors, such as cognitive impairment and negative symptoms, were particularly influential. Amador *et al.* (1993) showed that the number of previous admissions was associated with current awareness of mental disorder and acknowledgment of the possibility of future illness.

Peralta and Cuesta (1994) from Spain surveyed 115 inpatients and showed that, while awareness of illness and symptoms did not correlate significantly with global functioning or refusal of treatment, these insight parameters did correlate with the number of previous hospitalizations ($r = -0.23$ and -0.3, respectively). Amador *et al.* (1994) found modest negative correlations between most items of the SUMD and the GAS, for current functioning and GAS estimated for the preceding year, in their survey of around 400 patients. Rossi *et al.* (2000) assessed 30 schizophrenia patients using the SUMD and showed that those with poor outcome – as classified according to the Strauss–Carpenter scale had higher scores indicating lower awareness of symptoms, particularly, "negative" symptoms such as asociality and blunted affect. Young *et al.* (1998) combined samples from sites in Europe and North America in order to look at insight (using the SUMD) and neuropsychological deficits in 108 schizophrenia patients and 21 with bipolar disorder. They found that, for example, awareness of current symptoms correlated with activities of daily living competence in both groups; WCST performance may have confounded this relationship or it may be on the causal pathway (see Morgan and David Chapter 9 this volume). Finally, Trauer and Sacks (2000) showed clear relationships between clinician-rated social functioning and self-report insight measures in a large community sample.

Many of these studies shed light on the relevance of insight to the course of illness, but have tended to concentrate on chronic cases, whose course and outcome are by definition poor and did so at a single point in time (see David, *Insight and Psychosis*, 1998 for details).

Involuntary treatment

It is to be expected that refusal of treatment is reflected in measures of lack of awareness of illness or poor insight. McEvoy, Appelbaum *et al.* (1989) showed that 12 patients who required involuntary commitment had significantly lower ITAQ scores than the remainder and showed less improvement in such scores after treatment compared with their voluntarily treated counterparts. David *et al.* (1992) showed that, while voluntary and involuntary psychotic patients had similar levels of psychopathology the latter had clearly lower insight scores. Similar patterns have been found in manic patients (Ghaemi *et al.*, 1995).

On the other hand Weiler *et al.* (2000) found that while involuntary patients had significantly lower insight scores in the ITAQ than voluntary patients, improvement in insight between admission and discharge did not interact with civil status (i.e. they both improved to a similar extent). Ullrich and colleagues from Germany (1995) reported that certain changes in awareness of illness occurred with treatment but patients' "illness models" did not change. Unpublished data from a study carried out by Dr Dieneke Hubbeling and our group at the Maudsley Hospital, London (2001) examined measures of insight and psychopathology in relation to objective and subjective coercion. Like our previous study (David *et al.*, 1992) the levels of insight (as measured on the SAI-E) were significantly lower in the involuntary patients but on this occasion, psychopathology was also correspondingly higher. Insight improved in both groups by the end of the hospital stay. SAI-E scores between admission and discharge correlated significantly (r = 0.41, $P < 0.01$, n = 60) – a trait-like effect [see above]). The involuntary patients perceived much greater levels of coercion as assessed using the MacArthur Admission Experience Survey (AES) (Gardner *et al.*, 1993), but across the groups, the lower the insight, the higher the perceived coercion (r = −0.48, $P < 0.01$).

Going back to the pre-neuroleptic era, a survey of psychiatric admissions to an English county in the 1930s and 1940s analysed by Shepherd (1957) showed that approximately 50% of patients who were "certified" that is, involuntary admissions, failed to recover and leave hospital over a five-year period compared to just under 20% of those admitted voluntarily. There may be an element of self-fulfilling prophecy here, in that the act of certification may have determined the length of admission. However, the finding is also understandable in terms of a subgroup of patients lacking in insight having a poorer prognosis.

Insight and prognosis: Prospective studies

Table 18.2 summarizes studies with a prospective design from which the influence of insight on prognosis can be inferred. Soskis and Bowers (1969) must be credited with one of the first of these. Their patients were assessed three to seven years after discharge and it was found that those who viewed their illness as a personal experience to be learned from and integrated had better post hospital adjustment. These patients may not have met modern criteria for schizophrenia. McGlashan (1981) used methods devised by Soskis and Bowers (1969) to study the effects of attitudes toward recent illness on recovery and found that a realistic attitude regarding past illness correlated with more desirable employment and social outcomes after one year. Such work provoked interest in what is now known as recovery style, although not all contemporary authors accept that this is related to insight (Tait *et al.*, 2003).

Heinrichs, Cohen and Carpenter (1985) had the case records of 38 current outpatients rated, blind to course. Some 24 were regarded as having had early insight on their first relapse and of these, only two required readmission subsequently, compared to 7 of the remaining 14. The study was only quasi-prospective and there was no

Table 18.2 Prospective studies examining the relationship between insight and clinical outcome

Authors (year)	Subjects diagnostic criteria for schizophrenia	Follow-ups (yrs)	Relationship between insight and clinical outcome
Soskis and Bowers (1969)	32 "Schizophrenia" NB centre had psycho- therapeutic orientation	3–7	Posthospital adjustment if illness seen as learning experience (not no. of admissions)
McGlashan et al. (1981)	30 DSM-11	1	Soskis and Bowers scale predicted quality of work and less time in hospital
Heinrichs et al. (1985)	38 RDC schizophrenia or schizoaffective	Variable index adm to next adm	24 with "early insight on their first relapse" 2 required readmission, 7 of the remaining 14 readmitted
McEvoy et al. (1989)	52 DSM-111	2.5–3.5	Readmission sign associated with ITAQ; trend to predict compliance at 30 days post discharge
Buchanan (1992)	61 RDC	1 and 2	'Do you think you have been unwell/ become ill again?' Not associated with compliance Previous compliance predicted future compliance at 1 year.
McEvoy et al. (1993)	24 DSM-111 schizophrenia or schizoaffective	1	ITAQ did not predict exacerbation; 3 readmitted patients had lower intial insight

Lysaker and Bell (1995)	44 DSM-IIIR schizophrenia or Schizoaffective with impaired insight	26-week work placement	Poor insight (>4 on PANSS) improved in 61% of Ss after rehabilitation, predicted by cognitive function.
Van Os et al. (1996)	166 RDC	4 (mean)	Duration of hospitalization during follow-up and independent living
David et al. (1995)	150 RDC Psychotics (subset of van Os)	4 (mean)	PSE insight predictive of subsequent insight and attitudes to treatment
Schwartz et al. (1997)	23 DSM-IV chronic in-patients	1	SUMD. Psychosocial skills and GAF lower in 'poor' insight group, "good" insight predicted improvement on GAF
Weiler et al. (2000)	187 DSM-IIIR patients: 81 schizophrenia 40 bipolar	Admission vs. discharge	Change in ITAQ correlated with improvements on the BPRS

FRSF: Functional skills rating form

RDC: Research diagnostic criteria

DSM: *Diagnostic and Statistical Manual*

ITAQ: Insight and treatment attitudes questionnaire

PANSS: Positive and negative syndrome scale for schizophrenia

BPRS: Brief psychiatric rating scale

SUMD: Scale to assess unawareness of mental disorder

adjustment for person-years of follow-up. The findings were not explained by medication compliance or severity of illness. The same methodological weaknesses apply to Van Putten *et al.*'s 1976 study. They were especially interested in medication refusal. Seven cases who were later characterized as persistent refusers (out of 29) had insight as determined by a simple definition (similar to the PSE) rated on admission, while 18 out of 30 compliers were insightful. More recently Drake *et al.* (2000) studied predictors of the DUP in a first admission sample of 248 schizophrenia or schizophreniform patients. The insight item of the PANSS was the strongest single predictor (correlation coefficient of 0.35). Length of DUP itself predicted a poor treatment response.

A truly prospective study was undertaken by Buchanan (1992) on 61 patients from the Maudsley Hospital. Insight was judged on the basis of a number of questions, particularly, "Do you think you have been unwell during this admission?" And, "Do you think you will become ill again?" He found that the answers did not predict later compliance after one or two years, whereas more directly assessed beliefs in treatment efficacy and an optimistic outlook (e.g., faith in chances of recovery) were predictive, at least after one year.

McEvoy, Freter, Everett *et al.* (1989) followed 52 schizophrenic patients having rated them on the ITAQ. The authors demonstrated the predictive validity of the measure for rehospitalization (61% were admitted again at least once) as well as compliance. However, they emphasize the importance of other mediating factors, particularly the quality of the aftercare environment. A later study by McEvoy, Freter, Merritt *et al.* (1993) recruited 24 stable outpatients from the Western Psychiatric Institute and Clinic, Pittsburgh. Eleven had exacerbations over a one-year follow-up period, but initial insight scores, BPRS ratings and psychometric testing results did not differ between this group and the remainder. There is a hint that the three patients who required readmission were less insightful on the ITAQ measure. The small numbers involved preclude firm conclusions on this issue.

Predictors of outcome were examined by van Os *et al.* (1996) using their cohort of recent-onset psychotic patients (see above). Data were available on 166 cases. The authors carried out a factor analysis on the major categories of symptoms derived from the PSE. This revealed seven psychopathological dimensions that corresponded broadly to subsyndromes of acute and chronic schizophrenic illness, mania, depressive psychosis and delusional states, and explained 63% of the variance. A further factor was lack of insight, based on the PSE interviews, and explained 8% of the total variance. A variety of clinical and social outcome measures were obtained on the cohort. Using logistic regression techniques, van Os and colleagues (1996) found that initial lack of insight was predictive of the time spent in hospital and living independently over the follow-up period of four years on average and this effect was independent of DSM-III-R diagnosis, sociodemographic factors and other prognostic indicators.

Insight at index assessment was moderately, but significantly associated with later perceived helpfulness of hospitalization and medication (r = 0.21, $P < 0.05$) but not day care (r = 0.09; see David *et al.*, 1995). At follow-up (i.e., cross-sectionally), the correlations were much stronger (r's ranged from 0.54 to 0.61).

Schwartz *et al.* (1997) used the SUMD to investigate whether insight could predict responsiveness to an intensive skills-based rehabilitation program. Dividing their small group of chronic patients into "good" and "poor" insight subgroups they showed that while some baseline functioning measures were related to awareness of illness, insight was a more powerful predictor of psychosocial improvement. Whether this represents a truly causal association is not immediately clear.

Insight and suicide

Up until now the direction of the associations between insight and outcome have been positive – more insight, better outcome. However, as noted, many clinicians have raised concern that too much insight in major mental illness, may lead to depression, demoralization and even suicide. Although suicidal thoughts have been shown to increase with insight in some reports (Schwartz, 2000), no link with suicidal behaviour has been established unequivocally (Amador *et al.*, 1996). Indeed lack of insight has also been shown to predict suicide (Steblaj *et al.*, 1999). Thankfully suicide is a relatively rare outcome; this means that a true effect might easily by lost amidst statistical noise. In the largest study to date to address this issue on 333 schizophrenia patients, a secondary analysis of a multi-centre clozapine trial (Kim *et al.*, 2003), insight as measured on a single dimension was associated with more pathological scores on an index that combined suicidal thoughts and behaviour. However, it was one of many factors and did not remain significant in a multiple regression analysis, which revealed hopelessness to be the most important.

Conclusions

We have reviewed the clinical relevance of the insight concept. Most researchers have accepted the notion that it is a multidimensional construct and there is some empirical evidence to back this up.

There are now many insight–assessment instruments to assist (and confuse) researchers (see Amador and Kronengold, Chapter 1 this volume), fortunately they seem to be measuring a similar construct (Sanz *et al.*, 1998; Cuesta *et al.*, 2000). The time is ripe for a systematic comparison of all of these. I would favour those instruments that enable the components of insight to be scored separately.

The "domain specificity" of insight is only just beginning to be considered. This includes the traditional "psychiatric" areas such as awareness of and attribution for one's own behaviour versus that of another; awareness of and attribution for certain symptoms but not others; as well as awareness of cognitive impairment, interpersonal behaviours and involuntary movements.

Insight is associated with psychopathology and hence is influenced by clinical "state". This includes positive and negative psychotic symptoms as well as disorganization. An inverse relationship with depression (worse depression, better insight) is a frequent finding. All these associations are of an order that suggests they are closely but not intimately related.

Insight relates to familiar outcome variables, treatment compliance and voluntary versus involuntary commitment to hospital. This information needs to be bolstered by more prospective studies and is a relatively new addition to the psychiatric credo. It would be wrong to overemphasize the prognostic implications of insight, since it is only one factor among many and may be confounded by factors such as cognitive and executive dysfunction.

Some studies suggest that insight predicts symptomatic resolution and improvement in global and work functioning with treatment.

Regarding the stability of insight across illness episodes, insight at the beginning of an episode seems to correlate positively with insight at the end – it shows some trait-like behaviour. Insight early in a disorder may act by improving early warning systems and trigger early therapeutic interventions.

Insight has a relationship with depressed mood but the direction of causality is far from clear. It may be that they are simply two sides of the same coin and hence inseparable. A potential association with suicide has not been confirmed.

Yet again it is worth repeating Aubrey Lewis' words which ended his 1934 essay on insight: "I should be the last to suggest for these views finality or completeness." I am sure all contributors to this volume would echo that sentiment.

Acknowledgements

I am indebted to Dr Kevin Morgan for sharing some of his data (part of the south east London Aetiology and Ethnicity of Schizophrenia and other Psychoses (AESOP) study) with me and Dr Dieneke Hubbeling for her data on coercion (collected with collaborators Tony Pelosi, Alex Thom and Linda Findlay). Above all I thank my co-editor Xavier Amador for his continuing enthusiasm and good sense.

References

Adams, S. G. and Howe, J. T. (1993). Predicting medication compliance in a psychotic population. *Journal of Nervous and Mental Disease*, **181**, 558–60.

Aga, V. M., Agarwal, A. K. and Gupta, S. C. (1995). The relationship of insight to psychopathology in schizophrenia: a cross sectional study. *Indian Journal of Psychiatry*, **37**, 129–35.

Aguglia, E., De Vanna, M., Onor, M. L. and Ferrara, D. (2002). Insight in persons with schizophrenia: effects of switching from conventional neuroleptics to atypical antipsychotics. *Progress in Neuro-Psychopharmacology and Biological Psychiatry*, **26** (7–8), 1229–33.

Almeida, O. P., Levy, R., Howard, R. J., *et al.* (1996) Insight and paranoid disorders in late life (late paraphrenia). *International Journal of Geriatric Psychiatry*, **11**, 653–8.

Amador, D. F., Flaum, M., Andreasen, N. C., Strauss, D. H., Yale, S. A., Clark, S. C., *et al.* (1994). Awareness of illness in schizophrenia and schizoaffective and mood disorders. *Archives of General Psychiatry*, **51**, 826–36.

Amador, X. F., Friedman, J. H., Kasapis, C., Yale, S. A., Flaum, M. and Gorman, J. M. (1996). Suicidal behavior in schizophrenia and its relationship to awareness of illness. *American Journal of Psychiatry*, **153**, 1185–8.

Amador, X. F. and Seckinger, R. A. (1997). The assessment of insight: a methodological review. *Psychiatric Annals*, **27**, 798–805.

Amador, X. F., Strauss, D. H., Yale, S. A. and Gorman, J. M. (1991). Awareness of illness in schizophrenia. *Schizophrenia Bulletin*, **17**, 113–32.

Amador, X. F., Strauss, D. H., Yale, S. A., Flaum, M. M., Endicott, J. and Gorman, J. M. (1993). Assessment of insight in psychosis. *American Journal of Psychiatry*, **150**, 873–9.

Amador, X. F. and David, A. S. (1998). *Insight and Psychosis*. New York: Oxford University Press.

American Psychiatric Association (1987). *Diagnostic and Statistical Manual of Mental Disorders*, 3rd edn, revised. Washington, DC: American Psychiatric Association.

Andreasen, N. C. (1984). *Scale for the Assessment of Negative Symptoms (SANS); Scale for the Assessment of Positive Symptoms (SAPS)*. University of Iowa: Iowa City.

Arango, C., Adami, H., Sherr, J. D., Thaker, G. K. and Carpenter, W. T. (1999). Relationship of awareness of dyskinesia in schizophrenia to insight into mental illness. *American Journal of Psychiatry*, **156** (7), 1097–9.

Barr, W. B. (1998). Neurobehavioural disorders of awareness and their relevance to schizophrenia. In X. F. Amador and A. S. David (ed.) *Insight and Psychosis*, pp. 107–141. New York: Oxford University Press.

Bartkó, G., Herczeg, I. and Zador, G. (1988). Clinical symptomatology and drug compliance in schizophrenic patients. *Acta Psychiatrica Scandinavica*, **77**, 74–6.

Beck-Sander, A. (1998). Is insight into psychosis meaningful? *Journal of Mental Health*, **7**, 25–34.

Birchwood, M., Smith, J., Drury, V., Healy, J., Macmillan, F. and Slade, M. (1994). A self-report insight scale for psychosis: reliability, validity and sensitivity to change. *Acta Psychiatrica Scandinavica*, **89**, 62–7.

Blakemore, S-J. and Frith, C. D. (2003). Disorders of self-monitoring and the symptoms of schizophrenia. In T. Kircher and A. S. David (ed.) *The Self in Neuroscience and Psychiatry*, pp. 407–424. Cambridge: Cambridge University Press.

Brett-Jones, J., Garety, P. and Hemsley, D. (1987). Measuring delusional experiences: a method and its application. *British Journal of Clinical Psychology*, **26**, 257–67.

Buchanan, A. (1992). A two-year prospective study of treatment compliance in patients with schizophrenia. *Psychological Medicine*, **22**, 787–97.

Buchanan, A., Reed, A., Wessely, S., Garety, P., Taylor, P., Grubin, D., *et al.* (1993). Acting on delusions II. The phenomenological correlates of acting on delusions. I *British Journal of Psychiatry*, **163**, 77–81.

Buckley, P. F., Hasan, S., Friedman, L. and Cerny C. (2001). Insight and schizophrenia. *Comprehensive Psychiatry*, **42** (1), 39–41.

Budd, R. J., Hughes, I. C., Smith. J. A. (1997). Health beliefs and compliance with antipsychotic medication. *British Journal of Clinical Psychology*, **35**, 393–7.

Carni, M. A. and Nevid, J. S. (1992). Social appropriateness and impaired perspective in schizophrenia. *Journal of Clinical Psychology*, **48**, 170–7.

Carpenter, W., Bartko, J., Strauss, J. and Hawk, A. (1978). Signs and symptoms as predictors of outcome: a report for the international pilot study of schizophrenia. *American Journal of Psychiatry*, **135**, 940–5.

Carter, M. F. (2003). The relationship of a self-reported assessment of need in mental illness to insight. *Journal of Mental Health*, **12**, 81–9.

Carroll, A., Fattah, S., Clyde, Z., Coffey, I., Owens, D. G.C. and Johnstone, E. C. (1999). Correlates of insight and insight change in schizophrenia. *Schizophrenia Research*, **35**, 247–53.

Chen, E. Y., Kwok, C. L., Chen, R. Y. and Kwong, P. P. (2001). Insight changes in acute psychotic episodes: a prospective study of Hong Kong Chinese patients. *Journal of Nervous and Mental Disease*, **189**, 24–30.

Chung, K. F., Chen, E. Y., Lam, L. C., Chen, R. Y. and Chan, C. K. (1997). How are psychotic symptoms. perceived? A comparison between patients, relatives and the general public. *Australian and New Zealand Journal of Psychiatry*, **31**, 756–61.

Clare, L. (2003a). The construction of awareness in early-stage Alzheimer's disease: a review of concepts and models. *British Journal of Clinical Psychology* (in press).

Clare, L. (2003b). Awareness in early-stage Alzheimer's disease: a review of methods and evidence. *British Journal of Clinical Psychology* (in press).

Collins, A. A., Remington, G. J., Coulter, K. and Birkett, K. (1997). Insight, neurocognitive function and symptom clusters in chronic schizophrenia. *Schizophrenia Research*, **27**, 37–44.

Cormac, I., Jones. C. and Campbell, C. (2000). Cognitive behaviour therapy for schizophrenia.[update of Cochrane Database Syst Rev. 2000;(2):CD000524; PMID: 10796390]. Cochrane Database of Systematic Reviews. (1):CD000524, 2002.

Corrigan, P. W. (2002). Adherence to antipsychotic medications and health behaviour theories. *Journal of Mental Health*, **11**, 243–54.

Croghan, T. W., Tomlin, M., Pesosolido, B. A., Schittker, J., Martin, J., Ludell, K., *et al.* (2003). American attitudes toward willingness to use psychiatric medications. *Journal of Nervous and Mental Disease*, **191**, 166–74.

Cuesta, M. J. and Peralta, V. (1994). Lack of insight in schizophrenia. *Schizophrenia Bulletin* **20**, 359–66.

Cuesta, M. J., Peralta, V., Juan, J. A. (1996). Abnormal subjective experiences in schizophrenia: its relationships with neuropsychological disturbances and frontal signs. *European Archives of Psychiatry and Clinical Neuroscience*, **246**, 2, 101–5.

Cuesta, M. J. and Zarzuela, A. (1998). Psychopathological dimensions and lack of insight in schizophrenia. *Psychological Reports*, **83**, 895–8.

Cuesta, M. J., Peralta, V. and Zarzuela A. (2000). Reappraising insight in psychosis. Multi-scale longitudinal study. *British Journal of Psychiatry*, **177**, 233–40.

Cuffel, B. J., Alford, J., Fischer, E. P. and Owen, R. R. (1996). Awareness of illness in schizophrenia and outpatient treatment adherence. *The Journal of Nervous and Mental Disease*, **184**, 653–9.

David, A. (1990). Insight and psychosis. *British Journal of Psychiatry*, **156**, 798–808.

David, A., Buchanan, A., Reed, A. and Almeida, O. (1992). The assessment of insight in psychosis. *British Journal of Psychiatry*, **161**, 599–602.

David, A., van Os, J., Jones, P., Fahy, T., Harvey, I. and Förster, A. (1995). Insight and the course of psychiatric illness: cross-sectional and longitudinal associations. *British Journal of Psychiatry*, **167**, 621–6.

David, A. S. (1994). The neuropsychological origins of auditory hallucinations. In: *The Neuropsychology of Schizophrenia*. Lawrence Erlbaum: Hove, East Sussex.

David, A. S. (1998a). The importance of insight in psychosis. In X. F. Amador and A. S. David (ed.) *Insight and Psychosis*. New York: Oxford University Press.

David A. S. (1998b). Commentary on "Is insight into psychosis meaningful?" *Journal of Mental Health*, **7** (6), 579–83.

David, A. S., Owen, A. M. and Forstl, H. (1993). An annotated summary and translation of "On self-awareness of focal brain diseases by the patient in cortical blindness and cortical deafness" by Gabriel Anton. *Cognitive Neuropsychology*, **10**, 263–72.

David, A., van Os, J., Jones, P., Fahy, T., Forster, A. and Harvey, I. (1995). Insight and the course of psychiatric illness: cross-sectional and longitudinal associations. *British Journal of Psychiatry*, **167**, 621–6.

David, A. S. (1999). "To see oursels as others see us" Aubrey Lewis's insight. *British Journal of Psychiatry*, **175**, 210–16.

David, A. S., Kemp, R. (1998). Five perspectives on the phenomenon of insight in psychosis. *Psychiat Annals*, **27**, 791–7.

David A. S. (1999). On the impossibility of defining delusions. *Philosophy, Psychiatry and Psychology*, **6** (1), 17–20.

David, A. S., Morgan, K. D., Mallet, R., Leff, J. and Murray, R. M. (2003). Insight: unitary or multidimensional phenomenon? *Schizophrenia Research*, **60** (suppl.), 14.

Debowska, G., Grzywa, A., Kucharska-Pietura. K. (1998). Insight in paranoid schizophrenia – its relationship to psychopathology and premorbid adjustment. *Comprehensive Psychiatry*, **39** (5), 255–60.

Doyle, M., Flanagan, S., Browne, S., Clarke, M., Lydon, D., Larkin, C., *et al.* (1999). Subjective and external assessments of quality of life in schizophrenia: relationship to insight. *Acta Psychiatrica Scandinavica*, **99** (6), 466–72.

Drake, R. J., Haley, C. J., Akhtar, S. and Lewis, S. W. (2000). Causes and consequences of duration of untreated psychosis in schizophrenia. *British Journal of Psychiatry*, **177**, 511–15.

Eckman, T. A., Liberman, R. P., Phipps, C. C. and Blair, K. (1990). Teaching medication management skills to schizophrenic patients. *Journal of Clinical Psychopharmacology*, **10**, 33–8.

Eckman, T. A., Wirshing, W. C., Marder, S. R., Liberman, R. P., Johnston-Cronk, K., Zimmermann, K., *et al.* (1992). Technique for training schizophrenia patients in illness self-management: A controlled trial. *American Journal of Psychiatry*, **149**, 1549–55.

Endicott, J., Spitzer, R. L. and Fleiss, J. (1976). The Global Assessment Scale. *Archives of General Psychiatry*, **33**, 776–1.

Francis, J. L. and Penn, D. L. (2001). The relationship between insight and social skill in persons with severe mental illness. *Journal of Nervous and Mental Disease*, **189**, 822–9.

Fulford, K. W. M. (1989). *Moral Theory and Medical Practice*. Cambridge: Cambridge University Press.

Garavan, J., Browne, S., Gervin, M., Lane A. Larkin C. and O'Callaghan E. (1998). Compliance with neuroleptic medication in outpatients with schizophrenia; relationship to subjective response to neuroleptics; attitudes to medication and insight. *Comprehensive Psychiatry*, **39**, 215–19.

Gardner, W., Hoge, S., Bennett, N., Roth, L., Lidz, C., Monahan, J., *et al.* (1993). Two scales for measuring patients' perceptions of coercion during hospital admission. *Behavioral Sciences and the Law*, **20**, 307–21.

Garety, P. A., Kuipers, L., Fowler, D., Chamberlain, F. and Dunn, G. (1994). Cognitive behavioural therapy for drug-resistant psychosis. *British Journal of Medical Psychology*, **67**, 259–71.

Garety, P. and Hemsley, D. R. (1987). Characteristics of delusional experience. *European Archives of Psychiatry and Neurological Sciences*, **236**, 294–8.

Ghaemi, S. N. and Pope, H. G. (1994). Lack of insight in psychotic and affective disorders: a review of empirical studies. *Harvard Review of Psychiatry*, **2**, 22–3.

Ghaemi, S. N., Stoll, A.L. and Pope, H. G. (1995). Lack of insight in bipolar disorder. The acute manic episode. *Journal of Nervous and Mental Disease*, **183**, 464–7.

Goldberg, R. W., Green-Paden, L. D., Lehman, A. F. and Gold, J. M. (2001). Correlates of insight in serious mental illness. *Journal of Nervous and Mental Disease*, **189**, 137–45.

Greenfield, D. G., Anyon, W. R., Hobart, M., Quinlan, D. and Plantes, M. (1991). Insight into illness and outcome in anorexia nervosa. *Internal Journal of Eating Disorders*, **10**, 101–9.

Hayashi, N., Yamashina, M., Taguchi, H., *et al.* (2001). Schizophrenic outpatient perceptions of psychiatric treatment and psychotic symptomatology: an investigation using structural equation modeling. *Psychiatry and Clinical Neurosciences*, **55**, 587–93.

Heinrichs, D. W., Cohen, B. P. and Carpenter, W. T. (1985). Early insight and the management of schizophrenia decompensation. *Journal of Nervous and Mental Disease*, **173**, 133–8.

Hoge, S. K., Appelbaum, P. S., Lawlor, T., Beck, J. C., Litman, R., Greer, A., *et al.* (1990). A prospective, multicenter study of patients' refusal of antipsychotic medication. *Archives of General Psychiatry*, **47**, 949–56.

Holm, S. (1993). What is wrong with compliance? *Journal of Medical Ethics*, **19**, 108–9.

Hubbeling, D., Findlay, L., Thom, A., Pelosi. A. J. and David, A. S. (2001). Relationship between insight and compulsory admission. *Schizophrenia Research*, **49** (1–2), 15 Suppl.

Iqbal, Z., Birchwood, M., Chadwick, P. and Trower, P. (2000). Cognitive approach to depression and suicidal thinking in psychosis. 2. Testing the validity of a social ranking model. *British Journal of Psychiatry*, **177**, 522–8.

Jehkonen, M., Ahonen, J-P., Dastidar, P., Laippala, P. and Vilkki, J. (2000). Unawareness of deficits after right hemisphere stroke: double-dissociations of anosognosias. *Acta Neurologica Scandinavica*, **102**, 378–84.

Johnson, S. and Orrell, M. (1995). Insight and psychosis: a social perspective. *Psychological Medicine*, **25**, 515–20.

Joyce, C. R.B. (1993). Insight. *Lancet*, **341**, 213–14.

Kampman, O. and Lehtinen K. (1999). Compliance in psychoses. *Acta Psychiatrica Scandinavica*, **100**, 167–75.

Kampman, O., Laippala, P., Vaananen, J., Koivisto, E., Kiviniemi, P., Kilkku, N., *et al.* (2002). Indicators of medication compliance in first-episode psychosis. *Psychiatry Research*, **110**, 39–48.

Kane, J. M., Quitkin, F., Rifkin, A., Wegner, J., Rosenberg, G. and Borenstein, M. (1983). Attitudinal changes of involuntarily committed patients following treatment. *Archives of General Psychiatry*, **40**, 374–7.

Kay, S. R., Fiszbein, A. and Opler, L. A. (1987). The positive and negative syndrome scale (PANSS) for schizophrenia. *Schizophrenia Bulletin*, **13**, 261–76.

Keefe, R. S. E. (1998). The neurobiology of disturbances of self: autonoetic agnosia in schizophrenia. In X. F. Amador and A. S. David (ed.) *Insight and Psychosis*, pp. 142–73. New York: Oxford University Press.

Kemp, R. and David, A. (1997). Insight and compliance. In B. Blackwell (ed.) *Treatment Compliance and the Therapeutic Alliance in Serious Mental Illness*, pp. 61–84. The Netherlands: Harwood Academic Publishers.

Kemp, R. A. and Lambert, T. J. (1995). Insight in schizophrenia and its relationship to psychopathology. *Schizophrenia Research*, **18**, 21–8.

Kemp, R., Applewhaite, G., Hayward, P., Everitt, B. and David, A. (1996). Compliance therapy in psychotic disorders: randomised controlled trial. *British Medical Journal*, **312**, 345–9.

Kemp, R. and David, A. (1997). Insight and compliance. In B. Blackwell (ed.) *Treatment Compliance and the Treatment Alliance in Serious Mental Illness*, pp. 61–84. *The Netherlands: Harwood Academic Publishers.*

Kemp, R., Kirov, G.B., Hayward, P. and David, A. (1998). Randomised controlled trial of compliance therapy – 18 month follow-up. *British Journal of Psychiatry*, **172**, 413–19.

Kendler, K. S., Glazer, W. M. and Morgenstern, H. (1983). Dimensions of delusional experience. *Amercian Journal of Psychiatry*, **140**, 466–9.

Kiersky, J. E. (1998). Insight, self-deception and psychosis in mood disorders. In X. F. Amador and A. S. David (ed.) *Insight and Psychosis*, pp. 91–104. New York: Oxford University Press.

Kinsbourne, M. (1998). Representations of consciousness and the neuropsychology of insight. In X. F. Amador and A. S. David (ed.) *Insight and Psychosis*, pp. 174–90. New York: Oxford University Press.

Kim, Y., Sakamoto, K., Kamo, T. and Sakamura, Y. (1997). Insight and clinical correlates in schizophrenia. *Comprehensive Psychiatry*, **38**, 117–23.

Kim, Y., Sakamoto, K., Sakamura, Y., Kamo, T. and Kotoril, N. (1997 b). Subjective experience and related symptoms in schizophrenia. *Comprehensive Psychiatry*, **38**, 1, 49–55.

Kim, C. H., Jayathilake, K. and Meltzer, H. Y. (2003). Hopelessness, neurocognitive function and insight in schizophrenia: relationship to suicidal behavior. *Schizophrenia Research*, **60** (1), 71–80.

Kircher, T and David, A. S. (2003). Self-consciousness: an integrative approach from philosophy, psychopathology and the neurosciences. In T. Kircher and A. S. David (ed.) *The Self in Neuroscience and Psychiatry*, pp. 445–74. Cambridge: Cambridge University Press.

Kirov, G., Kemp, R., Kirov, K. and David, A. (1998). Religious faith after psychotic illness. *Psychopathology*, **31**, 5, 234–45.

Kjellin, L., Andersson, K., Candefjord, I. L., Palmstierna, T. and Wallsten, T. (1997). Ethical benefits and costs of coercion in short-term inpatient psychiatric care. *Psychiatric Services*, **48**, 1567–70.

Kraepelin, E. (1919). *Dementia Praecox and Paraphrenia* (trans R. M. Barclay). Edinburgh: E and S Livingston.

Kulhara, P., Basu, D. and Chakrabarti, S. (1992). Insight and psychosis: II. A Pilot study comparing schizophrenia in affective disorder. *Indian Journal of Social Psychiatry*, **8**, 45–8.

Kulhara, P., Chakrabarti, S. and Basu, D. (1992). Insight and Psychosis: I. An Empirical Inquiry. *Indian Journal of Social Psychiatry*, **8**, 40–4.

Lacro, J. P., Dunn, L. B., Dolder, C. R., Leckband, S. G. and Jeste, D. V. (2002). Prevalence of and risk factors for medication nonadherence in patients with schizophrenia: a comprehensive review of recent literature. *Journal of Clinical Psychiatry*, **63** (10), 892–909.

Lancet (Editorial). (1990). Real insight. **336**, 408–9.

Lam, L. C., Chan, C. K. and Chen, E. Y. (1996). Insight and general public attitude on psychotic experiences in Hong Kong. *International Journal of Social Psychiatry*, **42** (1), 10–17.

Lecompte, D. and Pelc, I. (1996). Cognitive-behavioural program to improve compliance with medication in patients with schizophrenia. *International Journal of Mental Health*, **25**, 51–6.

Lewis, A. (1934). The psychopathology of insight. *British Journal of Medical Psychology*, **14**, 332–48.

Lin, I. F., Spiga, R. and Fortsch, W. (1979). Insight and adherence to medication in chronic schizophrenics. *Journal of Clinical Psychiatry*, **40**, 430–2.

Löffler, W., Kilian, R., Toumi, M. and Angermayer, M. C. (2003). Schizophrenic patients' subjective reasons for compliacen and noncompliance with neuroleptic treatment. *Pharmcopsychiatry*, **36**, 105–12.

Lysaker, P. H., Bryson, G. J., Lancaster, R. S., Evans, J. D. and Bell, M. D. (2003). Insight in schizophrenia: associations with executive function and coping style. *Schizophrenia Research*, **59** (1), 41–7.

Lysaker, P. H., Bell, M. D., Bryson, G. and Kaplan, E. (1999). Personality as a predictor of the variability of insight in schizophrenia. *Journal of Nervous and Mental Disease*, **187**, 119–22.

Lysaker, P., Bell, M., Milstein, R., Bryson, G. and Beam-Goulet, J. (1994). Insight and psychosocial treatment compliance in schizophrenia. *Psychiatry*, **57**, 307–15.

Lysaker, P. and Bell, M. (1994). Insight and cognitive impairment in schizophrenia. Performance on repeated administration of the Wisconsin card sorting Test. *Journal of Nervous and Mental Disease*, **182**, 656–60.

Lysaker, P. and Bell, M. (1995). Work rehabilitation and improvements in insight in schizophrenia. *Journal of Nervous and Mental Disease*, **183**, 103–6.

Lysaker, P. H., Clements, C. A., Plascak-Hallberg, C. D., Knipscheer, S. J. and Wright, D. E. (2002). Insight and personal narratives of illness in schizophrenia. *Psychiatry*, **65** (3), 197–206.

MacPherson, R., Jerrom, B. and Hughes A. (1996). A controlled study of education about drug treatment in schizophrenia. *British Journal of Psychiatry*, **168**, 709–17.

Main, M. C., Gerace, L. M. and Camilleri, D. (1993). Information sharing concerning schizophrenia in a family member: adult siblings' perspectives. *Archives of Psychiatric Nursing*, **7**, 147–53.

Marder, S. R., Mebane, A., Chien, C-P., Winslade, W. J., Swann, E. and van Putten, T. (1983). A comparison of patients who refuse and consent to neuroleptic treatment. *American Journal of Psychiatry*, **140**, 470–2.

Markova, I. S. and Berrios, G. E. (1992). The meaning of insight in clinical psychiatry. *British Journal of Psychiatry*, **160**, 850–60.

Markova, I. S. and Berrios, G. E. (2001). The 'object' of insight assessment: relationship to 'structure'. *Psychopathology*, **34**, 245–52.

McCabe, R. and Quayle, E. (2002). Knowing your own mind. *Psychologist*, **15** (1), 14–16.

McCabe, R., Quayle, E., Beirne, A., Duane M. (2000). Is there a role for compliance in the assessment of insight in chronic schizophrenia? *Psychology, Health and Medicine*, **5**, 173–8.

McEvoy, J. P., Applebaum, P. S., Apperson, J., Geller, J. L. and Freter, S. (1989). Why must some schizophrenic patients be involuntarily committed? The role of insight. *Comprehensive Psychiatry*, **30**, 13–17.

McEvoy, J. P., Apperson, L. J., Applebaum, P. S., *et al.* (1989a). Insight into schizophrenia. Its relationship to acute psychopathology. *Journal of Nervous and Mental Disease*, **177**, 43–7.

McEvoy, J., Freter, S., Everett, G., Geller, J., Appelbaum, P. S., Apperson, J. *et al.* (1989c). Insight and the clinical outcome of schizophrenic patients. *Journal of Nervous and Mental Disease*, **177**, 48–51.

McEvoy, J. P., Freter, S., Merritt, M. and Apperson, L. J. (1993). Insight about psychosis among outpatients with schizophrenia. *Hospital and Community Psychiatry*, **44**, 883–4.

McEvoy, J. P., Schooler, N. J., Friedman, E., Steingard, S. and Allen, M. (1993). Use of psychopathology vignettes by patients with schizophrenia or schizoaffective disorder and by mental health professionals to judge patients' insight. *American Journal of Psychiatry*, **150**, 1649–53.

McFarlane, W. R. and Luken, E. P. (1998). Insight, families and education: an exploration of the role of attribution in clinical outcome. In X. F. Amador and A. S. David (ed.) *Insight and Psychosis*, pp. 317–31. New York: Oxford University Press.

McGlashan, T. (1981). Does attitude toward psychosis relate to outcome? *American Journal of Psychiatry*, **138**, 797–801.

Michalakeas, A., Skoutas, C., Charalambous, A., Peristeris, A., Marinos, V., Keramari, E., *et al.* (1994). A. Insight in schizophrenia and mood disorders and its relation to psychopathology. *Acta Psychiatrica Scandinavica*, **90**, 46–9.

Miller, W. R. and Rollnick, S. (1991). *Motivational Interviewing: Preparing People to Change*. New York: Guilford Press.

Mintz, A. R., Dobson, K. S. and Romney, D. M. (2003a). Insight in schizophrenia: a meta-analysis. *Schizophrenia Research*, **61** (1), 75–88.

Mintz, A. R., Addington, J. and Addington, D. (2003b). Insight in early psychosis: a 1-year follow-up. *Schizophrenia Research*, in press.

Mohamed, S., Fleming, S., Penn, D. L. and Spaulding, W. (1999). Insight in schizophrenia: its relationship to measures of executive functions. *Journal of Nervous and Mental Disease*, **187**, 525–31.

Mortimer, A. M., McKenna, P. J., Lund, C. E. and Mannuzza, S. (1989). Rating of negative symptoms using the High Royds Evaluation of Negativity (HEN) scale. *British Journal of Psychiatry*, (suppl. 7), **155**, 89–91.

Mullen, R., Howard, R., David, A. and Levy R. (1995). Insight in Alzheimer's disease. *International Journal of Geriatric Psychiatry*, **11**, 645–51.

Mullick, M., Miller, L. J. and Jacobsen, T. (2001). Insight into mental illness and child maltreatment risk among mothers with major psychiatric disorders. *Psychiatric Services*, **52**, 488–92.

Nayani, T. and David, A. (1996). The auditory hallucinations: a phenomenological survey. *Psychological Medicine*, **26**, 177–89.

Neumann, C. S., Walker, E. F., Weinstein, J. and Cutshaw, C. (1996). Psychotic patients' awareness of mental illness: implications for legal defense proceedings. *Journal of Psychiatry and Law*, Fall, 421–42.

Nosé, M., Barbui, C., Gray, R. and Tansella, M. (2003). Clinical interventions for treatment non-adherence in psychosis: meta-analysis. *British Journal of Psychiatry*, **183**, 197–206.

O'Connor, R. and Herrman, H. (1993). Assessment of contributions to disability in people with schizophrenia during rehabilitation. *Australian and New Zealand Journal of Psychiatry*, **27**, 595–600.

Overall, J. E. and Gorham, D. R. (1962). The brief psychiatric rating scale. *Psychological Reports*, **10**, 799–812.

Pallanti, S., Quercioli, L. and Pazzagli, A. (1999). Effects of clozapine on awareness of illness and cognition in schizophrenia. *Psychiatry Research*, **86** (3), 239–49.

Pan, P-C. and Tantum, D. (1989). Clinical characteristics, health beliefs and compliance with maintenance treatment: a comparison between regular and irregular attenders at a depot clinic. *Acta Psychiatrica Scandinavica*, **79**, 564–70.

Pekkala, E. and Merinder, L. (2000). Psychoeducation for schizophrenia.[update of Cochrane Database Syst Rev;(4):CD002831; PMID: 11034771]. Cochrane Database of Systematic Reviews. (2):CD002831, 2002.

Peralta, V. and Cuesta, M. J. (1994). Lack of insight: its status within schizophrenic psychopathology. *Biological Psychiatry*, **36**, 559–61.

Perkins, D. O. (2002). Predictors of noncompliance in patients with schizophrenia. *Journal of Clinical Psychiatry*, **63** (12), 1121–8.

Perkins, R. E. and Moodley, P. (1993a). Perception of problems in psychiatric inpatients: Denial, race and service usage. *Social Psychiatry and Psychiatry Epidemiology*, **28**, 189–93.

Perkins, R. and Moodley, P. (1993b). The arrogance of insight. *Psychiatric Bulletin*, **17**, 233–4.

Pini, S., Cassano, G. B., Dell'Osso, L., *et al.* (2001). Insight into illness in schizophrenia, schizoaffective disorder and mood disorders with psychotic features. *American Journal of Psychiatry*, **158**, 122–5.

Reid, J. R. and Finesinger, J. E. (1952). The role of insight in psychotherapy. *American Journal of Psychiatry*, **108**, 726–34.

Ritsner, M. (2003). Predicting changes in domain-specific quality of life of schizophrenia patients. *Journal of Nervous and Mental Disease*, **191** (5), 287–94.

Roback, H. B. and Abramowitz, S. I. (1979). Insight and hospital adjustment. *Canadian Journal of Psychiatry*, **24**, 233–6.

Roe, D. and Kravetz, S. (2003). Different ways of being aware of a psychiatric disability: a multifunctional narrative approach to insight into mental disorder. *Journal of Nervous and Mental Disease*, **191**, 417–24.

Rogers, R., Gillis, J. R., Turner, R. E. and Frise-Smith, T. (1990). The clinical presentation of command hallucinations in a forensic population. *American Journal of Psychiatry*, **147**, 1304–7.

Rossell, S. L, Coakes, J., Shapeleske, J., Woodruff, P. W. R. and David, A. S. (2003). Insight: its relationship with cognitive function, brain volume and symptoms in schizophrenia. *Psychological Medicine*, **33**, 111–19.

Rossi, A., Arduini, L., Prosperini, P., Kalyvoka, A., Stratta, P. and Daneluzzo, E. (2000). Awareness of illness and outcome in schizophrenia. *European Archives of Psychiatry and Clinical Neuroscience*, **250**, 73–5.

Sajatovic, M., Rosch, D. S., Sivec, H. J., Sultana, D., Smith, D. A., Alamir, S., *et al.* (2002). Insight into illness and attitudes toward medications among inpatients with schizophrenia. *Psychiatric Services*, **53** (10), 1319–21.

Sandyk, R., Kay, S. R., Awerbuch, G. I. (1993). Subjective awareness of abnormal involuntary movements in schizophrenia. *International Journal of Neuroscience*, **69** (1–4), 1–20.

Sanz, M., Constable, G., Lopez-Ibor, I., Kemp, R. and David, A. (1998). A comparative study of insight scales and their relationship to psychopathological and clinical variables. *Psychological Medicine*, **28**, 437–46.

Saravanan, B., Jacob, K. S., Prince, M., Bhugra, D. and David, A. S. (2004). Culture and insight revisited. *British Journal of Psychiatry*, **184**, 107–9.

Schwartz, R. C., Cohen, B. N. and Grubaugh, A. (1997). Does insight affect long-term inpatient treatment outcome in chronic schizophrenia? *Comprehensive Psychiatry*, **38**, 283–8.

Schwartz R. C. (1998). Insight and illness in chronic schizophrenia. *Comprehensive Psychiatry*, **39**, 249–54.

Schwartz, R. C. (2000). Insight and suicidality in schizophrenia: a replication study. *Journal of Nervous and Mental Disease*, **188**, 235–7.

Selten, J.-P. C. J., van den Bosch, R. J. and Sijben, A. E. S. (1998). The subjective experience of negative symptoms. In X. F. Amador and A. S. David (ed.) *Insight and Psychosis*, pp. 78–90. New York: Oxford University Press.

Selten, J. P., Wiersma, D. and van den Bosch, R. J. (2000). Distress attributed to negative symptoms in schizophrenia. *Schizophrenia Bulletin*, **26** (3), 737–44.

Seltzer, A., Roncari, I. and Garfinkel P. (1980). Effect of patient education on medication compliance. *American Journal Psychiatry*, **25**, 638–45.

Shepherd, M. (1957). A study of the major psychoses in an English county. *Maudsley Monographs, No 3*. London: Chapman and Hall Ltd.

Smith, C. M., Barzman, D. and Pristach, C. A. (1997). Effect of patient and family insight on compliance of schizophrenic patients. *Journal of Clinical Pharmacology*, **37** (2), 147–54.

Smith, T., Hull, J. and Santos, L. (1998). The relationship between symptoms and insight in schizophrenia: a longitudinal perspective. *Schizophrenia Research*, **33**, 63–7.

Smith, T. E., Hull, J. W., Goodman, M., Hedayat-Harris, A., Willson, D. F., Israel, L. M., *et al.* (1999). The relative influences of symptoms, insight and neurocognition on social adjustment in schizophrenia and schizoaffective disorder. *Journal of Nervous and Mental Disease*, **187**, 102–8.

Soskis, D. and Bowers, M. (1969). The schizophrenic experience: a follow-up study of attitude and post-hospital adjustment. *Journal of Nervous and Mental Disease*, **149**, 443–9.

Spitzer, R., Endicott, J. and Robins, E. (1978). Research diagnostic criteria: rationale and reliability. *Archives of General Psychiatry*, **35**, 773–82.

Startup, M. (1997). Awareness of own and others' schizophrenic illness. *Schizophrenia Research*, **26**, 203–11.

Startup, M. (1998). Insight and interpersonal problems in long-term schizophrenia. *Journal of Mental Health*, **7**, 299–308.

Steblaj, A., Tavcar, R. and Dernovsek, M. Z. (1999). Predictors of suicide in psychiatric hospital. *Acta Psychiatrica Scandinavica*, **100**, 383–8.

Stephens, J. H., Astrup, C. and Mangrum, J. C. (1966). Prognostic factors in recovered and deteriorated schizophrenics. *American Journal of Psychiatry*, **122**, 1116–21.

Stephens, J. H., Richard, P., and McHugh, P. R. (2000). Long-term follow-up of patients with a diagnosis of paranoid state and hospitalized, 1913 to 1940. *Journal of Nervous and Mental Disease*, **188** (4), 202–8.

Strauss, J. and Carpenter, W. (1974). The prediction of outcome in schizophrenia. *Archives of General Psychiatry*, **31**, 37–42.

Streicker, S. K., Amdur, M. and Dincin, J. (1986). Educating patients about psychiatric medication: failure to enhance compliance. *Psychiatric Rehabilitation Journal*, **4**, 15–28.

Surguladze, S., Timms, P., and David, A. S. (2001). Teaching psychiatric trainees "compliance therapy". *Psychiatric Bulletin*, **26**, 12–15.

Swanson, C. L., Freudenreich, O., McEvoy, J. P., Nelson, L., Kamaraju, L. and Wilson, W. H. (1995). Insight in schizophrenia and mania. *The Journal of Nervous and Mental Disease*, **193**, 752–5.

Takai, A., Uematsu, M. Hirofumi, U., Sone, K. and Kaiya, H. (1992). Insight and its related factors in chronic schizophrenic patients: a preliminary study. *European Journal of Psychiatry*, **6**, 159–70.

Tait, L., Birchwood, M., and Trower, P. (2003). Predicting engagement with services for psychosis: insight, symptoms and recovery style. *British Journal of Psychiatry*, **182**, 123–8.

Taylor, K. E. and Perkins, R. E. (1991). Identity and coping with mental illness in long-stay psychiatric rehabilitation. *British Journal of Clinical Psychology*, **30**, 73–85.

Tharyan, A. and Saravanan, B. (2000). Insight and psychopathology in schizophrenia. *Indian Journal of Psychiatry*, **42**, 421–6.

Trauer, T. and Sacks, T. (2000). The relationship between insight and medication adherence in severely mentally ill clients treated in the community. *Acta Psychiatrica Scandinvica*, **102**, 211–16.

Thompson, K. N., McGorry, P. D. and Harrigan, S. M. (2001). Reduced awareness of illness in first-episode psychosis. *Comprehensive Psychiatry*, **42**, 498–503.

Turkington, D., Kingdon, D. and Turner, T. (2002). Insight into Schizophrenia Research Group. Effectiveness of a brief cognitive-behavioural therapy intervention in the treatment of schizophrenia. *British Journal of Psychiatry*, **180**, 523–7.

Ullrich, J., Ulmar, G. and Starzinski, T. (1995). Disease models and change in attitude of involuntarily admitted schizophrenic patients. [German] *Fortschritte der Neurologie-Psychiatrie.* 63 (12), 480–6.

Vaillant, G. E. (1964). Prospective prediction of schizophrenic remission. *Archives of General Psychiatry*, **11**, 509–18.

Valenstein M., Copeland, L. A., Blow, F. C., McCarthy, J. F., Zeber, J. E., Gillon, L., *et al.* (2002). Pharmacy data identify poorly adherent patients with schizophrenia at increased risk for admission. *Medical Care*, **40** (8), 630–9.

van Os, J., Fahy, T. A., Jones, P., Harvey, I., Sham, P., Lewis, S., *et al.* (1996). Psychopathological syndromes in the functional psychoses: associations with course and outcome. *Psychological Medicine*, **26**, 161–76.

van Putten, T. (1974). Why do schizophrenic patients refuse to take their medication? *Archives of General Psychiatry*, **31**, 67–72.

van Putten, T., Crumpton, E. and Yale, C. (1976). Drug refusal in schizophrenia and the wish to be crazy. *Archives of General Psychiatry*, **33**, 1443–6.

Vaz, F. J., Bejar, A. and Casado, M. (2002). Insight, psychopathology and interpersonal relationships in schizophrenia. *Schizophrenia Bulletin*, **28**, 311–17.

Warner, R. (1985). *Recovery from Schizophrenia: Psychiatry and the political economy.* London: Routledge and Kegan Paul.

Warner, T., Taylor, D., Powers, M. and Hyman, J. (1989). Acceptance of the mental illness label by psychotic patients: effects on functioning. *American Journal of Orthopsychiatry*, **59**, 398–409.

Wechsler, D. (1955). *Wechsler Adult Intelligence Scale: Manual.* New York: Psychological Corporation.

White, R., Bebbington, P., Pearson, J., Johnson, S. and Ellis, D. (2000). The social context of insight in schizophrenia. *Social Psychiatry and Psychiatric Epidemiology*, **35** (11), 500–7.

Wing, J. K., Cooper, J. E. and Sartorius, N. (1974). *The Measurement and Classification of Psychiatric Symptoms.* Cambridge: Cambridge University Press.

Weiler, M. A., Fleisher, M. H. and McArthur-Campbell, D. (2000). Insight and symptom change in schizophrenia and other disorders. *Schizophrenia Research*, **45**, 29–36.

Yen, C. F., Yeh, M. L., Chen, C. S. and Chung, H. H. (2002). Predictive value of insight for suicide, violence, hospitalization and social adjustment for outpatients with schizophrenia: a prospective study. *Comprehensive Psychiatry*, **43**, 443–7.

Young, D. A., Davila, R. and Scher, H. (1993). Unawareness of illness and neuropsychological performance in chronic schizophrenia. *Schizophrenia Research*, **10**, 117–24.

Young D. A., Zakzanis, K. K., Bailey, C., Davilia, R., Griese, J., Sartory, G., *et al.* (1998). Further parameters of insight and neuropsychological deficit in schizophrenia and other chronic mental disease. *Journal of Nervous and Mental Disease*, **186**, 44–50.

Young, A. W., De Haan, E. H. F. and Newcombe, F. (1990). Unawareness of impaired face recognition. *Brain and Cognition*, **14**, 1–18.

Zygmunt, A., Olfson, M., Boyer, C. A. and Mechanic, D. (2002). Interventions to improve medication adherence in schizophrenia. *American Journal of Psychiatry*, **159**, 1653–64.

Index